THE CAMBRIDGE HISTORY OF
IRELAND

The thousand years explored in this book witnessed developments in the history of Ireland that resonate to this day. Interspersing narrative with detailed analysis of key themes, the first volume in *The Cambridge History of Ireland* presents the latest thinking on key aspects of the medieval Irish experience. The contributors are leading experts in their fields, and present their original interpretations in a fresh and accessible manner. New perspectives are offered on the politics, artistic culture, religious beliefs and practices, social organisation and economic activity that prevailed on the island in these centuries. At each turn the question is asked: to what extent were these developments unique to Ireland? The openness of Ireland to outside influences, and its capacity to influence the world beyond its shores, are recurring themes. Underpinning the book is a comparative, outward-looking approach that sees Ireland as an integral but exceptional component of medieval Christian Europe.

BRENDAN SMITH was born in Newport, Wales, of Irish parents and grew up in Ireland. He is a graduate of Trinity College Dublin and was Rooney Family Newman Scholar at University College Dublin before joining the University of Bristol in 1993. He was appointed Professor of Medieval History at Bristol in 2014. He is the author and editor of numerous books on medieval Ireland, including several collections of historical documents. His research focuses on the English colonists established in Ireland in the decades around 1200, and the relationship of their descendants with England and with their Irish neighbours. He is a Fellow of the Royal Historical Society and of the Society of Antiquaries of London.

THE CAMBRIDGE HISTORY OF
IRELAND

GENERAL EDITOR

THOMAS BARTLETT, professor emeritus of Irish history,
University of Aberdeen

This authoritative, accessible and engaging four-volume history
vividly presents the Irish story – or stories – from c.600 to the
present, within its broader Atlantic, European, imperial and
global contexts. While the volumes benefit from a strong political
narrative framework, they are distinctive also in including essays
that address the full range of social, economic, religious, linguistic,
military, cultural, artistic and gender history, and in challenging
traditional chronological boundaries in a manner that offers
new perspectives and insights. Each volume examines Ireland's
development within a distinct period, and offers a complete and
rounded picture of Irish life, while remaining sensitive to the
unique Irish experience. Bringing together an international team
of experts, this landmark history both reflects recent developments
in the field and sets the agenda for future study.

VOLUMES IN THE SERIES

VOLUME I
600–1550
EDITED BY BRENDAN SMITH

VOLUME II
1550–1730
EDITED BY JANE OHLMEYER

VOLUME III
1730–1880
EDITED BY JAMES KELLY

VOLUME IV
1880 to the Present
EDITED BY THOMAS BARTLETT

THE CAMBRIDGE HISTORY OF
IRELAND

*

VOLUME I
600–1550

*

Edited by

BRENDAN SMITH

University of Bristol

CAMBRIDGE
UNIVERSITY PRESS

University Printing House, Cambridge CB2 8BS, United Kingdom

One Liberty Plaza, 20th Floor, New York, NY 10006, USA

477 Williamstown Road, Port Melbourne, VIC 3207, Australia

314–321, 3rd Floor, Plot 3, Splendor Forum, Jasola District Centre, New Delhi – 110025, India

79 Anson Road, #06-04/06, Singapore 079906

Cambridge University Press is part of the University of Cambridge.

It furthers the University's mission by disseminating knowledge in the pursuit of education, learning, and research at the highest international levels of excellence.

www.cambridge.org
Information on this title: www.cambridge.org/9781107110670
DOI: 10.1017/9781316275399

© Cambridge University Press 2018

First published 2018
Reprinted 2018

Printed in the United Kingdom by TJ International, Padstow, Cornwall

A catalogue record for this publication is available from the British Library.

ISBN – 4-Volume Set 978-1-107-16729-2 Hardback
ISBN – Volume I 978-1-107-11067-0 Hardback
ISBN – Volume II 978-1-107-11763-1 Hardback
ISBN – Volume III 978-1-107-11520-0 Hardback
ISBN – Volume IV 978-1-107-11354-1 Hardback

Contents

Contents

Contents

Illustrations

Figures

Maps

Contributors

MICHAEL BENNETT, Emeritus Professor of History, University of Tasmania.

EDEL BHREATHNACH, Chief Executive Officer of the Discovery Programme: Centre for Archaeology and Innovation Ireland, Dublin.

JOHN CAREY, Professor of Early and Medieval Irish, University College Cork.

PETER CROOKS, Assistant Professor of Medieval History, Trinity College Dublin.

ROBIN FRAME, Emeritus Professor of Medieval History, University of Durham.

BETH HARTLAND, Independent Researcher.

JANE HAWKES, Reader in History of Art, University of York.

MARY ANN LYONS, Professor of History, Maynooth University.

CHRISTOPHER MAGINN, Professor of History, Fordham University.

RACHEL MOSS, Assistant Professor of History of Art and Architecture, Trinity College Dublin.

MARGARET MURPHY, Lecturer in History, Carlow College.

MÁIRE NÍ MHAONAIGH, Professor of Medieval and Celtic Studies, University of Cambridge.

COLMÁN Ó CLABAIGH OSB, Glenstal Abbey, Limerick.

KATHARINE SIMMS, Associate Professor Emerita of Medieval History, Trinity College Dublin.

Brendan Smith, Professor of Medieval History, University of Bristol.

Colin Veach, Senior Lecturer in Medieval History, University of Hull.

Nicholas Vincent, Professor of Medieval History, University of East Anglia.

Alex Woolf, Senior Lecturer in History, University of St Andrews.

General Acknowledgements

As General Editor of the Cambridge History of Ireland, I wish to express my gratitude to all those who assisted in bringing these four volumes to publication. My fellow editors, Brendan Smith, Jane Ohlmeyer and James Kelly have been unstinting with their time and unwavering in their determination to bring their respective volumes to completion as expeditiously as possible. John Cunningham offered vital editorial support at key points in this process. The team at Cambridge University Press, headed by Liz Friend-Smith, supported initially by Amanda George and latterly by Claire Sissen and Bethany Thomas, has been at all times enthusiastic about the project. It has been a great pleasure working with them. My thanks to the often unsung archivists whose documentary collections were freely drawn upon by the contributors in all volumes, to those who helped source images, and to those who drew the informative maps. Lastly, my warmest thanks to all the contributors who gave freely of their expertise in writing their chapters, and for their patience in awaiting publication of their efforts.

Thomas Bartlett, MRIA
General Editor, The Cambridge History of Ireland

Acknowledgements

I am grateful to Tom Bartlett for inviting me to be involved in the Cambridge History of Ireland project, and to Jane Ohlmeyer and James Kelly who along with Tom provided great support as fellow-editors. I have worked with an excellent team of contributors. Among them I owe special thanks to Edel Bhreathnach and Rachel Moss who pointed me towards the most suitable individuals to approach about the writing of certain chapters. (Seán Duffy's advice in this regard was also very helpful.) I am particularly indebted to Máire Ní Mhaonaigh who agreed to contribute a chapter at relatively short notice. The University of Bristol provided me with the time I needed to bring this volume to completion, and my Heads of School, Prof. Ronald Hutton and Prof. Hilary Carey deserve thanks for their support. My copy-editor, Denise Bannerman, has displayed remarkable patience, and I have enjoyed my dealings with Elizabeth Friend-Smith, Melissa Shivers, Claire Sissen and Bethany Thomas at Cambridge University Press. It is not the custom to dedicate works of this sort to individuals, but the late James Lydon was often in my thoughts as the volume came together. I hope he would approve.

Brendan Smith
University of Bristol
Autumn 2017

Abbreviations

Full references for the most frequently cited primary and secondary works are found below. These works are not included in the lists of sources to be found at the end of individual chapters.

AC *Annála Connacht. The Annals of Connacht (A.D. 1224–1544)*, ed. A. M. Freeman (Dublin: DIAS, 1983)

AFM *Annála Ríoghachta Éireann: Annals of the Kingdom of Ireland by the Four Masters from the Earliest Period to the Year 1616*, ed. and trans. J. O'Donovan. 7 vols. (Dublin, 1851; 3rd edn Dublin: De Burca rare books, 1990)

AI *The Annals of Inisfallen (MS Rawlinson B 503)*, ed. and trans. S. Mac Airt (Dublin: DIAS, 1951)

ALC *The Annals of Loch Cé: A Chronicle of Irish Affairs, 1014–1690*, ed. W. M. Hennessy. 2 vols. (London: RS, 1871)

Ann. Clon. *The Annals of Clonmacnoise, Being Annals of Ireland from the Earliest Period to AD 1408, Translated into English, AD 1627 by Conell Mageoghagan*, ed. D. Murphy (Dublin: RSAI, 1896)

Ann. Tig. *The Annals of Tigernach*, ed. W. Stokes. Reprinted from *Revue celtique*, 16–18 (1895–6) in 2 vols. (Felinfach: Llanerch, 1993)

ANS *Anglo-Norman Studies*

AU *Annála Uladh, Annals of Ulster*, ed. W. M. Hennessy and B. Mac Carthy. 4 vols. (Dublin, 1887–1901; 2nd edn Dublin: Edmund Burke, 1998)

AU (Mac Airt) *The Annals of Ulster (to AD 1131), Part I, Text and Translation*, ed. and trans. S. Mac Airt and G. Mac Niocaill (Dublin: DIAS, 1983)

BAACT British Archaeological Association Conference Transactions

Barry *et al.* (eds.), *Colony and Frontier in Medieval Ireland* T. B. Barry, R. Frame and K. Simms (eds.), *Colony and Frontier in Medieval Ireland: Essays Presented to J. F. Lydon* (London: Hambledon Press, 1995)

Bartlett, *Making of Europe*   R. Bartlett, *The Making of Europe: Conquest, Colonization, and Cultural Change, 950–1350* (London: Penguin, 1993)

Bartlett and Mackay (eds.), *Medieval Frontier Societies*   R. Bartlett and A. Mackay (eds.), *Medieval Frontier Societies* (Oxford University Press, 1989)

Bede's Ecclesiastical History   *Bede's Ecclesiastical History of the English People*, ed. B. Colgrave and R. A. B. Mynors (Oxford University Press, 1969)

BHL   Bibliotheca Hagiographica Latina

BJRL   *Bulletin of the John Rylands Library*

BL   British Library

Book of Magauran   *The Book of Magauran. Leabhar Méig Shamhr.gháin*, ed. and trans. L. McKenna (Dublin: DIAS, 1947)

Bracken and Ó Riain-Raedel (eds.), *Ireland and Europe in the Twelfth Century*   D. Bracken and D. Ó Riain-Raedel (eds.), *Ireland and Europe in the Twelfth Century* (Dublin: Four Courts Press, 2006)

Bradley (ed.), *Settlement and Society in Medieval Ireland*   J. Bradley (ed.), *Settlement and Society in Medieval Ireland: Studies Presented to Francis Xavier Martin O.S.A.* (Kilkenny: Boethius Press, 1988)

Browne and Ó Clabaigh (eds.), *Soldiers of Christ*   M. Browne and C. Ó Clabaigh (eds.), *Soldiers of Christ: The Knights Templar and the Knights Hospitaller in Medieval Ireland* (Dublin: Four Courts Press, 2015)

Bryan, *Gerald FitzGerald*   D. Bryan, *Gerald FitzGerald, the Great Earl of Kildare, 1456–1513* (Dublin: Phoenix Publishing, 1933)

Caithréim Thoirdhealbhaigh   *Caithréim Thoirdhealbhaigh: The Triumphs of Turlough*, ed. and trans. S. H. O'Grady. 2 vols. (London: ITS, 1929)

Cal.   *Calendar of [the]*

Cal. Gormanston Reg.   *Calendar of the Gormanston Register*, ed. J. Mills and M. J. McEnery (Dublin: RSAI, 1916)

CARD   *Calendar of Ancient Records of Dublin*, ed. J. T. Gilbert *et al.* 19 vols. (Dublin: Joseph Dollead, 1889–1944)

Carew   *Calendar of the Carew Manuscripts Preserved in the Archiepiscopal Library at Lambeth, 1515–1574* [etc.]. 6 vols. (London: Public Record Office, 1867–73)

C. Chart. R.   *Calendar of the Charter Rolls Preserved in the Public Record Office, Henry III, A.D. 1226–1257* [etc.] (London: HMSO, 1903)

CCR   *Calendar of Close Rolls* (London: HMSO, 1892–)

CDF J. H. Round (ed.), *Calendar of Documents Preserved in France, Illustrative of the History of Great Britain and Ireland* (London: HMSO, 1899)

CDI, *[1171–1251]* [etc.] *Calendar of Documents Relating to Ireland [1171–1251]*, ed. H. S. Sweetman. 5 vols. (London: Longman, 1875–86)

CFR *Calendar of Fine Rolls* (London: HMSO, 1911–)

CGG *Cogadh Gaedhel re Gallaibh: The War of the Gaedhil with the Gaill, or the Invasions of Ireland by the Danes and Other Norsemen*, ed. and trans. J. H. Todd (London: RS, 1867)

Chartul. St Mary's, Dublin *Chartularies of St Mary's Abbey, Dublin … and Annals of Ireland, 1162–1370*, ed. J. T. Gilbert. 2 vols. (London: RS, 1884–6)

Chron. Scot. *Chronicum Scotorum: A Chronicle of Irish Affairs … to 1135, and Supplement … 1141–1150*, ed. W. M. Hennessy (London: RS, 1866)

CIH *Corpus Iuris Hibernici*, ed. D. A. Binchy (Dublin: DIAS, 1978)

CIRCLE A Calendar of Irish Chancery Letters, *c.*1244–1509 http://chancery.tcd.ie/

CJRI, *[1295–1303]* [etc.] *Calendar of the Justiciary Rolls of Ireland … [1295–1303]* [etc.]. 3 vols. (Dublin: HMSO and the Stationery Office, 1905–56)

Clarke and Johnson (eds.), *Vikings in Ireland and Beyond* H. B. Clarke and R. Johnson (eds.), *The Vikings in Ireland and Beyond: Before and After the Battle of Clontarf* (Dublin: Four Courts Press, 2015)

Clarke *et al.* (eds.), *Ireland and Scandinavia* H. B. Clarke, M. Ní Mhaonaigh and R. Ó Floinn (eds.), *Ireland and Scandinavia in the Early Viking Age* (Dublin: Four Courts Press, 1998)

Clarke *et al.* (eds.), *Surveying Ireland's Past* H. B. Clarke, J. Prunty and M. Hennessy (eds.), *Surveying Ireland's Past: Multidisciplinary Essays in Honour of Anngret Simms* (Dublin: Geography Publications, 2004)

Close Rolls *Close Rolls of the Reign of Henry III Preserved in the Public Record Office 1227–[1272]*. 14 vols. (London: HMSO, 1902–38).

Clyn *The Annals of Ireland by Friar John Clyn*, ed. B. Williams (Dublin: Four Courts Press, 2007)

COD *Calendar of Ormond Deeds*, ed. E. Curtis. 6 vols. (Dublin: IMC, 1932–43)

Connolly, *Medieval Record Sources* P. Connolly, *Medieval Record Sources* (Dublin: Four Courts Press, 2002)

CPI *Chartae, Privilegia et Immunitates* (London: Record Commissioners of Ireland, 1889)

CPL, 1198–1304 [etc.]   *Calendar of Entries in the Papal Registers Relating to Great Britain and Ireland. Papal Letters, vol. i,* A.D. *1198–1304,* ed. W. H. Bliss (London: HMSO, 1893)

CPR   Calendar of Patent Rolls (London: HMSO, 1891–)

CPRI   Calendar of Patent and Close Rolls of Chancery in Ireland for the Reigns of Henry VIII to Elizabeth I, and Charles I, ed. J. Morrin (Dublin: HMSO, 1861–3)

CR   Close Roll

Crooks (ed.), *Government, War and Society*   P. Crooks (ed.), *Government, War and Society in Medieval Ireland: Essays by Edmund Curtis, A. J. Otway-Ruthven and James Lydon* (Dublin: Four Courts Press, 2008)

Crown Surveys of Lands, 1540–41   Crown Surveys of Lands, 1540–41, with the Kildare Rental begun in 1518, ed. G. Mac Niocaill (Dublin: IMC, 1992)

CSPI   Calendar of the State Papers relating to Ireland, 1509–1573 [etc.]. 24 vols. (London: Longmans, Green, Reader & Dyer, 1860–1912)

Davies, *First English Empire*   R. R. Davies, *The First English Empire: Power and Identities in the British Isles 1093–1343* (Oxford University Press, 2000)

Deeds of the Normans   The Deeds of the Normans in Ireland. La Geste des Engleis en Yrlande, ed. E. Mullally (Dublin: Four Courts Press, 2002)

DIAS   Dublin Institute for Advanced Studies

Diceto   The Historical Works of Master Ralph de Diceto, ed. W. Stubbs. 2 vols. (London: RS, 1876)

Doran and Lyttleton (eds.), *Lordship in Medieval Ireland*   L. Doran and J. Lyttleton (eds.), *Lordship in Medieval Ireland: Image and Reality* (Dublin: Four Courts Press, 2007)

Dublin Guild Merchant Roll   The Dublin Guild Merchant Roll, c.1190–1265, ed. P. Connolly and G. Martin (Dublin: Dublin Corporation, 1992)

Duffy (ed.), *Princes, Prelates and Poets*   S. Duffy (ed.), *Princes, Prelates and Poets in Medieval Ireland: Essays in Honour of Katharine Simms* (Dublin: Four Courts Press, 2013)

Duffy and Foran (eds.), *English Isles*   S. Duffy and S. Foran (eds.), *The English Isles: Cultural Transmission and Political Conflict in Britain and Ireland, 1100–1500* (Dublin: Four Courts Press, 2013)

EETS   Early English Texts Society

EHD, i   *English Historical Documents I c.500–1042,* ed. D. Whitelock (London: Eyre and Spottiswoode, 1955)

EHD, iii   *English Historical Documents III 1189–1327*, ed. H. Rothwell (London: Eyre and Spottiswoode, 1975)

EHR   *English Historical Review*

Ellis, *Ireland in the Age of the Tudors*   S. G. Ellis, *Ireland in the Age of the Tudors, 1447–1603: English Expansion and the End of Gaelic Rule* (London and New York: Longman, 1998)

Expugnatio   Gerald of Wales, *Expugnatio Hibernica. The Conquest of Ireland*, ed. A. B. Scott and F. X. Martin (Dublin: RIA, 1978)

Flanagan, *Irish Society*   M. T. Flanagan, *Irish Society, Anglo-Norman Settlers, Angevin Kingship* (Oxford University Press, 1989)

Flanagan, *Transformation of the Irish Church*   M. T. Flanagan, *The Transformation of the Irish Church in the Twelfth Century* (Woodbridge: Boydell Press, 2010)

Foedera   *Foedera, Conventiones, Litterae, et Cujuscunque Generis Acta Publica, inter Reges Angliae et Alios Quosvis Imperatores, Reges, Pontifices, Principes, vel Communitates*, ed. T. Rymer. 4 vols. (London: Londini, 1816–25)

Frame, *English Lordship*   R. Frame, *English Lordship in Ireland, 1318–1361* (Oxford University Press, 1982)

Frame, *Political Development of the British Isles*   R. Frame, *The Political Development of the British Isles 1100–1400* (Oxford University Press, 1990)

Frame *Ireland and Britain*   R. Frame, *Ireland and Britain, 1170–1450* (London: Hambledon Press, 1998)

Frame, *Colonial Ireland*   R. Frame, *Colonial Ireland 1169–1369*, 2nd edn (Dublin: Four Courts Press, 2012)

Gir. Camb. Op.   *Giraldi Cambrensis Opera*, ed. J. S. Brewer, J. F. Dimock and G. F. Warner. 8 vols. (London: RS, 1861–91)

Gwynn and Hadcock, *Medieval Religious Houses: Ireland*   A. Gwynn and R. N. Hadcock, *Medieval Religious Houses: Ireland* (London: Longman, 1970)

Hall, *Women and the Church*   D. Hall, *Women and the Church in Medieval Ireland, c.1140–1540* (Dublin: Four Courts Press, 2003)

Handbook and Select Calendar of Sources for Medieval Ireland   *Handbook and Select Calendar of Sources for Medieval Ireland in the National Archives of the United Kingdom*, ed. P. Dryburgh and B. Smith (Dublin: Four Courts Press and TNA, 2005)

Haren and de Pontfarcy (eds.), *Medieval Pilgrimage to St Patrick's Purgatory*   M. Haren and Y. de Pontfarcy (eds.), *The Medieval Pilgrimage to St Patrick's*

Purgatory: Lough Derg and the European Tradition (Enniskillen: Clogher Historical Society, 1988)

Herbert, *Iona, Kells, and Derry*   M. Herbert, *Iona, Kells, and Derry: The History and Hagiography of the Monastic Familia of Columba* (Oxford University Press, 1988)

HMSO   His/Her Majesty's Stationery Office

Howden, *Chronica*   *Chronica Rogeri de Houedene*, ed. W. Stubbs. 4 vols. (London: RS, 1868–71)

Howden, *Gesta*   *Gesta Regis Henrici Secundi et Ricardi Primi*, ed. W. Stubbs. 2 vols. (London: RS, 1867)

HSJ   *Haskins Society Journal*

IEP   *Irish Exchequer Payments 1270–1446*, ed. P. Connolly (Dublin: IMC, 1998)

IESH   *Irish Economic and Social History*

IHS   *Irish Historical Studies*

IMC   Irish Manuscripts Commission

IPR 14 John   *The Irish Pipe Roll of 14 John, 1211–1212*, ed. O. Davies and D. B. Quinn, *Ulster Journal of Archaeology*, 4, supplement (Belfast, 1941)

ITS   Irish Texts Society

JMH   *Journal of Medieval History*

JRSAI   *Journal of the Royal Society of Antiquaries of Ireland*

Kenny, *Anglo-Irish and Gaelic Women*   G. Kenny, *Anglo-Irish and Gaelic Women in Ireland, c. 1170–1540* (Dublin: Four Courts Press, 2007)

Letters and Papers   *Letters and Papers Illustrative of the Reigns of Richard III and Henry VII*, ed. J. Gairdner. 2 vols. (London, 1861–3)

Letters Henry II   *The Letters and Charters of Henry II King of England (1154–1189)*, ed. N. Vincent *et al.* (Oxford University Press, 2016)

Lydon, *Lordship*   J. F. Lydon, *The Lordship of Ireland in the Middle Ages* (Dublin: Gill & Macmillan, 1972; new edn Dublin: Four Courts Press, 2003)

Lydon (ed.), *England and Ireland*   J. F. Lydon (ed.), *England and Ireland in the Later Middle Ages: Essays in Honour of Jocelyn Otway-Ruthven* (Blackrock: Irish Academic Press, 1981)

Lydon (ed.), *English in Medieval Ireland*   J. Lydon (ed.), *The English in Medieval Ireland* (Dublin: RIA, 1984)

Lydon (ed.), *Law and Disorder*   J. Lydon (ed.), *Law and Disorder in Thirteenth-Century Ireland: The Dublin Parliament of 1297* (Dublin: Four Courts Press, 1997)

MacCotter, *Medieval Ireland*   P. MacCotter, *Medieval Ireland: Territorial, Political and Economic Divisions* (Dublin: Four Courts Press, 2008)

Mac Niocaill and Wallace (eds.), *Keimelia*   G. Mac Niocaill and P. F. Wallace (eds.), *Keimelia: Studies in Medieval Archaeology and History in Memory of Tom Delaney* (Galway University Press, 1988)

Metrical Dindshenchas   The Metrical Dindshenchas, ed. and trans. E. Gwynn. 5 vols. Todd Lecture Series 8–12 (Dublin: RIA, 1903–55)

Misc. Ir. Annals   Miscellaneous Irish Annals (AD 1143–1437), ed. S. Ó hInnse (Dublin: DIAS, 1947)

Moss (ed.), *Art and Architecture of Ireland*   R. Moss (ed.), *Art and Architecture of Ireland. Volume 1. Medieval c.400–c.1600* (Dublin, London and New Haven: RIA and Yale University Press, 2014)

Moss *et al.* (eds.), *Art and Devotion in Late Medieval Ireland*   R. Moss, C. Ó Clabaigh and S. Ryan (eds.), *Art and Devotion in Late Medieval Ireland* (Dublin: Four Courts Press, 2006)

Murphy and Potterton, *Dublin Region in the Middle Ages*   M. Murphy and M. Potterton, *The Dublin Region in the Middle Ages: Settlement, Landscape and Economy* (Dublin: Four Courts Press, 2010)

Murray, *Enforcing the English Reformation in Ireland*   J. Murray, *Enforcing the English Reformation in Ireland: Clerical Resistance and Political Conflict in the Diocese of Dublin, 1534–1590* (Cambridge University Press, 2008)

NAI   National Archives of Ireland

NCMH   The New Cambridge Medieval History, ed. P. Fouracre *et al.* 7 vols. (Cambridge University Press, 1995–2005).

Newburgh, 'Chronica'   William of Newburgh, 'Chronica', in *Chronicles of the Reign of Stephen, Henry II and Richard I*, ed. R. Howlett. 4 vols. (London: RS, 1885–9)

NHI i   A New History of Ireland I: Prehistoric and Early Ireland, ed. D. Ó Cróinín (Oxford University Press, 2005)

NHI ii   A New History of Ireland II: Medieval Ireland, 1169–1534, ed. A. Cosgrove (Oxford University Press, 1987)

NHI iii   A New History of Ireland III: Early Modern Ireland, 1534–1691, ed. T. W. Moody, F. X. Martin and F. J. Byrne (Oxford University Press, 1976)

NHI ix *A New History of Ireland IX: Maps, Genealogies, Lists*, ed. T. W. Moody, F. X. Martin and F. J. Byrne (Oxford University Press, 1989)

Nicholls, *Gaelic and Gaelicized Ireland* K. W. Nicholls, *Gaelic and Gaelicized Ireland in the Later Middle Ages* (Dublin: Gill & Macmillan, 1972; new edn Lilliput Press, 2003)

NLI National Library of Ireland

Ó Clabaigh, *Friars in Ireland* C. Ó Clabaigh, *The Friars in Ireland, 1224–1540* (Dublin: Four Courts Press, 2012)

ODNB *Oxford Dictionary of National Biography*, ed. H. D. G. Matthew and B. Harrison. 60 vols. (Oxford University Press, 2004); online at www.oxforddnb.com/

O'Neill, *Irish Hand* T. O'Neill, *The Irish Hand: Scribes and their Manuscripts from the Earliest Times to the Seventeenth Century with an Exemplar of Scripts* (Mountrath: Dolmen Press, 1984)

O'Neill, *Merchants and Mariners* T. O'Neill, *Merchants and Mariners in Medieval Ireland* (Blackrock: Irish Academic Press, 1987)

Orpen, *Normans* G. H. Orpen, *Ireland under the Normans*. 4 vols. (Oxford University Press, 1912–20)

Otway-Ruthven, *History of Medieval Ireland* A. J. Otway-Ruthven, *A History of Medieval Ireland* (London: Thames and Hudson, 1968)

Paris, *CM* Matthew Paris, *Chronica Majora*, ed. H. R. Luard. 7 vols. (London: RS, 1872–83)

Parls. & Councils *Parliaments and Councils of Medieval Ireland*, i, ed. H. G. Richardson and G. O. Sayles (Dublin: IMC, 1947)

Patent Rolls *Patent Rolls of the Reign of Henry III 1216–1232*. 2 vols. (London: HMSO, 1901–3)

PKCI *Proceedings of the King's Council in Ireland, 1392–3*, ed. J. Graves (London: RS, 1887)

PL *Patrologia Latina*, ed. J.-P. Migne. 221 vols. (Paris, 1844–64)

Pontificia Hibernica *Pontificia Hibernica: Medieval Papal Chancery Documents Concerning Ireland, 640–1261*, ed. M. P. Sheehy. 2 vols. (Dublin: Gill & Sons, 1962)

PR Patent Roll

PR 16 Henry II (etc.) Pipe Roll(s) published by the Pipe Roll Society

PRIA   *Proceedings of the Royal Irish Academy*

PROME   *The Parliament Rolls of Medieval England, 1275–1504*, ed. C. Given-Wilson (gen. ed.) *et al.* 16 vols. (Woodbridge: Boydell Press, 2005)

PRONI   Public Record Office of Northern Ireland

PRS   Pipe Roll Society

Purcell *et al.* (eds.), *Clerics, Kings and Vikings*   E. Purcell, P. MacCotter, J. Nyhan and J. Sheehan (eds.), *Clerics, Kings and Vikings: Essays on Medieval Ireland in Honour of Donnchadh Ó Corráin* (Dublin: Four Courts Press, 2015)

Red Book of the Earls of Kildare   *The Red Book of the Earls of Kildare*, ed. G. Mac Niocaill (Dublin: IMC, 1964)

Reg.   *Register [of]*

Reg. Mey   *Registrum Johannis Mey: The Register of John Mey, Archbishop of Armagh, 1443–1456*, ed. W. G. H. Quigley and E. F. D. Roberts (Belfast: HMSO, 1972)

Reg. Nicholas Fleming   *The Register of Nicholas Fleming, Archbishop of Armagh 1404–1416*, ed. B. Smith (Dublin: IMC, 2003)

Reg. Octaviani   *Registrum Octaviani, Alias Liber Niger. The Register of Octavian de Palatio, Archbishop of Armagh 1478–1513*, ed. M. A. Sughi. 2 vols. (Dublin: IMC, 1999)

Reg. St Thomas   *The Register of the Abbey of St Thomas, Dublin*, ed. J. T. Gilbert (London: RS, 1889)

Reg. Swayne   *The Register of John Swayne, Archbishop of Armagh and Primate of Ireland, 1418–1439*, ed. D. A. Chart (Belfast: HMSO, 1935)

Reg. Sweteman   *The Register of Milo Sweteman, Archbishop of Armagh 1361–1380*, ed. B. Smith (Dublin: IMC, 1996)

Rep. DKI   *Reports of the Deputy Keeper of the Public Records of Ireland* (Dublin: HMSO, 1869–)

RHF   *Recueil des historiens des Gaules et de la France*, ed. M. Bouquet and others. 24 vols. in 25 (Paris: Imprimerie royale, 1738–1904)

RIA   Royal Irish Academy

Rot. Chart.   *Rotuli Chartarum in Turri Londinensi Asservati*, ed. T. D. Hardy (London: Record Commissioners, 1837)

Rot. Litt. Claus.   *Rotuli Litterarum Clausarum*, ed. T. D. Hardy. 2 vols. (London: Record Commissioners, 1833–44)

Rot. Litt. Pat.   *Rotuli Litterarum Patentium in Turri Londinensi Asservati, 1201–1216*, ed. T. D. Hardy (London: Record Commissioners, 1835)

RS   Rolls Series

RSAI   Royal Society of Antiquaries of Ireland

s.a.   *sub anno*

Sayles, *Affairs*   *Documents on the Affairs of Ireland before the King's Council*, ed. G. O. Sayles (Dublin: IMC, 1979)

Sheehan and Ó Corráin (eds.), *Viking Age in Ireland*   J. Sheehan and D. Ó Corráin (eds.), *The Viking Age in Ireland and the West: Proceedings of the Fifteenth Viking Congress* (Dublin: Four Courts Press, 2010)

Simms, *From Kings to Warlords*   K. Simms, *From Kings to Warlords: The Changing Political Structure of Gaelic Ireland in the Later Middle Ages* (Woodbridge: Boydell Press, 1987, repr: 2000).

Simms, *Medieval Gaelic Sources*   K. Simms, *Medieval Gaelic Sources* (Dublin: Four Courts Press, 2009)

Smith, *Crisis and Survival*   B. Smith, *Crisis and Survival in Late Medieval Ireland: The English of Louth and their Neighbours, 1330–1450* (Oxford University Press, 2013)

Smith (ed.), *Britain and Ireland*   B. Smith (ed.), *Britain and Ireland 900–1300: Insular Responses to Medieval European Change* (Cambridge University Press, 1999)

Smith (ed.), *Ireland and The English World*   B. Smith (ed.), *Ireland and the English World in the Late Middle Ages: Essays in Honour of Robin Frame* (Houndmills: Palgrave Macmillan, 2009)

Smyth (ed.), *Seanchas*   A. P. Smyth (ed.), *Seanchas: Studies in Early and Medieval Archaeology, History and Literature in Honour of Francis J. Byrne* (Dublin: Four Courts Press, 2000)

Song of Dermot   *The Song of Dermot and the Earl*, ed. G. H. Orpen (Oxford University Press, 1892)

SP, Henry VIII   *State Papers, Henry VIII.* 11 vols. (London: Record Commissioners, 1830–52)

Stat. Ire., 1–12 Edw. IV   *Statute Rolls of the Parliaments of Ireland, 1st to 12th Years of the Reign of King Edward IV*, ed. H. F. Berry (Dublin: HMSO, 1914)

Stat. Ire., 12–22 Edw. IV   *Statute Rolls of the Parliament of Ireland, 12th and 13th to the 21st and 22nd Years of the Reign of King Edward IV*, ed. J. F. Morrissey (Dublin: The Stationery Office, 1939)

Stat. Ire., John–Hen. V Statutes and Ordinances and Acts of the Parliament of Ireland, King John to Henry V, ed. H. F. Berry (Dublin: HMSO, 1907)

Stat. Ire., Hen. VI *Statute Rolls of the Parliament of Ireland: Reign of King Henry VI*, ed. H. F. Berry (Dublin: HMSO, 1910)

Stat. Ire. Ric. III–Hen. VIII *Statute Rolls of the Irish Parliament, Richard III–Henry VIII*, ed. P. Connolly (Dublin: Four Courts Press for NAI, 2002)

Statutes at Large, Ireland *The Statutes at Large Passed in the Parliaments Held in Ireland [...]*, ed. W. Ball *et al.* 13 vols. (Dublin: Boulter Grierson, 1765–1801)

Statutes of the Realm *Statutes of the Realm*, ed. A. Luders, T. E. Tomlins and J. Raithby. 11 vols. (London: Record Commissioners, 1810–28)

TCD Trinity College Dublin

TNA The National Archives

Topographia Giraldus Cambrensis, *The History and Topography of Ireland*, ed. J. J. O'Meara (Mountrath and Harmondsworth: Penguin, 1982)

TRHS *Transactions of the Royal Historical Society*

Walter Bower, *Scotichronicon* Walter Bower, *Scotichronicon*, gen. ed. D. E. R Watt. 9 vols. (Aberdeen University Press, 1987–98)

Watt, *Church and the Two Nations* J. A. Watt, *The Church and the Two Nations in Medieval Ireland* (Cambridge University Press, 1970)

Watts, *Making of Polities* J. Watts, *The Making of Polities: Europe 1300–1500* (Cambridge University Press, 2009)

General Introduction

The aims of this four-volume History of Ireland are quite straightforward. First, we seek to offer students, and the general reader, a detailed survey, based on the latest research, of the history of the island from early medieval times to the present. As with other Cambridge histories, a chronological approach, in the main, has been adopted, and there is a strong narrative spine to the four volumes. However, the periods covered in each volume are not the traditional ones and we hope that this may have the effect of forcing a re-evaluation of the familiar periodisation of Irish history and of the understanding it has tended to inspire. A single twist of the historical kaleidoscope can suggest – even reveal - new patterns, beginnings and endings. As well, among the one hundred or so chapters spread over the four volumes, there are many that adopt a reflective tone as well as strike a discursive note. There are also a number that tackle topics that have hitherto not found their way into the existing survey literature. Second, we have sought at all times to locate the history of Ireland in its broader context, whether European, Atlantic or, latterly, global. Ireland may be an island, but the people of the island for centuries have been dispersed throughout the world, with significant concentrations in certain countries, with the result that the history of Ireland and the history of the Irish people have never been coterminous. Lastly, the editors of the individual volumes – Brendan Smith, Jane Ohlmeyer, James Kelly and myself – have enlisted contributors who have, as well as a capacity for innovative historical research, demonstrated a talent for writing lucid prose. For history to have a social purpose – or indeed any point - it must be accessible, and in these volumes we have endeavoured to ensure that this is the case: readers will judge with what success.

Thomas Bartlett, MRIA,
General Editor, The Cambridge History of Ireland

MAP 1. Selected Locations Mentioned in Part I.

MAP 2. Selected Locations Mentioned in Part II.

MAP 3. Selected Locations Mentioned in Part III.

Ireland

MAP 4. Map of Ireland showing Modern County Boundaries.

Introduction

BRENDAN SMITH

NO attempt to identify a theme that unites the 950 years covered by this volume will be entirely satisfactory, but one that gives primacy to the nature of the evidence used by historians to develop their interpretations has some merit.[1] While written records comprise only part of the source material at our disposal from these centuries, they remain our most important point of entry into the past. The period stretching from the early seventh century to the middle of the sixteenth was distinctive in Irish history in its relationship to the word and, by association, the Word. Examples from Ireland of writing in Irish – in *ogam* inscriptions – and Latin – most famously St Patrick's *Confessio* – can be found from before 600, but it is from that date onwards that the manuscripts produced in the island's scriptoria survive in any quantity. The new technology of writing inspired in Ireland by the introduction of Christianity prevailed throughout Europe until challenged by the advent of printing in the late fifteenth century. In Ireland, the first printed book was published in Dublin in 1551 – the year after the date at which the coverage of this volume ends. That the publication concerned was *The Boke of Common Praier* not only signifies continuity in terms of the centrality of religion to the Irish story over the intervening centuries, but also marks a moment of historical change. *The Boke* sought to propagate an interpretation of religious thought and life that would be contested in Ireland for centuries to come. As had been the case at the time of the coming of Christianity to the island, a technological breakthrough in the sphere of writing was linked inextricably in Ireland to competition between religious and intellectual ideas.[2]

---

1 A version of this essay was delivered as a lecture at the Irish Conference of Medievalists, Maynooth University, on 30 June 2016.
2 For writing in Ireland at the outset of this period, see John Carey's chapter in this volume. For printing in Ireland see M. Pollard, *Dublin's Trade in Books, 1550–1800* (Oxford University Press, 1990).

Ireland in the period covered by this volume experienced Christianisation, invasion, foreign settlement, economic growth and contraction, the development of administrative and political institutions, educational and intellectual advance, prolonged periods of warfare that were often related to contested notions of national and ethnic identity, and religious upheaval and fracturing. To observe that in this its history mirrored that of much of the rest of Western Europe in the same era is to state the obvious, but at least prompts consideration of how Ireland has featured in the historiography of medieval Europe. In choosing to approach this topic with reference to major works published since the 1980s, issues of manageability are clearly to the fore. But such an approach also reflects a belief that the decision of the peoples of the Republic of Ireland and the United Kingdom in 1973 to join what is now the European Union, and the end of the Cold War in 1989–90, encouraged important new thinking about both the recent and more distant past of the West.[3] In particular, these developments have prompted reconsideration of the nature of frontiers, and the relationship between core and peripheral regions, that have obvious relevance to the Irish situation.

Ireland is well represented in the coverage of the centuries between 600 and 900 contained in major edited series on the European Middle Ages published over the course of the last three decades, such as the *New Cambridge Medieval History* (7 volumes, 1995–2005), *The Cambridge Illustrated History of the Middle Ages* (3 volumes, 1986–97), and the single-volume *Oxford Illustrated History of Medieval Europe* (1988).[4] In these enterprises Irish evidence and examples have been frequently and imaginatively invoked, with particular attention being paid to Ireland's contribution to the development of monasticism and learning in the West, the nature of kingship on the island, and the impact on its people and culture of viking raids and settlements. Chris Wickham's *Framing the Early Middle Ages: Europe and the Mediterranean, 400–800*, published in 2005, is perhaps the best recent example of the extensive and successful integration of Irish material into a single-authored history of early medieval Europe. While Wickham is clear that Irish developments were to a large extent *sui generis*, he does not allow

---

3 On 23 June 2016 the UK voted to leave the European Union.
4 *NCMH*; R. Fossier (ed.), *The Cambridge Illustrated History of the Middle Ages*. 3 vols. (Cambridge University Press, 1986–97); G. Holmes (ed.), *The Oxford Illustrated History of Medieval Europe* (Oxford University Press, 1988). Earlier in the century the early volumes of *The Cambridge Medieval History* devoted considerable space to developments in Ireland: J. B. Bury (gen. ed.), *The Cambridge Medieval History*. 8 vols. (Cambridge University Press, 1911–36).

that to be used as a reason to exclude the island from his analysis of wider European developments.[5]

The vikings' integration of Ireland into the new trading zone they were establishing throughout Europe from the 800s onwards was the first step in a process – significantly enhanced and reshaped by English conquest – by which the links between the island and the rest of the Continent were greatly extended in depth and range. This drawing of Ireland into the European mainstream, however, is not particularly well reflected in the historiography of the later medieval centuries in the West. There is no mention of Ireland in *The Oxford Illustrated History of Medieval Europe* after 900, while the second and third volumes of *The Cambridge Illustrated History of the Middle Ages*, which examine the period between 950 and 1520, contain between them only one Irish reference.[6] Ireland, significantly, was not unique in virtually disappearing from sight after the ninth century in such historiographical ventures. The same could be said of Wales, Scotland, most of Scandinavia and other outlying parts of the Continent. In a view of the medieval West in which it was accepted as self-evident that all important developments occurred exclusively at the centre – France, England, Germany and Italy – more distant lands could for the most part simply be ignored.

A stake was put through the heart of this approach in 1993 with the publication of Robert Bartlett's *Making of Europe*: *Conquest, Colonization and Cultural Change, 950–1350*. Bartlett's thesis was that the integration of the kingdoms and nations on the edges of Europe into ways of thought and patterns of behaviour that prevailed in the core region of the West was not some side-show, but was instead the defining feature of European history at a key, expansionist, moment and signalled nothing less than 'the Europeanization of Europe'.[7] The importance of frontiers in an interpretation that recognised Western Europe as a region with a small core and an extensive periphery was obvious, and already in 1989 Bartlett had co-edited a volume of essays entitled *Medieval Frontier Societies* that fostered new thinking on this topic. Bartlett's own contribution to that volume, which compared the colonisation of Ireland and the eastern German lands in the decades around 1200, indicated the potential breadth of this new approach.[8]

---

5 C. Wickham, *Framing the Early Middle Ages: Europe and the Mediterranean, 400–800* (Oxford University Press, 2005), 5, 50–3, 354–64.

6 R. Fossier, 'Clouds Gather in the West', in Fossier (ed.), *Cambridge Illustrated History of the Middle Ages, 1250–1520* (Cambridge University Press, 1986), 19.

7 Bartlett, *Making of Europe*, especially ch. 11.

8 Bartlett and Mackay (eds.), *Medieval Frontier Societies*, especially the chapter by Bartlett, 'Colonial Aristocracies of the High Middle Ages', at 23–48. The frontier concept was revisited in D. Abulafia and N. Berend (eds.), *Medieval Frontiers: Concepts and Practices*

Medieval Frontier Societies also contained an important essay by Rees Davies that considered Ireland and Wales together in the context of their marcher experiences and characteristics.[9] This drew upon Davies's pioneering work in the area of medieval 'British Isles' history. In 1986 he had convened a conference at Gregynog in Wales on this theme that resulted in the publication two years later of a significant essay collection, *The British Isles 1100–1500: Comparisons, Contrasts and Connections*.[10] This was followed in 1990 by his ground-breaking *Domination and Conquest: The Experience of Ireland, Scotland and Wales 1100–1300*, which comprised the Wiles lectures delivered at Queen's University, Belfast, two years earlier.[11] The year 1990 also saw the publication of Robin Frame's *The Political Development of the British Isles 1100–1400*, which remains unsurpassed as a sustained exploration of its subject. Frame had already contributed essays to both *Medieval Frontier Societies* and *The British Isles 1100 1500*, and a collection of his essays published in 1998 as *Ireland and Britain 1170–1450* contained these and many other valuable chapters.[12]

It was in the context of these recent and continuing historiographical developments that Ireland was considered in the volumes of *The New Cambridge Medieval History* dealing with the period from the early eleventh to the late fifteenth centuries, published between 1998 and 2004.[13] Volume 4 part 2, published in 2004, which spanned the period from *c*.1024 to *c*.1198, contained a chapter on 'Scotland, Wales, and Ireland in the Twelfth Century' by Geoffrey Barrow – who had been a contributor to *Medieval Frontier Societies* – while volume 5, published in 1999, which covered the period from *c*.1198 to *c*.1300, included a chapter by Robert Bartlett on 'The Celtic Lands of the British Isles'.[14] Volume 6, which was published in 2000 and dealt with the period

(Aldershot: Ashgate, 2002). Irish concerns featured in the essay by B. Smith, 'The Frontiers of Church Reform in the British Isles, 1170–1230', at 239–53.

9 R. R. Davies, 'Frontier Arrangements in Fragmented Societies: Ireland and Wales', in Bartlett and Mackay (eds.), *Medieval Frontier Societies*, 77–100.

10 R. R. Davies (ed.), *The British Isles 1100–1500: Comparisons, Contrasts and Connections* (Edinburgh: John Donald, 1988).

11 R. R. Davies, *Domination and Conquest: The Experience of Ireland, Scotland and Wales 1100–1300* (Cambridge University Press, 1990).

12 Frame, *Political Development of the British Isles*; Frame, *Ireland and Britain*.

13 The relevant volumes of *The Cambridge Medieval History*, published between 1926 and 1936, had found space for Irish affairs. D. M. Stenton and F. M. Powicke included references to Ireland in their chapters on political developments in England in the seventy years after 1150, while G. H. Orpen contributed two chapters devoted solely to Irish history covering the entire period from the coming of Christianity to the late fifteenth century. Stenton, 'England: Henry II'; Powicke, 'England: Richard I and John'; Orpen, 'Ireland to 1315'; Orpen, 'Ireland 1315–*c*.1485'.

14 G. W. S. Barrow, 'Scotland, Wales and Ireland', in *NCMH*, iv, Part 2, 581–610; R. Bartlett, 'The Celtic Lands of the British Isles', in *NCMH*, v, 809–27.

from *c.*1300 to *c.*1415, contained a multi-authored chapter on 'The British Isles', which included a section on 'Ireland' by Robin Frame, while volume 7, published in 1998, covering the period from *c.*1415 to *c.*1500, included a multi-authored chapter on 'The Celtic World' to which Art Cosgrove contributed a section on 'Ireland'.[15] In short, to a greater or lesser extent, consideration of Ireland after 1100 in these volumes was integrated into analyses of larger historical arenas which shared the experience of 'Europeanisation' as mediated, for the most part, through the expansion of English power.

Historians of medieval Ireland were, in general, content to engage with this approach, not least because it did not preclude scholarship which continued to focus more particularly on the island itself. Seán Duffy, whose PhD thesis was examined by Rees Davies and whose research has deepened understanding of political links throughout the Irish Sea region, published *Ireland in the Middle Ages* in 1996; while the second edition of Robin Frame's *Colonial Ireland, 1169–1369*, first published in 1981, appeared in 2012.[16] For these historians there was no contradiction in accepting that many political, social, economic and cultural developments in late medieval Ireland were best understood when explored in wider contexts, while at the same time recognising that 'Ireland' remained a valid subject of historical investigation.

The 'British Isles' approach, however, was not without its critics, with some Scottish historians in particular arguing that it downplayed important developments that were especially relevant to the northern kingdom.[17] How to accommodate the role of Gascony within a 'British Isles' or 'first English empire' interpretation was an issue that also generated critical comment. As part of Aquitaine, it had come to King Henry II through marriage before he conquered Ireland, and it was not lost to France until 1453, long after the final conquest of Wales and attempted conquest of Scotland. Was it possible to give appropriate recognition to the importance of Gascony in contemporary English politics in an interpretation that was British Isles focused?[18] To a

---

15 R. Frame, 'Ireland', in *NCMH*, vi, 375–87; A. Cosgrove, 'Ireland', in *NCMH*, vii, 496–513.

16 S. Duffy, *Ireland in the Middle Ages* (Houndmills and Dublin: Macmillan, 1997); Frame, *Colonial Ireland*.

17 M. Hammond, 'Domination and Conquest?: The Scottish Experience in the Twelfth and Thirteenth Centuries', in Duffy and Foran (eds.), *English Isles*, 68–83; D. Broun, 'A Second England?: Scotland and the Monarchy of Britain in *The First English Empire*', in Duffy and Foran (eds.), *English Isles*, 84–102.

18 Davies, *First English Empire*; A. C. Ruddick, 'Gascony and the Limits of Medieval British Isles History', in Smith (ed.), *Ireland and the English World*, 68–88. See Robin Frame's observations on this issue in his 'Kingdoms and Dominions at Peace and War', in R. Griffiths (ed.), *The Fourteenth and Fifteenth Centuries* (Oxford University Press, 2003), 149–80.

significant extent, Robin Frame had already recognised and sought to address this concern in his *Political Development of the British Isles*. Whereas Rees Davies in *Domination and Conquest* had concentrated on how the Scottish, Welsh and Irish responded to English expansionism, Frame put development in the political society of England at the heart of his analysis. This required the ambitions of the English crown in France to be considered alongside its actions in the British Isles in any discussion of the spread of English power.

Frame thus anticipated a very recent historiographical development that has the potential to address the perceived deficiencies of the British Isles approach while still urging consideration of Ireland and its neighbours in wider contexts. The 'Plantagenet Empire' model takes as its chronological start- and end-dates the Treaty of Paris of 1259 on the one hand, and the expulsion of the English from France – with the exception of Calais – in 1453 on the other.[19] In so doing, it incorporates the British Isles perspective and at the same time extends it in both geographical and chronological terms. Although still at an early stage of development, the Plantagenet Empire approach can be viewed as contributing to larger and long-lasting debates about state-formation in European history. Rees Davies had implored historians of the medieval British Isles to shift their gaze from the state and its institutions, arguing that should they do so 'other solidarities and collectivities could come more clearly into focus'. Some of these, he added, 'seemed to have as great, if not occasionally greater, depth and historical resilience than did the nation state'. But Davies himself had written of 'the national shutters coming down' within the British Isles by the end of the thirteenth century, and many historians concerned with the period after 1300 have shown little inclination to question long-established, nation-based approaches to their subjects.[20]

The Plantagenet Empire model offers an alternative to national perspectives and any approach to the history of this European region in the later Middle Ages that gives pride of place to the supposed rise of the nation-state. It was undoubtedly the case that after 1300 some of the key experiences shared by England, Scotland, Wales and Ireland in the twelfth and thirteenth centuries – transnational magnate landholding and the migration of English-speaking

---

19 P. Crooks, D. Green and W. M. Ormrod (eds.), *The Plantagenet Empire, 1259–1453* (Donington: Shaun Tyas, 2016), especially the opening essay by the editors, 'The Plantagenets and Empire in the Later Middle Ages'.

20 The quotations from Davies are at 'The Peoples of Britain and Ireland 1100–1400. I. Identities', *TRHS*, 6th ser., no. 4 (1994), 1, and 'In Praise of British History', in Davies (ed.), *The British Isles 1100–1500*, 17. For a discussion of the historiography, B. Smith, 'The British Isles in the Late Middle Ages: Shaping the Regions', in Smith (ed.), *Ireland and the English World*, 7–19.

peasants, for instance – declined in significance. But, as Michael Brown argues in his 2013 survey, *Disunited Kingdoms: Peoples and Politics in the British Isles, 1280–1460*, viewing the history of the fourteenth and fifteenth centuries through a British Isles prism remains valuable. 'Looking for the state' in this part of north-west Europe in the late Middle Ages is, he suggests, a misdirection of energies which would be better spent analysing political arrangements and configurations that transcended regnal borders both within and beyond the archipelago. For example, in this period Gaelic Ireland deepened its already close ties with Gaelic Scotland, while the reach of the English government within the island was diminished, though never eradicated. These developments in turn reflected the extent to which the resources of both the Scottish and English kingdoms were concentrated on supporting or defeating the French.[21] Nation-based approaches were as likely to miss or underestimate the origins and consequences of such developments in the context of the fifteenth century as they had in the context of the thirteenth.

If Ireland refuses to sit comfortably in an analysis that identifies state-formation as the key historical development in the late medieval British Isles, within a broader European setting its apparent awkwardness can be seen as anything but untypical. 'When we turn to the fourteenth and fifteenth centuries', John Watts observes in his *The Making of Polities: Europe 1300–1500*, published in 2009, 'we enter a period with no meaningful political and constitutional narrative.' In a sentence that could have been written with Ireland in mind, he continues: 'Narratives of state growth … tend to neglect the frequent and dramatic collapse of central authority in this period … to understate the complexity of the world in which institutions operated, and to ignore the less state-like power structures that also held sway across Europe.'[22] Operating in the shadow of the huge and impressive edifice that is the historiography of medieval England, it is all too easy for historians of Ireland to lose sight of the extent to which English developments in this period were unusual within

---

21 M. Brown, *Disunited Kingdoms: Peoples and Politics in the British Isles 1280–1460* (Harlow: Pearson, 2013), esp. 5–6, 169–53; J. Watts, 'Looking for the State in Later Medieval England', in P. Coss and M. Keen (eds.), *Heraldry, Pageantry and Social Display in Medieval England* (Woodbridge: Boydell Press, 2002), 243–68.

22 Watts, *Making of Polities*, 1–42. Quotations at 1–2. Such an approach does not necessarily stand at odds with Steven Ellis's recent employment of a 'European state formation model' in assessing the worth of attempting to locate a point of transition from the medieval to the early modern in the British Isles: S. Ellis, 'From Medieval to Early Modern: The British Isles in Transition?', in R. Hutton (ed.), *Medieval or Early Modern: The Value of a Traditional Historical Division* (Cambridge: Cambridge Scholars Publishing, 2015), 10–28. For a critique of Ellis's approach see R. Hutton, 'The British Isles in Transition: A View from the Other Side', in Hutton (ed.), *Medieval or Early Modern*, 29–41.

the wider Western European context. Including the Irish experience as fully in interpretations of the later as of the earlier medieval centuries has the potential to both complicate and enrich our understanding of the British and European, as well as the Irish, past.

In planning this volume several considerations prevailed. The first of these was to present the reader with an account of Ireland's medieval past that was informative, fresh and accessible. At some points a political narrative appeared more necessary than others in seeking to achieve this end. Judgements of this type were of course made with reference to the nature of the current literature on the subject. It is, for instance, not much more than ten years since the publication of *A New History of Ireland I: Prehistoric and Early Ireland*, edited by Dáibhí Ó Cróinín.[23] The chapters in that impressive volume concerned with political developments between 400 and 1170, by Ó Cróinín, Francis John Byrne and Marie Therese Flanagan, are particularly strong, and it seemed an inefficient use of limited space to cover the same ground again in what is offered here.[24] On the other hand, scholarship on the socio-economic and cultural character of early medieval Ireland, the nature and impact of viking intervention, and the influence from *c*.1000 of new ideas related to the role of the Church and the nature of kingship, had advanced considerably even since 2005, and justified extensive discussion in the present volume. This was particularly the case because of the opportunity thus provided to include analysis of the wealth of archaeological evidence that had become available to scholars since the turn of the millennium. Government initiatives from that time to develop the Republic's transport infrastructure (and in particular its road-building schemes) included archaeological surveys of the areas affected. Managed by the Discovery Programme, which had been established by *An Taoiseach*, Charles Haughey, in 1991, and which now operates under the auspices of a statutory body, the Heritage Council, this process has yielded remarkable quantities of new information relevant to early Irish history.[25]

---

23 *NHI* i.
24 D. Ó Cróinín, 'Ireland, 400–800', in *NHI* i, 182–234; F. J. Byrne, 'The Viking Age', in *NHI* i, 609–34; F. J. Byrne, 'Ireland before the Battle of Clontarf', in *NHI* i, 852–9; F. J. Byrne, 'Ireland and her Neighbours, *c*.1014–*c*.1072', in *NHI* i, 862–98; M. T. Flanagan, 'High-Kings with Opposition', in *NHI* i, 899–933.
25 www.discoveryprogramme.ie/; www.heritagecouncil.ie/. The ongoing project 'Monastic Ireland', coordinated by the Discovery Project, is of particular importance: www.monastic.ie/. E. Bhreathnach, 'Review: Medieval Irish History at the End of the Twentieth Century: Unfinished Work', *IHS*, 32 (2000), 260–71.

The Heritage Council has also helped fund major research initiatives that have led to the public dissemination in print and online of a range of source materials relevant to the study of medieval Ireland. Among the most notable of these projects has been CELT: Corpus of Electronic Texts, hosted by University College Cork, and ISOS: Irish Script on Screen, which is hosted and for the most part funded by the Dublin Institute for Advanced Studies.[26] The study of medieval Irish history has also been boosted since the late 1990s by the release of new streams of state funding in the Republic for research into the Arts and Humanities, coordinated by the Irish Research Council for the Humanities and Social Sciences, and since 2012 by its successor, the Irish Research Council. As well as supporting the work of numerous doctoral and post-doctoral students, this body has also sponsored important research projects, such as the Material Culture of Irish Mendicant Orders project, hosted by the Mícheál Ó Cléirigh Institute at University College Dublin, and the Calendar of Irish Chancery Letters project, hosted by Trinity College Dublin.[27]

As the nature of the citations for the outcomes generated by these projects suggests, the study of medieval Irish history has benefited significantly from recent advances in computer science. By happy coincidence, the rise of Digital Humanities – the application of new information technologies to answer historical (and other) questions – has coincided with the growth in funding for historical research in Ireland.[28] This new mode of scholarship seems likely to continue to facilitate the development of exciting projects with a medieval focus. At the same time as web-based research has flourished, there has also been a noticeable increase in the quantity of scholarship on aspects of Ireland in the Middle Ages appearing in print. This may be attributed for the most part to the publication priorities of Four Courts Press.

In this context of significant developments over the past quarter of a century in both the historiography of the subject, and in our ability to gain access to an increased range of source materials relating to it, a fresh account of Ireland's medieval past seems timely. Our understanding of the period after *c.*1150 in particular stands to benefit as a result. *A New History of Ireland II: Medieval Ireland 1169–1534*, was published in 1987, almost twenty years before

26 www.ucc.ie/celt/; www.isos.dias.ie/.

27 www.ucd.ie/mocleirigh/; https://chancery.tcd.ie/. The UK funding agencies, AHRC and ESRC, also supported projects relating to late medieval Ireland: https://discover. ukdataservice.ac.uk/catalogue?sn=5570; www.researchcatalogue.esrc.ac.uk/grants/ R000239389/read.

28 www.cdh.ucla.edu/about/. I am grateful to my colleague at Bristol, Dr James Freeman, for his advice on this matter.

volume I, and while it contains innumerable insights that have stood the test of time, its appearance preceded some of the important developments just discussed.[29] The editor of the *New History of Ireland II*, Art Cosgrove, defended the hibernocentric approach of that volume in a convincing manner, and it is not the intention of the present enterprise to place Ireland anywhere but at the centre of our concerns.[30] It is in the belief that understanding of the Irish past is enriched by viewing it in wider contexts that I have taken the opportunity at certain points to invite historians whose primary area of scholarship is not Ireland to consider the Irish experience from an 'external' perspective. Appreciation of Ireland's place in the history of Western art before 1000, of viking expansion, and of Angevin and later English empire-building, for example, can be heightened when viewed from without.

I am grateful to the contributors concerned, who have been brave enough to venture beyond their usual scholarly domains, but in truth each chapter was conceived, and each contributor approached, with a view to stretching boundaries of expertise and moving beyond the familiar. This explains why traditional chronological turning points are challenged throughout the volume. Was the arrival of the English in 1169–70, for instance, as profound a moment of historical change as the death of Ragnall, king of Man, in 1229? With the latter died a species of politics that had come into being in the Irish Sea region long before 1066, and which continued to thrive for more than half a century after the events of 1170. In the same manner, to choose *c.*1460 and *c.*1550 as the start- and end-dates for chapters that analyse political and religious developments in Ireland as the period under review draws to a close is to beg reconsideration not only of the basis upon which we identify a change from the medieval to the early modern, but also of the very worth of attempting such an identification in the first place.

Gaelic society, the economy, and the Church, are obvious topics to consider in a volume such as this, but the goal has been not simply to present to the reader new information that has become available in recent decades, but also new ways of interpreting this information. Finally, while constitutional and institutional history are well represented in many accounts of late medieval Ireland, it is in this volume that medieval Irish political theory makes its historiographical debut.

Consensus should make the historian uneasy, and the reader will find many examples in this volume of differing interpretations of the same event or

---

29 *NHI* ii.
30 A. Cosgrove, 'The Writing of Medieval Irish History', *IHS*, 27 (1990), 97–111.

development. In this regard it will be clear that I have not sought to impose consistency in the choice of group-names used by contributors to describe the various inhabitants of the island in the later Middle Ages. Relatively unproblematic in this context are the descendants of those who possessed the island before 1169: there seems little difficulty in referring to them as 'Irish' or 'Gaelic Irish'. What to call those who invaded and settled in Ireland in the late twelfth century is less straightforward. 'Anglo-Norman' is clearly deemed satisfactory by most writers on the subject, though this was not a term ever used by newcomers of diverse geographical origins who from the outset referred to themselves simply as 'English'. This was still the term used by their descendants three hundred years later, though for reasons to do with a perceived diminution in contact with England and distancing from English customs on their part in the intervening centuries, some contributors prefer the designation 'Anglo-Irish'. Since the labels chosen in this matter reflect more fundamental views on the part of contributors about crucial issues to do with identity, I have preferred to allow a variety of practice than to insist on any one approach.

How to present the names of individuals or families mentioned in the text is also complicated. My guide has been the practice adopted in the *Dictionary of Irish Biography*, published under the auspices of the Royal Irish Academy by Cambridge University Press in 2009.[31] The surnames of Gaelic Irish individuals up to *c.*1200 are given in their Irish form, and thereafter in the English version. The surnames of Gaelic poets, annalists, scribes and clergy are generally given in Irish. Christian names are given in the Gaelic form. Turning to the settlers who arrived after 1170 and their descendants, and occasional visitors from England, I have not attempted to impose uniformity in the use of 'de' as part of surnames. Individuals belonging to families which did not use a settled surname until late in the period, such as the FitzGeralds, are identified by 'fitz' as the sons of their fathers.

This Introduction should be read in conjunction with Robin Frame's chapter at the end of this volume. This develops some of the themes touched upon here, and explores many others. I am very grateful to Professor Frame for his careful reading of each chapter, and for spotting many of my editorial lapses along the way. I would also like to thank my fellow editors, Professor Jane Ohlmeyer, Professor James Kelly and Professor Tom Bartlett, for their constant support and in particular for their suggestions as to how this Introduction might be improved.

---

31 J. McGuire and J. Quinn (eds.), *Dictionary of Irish Biography*, 9 vols. (Cambridge University Press and RIA, 2009), i, pp. xxv–xxvi.

PART I

*

CHRISTIANITY, INVASION AND CONQUEST: 600–1200

1

Communities and their Landscapes

EDEL BHREATHNACH

A Bé Find, in rega lim,
i tír n-ingnad hi fil rind?
Is barr sobairche folt and;
is dath snechtai corp co ind.

(Bé Find, will you go with me to a strange land where there is music? Hair there is like the primrose flower; on the smooth body there is the colour of snow.)

THE poem *A Bé Find, in rega lim?* 'O fair lady will you go with me?', extracted from the early Irish saga 'The Wooing of Étaín', is a moving expression of all that a man viewed as idyllic: a fair lady (*Bé Find*), beautiful hair and a healthy body, a fruitful and picturesque land, choice mead and wine, meat and milk, no sin or waywardness, and ultimately no death. The poet loves Ireland, but yearns for somewhere better: 'although the plain of Fál [Ireland] is fair to gaze upon, it is a wilderness after one has known the Great Plain; though you think the ale of the island of Fál good, the ale of the Great Land is stronger'. However charming the words of the poet and the images he conjures up, behind his poem lay the harsh reality of life; a reality that his audience tried to forget while momentarily enjoying a vision of the otherworld.[1]

What was that reality? The Irish lived on an island, mainly a temperate landmass although at times hit by powerful storms and periods of harsh cold winters or summer droughts. The sea and its main rivers offered the key points of access into inland communication networks, and coastal, island and riverine communities were the first to engage with traders, raiders and visitors, some of whom landed speaking a different language, offering novel goods or

---

1 *Early Irish Lyrics: Eighth to Twelfth Century*, ed. and trans. G. Murphy (Oxford University Press, 1956; repr. 1998), 104–7; J. T. Koch and J. Carey, *The Celtic Heroic Age; Literary Sources for Ancient Celtic Europe and Early Ireland and Wales* (Malden, MA: Celtic Studies Publications, 1995), 149.

believing in a different god. These same communities and their kings, saints and warriors ventured abroad and in their journeys were lost at sea, returned with foreign wives or with new ideas. Although an island, Ireland was not an isolated place at the edge of the earth and the Irish, or at least the ecclesiastical and literate classes, were acutely aware of the wider world and their place in it. The evidence for understanding actual living conditions and for visualising the landscape in early medieval Ireland is considerable, and once drawn together from various disciplines – archaeology, art history, history, language and literature, and the sciences – presents a fairly detailed picture of everyday life. This inter-disciplinary approach has been relatively slow in influencing commentaries on medieval Ireland as a more traditional emphasis on structures of authority – both secular and ecclesiastical – and the apparent hierarchical nature of society has dominated the discourse. In the past two decades, however, the exponential increase in archaeological evidence resulting from infrastructural and other development programmes, and the inclination of scholars of all disciplines to engage in theoretical debates, has moved the subject into a new arena, which this chapter is designed to reflect.[2]

The People of Ireland and the Wider World

As outlined by John Carey in the following chapter, the Irish literate class engaged throughout this period in developing an elaborate origin legend for the people of the island, drawing at once on their own traditional histories and on biblical and classical sources. This historiographical activity culminated in the eleventh century in the composite treatise known as *Lebor Gabála Érenn* 'The Book of the Invasions of Ireland'. In reality, the population on the island consisted of waves of people who had settled there since the Mesolithic era (*c*.8000 BC) and whose origins varied.[3] From Late Antiquity to the coming of the vikings, the island's main and most obvious interaction was with Britain. As might be expected, evidence for this interaction is primarily concentrated on the east coast, where personal names, dynastic names, origin legends, saints' names, military alliances and archaeology combine to suggest that the Irish Sea from Scotland to Cornwall was a busy highway. The Dumnonii, who occupied parts of Cornwall and Scotland, also lent their name to Inber Domnainn, now Malahide Bay, County Dublin, and appear

---

2 R. Schot, C. Newman and E. Bhreathnach (eds.), *Landscapes of Cult and Kingship* (Dublin: Four Courts Press, 2011).

3 J. P. Mallory, *The Origins of the Irish* (London and New York: Thames and Hudson, 2013).

to have been related to Fir Domnainn, a people who settled in north-west Mayo. To take another example, the name of the Llŷn peninsula in north-west Wales may derive from the name of the dominant people of the east and south-east regions of Ireland, the Laigin. This might suggest that parts of the west coast of Britain were ruled from time to time by Irish kings. The origin legend of the same Laigin centres on Labraid Loingsech, ultimately a deity and their eponymous ancestor, and a seventh-century poem containing a summary of Labraid's adventures sets out the scope of his ambitions. He campaigned in north-western Scotland as far as the Orkneys and even further: 'He fettered Gaulish hostages as far as the five peaks of the Alps; scores of fierce lords, of armoured legions, go into hiding.'[4]

This tale underlines the importance of seafaring to an island people but it also demonstrates two further recurring motifs: the successful hero conquering lands beyond Ireland, and the strong bonds that tied many Irish communities to various parts of Britain. Niall Noígiallach (Niall of the Nine Hostages), the eponymous ancestor of the dominant northern and midland dynasties, the Uí Néill, is depicted in later tales as conquering Britain as far as the English Channel (Muir nIcht) and even to the Alps in Roman military style.[5] None of this, of course, is true, but the tale hints at the Irish view of the world and the limits within which they operated. As to the connections with Britain, archaeology and art history confirm the existence of such connections. For example, it has been suggested that the distribution of fourth/fifth-century AD brooches and pins in Ireland and Britain, where there is a marked clustering in the lower Severn valley and in the northern half of the modern province of Leinster, may reflect the presence of Britons in eastern Ireland and the adoption of Romano-British dress styles at this time.[6] Following a universal pattern, women were the likely conduits of such material cultural transmissions as marriage, and military alliances were often concluded between dynasties on both sides of the Irish Sea. A study of early dynastic marriages to the late eighth century, some fictional, others historic and all based on the evidence of the text known as the *Banshenchas* ('Lore of Women'), shows that a fair

---

4 A. L. F. Rivet and C. Smith, *The Place-Names of Roman Britain* (London: Batsford, 1979; repr. 1981), 342–4; T. M. Charles-Edwards (ed.), *After Rome* (Oxford University Press, 2003), 32; Koch and Carey, *Celtic Heroic Age*, 45 §28.
5 K. Meyer (ed.), 'A Medley of Irish Texts 13: *Aided Néill Noígiallaig*', ed. K. Meyer, *Archiv für celtische Lexikographie*, 3 (1907), 323–4.
6 R. Ó Floinn, 'Patrons and Politics: Art, Artefact and Methodology', in M. Redknap *et al.* (eds.), *Pattern and Purpose in Insular Art: Proceedings of the Fourth International Conference on Insular Art held at the National Museum and Gallery, Cardiff 3–6 September 1998* (Oxford University Press, 2001), 6–8.

number of Ireland's royal women originated in Britain. As might be expected, the greatest concentration of these women was along the north-east and east coast. Historical military alliances between Irish kings and the Britons of the kingdoms of Strathclyde, Rheged and Wales are recorded in the seventh and eighth centuries. In 702, for example, Írgalach son of Conaing, king of the east midland dynasty of Síl nÁedo Sláine ('the descendant of Áed Sláine'), was killed by Britons on Inis Meic Nessáin (Ireland's Eye off the north county Dublin coast). His father-in-law, Cellach Cualann, king of Leinster, may have had a hand in the death of Írgalach, as he retained British mercenaries in his military retinue.[7] Frankish and Saxon connections with Ireland can be detected mainly in ecclesiastical associations. Bede's comments on the time of the plague of 664 are frequently quoted by scholars to demonstrate the extent of traffic across the Irish Sea:

> Many of the nobility, and of the lower ranks of the English nation, were there at that time, who, in the days of the Bishops Finan and Colman, forsaking their native island, retired thither, either for the sake of Divine studies, or of a more continent life; and some of them presently devoted themselves to a monastic life, others chose rather to apply themselves to study, going about from one master's cell to another. The Scots willingly received them all, and took care to supply them with food, as also to furnish them with books to read, and their teaching, gratis.[8]

Political connections are evident most especially in the relations between Bernician kings, among them Oswald, king of Northumbria (d. 642), and the Irish dynasty of Dál Riata, whose kingdoms straddled between the north-east of Ireland and the west of Scotland. Crucial to this relationship was the island monastery of Iona, whose monks educated these kings and had a considerable influence in Northumbria until the late seventh century.[9]

These inter-island connections, and others further afield, also find strong echoes in artistic influences and, to a lesser extent, in material culture. There is a general view that some of the best-known metal objects of the eighth century from Ireland, including the Ardagh Chalice and the so-called 'Tara' brooch, incorporate not only Anglo-Saxon motifs but also techniques

---

7 A. Connon, 'Prosopography II: A Prosopography of the Early Queens of Tara', in E. Bhreathnach (ed.), *The Kingship and Landscape of Tara* (Dublin: The Discovery Programme, 2005), 338–57 (Tables 1–9); *AU*, i, 151–3, 157.

8 *Bede's Ecclesiastical History*, ch. xxvii.

9 H. Moisl, 'The Bernician Royal Dynasty and the Irish in the Seventh Century', *Peritia*, 2 (1983), 103–26; H. Moisl, 'A Frankish Aristocrat at the Battle of Mag Roth', in M. Richter and J.-M. Picard (eds.), *Ogma: Essays in Celtic Studies in Honour of Proinséas Ní Chatháin* (Dublin: Four Courts Press, 2002), 36–47.

from contemporary Anglo-Saxon jewellery such as chip-carving and gold filigree inlays. And yet few imports from the Anglo-Saxon and Merovingian world have been discovered in Ireland. Among these few objects are two small glass Merovingian flasks, dated to the mid- to late seventh century, from the lake settlement (crannóg) at Moynagh Lough, County Meath, and two seventh-century Frankish gold coins found at Trim, County Meath, and Portlaoise, County Laois, respectively. The gold coins are significant in that they were minted on the Loire at Beaufray and Le Mans, possibly travelling along the same route as the glass vessels and pottery from western Gaul that reached Ireland. It is notable that they were discovered in a region well outside their normal area of distribution. Like the glass vessels, they may have been gifts or may have been destined for re-use for gilding or gold filigree.[10]

Apart from the conversion of Ireland to Christianity, a process that heralded considerable economic, intellectual and social changes, the other great upheaval to be wrought upon the island was the coming of the vikings in the late eighth century. Christianity had brought a new language and literacy and a new belief system to Ireland but had done so peacefully, and the Irish rarely had to endure hostility from outsiders. Indeed such was the infrequency of external attacks that much is made in the literature of an Anglo-Saxon raid on the east coast kingdom of Brega in 684. The arrival of the vikings on Irish shores must have been traumatic for many communities. The fear inspired by the raiders' disregard for Christianity is evident in vernacular ecclesiastical literature, such as the prayer surviving in the ninth-century Karlsruhe Bede *di thólu æchtrann et námat et geinte et fochide* 'against a flood of foreigners and foes and heathens and tribulations'. The newcomers appreciated only the financial value of the most sacred of church possessions, including the shrines and relics of their saints. Walahfrid Strabo (d. 849), abbot of Reichenau, recounted the death of Blathmac of Iona (d. 825) at the hands of the vikings for refusing to reveal the hiding place of the shrine of Columba (Colum Cille), Iona's founder (Illustration 1). The destruction of shrines and relics had reverberations throughout a neighbouring community, since these places and objects were often the medium through which ordinary people related most fervently with their church. While the military balance between the Irish and the vikings was not as unequal as portrayed in the past, it took time for

---

10 R. Ó Floinn, 'The Anglo-Saxon Connection: Irish Metalwork, AD 400–800', in J. Graham-Campbell and M. Ryan (eds.), *Anglo-Saxon/Irish Relations before the Vikings*. Proceedings of the British Academy 157 (Oxford University Press, 2009), 234–6.

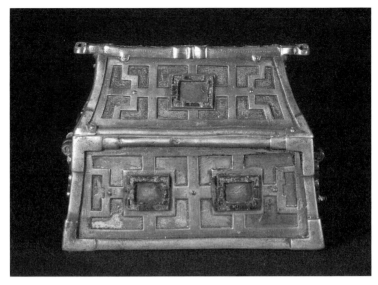

1. Ranvaiks casket shrine. © The National Museum of Denmark.

the Irish to master the new weapons, such as axes, that their attackers used against them. Once mastered, the axe became the classic Irish weapon of the medieval period.[11]

Within Ireland, communities were connected by a perceived or genuine common ancestry, by their mutual subjection to a king or kings, and by economic and trading links. One of the most powerful expressions of the construction of a common ancestry can be found in the literature of the Déssi 'the vassal tribes' or the *aithechthúatha* 'rent-paying peoples' of Ireland. Eoin MacNeill, in a seminal article on early Irish population groups, provided a comprehensive list of the peoples of pre-Norman Ireland that amounted to hundreds of names, some of them clearly ancient. He attempted to classify them by name formation (plural, collective and sept names) and on that basis to construct a chronology. Among the Déssi, for example, are people whose collective names end with -*r(a)ige* (< Celtic suffix –*rígion*).[12] There are two

11 M. Ní Mhaonaigh, 'Friend and Foe: Vikings in Ninth- and Tenth-Century Irish Literature', in Clarke *et al.* (eds.), *Ireland and Scandinavia*, 384–7; A. Halpin, 'Weapons and Warfare in Viking-Age Ireland', in Sheehan and Ó Corráin (eds.), *Viking Age in Ireland*, 124–35.

12 E. MacNeill, 'Early Irish Population-Groups: Their Nomenclature, Classification, and Chronology', *PRIA*, 29 C (1911), 59–109, esp. 67–9.

noteworthy aspects to some of these names. First, they are often associated with particular occupations, as in the case of the Semonrige 'people of the rivets' who inhabited the copper-mining region of the Waterford coast, or the Cerdraige 'the craft people' from another copper-mining region on the Beara Peninsula in west Cork. A second notable feature of these people was their dispersed geographical distribution throughout the island: the Gregraige (who may have had some involvement in rearing or herding horses), the Calraige and the Ciarraige (from which the name of County Kerry derives) were ubiquitous.

It is difficult to discern if those identified as belonging to such population groups actually realised that they either were associated through a common craft or were somehow related to people in another part of the country. What does survive is the existence of a collective sense of identity forged by traditional historians (*senchaid*) in the literature of the early medieval period. This is most forcefully expressed in the eighth-century text known as 'The Expulsion of the Déssi', which tells of the suppression of these peoples by the prehistoric kings of Tara.[13] This text may have been compiled in response to a genuine conquest of subject peoples by greater dynasties who were consolidating their territories and their grip on provincial kingships. Not that these people were completely annihilated. During the late ninth and early tenth century, the Dál Cais, a subject people whose territory straddled the Shannon region around Limerick and Killaloe, County Clare, rose from relative obscurity to produce Brian Bórama [Boru] (d. 1014), one of the most forceful kings of his era and the first of his dynasty to hold the kingship of Ireland.[14]

Affiliation to a dynasty, whether by claim of blood, by subjection or by fiction, echoes through the large corpus of surviving pre-Norman genealogies and law-tracts. The kin-group (*fine*) was the key social and economic unit in society and was normally composed of the male descendants of the same great-grandfather.[15] Women were tied to their own kin until they became part of their husband's kin, and if unmarried, widowed or cast aside for some

---

13 K. Meyer, 'The Expulsion of the Déssi', *Y Cymmrodor*, 14 (1901), 101–35; K. Meyer, 'The Expulsion of the Déssi', *Ériu*, 3 (1907), 135–42.

14 N. Ó Muraíle, 'Some Early Connacht Population-Groups', in Smyth (ed.), *Seanchas*, 161–77; E. Bhreathnach, 'Abbesses, Minor Dynasties and Kings *in clericatu*: Perspectives of Ireland, 700–850', in M. O. Brown and C. A. Farr (eds.), *Mercia: An Anglo-Saxon Kingdom in Europe* (London and New York: Leicester University Press, 2001), 119–21.

15 F. Kelly, *A Guide to Early Irish Law*, Early Irish Law Series 3 (Dublin: DIAS, 1988); T. M. Charles-Edwards, *Early Irish and Welsh Kinship* (Oxford University Press, 1993).

reason, they returned to their own kin. A maternal kin group maintained an interest in the children of their womenfolk and were compensated if they were killed. They could also participate in a blood-feud if not compensated by the culprits. The killing of kings by kinsmen is a frequent occurrence recorded in the early Irish annals, as is the process whereby such killings were avenged. In a typical entry, the Annals of Ulster record that in 963 Éicnech son of Dálach, king of Airgialla [mid-Ulster], and his son Dub Dara, were killed by his brother Murchad son of Dálach. The chronicle then comments that Murchad was promptly killed in the same month. This type of endemic violence, either within a kin-group or between neighbouring kin-groups, can be detected in the trauma evident from skeletons of the period. For example, the skeleton of an adolescent male from a familial cemetery at Faughart, County Louth, shows evidence of extreme violence, possibly sustained in battle, as the severe trauma to his body suggests that he had defended himself from attack.[16] Despite the desperate condition of his body, he seems to have been brought back to his kin's cemetery and given a proper burial. Given the oft-highlighted *Lex Innocentium*, the law instigated by Adomnán, ninth abbot of Iona (d. 704), to protect non-combatants such as clerics, children and women in battle, the archaeological record indicates that these people were far from safe from violence. A woman buried in Parknahown, County Laois, suffered thirteen sharp-force blows to her throat that caused her death, most likely the result of some form of domestic violence or of an attack on her settlement.[17]

A sense of affiliation could be constructed, mainly by the learned classes for their noble patrons, by linking dynasties to one common ancestor. This was the case with many of the dominant royal dynasties who found common cause through shadowy ancestors, some of whom were originally deities and others possibly prehistoric (or pseudo-historic) kings. Among the most prominent of these ancestors were Niall Noígiallach progenitor of the midland and northern Uí Néill dynasties, Eógan Mór and Conall Corc progenitors of the southern Eóganachta dynasties, and Conn Cétchathach progenitor of the

---

16 L. Buckley and C. McConway, 'Early Medieval Settlement and Burial Ground at Faughart Lower, Co. Louth', in C. Corlett and M. Potterton (eds.), *Death and Burial in Early Medieval Ireland in the Light of Recent Archaeological Excavations* (Bray: Wordwell, 2010), 49–59. See also www.mappingdeathdb.ie (Faughart).

17 D. Keating, 'An Analysis of the Human Skeletal Remains from Parknahown 5, Co. Laois (015/060)'. Unpublished report prepared for Archaeology Consultancy Services Ltd, 2008.

midland and western Connachta dynasties.[18] In turn, the obsession of the learned classes with fitting the Irish and their nobility into a biblical chronological framework generated an extensive corpus of origin legends, regnal poems and secular genealogies from the seventh century. As dynasties declined or rose to prominence, these texts were refreshed to reflect the new order but they did not erase the stories of older dynasties completely. Hence, many of these texts are like an archaeological stratigraphy consisting of layers of evidence. One of the most skilful insertions of a dynasty's right to a kingship by creating an affiliation with existing dynasties was that of Brian Bórama's dynasty of Dál Cais. Despite being outsiders, they wove their right to the kingship of Cashel (Munster) into traditional histories and genealogies so that when it came to writing the biography of Brian Bórama in the twelfth-century text *Cogad Gaedil re Gallaib* ('The war of the Gaedil with the Gaill'), Brian's great-grandson Muirchertach Ua Briain (d. 1119) could claim:

> There were then governing and ruling this tribe [Dál Cais] two stout, able, valiant pillars, two fierce, lacerating, magnificent heroes … the most eminent of the west of Europe, viz., Mathgamhain and Brian, the two sons of Cennedigh son of Lorcan, son of Lachtna, son of Corc [etc.] … son of Cas, son of Ailell Olaim, son of Mogh Nuadhat who divided Erinn with Conn of the hundred battles. This was one of the two houses that sustained the rule and sovereignty [*flaithes*] of Erinn, from the time of Eremon, son of Miledh, and Ebher, his brother, and from the beginning of the world.[19]

What was the reality that lay behind the propaganda of kinship and clientship, two social edifices that were so essential to this world? One way of engaging with the reality of early medieval Ireland is to draw together the evidence of the large canon of early medieval Irish laws with archaeological evidence. As illustrated recently by Teresa Bolger in an assessment of the patterns emerging from large-scale excavations of the past two decades, scholars are confronted with very complex and large fragments of relict landscapes. It is clear that these landscapes did not consist simply of ringforts of various sizes with their integrated enclosures and field systems at close proximity, or of large royal sites with their surrounding ceremonial landscapes often crowded with prehistoric monuments. Relict landscapes that have been exposed have revealed settlement enclosures that are atypical to the standard ringfort, more extensive field systems designed to organise the landscape, familial settlements with

---

18 F. J. Byrne, *Irish Kings and High-Kings* (London: Batsford, 1973; repr. Dublin: Four Courts Press, 2001, 2004); B. Jaski, *Early Irish Kingship and Succession* (Dublin: Four Courts Press, 2000).
19 *CGG*, 57–9.

adjacent cemeteries, and spaces for metallurgy, butchery and cereal processing. Ditches, pits, cisterns and evidence of fencing have been identified and
many of these settlements and associated features have a chronological horizon dating from the late sixth to the eleventh century.[20]

Rather than associating this busy landscape with the laws describing the
gradation of society such as the classic law on status *Críth Gablach*, Bolger
points to the subset of land laws such as those dealing with conducting water
through the landscape (*Coibnes Uisci Thairidne*), the law on bee-keeping
(*Bechbretha*) and the law on neighbourhood (*Bretha Comaithchesa*) as more
appropriate to interpreting the archaeological evidence now known to us.[21]
Strange as it may seem, the *Bechbretha*, a seventh-century law-tract that details
the obligations of owners of beehives and the compensations or penalties
due to the bees' trespassing into another's land or causing injury to others, at
times offers a delightful insight into the vagaries of rural life. It is clear that
swarms of bees were tracked and that this activity had to be regulated: if
a man found a stray swarm on another's green, one quarter of the honey
produced was taken by the finder and three-quarters by the owner of the
green in which the swarm was found. The definition of the 'lawful' green, the
faithche téchtae or area immediately around a settlement, according to Irish
law was 'as far as the sound of a bell or the crowing of a cock reaches'. Other
parts of the landscape covered by the law included a great forest (*ruud már*),
inaccessible country (*écmacht*), unshared land or commonage (*dírainn*). And
of course, bees could sting either their owners, those tracking them or just
an innocent passerby:

> Among the complete immunities in bee-judgements according to Irish law
> is the man on whom they have rushed when robbing them, moving them,
> seizing them [or] looking at them over their hives at the time when they are
> swarming.

> It is wrong for them, however, should they attack anyone going past them on
> his way who is doing them no harm or illegality.

---

20 M. Stout, *The Irish Ringfort* (Dublin: Four Courts Press, 1997); T. Bolger, 'Status,
   Inheritance and Land Tenure: Some Thoughts on Early Medieval Settlement in Light
   of Recent Archaeological Excavations', in C. Corlett and M. Potterton (eds.), *Settlement
   in Early Medieval Ireland in Light of Recent Archaeological Excavations* (Bray: Wordwell,
   2011), 1–10.
21 *Crith Gablach*, ed. D. A. Binchy, Mediaeval and Modern Irish Series 11 (Dublin: DIAS,
   1941); 'Coibnes Uisci Thairidne', ed. D. A. Binchy, *Ériu*, 17 (1955), 55–85; *Bechbretha: An
   Old Irish Law-Tract on Bee-Keeping*, ed. T. M. Charles-Edwards and F. Kelly. Early Irish
   Law Series 1 (Dublin: DIAS, 1983); *CIH*, i, 64.6–79.13; 191.1–205.21; Bolger, 'Status,
   Inheritance and Land Tenure', 6–8.

For this is an injury which entails his sufficiency of honey for the man who is stung there, with an oath from him that he did not kill the bee which stung him ...[22]

At least a painful bee-sting, as long as one survived it, guaranteed you a honey-comb!

Mruigrecht or land law as detailed in the law on neighbourhood (*Bretha Comaithchesa*) is a mine of information on the organisation of the farm settlement and the farmyard, outhouses, the garden, paths and pavements, gates and stiles, and a myriad of walls and fences. The complexity and layering of this early medieval landscape is best illustrated by examining particular relict landscapes. The crannóg (lake settlement) at Moynagh Lough, County Meath, for example, was a high-status residence – either of a king or of a noble craftsman – and was set in the centre of one such landscape. Close by to the immediate east at Nobber was an early church, to the west on high ground above the lake settlement was a cluster of eight ringforts or farmstead settlements while a further cluster of three ringforts was located on high ground to the south. A horizontal mill was located at the north-eastern tip of the lake. While all these farmsteads were not necessarily contemporary, it is likely that, as the excavator John Bradley surmised, several of these sites could have been dependencies of the central crannóg serving as farms of this dominant kin-group and as supply and preparation centres.[23]

An early medieval landscape built within an already crowded prehistoric landscape was revealed by excavations conducted at Glebe and Laughanstown in south County Dublin. The modern townlands are located where the foothills of the Dublin Mountains sweep into the floodplains of two local rivers, close to the coast. The Neolithic period is represented by a wedge tomb and the various phases of the Bronze Age by burials, including a cordoned urn burial, a cairn and an enclosure. Four fields were excavated and they revealed field ditches and cereal-drying kilns with associated structures of the sixth and seventh centuries and a ringfort complex with ditches defining a number of annexes dating to two centuries later (*c.*670–870). The excavators built a profile of life within the ringfort at Glebe: iron domestic and farm implements and objects (e.g. a knife, copper-alloy rings) were manufactured on site; a greater proportion of shellfish was in the diet than normal; seaweed was used as fertiliser; a spindle-whorl indicated the craft of spinning wool;

22 *Bechbretha*, 67–9 §§27–9, 82–3 §46, §48.
23 F. Kelly, *Early Irish Farming* (Dublin: DIAS, 1997), 360–8; J. Bradley, 'An Early Medieval Crannog at Moynagh Lough, Co. Meath', in Corlett and Potterton (eds.), *Settlement in Early Medieval Ireland*, 33 (Fig. 2.2).

and a small number of glass beads provided ephemeral evidence for personal adornment. Evidence for cereal processing was noticeable and small quantities of barley, oats and wheat were found. As with metal-working and butchery, cereal processing was a common activity in such settlements, and this might be expected given that *coirm Cualann* ('the ale of Cualu', Cualu being the kingdom in which Glebe and Laughaunstown were located) was regarded as a prized possession of the provincial kings of Leinster.[24]

While cattle dominated the animal bone assemblage at Glebe as elsewhere, there was a greater proportion of sheep and pigs than usual at the south Dublin site. This may have been due to the local terrain and environment. The Dublin Mountains provided suitable grazing for sheep and local woodlands were suitable for pannage. The cattle were butchered, skinned and dismembered on site and according to the analysis, the meat diet of the inhabitants would have included everything from offal to fillets of beef. A simple, although rare, expression of this community's literacy and Christianity turned up in the form of four animal bones that were inscribed with symbols and one word. One was inscribed with four backward S-motifs, which may symbolise a cross with expanded arms, and another, more significantly, was incised with several arcs and with the word DEO and a Chi-Rho. Cathy Swift has represented these small etchings on bone as possibly 'the practice attempts of a single pupil – his homework, as it were –' who was being taught literacy by a local priest attached to Tully or Rathmichael, the two main churches in the vicinity of Glebe. The life of the community living in this region was undoubtedly disturbed in the tenth century by Norse settlers who built long houses within an enclosure close to an existing cemetery nearby in the modern townland of Cherrywood. With the Scandinavians came a new material culture with new house architecture and a coin-based economy.[25]

Travel and Communication

Consideration of the communication networks that crossed Ireland is prompted by the information contained in early medieval tales such as *Scéla Mucce Meic Dathó* ('The Tidings of Mac Dathó's Pig'). This concludes with a

---

24 M. Seaver, 'Interchange: Excavations in an Early Medieval Landscape at Glebe and Laughanstown, Co. Dublin', in Corlett and Potterton (eds.), *Settlement in Early Medieval Ireland*, 261–87; Byrne, *Irish Kings*, 152–3, 161.

25 Seaver, 'Interchange', 284, 286–7; J. Ó Néill, 'Excavation of Pre-Norman Structures on the Site of an Enclosed Early Christian Cemetery at Cherrywood, County Dublin', in S. Duffy (ed.), *Medieval Dublin VII* (Dublin: Four Courts Press, 2006), 66–88.

chariot chase through modern County Kildare, providing details of one well-used route in the south-east of the island:

> Their flight turned southwards, over Bellaghmoon, past Reerin, over Áth Midbine in Maistiu, past Drum Criach which to-day is called Kildare, past Rathangan into Feighcullen to the Ford of Mac Lugna, past the hill of the two plains over Cairpre's Bridge. At the Ford of the Dog's Head in Farbill the dog's head fell from the chariot.[26]

This journey, which would have taken the charioteer over hills, through passes, woods and bogs, is typical of that described in many similar tales. Whether accurate or not, Ireland was represented in medieval literature, and in particular in the ninth-century tale *Airne Fíngein* (Fíngen's Vigil'), as being served by five main routeways which were said to have radiated from Tara.[27] These were:

Slige ('Road') Midluachra northwards to Emain Macha (Navan Fort, County
    Armagh)
Slige Cualann southwards to Dublin and beyond
Slige Asail north-westwards to Lough Owel near Mullingar, County
    Westmeath
Slige Dála south-westwards to Osraige (modern County Kilkenny)
Slige Mór ('The Great Road') which ran from east to west passing Uisnech
    (County Westmeath) and crossing the river Shannon

While it is unlikely that all these roads radiated from Tara – their most likely meeting-point was Dublin – place name and archaeological evidence supports the genuine existence of such major routeways. Located overlooking the monastic town of Kells, County Meath, is the Hill of Lloyd, easily identified today by the eighteenth-century inland lighthouse on its summit. The hill was known as Mullach Aite ('The Hill of Aite') and archaeological remote sensing surveys have identified evidence for extensive enclosures delineating its summit, possibly dating to the Late Bronze or Iron Age. The defence of this hill was presumably related to the fact that an important roadway passed nearby – probably the Slige Midluachra – and that it was a border-crossing into the significant kingdom of Brega in which Tara was located. Close by, to the north of the Hill of Lloyd is the church site of Castlekeeran, County Meath,

---

26 *Scéla Mucce Meic Dathó*, ed. R. Thurneysen, Mediaeval and Modern Irish Series 6 (Dublin: DIAS, 1935; repr. 1969), 19 §20; translation http://adminstaff.vassar.edu/sttaylor/MacDatho/

27 *Airne Fíngein*, ed. J. Vendryes, Mediaeval and Modern Irish Series 15 (Dublin: DIAS, 1953), 9–10 §VI; 44 (notes).

which was also known as Belach Dúin ('Road of the Fort').[28] References to Belach Dúin confirm that this was a boundary along a roadway. For example, there is a record of Cernach son of Flann, steward (*móer*) of Armagh, who ruled from Belach Dúin to the sea and from the river Boyne to Annagassan, County Louth. On one of his military campaigns through the northern half of Ireland, Brian Bórama travelled with his army in 1006 from Cenél nEógain (in mid-Ulster) and at Lugnasad (Lammas) reached Belach Dúin. Given the proximity of the monastery of Kells to the Hill of Lloyd and Belach Dúin, and that the place name Cenannas (anglicised to Kells) probably signifies a royal caput, it is no coincidence that the major Columban foundation was established there *c*.804. This territory had been a battleground in the late seventh/ early eighth centuries for local dynasties during fierce internecine struggles, and the aim of granting it to the church may have been to counteract its role as a borderland battleground.[29] A similar landscape existed around Freestone Hill, County Kilkenny, known in the literature as Belach Gabráin, a strategic pass and the site of a Bronze Age hillfort and a later cult shrine, with the Slige Dála probably passing along through a gap in the hills towards Munster.[30]

Archaeological evidence for paths and routeways (often designated in Ireland as toghers from Irish *tóchar* 'a way through a bog or wetland') is most commonly found in bogs and other wetland regions. The most spectacular of these is the Iron Age (*c*.148 BC) network of bog roads (over 100 toghers) discovered at Corlea, County Longford, which crossed the surrounding wet landscape. They were mainly made of woven hurdles heaped on brushwood or the larger trackways made of oakwood planks.[31] No early medieval toghers match the scale of the Corlea Trackway, but of the significant numbers that have been discovered some, such as the linear plank trackway and toghers unearthed at Castletown Bog, Castlearmstrong, County Offaly, have been dated to the late seventh century AD. This communications network seems to have coincided with the foundation of the monastery of Lemanaghan and may have linked this settlement with the greater monastery of Clonmacnoise, County Offaly.[32] The existence of river crossings and bridges can also be surmised from place name elements, *áth* 'ford' being the

28 See www.ucc.ie/locus/: New Historical Dictionary of Irish Place-Names.

29 *AU*, i, 289, 443, 445; *Chron. Scot., s.a.* 1006; Herbert, *Iona, Kells, and Derry*, 68–70.

30 R. Ó Floinn, 'Freestone Hill, Co. Kilkenny: A Reassessment', in Smyth (ed.), *Seanchas*, 12–29; C. Ó Lochlainn, 'Roadways in Ancient Ireland', in J. Ryan (ed.), *Féilsgribhinn Eoin Mhic Néill* (Dublin: Three Candles, 1940), 465–74.

31 B. Raftery, *Trackway Excavations in Mountdillon Bogs, Co. Longford, 1985–1991* (Dublin: Crannóg Publication, 1996).

32 www.excavations.ie (Lemanaghan).

most widespread element. Áth Cliath ('the ford of hurdles'), the alternative name for Dublin (*dublinn* 'black pool'), was a vital crossing between north and south over the river Liffey mentioned in Adomnán's seventh-century life of Columba (*ad vadum clied*).[33] The monastery of Clonmacnoise was located adjacent to the Slige Mór and the Esker Riada, a system of glacial ridges that crosses over the island between Dublin and Galway. The monastery's location served as a key crossing-point over the river Shannon, a function confirmed by the discovery in the river of a substantial wooden bridge which has been dated to 804. Control of such a crossing contributed to the dominant position of Clonmacnoise in the midlands and on the Shannon, but it also – along with the monastery's economic wealth – attracted the attention of competing provincial kings who realised its potential to enhance their status on the national stage. As a result, Clonmacnoise had to deal with the extremes of being endowed with lands, churches and valuables and being the location of royal burials at the same time as being the constant target of attacks by royal rivals.[34]

During the underwater exploration of the Clonmacnoise bridge, eleven dug-out canoes were found lying on the riverbed. Such a discovery draws attention to the other main form of communication in Ireland besides horse, cart and foot, that of boats and canoes. The skill and function of early medieval logboats is evident from a remarkable discovery at the bottom of Lough Corrib, County Galway. A finely crafted six-metre-long vessel, which would have easily navigated the lake, was propelled by four rowers. Dating to the eleventh century, the boat contained a slab of red sandstone, two iron spearheads, three battleaxes and an iron axe and apart from the settings for four rowers there was a fifth seat for another passenger.[35] This is probably the type of boat (*noe cúicses* 'a five-benched small boat') mentioned in the ninth-century saga *Togail Bruidne Da Derga* ('The Destruction of Da Derga's Hostel'). A large split in its hull caused the logboat to sink. It may have hit a rock in the lake or the cargo of red sandstone may have cut through the hull during a bout of bad weather. One wonders if the slab of sandstone was destined for a monastic island settlement on the lake such as Inchagoill – an island littered with early ecclesiastical remains – and was being transported there by a king, abbot

33 *Adomnán's Life of Columba*, ed. and trans. A. O. Anderson and M. O. Anderson (Edinburgh: Nelson, 1961; rev. by M. O. Anderson, 1991), 332: II 4.

34 A. O'Sullivan and D. Boland, *The Clonmacnoise Bridge*. Heritage Ireland guide no. 11 (Bray: Wordwell, 2000); A. Kehnel, *Clonmacnois – the Church and Lands of St. Ciarán: Change and Continuity in an Irish Monastic Foundation (6th to 16th century)* (Münster: Lit., 1995).

35 K. Brady, 'Secrets of the Lake: The Lough Corrib Longboats', *Archaeology Ireland*, 110 (2014), 34–8.

or more likely a master craftsman and his crew to fashion into a grave slab or something as mundane as a saddle quern.[36] The military aspect of lacustrine and riverine transport is evident from the annals, and the appearance of viking fleets, and the assembly of their own fleets by Irish kings, further enhanced its importance. An example of pre-viking activity is that recorded in the Annals of Ulster, where the midlands people known as Delbna were defeated on Lough Ree on the Shannon 'with thirty boats, and the crew of only one escaped'. An incident on Lough Corrib in 1027 demonstrates how kings must have used logboats as part of their military tactics: Muiredach Ua Flaithbertaig besieged Cathal, son of Ruaidrí, king of West Connacht, on Inishcraff and divided his kingdom.[37]

Although areas of the west of Ireland were probably sparsely populated, there were many pockets of fertile land even in the seemingly most barren landscapes which could support communities. The Burren in County Clare is a primary example of such a landscape. The extensive limestone plateau of Tullycommon/Glasgeivnagh Hill in the south-eastern part of the Burren was particularly rich for winter grazing. Over twenty cashels or stone enclosures have been recorded on the plateau, among them the spectacular stone forts of Cashlaungarr, Cahercommaun and Caherconnell. Cashlaungarr and Cahercommaun forts are located strategically on the plateau overlooking a fertile gorge and on the basis of a re-assessment of excavations undertaken by the Third Harvard Archaeological Expedition to Ireland led by Hugh O'Neill Hencken in 1934, it has been demonstrated that the latter was occupied intermittently from the fifth/sixth century to the tenth century, with the main occupation occurring in the ninth century. This was the likely caput of a kingdom, possibly that of a branch of the powerful Uí Fidgeinti, who ruled a territory from west Limerick to the Aran Islands, or their clients the Corcu Modruad, who were the dominant local kings.[38] Apart from the extent and defensive characteristics of its fortification, Cahercommaun yielded considerable evidence of economic activity and especially an exceptionally large number of spindle-whorls. This phenomenon suggests that its inhabitants – and particularly the women – were

---

36 P. Gosling, *Archaeological Inventory of County Galway. Vol. 1: West Galway* (Dublin: The Stationery Office, 1993), 96: nos. 548–50.

37 *AU*, i, 221; *AI*, 195.

38 M. Comber and G. Hull, 'Excavations at Caherconnell Cashel, the Burren, Co. Clare: Implications for Cashel Chronology and Gaelic Settlement', *PRIA*, 110 C (2010); C. Cotter, 'Cahercommaun Fort, Co. Clare: A Reassessment of its Cultural Context', *Discovery Programme Reports*, 5 (1999), 41–95, esp. 80–2 and 83–91 (contribution by E. Bhreathnach).

involved in wool processing, and even in intensive weaving of garments at some stage. According to an early Irish text, *Ceart ríg Caisil ó críchaib*, which lists the various tributes due to the provincial king of Munster from his client kingdoms and which in origin may date to the ninth century, the Corcu Modruad were expected to supply three hundred cloaks to their lord. Cloaks could be made of leather but more likely were woollen, and it may be that Cahercommaun was at the heart of the supply chain. Over five hundred whetstones were also discovered on the site along with a wide range of domestic and iron agricultural implements suggesting that this was possibly to do with the production or distribution of common objects such as iron knives, awls and slotted and pointed tools that may have been used for weaving.[39]

A site at Lowpark near Charlestown in north-eastern County Mayo provides us with a comparative and contemporary landscape from the west. This site was not visible prior to the building of a road bypass, and when excavated revealed the remains of an industrial landscape. Four iron-working areas were uncovered which spanned a period from 560 to 970. These were the remains of iron workshops, and evidence for the essential elements of such a workshop survived: a hearth or fireplace, a bellows, water, fuel and waste deposit. Other structures discovered on-site revealed that this was a substantial settlement consisting of ditches and a palisade, an entrance, a possible round house with a key-hold pit inside and two well-constructed souterrains (subterranean man-made passages built of stone and roofed that were probably used for storage and refuge) built sometime between the mid-sixth and mid-seventh centuries. This settlement could have been the homestead of a family of smiths, whose craft was highly regarded in early Ireland and often associated with magical properties. There was a distinction between the *gobae* who worked with iron and the *cerd*, a craftsman of higher grade who worked with precious metals as described in the law on smithing *Blaí Ord Indeóin* ('The exemption of hammers is the anvil'):

> Gold, silver, and copper-alloy are unindemnified in the forge of a smith, but not in the workshop of a *cerd*, since they are inappropriate to a blacksmith's forge but not to the workshop of a *cerd*.[40]

---

39 B. Hodkinson, 'A Reappraisal of the Archaeological Evidence for Weaving in Ireland in the Early Christian Period', *Ulster Journal of Archaeology*, 50 (1987), 49; Cotter, 'Cahercommaun Fort', 71–2 and 85 (Bhreathnach).

40 R. F. Gillespie, 'An Early Medieval Settlement at Lowpark, Co. Mayo', in Corlett and Potterton (eds.), *Settlement in Early Medieval Ireland*, 181–211; B. G. Scott, *Early Irish Ironworking* (Belfast: Ulster Museum, 1990), 184–97; *CIH*, I, 268.10f.

It is possible, although not definite, that at least one smith working at Lowpark was a *cerd* as a rolled up gold filigree panel dating to the sixth or seventh century was discovered there, and in that condition it was more likely for the melting pot than for wearing.[41]

Lake islands, natural and man-made, and lakeshore dwellings known as crannógs were common especially in the lakelands of the midlands and the north of Ireland, and were also to be found in Scotland and Wales.[42] Excavations and surveys of Irish crannógs have shown that these dwellings were constructed and inhabited from early prehistory to the seventeenth century. Many of them belong to the early medieval period and often consist of clusters on a single lake or of a string of settlements, both on the lakeshore and in the lake, consisting not just of habitations but also of fishing platforms and industrial centres. Some of the richest cultural assemblages have come from lacustrine sites such as Lagore, County Meath, Ballinderry 1 and 2, County Westmeath, and Lough Gara, County Sligo. These were royal residences. Kings of Lagore (Loch Dá Gabor), mainly of the Síl nÁedo Sláine dynasty in the east midlands, were often kings of Tara from the eighth century until the mid-ninth century when the crannóg was destroyed:

> Cináed son of Conaing, king of Cíanacht, rebelled against Máel Sechnaill with the support of the foreigners, and plundered the Uí Néill from the Sinann to the sea, both churches and states, and he deceitfully sacked the island of Loch Gabor, levelling it to the ground, and the oratory of Treóit, with seventy people in it, was burned by him.[43]

Not all crannógs were major royal residences and Aidan O'Sullivan, has recently described the crannógs of Coolure Demesne, County Westmeath, as 'representing the dwellings of a community who resided around their lord or gathered for public assemblies, hosting, feastings or other activities associated with kingship'.[44]

Communities in early Ireland gathered in assemblies, of which there were many different types. As a rural society depending on the produce of the land, seasonal gatherings were part of the year's cycle, be they the communal gathering of the harvest and the festivities that went with that or the

---

41 Gillespie, 'Early Medieval Settlement', 205, 208; N. Whitfield, 'The Gold Filigree Panel', in R. F. Gillespie and A. Kerrigan (eds.), *Of Troughs and Tuyères: The Archaeology of the N5 Charlestown Bypass* (Dublin: National Roads Authority, 2010), 296–303.
42 A. O'Sullivan, *Crannogs: Lake-Dwellings in Early Ireland* (Dublin: Country House, 2000).
43 *AU*, i, 359 [*s.a.* 840].
44 A. O'Sullivan, R. Sands and E. P. Kelly, *Coolure Demesne Crannog, Lough Derravaragh: An Introduction to its Archaeology and Landscapes* (Bray: Wordwell, 2007), 71.

darker and somewhat chaotic Samain celebration in winter. With the adoption of Christianity, the feast-days of saints or the procession of relics through the countryside often attracted a crowd. This may be the reason why, for example, the Norse of Dublin attacked Armagh on 10 November – the Saturday before the feast of St Martin – in 921, knowing that the place would be preparing for the feast-day and that people and supplies would be coming in from the surrounding districts. Equally, the sight of a procession of relics and processing dignitaries – bishops, abbots, kings and nobles – along a road or through the countryside would have attracted a crowd. Convening assemblies might have been a measure taken by rulers to calm the people and to engender stability in society at times of distress, such as periods of famine or disease. It is noteworthy that the taking of relics on tour (*comotatio martirum/reliquarum*) was particularly prevalent in the late eighth century, when the country was struck by successive diseases, famine, bad weather and loss of stock. During the same period, kings went on pilgrimages and ecclesiastical 'laws' (*cánai*) – a means by which major churches exacted tributes – were enacted. Like the processions of relics, the promulgations of saints' laws must have been dramatic public spectacles. Although we are not certain as to the form of ceremony referred to, the entry in the Annals of Ulster under 793 speaks of an exceptional occasion that may not have been open to the wider public in Munster: 'the law of Ailbe [of Emly, County Tipperary] promulgated in Munster and Artri son of Cathal ordained (*ordinatio*) king of Munster'. The record suggests that this ceremony took place in Imlech Iubair (Emly), the *eigenkirche* of the Eóganacht kings of Munster, and that the abbot of Emly, if not also the abbot of Armagh, was present.[45]

The gatherings and ceremonies of the powerful, be they recurring royal provincial assemblies such as the *óenach Tailten*, held in Teltown, County Meath, or great meetings called by particularly powerful kings to exact submission or tribute or to confirm an alliance, litter the annalistic records. The king of Tara, Máel Sechnaill son of Máelruanaid (d. 862), stamped his authority on a national scale by holding a series of major royal assemblies (*rígdála*). In 851, the *rígdál* he convened at Armagh affirmed the submission to him of the Ulaid kings of the north-east. He was accompanied by the nobles of the northern half of Ireland (Leth Cuinn), by the joint abbots of Armagh and their company, and by the clerics of Mide – his own core territory – led by Suairlech, abbot of Clonard. He convened another *rígdál* in a very different

---

45 On the general context of *cánai* see T. M. Charles-Edwards, *The Early Mediaeval Gaelic Lawyer* (Cambridge: Department of Anglo-Saxon, Norse and Celtic, 1999), 48–54.

setting in 859. This assembled at Ráith Áeda Meic Bric (Rahugh, County Westmeath) in his own core kingdom, in order to impose peace throughout the country, and again was attended not only by the king of Tara but also the abbots of Armagh and Clonard. A more specific objective of this particular royal assembly was to alienate the strategic kingdom of Osraige from Munster to Leth Cuinn (northern half of Ireland) and to ensure that the king of Osraige paid his dues to Armagh. This alienation was accepted by the king of Munster, who had lost out to Máel Sechnaill in the previous year: this was the price of his submission.[46] *Críth Gablach*, the law on status, refers to various reasons why the king of the smaller, local kingdom, the *túath*, might also hold an *óenach* 'assembly'. Among them was the need to gather together a *slógad* 'military hosting', to deal with a plague or when defeated in battle (*rechtge*) and to confirm a treaty (*cairde*). There were also more mundane practical reasons why a king would call upon various groups in his community to assemble: judges and elders were to assist him in administering justice, labourers to build or renovate his residence and vassals to build roads.[47]

Violence and Peace-Keeping

The Irish annals are full of references to military hostings and raids, small and large. Aristocratic violence was endemic in early Irish society, with consequences for the wider population. Certain parts of the country experienced constant warfare, the most obvious being the eastern kingdom of Brega. Struggles within dynasties were particularly fierce and often involved a series of revenge killings and expulsions from kingships. One of the bloodiest feuds recorded in the annals was that fought among the Síl nÁedo Sláine of Brega in the early decades of the eighth century. It involved the descendants of the seventh-century kings Cernach Sotal and Conaing son of Congal. They were contesting for supremacy of the dynasty and the kingdom, and also the ultimate prize of the kingship of Tara which had been theirs for long periods during the seventh century. However, so intense was the rivalry that they lost their claim to that supreme kingship and from the eighth to the late tenth centuries the title mainly alternated between the dynasties of Clann Cholmáin

---

46 E. Bhreathnach, 'Transforming Kingship and Cult: The Provincial Ceremonial Capitals in Early Medieval Ireland', in Schot, Newman and Bhreathnach (eds.), *Landscapes of Cult and Kingship*, 126–48; E. FitzPatrick, 'The Landscape of Máel Sechnaill's *rígdál*, 859 AD', in T. Condit and C. Corlett (eds.), *Above and Beyond: Essays in Memory of Leo Swan* (Bray: Wordwell, 2005), 267–80.

47 T. M. Charles-Edwards, 'A Contract between King and People in Early Medieval Ireland? *Críth Gablach* on Kingship', *Peritia*, 8 (1994), 107–19.

(midlands), Cenél Conaill (north-west) and Cenél nEógain (north), with an occasional challenge from a king of Munster. Some impression of the misery wrought by this type of dynastic warfare on a region and its inhabitants can be gained from descriptions such as the preface to the previously mentioned *Cáin Adomnáin* 'The law of Adomnán', which although later than the seventh-century law itself – possibly written in the tenth century – is an evocative description of the cruelty of war:

> Then she [Adomnán's mother] went up on her son's back, till they came upon a field of slaughter. This was how thick the carnage was on which they came: the two feet of one woman reached the headless neck of the next one. Of all they saw on the battlefield, they saw nothing which they found more touching or more wretched than the head of a woman lying in one place and her body in another, and her infant on the breast of her corpse. There was a stream of milk on one of its cheeks and a stream of blood on the other cheek.[48]

The brutality of violence to both men and women emerges starkly from archaeological burial evidence. Two male skeletons – one young and one aged around forty – in a familial cemetery at Millockstown, County Louth, for example, died of blows to the head. The older man died of a blow to the back of his head with a sharp instrument, having survived an earlier blow to his forehead.[49]

Not all wars or battles involved petty and ferocious feuding in a confined territory. The greater campaigns of provincial kings, which often necessitated a king and his army travelling long distances, appear to have been more professional and subject to legal agreements with their allies. How else could kings of Cenél Conaill who resided in modern County Donegal or their neighbours Cenél nEógain who came from modern mid-Ulster claim and hold the distant kingship of Tara, and withstand challenges from midland and southern kings and, from the ninth century onwards, deal with the ever-increasing power of the vikings? An eighth-century metrical legal text that details the arrangements between the Uí Néill dynasties, particularly the northern branches, and a group of dynasties known as the Airgíalla, who rendered them formal military services, affords us some idea of the mutual obligations of such an alliance. In his commentary on this text, Thomas Charles-Edwards has listed the terms used in early Irish texts for royal rights and privileges – taxes and

---

48 *Adomnán's 'Law of the Innocents': Cáin Adomnáin*, ed. G. Márkus (Glasgow: Blackfriars Books, 1997), 9§7.

49 C. Manning, 'Archaeological Excavation of a Succession of Enclosures at Millockstown, County Louth', *PRIA*, 86 C (1986), 135–81.

other renders, specific commodities, purveyance, hospitality, labour, military services, legal immunities and acknowledgement of rank. Terms relating to military service include *dúnad* 'encampment', *fecht* 'military service', *forbanda* 'extra exactions after desertion (*élud*)', *fubae* (*rubae*) 'local police duties, hunting down pirates, horse-thieves, wolves, and *slógad* 'hosting'. In Charles-Edwards's words, 'war was as much subject to law as was any other department of life'.[50] In the grand alliance between the Uí Néill, especially Cenél nEógain, and the Airgíalla, the hosting was required to follow selected roads to designated encampments in the territory of the Airgíalla. Scouts familiar with the terrain were available to guide the army and any loss of livestock was penalised as if it were theft, except at a higher rate. The Airgíalla were not obliged to provide military service in the spring or autumn, the season of sowing and reaping, although the annals show that this restriction was not always adhered to either between the Uí Néill and the Airgíalla or other similar allies.

A Sense of Place

No matter where one stands in Ireland, place names and monuments speak volumes about the history of the locality. In a society in which religious beliefs were embedded in places, their names and their associations, the landscape consists of a rich deposit through which we can begin to understand the complexities of the Irish belief system, Christian and probably pre-Christian. In her study of place names and the understanding of monuments, Kay Muhr considers a series of place names that are associated with supernatural beings and with particular landmarks in a country in which 'the old hag may be a sovereignty goddess, a hill or cairn a manifestation of the boundary with the Otherworld, a hole in the ground a telluric womb'. She quotes Proinsias Mac Cana's view that the Irish were among societies for whom the landscape itself was the key: 'the Irish landscape and the *dindshenchas* "the history of places", which was its collective reflex in tribal myth and history, served together as an effective mnemonic index and treasury of a great part of native tradition'.[51]

The written corpus of poems and prose known as the *dindshenchas*, in its current form mainly dating from the eleventh century with subsequent

---

50 T. M. Charles-Edwards, '*The Airgíalla Charter Poem*: The Legal Content', in Bhreathnach (ed.), *Kingship and Landscape of Tara*, 100–23, esp. 109–12, 119.

51 K. Muhr, 'Place-Names and the Understanding of Monuments', in Schot, Newman and Bhreathnach (eds.), *Landscapes of Cult and Kingship*, 255; P. Mac Cana, *The Learned Tales of Medieval Ireland* (Dublin: DIAS, 1980), 27.

re-workings to the fifteenth century, seeks to explain the names of the prominent natural and man-made features in the countryside including lakes, mountains, rivers, forests, estuaries, prehistoric tombs and other types of funerary monuments and prehistoric forts. Place names were associated with mythical beings, warriors, heroic kings, beautiful and scheming women, and even saints. Some characters are historical, others mythological and a few belong to folklore. It covers most of the country but there is a heavy concentration on the east, the midlands and Connacht. This fervent interest in toponyms is not confined to the *dindshenchas*, however, as it also pervades genealogies, saints' lives and sagas.[52]

One of the most evocative of such places is *Úaimh na gCat* (Oweynagat) 'Cave of the Cats', otherwise known from early sagas as *Úam Chrúachain* 'Cave of Cruachain' the ceremonial landscape of Rathcroghan, County Roscommon. Of Oweynagat in today's landscape John Waddell in his description of the monument comments: 'The inconspicuous nature of the site, a small natural cave with a souterrain attached, stands in stark contrast to other large earthworks in the area and to its literary status with a remarkable wealth of associated legend.' Despite being unimpressive and dilapidated, once entered, even today, the cave is a fascinating cavern of passages, natural and man-made, the main artificial passage of which descends steeply to join a limestone cave. There are two ogham inscriptions in one of the artificial passages, one of which reads VRAICCI MAQI MEDVVI '[the stone] of Fróech, son of Medb'.[53] This is remarkable as both names – Fróech and Medb – are those of characters intimately associated with the mythology of Rathcroghan. The form MEDVVI is problematic as it is masculine genitive, and not feminine MEDVVIAS, which would be expected if referring to the great goddess/queen Medb. It might be an antiquarian forgery, although the physical evidence suggests otherwise. If genuine, the appearance of characters from mythology on an inscription in Oweynagat is unsurprising as this cave was the entrance to the Otherworld or, as described in the ninth-century tale *Cath Maige Mucrama* 'The Battle of Mag Muccrama', it was 'Ireland's gate to Hell' (*dorus iffirn na Hérend*):

> Now Mag Mucríma [was so called from] magic pigs that had come out of the cave of Crúachain. That is Ireland's gate to Hell. Out of it too came the swarm of three-headed creatures that laid Ireland waste until Amairgene

---

52 *Metrical Dindchenchas*.
53 J. Waddell, *Archaeology and Celtic Myth: An Exploration* (Dublin: Four Courts Press, 2014), 62–4.

father of Conall Cernach, fighting alone (?), destroyed it in the presence of the Ulaid.

Out of it also came the saffron-coloured(?)bird-flock and they withered up everything in Ireland that their breath touched until the Ulaid killed them with their slings.[54]

This cave is also the setting for one of the most bizarre early Irish tales *Echtra Nerai* 'The Adventure of Nera' in which the hero Nera is tricked at Samain into entering *Úam Chrúachain*, in essence the Otherworld, where he encounters weird and wonderful beings.[55]

Oweynagat was only one of many places throughout the Irish countryside that would have evoked fear among the general populace and would have excited the imaginations of storytellers. In exploring this topic I will focus not only on the well-known site of Tara, but also on the less celebrated but still fascinating ancestral burial site at Fartagh, County Galway; the church site at Knockboy, County Waterford; and the kingdom of Cualu in which the previously mentioned Glebe and Laughaunstown, County Dublin, were located.

Tara (Illustration 2) is one of the most puzzling landscapes in Ireland, not least because despite its appearance as a ridge of grassy mounds and a nineteenth-century church, it has captivated the Irish imagination for the entire period for which we have written records. Patrick Pearse wanted the Proclamation of the Republic declared there in 1916, as he considered the site 'all-important for historical reasons'. In the late 1890s, prominent members of the Irish cultural nationalist movement, among them the poet W. B. Yeats and nationalist activist Maude Gonne, led a public campaign against the British Israelites who had dug their way through the Rath of the Synods, one of the hill of Tara's most significant monuments, in their search for the Ark of the Covenant.[56] What is the attraction of this otherwise relatively uninspiring low ridge? From it on a good day one can see well into the midlands, south to the Wicklow Mountains, north to the Mountains of Mourne and east to the Boyne valley. For a long time scholars accepted the early medieval derivation of the name *Temair* (anglicised Tara) as meaning 'a place with a view'. Recently, however, a more scientifically acceptable derivation has been postulated and this explanation goes to the heart of Tara's importance. In his study on the significance of the place name *Temair*, Dónall Mac Giolla Easpaig proposed that

54 *Cath Maige Muccrama*, ed. M. O'Daly (Dublin: ITS, 1975), 48; Waddell, *Archaeology and Celtic Myth*, 58–9.

55 Koch and Carey, *Celtic Heroic Age*, 117–22.

56 C. Townshend, *Easter 1916. The Irish Rebellion* (London: Allen Lane, 2005), 222; M. Carew, *Tara and the Ark of the Covenant* (Dublin. RIA, 2003).

2. Tara, County Meath. Courtesy of Discovery Programme: Centre for Archaeology & Innovation Ireland.

it derived regularly from Indo-European *tem-r-i-s* and reflected the e-grade of the root *tem-* 'cut', along with -*r*- suffix, therefore signifying 'an area cut off, undoubtedly one that had been demarcated for sacred purposes'. Hence *Temair* is related to Greek *temenos* and Latin *templum* in both signification and etymology. All three terms imply the existence of some form of sacred precinct at a given site, be it a space marked off for kings or dedicated to a god or a space demarcated by the augurs from which the auspices might be taken.[57]

A companion study to Mac Giolla Easpaig's was compiled by Nollaig Ó Muraíle, in which he located over twenty-five possible other places in Ireland with the same name, many of which are also hilltop sites with prehistoric monuments. It is possible, although yet to be proven, that the name *temair* was given to a particular type of cultic site, as *nemeton* (Old Irish *nemed*) was often associated with groves of trees.[58] But the literature makes clear that Tara, in Meath was the greatest of all and as a result was designated as *Temair na Ríg* 'Tara of the Kings'. The scale of the monuments on the hill and in its environs confirm this status and also confirm that the concept of the sacred precinct was a crucial element to the architecture of this landscape. Two such extensive prehistoric precincts have so far been discovered on the hill. A massive oval ditched pit enclosure was discovered in the 1990s

---

57 *Sanas Cormaic (Cormac's glossary)*, ed. K. Meyer (Halle and Dublin, 1913; Felinfach, 1994), 105 §1212; D. Mac Giolla Easpaig, 'Significance and Etymology of the Placename *Temair*', in Bhreathnach (ed.), *Kingship and Landscape of Tara*, 448; M. Eliade, *The Sacred and the Profane* (San Diego and London: Harcourt, Brace & Co., 1959).

58 N. Ó Muraíle, '*Temair*/Tara and Other Places of the Name', in Bhreathnach (ed.), *The Kingship and Landscape of Tara*, 449–77; R. Latvio, '*Neimed*: Exploring Social Distinctions and Sacredness in Early Irish Legal Sources', in K. Ritari and A. Bergholm (eds.), *Approaches to Religion and Mythology in Celtic Studies* (Cambridge: Cambridge Scholars Publishing, 2008), 220–42.

through remote surveying. This monument is draped over the spine of the hill (Illustration 2), and on the basis of its relation to the other monuments around it is likely to date to the Bronze Age or earlier. The equally large monument known as *Ráith na Ríg* ('Rath of the Kings') which encompasses the brow of the hill and encloses the earliest monument at Tara, a Neolithic passage tomb (*Duma na nGíall* 'The Mound of the Hostages') and the likely inauguration mound (*Forrad*), was excavated in the 1950s and in 1997. The excavations demonstrated that its chronological horizon was from *c.*370 BC to *c.*AD 406. For the purposes of the discussion here, two features of particular significance were discovered. One was an impressive rock cut ditch that reached a depth of up to 3 m and a width of 7 m quarried out of boulder clay into a seam of underlying shale with edges that had been cut in a series of narrow shelves or steps.[59]

Visitors to the excavation site in 1997 were astounded by the scale of this ditch and, given the etymology of *Temair* incorporating the root *tem-* 'to cut', it would be easy to link the two. This was the cutting of the hill that created the sacred precinct inside, a place where only the privileged could enter and a place where they negotiated with the supernatural, at times to keep malevolent forces outside. Human remains were found from the basal layers of the ditch including the skeleton of a six-month-old child buried with a scatter of dog bones and sealed under sods. By analogy with other deliberate depositions at similarly exceptional sites – varying between adult and animal remains – it would appear that this child burial was some form of foundation deposit; part of the sanctification of the precinct. The importance of burials at Tara is underscored by the apparent mass of graves – predominantly Bronze Age barrows – that seem to cover the hill. This was a necropolis as well as a sacred precinct where the dead and their power of legitimising the claims of the living were paramount. This prehistoric practice and belief was translated into early medieval literature and conveyed in texts relating to Tara's monuments, many of which were correctly designated as burial sites, among them the *Clóenfherta* 'Sloping ancestral graves' and *Ráith Gráinne* 'Rath of Gráinne'.[60]

---

59 J. Fenwick and C. Newman, 'Geomagnetic Survey on the Hill of Tara, Co. Meath, 1998–9', *Discovery Programme Reports*, 6 (2002), 1–17; H. Roche, 'Excavations at Ráith na Ríg, Tara, Co. Meath, 1997', *Discovery Programme Reports*, 6 (2002), 19–82, esp. 23, 71.

60 J. Carey, 'Tara and the Supernatural', in Bhreathnach (ed.), *Kingship and Landscape of Tara*, 32–48, esp. 45. For the nature of infant burial in another culture see S. Crawford, 'Special Burials, Special Buildings? An Anglo-Saxon Perspective on the Interpretation of Infant Burials in Association with Rural Settlement Structures', in K. Bacvarov (ed.), *Babies Reborn: Infant/Child Burials in Pre- and Protohistory* (Oxford: Archaeopress, 2008), 197–204.

But what of the mythical and religious landscape other than that of the great ceremonial sites? One place name that conveys a tangible and widespread manifestation of the power of the ancestors and the dead throughout the countryside is that derived from the term *fert(a)* 'an ancestral grave'. Hence one comes across place names such as Farta(gh), Fertagh, Ardfert, Clonfert and Kilfert, many of them now the sites of medieval ecclesiastical ruins with their names signifying more ancient origins. Some very intriguing sites were never incorporated into an ecclesiastical landscape and could well have marked territorial boundaries or assembly sites. An extraordinary *ferta* worth noting was discovered at Farta, County Galway. This site contained a female extended inhumation inserted into a mound that already contained a Bronze Age cinerary urn. The woman was buried with the complete skeleton of a horse. Carbon-14 dating of the woman and the horse confirm that they are contemporary and date to sometime in the fifth or sixth century AD.[61] What is more dramatic about this burial is that the mound is close to the Rath of Feerwore, the original location of the highly decorated Turoe Stone. In this place in the fifth or sixth century all the facets of kingship and sovereignty were visible to the community: an ancestral grave, probably an inauguration site and stone, and a woman and horse buried in the same mound, the very core symbols associated with prehistoric sacral kingship of sovereignty goddess and equine characteristics interwoven.[62]

Places such as Ardfert, County Kerry, and Clonfert, County Offaly, continued to function as sacred places after the acceptance of Christianity and became churches or monastic foundations. Writing in the seventh century, Bishop Tírechán narrates how this Christianisation happened. He tells of St Patrick meeting the daughters of the king of Tara near Rathcroghan. He instructed them in the teachings of Christianity, baptised them and on receiving the body of Christ they both died. Even though they were Christians on their deaths, their household waked them in the traditional manner and 'they made a round ditch after the manner of a *ferta*, because that is what the heathen Irish used to do, but we call it *relic*' (*et fecerunt fossam rotundam in similitudinem fertae, quia sic faciebant Scotici homines et gentiles, nobiscum autem relic uocatur*). Tírechán does not end his story there. He notes that the girls'

---

61 E. O'Brien and E. Bhreathnach, 'Irish Boundary *Ferta*: Their Physical Manifestation and Historical Context', in F. Edmonds and P. Russell (eds.), *Tome: Studies in Medieval Celtic History and Law in Honour of Thomas Charles-Edwards* (Woodbridge: Boydell Press, 2011), 53–64; G. Coffey, 'On the Excavation of a Tumulus near Loughrea, Co. Galway', *PRIA*, 25 C (1904), 14–20; www.mappingdeathdb.ie (Fartagh: see Dr E. O'Brien's comments).
62 Waddell, *Archaeology and Celtic Myth*, 82–109.

grave became a venerated site because of their sanctity and that a church was founded on the site, and that this church was subject to Armagh and St Patrick. Thus a mound or a ring barrow associated with two royal princesses, or more likely sovereignty goddesses given that their names were Eithne and Fedelm, shifted in function from one belief system to another, from ancestral grave (*ferta*) to saintly shrine (*relic* < *reliquiae*).[63]

The fusion of myth and probably pre-Christian ritual, early literacy and Christianity is visible in the landscape around the late medieval parish church of Seskinan in Knockboy, County Waterford. All window lintels and the south door lintel, six stones in total, have ogham inscriptions, and a seventh ogham stone stands in the church.[64] It is remarkable that as late as the fifteenth century the antiquity of the ogham inscriptions was recognised. These stones were ideal for use as lintels, being long and flat in comparison to the fabric of the church walls, but their inscriptions were not hidden. They were clearly visible and probably intelligible to some who visited the church at the time. The late medieval church is on the site of an earlier church, the foundations of which may be in the surrounding graveyard, and one of the ogham inscriptions commemorates a descendant of Nia Segemon (NETA-SEGAMONAS), a mythical king of Munster. There are two other NETA-SEGAMONAS inscriptions in the same part of County Waterford, one at the monastic site of Ardmore (Illustration 3), the other from an early church site at Island. These stones must reflect the extent of a kingdom that stretched from the coast to the strategic pass between the Knockmealdown and Monavullagh Mountains (Slíab Cua) in which Knockboy is located.[65] The immediate site is surrounded by other monuments including a possible embanked stone circle and a three-stone alignment within a small enclosure. Both are probably prehistoric monuments with some form of religious associations. Close to the church is the site of Tobaratempall Well ('The Well of the Church'). There is no cult of a local saint. The dedication appears to be to the Blessed Virgin of Knockboy. A fair was held there on 8 September, the feast of the Nativity of the Virgin.[66]

---

63 *The Patrician Texts in the Book of Armagh*, ed. L. Bieler. Scriptores Latini Hiberniae 10 (Dublin: DIAS, 1979), 144–5§26.

64 M. Moore, *Archaeological Inventory of County Waterford* (Dublin: The Stationery Office, 1999), nos. 1407, 1495. See John Carey's chapter for observations on ogham.

65 R. A. S. Macalister, *Corpus Inscriptionum Insularum Celticarum*. vol. 1 (Dublin: IMC, 1945; repr 1996), nos. 263, 292, 300; Moore, *Archaeological Inventory ... Waterford*, nos. 1481, 1490; E. Breathnach, *Ireland in the Medieval World, AD 400–1000: Landscape, Kingship and Religion* (Dublin: Four Courts Press, 2014), 44–5.

66 P. Power, 'Ancient Ruined Churches of Co. Waterford', *Waterford Archaeological Journal*, 4 (1898), 83; Moore, *Archaeological Inventory ... Waterford*, no. 1407; P. Power, *The Place-Names of Decies* (Cork University Press, 1952), 172.

3. Ogham stone, Ardmore Cathedral, County Waterford. Courtesy of Discovery Programme: Centre for Archaeology & Innovation Ireland/Dublin Institute for Advanced Studies.

One wonders if the mundane explanation of the place name Knockboy as *Cnoc Buí*, 'the yellow hill', does not conceal a dedication to the supernatural woman, Baoi, who is also associated with the great passage tomb of Knowth, County Meath, and with Dunboy on the Beare Peninsula, County Cork. In the literature Baoi is also the Caillech Béarra 'The Hag of Beare' who is a manifestation of the sovereignty goddess and whose memory survives into modern folklore and is linked with places throughout Ireland. A well-known early poem is a lament by her about her loss of beauty and her power to attract men – possibly a reflex of a genuine downgrading of the sovereignty goddess that occurred as the medieval period progressed.[67]

Earlier in this chapter, reference was made to the Christian landscape of Cualu, the kingdom in which the sites of Glebe and Laughanstown settlements were located. This area became a busy centre for Christian activity, probably from the fifth or sixth century. Dalkey Island is located off the mainland and on the evidence of excavation was a trade emporium. Among the

---

67 T. Ó Cathasaigh, 'The Semantics of *Síd*', *Éigse*, 17 (1978), 137–55; G. Ó Crualaoich, *The Book of the Cailleach: Stories of the Wise-Woman Healer* (Cork University Press, 2003); Muhr, 'Place-Names', 242–3; K. Ritari, 'Images of Ageing in the Early Irish Poem *Caillech Bérri*', *Studia Celtica Fennica*, 3 (2006), 57–70.

items discovered there were sherds of late antique Mediterranean pottery, suggesting that imports of oil or wine were landed.[68] From the coast to the mountains there is a myriad of stone churches mainly dated to the eleventh century or later, but which stand on the sites of earlier foundations.[69] The corpus of saints' genealogies, along with the secular genealogies and local place names, preserve information about the holy men and women associated with these earlier churches. The name of the coastal suburb of Killiney, County Dublin, derives from *Cill Ingine Lenéni*, 'The church of the daughters of Lenéni'. These women belonged to the Catraige, a people to whom the early saint Colmán of Cloyne, County Cork, (d. 606) belonged and who were associated with royal ceremonies at Cashel. As previously mentioned, two important churches are situated along the same ridge as Glebe and Laughanstown, namely, Tully and Rathmichael. Tully appears in the sources as *Telach na nEscop*, 'The hill of the bishops' and had associations with St Brigit and Kildare.[70]

Rathmichael is an impressive site, with the remains of a church and round tower located downhill from a substantial ringfort. The dedication to St Michael could be original, as such dedications, although rare, are known elsewhere in Ireland, the most famous being Skellig Michael, County Kerry. The more likely dedication, however, is to Máel Ruain of Tallaght (County Dublin), the head of an ascetic monastic movement known as the *Céli Dé* ('clients of God') who died in 792. Máel Ruain and his companions' influence was widespread and it would not be unusual to find a church dedicated to him in this area. His particular association with Michael the Archangel is explained in the later preface to the ninth-century Martyrology of Óengus.

> Now it is that Maelruain who decided that he would not take land in Tamlachtu until Michael [the Archangel], with whom he had a friendship, should take it; and because of that agreement there are in Tamlachtu relics consecrated to Michael.[71]

---

68 I. W. Doyle, 'The Early Medieval Activity at Dalkey Island: A Reassessment', *Journal of Irish Archaeology*, 9 (1998), 89–103.

69 T. Ó Carragáin, 'Church Buildings and Pastoral Care in Early Medieval Ireland', in E. FitzPatrick and R. Gillespie (eds.), *The Parish in Medieval and Early Modern Ireland: Community, Territory and Building* (Dublin: Four Courts Press, 2006), 91–123.

70 E. O'Brien, 'Churches of South-East County Dublin, Seventh to Twelfth Century', in G. Mac Niocaill and P. F. Wallace (eds.), *Keimelia: Studies in Medieval Archaeology and History in Memory of Tom Delaney* (Galway: Galway University Press, 1988), 504–24; P. MacCotter, *Colmán of Cloyne. A Study* (Dublin: Four Courts Press, 2004), 23–30; J. Stokes and J. Strachan, *Thesaurus Palaeohibernicus*, 2 vols. (Cambridge University Press, 1901–2), ii, p. 334.

71 *Félire Óengusso Céli Dé: The Martyrology of Oengus the Culdee*, ed. and trans. W. Stokes (London: Henry Bradshaw Society, 1905; repr. 1984), 12–13.

The overall structure of the network of churches in south Dublin and elsewhere, and how they related to one another, is unclear. It is suggested that possibly in the eleventh century and certainly by the twelfth century, due to Dublin's influence, such a network operated as a proto-parochial system. Prior to that period it would appear that at least some of these churches were allied to much greater churches, including Glendalough, Kildare or Tallaght, through dynastic or cult connections. Many of the saints of the area reputedly belonged to the Dál Messin Corb, a dynasty of which St Cóemgen (Kevin) of Glendalough was a member, and which contested the provincial kingship of Leinster until the seventh century.[72] The cartularies of later Dublin monastic foundations, especially St Mary's Abbey (Cistercian) and St Thomas's Abbey (Augustinian Canons/Victorines), and of the archdiocese of Dublin itself show that these churches and their lands were alienated either to the diocese or these powerful foundations. If Tully was an episcopal church subject to Kildare it may have held a superior status among the churches of the area, while Rathmichael may have been a monastery housing a community following the monastic rule of the *Céli Dé* linked to Tallaght.[73]

In addition, a Scandinavian population appears to have settled in this area. Documentary sources confirm their presence, as Tully was granted to Christ Church Cathedral by Sitric son of Torcall (Thorkettle) in the twelfth century and the land of Rathmichael was in the possession of an Ostman, MacDuel, in 1264. Distinctive grave slabs, commonly known as 'Rathdown slabs', survive in many of the small medieval churchyards of the area, and are associated with the Christianisation of the Mac Torcaill dynasty. Three such slabs survive in Tully churchyard while ten of them have been recorded at Rathmichael.[74] Excavations at Cherrywood, County Dublin, close to Tully and also to Laughaunstown and Glebe, demonstrated the complexity of settlement and cultural identity in this area. An enclosure contained evidence for a sixth-/seventh-century cemetery which was replaced by a series of houses and a kiln, dated to various points between the ninth and twelfth centuries. The structure of the houses has similar features to house-types found in Dublin, and the Scandinavian associations were also somewhat strengthened by the discovery of the fragment of a whalebone plaque often found in ninth-century women's graves in Norway

72 Ó Carragáin, 'Church Buildings'; A. S. MacShamhráin, *Church and Polity in Pre-Norman Ireland: The Case of Glendalough* (Maynooth: An Sagart, 1996).
73 For a comprehensive survey of the medieval church and church lands in the Dublin region, see Murphy and Potterton, *Dublin Region in the Middle Ages*, 209–63.
74 J. Bradley, 'The Interpretation of Scandinavian Settlement in Ireland', in Bradley (ed.), *Settlement and Society in Medieval Ireland*, 56; P. Healy, *Pre-Norman Grave-Slabs and Cross-Inscribed Stones in the Dublin Region*, ed. K. Swords (Dublin: Local Studies Section, South Dublin Libraries, 2009): Tully: nos. 28, 39, 42; Rathmichael: nos. 17–8, 22–4, 31–3, 35–6.

and Scotland.[75] Thus in the early kingdom of Cualu, archaeological and histor-ical evidence reveals a busy coastal region trading with the outside world and absorbing cultural and religious influences, and a landscape probably settled by people of diverse origin, among them British and Scandinavian, active in grain production and sheep rearing, and in metal-working and other crafts.

In attempting to explore the shape and reality of life and the land-scape in Ireland from *c*.400 to 1000 this chapter has suggested that Ireland, although an island undoubtedly far from the great centres of power – Rome, Constantinople, Aachen – and immersed in its own vibrant culture, was nevertheless not an isolated place. Rome and Aachen (and other centres of imperial power) attracted many Irishmen to their courts and these scholars in turn contributed to the intellectual life of these places. No doubt few of the inhabitants of Ireland were aware of Columbanus' correspondence with the Pope or Johannes Scottus Eriugena's philosophical tracts being expounded in the Carolingian court school, but all shared in the high reputation of Ireland engendered on the Continent by such men. Many commentaries on early Irish society depend on the huge amount of information available in early Irish laws and indeed these texts offer a very detailed profile of society. But all legal tracts operate at a certain remove from the reality of living. Increased archaeological activity has led to the discovery of otherwise unknown sites, and as a result a palimpsest of human activity from prehistory to the modern period has been uncovered throughout Ireland. Discoveries from the early medieval period have been particularly plentiful. There is now a challenge for archaeologists and historians to combine their disciplines to deepen our understanding of the economy, social hierarchies, *mentalités* and even the health index of early Irish society from this new evidence.

75 Ó Néill, 'Excavation of Pre-Norman Structures'.

2

Learning, Imagination and Belief

JOHN CAREY

OUR two primary sources for the conversion of the Irish to Christianity are very different in kind. Each is of fundamental importance, both for our own understanding and in terms of its influence on the medieval tradition. But each is also acutely tantalising, in the number of important questions that it leaves unanswered. First, there is Prosper of Aquitaine's *Chronicon* entry for the year 431:

> To the Irish believing in Christ, ordained by Pope Celestine, Palladius is sent as [their] first bishop.[1]

Prosper wrote not merely as a contemporary, but as a churchman moving in the circles most directly involved in Palladius' mission: as far as it goes, therefore, we can accord this brief statement considerable confidence. It tells us that, by the year 431, there existed not only enough Irish Christians to require a bishop, but also a community sufficiently organised to request one, and to communicate that request to Rome.[2] That Prosper speaks of 'the Irish (*Scotti*) believing in Christ' rather than of 'those believing in Christ in Ireland' suggests that this community already consisted largely of native Gaels rather than of transplanted Britons, slave or free; but it may not be possible to place so much weight on the details of his wording. This is precious information; but it is very nearly all that Prosper has to tell us.[3]

---

1 *Ad Scottos in Christo credentes ordinatus a papa Caelestino Palladius primus episcopus mittitur: Chronica Minora*, i, ed. T. Mommsen, Monumenta Germaniae Historica, Auctores Antiquissimi 9 (Berlin: Weidmann, 1892), 473. Except where otherwise noted, all translations are my own.

2 T. M. Charles-Edwards, *Early Christian Ireland* (Cambridge University Press, 2000), 204–5. Celestine himself had stipulated that 'no bishop should be sent to the unwilling'; E. A. Thompson, *Who was Saint Patrick?* (Woodbridge: Boydell Press, 1985), 61.

3 Somewhat more can be inferred with respect to the considerations which prompted Celestine to dispatch Palladius: T. M. Charles-Edwards, 'Palladius, Prosper, and Leo the Great: Mission and Primatial Authority', in D. N. Dumville (ed.), *Saint Patrick, A.D. 493–1993* (Woodbridge: Boydell Press, 1993), 1–12; Charles-Edwards, *Early Christian Ireland*, 202–14.

Our other source for this period is the writings of Saint Patrick: the *Confessio*, his spiritual autobiography; and the briefer *Epistola ad milites Corotici*. In prose which manages to combine a bricolage of biblical citations with intense emotional power, Patrick gives an account of his experiences of divine grace and of his own mission. This includes vivid narratives of incidents from his inner life, and of some of his early adventures; but Patrick is not concerned with what we would be inclined to call history. He does not mention the dates of any of the events described; or name any of his converts, any of the kingdoms or peoples among which he preached, or any of the churches that he founded. He does however, although often only in passing, give us several indications of the nature of his mission. It extended 'to the outer regions, beyond which there was no one', where Christianity had never been preached before (*Confessio* §51). Patrick speaks of having baptised 'many thousands' (*Confessio* §§14, 50; cf. *Epistola* §2), including female slaves and women of royal birth, together with the sons of kings; he was particularly concerned to inspire his converts to embrace a monastic vocation (*Confessio* §§41–2; *Epistola* §12). It does not appear that any of his converts died for their faith, although Patrick himself prays for the grace of martyrdom (*Confessio* §§57, 59). But he does speak of twelve occasions on which his own life was threatened (§35), and further of having been mocked, harassed and imprisoned (§§37, 52). Among his converts it was the women and especially the female slaves who suffered most, on account of their vows of virginity (§42). At one point Patrick claims to expect death, or slavery, every day (§55), and at another he speaks of acting cautiously for fear of stirring up persecution (§48). In order to be allowed to preach he made payments to local kings, and perhaps to other officials, and travelled with an escort of royal youths (§§52–3).[4]

The Church and Native Society

It was into this hierarchical, brutal, but also receptive environment that the new faith was introduced, and here that it came ultimately to prevail. The details of this process are largely unknown to us: after the crucial fifth-century testimony of Prosper and Patrick, the literary record is virtually silent for two hundred years. Patrick has almost nothing to tell us about the religion which his message sought to supplant: he refers to the worship of 'idols and

---

4 I use the standard paragraph-divisions, as found in *Libri Epistolarum Sancti Patricii Episcopi*, ed. L. Bieler (Copenhagen: Librairie Gyldendal, 1950–1). On those 'who used to judge' (*qui iudicabant*), to whom Patrick made payments on his journeys (*Confessio* §53), see now D. Ó Corráin, 'St Patrick and the Kings', in Duffy (ed.), *Princes, Prelates and Poets*, 211–20.

unclean things' (§41), and to 'all those who adore' the sun (but without saying in so many words that this includes the pagan Irish; §60); but that is all. Yet he, and other missionaries active in Ireland, would have confronted a society which had never been subordinated to the cultural homogenisation which came with Roman rule – although Ireland was not isolated from contact with the Roman world – and with its indigenous ethos and belief structures correspondingly intact. There are however indirect indications of what some of the strategies of conversion may have been; some of these we can now consider.

Among the oldest texts in the Irish language to have survived, dating perhaps from the early seventh century, are dynastic poems celebrating the forebears of the kings of Leinster. Two of these are brief compositions in praise of the legendary ruler Labraid Loingsech: in one, his supremacy is likened to that of 'the one God to the gods' (*deeib dia oen*), while in the other he is called 'a mortal loftier than gods' (*airddiu deeib doen*). In each instance, however, Labraid's sovereignty is also subordinated to that of the God of Christianity: explicitly in the former case, where he is said to have been 'higher than men save for the holy King of heaven'; implicitly in the latter, which states that it was only 'beneath the heavens' that Labraid had no equal. Three elements are present here: the real existence of 'gods' is taken for granted; they are however regarded as being inferior to 'the one God', and even to the greatest among men; and the assertion of this one God's supremacy is juxtaposed with the assertion of the supremacy of an earthly king.[5] Precisely these elements can be found juxtaposed in the Old Testament, particularly in the Book of Psalms: there, the omnipotence of Yahweh vis-à-vis lesser gods is linked with the claims of the Davidic kings of Israel, and with the conjunction of Temple and palace in Jerusalem. The Bible appears to have been used in Ireland to justify a missionary argument which was only 'monotheistic to a certain extent':[6] although the native gods were immeasurably lower than the God of Christianity, who was conceived as the God 'of heaven', they did nevertheless exist. Traces of a linkage between Christian preaching and royal ideology may remain in the archaic compounds *ardri* and *ríched*: originally, these meant 'high-king' and 'king's seat'; but they are only

---

5　On dating: D. Ó Corráin, 'Irish Origin Legends and Genealogy: Recurrent Aetiologies', in T. Nyberg *et al.* (eds.) *History and Heroic Tale: A Symposium* (Odense University Press, 1985), 60–3. Texts cited from, 'The Rhymeless "Leinster Poems": Diplomatic Texts', ed. J. Corthals, *Celtica*, 24 (2003), 84, 87.

6　The phrase appears in J. Borsje, 'Monotheistic to a Certain Extent: The "Good Neighbours" of God in Ireland', in A.-M. Korte and M. de Haardt (eds.), *The Boundaries of Monotheism: Interdisciplinary Explorations into the Foundations of Western Monotheism*, Studies in Theology and Religion 13 (Leiden: Brill, 2009), 53–81.

attested, respectively, as a purportedly pre-Christian designation for the one God and as a word for 'heaven'. As had been the case in Israel, the image of a single God exalted utterly above other deities could readily form the basis of a political analogy: the promulgation of a form of monotheism could have been coupled with propaganda for secular hegemony.

Apart from such oblique indications, the details of the conversion are almost entirely unknown to us; but it must have been a complex process. In later tradition, however, the Christianisation of Ireland was largely identified with the career of Patrick, and was held to have been in all essentials accomplished by the time of his death. The story of the national apostle and the story of the conversion were accordingly the same story; and the form given to that story by Muirchú and Tírechán remained normative throughout the Middle Ages. Each of their accounts has a distinct character, and unique features; but many of the same elements can be found in both. Some of Patrick's converts are portrayed as embracing the new religion out of innate goodness (the 'natural good' or *bonum naturae*), but others are swayed by his miracles. The druids have foreknowledge of Patrick's inevitable victory; those who nevertheless defy him are annihilated, while others accept baptism and indeed enter the priesthood. The new religion's authority is also asserted in the political arena: those lineages which do not show due reverence to the saint will fail or lose power, while those which grant him favour will prosper.[7]

Other sources, however, show that the retreat of the old beliefs was a slower and more piecemeal affair. This is even apparent from other saints' Lives: in the Life of Brigit written by Muirchú's teacher Cogitosus, there is an anecdote concerning a druid who lived at some point after the saint's death, traditionally assigned to the year 524. A collection of precepts known as the *Sinodus episcoporum*, of uncertain date but evidently compiled at a time when Christianity had established itself reasonably securely on the island, is still obliged to legislate against assuming legal obligations on behalf of a pagan (*gentilis homo*), against accepting alms from pagans (*gentes*), against having a soothsayer (*haruspex*) as guarantor of an oath 'in the pagan manner', and against belief in witches.[8] Of particular interest is the evidence

---

7 J. Carey, 'Saint Patrick, the Druids, and the End of the World', *History of Religions*, 36 (1996), 42–53. References to Muirchú and Tírechán: *The Patrician Texts in the Book of Armagh*, ed. L. Bieler, Scriptores Latini Hiberniae 10 (Dublin: DIAS, 1979), 76, 80, 86, 96–8, 100, 104, 116, 126, 130–2, 136, 140, 144, 148, 150, 156; Cf. D. Ó Corráin, 'Irish Vernacular Law and the Old Testament', in P. Ní Chatháin and M. Richter (eds.), *Irland und die Christenheit* (Stuttgart: Klett-Cotta, 1987), 290–4.

8 Cogitosus in J. Colgan, *Trias Thaumaturga* (Louvain: apud Cornelium Coenestenium, 1647; repr. Dublin: Éamonn de Búrca, 1997), 523. Considerations summarised by Charles-Edwards, *Early Christian Ireland*, 246–7 point to a date for the *Sinodus* in the late fifth

for the continuing existence of druids. A theologian of the mid-seventh century alludes to the 'laughable fables' related by druids in his time; and penitentials and legal writings of this and the subsequent century condemn druids together with other classes of grievous sinner. In other legal texts of the eighth century the existence of druids is acknowledged, but not treated as a social problem: the status tract *Uraicecht Becc* includes them in a list of craftsmen with non-noble status (*dóernemed*), while according to the compilation *Bretha Nemed Tóisech* this status depends on their ability to use magic for military ends.[9]

Even if druids remained in existence thus long, however, the hierarchy of religious authority which they had once dominated was by then a thing of the distant past: Christianity's triumph brought Ireland, in this most essential respect, into line with the lands of the former Roman empire.[10] But what was the nature of the Church which had taken that hierarchy's place? For a considerable time the consensus view, most influentially formulated by Kathleen Hughes, was that an originally episcopal institution assumed an increasingly monastic character; but the work of more recent historians has challenged both the polarity and the evolutionism inherent in this model.[11] Patrick himself, after all, insisted on his own status as a bishop (*Confessio* §26; *Epistola* §1), while at the same time regarding the ordination of monks and nuns as the crowning success of his mission (*Confessio* §§41–2; *Epistola* §12). After an extended review of the evidence for our period, Colmán Etchingham has concluded that it reflects 'a single, multi-faceted organisational model' which 'comprehended a diversity of realities; … an integrated and undifferentiated ecclesiastical structure, in which distinctions between monastic and non-monastic are misleading'. Thomas Charles-Edwards emphasises plurality rather than non-differentiation, but agrees with Etchingham in insisting

---

century or the early sixth. References are to *The Irish Penitentials*, ed. L. Bieler. Scriptores Latini Hiberniae 5 (Dublin: DIAS, 1963), 54–9 §§8, 13–14, 16.

9 Augustinus Hibernicus, *De Mirabilibus Sacrae Scripturae* i.17: *PL*, xxxv.2164; *Irish Penitentials*, 160 §4; '*Bretha Crólige*', ed. D. A. Binchy, *Ériu*, 12 (1938), 40 §51; 'The Old-Irish Table of Penitential Commutations', ed. D. A. Binchy, *Ériu*, 19 (1962), 58 §5; *CIH*, 1612.8–9, 2220.14–15.

10 This is the message of the often-quoted 'downfall of heathendom' section in the prologue to *Félire Óengusso Céli Dé*, ed. W. Stokes (London: Henry Bradshaw Society, 1905), 20–6: just as Peter has displaced Nero as master of Rome, so the great churches of Ireland flourish while its ancient royal strongholds are desolate.

11 K. Hughes, *The Church in Early Irish Society* (London: Methuen, 1966), chs. 5–8. An alternative view was first given in R. Sharpe, 'Some Problems Concerning the Organization of the Church in Early Medieval Ireland', *Peritia*, 3 (1984), 230–70. More recently, see severally C. Etchingham, *Church Organisation in Ireland AD 650 to 1000* (Naas: Laigin, 1999), and W. Follett, *Céli Dé in Ireland: Monastic Writing and Identity in the Early Middle Ages* (Woodbridge: Boydell Press, 2006).

on the coexistence of multiple elements within a single Church; it was for precisely this reason, in his view, that the synod or ecclesiastical assembly was so important as the supreme arbiter in matters of religion:

> The synod shows us an Irish Church which allowed for several sources of authority: the orders of a bishop; the prestige which flowed from being the abbot of a major monastery; the learning of the scribe and the scholar; the asceticism of the anchorite ... Only by focusing these different authorities in the one institution could cohesion be maintained.[12]

Considerable scholarly attention has been devoted to the dynastic affiliations and territorial claims of Irish religious foundations in the pre-Norman period; these are matters of interest and importance, but pertain to ecclesiastical politics rather than to religion as such. More germane to the concerns of this chapter are the questions – intimately connected in their essence, but curiously disjunct in the sources – of the Church's pastoral ministry and its inner life.

The relationship between a church and its lay community is portrayed in contractual terms, as a reciprocal obligation of spiritual services bestowed in exchange for material support. According to the eighth-century *Ríagal Phátraic*, every church is responsible for providing 'baptism and communion and the recitation of intercession [for the dead], for every person whose rightful church it is; and that there should be the offering of the body of Christ upon every altar' (§7; cf. §§5, 8, 9, 12). The local bishop was also charged with administering the sacrament of confirmation (§§1–3), with giving spiritual instruction (*anmchairdes* 'soul-friendship') to the nobility and clergy (§§1, 6), and with ensuring the ritual purity and proper furnishing of church and burial ground (§6). For the 'instruction or spiritual direction' (*forcetul no anmchairdes*) of others, the 'man in orders' was responsible (§12). A negative formulation of the same obligations is found in *Bretha Nemed Toísech*, which gives a list of the failures which deprive a church of its status, beginning 'being without baptism, without communion, without mass, without praying for the dead, without preaching'.[13]

The scope of such legislation, and the density of early ecclesiastical sites on the ground as indicated by archaeological and place-name evidence, have led Richard Sharpe to attribute to Ireland at this time 'one of the most comprehensive pastoral organisations in northern Europe'. This is certainly affirmed

---

12 Etchingham, *Church Organisation*, 456–7; Charles-Edwards, *Early Christian Ireland*, 277.
13 *CIH* 2129.6–2130.37; 'The First Third of *Bretha Nemed Toísech*', ed. and trans. L. Breatnach, *Ériu*, 40 (1989), 10 §6; cf. *CIH*, 2100.38–9, 2211.27–8.

in several of the sources: thus Etchingham cites the statement of the law tract *Córus Aithni* that 'the church is mother of baptism and communion to all'. Not all indications support such a picture, however, and several scholars have suggested that these claims were largely aspirational. In the contemporary legal treatise *Córus Bésgnai*, sacraments and preaching are not available to 'everyone' without qualification, but rather to 'everyone' whose piety merits such ministry. The provisions of *Ríagal Phátraic* are even more telling. While this text is emphatic in asserting that sin and damnation are inevitable without access to the sacraments and to spiritual direction, the priest's responsibility to provide these services is restricted: they are due 'from every church to the *manaig* who belong to it' (§5; cf. §8), 'for every person whose rightful church it is' (§7), for 'the *manaig* both living and dead' (§9).[14]

The term *manaig* (singular *manach*), so crucial in *Ríagal Phátraic*, is a borrowing from Latin *monachus* 'monk', which it can sometimes translate. It has however also undergone an important extension of its sense, in that *monachus* or *manach* was used to designate the lay tenant of a religious establishment.[15] Such a tenant owed dues to the foundation (*monasterium*) to which he was attached, was to varying degrees subordinate in his legal capacity to that foundation's superior, and was obliged to observe a behavioural regime involving regular religious observance as well as dietary and sexual restraint. This way of life was contrasted with the sinful ways of the rest of society (often called simply 'laity'), characterised by promiscuity and bloodshed; and indeed *manaig* were often *conuersi* 'converts' or *athlaíg* 'ex-laymen', engaged in penance for the faults of their former life.[16]

We are accordingly presented with three categories: the clergy; the *manaig* to whom they were obliged to minister; and the lay population more generally, condemned by the Church and not entitled to such ministry. These distinctions were not absolute: there was of course no question of kings and the nobility, albeit they were certainly not *manaig*, being denied spiritual

---

14 R. Sharpe, 'Churches and Communities in Early Medieval Ireland: Towards a Pastoral Model', in J. Blair and R. Sharpe (eds.), *Pastoral Care before the Parish* (Leicester University Press, 1992), 109; Etchingham, *Church Organisation*, 248–9. *CIH*, 529.20–3, 2109.28–9.

15 Other terms received similar treatment in Ireland: Lat. *abbas*/Ir. *ap* can mean 'religious superior' in general, not only 'abbot'; and Lat. *monasterium*/Ir. *mainistir* can apply to a religious foundation of any kind, not only to a monastery.

16 For dues, see the tract *Synodus Sapientium* §5; *Irish Penitentials*, 168. T. M. Charles-Edwards, 'The Church and Settlement', in Ní Chatháin and Richter (eds.), *Irland und Europa*, 171–5; Etchingham, *Church Organisation*, 363–93. For the lifestyle of the *manaig* see the references provided by Ó Corráin in D. Ó Corráin, L. Breatnach and A. Breen, 'The Laws of the Irish', *Peritia*, 3 (1984), 404–5. Etchingham uses the term 'paramonasticism' for 'a penitential or quasi-penitential regime of periodic abstinence and sexual continence'. Etchingham, *Church Organisation*, 292–8, 306–18, quotation at 290.

direction or the sacraments.[17] All the same, it appears likely that large segments of the population would have had little if any experience of the
Church's teaching, or access to its rituals. Etchingham suggests that

> early medieval Irish society was beset by a chronic tension between two ten-
> dencies. On the one hand, the Christian church offered the only coherent,
> respectable, endowed religious system. On the other hand, the extent of
> devotion among the laity seems to have been limited and there were intrinsic
> features of society which carried anti-Christian resonances for churchmen.[18]

But what were 'those things which pertain to a monk'? What spiritual life
was lived within the ecclesiastical enclosures? While the terms *monachus* and
manach could, as we have seen, be applied to individuals who were not monks
in the conventional sense, this is not of course to say that such monks did not
exist. Some texts recognise the terminological ambiguity at the same time
that they attempt to resolve it: thus the Old Irish glossator of the legal tract *Di
Dligiud Raith ⅂ Somaíne la Flaith* distinguishes between *fírmanaig* 'true manaig', qualified by the adjectives *glan* 'pure' and *nóeb* 'holy', and *túathmanaig* 'lay
manaig'. The expression *fírmanach* is likewise found in the text called 'the Old
Irish Penitential', which also speaks of *bráithre* 'brothers' in contexts where
monks *sensu stricto* are evidently being referred to. It will not be possible to
give a comprehensive account of early Irish monasticism here, but it may be
useful to indicate some of its guiding principles and ideals.[19]

The great eighth-century compilation known as the *Collectio canonum
Hibernensis* attributes to Jerome the statement that 'There are three things
which a church protects and maintains: the contemplative [life], and the active,
and the penitent (*theoricam et actualem et penitentem*); a church neither receives
nor protects beyond [that]' (xlii.1). In *Bretha Nemed Toísech*, similarly, the list
of failings in a church which has been cited earlier goes on to include '[being]
without penitents, without the active life, without the contemplative life' (*cen
áes n-aithrige, cen achtáil, cen teoir*); and maintenance of the contemplative and
active lives, and of penitents, are subsequently described as the 'three lights'
which distinguish sanctuaries (*nemid*).[20] That a Christian life should have both

---

17 Their entitlement to these is specified in *Ríagal Phátraic* §§1–2, *CIH* 2129.6–2130.37.
   Charles-Edwards, *Early Christian Ireland*, 118–19.
18 Etchingham, *Church Organisation*, 315.
19 *CIH*, 918.12–16; Etchingham, *Church Organisation*, 340–1, 432–3; cf. 'An Irish Penitential',
   ed. and trans. E. J. Gwynn, *Ériu*, 7 (1914), 150.
20 *Die irische Kanonensammlung*, ed. H. Wasserschleben (Giessen: J. Ricker'sche
   Buchhandlung, 1874), 187; Breatnach, 'First Third', 10 §6, 12 §12 (where the editor renders *sluindte nemthiu* as 'which characterise privileged ecclesiastics').

active and contemplative aspects was a patristic commonplace, and this doctrine is reflected in Irish religious writings also. Elsewhere, however, contemplative and active are seen as two categories of person: in pseudo-Hilary's commentary on the Catholic Epistles, humans and birds respectively symbolise 'men of the active and of the contemplative life', while Old Irish glosses on the discussion of the different members of the Church in Corinthians 1:12 identify the foot and hand as 'people of action' (*óis achtáil*) and the eye as 'people of contemplation' (*óis teoáir*). A Middle Irish Life of Colum Cille makes the division even clearer, stating that when the saint established a church on Iona he had 'three fifties for the contemplative life in monastic service in it, and sixty for the active life'.[21]

Besides communities of clerics and monks, and the *manaig* who supported them, there were hermits and recluses: some living in entire solitude, others remote from their fellows but still in connection with a religious house. The *Collectio canonum* states that after thirty years subject to 'all of the discipline of a monastery' it was permissible to withdraw in this way, 'living only in meditative contemplation' (*in sola contemplatione theorica uiuentes*) (xxxix.3); in other cases such a life was undertaken as a temporary retreat. The hermit or anchorite, also called the *deórad Dé* or 'outcast of God', was accorded extremely high rank, and could be resorted to as an arbiter and worker of miracles; figures called 'anchorites' exercised various other religious offices and may have had 'overall responsibility for those members of a community living a life of more advanced ascetic discipline', and Cogitosus relates that when Brigit needed a bishop for Kildare she summoned 'a solitary … from the wilderness and from his lone existence' (*solitarium … de eremo et de sua uita solitaria*). The celebrity status accorded to such figures in the Church and in society as a whole would have undermined the anchoritic vocation: as Charles-Edwards has observed, 'the *peregrinus* might have renounced the world, but the power which he held prevented the world from renouncing him'.[22]

---

21 For an example of this patristic commonplace, see the late seventh-century *Expositio quatuor euangeliorum* (*PL*, xxx.577); cf. the Leabhar Breac copy of the glossary *Sanas Cormaic*: *Three Irish Glossaries*, ed. W. Stokes (London: Williams and Norgate, 1862), 15. Pseudo-Hilary: *Scriptores Hiberniae Minores*, Pars I, Corpus Christianorum Series Latina 108B, ed. R. E. McNally (Turnhout: Brepols, 1973), 91. Glosses: W. Stokes and J. Strachan, *Thesaurus Palaeohibernicus*, 2 vols. (Cambridge University Press, 1901–2), i, 572 (Wb 12a23-4). The same interpretation is offered by Sedulius Scottus: *PL*, ciii.153. Life of Colum Cille: Herbert, *Iona, Kells, and Derry*, 237.

22 F. Kelly, *A Guide to Early Irish Law*, Early Irish Law Series 3 (Dublin: DIAS, 1988), 41. The suggestion concerning responsibility is that of A. MacDonald, 'Notes on Monastic Archaeology and the Annals of Ulster, 650–1050', in D. Ó Corráin (ed.), *Irish Antiquity: Essays and Studies Presented to M. J. O'Kelly* (Cork: Tower Books, 1981), 316.

The ultimate purpose of both communal and solitary religious life was to bring people into relationship with God. Mixed and compromised as the motives of many religious undoubtedly were, many others surely gave themselves unreservedly to this highest goal. One of the richest and most distilled expressions of the spiritual ideal is the collection of maxims entitled *Aipgitir Chrábaid* and attributed to Colmán mac Beógnai (died 611); while this attribution, and the age of the text, are matters of debate, the *Aipgitir* certainly formed an important part of the dossier of the *Céli Dé* communities in the later eighth century. Salvation is to be found by turning the heart from the world and its desires: 'the four redemptions of the soul' are fear and repentance with respect to temporal things, love and hope for things eternal. Love is also to be felt for one's fellows: 'it is when full of charity that one is holy'; 'watching over the sick' and 'compassion for a neighbour' are integral to the Christian life, and one should be prepared to seek to bring 'the people of the whole world' to God. 'It is when his heart is as it should be that truth is therein', arising 'as a lamp brings forth its light in a dark house'. The monk is warned against a pharisaical, unbalanced piety, in which vices can easily disguise themselves as virtues; rather, he should observe 'devotion subject to moderation according to God's will', in the confidence that a loving and humble heart is the crossroad where all the commandments pass. 'Wisdom without learning is better than learning without wisdom.'[23]

Even if learning (*suíthe*) is inferior to wisdom (*ecnae*) in the eyes of God and the saints, it enjoyed high esteem among both ecclesiastics and laity in early Ireland. *Uraicecht Becc* decrees that 'a sage of scripture (*suí litre*) has equal nobility with the king of a single kingdom', while the legal compilation *Bretha Nemed Déidenach* states that no kingdom can rightly be so called 'without a sage (*ecnae*), without a church, without a king, without a poet'.[24] The Old Irish introduction to the legal collection *Senchas Már* assigns 'equal payment to a king and a bishop and an expert in the law of scripture and a sage of poetry... and to a hospitaller'.[25] That an ecclesiastical scholar of the highest rank (in Latin *sapiens* or *scriba*) had the same rank as a bishop or a king appears from the decrees of an Irish synod; and the law tract *Cethairslicht Athgabálae*

Cogitosus: Colgan, *Trias Thaumaturga*, 518. T. M. Charles-Edwards, 'The Social Background of Irish *Peregrinatio*', *Celtica*, 11 (1976), 53.

23 Follett, *Céli Dé*, 140–3. Aipgitir: I cite my own translation, in J. Carey, *King of Mysteries: Early Irish Religious Writings*, rev. edn. (Dublin: Four Courts Press, 2000), 231–45; for the text, see '*Apgitir Chrábaid*: The Alphabet of Piety', ed. trans. V. Hull, *Celtica*, 8 (1968), 44–89.

24 *CIH*, 1615.4, 2279.16–17, 2331.28, 1123.32. The sense of *ecnae* in this context is made clear a few lines below: 'He will not be an *ecnae* who does not rightly emend scripture' (35).

25 *CIH*, 348.24–349.25.

classes the *suí* together with the bishop and the *deórad Dé* as the three whose testimony a king could not overrule. Like the king, the bishop and the master poet, the chief scholar occupied the apex of a sevenfold hierarchy.[26]

The exceptionally high legal status accorded to ecclesiastical learning is striking, and seems to have been a distinctive feature of early Irish society. Equally striking, and equally distinctive, is the placing of the *fili* (plural *filid*) or professional poet on the same level: like the passage just quoted from the introduction to the *Senchas Már*, *Uraicecht Becc* affirms that 'a master poet (*ollam filed*) and a master of wisdom and a master hospitaller have equal nobility with the king of a single kingdom'. To obtain the highest rank in his profession, the *fili* was required not only to be expert in all of the varieties of poetry, but also to have knowledge of 'the placename lore (*dindšenchas*) and the chief stories of Ireland besides that, to relate to kings and lords and noble folk; for a *fili* is not complete without that'.[27] The formulation cited from *Bretha Nemed Déidenach* in the preceding paragraph associates the scholar with the Church and the *fili* with the king, portraying them as the supreme representatives of ecclesiastical and secular erudition respectively.

Interpretations of the nature of the *filid* have varied. Hector and Nora Chadwick, and Gerard Murphy, saw them as having originated as a part of the druid hierarchy, while Eoin MacNeill held that the *filid* were simply druids under another name; in the second half of the twentieth century, James Carney described the *ollam* or master *fili* as 'most significantly the shadow of a high-ranking pagan priest or druid', and Proinsias Mac Cana spoke of *filid* as being '(culturally) pagan' throughout the early medieval period. Reacting against this view, other scholars have argued that the *filid* were closely associated with, if not indeed a part of, the ecclesiastical establishment. Surveying evidence that Irish canon lawyers conceived of the priesthood as belonging to a larger caste, modelled on the levites of the Old Testament, Donnchadh Ó Corráin has concluded that 'poets were levites and had the privileges as well as the obligations of clergy'. Kim McCone similarly speaks of the

---

26 On the distinction and overlap of *sapiens* and *scriba* see Charles-Edwards, *Early Christian Ireland*, 265–7. Synodal decree: *Irish Penitentials*, 170 §9: the same penalty is exacted for theft from a king, a bishop or a *scriba*. *Cethairslicht Athgabálae: CIH*, 357.25–7. There are several versions of the poetic hierarchy: *Uraicecht na Ríar: The Poetic Grades in Early Irish Law* ed. and trans. L. Breatnach, Early Irish Law Series 2 (Dublin: DIAS, 1987), 84.

27 *Uraicecht Becc: CIH*, 1618.11–13; cf. 2334.38–2335.1. One metrical treatise states that twelve years were required to gain this poetic training: 'Mittelirische Verslehren', ed. R. R. Thurneysen, *Irische Texte*, 3.1 (1891), 31 §1; 50 §91. The text goes on to cite a poem which claims that 'without stories he will not be a *fili*'.

'incorporation of the *fili* and his profession into the ecclesiastical network', and Liam Breatnach of the 'ecclesiastically-educated lawyer or *fili*'.[28]

A substantial body of evidence indicates that the *filid* were closely associated with the Church by the eighth century, and increasingly so thereafter. Thus a Middle Irish discussion of ecclesiastical grades states that every *cathair* or religious settlement has its own *fili*, and the Middle Irish preface to the law tract *Bretha Éitgid* speaks of the monastery of Túaim Drecon as having had a 'school of *filid*' as well as schools of law and ecclesiastical learning.[29] Occasional references to *filid* with ecclesiastical rank, or to ecclesiastics with expertise in *filedacht*, are found in the annals from the ninth century onward, and already in the eighth century we find *filid* belonging to the same families as high-ranking clerics.[30] Describing the non-elite poets known as *baird*, *Bretha Nemed Déidenach* says that they are not required to have 'knowledge in letters or in [syllabic] metres' – types of learning originating in the Church. Such knowledge is however required of *filid* in the first Middle Irish metrical tract, dated to the tenth century; and the second of these tracts, also assigned to the tenth century, gives literacy, grammar and the basics of syllabic prosody a fundamental place in a *fili*'s training. As already noted, several categories in early Irish society were assigned a sevenfold ranking by analogy with the grades of the Church; the hierarchy of the *filid* is in some texts made to correspond to the ecclesiastical hierarchy even more closely, having three sub-grades as well as seven main grades. In *Uraicecht na Ríar*, a legal text assigned by its editor to the second half of the eighth century, a *fili* is required to have only a single sexual partner, and to limit his relations with her to 'lawful nights': prescriptions reminiscent of the regime observed by laymen under close clerical supervision.[31]

28 H. M. and N. K. Chadwick, *The Growth of Literature*, 3 vols. (Cambridge University Press, 1932–40), i, 607–15; G. Murphy, 'Bards and Filidh', *Éigse*, 2 (1940), 200–1; E. MacNeill, *Early Irish Laws and Institutions* (Dublin: Burns Oates and Washbourne, 1935), 82; J. Carney, *The Irish Bardic Poet* (Dublin: DIAS, 1985), 8; P. Mac Cana, '*Regnum* and *Sacerdotium*: Notes on Irish Tradition', *Proceedings of the British Academy*, 65 (1979), 478. Cf. 446: 'The druid dies and yet he lives'. Ó Corráin, Breatnach and Breen, 'Laws of the Irish', 403, 429; K. McCone, *Pagan Past and Christian Present in Early Irish Literature*, Maynooth Monographs 3 (Maynooth: An Sagart, 1990), 25.

29 *CIH* 2102.5; cf. Breatnach, *Uraicecht na Ríar*, 91; *CIH* 250.42, 926.13.

30 McCone, *Pagan Past*, 24–5; K. McCone, 'Dán agus Tallann', *Léachtaí Cholm Cille*, 16 (1986), 12–13. For case studies see *Corpus Genealogiarum Sanctorum Hiberniae*, ed. P. Ó Riain (Dublin: DIAS, 1985), §§690.4, 722.74 (Ruman mac Colmáin), and L. Breatnach, 'Canon Law and Secular Law in Early Ireland: The Significance of *Bretha Nemed*', *Peritia*, 3 (1984), 439–59 (Máel Tuile úa Búirecháin).

31 *CIH*, 1132.20–21, 1495.19–20. Thurneysen, 'Mittelirische Verslehren', 6 §3, 32 §2; on dating see 'The First Middle Irish Metrical Tract', ed. and trans. D. Ó hAodha, in H. Tristram (ed.), *Metrik und Medienwechsel / Metrics and Media*, ScriptOralia 35 (Tübingen: Gunter Narr, 1991), 207–8. Breatnach, *Uraicecht na Ríar*, 81–9, 104 §6; cf. Etchingham, *Church Organisation*, 65–6.

All of these indications reflect a situation in which the *filid* were in intimate association, amounting in some cases to identity, with the clergy: there is nothing surprising here, as the same was the case for men of learning throughout medieval Europe. On the other hand, none of this evidence belongs to the earliest period; and it increases in bulk and emphasis with the passage of time. There are moreover further factors to be taken into account in assessing the *filid*'s background and character. Several scholars have found significance in the etymology of the word *fili*, which originally meant 'seer'; its synonym *éices* originally meant something like 'inner seer', denoting the same faculty with another verbal root. While it is valid to object that a word's etymology is not necessarily relevant to its contemporary meaning, this evidence is certainly strongly suggestive of the *filid*'s antecedents; and in fact Old Irish sources make the possession of *imbas*, a type of inspired clairvoyance associated with the native supernatural, an essential qualification of the master *fili*.[32] The *fili* had other powers as well, being able to protect the king against supernatural attack and also to practise destructive sorcery. The glossary *Sanas Cormaic* (*c.*900) says of the deity Brigit not only that she is 'a goddess whom *filid* used to worship' (using the imperfect tense) but that 'they call her the goddess of poets' (using the present): whether or not this is a statement of fact, it reflects the way in which *filid* were regarded at the time.[33] The great *filid* of Irish tradition are figures of the pagan period. Moreover, the system of poetic grades modelled on the ecclesiastical hierarchy appears to be secondary. Liam Breatnach has called attention to another scheme, in which he suggests that 'we have a trace of an earlier state of affairs': here there are six grades, including both *filid* and *baird*, and the highest rank is designated either *fili* or *deán* 'little god'.[34]

The *filid* are accordingly portrayed as figures originating in and still to a great extent identified with the pagan past, possessed of supernatural powers which had little if anything to do with Christianity. In the course of the eighth century, a time which also witnessed condemnation and demotion of the druids in legal sources, there is evidence of rapprochement and

32 L. Breatnach, 'Poets and Poetry', in K. McCone and K. Simms (eds.), *Progress in Medieval Irish Studies* (Maynooth: Department of Old Irish, Saint Patrick's College, 1996), 76; J. Carey, 'The Three Things Required of a Poet', *Ériu*, 48 (1997), 41–58.

33 Protection: *CIH*, 668.12–13. Sorcery: Breatnach, *Uraicecht na Ríar*, 114 §§23–4. Brigit: 'Sanas Cormaic... Edited from the Copy in the Yellow Book of Lecan', ed. K. Meyer, *Anecdota from Irisvh Manuscripts*, 4 (1912), 1–128: §150: *bandea no adratis filid... deam uocant poetarum.*

34 On legendary poets, see for example the selection of texts translated in P. Ford, *The Celtic Poets: Songs and Tales from Early Ireland and Wales* (Belmont, MA: Ford and Baillie, 1999), 3–52. Six-grade scheme: Breatnach, *Uraicecht na Ríar*, 99–100.

partial assimilation with the Church: in Breatnach's words, an initiative to move beyond 'the conflicting views of the native learned classes and of the ecclesiastics'. Muirchú portrays the *fili* Dubthach moccu Lugair as one of the first of the pagan Irish to welcome Patrick; and in subsequent tales the Holy Spirit utters from his mouth a reconciliation of the old law and the new, and Dubthach himself offers Patrick his own chief disciple as a bishop. Our own understanding can be guided by that of the native tradition: the *filid* appear neither as the shadows of pagan priests nor as quasi-clerical 'levites', but as figures bridging two spiritual worlds.[35]

The Written Word

What we know about the *filid*, and indeed virtually everything that we know about the culture of medieval Ireland, comes to us, however, in written texts, produced in an ecclesiastical milieu. Literacy in the Roman alphabet came to Ireland early; but this was not the first kind of writing that the Irish employed. Like the Germanic peoples, who had devised runes in order to produce inscriptions in their own languages, the Irish invented a writing system named *ogam* which they used for epigraphic purposes well before there is any evidence of their adoption of Roman script. While the creation of *ogam* was evidently inspired by the example of the Roman alphabet, it was constructed on an entirely different basis, consisting of strokes and notches on the ascending edge (or arris) of a standing stone; nor was it simply a cryptographic counterpart of its model, being designed as a vehicle for the sound system of the Irish language, not of Latin. *Ogam* inscriptions are found not only in Ireland, with a concentration in the southwest, but also in regions of Irish settlement in Britain: of particular interest are *ogam* inscriptions in Wales, which appear juxtaposed with British Latin inscriptions in the Roman alphabet. *Ogam* reflects the Irish language at its earliest recorded stage (apart from the scant and often ambiguous testimony of classical geographers): there is general agreement that the oldest specimens go back at least to the fifth century. Very brief, the inscriptions consist exclusively of personal names (almost always male) in the genitive case – a usage which accords with medieval references to their function as boundary and/or funerary markers. There is no telling

---

35 ' "The Caldron of Poesy" ', ed. and trans. L. Breatnach, *Ériu*, 32 (1981), 51. Dubthach: Bieler, *Patrician Texts*, 92, 176; 'An Edition of the Pseudo-Historical Prologue to the *Senchas Már*', ed. J. Carey, *Ériu*, 45 (1994), 1–32.

evidence to indicate that the script was of pagan or of Christian origin, although both scenarios have their advocates.[36]

These inscriptions continued to be executed into the seventh century; thereafter, *ogam* survived only as an antiquarian curiosity. The Roman alphabet in Ireland belonged to scriptoria from the outset, and bookhand rather than monumental script was used even when it was carved into stone.[37] A very few specimens of manuscript practice appear to survive from the sixth century, from which it is apparent that a distinctively Insular form of script was only just beginning to emerge at this time; by the end of the seventh, however, it was fully developed.[38] Although relatively little which can be dated with any confidence to the sixth century survives, there is enough to make it clear that Irish writers of Latin in this period could express themselves with confidence and sometimes with elegance: clear evidence of this is provided by the writings of Columbanus, and the hymn to Patrick traditionally attributed to his follower Secundinus is very likely of sixth-century date as well. From the seventh century we have a wealth of material, including grammars, computistic tracts, biblical exegesis, penitentials, saints' Lives and hymns.[39] Less is preserved from the eighth century, what there is belonging mainly to the last two of these categories; while the ninth century affords almost no evidence of writing in Latin in Ireland, although (as will be discussed more fully below) this was a time when Irish Latin scholarship was flourishing in Carolingian Europe. This has led Sharpe to argue that 'by this date, Ireland had effectively exported her Latin culture to Francia'.[40] The picture is doubtless skewed by the fact that Irish Latin works survive almost exclusively outside Ireland itself; and the Irish scholars whose learning made such an impact on the Continent

---

36 The first attested Germanic runes date from c.AD 200: R. I. Page, *Runes* (London: British Museum, 1987), 23. D. McManus, *A Guide to Ogam*, Maynooth Monographs 4 (Maynooth: An Sagart, 1991). Divergent assessments: E. MacNeill, 'Archaisms in the Ogham Inscriptions', *PRIA*, 39 C (1931), 33–53; C. Swift, *Ogam Stones and the Earliest Irish Christians*, Maynooth Monographs Series Minor 2 (Maynooth: Department of Old and Middle Irish).

37 The earliest example is a sixth-century (?) inscription from Inchagoile, County Galway: F. J. Byrne, 'Introduction', in O'Neill, *Irish Hand*, xi–xii.

38 Discussion in D. N. Dumville, *A Palaeographer's Review: The Insular System of Scripts in the Early Middle Ages*, vol. 1, Institute of Oriental and Occidental Studies Sources and Materials Series 20–1 (Suita: Kansai University Press, 1999), 17–40.

39 *Sancti Columbani Opera*, ed. G. S. M. Walker, Scriptores Latini Hiberniae 2 (Dublin: DIAS, 1957); now also M. Lapidge, 'Columbanus and the "Antiphonary of Bangor"', *Peritia*, 4 (1985), 104–16; ' "Audite omnes amantes": A Hymn in Patrick's Praise', ed. and trans. A. Orchard, in Dumville (ed.), *Saint Patrick*, 153–73; F. J. Byrne, 'Seventh-Century Documents', *Irish Ecclesiastical Record*, 5th ser. 108 (1967), 170–8.

40 R. Sharpe, *Medieval Irish Saints' Lives: An Introduction to Vitae Sanctorum Hiberniae* (Oxford University Press, 1991), 19.

must have received a sound training before they went abroad. Nevertheless, the story of Irish literature from the eighth century onward is one in which writing in the vernacular increasingly predominates.

Apart from the inscriptions already referred to, it is not certain that any of the writing in Irish that has come down to us dates from the sixth century. Various scholars have held that some items at least in the corpus of dynastic poetry associated mainly with Leinster may go back this far; but the only concrete indications point no earlier than the seventh century. If correctly attributed, the poems associated with Colmán mac Lénéni (d. 604) and the devotional tract *Aipgitir Chrábaid* (sometimes as we have seen assigned to Colmán mac Beógnai; d. 611) could belong to the end of the sixth century; but neither ascription is beyond doubt. The tradition that the elegy *Amra Coluim Chille* was composed shortly after the death of Colum Cille in 597 has been accepted by most scholars for well over a century, but has recently been called into serious question by Jacopo Bisagni.[41] No such doubt attaches however to the seventh century. Besides the 'Leinster poems' already referred to, a seventh-century date seems likely and in some cases certain for other poems preserved in genealogical collections, for religious poems,[42] for religious texts in prose,[43] for legal treatises and the opening sections of chronicles, and for compositions relating to kingship.[44] The situation with regard to narrative is uncertain: a case has been made for assigning the tale *Echtrae Chonnlai* to the reign of Fínnachta Fledach (d. 695), but this has met with

41 For cautious acceptance of Thurneysen's positive view of Colmán mac Lénéni's authorship: Breatnach, 'Poets and Poetry', 75. Contrasting views on the *Aipgitir*: Hull, 'Apgitir Chrábaid', 50–2; P. Ó Néill, 'The Date and Authorship of *Apigitir Chrábaid*: Some Internal Evidence', in P. Ní Chatháin and M. Richter (eds.), *Irland und die Christenheit: Bibelstudien und Mission* (Stuttgart: Klett-Cotta, 1987), 203–15. J. Bisagni, 'The Language and the Date of *Amrae Coluimb Chille*', in S. Zimmer (ed.), *Kelten am Rhein: Akten des dreizehnten Internationalen Keltologiekongresses*, 2 vols. Beihefte der Bonner Jahrbücher 58 (Mainz am Rhein: Philipp von Zabern, 2009), ii, 1–11.

42 See the discussion of the date of the poem 'Ba mol Mídend midlaige' in *Two Texts on Loch nEchach*, ed. R. de Vries, ITS 65 (Dublin: ITS, 2012), 63–78. Especially noteworthy are two poems in honour of Colum Cille, which meet the metrical requirements both of stress-based verse and of the syllabic verse introduced from Latin hymnody: 'Tiughraind Bhécáin', ed. and trans. F. Kelly, *Ériu*, 26 (1975), 75.

43 Of particular importance is the bilingual 'Cambrai Homily': Stokes and Strachan, *Thesaurus*, ii, 244–7.

44 Both *Cáin Ḟuithirbe* and *Cáin Adomnáin* date from the close of the century: L. Breatnach, 'The Ecclesiastical Element in the Old Irish Legal Tract *Cáin Fhuithirbe*', *Peritia*, 5 (1986), 36–52; M. Ní Dhonnchadha, 'The Guarantor List of *Cáin Adomnáin*, 697', *Peritia*, 1 (1982), 178–215. On the chronicles: A. P. Smyth, 'The Earliest Irish Annals: Their First Contemporary Entries, and the Earliest Centres of Recording', *PRIA*, 72 C (1972), 1–48. '*Baile Chuinn Chétchathaig*: Edition', ed. E. Bhreathnach and K. Murray, in E. Bhreathnach (ed.), *The Kingship and Landscape of Tara* (Dublin: The Discovery Programme, 2005), 73; *Audacht Morainn*, ed. F. Kelly (Dublin: DIAS, 1976), xxix.

some scepticism.[45] For most of these texts, an origin in a literate (and ecclesiastical) milieu is evident; but oral composition seems a legitimate possibility for some of the secular poems.

Vernacular literacy, accordingly, emerged very early in Ireland by comparison with most of the rest of Christian Europe. This development was not unique: the recording of laws among the Anglo-Saxons goes back at least to the beginning of the seventh century, and the earliest Welsh heroic poetry is held by many scholars to date from the sixth. The standard orthography of Old Irish in fact corresponds to that of Old Welsh in ways which reflect the phonology of the latter, indicating that when the Irish first began writing their own language they were following the example of the Britons.[46] This seed fell however on fertile ground: as can be seen from the invention of *ogam*, the Irish had a keen sense of the value of their own language from an early date. It is in Ireland that we find the first evidence of a vernacular language (as opposed to Latin or the more exotic 'sacred languages' Greek and Hebrew) being taken as an object of scholarly study. Such study is reflected in an extensive corpus of glossaries dealing with the purported etymologies and meanings of Irish words and phrases, the earliest stratum in the oldest of which – the collection *De origine Scoticae linguae*, usually designated 'O'Mulconry's Glossary' – can be assigned to the seventh century.[47] This is much earlier than anything comparable to be found elsewhere in Europe; as is the first attempt at a grammatical description of the Irish language, the treatise *Auraicept na nÉces*. The core of the latter work, to which much material was subsequently added, may date from 'a fairly early stage of the Old Irish period'; as the editor of this 'canonical' portion has rightly emphasised, the *Auraicept* 'must be one of the very first texts in the Western grammatical

45 J. Carey, 'On the Interrelationships of Some *Cín Dromma Snechtai* Texts', *Ériu*, 46 (1995), 88–9; *Echtrae Chonnlai and the Beginnings of Vernacular Narrative Writing in Ireland*, ed. K. McCone, Maynooth Medieval Irish Texts 1 (Maynooth: Department of Old and Middle Irish, 2000), 45, 48.

46 Anglo-Saxon and Welsh: L. Oliver, *The Beginnings of English Law* (University of Toronto Press, 2002), with reference particularly to the laws of Æthelberht of Kent (*c*.600). J. T. Koch, 'When was Welsh Literature First Written Down?', *Studia Celtica* 20/21 (1985–6), 43–66. Spelling: A. Harvey, 'Some Significant Points of Early Insular Celtic Orthography', in D. Ó Corráin, L. Breatnach and K. McCone (eds.), *Sages, Saints and Storytellers: Celtic Studies in Honour of Professor James Carney*, Maynooth Monographs 2 (Maynooth; An Sagart, 1989), 56–66; K. McCone, *Towards a Relative Chronology of Ancient and Medieval Celtic Sound Change*, Maynooth Studies in Celtic Linguistics 1 (Maynooth: Department of Old and Middle Irish, Saint Patrick's College, 1996), 30–2.

47 'O'Mulconry's Glossary', ed. W. Stokes, *Archiv für celtische Lexikographie*, 1 (1900), 232–324; discussion of dating by E. MacNeill, 'De Origine Scoticae Linguae', *Ériu*, 11 (1930–2), 112–29. On the glossary literature as a whole, see P. Russell, 'The Sounds of a Silence: The Growth of Cormac's Glossary', *Cambridge Medieval Celtic Studies*, 15 (1988), 1–30.

tradition that ever even tried to contrast a classical language with the vernacular of the writer'. Nothing similar was to appear until the composition of an Icelandic grammar in the eleventh century, followed by an Occitan grammar in the twelfth.[48]

Perhaps the most striking expression of this esteem for the Irish language is the legend of how it was invented by Fénius Farsaid, legendary forefather of the Gaels, after the division of languages at the Tower of Babel: 'what was best then of every language and what was widest and finest was cut out into Irish'. This story introduces the *Auraicept*, and may have formed part of the original composition; it is considerably expanded in the later sections of the work, and also in texts of the eleventh century and subsequently which lie beyond the scope of this discussion. The idea that Irish had been extracted from other languages is already present in the glossary *De origine Scoticae linguae*, where it is stated that 'the Irish derived their origin from the Greeks, [and] thus also their language'. The roots of the tale of the construction of the Irish language may lie, again, in Britain: some versions state that the universal language spoken before Babel was called *Goirtigernn*, a Brittonic word meaning 'overlord'.[49]

The literary use of the vernacular was particularly apt as a vehicle for secular narrative, and especially for stories drawing some at least of their materials from indigenous tradition. As mentioned above, we may have some evidence for the writing of tales in Irish from as early as the seventh century; by the eighth century there is a substantial corpus, reflecting a saga tradition which is already vigorous and sophisticated; and productivity in this area continued, and gained momentum, throughout the remainder of our period and beyond. It may again be noted that there are no contemporary European parallels for this phenomenon, with narrative prose only emerging in the twelfth century, and becoming firmly established in the course of the thirteenth. By contrast, Old Irish lacks a tradition of narrative

---

48 *The Early Irish Linguist: An Edition of the Canonical Part of the Auraicept na nÉces*, ed. and trans. A. Ahlqvist, Commentationes Humanarum Litterarum 73 (Helsinki: Societas Scientiarum Fennica, 1982), 36, 19; the expanded text in *Auraicept na n-Éces: The Scholars' Primer*, ed. G. Calder (Edinburgh: John Grant, 1917). *First Grammatical Treatise: The Earliest Germanic Phonology*, ed. and trans. E. Haugen (London: Longman, 1972); *Grammaires Provençales de Hugues Faidit et de Raymond Vidal de Besaudun*, ed. F. Guessard, 2nd edn (Paris: Brunsvic, 1858). Cf. W. K. Perceval, 'The Grammatical Traditions and the Rise of the Vernaculars', *Current Trends in Linguistics*, 13 (1975), 231–75.

49 Invented language: Ahlqvist's trans., *Early Irish Linguist*, 48. His view that the passage is original, has been questioned by H. Roe in his review of this work: *Peritia* 6/7 (1987–8), 338; Stokes. 'O'Mulconry's Glossary', 235; *Goirtigernn*: J. T. Koch, 'On the Origins of the Old Irish Terms *Goídil* and *Goídelc*', in G. Evans et al. (eds.), *Origins and Revivals: Proceedings of the First Australian Conference of Celtic Studies* (University of Sydney, 2000), 5–6.

poetry comparable to that of Old English: poems which actually tell stories, rather than merely alluding to them or accompanying them, do not appear to antedate the tenth century.[50]

The prestige and importance of such tales is reflected in the requirement, already mentioned, that they form part of the repertoire of the elite professional poet or *fili*, with one text going so far as to claim that a *fili* should know 350 stories. An Old Irish anecdote describes a master poet as being able to recite 'a tale every night ... from Samain to Beltaine', in other words for six months: a less inflated but still impressive figure. Versions of a tale-list have been preserved, the 'common core' of which (comprising rather less than 200 items) appears to derive from the tenth century.[51] The subjects of these stories are various. Many concern the semi-divine warrior Cú Chulainn and his contemporaries in pre-Christian Ulster, and there are tales of kings, sages and poets belonging both to the pagan and to the early Christian periods. Several stories feature the supernatural inhabitants of the *síde* (the hollow hills or the Otherworld; singular *síd*), and in a few these beings are the only characters. There are only a few texts relating to Find mac Cumaill, the other great hero of Gaelic tradition, although he was surely already prominent in oral narrative; subsequent to the time covered in the present chapter, the literature concerning Find proliferated enormously.[52]

The literary interests of one man of learning are reflected in *Cín Dromma Snechtai*, a collection of tales and other materials which appears to have been compiled at the church of Drumsnat, in County Monaghan, perhaps in the eighth century. The manuscript itself has not survived, but its contents have been reconstructed on the basis of references to it in later sources. It appears to have contained genealogical lore, and some account or accounts of the legendary settlements of Ireland. The compiler also assembled stories from the Ulster heroic cycle, as well as lore concerning the origins of Lough Foyle, and texts relating to early kings of Tara and the ideology of the Tara kingship. Having brought these together, he then

---

50 T. O. Clancy, 'Before the Ballad: Gaelic Narrative Verse before 1200', *Scottish Gaelic Studies*, 24 (2008), 115–31.

51 P. Mac Cana, *The Learned Tales of Medieval Ireland* (Dublin: DIAS, 1980), 83, 111–15; *Compert Mongáin and Three Other Early Mongán Tales*, ed. N. White, Maynooth Medieval Irish Texts 5 (Maynooth: Department of Old and Middle Irish, 2006), 73 §1.

52 R. Thurneysen, *Die irische Helden- und Königsage bis zum siebzehnten Jahrhundert* (Halle: Niemeyer, 1921). Published nearly a century ago, this 700-page survey has never been surpassed. D. M. Wiley, *Essays on the Early Irish King Tales* (Dublin: Four Courts Press, 2008), 54–67. K. Murray, 'Interpreting the Evidence: Problems with Dating the Early *Fíanaigecht* Corpus', in S. J. Arbuthnot and G. Parsons (eds.), *The Gaelic Finn Tradition* (Dublin: Four Courts Press, 2012), 31–49.

combined them to create new narratives, all of them with a pronounced supernatural dimension, and all of them localised in the north of Ireland. *Cín Dromma Snechtai* as a whole is accordingly a witness both to a keen interest in the pre-Christian past, and to a readiness to make creative use of traditional materials. Some scholars have been inclined to view the surviving tales as no more than 'inartistic manuscript versions' which, in all essentials, present 'a fair reflection of the oral narrative of pre-literate tradition'.[53] Quite apart from failing to do justice to the literary merits of many of these texts, such assessments ignore fundamental aspects of their style, structure and content. To this, James Carney had already made the succinct objection that 'early Irish written work has the character of written work', going on to state that 'it is a literature based in part upon oral tradition, but the assumption that it is oral tradition in any very full sense cannot be made'. Subsequent research has gone further, arguing persuasively that Christian Latin models, and the stories of the Vulgate Bible in particular, provided a starting point for Irish writers attempting to compose stories in their own language.[54]

Such correctives are of crucial importance. But it is at least equally important not to allow this revisionist perspective to obscure the fact that, as Carney freely acknowledged, 'without any doubt this literature was based in part upon an oral tradition going back to the remote pre-Christian past'. It is this which is remarkable: that the clerically trained literate elite of a Christian society should have been so imaginatively preoccupied with their pagan antecedents. Nor were such tales 'mere' entertainment; both annals and genealogies affirmed an unbroken, factual continuity between the kings and heroes of ancient times and the medieval Irish.[55] An elaborate scheme of legendary history, documenting both the primeval settlements of Ireland and the origins of the Gaels, was in the process of development throughout our period. This system was given its most influential expression in the prosimetrum treatise *Lebor Gabála Érenn*, composed in the second half of the eleventh

---

53 G. Murphy, *Saga and Myth in Ancient Ireland* (Dublin: Three Candles, 1961), 8; P. Mac Cana, 'Conservation and Innovation in Early Celtic Literature', *Études celtiques*, 13 (1971), 98.

54 J. Carney, *Studies in Irish Literature and History* (Dublin: DIAS, 1955), 322; McCone, *Pagan Past*, 48–52.

55 Carney, *Studies*, 321. Mere entertainment: *Ad delectationem stultorum*, in the cutting words of the Latin colophon to the Book of Leinster *Táin*. Factual continuity G. Toner, 'The Ulster Cycle: Historiography or Fiction?', *Cambrian Medieval Celtic Studies*, 40 (2000), 1–20. The relevant entries in the annals may however not antedate the tenth (or indeed the eleventh) century: thus D. N. Dumville, 'The *Táin* and the Annals: A Caveat', *Éigse*, 17:1 (1977), 47–54.

century, but had already more or less crystallised by the time of the Armagh scholar Eochaid úa Flainn (*c*.936–1004).[56]

The strong desire for a sense of connection with the deeper past is vividly reflected in stories which ascribe knowledge of that past to a first-hand witness. This may be a revenant come back from the dead, like Find mac Cumaill's follower Caílte in one of the stories concerning the seventh-century ruler Mongán, or the Ulster heroes Fergus mac Roich and Cú Chulainn.[57] From at least the tenth century there are many references to the immortal historian Fintan mac Bóchrai, said to have come to Ireland before the Flood and then to have lived on until the time of the early Irish saints.[58] Apparently earlier (ninth century?), and still more unusual, is the story of Tuán mac Cairill, who lived through all of the settlements of Ireland by periodically changing into different animals. He was rejuvenated with each metamorphosis, and at last reborn as a human being, possessing all of the knowledge accumulated in the course of his previous lives: 'Whatever history and genealogy there is in Ireland, its origin is from Tuán son of Cairell.' This sequence of metamorphoses culminating in a rebirth, together with the image of a sage who recalls his former lives, shows analogies with the doctrines ascribed to Pythagoras, with whose teachings those of the druids of Gaul had been compared. Yet more remarkable is a brief Old Irish text purporting to recount a conversation between Saint Colum Cille and a youth perhaps to be identified as Mongán: not only does the youth also claim to be able to remember the distant past, thanks to having existed as several different creatures, but he speaks of reincarnation as the common lot of humanity. Dialogue with a saint places these ideas within a Christian framework, but the ideas themselves are anything but Christian.[59]

56 *Lebor Gabála Érenn*, ed. R. A. S. Macalister, ITS 34, 35, 39, 41, 44 (London: ITS, 1938–56). On the question of Eochaid's identity, see most recently M. Ó Mainnín, 'Eochaid Ua Flainn agus Eochaid Ua Flannucáin: Súil Úr ar an bhFianaise', *Léann*, 2 (2009), 75–105.

57 Caílte and Fergus: *Compert Mongáin*, 73–4, 79–81; 'The Finding of the *Táin*', ed. and trans. K. Murray, *Cambrian Medieval Celtic Studies*, 41 (2001), 17–23. In the absence of a critical edition of the tale *Síaburcharpat Con Culainn*, the most conveniently accessible text is probably that in *Lebor na hUidre: Book of the Dun Cow*, ed. R. I. Best and O. Bergin (Dublin: RIA, 1929), 278–87; an abridged and emended version of the flawed translation by J. O'B. Crowe was published in E. Hull, *The Cuchullin Saga in Irish Literature* (London: David Nutt, 1898), 275–88.

58 Of the many texts referring to Fintan, only *Airne Fíngein* seems clearly to fall within our period: *Airne Fíngein*, ed. J. Vendryes, Mediaeval and Modern Irish Series 15 (Dublin: DIAS, 1953), 5–7. See also 'The Settling of the Manor of Tara', ed. and trans. R. I. Best, *Ériu*, 4 (1908–10), 162–4; and J. Carey, 'Origin and Development of the Cesair Legend', *Éigse*, 22 (1987), 37–48.

59 'Scél Tuáin meic Chairill', ed. and trans. J. Carey, *Ériu*, 35, (1984), 93–111; 'The Lough Foyle Colloquy Texts: *Immacaldam Choluim Chille ⁊ ind Óclaig oc Carraic Eolairg* and *Immacaldam in Druad Brain ⁊ inna Banḟáṫho Febuil ós Loch Ḟebuil*', ed. and trans. J. Carey, *Ériu*, 52 (2002), 54–71.

Above, we have seen evidence that there were still druids in Ireland in the eighth century: a text like the youth's colloquy with Colum Cille suggests that other elements of paganism may have endured this late, or even later. Such survivals would have belonged mainly to oral, popular culture, and are consequently irrecoverable from the medieval written record; but there are a few suggestive indications. Falling just after our period, but surely reflecting customs inherited from the first millennium, are the statement in one eleventh-century tale that 'women and the common people' pray on the night of Samain or Hallowe'en to 'Mongfind the *síd*-woman'; and the reference in the Annals of Tigernach under the year 1084 to a man 'who used to visit the *síd* every year on the night of Samain', apparently to obtain knowledge of the future. *Bethu Phátraic*, a composite text, most of which appears to date from around the end of the ninth century, speaks of immortal 'guardians' existing in various parts of Ireland, one of whom receives every Easter the offering of 'a haunch of meat together with its trimmings, and a pitcher of ale'. Although these beings are said to be followers of Patrick, and to owe their deathlessness to his miraculous powers, their origin is evidently pre-Christian; it is noteworthy that one of them was still the recipient of offerings at this late date, however domesticated and reinterpreted by the Church.[60]

That the native supernatural should have remained important for the laity is not surprising – especially given that, as we have seen above, extensive segments of the lay population may have received little if any pastoral supervision. The popular beliefs of which traces can be found in medieval sources are indeed abundantly attested in the 'fairy faith' of modern times. More curious is evidence that the old gods also had some kind of ongoing role in the mental world of the literate clergy. Thus references to the divinities Goibniu, Dían Cécht and Flidais figure in the manuscripts side by side with Christian prayers and with appeals to Christ, saints and angels. Sometimes these allusions seem to be to events in the past, like the *historiolae* or magical anecdotes featuring the Germanic god Woden/Wotan which are attested in Old English and Old High German; but in other cases the non-Christian powers are addressed directly, with the formulaic word *ad-muiniur*, 'I invoke'.[61] Especially remarkable is an extended composition which calls on the persons of the Trinity, but

60 S. H. O'Grady (ed. and trans.), *Silva Gadelica*, 2 vols. (London: Williams and Norgate, 1892), i, 332; *Ann. Tig.*, 416–17; *Bethu Phátraic*, ed. K. Mulchrone (Dublin: RIA, 1939), 75.
61 For an edition of the Old English 'Nine Herbs Charm', see *The Anglo-Saxon Minor Poems*, ed. E. V. K. Dobie, Anglo-Saxon Poetic Records 6 (New York: Columbia University Press, 1942), 119–21; for the Old High German Merseburg charm, see R. Ködderitzsch, 'Der 2. Merseburger Zauberspruch und seine Parallelen', *Zeitschrift für celtische Philologie*, 33 (1974), 45–57.

also and more conspicuously on 'the seven daughters of the sea who form the threads of the long-lived youths', 'my silver champion, who has not died, who will not die' and 'Senach of the seven ages, whom fairy women fostered on the breasts of inspiration'. If the Fer Fio to whom this invocation is attributed was the same as the *sapiens* and religious superior of that name who died in 762, this is evidence that syncretistic attitudes could obtain even among the clerical elite.[62]

For anyone of a thoughtful turn of mind, such an anomalous juxtaposition of beliefs would require some justification; and attempts at such justification are in fact to be found in the early literature. We have already seen that the Old Testament may have provided a precedent for the coexistence of one supreme God with a plurality of lesser gods. There is also evidence of further speculations: that the gods of the pagan Irish were angels exiled from heaven but not condemned to hell; or alternatively, that they were a branch of the human race which had escaped the effects of original sin; and that their Otherwordly habitation, often portrayed as lying 'in the hills' or beneath the earth, was located in the southern hemisphere. A passage in the hymn *Altus Prosator*, probably composed on Iona early in the seventh century, appears to equate the native immortals with 'those beneath the earth' (*inferni*) in Philippians 2:10 (cf. Revelation 5:3: *subtus terram*). From the ninth century onward, we also find references to views widely attested elsewhere in Christendom: that the gods of paganism were devils, or great figures of the past whose deeds had been exaggerated by posterity.[63]

This many-sided engagement with indigenous tradition on the part of the ecclesiastical intelligentsia is a remarkable aspect of medieval Irish culture; but it should not be imagined that enthusiasm for what was native entailed indifference toward what was foreign. From the earliest period for which we have evidence, it is clear that the Irish had a voracious enthusiasm for the learning of the wider world. Besides the Bible, many of the Church Fathers and the acts of Church councils, Irish literature reflects extensive familiarity with (for instance) the literature of time-reckoning (important because of its relevance to calculating the date of Easter, but also valued in the context of an interest in cosmology), and with treatises on Latin grammar. Scholars made use of the encyclopaedic writings of the Spanish bishop Isidore of Seville

---

62 J. Carey, 'Téacsanna Draíochta in Éirinn sa Mheánaois Luath', *Léachtaí Cholm Cille*, 30 (2000), 98–117.

63 J. Carey, 'Ireland and the Antipodes: The Heterodoxy of Virgil of Salzburg', *Speculum*, 64 (1989), 1–10; J. Carey, *A Single Ray of the Sun: Religious Speculation in Early Ireland*, 2nd edn (Aberystwyth: Celtic Studies Publications, 2011), 1–38.

(*c*.560–636), especially of his *Etymologiae*, and also of the earlier secular compendia by Pliny the Elder (*Historia naturalis*) and Servius (commentary on the *Aeneid*).[64]

Some of the works available to the Irish were rare elsewhere: thus, with a single exception, all but one of the surviving copies of Servius appear to go back to an Irish exemplar.[65] Ireland has a notably rich apocryphal literature, best attested from the later Middle Ages but clearly already flourishing in our period; this includes texts, or traces of texts, which are not otherwise attested in Latin Christendom, and sometimes not otherwise attested at all. M. R. James was exaggerating somewhat when he stated that 'the transmission of apocryphal writings, otherwise unknown, in the Irish vernacular would be a proper subject for a small monograph', but there are certainly some noteworthy specimens. Thus the Old Irish cosmological treatise *In Tenga Bithnúa* is based in part on the apocryphal *Acts of Philip*, a work otherwise attested only in Greek, and in part apparently on a lost Egyptian Gnostic apocalypse.[66] Among other examples is the work known as the Ethiopic Book of Enoch: its catalogue of fallen angels provided the basis for a list of archangels in the Middle Irish poem-cycle *Saltair na Rann*, and the only direct evidence for a Latin version is an extract preserved in a Breton manuscript with Hiberno-Latin contents. David Dumville has made the attractive suggestion that a significant number of apocryphal texts may have reached Ireland from Spain, where they had been collected by the followers of the schismatic Priscillian of Avila. According to this scenario, the same channels which brought the Irish into the cultural mainstream by transmitting the works of Isidore were also responsible for introducing them to knowledge of more deviant kinds.[67]

64 For Irish computistic knowledge in the early seventh century, see *Cummian's Letter De Controversia Paschali and the De Ratione Conputandi*, ed. M. Walsh and D. Ó Cróinín (Toronto: Pontifical Institute of Medieval Studies, 1988). For general discussion of grammar, see V. Law, *The Insular Latin Grammarians* (Woodbridge: Boydell Press, 1982). M. Herren, 'Classical and Secular Learning among the Irish before the Carolingian Renaissance', *Florilegium*, 3 (1981), 118–57.
65 J. J. H. Savage, 'The Manuscripts of the Commentary of Servius Danielis on Virgil', *Harvard Studies in Classical Philology*, 43 (1932), 120; J. J. H. Savage, 'The Manuscripts of Servius's Commentary on Virgil', *Harvard Studies in Classical Philology*, 45 (1934), 157.
66 D. N. Dumville, 'Biblical Apocrypha and the Early Irish: A Preliminary Investigation', *PRIA*, 73 C (1973), 299–338; M. R. James, 'Irish Apocrypha', *Journal of Theological Studies*, 20 (1919), 9; *In Tenga Bithnua: The Ever-new Tongue*, ed. J. Carey, Corpus Christianorum Series Apocryphorum 16 (Turnhout: Brepols, 2009), 58–63.
67 R. Thurneysen, 'Mélanges irlandais', *Revue celtique*, 6 (1883–5), 371–3; J. Carey, 'Angelology in *Saltair na Rann*', *Celtica*, 17 (1987), 6–7; 'A Fragment of the Book of Enoch in Latin', ed. M. R. James, *Apocrypha Anecdota*, Texts and Studies 2:3 (Cambridge University Press, 1893), 146–50; Dumville, 'Biblical Apocrypha', 322.

Irish Influence Abroad

Assiduous study led to the rise of eminent schools, celebrated not only in Ireland but also overseas. Bede, in a famous passage, describes many of the English as travelling to Ireland in the seventh century 'for the sake of religious study' (*diuinae lectionis … gratia*); and elsewhere he speaks of the bishop Agilbert, born in Gaul, having 'dwelt for no short time in Ireland in order to study the scriptures'. Writing in the latter part of the seventh century, Aldhelm of Malmesbury also attests (albeit disapprovingly) to the attraction which Irish schools had for English students: besides scriptural exegesis, he indicates that instruction in grammar, geometry, physics and classical mythology was available. That this reputation endured, at least in Wales, is apparent from the poet Ieuan of Llanbadarn Fawr's account of his father Sulien (1011–1091): moved by the example of 'the fathers', Sulien spent years studying with 'the Irish, illustrious in marvellous wisdom … a race famous for scriptures and teachers'.[68]

Many important parts of the Irish story have lain beyond the confines of the island: this chapter will conclude with a brief consideration of the Irish overseas in the first millennium. Various Irish settlements were established in western Britain in the sub-Roman period; but these were political developments and lie outside the remit of this chapter. More germane were the travels of Irish ecclesiastics. Inspired perhaps in part by Patrick's own situation as a 'newcomer and exile' (*proselitus et profuga*) dwelling among barbarians for the love of God (*Epistola* §1), in part by the example of the Desert Fathers, and in part by an ascetic desire to embrace the degradation which outcast status entailed in native Irish society, Irish ecclesiastics came to cultivate an ideal of *peregrinatio pro amore Dei*: a spiritually motivated self-banishment from one's own land and kindred, and from that anchorage in the world and its concerns which contact with these gave.[69] Such *peregrini* might simply travel to another territory in Ireland, but others felt the need to undertake a 'mightier pilgrimage' (*potior peregrinatio*) and leave Ireland altogether. The most famous of these were Colum Cille (d. 597), a member of the Cenél Conaill dynasty who founded a monastery

---

68 *Bede's Ecclesiastical History*, 234; *Aldhelmi Opera*, ed. R. Ehwald. Monumenta Germaniae Historica, Auctores Antiquissimi 15 (Berlin: Weidmann, 1919), 479, 490–1. *Hibernos sophia mirabili claros … famosam gentem scripturis atque magistris*: 'The Welsh-Latin Poetry of Sulien's Family', ed. and trans. M. Lapidge, *Studia Celtica*, 8/9 (1973–4), 84–6.

69 For outcast status see T. M. Charles-Edwards, 'The Social Background of Irish Peregrinatio', *Celtica*, 11 (1976), 43–59. *Peregrinatio pro amore Dei*: I have not been able to find an early source for this frequently quoted phrase. Some close approximations from *uitae* of Walaric and Gall are cited by L. Gougaud, *Christianity in Celtic Lands*, trans. M. Joynt (London: Sheed and Ward, 1932), 130 n. 2.

on the Hebridean island of Iona, preached among the Picts, and established a *familia* or network of monasteries ranging across Ireland and Britain; Columbanus (d. 615), a Leinsterman who left home to study in Ulster, then travelled to France and ultimately to Italy, founding a series of monasteries which disseminated Irish conceptions of penance and monastic discipline; and Fursa (d. *c*.648), a nobleman from eastern Ulster who founded a monastery among the East Angles before crossing to the Continent to establish the monastery of Lagny in France, and whose burial-place of Péronne became the home of an Irish community which endured until its destruction by vikings in 880 (see Map 5).[70]

Toward the end of the seventh century, English clerics began journeying to the Continent to evangelise their Germanic kin; it is interesting that this missionary initiative originated among English monks resident in Ireland. Irish monks preached in the same territories: thus Kilian and two of his companions were martyred at Würzburg around the year 689.[71] The Irish were also instrumental in establishing Christianity in Bavaria. Bruno Krusch's argument that the missionary Corbinian, first bishop of Freising, was an Irishman has not met with universal agreement, but there can be no doubt that in the mid-eighth century the Bavarian Church was under the authority of the Irish bishop Virgil of Salzburg, notorious for his alleged advocacy of the idea that 'another world and other men' (*alius mundus et alii homines*) exist beneath the earth. The oldest *liber confraternitatum* or necrology for the church of St Peter at Salzburg, evidently begun by Virgil, contains a list of the abbots of Iona extending from Columba down to Virgil's own contemporary Slébéne (d. 767): it accordingly seems likely that Virgil himself had belonged to a Columban community.[72] Irish monks travelled further afield as well. Writing in the year 825, the Irish geographer Dicuil speaks of having been told by *clerici* thirty years previously (i.e. in 795) of their visit to 'Thule' or Iceland, this being our earliest evidence for any human presence in that country, and

70 Jonas of Bobbio, *Vita Columbani Discipulorumque Eius*, in *Passiones Vitaeque Sanctorum Aevi Merovingici*, ed. B. Krusch, Monumenta Germaniae Historica, Scriptores Rerum Merovingicarum 4 (Hannover and Leipzig: Hahn, 1902), 68. The fundamental treatment of Colum Cille is Herbert, *Iona, Kells, and Derry*. For Fursa: *Transitus Beati Fursei: A Translation of the 8th Century Manuscript*, ed. O. Rackham (Norwich: Fursey Pilgrims, 2007).

71 *Bede's Ecclesiastical History*, 312; cf. D. Ó Cróinín, 'Rath Melsigi, Willibrord, and the Earliest Echternach Manuscripts', *Peritia*, 3 (1984), 17–49. F. Emmerich, *Der heilige Kilian, Regionarbischof und Märtyrer* (Würzburg: A. Göbel, 1896), with an edition of the earliest *uita* at 3–10.

72 Discussion in L. Vogel, *Vom Werden eines Heiligen: eine Untersuchung der Vita Corbiniani des Bischofs Arbeo von Freising* (Berlin: Walter de Gruyter, 2000), 80–125; Carey, 'Ireland and the Antipodes'; *Dioecesis Salisburgensis*, ed. S. Herzberg-Fränkel, Monumenta Germaniae Historica, Necrologia Germaniae 2 (Berlin: Weidmann, 1904), 27.

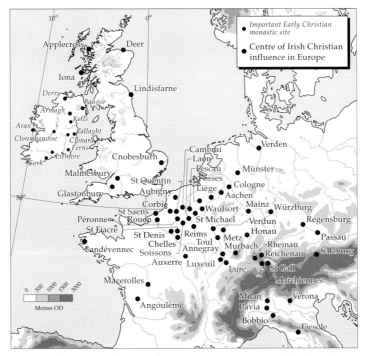

MAP 5. The Travels of Early Irish Missionaries. Courtesy of Matthew Stout, School of History and Geography, DCU.

of having heard one 'brother Fidelis' relate to 'my master Suibne' an account of a journey to Egypt.[73]

The nature of the Irish presence on the Continent was modified in the ninth century. Responding both to the vulnerability of their communities to viking attack, and to the vigorous patronage of learning offered by Carolingian rulers, many Irish scholars emigrated in order to seek careers as teachers rather than in obedience to an ascetic and/or missionary vocation; the scale of this phenomenon was such that a writer like Heiric of Auxerre could say, albeit with some exaggeration, that 'almost the whole of Ireland, setting the obstacle of the sea at nought, is migrating to our shores with a herd of philosophers (*cum grege philosophorum*)'.[74] The expertise in such subjects as grammar, biblical studies and computistics which had made Irish schools so attractive two centuries

73 *Dicuili Liber de Mensura Orbis Terrae*, ed. J. J. Tierney. Scriptores Latini Hiberniae 6 (Dublin: DIAS, 1967), vi.12–19; vii.11, pp. 62–3, 74–5.
74 From the dedication to Charles the Bald introducing his Life of Germanus of Auxerre: *PL*, cxxiv.1133.

before were assets to Irish men of learning now. Dicuil, mentioned above, was only one of the scholars from Ireland active under Charlemagne; and the Irish contribution to continental learning continued under Charlemagne's successors. Two particularly notable intellects distinguished the reign of his grandson Charles the Bald: Sedulius Scottus, celebrated as a teacher, as the author of a treatise on kingship, as a sophisticated poet in the manner of Horace, and as 'a scholar of universal interests'; and Johannes Eriugena, remarkable for his knowledge of Greek and more remarkable still for the power of his speculative intellect, which rendered him the greatest philosopher of the early Middle Ages. But the Irish literati of this period were not only purveyors of what we would regard as enlightenment: of the magical texts mentioned earlier, several are preserved in manuscripts in Switzerland and Austria.[75]

With the passing of the Carolingians the centre of power shifted eastward, to the Saxon dukes who established the Holy Roman Empire. Irish churchmen were recognised as having an important place in the contemporary climate of ecclesiastical reform: thus the emperor Otto the Great, by a charter dated 946, assigned the Lotharingian monastery of Waulsort to 'servants of God coming for the sake of pilgrimage from the land of *Scotia*, and wishing to live under the rule of Benedict', and expressed his hope that the community would remain 'under the authority of the *Scoti*'; while Otto's brother Bruno, bishop of Cologne, had as his teacher a certain *Israel episcopus Scotigena*.[76] An Irish and Scottish monastic presence continued in the region into the second half of the century and beyond.[77] This may seem a rather anticlimactic point at which to end this survey, but in fact tenth-century Lotharingia provided the setting for one of the most far-reaching contributions which medieval Ireland was to make to the Western imagination. The two oldest manuscripts of *Nauigatio Sancti Brendani*, 'the best known legend of the Middle Ages', have a 'Lotharingian-Rhenish provenance'; and the *Nauigatio*'s editor, Carl Selmer, went so far as to place it 'among the outstanding literary products of the so-called Ottonian period'.[78] The *Nauigatio* is now regarded as being in fact of earlier date, and as

75 L. Bieler, *Ireland Harbinger of the Middle Ages*, rev. edn (Oxford University Press, 1966), 124. A brief and lucid study is J. J. O'Meara, *Eriugena* (Oxford University Press, 1988). Magical texts: Stokes and Strachan, *Thesaurus*, ii.248–9, 293; Stokes, 'Mélanges', 112–15.

76 *Diplomata regum et imperatorum Germaniae* pars II, ed. E. Sickel (Berlin: Weidmann, 1879–84; repr. Munich, 1980), i, 160–1; cited with discussion in D. N. Dumville, 'St Cathróe of Metz and the Hagiography of Exoticism', in J. Carey, M. Herbert and P. Ó Riain (eds.), *Studies in Irish Hagiography: Saints and Scholars* (Dublin: Four Courts Press, 2001), 179–80. Ruotger, *Vita Brunonis*, cap. 7: *PL*, cxxxiv.946.

77 There is a helpful discussion in Dumville, 'St Cathróe'.

78 *Navigatio Sancti Brendani abbatis*, ed. C. Selmer (South Bend: University of Notre Dame Press, 1959), xxvii–xxix.

probably having been composed in Ireland, but it remains the case that it was from a continental point of dissemination, at the very end of our period, that the tale spread across Europe in a proliferation of copies, translations and adaptations. Brendan's search for an earthly Paradise beyond the sea, while it was regarded by Romantic writers as quintessentially Celtic, has also been held to have inspired figures as diverse, and as pivotal, as Dante and Columbus.[79]

79 *Navigatio Sancti Brendani*, ed. G. Orlandi. 2 vols. (Milan and Varese: Istituto Editoriale Cisalpino, 1968), i, 72–3 (ninth century); D. N. Dumville, 'Two Approaches to the Dating of *Navigatio Sancti Brendani*', *Studi medievali*, 3rd ser., no. 29 (1988), 87–102, and Sharpe, *Medieval Irish Saints' Lives*, 17–18, argue for a late eighth-century date at latest. Ernest Renan, *Essais de morale et de critique* (Paris: Michel Lévy Frères, 1859), 442: 'La légende de saint Brandan est sans contredit le produit le plus singulier de cette combinaison du naturalisme celtique avec le spiritualisme chrétien'; cf. C. Labitte, 'La *Divine Comédie* avant Dante', *Revue des Deux Mondes*, 31 (1842), 727.

3

Art and Society

JANE HAWKES

THE early medieval era has often been referred to as 'The Golden Age of Irish Art'. The term emerged from a scholarly tradition that examined artistic material within a discourse of independence and nationalism. This discourse invoked art to demonstrate the nature of Irish culture prior to the incorporation of the island into the English and later British Empire. This approach has coloured observations made about material which in its own terms is a vibrant strand within the broad traditions of early medieval Christian and Western European art histories. Indeed, the art of early medieval Ireland has long been viewed as deeply significant within these histories. Its decorated metalwork, illuminated manuscripts and carved stone sculptures feature in almost every discussion of the art of the Western European tradition. In part this is due to the nature of the material itself – technically sophisticated, artistically proficient and intellectually complex. It is these aspects that deserve further examination.

The Christianisation of Early Irish Art

The traditional art of Ireland, like that of the early Britons and 'Celtic' peoples of mainland Europe, was that used primarily to decorate metalwork objects, and was characterised, broadly speaking, by curvilinear patterns and a sophisticated appreciation of positive and negative (foreground and background) spaces, of surface texture and visual paradox. The patterns themselves were composed from a set of formulaic shapes, such as the pelta, triskele, spiral and running-scroll, but the ways in which these were arranged together on the given field of decoration, such as the circular field of a disc-shaped mount, could vary almost infinitely. Thus, for example, the discs mounted on the bronze sheet of the so-called Petrie 'crown' (Illustration 4), which has been dated to the second century AD, are decorated with a series of spirals that in one case terminates in flourishes recalling an extremely stylised bird head.

4. 'Petrie Crown' – bronze headdress, second century A D. Reproduced courtesy of the National Museum of Ireland, NMI – IA:P869, IA:P870.

The areas that are left plain between the repoussé lines forming the linear pattern of the spirals can themselves be seen to form pelta or curved triangular shapes. Thus the overall design presents at least two patterns: one of spirals formed by raised lines; the other of pelta shapes formed by the 'negative' spaces between those lines. The eye of the viewer is thus required to move over a series of patterns that constantly re-form, encouraging the eye to rest on one point in an attempt to 'see' it, that point then being undermined or disappearing as the eye moves on to the next. In this way the focus of the design becomes the arrangement of the strands of the linear patterns and the spaces between them.

In this respect such early metalwork rarely involves the use of highly coloured insets; colour, when it is employed, is often limited to a red enamel-like substance which is used to infill the spaces between the pattern formed by the raised lines to present the 'negative' or background pattern in colour. For modern viewers the phenomenon is familiar since the work of the Danish psychologist Edgar Rubin, in 1915, in his study of figure/ground reversal, and the recognition that the human brain needs to be able to interpret patterns in terms of external objects.[1] To do this, the eye distinguishes objects (the 'figure') from their background (the 'ground'); the now-familiar vase-profile illusion (Illustration 5) illustrates the dynamic nature of the processes involved

---

1 E. Rubin, *Experimenta Psychologica: Collected Scientific Papers in German, English and French* (Copenhagen: Munksgaard, 1949).

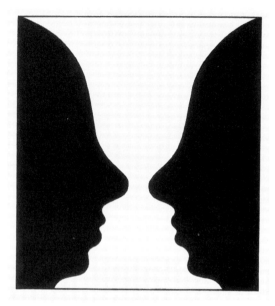

5. Vase-profile illusion. Dorling Kindersley / Getty Images.

in perceiving the spontaneous reversals of patterns – such as those employed by the artists working with the designs traditionally used for decorating metalwork in early (Iron Age) Ireland.

This well developed and sophisticated visual tradition was found to be highly appropriate for development by Christian artists from the sixth and seventh centuries onwards. In the early Church across Europe and the eastern Mediterranean world there was considerable debate about the role of art in sacred contexts, given the biblical Old Testament prohibition of the use of 'graven images' (Exodus 20:4–5). Those who supported the use of art to decorate churches and the objects used within them, such as liturgical vessels and manuscripts, argued that images should not be prohibited; only the adoration of them. Thus Pope Gregory the Great (d. 604) wrote to one of his bishops, in Marseilles, in AD 600 to clarify that the clergy should admonish the congregation 'that from the sight of the event portrayed they should catch the ardour of compunction, and bow themselves down in adoration of the One Almighty Holy Trinity'.[2] 'Compunction' was understood to be the

---

2 *The Letters of Gregory the Great*, ed. J. R. C. Martyn. 3 vols. (Toronto: Pontifical Institute of Medieval Studies, 2004). Letter 11.10 at iii, 744–6; see also Letter 9.209 at ii, 674.

initial emotional reaction elicited by the sight of the image, and was deemed to inspire contemplation of that which was signified by the image. In turn, it was thought, this would lead to a fuller understanding of the processes of salvation and so to 'adoration of the One Almighty Holy Trinity'. In this context, the visual tradition of early Irish artists lent itself to 'contemplation' in the demands it placed on the viewer to decipher the spontaneous reversal of patterns presented simultaneously on the field of decoration.

With the establishment of the Church across Britain during the course of the seventh century as a result, in part, of the mission sent from the Columban foundation on Iona to Anglo-Saxon Northumbria in 637, and the extensive network of monasteries founded by Irish missions across northern Europe, the work of artists decorating ecclesiastical objects in Ireland began to incorporate elements of visual traditions current elsewhere. That produced by early Christian artists across mainland Europe and in the lands of the Eastern Mediterranean continued the so-called classical tradition of late antiquity. This was an art very different to that traditionally worked by artists in Ireland in that even if presented in a highly stylised manner, it prioritised the representation of objects and figures encountered on a daily basis (Illustration 6). Objects decorated within this tradition were sometimes appropriated for use by the early Irish Church. Consular diptychs, for instance, carved in the rare and precious material of elephant ivory, were painted on the reverse with prayers and the names of those members of the community who were remembered in the course of the liturgy, and displayed on the altar.

The visual tradition of the Germanic peoples of north-western Europe, including the Anglo-Saxons who had come to settle in Britain, was more analogous to that of the artists working in early medieval Ireland. This was an art primarily developed in the field of metalwork which, being devoted to linear patterning and textured surfaces, was non-representational and exploited visual paradoxes. Unlike the curvilinear motifs of early Irish art, however, those of early Germanic art formed stylised zoomorphs (attenuated animal forms): birds of prey, serpents, boars, or anonymous quadrupeds and bipeds. Rather than favouring the use of patterns presented simultaneously, the Anglo-Saxon artists also tended to fill the field of decoration in such a way that the multiplicity of interlacing animal forms worked together to confuse the eye. Individual components, such as the curved beak of a bird of prey, were at the same time highlighted to enable the viewer to decipher the menagerie being presented (Illustration 7). Patterns were thus formed that served to hide their component parts, while at the same time revealing them. Moreover, the edges of an object, such as a square-headed

6. Diptych of Aerobindus. Elephant Ivory, Constantinople AD 506. © Musée national du Moyen Âge–Thermes et hôtel de Cluny, Cl 13135.

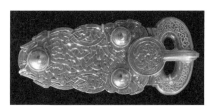

7. Belt buckle from Sutton Hoo, Suffolk. Gold, niello, *c.*AD 625. British Museum, acc. no.1939,1010.1. Universal History Archive / Getty Images.

brooch, could incorporate adjunct creatures, and the object itself could appear to morph into an animal in its own right. Furthermore, the surfaces of the objects decorated in this way could be highly coloured, textured and variegated, with niello (silver sulphate) offsetting gold or gilt bronze, and minute garnets being laid over stamped foils of gold allowing light to refract off the surfaces.

By such means, the patterns constantly shift and change, forever transforming and metamorphosing into something other. Thus, with the emphasis on surface pattern, colour and texture, on variegated surface and refraction, on shifting shapes and patterns constantly in flux, the eye is required to move over a series of patterns that constantly re-form, in a manner analogous to what Mary Carruthers has termed poly-focal perspective.[3] Here, it is the apparent chaos of the design that fills the field of decoration which encourages the eye to rest on a single point in an attempt to 'see' it, that point being then undermined or disappearing, as the eye moves on to the next. Although engendered by means totally distinct from those employed by the early Irish artists, the effect is not dissimilar, in that the viewer is required to 'contemplate' the design in order to decipher and resolve the patterns.

'Insular Art': The Manuscript Tradition

Increased contacts with such visual traditions, fostered by the Church, encouraged artists working in early medieval Ireland and Britain to develop a new and vibrant artistic style – the style usually termed 'Insular Art' (the art of these islands). This is perhaps the art style most usually associated with early medieval Ireland, but in its turn it influenced the art produced in Western Europe more widely. The cross-cultural connections at play, ecclesiastically and diplomatically, between Ireland, Anglo-Saxon England, Carolingian Gaul and early medieval Italy ensured that this was the case. It is an art that is highly complex and sophisticated and was exploited to communicate and celebrate the complexities of Christian thought and theology in the media of manuscript and stone – media less traditionally used for visual display in the region.

To take an example, the Book of Durrow,[4] one of the earliest surviving gospel manuscripts from the region, probably produced in *c*.700 by the Columban Community, opens and closes with two carpet pages, folios filled with coloured patterns, that encourage the viewer to focus on the sign of the cross (for the first carpet page, fol. iv, see Illustration 8). They achieve this by means of a palette dominated by red and yellow, colours evocative of the materials (gold and red enamel or garnet inlay) traditionally associated with

---

3 M. Carruthers, *The Experience of Beauty in the Middle Ages* (Oxford University Press, 2013).
4 Dublin: Trinity College Library, MS 57 (J. J. G. Alexander, *Insular Manuscripts, 6th to the 9th Century* (London: Harvey Miller, 1978), cat. no. 6, pp. 30–2).

8. Book of Durrow, Carpet Pages. TCD, MS 57, fol. 1v.

the precious metalwork circulating in the Insular world. Thus, the significance of the cross as 'the' sign of Christ and his salvation, and the value invested in those concepts within the Church are signified by means long familiar to viewers, and in the process the 'value' of the Word contained within the manuscript between the two carpet pages is indicated. On the carpet pages preceding the gospels of Mark (fol. 85v) and Luke (fol. 125v) the theme of the cross is continued, but in these instances the eye is forced to decipher the shape within the plain (non-zoomorphic) interlace patterns that fill the pages (Illustration 9a–b). On the Mark carpet page, the interlace is arranged as a series of linked medallions, framed variously with red and yellow so that the medallions themselves form a double-barred cross (yellow) and X-shapes (red), with the X comprising the first letter of Christ's name in the Greek alphabet (*Chi*); the central medallion is filled with three crosses superimposed on one another with that at the centre, coloured yellow, being the smallest.

The Luke carpet page offers a slightly different visual approach, using a bifurcated frame of black and white patterns recalling fretwork inlays found in contemporary metalwork, that overlays the field of interlace knots coloured red, yellow and green. As the eye focuses on the eight interlace knots in the central panel, they move behind and in front of the black and white

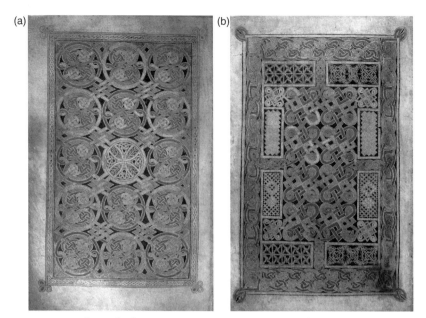

9. (a–b) Book of Durrow, Carpet pages. TCD, MS 57, fols. 85v; 125v.

frame, while the spaces between them, revealing the black background of the entire page, open up to form three crosses running vertically down the panel. The whole design incorporates motifs found in metalwork decoration and operates in the ways familiar in the art of Ireland, while invoking the '*horror vacuii*' of Germanic art, to reveal the 'hidden' patterns of the crosses. Here, the 'new' medium of parchment has been transformed by colour and pattern to look and function like the art displayed traditionally on metalwork – a process of borrowing and imitation across media known as skeuomorphism – in order to signify the value of Christian salvation articulated by the gospel manuscript in terms that were known and recognised.

The early Christian art of Ireland, however, did not just incorporate motifs and ways of viewing from other visual traditions and amalgamate them with those long familiar in the region in order to 'reveal' new symbols and significances. In the new medium of the manuscript it also developed wider schemes through which the Word could be revealed. Little survives of the biblical manuscripts produced in northern Europe, Italy and the Eastern Mediterranean before the late sixth century, but what does remain indicates that it was not unknown to open the gospel with an image of the evangelist – an author portrait – followed by an enlarged or elaborated initial letter marking the opening of the gospel text. The Augustine Gospels,[5] for instance, produced in southern Italy in the later sixth century and thought to have been brought into England at the turn of the seventh century, contain a full-page portrait of the evangelist Luke seated with his gospel open on his knee. Less common were the carpet pages, although one from Cassiodorus' scriptorium at Vivarium (outside Naples), which has been dated to the sixth or seventh century, has survived, reused as a cover for an eighth-century manuscript produced in Corbie in France.[6] Filled with panels of interlacing ribbons like those found in floor mosaics across the Roman world, no attempt is made to arrange the knots in order to reveal the spaces between them as can be seen in the Book of Durrow. Nevertheless, it seems that pages decorated with images, patterns and elaborate letter forms, although known, were not overly common in the manuscripts produced in early Christian Europe and the Eastern Mediterranean world.

In Irish scriptoria, however, such ornamentation was quickly adopted and developed. The opening of each Psalm in the Cathach of St Columba, a late sixth-century Psalter, for instance, is marked by an elaborate initial letter with the first word gradually diminishing in size for the remainder of the line, a distinctive practice identified with Irish and Insular scriptoria known as 'diminuendo'.[7] Although not picked out in colour, each initial letter is decorated with trumpet, pelta, spiral and guilloche patterns, and often outlined with orange dots (another practice that seems to have been adopted by Irish scriptoria). The terminal of the initial Q of the opening of Psalm 90 (*qui habitat in adiutorio Altissimi*), for instance, extends to form a spiral that opens in an animal head on which stands an open-armed cross (fol. 48). Equally importantly, the shapes of the initial letters in the Cathach are distorted by the decorative forms they take – not simply enlarged: thus the opening M of Psalm 6 (*miserere mei*) takes the form of two conjoined and confronting open spirals emerging from a central double curved stem, which each terminate in smaller spirals that evolve into double confronting trumpet peltas and return to the central stem of the letter. In its entirety this single letter takes up the equivalent space of four to five words in the lines of text below (fol. 21). Elsewhere, an early seventh-century Irish gospel manuscript (Codex Usserianus Primus) marks the transition between one gospel and the next with half the folio at the end of Luke filled with a cross, the upper arm of which terminates in a

5 Cambridge: Corpus Christi College Library, MS 286, fol. 129v.
6 Paris: Bibliothèque Nationale de France, MS lat. 12190.
7 Dublin: Royal Irish Academy, MS 12 R 33.

loop, transforming the shape into a *Chi-Rho* (the first two letters of Christ's name in the Greek alphabet), which is flanked by the letters *Alpha* and *Omega*, the first and last letters of the Greek alphabet: invoking the Christ as Judge at the end of time (Revelation 1:8).[8]

Irish centres on the Continent, such as Columbanus' monastery at Bobbio in Northern Italy (founded in 614), also produced manuscripts that seem to have favoured even more elaborate decoration in their pages. A seventh-century copy of Paulus Orosius' early fifth-century *Chronicon*, for instance, opens with a carpet page, considered to be the earliest produced in an Irish/Insular context; this faces the first page of the text, the initial letter of which and the opening words *Praeceptis tuis par(rui)* are many times larger than the rest of the text, with the stem of the P descending the entire length of the text block.[9] Here, however, the palette is dominated by pink and orange pigments – markedly different from that selected for the slightly later Book of Durrow.

With such elaborations evolving in the decoration of early Christian Irish manuscripts as a result of renewed and increasing contacts with the wider Christian world, the opening of each gospel came to be highly elaborated. In the Book of Durrow, for instance, like those in other gospel manuscripts produced in Insular scriptoria from the seventh century onwards, the opening of each gospel text is marked with a triplicate of decorated pages: that depicting the evangelist, followed by a carpet page facing the opening initial page. The development of this gathering of highly decorated pages serves to effectively mark the gospels in a manner that encourages the viewer to contemplate that which will follow in the text. In this respect the pages devoted to the evangelists and the initial pages became ever more complex.

The idea of portraying the evangelists in Christian art had a long history, emerging from early attempts to establish the authenticity of scriptural text by explaining apparent inconsistencies, not only between the Old and New Testament, but between the accounts of the gospels themselves. Thus, in the second century Tatian had combined all four gospel accounts into a single harmonised version, the *Diatessaron*. Eusebius' development of a series of ten canon tables in the fourth century represented a further attempt to 'illustrate' parallels between the gospels, which was incorporated into the prefatory material of all Insular gospel manuscripts, often accompanied by an

8 Dublin: Trinity College Library, MS 55, fol. 149v (Alexander, *Insular Manuscripts*, cat. no. 1, p. 27).
9 Milan: Biblioteca Ambrosiana, MS D. 23. sup., fols 1v–2r (Alexander, *Insular Manuscripts*, cat. no. 3, p. 28).

explanatory letter from Jerome to Pope Damasus written in the later fourth century (the *Novum Opus*). Augustine also wrote a treatise, *De Consensu evangelistarum* (*c*.400–5), on the subject, the greater part of which is devoted to listing and explaining the apparent discrepancies between the gospel texts.

As part of these exegetical activities the idea emerged that the four evangelists and their gospels were prefigured by the four 'living creatures' encircling the heavenly throne in the visions recounted by Ezekiel in the Old Testament (Ezekiel 1:4–16) and John at the end of the New Testament in the Book of Revelation (Revelation 4–7). These are described as winged and each bearing four aspects: the likenesses of a man, a lion, an ox/calf and an eagle. At the end of the second century, Irenaeus of Lyons had associated the creatures with the evangelists, but it was Jerome who identified them as symbols of the gospel writers in his Prologue to the gospels (the *Plures fuisse*), associating the man with Matthew because his gospel opens with an account of Christ's human ancestry, the lion with Mark because his text opens with an account of John the Baptist as a voice 'crying in the desert', the ox or calf with Luke because that narrative opens with an account of Zachariah, a priest of the Temple, and the eagle with John because of the soaring nature of the opening of his gospel.[10]

Although Jerome's associations were not the only ones circulating in the Insular world, they came to dominate the art. Further informing his pairings and their significances was the relationship of the creatures and their respective gospels to different aspects of the nature of Christ. This association had been widely circulated in Augustine's *De Consensu* and Gregory the Great's late sixth-century Homilies on Ezekiel. Thus Augustine (framing his argument with a different set of pairings) understood Matthew to epitomise Christ's kingly aspect, Mark, his mortal aspect, Luke his sacrificial and priestly roles, and John, his divine nature. Gregory, on the other hand, examined the ways in which each gospel signified one of the four mysteries of Christ – those events that brought about human redemption: Matthew thus represented his birth, Luke his death, Mark his resurrection, and John his ascension. Moreover, underlining such 'harmonies' was a complex scheme that related the gospels to an all-encompassing quarternity defining the divinely created universe; in this way the evangelists were paralleled by such phenomena as the four

---

10 J. O'Reilly, 'Patristic and Insular Traditions of the Evangelists: Exegesis and Iconography', in A. M. Luiselli Fadda and É. Ó Carragáin (eds.), *Le Isole Britanniche e Roma in Età Romanobarbarica* (Rome: Herder Editrice e Libreria, 1998), 56–7; N. G. Baker, 'The Evangelists in Insular Culture, *c*.600–*c*.800 AD'. PhD thesis, 2 vols. University of York (2011), 24, 45, 139.

cardinal points, the four corners of the world, the four rivers of paradise, the four winds, the four elements and the four seasons, as well as the four epochs of human history and the four humours of the human body. Thus, the gospels and their evangelists were considered integral to God's harmonious and geometrically perfect creation. These ideas circulated throughout the Insular world and were drawn on by Irish exegetes, who further amalgamated them with ideas drawn from the apocrypha.[11]

With such ideas informing the figures of the evangelists and their gospels, it is hardly surprising that their images came to be developed and elaborated in Insular gospel art. In the Book of Durrow all four are depicted on a single folio: that facing the opening carpet page. Preceded by the yellow double-barred cross of the carpet page (fol. 1v), the evangelists, denoted by their symbols, are positioned in the arms of a decorated cross (fol. 2r). Set within a narrow, coloured frame surrounded by a wide border filled with small (primarily) red and yellow squares resembling millefiore work arranged in cross and lozenge shapes, the cross, decorated with plain interlace, fills and quarters the field of the page with the evangelist symbols set in the quadrants. The cross-arms terminate in flared 'cup'-shapes with that at the base being significantly larger and picked out by a double red outline. Here, the quarternities are clearly articulated, while the enlarged cross base references the cross of the Crucifixion set on Calvary, and the way in which the cross fills the space refers to 'the breadth, and length, and height, and depth' of the salvation of Christ (Ephesians 3:18). This was a scheme that found considerable favour among Irish manuscript artists who seem to have regarded it as a suitable revelatory opening. In the eighth-century Trier Gospels and the later ninth-century Macdurnan Gospels it forms the first decorated page of the manuscript, encapsulating all that will follow in the text of the four gospels,[12] while in the early ninth-century Book of Armagh it marks the transition between the prefatory material and the opening of Matthew, the first of the gospel texts;[13] In the *c.*800 Book of Kells (Illustration 10), it survives at the opening of three of the four gospels (Matthew, Mark and John), preceding – where they still survive – the

---

11 J. O'Reilly, 'The Hiberno-Latin Tradition of the Evangelists and the Gospels of Mael Brigte', *Peritia*, 9 (1995), 292–3; O'Reilly, 'Patristic and Insular', 67.
12 Trier Gospels (Trier: Domschatz Codex 61 (Bibliotheksnummer 134)), fol. 1v; Macdurnan Gospels (London: Lambeth Palace Library, MS 1370), fol. 1v; see Alexander, *Insular Manuscripts*, cat. nos. 26, 70, pp. 52–4; 86–7.
13 Dublin: Trinity College Library, MS 52, fol. 32v (Alexander, *Insular Manuscripts*, cat. no. 53, pp. 76–7).

10. Book of Kells, Matthew, Four-Symbols Page. TCD, MS 58, fol. 27v.

evangelist portraits; it is assumed that Luke opened in a similar manner but the page has since been lost.[14]

This latter manuscript also demonstrates the way in which the initial pages of biblical manuscripts came to be given over primarily to highly elaborate patterned forms. Thus, the Gospel of Matthew, following the four-symbols page (fol. 27v), presents the portrait of Matthew on the left of a double-page spread opposite the opening of the gospel text on the right (fols. 28v–29r), which contains only two words, *Liber generationis*: The Book of the Generations (of Christ). It thus functions as the 'title page' of the gospel, with the two words contained in discrete panels (Illustration 11). Above, in a panel framed on the left by the vertical of the L and the lower extension of the I, the LI of Liber intersect with each other, with the horizontal of the L extending into the bowl of the b, where it morphs into the E and intertwines with the R. Below, in a separate panel, GENERATIONIS in purple letters set against an orange-scarlet background runs over three lines enclosed in a series of frames that open on the far right to lead the eye notionally over to the next page which contains only two columns of text listing the genealogy (fol. 29v). Here, the extreme elaboration of the preceding three pages is replaced

14 Dublin: Trinity College Library, MS 58, fols. 27v, 129v, 290v (Alexander, *Insular Manuscripts*, cat. no. 52, pp. 71–6).

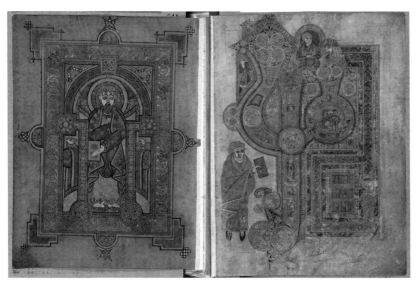

11. Book of Kells, Matthew, Portrait and Initial page. TCD, MS 58, fols. 28v–29r.

by a comparatively sparse page; the eye has no option but to focus on the words: the names of the human forefathers of Christ.

Following the seventeen verses filled by the genealogy (Matthew 1:1–17), a second triplicate of decorated pages marks the opening of the remainder of the gospel text (Illustrations 12–13). The first depicts a book-bearing human figure before a bench throne with a cross over his head, dependant from the arched frame surrounding him, flanked at each shoulder by peacocks entwined in fruited vines emerging from chalices, and by two pairs of angels below (fol. 32v). Here, Christ, whose humanity has been established by the text of the preceding six pages, is presented in terms of his divine nature (by means of the angels flanking the throne), and his salvific sacrifice within which the faithful Christian can partici-pate through the Eucharist (by means of the peacocks, signifying the body of Christ; the vines, signifying the blood of Christ; and the dependant cross). Facing this image, with its complex presentation of the matrix of interconnected ideas relating to the gospel, Christ, his nature and his sal-vation, is a carpet page filled with a double-barred cross whose interstices and terminals form eight elaborate medallions, referencing the eight ages of human history – the eighth being that which follows the general resur-rection at the end of time, prefigured by the eighth day following creation

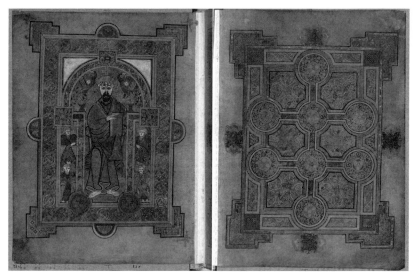

12. Book of Kells, Christ and Matthew, Carpet Page. TCD, MS 58, fols. 32v–33r.

and the day on which the Lord rested, both of which were articulated in the rituals of death and rebirth re-enacted during baptism. Thus the salvific nature of Christ's humanity and the means of participating in that mystery are symbolically presented over these two pages which, when turned, reveal the word 'Christ': in symbolic form, being articulated by the three initial Greek letters of his name: *Chi, Rho* and *Iota* (Illustration 13). Here, on a page that marks the opening of the narrative of Mathew's gospel with the account of the nativity – *XPI autem generatio* (Now the generation of Christ …) – the entire nature of Christ and his salvation is signified in a crescendo of curvilinear motifs, zoomorphs and angels (on the far left). The interstice of the X (*Chi*) forms an elaborate lozenge filled with yellow zoomorphic and human interlace framed in purple and orange – an aniconic motif referring to Christ and the universal nature of his salvation – while a small human face set over the lozenge has been identified as Christ's face. Here, the form of the letter has been transformed into a patterned shape that incorporates in its entirety and in its composite decoration, not only the motifs familiar to Insular art, but arranges them in such a way that, through the act of contemplation, the entire message of the gospel is revealed – made visible – before the words that follow with each turning of the page.

13. Book of Kells, *Chi-Rho* Page. TCD, MS 58, fol. 34r.

Artistic Expression in Metal and Stone

Early Christian Irish art did more than amalgamate and develop motifs and ways of viewing from visual traditions long familiar in the region in order to 'reveal' new symbols and significances in the new medium of the manuscript. It also continued to flourish in the art of decorated metalwork used in the service of the Church, with the production and elaboration of objects such as liturgical vessels, reliquaries and ecclesiastical attributes. The hoard of eighth- or ninth-century liturgical vessels found within the monastic enclosure of Derrynaflan in County Tipperary in 1980, for instance, includes a paten, paten stand, wine strainer and chalice – a *calix ministerialis* used to administer the Eucharist to the congregation – as opposed to smaller chalices, *calix minor*, used by the celebrant of the Mass (Illustration 14). All these vessels were made of silver and decorated with panels of applied metalwork. On the chalice these are filled with gold filigree and set round the rim of the bowl, the handles and escutcheons, the stem, the foot and the foot ring and are filled with highly stylised patterns composed of various zoomorphs, human figures, lozenge- and cross-shapes, and are interspersed with amber studs. The underside of the foot is further decorated with an interlace pattern within which are further amber studs. Composed and decorated in this way

14. Derrynaflan Hoard, eighth to ninth century. Reproduced courtesy of the National
Museum of Ireland, NMI: IA:1980.

the chalice can be compared with the contemporary large silver chalice found
in Ardagh, County Limerick, in 1863, also as part of a hoard of liturgical vessels and elaborate brooches.[15]

It is generally accepted that the analogue for these elaborate silver chalices,
used to dispense the Eucharist to the congregation, were those produced in
the Eastern Mediterranean world; indeed an account of the holy sites of the
Holy Land, apparently transmitted to the Iona community under the abbacy
of Adamnán (c. 624–704; abbot: 679–704), included an account of the chalice
then believed to have been used at the Last Supper.[16] Preserved in Jerusalem,
it is described as silver, with two handles and having a bowl of considerable
size; comparable examples survive from Syria decorated with bands of contrasting materials containing images and patterns in their design. It has been
suggested that knowledge of such vessels could have been transmitted to
Ireland through the aegis of the Irish monasteries and missions established
in areas of northern Italy where large, elaborate two-handled silver chalices
were known to have been used.[17] Thus, continued contacts with the wider
Christian world inspired the creation of an elaborate form of chalice decorated with motifs familiar to the Insular region, articulated in a highly stylised
manner that serves to render them as patterns that need to be deciphered,
but which can be deemed to have symbolic significance in the context of the

15 E. Bhreathnach, 'The Cultural and Political Milieu of the Deposition and Manufacture
    of the Hoard Discovered at Reerasta Rath, Ardagh, Co. Limerick', in M. Redknap, N.
    Edwards, A. Lane and S. Youngs (eds.), *Pattern and Purpose in Insular Art: Proceedings of
    the Fourth International Conference on Insular Art held at the National Museum and Gallery,
    Cardiff, 3–6 September 1998* (Oxford: Oxbow Books, 2001), 15–23.
16 *Adamnán's De Locis Sanctis*, ed. and trans. D. Meehan. Scriptores Latini Hiberniae 3
    (Dublin: DIAS, 1958), 51.
17 M. Ryan, *The Derrynaflan Hoard, I: A Preliminary Account* (Dublin: National Museum of
    Ireland, 1983), 15.

rituals and performance of the Mass. The filigree animals set round the edge of the paten, for instance, include serpents, stags, kneeling figures, birds of prey: all of which are interspersed by panels of curvilinear motifs and plain interlace forming cross-shapes: the stag had long been featured in Christian art as a symbol of the faithful Christian, while the serpent was invoked in the light of Christ's admonition to his disciples to be 'wise as serpents' (Matthew 10:16).

The reliquary containers made for the early Irish Church were also highly decorated. The use of relics in Ireland dates to the introduction of Christianity in the fifth century, with Palladius bringing relics of Peter and Paul to Ireland from Rome; by the early seventh century the church of St Patrick at Armagh was distributing its relics of early continental saints and martyrs to other churches. In part the demand for such objects was due to the need to dedicate churches on the remains of saints, and while the remains of the host (the body of Christ), used in the dedication rituals could be substituted, the bodies of the saints also served to link the earthly to the heavenly, the presence of their human remains providing the faithful with a 'portal' through to the divine. Such relics were thus highly prized and clearly in short supply, but by the seventh century the remains of local saints were also circulating and the containers made to house them took many forms.

Perhaps the most familiar reliquary form associated with the early Irish Church is that of the house-shaped reliquary shrine (Illustration 15a). These were extremely small boxes, some entirely made of metal, others of wood encased in elaborately decorated metal sheets, with a hinged trapezoidal lid – providing the eponymous house-shape – that was locked by means of a key inserted into the side of the box (rather than its front), and which could incorporate hinge attachments allowing them to be carried suspended around the neck. This perhaps indicates that they played a part in ecclesiastical circuits, such as the promulgation of the 'laws' of a saint, a practice enacted from the seventh century onwards. The ecclesiastical laws of Patrick, for instance, were promulgated in Connacht and Munster by Armagh, along with the levying of taxes and collection of tribute; the outbreak of smallpox in 742–3 also coincided with the circuit of the relics of Kildalkey, County Meath.[18]

The diminutive dimensions of these shrines speak to the distribution of the minute (and extremely precious) portions of the relics that were contained within the boxes, usually wrapped in textiles. The fact that access

18 R. Ó Floinn, *Irish Shrines and Reliquaries of the Middle Ages* (Dublin: Country House, 1994), 11

15. a) Emly Shrine, late seventh–early eighth century. © Boston Museum of Fine Art, 52.1396.

could be gained to the earthly remains of the saint distinguishes them from their continental counterparts that could be house-shaped but whose contents were generally inaccessible. One explanation for the distinctive house-shape adopted for so many of the early Irish reliquary shrines is that they were designed as miniature versions of late antique sarcophagi (which held the bodies of continental saints and martyrs), and so should be referred to as tomb-shaped reliquaries. Indeed, the extremely large dimensions of a pair of eighth-century gilt bronze finial mounts preserved in the Musée Nationale at St Germain, near Paris, indicate the presence of a large tomb shrine decorated with ornamental metalwork – perhaps like those described in Cogitosus' seventh-century *Life of St Brigid*, which records the elaborately decorated tombs of Brigid and Archbishop Conled standing on either side of the altar in the church at Kildare;[19] the finial mounts would have formed the gable ends of a tomb of this type. A twelfth-century stone tomb shrine with skeuomorph finials survives at Clones, County Monaghan.

The house-shape was not one commonly associated with late antique sarcophagi in Europe, however, and it is possible that elaborate tombs for high-status ecclesiastics and saints in early medieval Ireland were designed, not as replicas of Irish houses, but rather in imitation of the earliest ecclesiastical stone buildings, such as 'Temple Ciarán' at Clonmacnoise, County Offaly, or 'St Columba's Cell' at Kells, County Meath, which were exceedingly small

19 S. Connolly and J.-M. Picard, 'Cogitosus's "Life of St Brigit" Content and Value', *JRSAI*, 117 (1987), 25.

15. b) Book of Kells, Temptation of Christ. TCD: MS 58, fol. 202v.

single-cell buildings with high-pitched roofs. Furthermore, the Temple of Solomon in Jerusalem is depicted in the Book of Kells (fol. 202v) as just such a structure: a small, single-cell building with a high-pitched roof, and elaborate zoomorphic gable terminals (Illustration 15b). This is particularly instructive as it forms a visual commentary on the idea, common in the Insular world, that the Temple of Solomon signified the Church. As Bede put it at the opening of his early eighth-century commentary on the Temple: 'The house of God which King Solomon built in Jerusalem was made as a figure of the holy universal Church which, from the first of the elect to the last to be born at the end of the world, is daily being built through the grace of the king of peace, namely, its redeemer.'[20] In other words, the house-shaped shrines were likely inspired by the idea that the 'house of God' was the universal Church, of which that in Ireland was an integral part, with each individual church being a member of that Church, whose congregation, past, present and future, was the community of saints.

Considered in this way, the house-shaped shrine becomes an extraordinarily evocative object that evokes the universal Church and its congregation, made present in the earthly remains of the saint that it contains, in the environs of the church in which it was housed. Furthermore, many of the house-shaped shrines, like the late seventh- or early eighth-century Emly shrine (Illustration 15a), have a small house-shape placed centrally on the ridge pole of the 'roof' flanked by diminutive zoomorphs, set at the gable ends. While

20 *Bede: on the Temple*, ed. S. Connolly with introduction by J. O'Reilly (Liverpool University Press, 1995), 5.

the figure of Christ forms the pinnacle of the roof of the Temple in the Book of Kells image, it can be suggested that the house-shape forming the pinnacle of the roof of the shrine may also have been intended to signify Christ, within the context of the Old Latin verse from the Canticle of Habbakkuk that was recited each day as part of the celebration of Lauds, the office that coincided with the dawn of each new day, as well as during the rites of Good Friday: namely, that 'in the midst of two beasts you will be recognised'. The form and decoration of these reliquaries were thus designed in keeping with a rich matrix of ideas associating the Church and its saints with Christ, his salvation, the liturgy and the sacraments, while incorporating ideas of death, enshrinement and resurrection.

Other early Irish reliquaries were equally innovative in their design, replicating the shapes of the relic contained within. Thus the eighth-century Moylough belt-shrine is a skeuomorph belt and buckle composed of four pairs of strips of sheet bronze, linked by hinges, that contain strips of plain leather, thought to be the belt or girdle of a local saint which, by association with the saint, was as much a relic of their human existence as their body. Many such objects are recorded as performing miraculous cures and being used in the swearing of oaths. The girdle of St Brigid, for example, would heal any disease or illness, while that of St Mobhí (St Berchan) of Glasnevin 'never closed around lies'. The surface of the Moylough belt-shrine is considerably worn and shows signs of repair, suggesting that it was in regular use before coming to rest in the bog at Moylough, County Sligo, probably in the later Middle Ages (given the depth at which it was recovered from the bog in 1945).[21] Originally tinned, so as to appear silver, the outer face of each bronze segment of the belt is decorated with a cast ringed cross of bronze inset with enamel and glass, two of which (flanking the buckle) were additionally highlighted with silver foil decorated with traditional spiral patterns. The ends of each segment are further elaborated with stamped silver foil or panels of openwork bronze laid over thin sheets of mica, a glittering rock found in granite. The skeuomorph buckle and buckle plate were also richly decorated with silver foils, glass and enamel, but the overall shape of this element is further elaborated so that the tongue of the buckle takes the form of two birds' heads, while the buckle and buckle plate are cast as animal heads which grasp the coloured glass studs with their silver inlays. The contrast between the bronze panels, red and yellow enamel, blue and white glass, silver foils, glittering mica and the silvered appearance of the bronze plates would have been

21 R. Ó Floinn, *The Moylough Belt-Shrine* (Bray: Wordwell, 2008), 14–15.

striking to say the least, while the object itself speaks to a rich and influential ecclesiastical culture, perhaps centred on the church of Achonry, founded by St Finnian of Clonard, where the remains of St Nathí were buried. It was certainly a centre which was actively promoting the cult of (local) saints in keeping with practices current across Europe by this time, and employing the skills of metalworkers well-versed in traditional and Christian art to present their status and value in order to reflect not only the preciousness of the object enshrined within, but also that of the divine with which it provided contact.

The idea of enshrinement was particularly potent in the early Irish Church, with all types of objects being presented as relics by virtue of association and encasement in elaborately decorated metalwork containers. In addition to the girdles of local saints, objects such as bells and croziers associated with early ecclesiastics were similarly enshrined, as were books that had come to be linked with such figures. The iron bells used by early churches, some plain and others, like the Bernán Conaill bell, incised with a cross, were frequently associated with ecclesiastics whose remains became sites of pilgrimage and veneration. Thus, a plain eighth- or ninth-century bronzed iron bell was connected from an early date with St Patrick and, like the Bernán Conaill bell, was subsequently (in the twelfth century) encased in a shrine that replicated the shape of the bell within (Illustration 16a–c). Formed of a series of bronze plates, the shrine is topped by a curved crest that covers the handle of the bell, while the front is covered with a silver-gilt frame which originally held thirty panels of gold filigree and the back is decorated with an openwork silver plate. Overall, the decoration involves the use of up-to-date motifs associated with the Urnes style of Scandinavian art, characterised by long swirling tendrils terminating in spiraliforms that emerge from the bodies of zoomorphs. But it also incorporates the interlacing and curvilinear motifs of earlier Insular art, arranged in panels over the front of the shrine to form a central cross, while interlocking crosses recalling those of the final carpet page of the Book of Durrow fill the back of the shrine, and the Urnes style zoomorphs are set as terminals to the skeuomorph handle of the shrine.

The inscription along the edge of the back-plate records the name of the craftsman and his sons who made the shrine, and the king who commissioned it: Domnall Mac Lochlainn (reg. 1094–1121). Cathalan Ua Maelchallain, the keeper of the bell, is also mentioned. The art of the earlier Irish Church with which the bell was associated, has been invoked here, under royal patronage in the context of ecclesiastical reform, to articulate the perceived sanctity of

(a)  (b)  (c)

16. (a, b and c) St Patrick's Bell and shrine, front and back with sides. Reproduced courtesy of the National Museum of Ireland, R4010-1.

that Church and the value invested in it in the early twelfth century. The loss of some of the metalwork panels from this later shrine is explained by the fact that they were removed as late as the nineteenth century when the bell was still in the possession of the family of Cathalan Ua Maelchallain, 'to be used as charms against disease and other evils'.[22] By means of a series of associations that traverse temporal and geographical boundaries, the sanctity of the saint assumed by the bell has subsumed the shrine. Books, such as the Cathach of Columba, were similarly enshrined, often during the eleventh century, with the shrines being successively elaborated through to the fifteenth century.

So dominant was the art of the metalworker and its associations in the early Irish Church that it was used not only to decorate the objects displayed within the churches, and as a means of signifying the value of Christian objects, such as the manuscripts, but also to enhance the art of stone carving. In this respect the metalwork aspect of a number of the high crosses, such as those at Ahenny in County Tipperary, has been invoked to explain an early (perhaps eighth-century) date of production (Illustration 17a). These crosses are now, however, dated to the tenth century and their production is explained in the context of displays of regional and royal power at the point where the kingdom of Ossory bordered on that of Munster, from which it achieved formal independence under Cerball mac Dúnlainge in 859.[23] The decoration of the North Cross at Ahenny is particularly redolent of metalwork, not only

22 Ó Floinn, *Irish Shrines*, 18
23 R. Ó Floinn, 'Patrons and Politics: Art, Artefact and Methodology', in M. Redknap, N. Edwards, A. Lane and S. Youngs (eds.), *Pattern and Purpose in Insular Art: Proceedings of the Fourth International Conference on Insular Art held at the National Museum and Gallery, Cardiff, 3–6 September 1998* (Oxford: Oxbow Books, 2001), 1–14.

(a)

(b)   (c)   (d)

17. (a) South Cross (left) and North Cross (right), Ahenny, County Tipperary, tenth century [Photo © Humphrey Bolton (cc-by-sa / 2.0)]; (b–d) North Cross, Ahenny, details: (b) centre of cross-head; (c) shaft; (d) end of cross-arm.

in its use of motifs (which were also invoked in manuscript art), but in the manner in which it is carved, so that it replicates, in three dimensions, the cast and filigree metalwork plaques ornamenting liturgical vessels and high-status brooches, such as the so-called Tara brooch, an eighth-century silver-gilt annular brooch found at Bettystown, County Meath, in 1850. Decorated in cast and gilt silver, this is elaborately decorated on both faces with a series of fine gold filigree panels depicting animal motifs and scrolls and triple spiral motifs separated by studs of glass, enamel and amber (Illustration 18). On the Ahenny Cross, the boss at the centre of the cross-head (Illustration 17b) is carved in very high relief against a ground of extremely low-relief traditional spiral and pelta ornament replicating a cast metalwork plaque

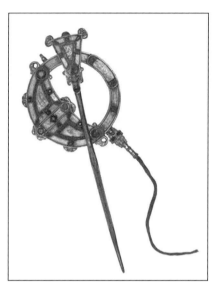

18. 'Tara' brooch, eighth century. Reproduced courtesy of the National Museum of Ireland.

inset with a stud of millefiore work, which incorporates a void that perhaps once did hold a paste-glass inset, such as those that have recently been identified on an early medieval cross-shaft at Aberlady in Scotland. The base of the shaft is filled with a panel of fretwork that is inset with a small panel of high-relief interlace, replicating filigree work, that incorporates the hidden form of a cross in the spaces between the knots forming the interlace (Illustration 17c), while the ends of the cross-arms are decorated with a small panel of 'cast' spiral motifs surrounded by high-relief mouldings replicating the filigree rope-twists used to frame panels of decorated metalwork (Illustration 17d).

Throughout, the North Cross and its counterpart to the south present the viewer with stone skeuomorphs of highly decorated metalwork crosses. This can be understood, as was common across the Insular world, as an extremely elaborate presentation of the metalwork crosses that stood on the altars of the churches and which were carried in procession, which, in turn, look to the *crux gemmata*: the cross which, it was understood, would appear in the heavens at the end of time. Many versions of such crosses survive from early medieval Ireland, the most notable perhaps being the twelfth-century Cross of Cong (Illustration 19), associated with Cong, County Mayo, and acquired by Tairdelbach Ua Conchobair, the High King of Ireland (1106–56). Made of oak, it is covered with plates of copper-alloy decorated with gold, silver, niello, glass and enamel, and it enclosed a relic of the True Cross behind an

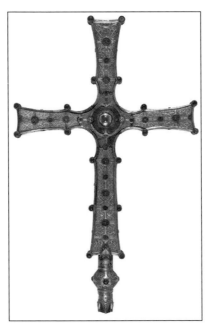

19. Cross of Cong, twelfth century. Reproduced courtesy of the National Museum of
Ireland, NMI: R2833.

elaborate stud of large polished rock crystal at the centre of the cross-head.
Although the relic is missing, the wood behind the rock crystal is engraved
with a double-barred cross, the traditional sign of the True Cross in early medieval art, particularly that of the Insular world. The metal plates are decorated
with ribbon-shaped intertwined animals in the Scandinavian-derived Urnes
style. Inscriptions, set around the sides of the cross, identify Tairdelbach Ua
Conchobair as the patron and Máel Ísú mac Bratáin Uí Echach as the craftsman; two further prominent churchmen are also mentioned: Muiredach Ua
Dubthaig and Domnall mac Flannacáin Uí Dubthaig. The inscription, which
is in Irish, is framed by two identical lines in Latin that translate as: 'by this
cross is covered the cross on which the creator of the world suffered'.[24] It is
recorded in the Annals of Tigernach for the year 1123 that 'a great circuit was
given to [Christ's Cross] by the king of Ireland, Toirdelbach Húa Conchobáir,
and he asked for some of it to keep in Ireland, and it was granted to him,
and it was enshrined by him at Roscommon'.[25] The Cross of Cong has thus
been identified as the 'shrine' made for the relic at Roscommon and dated to

24 G. Murray, *The Cross of Cong: A Masterpiece of Medieval Irish Art* (Dublin: Irish Academic
Press, 2014).
25 *Ann. Tig.* ii, 43–4; Murray, *Cross of Cong*, 41.

1123. It provides a clear insight into the ways in which a cross could be elaborated by decorated and gem-encrusted precious metals, denoting not only the value placed on the object it signified (or in the case of the Cross of Cong, enshrined), but also the *crux gemmata*, which it prefigured.

This was a common motif in the mosaic decoration of early churches in Italy, such as those in Ravenna and Rome dated to between the fifth and ninth centuries, where it was often set against a starry sky or the clouds of the setting sun and flanked by the beasts surrounding the heavenly throne – settings that made its apocalyptic nature clear while the glass tesserae used to make up the mosaic would have glittered in the shifting light of the candles and torches used to light the churches, thus adding to the appearance of shining metalwork in the medium of glass. In this context it is worth noting that the early medieval stone sculptures of the Insular world were originally highly coloured, in addition to the paste-glass and metalwork insets that would have enhanced their precious and elaborate appearance. Originally therefore, the high crosses, like those at Ahenny, but also the twelfth-century versions set up at Tuam (in County Galway) and Dysert O'Dea, County Clare, that deliberately replicate the metalwork crosses set up inside the churches, would have been extremely eye-catching, recalling not only the sign of the cross, the means of Christian salvation, but also the *crux gemmata* of the end of time, and so would have further denoted the reward of life eternal that all faithful Christians were encouraged to bear in mind.

Dated to the ninth and tenth centuries, the high crosses of the Irish midlands, at Clonmacnoise and Durrow (County Offaly), Kells (County Meath) and Monasterboice (County Louth), have tended to be discussed in terms of the panels of relief figural carving that cover their surfaces. However, these monuments, like those at Ahenny, Tuam and Dysert O'Dea, also reference other media in their design. The narrow sides of the so-called Cross of Muirdach at Monasterboice, for instance, are filled with panels evoking the filigree interlace and cast spiraliform plates decorating the metalwork, while the upper cross-arm, like that of the Tall (West) Cross at the same site and the Durrow High Cross, terminates in a house-shaped cap-stone with gable terminals that replicates the small metalwork house-shaped reliquaries that were intended to evoke the idea of the Church (Illustration 20). The setting of this particular cap-stone thus indicates that the cross was being publicly and visibly presented as the foundation of the Church: the Church is literally established on the cross of the crucifixion, based on the sign of universal salvation; immediately below the cap-stone, the cross-head is filled on the west face with the crucifixion itself, while on the east face is the image of Christ as Judge.

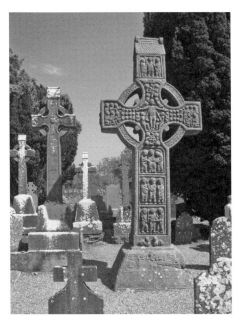

20. Muirdach's Cross, Monasterboice, County Louth, ninth century. Photo courtesy of J. Hawkes.

The figural panels filling the shafts of these crosses, moreover, are carved in such high relief that they physically obtrude into the space of the viewer from the surface of the cross (Illustration 21a); at Durrow and Kells this phenomenon of 'breaking the frame' is taken one step further by opening the frames surrounding the figural panels, allowing one event to 'flow' into another. The entirety of the iconographic programme is thus yoked together by a continuous border that encloses, separates, and yet links the images of salvation presented to the viewer, allowing them to become a single continuum embracing time and place (Illustration 21b). The same process is used for the non-figural motifs on the narrow sides of the cross shafts; thus at Kells, the cross presented in the spaces between the spiraliform linear patterns of the 'Broken Cross' flows vertically into the panel above (Illustration 21c).

With this in mind, it seems that these sculpted relief panels were intended to function in a manner analogous to that generally associated in the scholarship today with painted panels understood to be devotional images, otherwise known as 'icons'. While these are generally understood to be wooden panels painted with wax encaustic (sometimes edged by painted borders), framed

21. (a) Muirdach's Cross, Monasterboice, side view; (b–c) Broken Cross, Kells, showing linked frames; (d) Durrow High Cross, Resurrection of Christ. Photos courtesy of Jane Hawkes.

paintings were also familiar in other media and they could be enhanced with other materials; the panel painting housed in Santa Maria in Trastevere in Rome originally bore a metalwork cross. In his early eighth-century discussion of imagery Bede, following the writings of Gregory the Great, argued that sight of sacred subject-matter elicited great compunction in the viewers.[26] In the act of viewing an image, a person or event from the past was called to mind in the present, enabling the future significance of that event

26 *Bede: on the Temple*, 91.

or person in the process of salvation to be recalled. Put another way: images functioned as portals through which the viewer could gain proper understanding of the Divine, through contemplation and remembrance – processes that made present the past and future. Thus, a panel carved with the image of Christ in his tomb, which is preserved on the cross-shafts at Clonmacnoise, Monasterboice, Kells and Durrow (Illustration 21d), has been demonstrated to have operated by means of a complex matrix of references, visual and textual, which would have been revealed through the process of contemplation, to the history of redemption through the incarnation, death, resurrection of Christ, and the future Parousia, the full revelation of Christ in Glory at the Day of Judgement.[27]

The act of viewing the stone carvings of the early Irish Church thus enabled imagined movement through time and planes of existence: between past, present and future; between the (tangible, material) human, and the (intangible, uncontainable, immaterial) Divine. That the carved relief panels of the Irish high crosses can be understood in this manner is certainly implied by Bede, who refers to the relief carvings of Solomon's Temple as appearing 'as if they were coming out of the wall'.[28] In other words, the three-dimensional nature of relief carving can be understood to enact the processes of viewing imagery. Encounters with the figural carvings, arranged in panels, polychromed and carved in deep relief, were probably intended to elicit contemplation of the painted images, while viewing the panels carved as skeuomorphs of precious metalwork associated with liturgical vessels, altar and processional crosses may equally have inspired contemplation of the *crux gemmata* and the salvation available to those participating in the mystery of Christ at every celebration of the Mass.

Whether considering the art of the decorated manuscripts, metalwork or stone carvings of early medieval Ireland, it is clear that the early visual traditions of the region, current in the pre-Christian period, which capitalised on visual paradoxes presented through sophisticated curvilinear patterns, variegated surfaces and hidden shapes, continued to be invoked and exploited, along with the other visual traditions current in the Insular world, to considerable effect, visually and conceptually, in secular and ecclesiastical contexts throughout the period. While the form, medium and context of the

---

27 É Ó Carragáin, 'Recapitulating History: Contexts for the Mysterious Moment of Resurrection on Irish High Crosses', in J. Hawkes (ed.), *Making Histories: Proceedings of the Sixth International Conference on Insular Art, York 2011* (Donington: Shaun Tyas, 2013), 246–61.
28 *Bede: on the Temple*, 54.

art varied across the period, it remained consistently sophisticated, artistically proficient and intellectually complex, perhaps deserving of the attribution given it by Gerald of Wales at the end of the twelfth century as 'the work of angels'.[29]

---

29 *Topographia*, 84.

4

The Scandinavian Intervention

ALEX WOOLF

FOLLOWING the introduction of Christianity in Late Antiquity the next major phase in Irish history resulted from the interaction between native Irish and Scandinavians, and, subsequently, the development of communities of Scandinavian origin established within Ireland and her peripheral territories (such as the Scottish islands, south-west Scotland, north-west England, the Isle of Man and coastal Wales). These interactions began as part of the wider phenomenon of Scandinavian diaspora in what is often termed the Viking Age. The concept of a Viking Age is not entirely unproblematic since, as Scandinavian archaeologists have argued, its beginnings, usually dated to the 790s, do not correspond to any major changes in domestic Scandinavian society.[1] Indeed, the widely accepted chronological brackets of the Viking Age, c.790–1066, are derived entirely from the English experience, with the earliest recorded raid on Lindisfarne in 793 and the Battle of Stamford Bridge, in which the Norwegian king Harald Hardrada was slain in September 1066, providing the book-ends. It is thus questionable whether they should be exported to other countries. Even for England this chronology is tendentious, since although the raid on Lindisfarne may well be the earliest firmly dated Scandinavian attack, the Norwegian invasion of 1066 was followed up over the next decade by more than one Danish invasion under Sven Estridsson and the Domesday survey of 1086 seems to have been prompted by a planned invasion by Sven's son Cnut the Holy. Later still, Earl Hugh of Shrewsbury was killed by Scandinavian raiders in 1098. The concept of a discrete Viking Age can also be critiqued on the grounds that the invasions led by national kings leading national armies of the eleventh century were very unlike anything

---

1 B. Myhre, 'The Beginning of the Viking Age – Some Current Archaeological Problems', in A. Faulkes and R. Perkins (eds.), *Viking Revaluations* (London: Viking Society, 1993), 182–203. I would like to thank Lesley Abrams and Helen Foxhall Forbes for reading this chapter in draft and supplying comments and references. Errors and eccentricities remain my own.

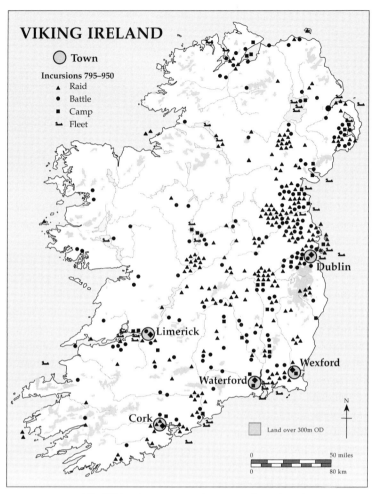

MAP 6. The Viking Intervention. Courtesy of Matthew Stout,
School of History and Geography, DCU.

that had occurred earlier. Indeed, the earlier centuries of the Viking Age can also be broken down into numerous distinct phases (see Map 6).

Within Irish historiography the Battle of Clontarf, fought in April 1014, has fulfilled a similar role to Stamford Bridge as the 'final defeat of the vikings' but in reality it was no such thing. Sitriuc, the Scandinavian king of Dublin, remained in control of the city after the battle and continued to rule there for a further twenty years or so. The posthumous victor of the battle, Brian

Bórama [Boru], certainly did have a military career that was transformative within Irish history; however, its legacy was not the defeat of the vikings but the ending of the Uí Néill [O'Neill] monopoly on claims to the king-ship of Ireland. From his time until the Anglo-Norman conquest, the king-ship of Ireland was claimed and disputed by dynasts from all the provinces of Ireland, not simply by branches of the descendants of Niall of the Nine Hostages.[2]

Perhaps more significant than Clontarf in curtailing the aspirations of the Dublin dynasty to dominate Ireland was the Battle of Tara, fought in 980, a generation earlier, in which Sitriuc's father, Olaf Cuarán, was defeated by Máel-Sechnaill of Meath.[3] This said, the Dubliners and their allies who fought at Tara, and indeed at Clontarf, were very different in identity, origins and aspirations from the earliest raiders of the 790s. Sitriuc and Olaf, despite their ultimate paternal ancestry, were probably both natives of Ireland and were certainly Christians whose kinship networks were deeply intertwined with those of their contemporary Irish kings.[4] Their descendants continued to play an important part in Irish history up to and beyond the Anglo-Norman invasion.[5]

This chapter describes the changing nature of the Scandinavian contri-bution to the history of Ireland from the initial attacks *c.*800 through to the twelfth century. Topics covered will include the motivation for those first expe-ditions, the establishment of Ireland's first towns, the changing nature of those communities, the rate at which, and extent to which, a distinct Hiberno-Norse identity emerged, and the extent to which continued influx from Scandinavia influenced their development. The transformative nature of the interaction between the Scandinavians and the natives across Irish society, particularly in relation to slavery, will also be explored. I will avoid over-using the 'v-word', since 'viking' was not a commonly used early medieval term, and its meaning and etymology are far from clear. It appears both as a personal name and as a verb which seems to mean something like 'engaging in piracy' as well as a

2 M. Ní Mhaonaigh, *Brian Boru: Ireland's Greatest King?* (Stroud: Tempus, 2007); S. Duffy, *Brian Boru and the Battle of Clontarf* (Dublin: Gill & Macmillan, 2013).

3 A. Woolf, *From Pictland to Alba, 789–1070* (Edinburgh University Press, 2007), 214–16.

4 A. Woolf, 'Amláib Cúarán and the Gael, 941–81', in S. Duffy (ed.), *Medieval Dublin III* (Dublin: Four Courts Press, 2002), 34–42; H. B. Clarke, 'King Sitriuc Silkenbeard: A Great Survivor', in Clarke and Johnson (eds.), *Vikings in Ireland and Beyond*, 253–67.

5 S. Duffy, 'Irishmen and Islesmen in the Kingdoms of Dublin and Man, 1052–1171', *Ériu*, 43 (1992), 93–133; S. Duffy 'The Royal Dynasties of Dublin and the Isles in the Eleventh Century', in S. Duffy (ed.), *Medieval Dublin VII* (Dublin: Four Courts Press, 2006), 51–65.

common noun for someone involved in that activity. It was certainly not an ethnic label and owes its popularity as a catch-all descriptor to eighteenth-century romanticism. Its over-use in modern times has created an unhelpful image of a homogeneous cultural identity over several hundred years and thousands of square miles. It is much more helpful to consider the various cultural phenomena in their local contexts.[6]

Scandinavian Identity and Motivations

The core of Scandinavian identity in the early Middle Ages was a shared language and those aspects of oral culture that went with that shared language. The Scandinavian language, or cluster of dialects, began to emerge in the period *c*.400–700 as the Germanic dialect continuum of north-central Europe began to polarise into two clusters, a northern one, the ancestor of Scandinavian, and a western group ancestral to modern English, Dutch and German.[7] These clusters probably reflect the competing attraction of the two most successful Germanic-speaking courts of the time; that of the Franks, established in northern Gaul and the Rhineland, and that of the Danes, based on the islands of the western Baltic and the province of Skåne (part of Sweden since 1658). The Danish kingdom was less powerful than the Frankish but within its region was nonetheless overwhelmingly significant. In contrast to the modern stereotype of Scandinavian landscape, which draws on images of the fjords of western Norway, the Danish islands and Skåne in many ways more closely resemble the Irish east midlands or East Anglia, relatively flat rolling countryside comprising fertile fields separated by bosky hedgerows. This landscape had been settled for millennia and the islands had been cleared of bears, wolves and other such beasts long before the Viking Age. It was anything but wild. This Danish heartland was far more populous than any other region of Scandinavia, indeed its population probably exceeded that of the rest of Scandinavia put together, and since the last centuries BC it had supported a relatively stable settlement hierarchy and presumably political structures to match. Across Scandinavia as a whole, local ecologies, subsistence strategies, settlement patterns and funerary customs varied enormously but the presence of a wealthy elite class of Danish aristocrats provided a model for emulation and a potential source of patronage. Their geographical location also gave the

---

6 For a discussion of the term, see J. Jesch, *Ships and Men in the Late Viking Age: The Vocabulary of Runic Inscriptions and Skaldic Verse* (Woodbridge: Boydell Press, 2001), 44–56.

7 M. P. Barnes, 'The Scandinavian Languages in the Viking Age', in S. Brink (ed.), *The Viking World* (London: Routledge, 2008), 274–80.

Danes the ability to control most of the exotic goods travelling north from Western and Central Europe, including wine, high-quality weapons, fine textiles and so forth. This central position of the Danes was one of two major factors contributing to Scandinavian identity, providing a hub, as it were, around which the other groups of North-Germanic speakers circled.[8] The other major factor was the outer world, particularly those regions where Germanic was not spoken such as the Gaelic-speaking West, the Slavic-speaking south-east and the Finnish-speaking north-east and of course Romance-speaking Europe beyond the Franks. On journeys into these regions Scandinavian-speakers from different and quite distinct regions, who might have felt they had little in common while in the North, will have recognised shared elements in their identity and culture when surrounded by speakers of alien tongues. Thus, to some extent, the expansion of the Viking Age may have helped the Scandinavians to discover themselves and to create or reinforce a common identity.[9]

A number of factors contributed to the expansion out of the Scandinavian homelands in the late eighth and early ninth centuries. While the Danes controlled access to the North Sea trading network, largely operated by Frisians, which linked Scandinavia to the Frankish and Anglo-Saxon worlds, the most northerly Scandinavians traded, via the Russian rivers, with the Islamic World; exporting furs, amber and fair-skinned slaves in return for silver. This silver was then used to engage in commerce via the Danish and Frisian networks that could bring Rhenish wine and sword blades to the North. The earliest raids on northern Britain and Ireland seem to have resulted from disruption to these networks which had ensured relative stability through the eighth century. A combination of fluctuations in the silver supply coming from the east, due to political crises in the Caliphate, and increased Frankish royal intervention in Frisia and Saxony, the Danes' southern neighbours, created economic instability which prompted not only direct military conflict between Danish and Frankish kings but also from the most marginalised Scandinavian communities, those in western Norway, desperate attempts to find new and more reliable sources of wealth.[10]

---

8 For the rise of the Danish kingdom: U. Näsman, 'The Ethnogenesis of the Danes and the Making of a Danish Kingdom', *Anglo-Saxon Studies in Archaeology and History*, 10 (1999), 1–10; M. Axboe, 'Towards the Kingdom of Denmark', *Anglo-Saxon Studies in Archaeology and History*, 10 (1999), 109–18.

9 For the impact of the diaspora on the appearance of a Scandinavian identity: L. Abrams, 'Diaspora and Identity in the Viking Age', *Early Medieval Europe*, 20.1 (2012), 17–38; J. Jesch, *The Viking Diaspora* (London: Routledge, 2015), appeared too late to be fully consulted in the writing of this chapter.

10 J. H. Barrett, 'What Caused the Viking Age?', *Antiquity*, 82 (2008), 671–85.

It is unlikely that the Norwegian Westlanders 'discovered' the lands 'West Overseas' in this period. Shetland is extremely close to Norway (Bergen is the nearest railway station to Lerwick, the island's capital) and it is implausible that the populations of both these territories, who had long depended on boats for their livelihood, were not aware of the land just beyond the horizon. There had probably been sporadic contact since the Bronze Age. What had changed was motivation. For most of prehistory the northern parts of Scotland, with which Scandinavians might have been familiar, probably had little to offer. They had a sparse population, poor agricultural potential and a low level of material wealth. What had changed between the sixth century and the ninth, however, was the arrival of Christianity and innovative Christian institutions, largely spreading up the west coast from Ireland, famously to places such as Iona, Applecross and Lismore but also to undocumented sites such as those discovered by archaeological investigation at Portmahomack in Easter Ross, Birsey on Orkney or St Ninian's Isle and Papil on Shetland. Shetland was no longer a remote and unappealing timberless land of sheep-farmers and fishermen, miles from anywhere, but a gateway into a world beyond connecting western Scandinavia, on the fringes of Europe, with wealthy and exotic places such as Armagh, Clonmacnoise and Monkwearmouth–Jarrow, the great 'monastic cities' of the Insular World. For the hardy sea-faring inhabitants of western Norwegian territories like Hordaland and Møre, directly accessing this new source of wealth must have seemed preferable to the unreliable trickledown of southern silver which came to them via Danish- and Swedish-controlled networks to the south and east.[11] This, then, is almost certainly the context for the earliest raids, a search for start-up capital, in slaves and precious metals, which would allow the raiders to enter into trading relations that would bring them wine, weapons and fancy clothing from the Frankish Empire. The Danes, on the other hand, had become increasingly involved in direct conflict with the Franks over Saxony and particularly Frisia and this had led to Frankish intervention in internal Danish politics resulting in a series of coups and civil conflicts. The losers in these conflicts, often accompanied by large fleets of supporters, began to engage in larger-scale military activity in Gaul and England.[12] Thus even in

---

11 M. Heen-Pettersen, 'Insular Artefacts from Viking-Age Burials from mid-Norway: A Review of Contact between Trøndelag and Britain and Ireland', *Internet Archaeology*, 38 (2014) http://dx.doi.org/10.11141/ia.38.2.

12 For Danish–Frankish relations see K. L. Maund, 'Turmoil of Warring Princes: Political Leadership in Ninth-Century Denmark', *HSJ*, 6 (1994), 29–47.

its earliest phase, 'viking' activity had at least two distinct origins and sets of characteristics.

Raids and Settlement

Scholars working on the activities of Viking-Age Scandinavians in Ireland have over the past decade or so begun to re-assess their views about the rate at which sporadic raiding turned into settlement. The traditional view was that serious settlement began in the 840s but in the last few years new archaeological discoveries and re-examination of some of the chronicle records has led this view to be questioned. As early as 798, we are told that a group of heathens burned Inis Pátraic (County Dublin) and 'took the cattle tribute from the territories'. This last detail does not sound like an element in a smash and grab raid. It is unlikely that large numbers of cattle could have been taken away on ship-board and so the extraction of cattle tribute was more likely intended for local consumption over a period of time. This suggests that the 'raiders' were perhaps based for several months, at least, somewhere in the Dublin area. Developer-funded archaeology in and around Dublin has also begun to uncover Scandinavian-style burials with carbon-14 dates centring on the late eighth or very early ninth centuries. As more such evidence is recovered and analysed it may well be that we have to revise received ideas about the origins of Scandinavian settlement in Ireland.[13]

Whatever the precise chronology, by the middle of the ninth century long-term and in some cases permanent (as it transpired) Scandinavian settlements began to appear in Ireland. This type of settlement, termed *longphuirt* (singular *longphort*) in the scholarly literature, was not introduced from Scandinavia but developed in the colonial context. The most famous of them became the medieval and modern cities of Dublin, Limerick and Waterford, but a number of others are mentioned in contemporary annals and yet more have begun to be identified in the archaeological record and investigated.[14] The best known and largest of these is the site known as Woodstown, located upstream of Waterford on the south bank of the River Suir. This site was almost certainly

---

13 L. Simpson, 'The First Phase of Viking Activity in Ireland: Archaeological Evidence from Dublin', in Sheehan and Ó Corráin (eds.), *Viking Age in Ireland*, 418–29.

14 E. P. Kelly, 'The *longphort* in Viking-Age Ireland: The Archaeological Evidence', in Clarke and Johnson (eds.), *Vikings in Ireland and Beyond*, 55–92. For a critical approach see S. H. Harrison, 'Beyond *longphuirt*? Life and Death in Early Viking-Age Ireland', in D. M. Hadley and L. ten Harkel (eds.), *Everyday Life in Viking-Age Towns: Social Approaches to Towns in England and Ireland, c.800–1100* (Oxford: Oxbow, 2013), 61–72; J. Sheehan, 'The Longphort in Ireland', *Acta Archaeologica*, 79 (2008), 282–95.

a precursor to Waterford, though there are no certain annalistic references to it, and initial investigation suggests that it was occupied from the mid-ninth to the mid-tenth century. Sites like Woodstown, which did not develop into later towns, are particularly useful as they give us an opportunity to assess the early layout of Scandinavian settlements in Ireland.[15] The ground-plans of these *longphuirt*, while making allowances for local topography, seem to have been fairly consistent. Their principal initial function seems to have been to protect the ships of the invaders while plundering expeditions were made overland, presumably on captured ponies. Consequently they mostly conform to a plan comprising a D-shaped ditch and bank (probably originally surmounted by a palisade) enclosing a significant stretch of shelving river bank, in the case of Woodstown some 500 m. Some seem to have been occupied for very brief periods, perhaps as little as a few days or weeks, others on what must have seemed a permanent basis and yet others, perhaps, periodically revisited. Most seem to have been located on or very near to pre-existing political boundaries, either exploiting under-utilised march land or perhaps established in collaboration with one of the neighbouring kingdoms in return for shared defence, or aggression, against the other.

The story of Hiberno-Norse settlements can be characterised as the evolution of pirate bases into medieval cities. Whilst few scholars would disagree with this notion in its broadest terms, there has been much debate about certain aspects of this evolution. Was it, for example, gradual or should archaeologists be able to pinpoint the moment at which a particular settlement became a 'real' town?[16] The debate has at times become polarised between those who see the Scandinavian colonists as principally traders and those who see them as principally raiders.[17] Increasingly, however, the inextricable relationship between these two activities has been recognised. As noted above, when discussing the motivation for raiders coming from the Norwegian Westland, predation was principally undertaken for the purpose of accruing

---

15 I. Russell and M. F. Hurley (eds.), *Woodstown: A Viking-Age Settlement in Co. Waterford* (Dublin: Four Courts Press, 2014).

16 H. B. Clarke, 'Proto-Towns and Towns in Ireland and Britain in the Ninth and Tenth Centuries', in Clarke *et al.* (eds.), *Ireland and Scandinavia*, 331–80; D. M. Hadley and L. ten Harkel, 'Preface', in Hadley and ten Harkel (eds.), *Everyday Life in Viking-Age Towns*, vii–xii.

17 For a study emphasising trade: M. A. Valante, *The Vikings in Ireland: Settlement, Trade and Urbanization* (Dublin: Four Courts Press, 2008). For a somewhat bloodier perspective: D. N. Dumville, *The Churches of North Britain in the First Viking Age* (Whithorn: Whithorn Trust, 1997); A. P. Smyth, 'The Effect of Scandinavian Raiders on the English and Irish Churches: A Preliminary Reassessment', in Smith (ed.), *Britain and Ireland*, 1–38.

start-up capital that could be used to engage in trade. The most sought-after commodities in Scandinavian communities, such as wine, high-quality weapons, silver, and fine textiles, were not, by and large, available in places like Ireland and Britain, but had to be obtained from much more developed economies such as those of the Frankish Empire or the Islamic Caliphate. These polities, however, had an unceasing demand for cheap labour, and thus slaves, captured or purchased from less powerful polities, could be used to engage in trade with the economic superpowers of the day.[18]

For most of the ninth and tenth centuries, the basic currency in use amongst Scandinavians, at home and abroad, was bullion, often in the form of what modern scholars term hack-silver. Hack-silver is made up of fragments of silver artefacts, including ingots and fragmentary coins, which have been chopped up into small pieces to allow them to function as currency. Because, unlike coins, these fragments are not standard weights, sizes and values, those engaging in hack-silver economic practices also require scales and standardised weights. Complete coins were also used in this bullion economy but were valued purely by weight and purity of silver content rather than for any notional 'face value'.[19] Fragments of hack-silver, scales and weights and coins were recovered scattered across the interior of the Woodstown enclosure, the most intensively investigated of the *longphort* sites. This phenomenon has given support to the view that trade and exchange was a major function of these sites even before they began to transform into fully fledged towns. It should be noted that the coins from the site were all Anglo-Saxon and Islamic. Coinage of this sort is very rare in pre-Viking-Age Ireland and thus it is likely that it was brought into the country by the Scandinavians. The same seems to be the case with the hack-silver, much of which derives from artefacts fashioned overseas. Some of the silver, however, would appear to derive from ingots smelted on the site itself and its ultimate provenance is thus unclear (most silver circulating in northern Europe came from elsewhere and had often been melted down and refashioned several times before

18 M. McCormick, *The Origins of the European Economy: Communications and Commerce, AD 300–900* (Cambridge University Press, 2001), 729–77; M. McCormick, 'New Light on the "Dark Ages": How the Slave Trade Fuelled the Carolingian Economy', *Past and Present*, 177 (2002), 17–54.

19 B. Hårdh, *Silver in the Viking Age: A Regional Economic Study* (Stockholm: Almquist and Wiksell International, 1996); J. Graham-Campbell, '"Silver Economies" and the Ninth-Century Background', in J. Graham-Campbell, S., M. Sindbæk and G. Williams (eds.), *Silver Economies, Monetisation and Society in Scandinavia, AD 800–1100* (Aarhus University Press, 2011), 29–40.

entering the archaeological record in whatever form it survives in today).[20] What is significant about this is that whilst the popular image is of vikings stripping Ireland of her material wealth, the archaeological evidence would seem to indicate that the Scandinavians were in fact net importers of precious metal into the country. With regard to the currency function of this material, attested by the presence of scales and weights, an important question is whether the exchange it attests to was principally between Scandinavians and native Irish or simply amongst the Scandinavians themselves.

Slavery

Due to the objectification of Scandinavians in Ireland simply as vikings, and to the tendency to create, consciously or unconsciously, rather simplistic binary categories of Norseman and native, too little attention has been paid to the nature of social and economic relations between Scandinavian groups and individuals within Ireland. Most of the plunder taken by raiders in the ninth and tenth centuries comprised livestock and people. The livestock were probably mostly used to supply the armies with food and hides for clothing and equipment, or as mounts for expeditions, but the people were either ransomed back to their communities, if of sufficiently high status, or sold overseas.[21] The logistics of the slave trade probably require a little more thought than has often been given them. Each warrior was in a position to capture slaves, or receive his share of a joint predation, but it is unlikely that these individuals would carry through the entire exportation process themselves. We should probably consider then that much of the market activity that occurred at *longphort* sites such as Woodstown consisted of slaves being purchased from individuals or small groups of warriors either by professional traders or, perhaps more likely, by their own commanders. In this way the principle of a distribution of spoils and the practicalities of long-distance commerce could be reconciled. This may suggest that the presence of scales and weights on these sites attests to the practicalities of soldiers' pay and division of spoils rather than mercantile entrepreneurism. The silver itself must have been brought into Ireland by the invaders. If any of it made its way into the hands of native Irish groups it must have done so either through

---

20 J. Sheehan, 'Silver', in I. Russell and M. F. Hurley (eds.), *Woodstown: A Viking-Age Settlement in Co. Waterford* (Dublin: Four Courts Press, 2014), 194–221.
21 P. Holm, 'The Slave Trade of Dublin, Ninth to Twelfth Centuries', *Peritia*, 5 (1986), 317–45.

successful assaults on viking encampments or through the purchase of slaves from Irish warriors who had preyed upon their neighbours.[22]

This last point should encourage us to consider the nature of slavery and the transformative nature of the viking engagement in the slave trade in Ireland. Slavery was endemic to Ireland: the *cumal*, a slave girl, was one of the standard units of value. It is likely that many, perhaps most, households would have owned a handful of slaves who would have helped with the agrarian and household chores. These slaves, however, will have mostly been Irish-born and the households they served in would have been very like those into which they had been born; in language, custom and economy. They will, for the most parts have been recruited through the widespread local warfare which makes up most of the entries in the Irish chronicle record. What changed with the arrival of the vikings was both the nature of the fate of the enslaved and the motivation of the enslavers. There is very little evidence of a slave trade in pre-viking Ireland and most slaves were probably allocated to the households of those who had engaged in the fighting or distributed by the local kings and lords as part of the practice of redistributive chieftaincy that characterised the Irish political system. Cattle and ponies would have been passed on in much the same way. Kings or their kinsmen led predatory raids on neighbouring territories and redistributed the spoils amongst their neighbours. Slaves taken or sold to the Scandinavians, however, would mostly have gone out of the country and found themselves, ultimately, in households or labour gangs where Irish was not the language of the community, where customs, foodstuffs and perhaps even climate and social norms were completely different.

We can compare this to the trans-Atlantic and trans-Saharan slave trade of more recent centuries which transformed the endemic and localised West African slavery, very similar to early Irish slavery, into something far less humane. The other similarity to this modern phenomenon was the way in which the willingness of the foreigners to pay for slaves with exotic and very valuable currency encouraged the development of native polities which engaged in commercial slaving rather than simply supplying their own domestic needs.[23] This may lie behind the appearance in the later ninth and tenth

---

22 E. Purcell and J. Sheehan, 'Viking Dublin: Enmities, Alliances and the Cold Gleam of Silver', in Hadley and ten Harkel (eds.), *Everyday Life in Viking-Age Towns*, 35–60.

23 R. J. Reid, *Warfare in African History* (Cambridge University Press, 2012), 79–90. For the centrality of slave-raiding in a modern African kingdom, see S. P. Reyna, *Wars without End: The Political Economy of a Pre-Colonial African State* (Hanover, NH: University Press of New England, 1990).

centuries of large hoards of silver, ultimately deriving from the Hiberno-Norse communities, in the territories of some of the more politically active and dominant Irish dynasties such as Mide, northern Brega and the lands of the Cenél Eógain. The opportunities for wealth that this trade provided may also have created the conditions which led to the breakdown of the relative political stability of Uí Néill and Eoganacht hegemonies which had existed at the beginning of the Viking Age, and may explain why even when Irish kings were in a position to snuff out the Hiberno-Norse towns they increasingly declined to do so, from Cerball mac Murecáin's conquest of Dublin in 902, to the capture of Limerick by Mathgamain mac Cennétig in 967 and beyond. Whilst they wished to call a halt to Scandinavian predation on their own lands and the rivalry of the Hiberno-Norse dynasties within Irish politics, they did not wish to kill the goose which laid the silver egg.[24]

Dublin

The ability of Hiberno-Norse towns to survive even when their ruling dynasties were expelled should encourage us to consider what the political structures of such places were and how they related to kings. Whilst modern scholarship tends to use the term 'king of Dublin' quite freely, its Irish equivalent *rí Atha Cliath* appears very rarely, and late, in the chronicle record and usually seems to be applied to a ruler who acknowledged another king as his overlord.[25] More usually, the kings whom scholarship designates as kings of Dublin are simply titled *rí Gall*, 'king of the foreigners'.[26] This ought to encourage us to consider whether we are correct in seeing their polity as Dublin or whether Dublin was not merely one province that sometimes fell under their sway. Scandinavian polities tended to be somewhat federal in structure with autonomous districts governed by local assemblies and having their own customary law. Kings, leading a largish military household, tended to itinerate between them, spending a few weeks in each before moving on to consume tribute elsewhere. Different provincial assemblies often elected

---

24 Reid, *Warfare in African History*, 101–5. *AU*, i, 417, 483. See also *Íslendingabók, Landnámabók*, ed. J. Benediktsson (Reykjavík: Hid islenzka fornritafelag, 1986), 32–3, which synchronises the settlement of Iceland with a list of kings ruling elsewhere in Europe including 'Kjarvalr at Dyflinni'.

25 So far as I have been able to ascertain, the first appearance of the term is in 1075 (*AU*, ii, 27); a notice of the death of Godred Olafsson.

26 The Irish word *Gall* (pl. *Gaill*) actually means something slightly more nuanced than its conventional translation 'foreigner'. It derives from Latin *Gallus*, 'a Gaul', and was used of those deemed to be from continental Europe. Saxons, Britons and Picts were not termed *Gaill*.

rival members of the ruling dynasty as king when the succession came into question, leading to protracted periods of civil war.[27] The dynasty of Ímar [Ivar], which dominated Dublin and perhaps the other Hiberno-Norse towns from the late ninth century onwards, also had strong interests in Britain and perhaps in the Scottish islands, and we are probably being misled by the relative volume of the Irish sources if we assume that Dublin was their principal residence and that the Uí Ímair *imperium* was ruled from Dublin. Whilst it was undoubtedly a very important part of their kingdom, and its loss over the course of the eleventh century dealt them a fatal blow, the manpower they deployed in the ninth and tenth centuries must have been drawn from a much wider area and the eventual Irish domination of Dublin may have been facilitated by the men of Dublin themselves if they found the presence of the Uí Ímair king and his retinue somewhat inconvenient and oppressive.[28] The Isle of Man immediately leaps to mind as a possible major component in this polity. It is the only part of these islands which has so far yielded significant viking ship burials and it plays host to its own distinctive school of very high-quality Scandinavian sculpture. A number of eleventh-century 'Dublin' kings are found ruling there after their expulsion from the city, and in the twelfth century it was clear that 'Manx' kings felt they had a claim on Dublin. Man is almost completely absent from our sources during the height of the power of the Uí Ímair and re-emerges as Dublin falls under the dominion of native rulers.[29] It is, in some sense, the Heart of Darkness of the Irish Sea in the Viking Age. Around it lay parts of northwest England and southwest Scotland that were very late being incorporated into the nascent Scottish and English kingdoms and which for much of the Viking Age were probably component parts of the Uí Ímair *imperium*, much as Man, Dublin and at least some of the other Hiberno-Norse towns were.[30]

27 S. Brink, 'Law and Legal Customs in Viking-Age Scandinavia', in J. Jesch (ed.), *The Scandinavians from the Vendel Period to the Tenth Century: An Ethnographic Perspective* (Woodbridge: Boydell Press, 2003), 87–115; S. Brink, 'Legal Assemblies and Judicial Structure in Early Scandinavia', in O. S. Barnwell and M. Mostert (eds.), *Political Assemblies in the Earlier Middle Ages* (Turnhout: Brepols, 2003), 61–72.

28 For the narrative of the dynasty of Ívarr see B. Hudson, *Viking Pirates and Christian Princes: Dynasty, Religion and Empire in the North Atlantic* (Oxford University Press, 2005), and C. Downham, *Viking Kings of Britain and Ireland: The Dynasty of Ívarr to AD 1014* (Edinburgh: Dunedin Academic Press, 2007).

29 D. M. Wilson, *The Vikings in the Isle of Man* (Aarhus University Press, 2008).

30 The best account of the Irish Sea as an interconnected set of provinces in this period is D. Griffiths, *Vikings in the Irish Sea: Conflict and Assimilation, AD 790–1050* (Stroud: Sutton Publishing, 2010), which includes detailed discussion of patterns of Scandinavian-style burial around the region, including the Manx ship burials, at 72–99.

What then of Dublin itself, and by analogy perhaps, the other Hiberno-Norse towns which are less well accounted for in either the chronicle or the archaeological record? The interior layout of the towns is not well known since all lie under modern urban centres and so full plans cannot be drawn out. However, one distinctive feature is clear and that is that wherever it has been possible to investigate the interior, it has become apparent that from the late ninth century onwards regular plots, similar to later medieval burgage plots, had emerged and that the boundaries of these plots remained very stable for several hundred years, even when the buildings within them were replaced or destroyed. During the ninth to eleventh centuries the dominant type of building within each plot was also remarkably stable. This is what has been termed the Dublin 'Type 1' house; a rectangular building with a total floor space of about 40 m² with a door at each end, one opening onto the street and the other onto the plot, a hearth in the middle, impeding clear access between the doors, and raised sitting and sleeping areas on either side. The tripartite structure of the building was also marked out by a line of roof supports separating the floor space from each of the raised areas. In the rear of the plot there might be a range of secondary building and also metalled or decked pathways leading between buildings and alongside plots that were probably garden beds or small livestock pens. The plots were almost certainly the garths or *gardda* mentioned in the textual sources which formed the basis for taxation within the town.[31]

When trying to visualise these domestic units we should remember that the vast majority of early medieval buildings had only one room and that therefore collections of detached buildings on a single plot may have fulfilled a range of domestic functions similar to the rooms in a more modern house. Thus we have to wonder whether all members of the household slept on the raised areas of the Type 1 house, or whether the householder and his wife might have had a separate chamber in the yard out back. It is quite likely that the answer to such questions would vary according to the demography and wealth of the household. What we can be fairly certain of is that these domestic units represent the habitations of the Dubliners themselves rather than the itinerant followers of the king. So far, no royal hall or compound

---

31 R. Boyd, 'From Country to Town: Social Transitions in Viking Age Housing', in Hadley and ten Harkel (eds.), *Everyday Life in Viking-Age Towns*, 76–9; P. F. Wallace, '*Gardda* and *Airbeada*: The Plot Thickens in Medieval Dublin', in Smyth (ed.), *Seanchas*, 261–74. For scepticism regarding the equation of *gardda* with these plots: P. Holm, 'Manning and Paying the Hiberno-Norse Dublin Fleet', in Purcell *et al.* (eds.), *Clerics, Kings and Vikings*, 76.

has been located by the archaeologists though it is widely speculated that such a site might have lain on the site of the present-day Dublin Castle. This seems quite likely, though we should not exclude the possibility that the royal compound lay outside the town, as the Earl's hall at York did. Were a royal compound to exist, it would probably not contain enough space for the whole of the retinue of the king and, by analogy with later Scandinavian, Irish and Welsh practice, it is likely that some of the king's soldiers would be billeted upon townsmen. In some cases these might have been people with whom they had good social and perhaps familial links, in other cases this might have been a duty which householders, particularly those with teenage daughters, might have resented. A local *rí Atha Cliath* with a much smaller retinue who depended on the Dubliners themselves for his military support might have been more welcome to the locals.

We have no textual evidence for the social organisation of Dublin or any of the other Hiberno-Norse towns in this period, but a useful piece of comparative material survives in a text from the very late tenth century known as the Cambridge Thegns' Guild.[32] Like Dublin, Cambridge was a settlement founded by a viking army in the ninth century and gradually came to be incorporated into the English kingdom as its townsmen accepted the overlordship of the West-Saxon kings who were in the process of uniting the country. In crude terms its basic history was broadly similar to that of Dublin or Limerick in the period between the mid-ninth and early eleventh centuries. The Cambridge document is very short and was written onto a blank leaf of a Gospel book between 970 and 999:

> Here in this writing is the declaration of the enactment which this fellowship has determined in the thegns' guild in Cambridge. Firstly, that each was to give to the others an oath of true loyalty, in regard to religious and secular affairs, on the relics; and all the fellowship was ever to aid him who had most right. If any guild-brother die, all the guildship is to bring him to where he desired, and he who does not come for that purpose is to pay a sester of honey; and the guildship is to supply half the provisions for the funeral feast in honour of the deceased; and each is to contribute two pence for the alms-giving, and from it the fitting amount is to be brought to St Æthelthryth's.[33] And if then any guild-brother have need of his fellows' help and it is made known to the reeve of the nearest guild-brother – unless the guild-brother himself be at hand – and the reeve neglects it, he is to pay one pound. If the

---

32 *Diplomatarium Anglicum Aevi Saxonici*, 610–13; translated in *EHD*, i, 557–8.

33 Probably the monastery at Ely, fourteen miles north of Cambridge (one might like to compare the relationship between Dublin and the church at Swords in the eleventh century).

lord neglects it, he is to pay one pound, unless he is engaged on the necessary business of his lord, or is on a bed of sickness. And if anyone kill a guild-brother, nothing other than eight pounds is to be accepted as compensation. If the slayer scorn to pay the compensation, all the guildship is to avenge the guild-brother and all bear the feud. If then one avenges him, all are to bear the feud alike. And if any guild-brother slays a man and does it as an avenger by necessity and to remedy the insult to him, and the slain man's wergild is 1200 [shillings], each guild-brother is to supply half a mark to his aid; if the slain man is a *ceorl*, two ores; if he is Welsh, one ore. If, however, the guild-brother kill anyone foolishly and wantonly, he is himself to be responsible for what he has done. And if a guild-brother slay a guild-brother through his own folly, he is himself to be responsible towards the kindred for the offence he has committed, and to buy back his membership of the guild with eight pounds, or he is to forfeit for ever fellowship and friendship. And if a guild-brother eats or drinks with the man who slew his guild-brother – unless it be in the presence of the king, or the bishop of the diocese, or the ealdorman[34] – he is to pay one pound, unless he can deny with two of his bench-fellows that he knew him.[35] If any guild-brother insults another, he is to pay a sester of honey, unless he can clear himself with two of his bench-fellows. If a retainer draws a weapon, the lord is to pay one pound, and the lord is to get from him what he can, and all the guildship is to assist him to recover his money. And if a retainer wound another, the lord is to avenge it, and all the guildship together; that – no matter what advocacy he seek – he shall not keep his life. And if a retainer sits within the aisle he is to pay a sester of honey. And if anyone has a *fotsetla*,[36] he is to do the same. And if any guild-brother dies outside the district, or is taken ill, his guild-brothers are to fetch him and bring him, dead or alive, to where he wishes, on pain of the same fine which has been stated in the event of his dying at home and a guild-brother failing to attend the body. And the guild-brother who does not attend his m ... [lacuna in the manuscript] is to pay his sester of honey.

As can be seen, the Cambridge Thegns' Guild is an association of equals, who own property and might have armed retainers and servants. The references to the aisle, and to bench-fellows, suggests that the Guild had a commonly held drinking hall, something which was a standard feature of guilds in this period. Such a guild hall at Dublin may even be mentioned by Gerald of Wales.[37] The Guild served, to some extent, to provide the urban dwellers with the

---

34 Each of these dignitaries is recognised as being able to 'impose peace' within their presence.
35 That is, that he sat down to eat with him not knowing him to be the killer of his guild-brother.
36 A personal attendant.
37 *Expugnatio*, 67–9.

same kind of protection a kinship network would provide in the rural society that was more normal at the time. The emphasis put on vengeance and burial is particularly noteworthy. What I would suggest is that this short text gives us an impression of the kind of 'constitution' that would have bound the householders of Dublin, and the other Hiberno-Norse towns, together. In 917 the 'army that belonged to Cambridge' chose Edward the Elder 'as their lord and protector' when he led his forces into East Anglia and it is very likely that the men of Dublin behaved in like fashion that same summer when Sitriuc, grandson of Ímar, arrived at their gates.[38] The corporate interests of each viking town would be governed by such guilds with regular meetings to hear court cases and decide on policy at established assembly sites like the Thingmote across the Poddle from the town of Dublin, probably located somewhere near where the Olympia theatre stands today. It would be at such assembly sites that kings would be acclaimed.[39]

The 'Hiberno-Norse'

When viking raids began in the eighth century we can clearly distinguish Scandinavian raiders from native Irish, but as time went by this distinction becomes less simple. By the time of the Anglo-Norman invasion in the later twelfth century some Norse kindreds might have been established in Ireland for over 300 years. Given that popular accounts of invasions and migrations often take a very simplistic, even irrational, view of ethnic identity, there is a need to re-examine what it meant to be Hiberno-Norse. In modern scholarship, 'ethnicity' refers to social identity whilst 'race' refers to biological identity. These terms are often confused in public discourse, with 'ethnicity' simply being used as a polite alternative for 'race'. The easiest way to get to grips with the distinction is to think of an individual who has been adopted abroad in infancy, such as one of the many Chinese or African orphans who have been coming to Europe and North America in recent times. They will grow up with the social attitudes of their adopted parents and the community they live in, even though they do not share their biological heritage. The biological heritage is often referred to as 'race', but this term is problematic: the old idea that there were discrete races is not founded on good

---

38 *Anglo-Saxon Chronicle 5, MS C*, ed. K. O'Brien O'Keeffe (Woodbridge: Boydell Press, 2000), *s.a.* 917 A: *AU*, i, 435.
39 S. Duffy, 'A Reconsideration of the Site of Dublin's Viking Thing-mót', in T. Condit and C. Corlett (eds.), *Above and Beyond: Essays in Memory of Leo Swan* (Bray: Wordwell, 2005), 351–60.

science, since most population groups have undergone considerable mixing throughout history and the variation within and between them cannot be scientifically defined. Furthermore, in many historical texts, such as the Bible and much medieval literature, the terms generally translated into modern English as 'race' referred to unilineal descent, usually in the direct male line, taking no account of the ancestry of all the mothers. This is the case when we talk about early Irish dynasties such as the Uí Néill or indeed the Uí Ímair. Unilineal descent can of course have little relationship to either one's ethnic identity or one's physical appearance. A useful term that might replace the popular usage of race is 'phenotype', which means genetically-determined physical appearance.[40]

These issues are of particular significance for the Viking-Age Scandinavian diaspora. To what extent and in what sense did the populations of the colonies remain Scandinavian over time? In multicultural metropoloi like twenty-first-century Dublin, London or New York, it is very easy to think of cultural choices as individual, personal and varied. In such societies generational differences are often as great as inherited differences. The early medieval world was very different. It was overwhelmingly rural. There were no towns in Ireland before the Norse arrived, and even on the eve of the Anglo-Norman invasion only a tiny percentage of the population lived in towns. The same was true in Scandinavia. In rural societies men could usually only marry if they held enough agricultural land, either in allodial, inherited, tenure, or in some sort of relatively secure tenancy. This meant that most men lived close to their patrilineal brothers and cousins, who would be potential heirs to their land if they died without issue. There was no monetised economy and most material culture, from clothes and tools to houses and furniture, was made locally either by members of one's own household or by neighbours. A very small amount of relatively exotic material might filter down through society from chieftains who engaged in gift-exchange, raiding and perhaps some small-scale trade, and who may have patronised a very small number of specialist craftsmen. Wives were also often cousins or at least neighbours. This meant that in times of stability social choices were limited and individuals had little scope to be culturally innovative. Tradition – that is ideas and stories handed down the generations – dominated ideas of identity.

---

40 A German colleague describes her adopted sister as 'phenotypically Chinese'. The woman in question resembles the Chinese stereotype physically and draws her biological heritage from China, but has grown up in Germany, in a German-speaking family, so her attitudes, prejudices and tastes reflect her German ethnicity.

When groups of individuals engaged in long-distance migration, however, as the early viking raiders and invaders did, things were different. The first generation of warriors to cross the sea had grown up in conservative societies. They were now encountering new sets of challenges without their elders on hand to advise them on how to deal with them. For the most part, ships' crews were entirely male and reflected a relatively limited age profile, perhaps between about fourteen and thirty years of age, with a bias towards the younger end of the scale. From a very early stage these groups may have begun to recruit locals into their forces. We have seen that slave-raiding was a major part of the activities of viking expeditions and it is likely that the majority of slaves taken were younger women and children. Whilst women, particularly those whose virginity had been preserved, could probably be sold on for a very high premium, it is quite likely that some of the male children might have been retained as personal servants, to cook, clean weapons and so forth. As happens, notoriously, in many militias in central Africa today, such boys might graduate to become child soldiers.[41] This brings us back to questions of ethnicity and race. When discussing Chinese babies adopted by European couples it is easy to see that the children will retain none of their biological parents' ethnic traits, but what of someone who moves from one ethnic community to another aged eight or twelve? To what degree will he retain the social identity of his natal home? The answer is probably entirely situational; down to the individual himself or the attitude of his new messmates. Perhaps one viking warrior slaps his boy if he catches him speaking Irish or talking about his family, while another shows curiosity or empathy. In the end, however, the corporate identity of the group in which the young person continues to mature, be it a household or a ship's crew, will be the main factor governing his daily speech, his diet and his clothing choices. By the time he is in his twenties he will be a viking, regardless of the circumstances of his birth. Irish, English and continental annals make it quite clear that some viking fleets and armies remained on the move for decades and life histories like those just hypothesised were probably a significant factor in allowing them to recruit fresh soldiers. Such conditions, of course, play havoc with attempts to identify vikings or their descendants using genetic markers. Recently excavated warrior burials from the earliest phases of viking Dublin contain individuals, some of whom were probably raised in Scandinavia and

---

41 A. Honwana, *Child Soldiers in Africa* (Philadelphia: University of Pennsylvania Press, 2006); M. A. Drumbl, *Reimagining Child Soldiers in International Law and Policy* (Oxford University Press, 2012).

others almost certainly in Ireland or western Scotland. These young men may have begun their career in the fashion just described.[42]

The dynamics of viking armies on the move were undoubtedly different from those of settled Hiberno-Norse communities. One major factor underpinning the development of the urban communities was necessarily their relationship with their immediate hinterlands. In the early days, when the *longphuirt* were simply pirate camps, local people probably fled from their occupants who were left to steal what they could find. Over time, however, tributary relations (doubtless still viewed as predation) will have developed, and then ultimately, where the camps became towns, a sense of mutual obligation will have arisen. The underlying structures for such a relationship were already in play in Irish society. Many *túatha* regularly paid tribute to neighbouring kings or indeed to a king of their own who spent little time among them. The hinterland of Dublin, which came to be known in Irish as Fíne Gall, the 'kindred of the foreigners', seems to have been constructed out of two pre-existing *túatha*, both lying north of the Liffey: Saithne, in the south, and Túath Tuirbe to the north, divided from one another by the Broad Meadow Water.[43] These had originally been component parts of the kingdoms of southern Brega. No detailed accounts survive of how these territories evolved from oppressed tributaries to suburban hinterlands but the transition doubtless happened. Immediately south of Dublin the local *túatha* seem to have remained under the control of the Uí Dúnchada dynasty, which continued to compete for the over-kingship of the Láigin until at least 1003, but it is hard to believe this would have been possible without some level of collaboration. By the twelfth century, and perhaps long before, some farms in the area were owned by men with Norse names though Irish appears to have remained the most widespread language.[44] Whether individual Dubliners bought land from their Irish neighbours or whether the tribute of the territory was shared out into plots, as happened with the viking-founded towns in Russia at about the same time, is unclear.[45] It is very likely that intermarriage occurred and some land may have changed hands in such transactions. The regulations of the Cambridge Thegns' Guild, cited above, mention a guild-brother having a reeve and this would seem to imply that the townsmen

42 L. Simpson, 'A Viking Warrior Grave from Dublin', in Clarke and Johnson (eds.), *Vikings in Ireland and Beyond*, 142–5.

43 MacCotter, *Medieval Ireland*, 165–6.

44 J. Bradley, 'The Interpretation of Scandinavian Settlement in Ireland', in Bradley (ed.), *Settlement and Society in Medieval Ireland*, 49–78.

45 J. Blum, *Lord and Peasant in Russia: From the Ninth to the Nineteenth Century* (Princeton University Press, 1961), 29–42.

might, or perhaps normally would, own rural estates. The basic taxable unit in rural Ireland in this period, the *baile* (ancestral to the modern townland), may well have been transferred to Hiberno-Norse landlords who initially resided in Dublin and simply lived off the agricultural renders, but who may have increasingly taken an interest in managing their estates. At the same time inhabitants of these territories may have increasingly entered the town to avail themselves of market opportunities and relationships of fosterage may even have been entered into across the ethnic divide. Bilingualism will have presumably become increasingly common as time went on.[46]

Had the Norse simply left Scandinavia in the ninth century, settled in Ireland and turned their backs on their homeland we might have expected a more rapid assimilation and adoption of the Irish language. The people of the rural hinterland, the servants and probably many of the wives of the townsmen, would have spoken Irish as their first language. Norse, however, remained useful as long as commercial relations underpinned the prosperity of the towns. Irish was not a language of commerce, whilst Norse was spoken widely in the ports of the North Sea and the Channel littoral and beyond. It is probably also the case that Hiberno-Norse towns continued to attract fresh migrants from Scandinavia seeking their fortune either as merchants or mercenaries, or as both. Nonetheless by the end of the tenth century we begin to see Gaelic names appearing even in the ruling dynasty and this, together with the veneration of Gaelic saints, probably signals the emergence of a distinctive Hiberno-Norse identity. To some extent the break-up of the Uí Ímair *imperium* may have reflected the emergence of distinct hybrid cultures in its different territories, as many who shared a common patrilineal descent from viking raiders of the ninth century came to be thought of as more Irish or English. In modern scholarship we use the terms Hiberno-Norse and Anglo-Danish to describe these new hybrid colonial cultures: such terms were alien to the men and women of the tenth and eleventh centuries but the underlying distinctions would have been very apparent to them. In Rouen and Bayeux the Normans were undergoing a similar process, as were the Rus in Novgorod and Kiev. What we do see throughout the Scandinavian diaspora in this period is the reinforcing of certain specific cultural features, be it toy ponies of remarkably similar design across the whole of the viking world, images reflecting the story of Sigurðr the Dragon-slayer, or the spread of the innovative Ringerike art style. In some ways explicit appeals to a common stock of Scandinavian signifiers appear to have become more prevalent

---

46 For *bailte* see MacCotter, *Medieval Ireland*, 45–87.

in the decades around the year 1000, when colonial communities were nativising apace.[47]

One factor intimately connected with this nativisation was the conversion to Christianity. There are no dramatic conversion narratives surviving for the Hiberno-Norse like those recounted in Bede's *Historia Ecclesiastica* or Muirchú's *Life of Patrick*. Indeed Irish sources tell us of no such conversion. In the second quarter of the tenth century, three kings of the dynasty of Ívarr were pressured into undergoing conversion ceremonies by West-Saxon kings in England but the extent to which these events contributed to any real Christianisation is unclear.[48] The use of the term *geinte* ('heathens') to describe the Norse in Ireland declines rapidly in the Irish chronicles in the same period. Olaf Cuarán, the dominant figure in the mid-tenth century, retired to Iona, where he died, after his defeat at the Battle of Tara in 980, and his son Sitriuc went on pilgrimage to Rome in 1028.[49] Other evidence for Christianisation comes in the use of Irish names for adult Norsemen from the last quarter of the tenth century. Some of these may not indicate that the bearer is Christian, though it seems likely, but others, compounds of *Mael* and *Gilla* with a saint's name, are explicitly so and there is some indication that the *Gilla* names, which seem to occur earliest and most frequently amongst Hiberno-Norse and Hebridean individuals, may even have been coined in this context.[50] The conversion of the Uí Ímair rulers, however, need tell us little of the confessional history of the bulk of Hiberno-Norse individuals. Many of the inhabitants of the Hiberno-Norse towns, servants, wives and hostages, must have been born and raised in Christian households and may have continued to practise and even proselytise in their new homes. Many a Christian hand may have rocked a pagan cradle, and during the period when Dublin was ruled by the Leinster kings Cerball and Augaire (902–17) there must have been social, if not political, pressure to accommodate Christianity. Dublin seems not to have gained its own bishop until late in Sitriuc Olafsson's reign but its location on the south side of the Liffey will have put it, at least notionally, in the cure of the bishops of Uí Dunchada; the obits of these prelates, based at Tallaght, are noted in 915, 964, 966 and 968. Within the tributary territories north of the

---

47 D. McAlister, 'Childhood in Viking and Hiberno-Scandinavian Dublin, 800–1100', in Hadley and ten Harkel (eds.), *Everyday Life in Viking-Age Towns*, 92–4; L. Abrams, 'Diaspora and Identity in the Viking Age', *Early Medieval Europe*, 20.1 (2012), 23–4, 29–30.

48 L. Abrams, 'The Conversion of the Scandinavians of Dublin', *ANS*, 20 (1997), 1–29.

49 Dumville, *Churches of North Britain*, 37; *Ann. Tig.*, 342, 368.

50 L. Abrams, 'Conversion and the Church in Viking-Age Ireland', in Sheehan and Ó Corráin (eds.), *Viking Age in Ireland*, 5.

Liffey episcopal obits are noted for Lusk in 907, 909, 929 and 967.[51] In the early eleventh century, shortly before Sitriuc's expedition to Rome, we have an obit for a bishop of Swords, the Columban church patronised by the dynasty of Ívarr. The first bishop based in Dublin, appears to have been Dúnan, who died in 1074.[52]

Sitriuc Silkenbeard (d. 1042) was the last significant ruler to be based in Dublin. By his time the city had far surpassed all the other Hiberno-Norse towns with Limerick, its closest rival, having been securely within the Dál gCais kingdom of Thomond since his childhood. He should probably also be compared with some of his Scandinavian peers in the actions he took to promote a more 'European' character to his kingdom. In the latter part of the 990s he began to mint his own coins, the first in to be minted in Ireland. They closely followed the model of English contemporary coinage, and his desire to produce coins with his own name on them (since foreign coins had long been in circulation) may reflect the need of kings based primarily in Dublin, and lacking a British hinterland from which to draw troops, to supplement the levy of the townsmen with mercenary forces. Elsewhere in the world, from the ancient Aegean onwards, coinage frequently first appeared hand-in-hand with the payment of mercenaries, and in the literary accounts of Sitriuc's great showdown with his father-in-law Brian Bórama at Clontarf his reliance on troops drawn from outwith his own lordship is always emphasised. A mercenary army, pilgrimage to Rome, and the establishment of an episcopal seat in his capital marked Sitriuc out as a modern European ruler.[53]

A major problem is knowing to what extent the history of Dublin, so well documented both by medieval texts and archaeological excavation, can be used to understand the other Hiberno-Norse towns. Limerick seems to have shared a broadly similar, if less auspicious, history in the tenth and eleventh centuries but has so far delivered far less archaeological evidence. Its name, derived from Loch Luimnech, the broad island-dotted stretch of water where the River Fergus joins the lower Shannon now dominated by Shannon International Airport, suggests that the present site is a late development. How late is difficult to say, and no site comparable to Woodstown has so far

---

51 C. Etchingham, *Church Organisation in Ireland AD 650 to 1000* (Naas: Laigin, 1999), 483.

52 *AFM,* ii, 805, 907. Note that in recording Dúnan's death *AU,* ii, 27 makes no mention of Dublin, describing him instead as Archbishop of the *Gaill.* This may indicate a wider remit in the Irish Sea region: A. Woolf, 'The Diocese of the Sudreyar', in S. Imsen (ed.), *Ecclesia Nidrosiensis, 1153–1537* (Trondheim: Senter for middelalderstudier, 2003), 171–2.

53 D. Schaps, 'The Invention of Coinage in Lydia, in India, and in China', *XIV International Economic History Congress* (Helsinki, 2006), session 30, www.helsinki.fi/iehc2006/papers1/Schaps.pdf.

been identified in Loch Luimnech. It is hard to demonstrate, on the basis of either archaeological or textual evidence, that the smaller towns of Cork and Wexford existed prior to the later eleventh century and they may belong entirely to the period when the Hiberno-Norse operated within native Irish kingdoms. Elsewhere re-analysis of earlier finds and more critical readings of the textual evidence continue to modify our view of the subject.[54]

---

54 S. H. Harrison and R. Ó Floinn, *Viking Graves and Grave-Goods in Ireland* (Dublin: National Museum of Ireland, 2015) reviews all of the cemetery evidence recovered in the last three hundred years, whilst C. Etchingham is currently working on a full-length monograph updating his insightful volume *Viking Raids on Irish Church Settlements in the Ninth Century* (Maynooth: An Sagart, 1996).

5

Perception and Reality: Ireland c.980–1229

MÁIRE NÍ MHAONAIGH

Hi Kalaind Auguist cen ail
tiagtís ind cech tress blíadain;
agtís secht ngraifne im gním nglé
secht laithe na sechtmaine.

And luaitís fri bága bil
certa ocus cána in cóicid,
cech recht ríagla co rogor
cech tress blíadna a chórogod.

On the kalends of August free from reproach
they would go thither every third year:
they would hold seven races, for a glorious object,
seven days in the week.

There they would discuss with strife of speech
the dues and tributes of the province,
every legal enactment right piously
every third year it was settled.[1]

THIS eleventh-century depiction of a gathering (*óenach*) held at regular intervals at Carmain provides an imagined glimpse of medieval Ireland at work and play. Conventionally but misleadingly translated 'fair', the *óenach* was an institution in which the wider community played a part. Among those said to have been assembled on this particular occasion were 'the clerics and laity of the Leinstermen, as well as the wives of the nobility' (*clérig, láeich Lagen ille, mnái na ndagfher*). Fasting was undertaken there 'against wrong and oppression' (*ra anrecht, ra écomlund*).[2]

---

1 *Metrical Dindshenchas*, iii, 18–19 (lines 208–16). I am grateful to Dr Fiona Edmonds of the University of Lancaster, for perceptive comments on what follows.
2 *Metrical Dindshenchas*, iii, 20–1 (lines 280–2).

Misconduct was forbidden;[3] knowledge was imparted of various kinds.[4] Kings controlled these occasions, convening an *óenach* for a variety of reasons. It was to celebrate his accession to the kingship of Leinster that the *óenach* at Carmain was held by Donnchad mac Gilla Phátraic in 1033 and this poem may mark that specific event.[5] Máel Sechnaill mac Domnaill, king of Mide, had earlier hosted a similar assembly at Tailtiu [Teltown, County Meath] in 1007, when he had already been ruling for more than a quarter of a century and had achieved considerable success.[6] His revival of *óenach Tailten* was designed to bolster his authority further, and it too was commemorated in a composition attributed to Máel Sechnaill's court-poet, Cúan ua Lothcháin. In rejuvenating Tailtiu, Ireland's premier *óenach* (*prím-óenach hÉrend*), this midland ruler takes his place in a long line of ancestral kings. Hailed as 'the glory of the noble West' (*orddan íarthair domuin duind*), he is claimed to occupy by right the royal seat (*forud flatha*).[7]

Underlying these carefully choreographed descriptions is a social reality, which is both mediated and informed by the constructed text. A focus on what has been called the 'social logic of the text' is important as we commence an evaluation of selected aspects of a transformative period in Irish history, for which the rich and varied sources at our disposal form the very fabric of the transformation itself.[8] Máel Sechnaill had earned his kingship, in Cúan ua Lothcháin's words, 'since he raised the fair of Tailtiu from the sod; though of ancestral use, it was unknown' (*tuc óenach Talten a feór / ciarb atharda, rop aneól*). His power is thus presented as deep-rooted, but his learned advocate is also of the view that Máel Sechnaill 'king of Tara' (*rí Temra*) and 'singular champion of Europe' (*oen-milid na hEorapa*) are one.[9] The historical world encapsulated

---

3 *Acra, tobuch frithir fíach / écnach, écraite, anríad / ní lámar … mad aithed and, nír chlunter …*: 'Suing, harsh levying of debts, satirising, quarrelling, misconduct is not dared … as for elopement, it is not to be heard of there': *Metrical Dindshenchas*, iii, 18–19 (lines 221–3, 227).

4 This included *cach rand rorannad Héreo* 'every division into which Ireland has been divided'; *fis cech trichat in Hérind* 'the knowledge of every cantred in Ireland'; *coimgne cinte cóem-cheneóil* 'the exact synchronising of the goodly race': *Metrical Dindshenchas*, iii, 20–1 (lines 247, 249, 265).

5 *AU* (Mac Airt), *s.a.* 1033.4; D. Ó Corráin, 'Viking Ireland – Afterthoughts', in Clarke *et al.* (eds.), *Ireland and Scandinavia*, 421–52, at 443–4.

6 *Chron. Scot.*, *s.a.* 1007. Reference to it was added in a different hand in *AU* (Mac Airt), *s.a.* 1007.10; for discussion, see M. Ní Mhaonaigh, 'A Man of Two Faces: Máel Sechnaill mac Domnaill in Middle Irish Sources', in Clarke and Johnson (eds.), *Vikings in Ireland and Beyond*, 232–52, at 249–50.

7 *Metrical Dindshenchas*, iv, 146–63, esp. 150–1 (line 48) and 160–1 (lines 201 and 203). For a discussion of the term *forad*, see C. Swift, 'The Local Context of *Óenach Tailten*', *Ríocht na Midhe*, 11 (2000), 24–50, at 31–3.

8 G. M. Spiegel, 'History, Historicism and the Social Logic of the Text in the Middle Ages', *Speculum*, 65 (1990), 59–86.

9 *Metrical Dindshenchas*, iv, 160–1 (lines 207–8, 197 and 200).

in this literary creation thus looks inwards and out, marking what Spiegel has termed the 'moment of inscription', by which she means the process through which the text's meaning becomes fixed.[10] As part of learned discourse, 'Tailtiu' itself shaped social ideology and in this way could have informed 'Carmain', a comparable literary representation from a similar milieu. In the case of these two poems, verbal parallels in fact suggest a direct relationship.[11] In his rise to supremacy in Osraige and Leinster, Donnchad mac Gilla Phátraic overcame opposition from the celebrant of *óenach Tailten*, Máel Sechnaill mac Domnaill, as well as from his son.[12] The pen served as an effective weapon alongside the sword. In presenting Donnchad as master of a gathering echoing that of Tailtiu, a partisan author buttressed that king's position through the power of the word.

Twelfth-century kings employed *óenach Tailten* to similar effect, specifically the king of Connacht, Tairdelbach Ua Conchobair and his son and royal successor, Ruaidrí, who each convened this intensely symbolic gathering to emphasise acquisition of actual gains.[13] In cultivating a gathering like an *óenach*, recourse was had to a sense of community and identity, and an appeal made to a polity as a whole.[14] The communicative force itself, however, was harnessed by the influential few, and the cultural reality refracted represents that of elite society. In delineating the world in which *óenaig* functioned, many of its contours are obscured from view. Notwithstanding this, the mediators-*cum*-moulders of eleventh- and twelfth-century Ireland revealed much of their present through elaborate depiction of their past and alleged projection of a specific future. They operated in centres of learning that formed part of ecclesiastical establishments. Throughout the period with which we are concerned, the mutual dependency of cleric and king ensured that written

---

10 Spiegel, 'History', 84.
11 See *Metrical Dindshenchas*, iv, 150–1 (lines 65–8), 152–3 (lines 71–2), and iii, 18–19 (lines 225–8), 10–11 (lines 103–4). These parallels were discussed by Denis Casey in a lecture he presented on 'Carmain' at a conference arising out of 'The Óenach Project' in Cork, March 2012. I am grateful to Dr Casey for sending me a draft version of his work on the poem.
12 See, for example, *AU* (Mac Airt), *s.a.* 1016.6, on which occasion Donnchad killed the Leinster ruler with whom Máel Sechnaill had formed an alliance (and *Chron. Scot., s.a.* 1013; *AU* (Mac Airt), *s.a.* 1015.2). See also *Ann. Tig., s.a.* 1039.
13 D. Ó Corráin, 'Nationality and Kingship in Pre-Norman Ireland', in T. W. Moody (ed.), *Nationality and the Pursuit of National Independence. Historical Studies* XI, (Belfast: Appletree, 1978), 1–35; T. M. Charles-Edwards, 'Ireland and its Invaders, 1166–1186', *Quaestio Insularis: Selected Proceedings of the Cambridge Colloquium in Anglo-Saxon, Norse, and Celtic*, 4 (2003), 1–34, at 23–4.
14 P. Gleeson, 'Kingdoms, Communities and Óenaig: Irish Assembly Practices in their Northwest European Context', *Journal of the North Atlantic*, 8 (2015), 33–51 (http://dx.doi.org/10.3721/037.002.sp801). For the audience of these works see E. Johnston, *Literacy and Identity in Early Medieval Ireland* (Woodbridge: Boydell Press, 2013).

records encompassed religious and secular affairs.[15] Court literacy became more prominent as the administrative support required by rulers in control of larger territories grew. Lay learned families are a feature of the later part of our period, serving eulogy to royal patrons and memorialising significant events.[16] Yet irrespective of this development, the Church maintained an active interest in the transmission of knowledge more generally, even after the introduction of new religious orders in the twelfth century. The set of annals known as the Cottonian Annals or 'Annals of Boyle' deals with a wide range of events and was recorded in the Cistercian monastery of Boyle, County Roscommon, until 1228, before being continued elsewhere.[17] Moreover, the association with the new orders was deemed significant, at least by some kings: Cathal Crobderg Ua Conchobair was buried in the Cistercian abbey of Knockmoy on his death in 1224, rather than in the traditional burial ground and site of a significant cultural centre, Clonmacnoise.[18] Notwithstanding the increasing variety of loci for scholarly production, some continuity, as far as ecclesiastical participation in literary cultivation is concerned, was undoubtedly maintained.[19]

Literary production was thus supported and promoted by secular and religious elites alike, and extant texts – whether chronicle or genealogy, legal commentary or imaginative tale – must be evaluated as the ideological documents that they so often are. This pseudo-historical record can be relativised with reference to other valuable source material, archaeological, art historical, linguistic, onomastic, to allow a multi-dimensional picture of the past to be drawn. Loan-words, place names, coins, as well as arm-rings and the like, provide other types of commentary with which the evidence of written compositions should, where possible, be meshed. Recent scholarship on óenaig, for example, places landscape and literature on the same page.[20] Yet as the óenach example highlights, we may glean why something happened without

---

15 See M. Ní Mhaonaigh, 'The Literature of Medieval Ireland, 800–1200: From the Vikings to the Normans', in M. Kelleher and P. O'Leary (eds.), The Cambridge History of Irish Literature, Volume I: to 1890 (Cambridge University Press, 2006), 32–73, especially 36–7.

16 The earliest examples of their poetry are discussed by P. Ó Macháin, 'Aspects of Bardic Poetry in the Thirteenth Century', in C. Breatnach and M. Ní Úrdail (eds.), Aon don Éigse: Essays Marking Osborn Bergin's Centenary Lecture on Bardic Poetry (1912) (Dublin: DIAS, 2015), 91–125.

17 'The Annals in Coton MS Titus A xxv', ed. and trans. A. M. Freeman, Revue celtique, 41 (1924), 301–30; 42 (1925), 283–505; 43 (1926), 358–84; 44 (1927), 336–61.

18 AC, s.a. 1224.2.

19 K. Simms, 'An Eaglais agus Filí na Scol', in P. Ó Fiannachta (ed.), An Dán Díreach. Léachtaí Cholm Cille XXIV. (Maigh Nuad: An Sagart, 1994), 21–36.

20 This is the explicit aim of the Óenach Project, for which see https://theoenachproject.wordpress.com.

determining how it functioned on the ground.[21] The tapestry of surviving evidence contains strands of varying thickness alongside its threadbare gaps.

King of Tara, Ruler of the Irish, Emperor of the Western World

Whatever about its physical manifestation, the *óenach's* ideological significance was great. By convening *óenach Tailten* in particular, a king's authority was underlined through association with the kingship of Tara. Celebrated in the literature of this period as the prerogative of the ideal sovereign, *rí Temra(ch)* 'king of Tara', as Máel Sechnaill is termed in the poem 'Tailtiu', marked the addressee out as an aspirant to recognition as most powerful king. Uí Néill, to whose southern branch of Clann Cholmáin Máel Sechnaill belonged, had long been inextricably linked with this prestigious kingship, though its kings were also accorded the title *rí Érenn* 'king of Ireland' from the time of its first known usage in the ninth and tenth centuries.[22] In the account of the rivalry between Máel Sechnaill and his Munster opponent, Brian Bórama, with which our period opens, the term 'king of Tara' is subservient to 'king of Ireland', at least in the pro-Brian record of events. Thus, while both Brian and Máel Sechnaill are included in a list of Tara kings, as *rí Temrach*, the midlands ruler is clearly subordinate to his southern contemporary, *rí Érenn*, as the two march at the head of an army to Dublin in an encounter that will become known as the Battle of Clontarf.[23] The resonances of the sovereignty of Tara remained useful and it retained its force as a legitimising label throughout our period. An eleventh-century narrative, *Echtra mac nEchach Mugmedóin* ('The Adventure of the Sons of Echaid Mugmedón'), set out Uí Néill claims to rule, with reference to how their eponymous ancestor, Níall Noígíallach (Niall of the Nine Hostages), acceded to Tara.[24] Appropriating the same story more

21 For discussion of activities at an *óenach*, see C. Etchingham, *The Irish 'Monastic Town': Is this a Valid Concept? Kathleen Hughes Memorial Lecture VIII* (Cambridge: Department of Anglo-Saxon, Norse and Celtic, 2010).

22 M. Herbert, '*Rí Érenn, Rí Alban*: Kingship and Identity in the Ninth and Tenth Centuries', in S. Taylor (ed.), *Kings, Clerics and Chronicles in Scotland 500–1297: Essays in Honour of Marjorie Ogilvie Anderson on the Occasion of her Ninetieth Birthday* (Dublin: Four Courts Press, 2000), 62–72. The concept of a kingship of Ireland itself is attested earlier: E. Breathnach, 'Temoria: Caput Scotorum?', *Ériu*, 47 (1996), 67–88.

23 *CGG*, 4–5 (§III); *AU* (Mac Airt), *s.a.* 1014.1. The account of the battle in the Annals of Ulster has been augmented in favour of Brian: see M. Ní Mhaonaigh, *Brian Boru: Ireland's Greatest King?* (Stroud: Tempus, 2007), 55–6.

24 'The Death of Crimthann son of Fidach and the Adventures of the Sons of Eochaid Mugmedón', ed. and trans. W. Stokes, *Revue celtique*, 24 (1903), 172–207, at 190–203; 'Echtra maic Echdach Mugmedóin', ed. and trans. M. Joynt, *Ériu*, 4 (1910), 91–111; for discussion, see C. Downey, 'Literature and Learning in Early Medieval Meath', in F.

than a century later, Uí Chonchobair of Connacht employed it with a twist to claim Tara and thus legitimacy for King Cathal Crobderg, descendant of Niall's brother, Brión.[25]

It is, however, as 'king of Connacht and king of the Irish of Ireland' (*ri Connacht 7 ri Gaidhel Erenn*), that Cathal is described in his death notice of 1224.[26] Indeed, even the Ua Néill ruler, Máel Sechnaill, was described as *airdri Erenn* in his obit, some two hundred years previously. Almost a decade earlier than that, Brian Bórama had been hailed in death, not simply as *ardrí Gaidhel Erenn* ('chief ruler of the Irish of Ireland') but of the foreigners (*gaill*) and Britons, and 'the Augustus of the whole of north-west Europe' (*August iartair tuaiscirt Eorpa uile*) as well.[27] As rulers of a physical domain, the designation 'king of Ireland' and the depiction as leader of a single geographically defined people reflected the territorial basis of rule.[28] The importance of the ideological dimension of sovereignty endured, tales of royal ancestry forming part of the literary arsenal of kings whose ambition often extended beyond island-wide rule. The imperial accolade accorded Brian by a later commentator in the Annals of Ulster is matched by his assignation as *imperator Scottorum* ('emperor of the Irish') by his confessor, Máel Suthain, in a marginal addition penned in the Book of Armagh during the king's own life.[29] It was with the claim to the kingship of Ireland, however, that all further aspiration commenced.

The parallel between Brian's title, *imperator Scottorum*, and that of his contemporary, Otto III, *imperator Romanorum*, has long been noted. The imitation could certainly be deliberate, given Ireland's ongoing connections with the Frankish world. Ottonian style may also have informed the later writer who deemed Brian Augustus, since it was as *Romanorum imperator augustus*

Ludlow and A. Crampsie (eds.), *Meath, History and Society: Interdisciplinary Essays on the History of an Irish County* (Dublin: Geography Publications, 2015), 101–34.

25 'A Poem Composed for Cathal Croibhdhearg Ó Conchubair', ed. and trans. B. Ó Cuiv, *Ériu*, 34 (1983), 157–74; D. Ó Corráin, 'Historical Need and Literary Narrative', in D. Ellis Evans, J. G. Griffith and E. M. Jope (eds.), *Proceedings of the Seventh International Congress of Celtic Studies, Oxford 1983* (Oxford: Cranham Press, 1986), 141–58, at 146; and D. Ó Corrain, 'Legend as Critic', in T. Dunne (ed.), *The Writer as Witness: Literature as Historical Evidence. Historical Studies, XVI* (Cork University Press, 1987), 23–38.

26 *AU*, ii, *s.a.* 1224. He is enumerated as one of the 'kings of Ireland' in his obit in *AC*, *s.a.* 1224.2.

27 *AU* (Mac Airt), *s.a.* 1022.3 and 1014.1.

28 Herbert, 'Rí Érenn, Rí Alban', 71.

29 *Liber Ardmachanus: The Book of Armagh*, ed. J. Gwynn (Dublin: Hodges Figgis & Co., 1913), fol. 16v; D. Casey and B. Meehan, 'Brian Boru and the Book of Armagh', *History Ireland*, 22:2 (2014), 28–9.

that Otto II was known from the 980s.[30] Inspired by its use in antiquity, Anglo-Saxon kings had earlier been termed *imperator*, including King Æthelstan in 930, and a later successor, Edgar, who was deemed *basileus et imperator omnium regnum Anglorum*.[31] A number of Irish books have been associated with Æthelstan's court, and contacts across the Irish Sea continued after his death.[32] Thus, available models could have been manifold for the expression of Brian's imperial power. The Munster ruler was not unusual in the scale of his ambition and in this can be compared with Cnut the Great whose imperial tendencies have also been observed.[33] In a hyperbolic claim, comparable with Brian Bórama's description as emperor of the western world, Cnut was celebrated as 'king of the Danes, of the Irish, and of the English and of the Island dwellers [Orcadians]' (*konung Dana, Íra ok Engla ok Eybúa*) by one of his most prolific skalds, Óttarr svarti (the black). Nonetheless, in the realm of eulogistic poetry, the description is far from outlandish and Óttarr's desire 'that his [Cnut's] praise may travel with heavenly support more wisely through all the lands' (*at hans fari / með himinkrǫptium / lǫndum ǫllum / lof víðara*) could have encompassed, in the poet's mind, Ireland too.[34]

Similar titles were applied to Irish kings in the twelfth century, including Tairdelbach Ua Conchobair, ruler of Connacht, who was described on his death in 1156 as 'king of all Ireland and the Augustus of western Europe (*rí Erenn uile 7 Auguist iarthair Eorpa*).[35] Brian and Tairdelbach bear further

---

30 A. Gwynn, 'Brian in Armagh (1005)', *Seanchas Ard Mhacha*, 9 (1978), 38–51; K. Leyser, '*Theophanu Divina Gratia Imperatrix Augusta*: Western and Eastern Emperorship in the Later Tenth Century', in A. Davids (ed.), *The Empress Theophano: Byzantium and the West at the Turn of the First Millennium* (Cambridge University Press, 2002), 1–48, at 35.

31 Flanagan, *Irish Society*, 179; S. Duffy, *Brian Boru and the Battle of Clontarf* (Dublin: Gill & Macmillan, 2013), 143–4 (and references therein). Irish scholars also noted imperial rule before the Ottonian period, as indicated by a reference to 'the emperor of the whole world' (*impir in beatha uile*) in the eighth-century law tract, *Míadshlechta*: see C. Etchingham, 'Review Article: The "Reform" of the Irish Church in the Eleventh and Twelfth Centuries', *Studia Hibernica*, 37 (2011), 215–37, at 222.

32 M. Herbert, 'Crossing Historical and Literary Boundaries: Irish Written Culture around the Year 1000', in *Crossing Boundaries, Croesi Ffiniau: Proceedings of the XIIth International Congress of Celtic Studies 24–30 August 2003, University of Wales, Aberystwyth* (= *Cambrian Medieval Celtic Studies*, 53/54 [2007]), 87–101, at 90.

33 See T. O'Donnell, M. Townend and E. M. Tyler, 'European Literature and Eleventh-Century England', in C. A. Lees (ed.), *The Cambridge History of Early Medieval English Literature* (Cambridge University Press, 2013), 607–36, at 614–15.

34 M. Townend, 'Contextualising the *Knútsdrápur*: Skaldic Praise Poetry at the Court of Cnut', *Anglo-Saxon England*, 30 (2001), 145–79, at 157–9. The poem in question is edited by him in *Poetry from the Kings' Sagas 1: From Mythical Times to c. 1035*, ed. D. Whaley, Skaldic Poetry of the Scandinavian Middle Ages, 1 (Turnhout: Brepols, 2012), 786–9; see also O'Donnell *et al.*, 'European Literature', 615.

35 *Ann. Tig.*, s.a. 1156. Ua Conchobair's rival, Muirchertach Mac Lochlainn, who died a decade later is also termed 'the Augustus of all of north-western Europe' (*August iarthair tuairscirt Eorpa uile*): *AU*, ii, s.a. 1166.

resemblances. Both built fortifications for defence purposes and were engaged in conflict and communication by water, as well as land.[36] The two rulers imposed their own candidates over subordinate territories, where possible, Tairdelbach doing so with great frequency throughout his reign.[37] Each was intimately associated with the Church, using it to advance political ambition. Brian's ostentatious gift of twenty ounces of gold on Patrick's altar at Armagh is linked in the annalist's view to his return homewards 'bringing with him the pledges of the men of Ireland' (*co n-etire fer nErenn laiss*). In his will, Tairdelbach left the majority of his not inconsiderable moveable wealth to various churches, the culmination of his extensive involvement in ecclesiastical affairs during his lifetime.[38]

The connection between his son, Cathal Crobderg, and the Cistercians has already been noted. Moreover, Pope Innocent III recognised the latter's royal authority.[39] In terms of fortifications, Cathal is better known for his destruction rather than his construction of castles, as part of his campaign against English rule. His relationship with the settlers was more complex, however, than these destructive acts would suggest. He was granted a charter by King John, received royal protection and invoked primogeniture in an effort to secure the succession of his eldest son, Áed. His outward-looking attitude is also reflected in the image of him carved about the time of his death, curly-haired and surrounded by fleur-de-lis.[40] Throughout the eleventh and twelfth centuries and later, Irish kings and their image-makers continued to be influenced by their interaction with English and continental royal rule.

These cross-channel connections had a practical basis. As one of the chosen few of the generous host of Brión (brother of Níall Noígíallach), Cathal Crobderg is depicted in one of a number of contemporary poems on his rule as 'a beautiful salmon' (*éicne án*) destined to defeat 'the British with abundance of weapons and the English and French from over the fair sea' (*Bretnaig co n-imat n-arm … Sacsain, Francaig tar finnmuir*).[41] Ignoring the political reality of that king of Connacht's day, the author does not make reference to Cathal's support of King John against the de Lacys, nor his recourse to English

---

36 For fortifications: *AI*, *s.a.* 995.6; *Ann. Tig.*, *s.a.* 1124. For naval warfare: *AI*, *s.a* 993.2; *Ann. Tig.*, *s.a.* 1127, 1140.

37 E.g. *AU* (Mac Airt), *s.a.* 1125.3, 1126.7.

38 *AU* (Mac Airt), *s.a.* 1005.7; *Ann. Tig.*, *s.a.* 1156.

39 P. J. Dunning, 'Pope Innocent III and the Irish Kings', *Journal of Ecclesiastical History*, 8 (1957), 17–32.

40 *AI*, *s.a.* 1195.2; H. Perros, 'Crossing the Shannon Frontier: Connacht and the Anglo-Normans, 1170–1224', in Barry *et al.* (eds.), *Colony and Frontier in Medieval Ireland*, 177–200. Perros [Walton], 'Ó Conchobhair, Cathal', in *ODNB*.

41 'A Poem for Cathal Croibhdhearg', ed. and trans. Ó Cuív, 166–7, stanzas 41, 47 and 50.

military allies. At Clontarf, over two hundred years earlier, according to the augmented account in the Annals of Ulster, 'the earl of Marr in Scotland' (*mormhaer Marr i nAlbain*) was killed in the battle fighting on Brian's side.[42] His presence reflects contacts, real or desired, on the part of Brian's descendants in an extended northern world.

Leinster too had recourse to outside assistance, as indicated by a reference in a mid-eleventh-century poem to *Frainc*, in the meaning 'Normans', in the service of Diarmait mac Maíl na mBó.[43] Moreover, the latter's relationship with the prominent dynasty of Earl Godwine of Wessex was ongoing and intense. His sons, Harold and Leofwine, found political refuge in Leinster under Diarmait's protection in 1051. After Harold's death at the Battle of Hastings in 1066, bringing his short reign as king of England to an end, his sons too were harboured by Diarmait.[44] Their gratitude may be indicated by the gift of Edward the Confessor's standard which Diarmait presented to Tairdelbach Ua Briain, king of Munster, in 1068.[45] Given these dealings, it is scarcely surprising that Harold's sister, Edith, wife of Edward the Confessor, was said by the biographer of her husband to have been proficient in Irish, as well as Danish and perhaps French and Latin.[46] Even if not factual (though there could be some truth to it), reference to her fluency in Irish is explicable against the general backdrop of this broader integrated Irish Sea world.

Notwithstanding the intensive contacts across the Irish Sea in this period, no record of the Battle of Hastings is preserved in extant contemporary Irish

---

42 *AU* (Mac Airt), *s.a.* 1014.2. He is accorded a prominent role in the encounter in an early twelfth-century literary account of the battle, *CGG*, 175–7. That text also includes Normans among the battle roll of the dead, but this evidence, and that suggesting their battle-involvement in the Annals of Loch Cé, is not contemporary: see Ní Mhaonaigh, *Brian Boru*, 67.

43 'Mittelirische Verslehren', ed. R. Thurneysen, in *Irische Texte mit Wörterbuch*, ed. E. Windisch and W. Stokes, 4 vols., vol. 3:1 (Leipzig: Verlag von S. Hirzel, 1891), 1–82, and *Bruchstücke der älteren Lyrik Irlands*, ed. K. Meyer (Berlin: Walter de Gruyter, 1919), 18 (no. 36). For discussion, F. J. Byrne, 'The Trembling Sod: Ireland in 1169', in *NHI* ii, 22; and P. Wadden, 'Some Views of the Normans in Eleventh- and Twelfth-Century Ireland', in Duffy and Foran (eds.), *The English Isles*, 26–7.

44 B. Hudson, *Irish Sea Studies 900–1200* (Dublin: Four Courts Press, 2006), 100–8; K. L. Maund, *Ireland, Wales and England in the Eleventh Century* (Woodbridge: Boydell Press, 1991), 164–5; S. Duffy, 'Ostmen, Irish and Welsh in the Eleventh Century', *Peritia*, 9 (1995), 378–96 (at 387); C. Etchingham, 'North Wales, Ireland and the Isles: The Insular Viking Zone', *Peritia*, 15 (2001), 145–87 at 154.

45 *AI*, *s.a.* 1068.5; the reference is to *merge ríg Saxan* 'the standard of the king of the Saxons'.

46 *The Life of King Edward who rests at Westminster attributed to a Monk of Saint-Bertin*, ed. and trans. F. Barlow (Oxford University Press, 1992), 22–3; E. M. Tyler, 'The *Vita Edwardi*: The Politics of Poetry at Wilton Abbey', *ANS*, 31 (2009), 131–56; M. Ní Mhaonaigh, '*Carait tairisi*: Literary Links between Ireland and England in the Eleventh Century', in A. and N. Harlos (eds.), *Adapting Texts and Styles in a Celtic Context* (Münster: Nodos Publikationen, 2016), 265–88.

annalistic sources.[47] It is noted by Marianus Scotus, alias Máel Brigte, a monk who received his early education in Moville, County Donegal, before going to the Continent in 1056 in his late twenties. He spent time in such learned centres as Cologne and Fulda, but his *Chronicon*, a universal history similar in concept to that of the early eleventh-century chronicler, Thietmar, bishop of Merseburg, was produced in Mainz where he had access to that monastery's considerable bibliographical resources, as well as to books he had brought with him from Ireland.[48] These too informed his writing: among the Chronicle's prefatory material is a list of Irish kings, nestling alongside a catalogue of popes.[49] Three stanzas of a versified biblical history by an early eleventh-century Irish scholar, Airbertach mac Coisse, are quoted in one of the margins, while the obits of some Irish and Scottish kings who had died after his departure for the Continent are also recorded.[50] For Marianus, and others like him, the learned activity in which he engaged in ecclesiastical centres abroad was a continuation of that he had practised at home.

The Chronicle of Marianus Scotus proved influential and his work was drawn on by the twelfth-century English historian, John of Worcester, whose *Chronicon ex chronicis* continued the Irishman's history, augmenting it considerably with English affairs. Another English historian of the same period, Henry of Huntingdon, a secular cleric and one-time bishop of Lincoln, produced for England an historical mythology, the *Historia Anglorum*, that bears comparison in approach and outlook with *Lebor Gabála Érenn* (The Book of the Taking(s) of Ireland), which was being revised and written across the Irish Sea just as the Englishman was composing his account.[51] What links these disparate texts despite their many differences is their focus on what Rees Davies called 'the unity, the identity, the ethnic homogeneity of a people';[52] each eloquently bears

---

47 In addition to the high-level contacts just discussed, trade between Chester, Bristol and Dublin should also be noted: D. Griffiths, *Vikings of the Irish Sea: Conflict and Assimilation AD 790–1050* (Stroud: History Press, 2010), 119–39.

48 Marianus Scottus, *Chronicon*, ed. G. Waitz, Monumenta Germaniae Historica, Scriptores 5 (Hannover, 1844), 559. For his account of the Battle of Hastings, see Wadden, 'Some Views of the Normans', 17–18.

49 B. Mac Carthy, *The Codex Palatino-Vaticanus, No. 830*, Todd Lecture Series III (Dublin: RIA, 1892), 7–8.

50 B. Ó Cuív, 'The Irish Marginalia in Codex Palatino-Vaticanus No. 830', *Éigse*, 24 (1990), 45–67. The biblical poem in question is edited by P. Ó Néill, 'Airbertach mac Cosse's Poem on the Psalter', *Éigse*, 17 (1977–78), 19–46.

51 The text is commonly known as the Book of Invasions: J. Carey, *A New Introduction to Lebor Gabála Érenn, The Book of the Taking of Ireland* (Dublin and London: ITS, 1993).

52 R. R. Davies, 'The Peoples of Britain and Ireland, 1100–1400: IV, Language and Historical Mythology', *TRHS*, 6th ser., no. 7 (1997), 1–24, at 20.

witness to a shared intellectual strand. In any exploration of Ireland's history in this vibrant era, this broader cultural heritage has an important part to play.

God's Chosen People: Gaídil and Gaill

At the heart of what was a broader Christian learned heritage was the biblical concept of a people chosen by God.[53] This idea underpins the elaborate history of Ireland set out in *Lebor Gabála Érenn* in which the wandering Irish (*Gaídil* 'Gaels') are identified with the exodus of the Israelites, *túatha Dé* (the peoples of God). Descended from Japheth son of Noah, the Irish too are accorded their place among the nations of the earth.[54] Read in conjunction with another medieval staple text, *Sex Aetates Mundi*, with which it is often associated in manuscripts, *Lebor Gabála* elucidated and embedded the Irish strand in the universal history of mankind.[55] This is mirrored in microcosm in the *Banshenchas* (Lore of Women), a metrical version of which was composed by Gilla Modutu Ua Casaide who died in 1147. Concerned primarily with Irish women who were wives and mothers of kings, the text takes as its starting point Eve and other notable females from biblical and apocryphal sources.[56] The self-awareness and self-confidence this approach necessitated is evident in Irish learning from a much earlier period. The developed vernacular literature that has been posited as key to the growth of nationhood had

53 M. Garrison, 'Divine Election for Nations – a Difficult Rhetoric for Medieval Scholars?', in L. B. Mortensen (ed.), *The Making of Christian Myths in the Periphery of Latin Christendom (c.100–1300)* (Copenhagen: Museum Tusculanum Press, 2006), 275–314.

54 J. Carey, '*Lebor Gabála* and the Legendary History of Ireland', in H. Fulton (ed.), *Medieval Celtic Literature and Society* (Dublin: Four Courts Press, 2005), 32–48 and the essays in his *Lebor Gabála Érenn: Textual History and Pseudo-History* (Dublin and London: ITS, 2009). This is but one strand in a complex text. See M. Clarke, 'The *Leabhar Gabhála* and Carolingian Origin Legends', in P. Moran and I. Warntjes (eds.), *Early Medieval Ireland and Europe: Chronology, Contacts, Scholarship. A Festschrift for Dáibhí Ó Cróinín* (Turnhout: Brepols, 2015), 441–79.

55 *The Irish Sex Aetates Mundi*, ed. and trans. D. Ó Cróinín (Dublin: DIAS, 1983); another edition with commentary is found in *Sex Aetates Mundi. Die Weltzeitalter bei den Angelsachsen und den Iren. Untersuchungen und Texte*, ed. H. L. C. Tristram. Anglistische Forschungen, 165 (Heidelberg, 1985). For comment, M. Herbert, 'The Irish *Sex Aetates Mundi*: First Editions', *Cambridge Medieval Celtic Studies*, 11 (1986), 97–112, and more generally P. Geary, 'Reflections on Historiography and the Holy: Center and Periphery', in Mortensen (ed.), *Making of Christian Myths*, 323–9.

56 A. Connon, 'The *Banshenchas* and the Uí Néill Queens of Tara', in Smyth (ed.), *Seanchas*, 98–108, at 98. For the edited text, see 'The Ban-shenchus', ed. and trans. M. C. Dobbs, *Revue celtique*, 47 (1930), 283–339; 48 (1931), 163–233; and 49 (1932), 437–89. For Gilla Modutu's authorship, see K. Murray, 'Gill Mo Dutu Ua Casaide', in J. Carey, M. Herbert and K. Murray (eds.), *Cin Chille Cúile, Texts, Saints and Places: Essays in honour of Pádraig Ó Riain* (Andover, MA and Aberystwyth: Celtic Studies Publications, 2004), 150–62, at 158–9.

been present in Ireland from the seventh century or so.[57] Yet exploration of group identity and nationality acquired renewed emphasis in Irish writing in the period under consideration here.[58]

In this, Ireland was not unusual. Susan Reynolds has documented the extent to which historical writing in general and myths of common descent in particular acquired a new purpose from the tenth century. As stories binding a particular people, they came to epitomise the unity of a group owing loyalty to what was an increasingly powerful leader, contributing to the construction of newly evolving kingdoms in the process.[59] The eleventh- and twelfth-century Irish phase of this development saw provincial rulers – the so-called *ríg co fressabra* (kings with opposition) – jockeying with each other for supreme position of *rí Érenn* (king of Ireland) or *rí Temra* (king of Tara) in turn.[60] Fostering a shared identity by means of a universal origin myth enhanced a sense of communal solidarity. A powerful ruler, be he Ua Briain of Munster, Ua Conchobair of Connacht or Mac Lochlainn of Cenél nÉogain, could turn the conceit of collective ancestry articulated in such texts as *Lebor Gabála* to his advantage when his place in the political pecking order allowed. Writing this particular brand of history flourished as a medieval industry precisely because aspiring, ambitious rulers had a vested interest in its promotion.

Lebor Gabála Érenn was first written and then re-written in the eleventh and twelfth centuries, drawing on the work of contemporary poets, including a mid-eleventh-century lector of Monasterboice, Flann Mainistrech. Of note is the fact that texts concerning other peoples, such as Bede's 'Ecclesiastical History of the English People' and *Historia Brittonum* ascribed to Nennius, were also translated into Irish at this time.[61] A ninth-century Frankish text,

---

57 See, for example, D. Ó Corráin, 'The Church and Secular Society', in *L'irlanda e gli irlandesi nell'alto medioevo, Spoleto, 16–21 aprile 2009*, Atti delle settimane, CVII (Spoleto, 2010), 261–321, especially 261, 266; Johnston, *Literacy and Identity*; and A. Hastings, *The Construction of Nationhood: Ethnicity, Religion and Nationalism* (Cambridge University Press, 1997), 2–3.

58 David Dumville evaluates the general context in his article, 'Did Ireland Exist in the Twelfth Century?', in Purcell *et al.* (eds.), *Clerics, Kings and Vikings*, 115–26.

59 S. Reynolds, 'Medieval *origines gentium* and the Community of the Realm', *History*, 68 (1983), 375–90.

60 M. T. Flanagan, 'High-Kings with Opposition, 1072–1166', in *NHI* i, 899–933.

61 P. Ní Chatháin, 'Bede's Ecclesiastical History in Irish', *Peritia*, 3 (1984), 115–30. Thomas Owen Clancy has argued that the translation of *Historia Brittonum* was undertaken in Abernethy, whence it was transmitted to the Cistercian monastery at Sawley in Lancashire: 'Scotland, the "Nennian" Recension of the *Historia Brittonum*, and the *Lebor Bretnach*', in Taylor (ed.), *Kings, Clerics and Chronicles*, 87–107. If so, the text was certainly in Ireland by the late eleventh century as it forms part of the earliest extant

De proprietatibus gentium, describing the defining characteristics of particular *gentes* was similarly cast into vernacular form as *Cumtach na nIudaide nard.*[62] Literary enterprises were often perceived as island-wide. The landscape captured in story in *Dindshenchas Érenn* (The Lore of Ireland's Notable Places), for example, which contains the poems on 'Tailtiu' and 'Carmain' with which we commenced, extended throughout Ireland. The Church too came to form a unit of interlinked dioceses, as the 'reform' of the long twelfth century progressed. In the person of Patrick, it was granted access to past knowledge by means of a journey throughout Ireland, according to the narrative, *Acallam na Senórach* (The Colloquy of the Ancients), which may have been written in Cathal Crobderg of Connacht's reign.[63]

By then the arrival of the English had introduced a different dimension, but one which a malleable sense of community could accommodate. *Gaill*, originally signifying Gauls, came later to mean vikings; in its third reincarnation, it was applied to English settlers, though *Saxain* was also used, as well as *Engleis* in French texts.[64] The separateness signalled by such terminology underplayed the links forged between different groups from the outset of the conquest. Thus, in the late twelfth-/early thirteenth-century 'Song of Dermot and the Earl', which focuses on the activities of the Leinster king, Diarmait Mac Murchada, and Richard fitz Gilbert de Clare (Strongbow), a clear distinction is drawn between *nos Engleis* 'our English' and *les Yrreis* 'the Irish'.[65] Subcategorisation of the latter, in terms of dynastic affiliation, reveals more detailed knowledge. Nonetheless, King Diarmait apart, the Irish for the most part are rebel tyrants who oppose an altogether more civilised, chivalrous host.[66] A contemporary of the author of this French poem, Gerald of Wales (Giraldus Cambrensis), expresses it more vividly, the Irish 'live like

---

vernacular manuscript, *Lebor na hUidre*: see D. N. Dumville, 'The Textual History of "Lebor Bretnach": A Preliminary Study', *Éigse*, 16 (1975/6), 255–73, at 255.

62 'Two Middle Irish Poems', ed. K. Meyer, *Zeitschrift für celtische Philologie*, 1 (1897), 112–13.

63 'Acallam na Senórach', ed. and trans. W. Stokes in *Irische Texte mit Wörterbuch*, ed. E. Windisch and W. Stokes, 4 vols., vol. 4:1 (Leipzig: Verlag von S. Hirzel, 1900). For a translation, see A. Dooley and H. Roe, *Tales of the Elders of Ireland* (Oxford University Press, 1999). For discussion, see A. Dooley, 'The Date and Purpose of *Acallam na Senórach*', *Éigse*, 34 (2004), 97–126.

64 M. T. Flanagan, 'Strategies of Distinction: Defining Nations in Medieval Ireland', in H. Tsurushima (ed.), *Nations in Medieval Britain* (Donington: Shaun Tyas, 2010), 104–20, at 112–14.

65 The text continued to be revised for a further quarter of a century after its initial composition in the 1190s: *Deeds of the Normans*, 27–32.

66 Thus, *les Yrreis de O Kenselath* 'the Irish of Uí Chennselaig' (line 11740), alongside *tut Yrlande les Yrreis* 'all the Irish of Ireland' (line 1745): *Deeds of the Normans*, 22–3; Charles-Edwards, 'Ireland and its Invaders', 10–15.

beasts' (*bestialiter vivens*). Much superior to them are the new settlers with whom this Cambro-Norman cleric identified, and whose conquest he sought to justify.[67] Notwithstanding the fact that Gerald had come to Ireland in 1185 with Henry II's son, John, who was later himself to become king, his colourful commentary owes as much and more to his own specific bias and the ethnographic tradition within which he was writing.[68]

Nor was his negative view anything new.[69] A satirical Latin poem written around the year 1000 by Warner of Rouen, whose principal subject is a slow-witted (*stultus*) Irishman, Moriuht, ascribes bestial behaviour to the latter's countrymen.[70] In his castigation of their ignorance of God, Warner foreshadows the twelfth-century Cistercian, Bernard of Clairvaux, who considered the Irish pagan in all but name.[71] Similar aspersions continued to be cast on what was perceived as a peculiar brand of Irish Christianity in the thirteenth century, as shown by the remark in 1229 of an abbot of Savigny who later followed in Bernard's footsteps as abbot of Clairvaux, Stephen of Lexington: 'How can anyone love the cloister of learning who knows nothing but Irish?'[72] Stephen's concern in this regard, however, must be read in the context of what was perceived to be a more general crisis of the Cistercians in Ireland. Attempting to impose uniformity, he was opposed to difference

---

67 *Gir. Camb. Op.* i, 151; *Topographia*, 101; Flanagan, 'Strategies of Distinction', 105–6.

68 According to Gerald himself, he was 'specially sent with John by his father': *Expugnatio*, 229. On the ethnographic traditions, see R. Bartlett, *Gerald of Wales: A Voice of the Middle Ages* (Stroud: Tempus, 2006) and his *Gerald of Wales and the Ethnographic Imagination*, Kathleen Hughes Memorial Lectures, 12 (Cambridge: Department of Anglo-Saxon, Norse and Celtic, 2013).

69 J. Gillingham, 'Conquering the Barbarians: War and Chivalry in Twelfth-Century Britain', in his *The English in the Twelfth Century: Imperialism, National Identity and Political Values* (Woodbridge: Boydell Press, 2000), 41–58; L. Ashe, *Fiction and History in England, 1066–1200* (Cambridge University Press, 2007), 117, 175 (the latter reference I owe to Fiona Edmonds).

70 *Warner of Rouen, Moriuht: A Norman Latin Poem from the Early Eleventh Century*, ed. and trans. C. J. McDonough (Toronto: Pontifical Institute of Mediaeval Studies, 1995), 74–5. The author claims that though 'many facts have been reported to me about these Irish, it is immoral to record them and it shames (me) to recount (them)' (*de his Scottis mihi multa relata / scriber quod nefas est quodque referre pudet*).

71 *Warner of Rouen*, 74–5, line 38: *et ignari luminis [et] Altithroni* 'They are also unaware of the light of God enthroned on high.' Bernard's remark (*Christiani nomini, re pagani*) is the culmination of a long diatribe against the uncivilised Irish: *Vita Sancti Malachiae*, in *Sancti Bernardi Opera*, ed. J. Leclercq, H. M. Rochais and C. H. Talbot. 8 vols. (Rome: Editiones Cistercienses in World Cat., 1957–77), iii, 307–78, 325. D. Scully, 'Ireland and the Irish in Bernard of Clairvaux's Life of Malachy', in Bracken and Ó Riain-Raedel (eds.), *Ireland and Europe in the Twelfth Century*, 239–56.

72 *Stephen of Lexington, Letters from Ireland*, ed. B. W. O'Dwyer (Kalamazoo: Cistercian Publications, 1982), 68, 91, 162. Davies, 'The Peoples of Britain and Ireland, IV', 13–14.

in language as in other spheres, wishing to promote Latin as the language of the Church, or French as the vernacular of the Cistercians' spiritual home.[73]

Yet Cistercian houses embodied connections too. The foundations of John de Courcy were affiliated with Furness in Lancashire. His involvement with that abbey is further indicated by his role as one of a trio of patrons to commission Jocelin, a monk of Furness, to write a biography of Patrick.[74] One of de Courcy's Irish monasteries was Inch Abbey, County Down. In relative proximity to it was Grey Abbey founded as a daughter-house of Holm Cultram in 1192 by his wife, Affreca, daughter of Gofraid mac Amlaíb, king of Man. De Courcy's liaison with Gofraid's daughter was a major part of his political strategy and had happened by 1180, if not before. In allying with the Manx ruler who was linked to the northern dynasty of Mac Lochlainn, de Courcy sought to invoke the support of his two powerful neighbours.[75] While the Isle of Man was pivotal to de Courcy, the Isles, under the leadership of Gofraid's enemies, Meic Shomhairle, were also increasingly drawn into Irish politics. Along with Gofraid of Man, they came to the aid of the king of Connacht, Ruaidrí Ua Conchobair, in his blockade of Dublin against Henry II in 1171. They became increasingly enmeshed in internal Irish struggles, supporting Ruaidrí's sons in their succession struggle against their uncle, Cathal Crobderg, after their father's death in 1183. John de Courcy himself, too, was drawn into this contest after 1185, the year in which he was entrusted with the administration of Ireland by King John.[76] In this justiciar, Gofraid of Man had a powerful ally in his final years and the association between the two men exemplifies how the English conquest of Ireland influenced insular, and not just Irish, politics in a range of spheres.

Gofraid himself had been active in Ireland and he undertook what was ultimately an unsuccessful expedition to Dublin sometime in the 1150s. According to the Chronicle of Man, his expedition there was in response to an invitation by the men of Dublin to become their overlord and he was appointed king by them of one voice.[77] Opposed by Muirchertach Mac Lochlainn, the most

---

73 Watt, *Church and the Two Nations*, 106.

74 S. Duffy, 'The First Ulster Plantation: John de Courcy and the Men of Cumbria', in Barry *et al.* (eds.), *Colony and Frontier in Medieval Ireland*, 1–27, at 8 and n. 37; Flanagan, 'John de Courcy, the First Irish Plantation and Irish Church Men', in Smith (ed.), *Britain and Ireland*, 154–78; M. T. Flanagan, 'Jocelin of Furness', in C. Downham (ed.), *Jocelin of Furness: Essays from the 2011 Conference* (Donington: Shaun Tyas, 2013), 45–66.

75 Duffy, 'First Ulster Plantation', 25, 26, and n. 167.

76 *Expugnatio*, 78–9, 243; S. Duffy, 'The Bruce Brothers and the Irish Sea World, 1306–29', *Cambridge Medieval Celtic Studies*, 21 (1991), 55–86, at 60 and n. 6.

77 *Cronica Regum Mannie et Insularum*, transcribed and trans. G. Broderick (Douglas: Manx Museum and National Trust, 1979), fol. 37r.

powerful king in Ireland at the time, he retreated to Man, despite being victorious in battle, according to the *Cronica*.[78] A later alliance with Mac Lochlainn is indicated by his marriage to a member of that dynasty, Finnguala. The precise date of that union is not known, though it is frequently placed in the period between 1170 and 1172, since their son, Amlaíb, was around three years of age at the time of their canonical union in 1176.[79] This coincides with Gofraid's known involvement in the siege of Dublin organised by King Ruaidrí Ua Conchobair in 1171 as noted above.[80]

Gofraid's grandfather, Gofraid Méránach, had ruled Dublin and Man though he was expelled as *rí Gall* in Dublin by Muirchertach Ua Briain, great-grandson of Brian Bórama, in 1094.[81] Gofraid died the following year, the victim of a widespread plague, according to some sources.[82] On his death, the Munster ruler became king-maker in Man, installing a family member, Domnall mac Taidc, in the kingship there.[83] The allegedly tyrannous rule of Domnall was interrupted by the assumption of control in the region by King Magnús Berfœttr (Barelegs) of Norway, who was allied with and opposed to Muirchertach Ua Briain in turn.[84] The backdrop to the shifting allegiances between Magnús, Muirchertach and Normans of Shrewsbury was control over Gwyned.[85] Marriage alliances bolstered relations: a truce between Muirchertach and

---

78 *Cronica regum Mannie*, fol. 37r. The dating of the episode is far from certain; see I. Beuermann, *Masters of the Narrow Sea: Forgotten Challenges to Norwegian Rule in Man and the Isles, 1979–1266*, Acta Humaniora (Oslo: Faculty of Humanities, University of Oslo, 2006), 100–22 and S. Duffy, 'Irishmen and Islesmen in the Kingdom of Dublin and Man, 1052–1171', *Ériu*, 43 (1992), 93–133, at 126–8.

79 Beuermann, *Masters of the Narrow Sea*, 150–6.

80 Gerald of Wales writes that both Ruaidrí and Lorcán Ua Tuathail, archbishop of Dublin, sent letters to Gofraid seeking assistance in return for financial reward: *Expugnatio*, 78–9.

81 *AU* (Mac Airt), *s.a.* 1094.2; *AI*, *s.a.* 1094.2. He is termed *rí Átha Cliath 7 Inse Gall* on his death: *AI*, *s.a.* 1095.13.

82 *AI*, *s.a.* 1095.13. The Annals of Ulster mention his death and the plague separately: *AU* (Mac Airt), *s.a.* 1095.8 and 1095.11.

83 See Duffy, 'Irishmen and Islesmen', 108–10. Domnall may have been the son of Muirchertach's brother Tadc, and hence was also the Munster king's nephew and grandson of an earlier king of Man, Echmarcach mac Ragnaill. According to the Manx Chronicle, Muirchertach was requested to intervene by the people of Man and grant them a ruler 'until Óláfr son of Guðrøðr should have grown up' (*donec olauus filius godredi cresceret*), as a result of strife between Gofraid's two adult sons: *Cronica Regum Mannie*, fol. 33v. This period is also discussed in various contributions in S. Duffy and H. Mytum (eds.), *A New History of the Isle of Man*, vol. III, *The Medieval Period, 1000–1406* (Liverpool University Press, 2015), for which reference I am indebted to Fiona Edmonds.

84 According to the *Cronica* (fol. 33v), Domnall 'reigned ruthlessly for three years' (*tribus annis enormuiter regnavit*). On Magnus Barelegs, see Etchingham, 'North Wales, Ireland and the Isles', 148–50 (with references to earlier literature), and R. Power, 'Meeting in Norway: Norse–Gaelic Relations in the Kingdom of Man and the Isles', 1090–1270', *Saga-Book*, 29 (2005), 5–66.

85 Etchingham, 'North Wales, Ireland and the Isles', 150–1.

Magnús in 1102 was symbolised by a union between the latter's nine-year-old son, Sigurd, and the Irish ruler's five-year-old daughter, called Bladmynja in the saga of Magnus Barelegs.[86] Around the same time, another of Muirchertach's daughters was married to Arnulf de Montgomery, brother of Robert de Bellême, Earl of Shrewsbury, who sought the assistance of the Munster king in his rebellion against Henry I.[87] That Muirchertach was involved is indicated by a letter written by him to Anselm of Canterbury, in which he gives thanks to the archbishop for interceding with the king on his son-in-law's behalf.[88]

Muirchertach's correspondence with Anselm, like that of his father, Tairdelbach, before him, highlights once more the ecclesiastical dimension of Ireland's contacts with the wider world. Tairdelbach had also exchanged letters with Pope Gregory VII, as well as with Anselm's predecessor, Lanfranc, the latter considering him king of Ireland, as suggested by his address to him as *magnifico Hibernie regi Terdeluaco*.[89] Lanfranc was closely associated with William the Conqueror, with whom Tairdelbach may also have had links through a shared interest in encouraging trade across the Irish Sea.[90] In this connection, we may note the visitation to Tairdelbach in 1079 by a group of five Jews who may have had commercial interests. For whatever reason, their gifts were repudiated and 'they were sent back again across the sea' (*a ndíchor doridisi dar muir*).[91] Tairdelbach, and in particular his son, were heavily associated with ecclesiastical development in the period. Muirchertach convened the first of what are deemed to be the reforming synods at Cashel in 1001. He was closely connected with Gille, bishop of Limerick and papal legate, whose treatise, *De statu ecclesia*, set out in detail the structured hierarchy of a reformed Church. Alluding to secular ranks also, his unitary structure, which implicitly extended to the kingdom within which this unified Church operated, would certainly have appealed to his patron, Muirchertach Ua Briain.[92]

---

86 *AU* (Mac Airt), *s.a.* 1102.7; *Heimskringla*, ed. Bjarni Aðalbjarnarson. 3 vols. Íslenzk fornrit 26–8 (Reykjavík: Hið ílenzka fornritafélag, 1941–51), iii, 224–5.

87 Flanagan, *Irish Society*, 67–8; E. Curtis, 'Murchertach O'Brien, High-King of Ireland and his Norman Son-in-Law, Arnulf de Montgomery, *circa* 1100', *JRSAI*, 51 (1921), 116–34.

88 A. Candon, 'Muirchertach Ua Briain: Politics and Naval Activity in the Irish Sea 1075–1119', in Mac Niocaill and Wallace (eds.), *Keimelia*, 397–415 at 411–13.

89 *The Letters of Lanfranc, Archbishop of Canterbury*, ed. and trans. H. Clover and M. T. Gibson (Oxford University Press, 1979), 70–1 (no. 10).

90 A. Candon, '"Barefaced Effrontery": Secular and Ecclesiastical Politics in Early Twelfth-Century Ireland', *Seanchas Ard Mhacha*, 14 (1991), 1–25, at 4; B. Hudson, 'William the Conqueror and Ireland', *IHS*, 29 (1994), 145–58, at 149–51.

91 *AI*, *s.a.* 1079.3. Hudson speculates that they were requesting permission for a settlement at Dublin, 'William the Conqueror', 154.

92 J. Fleming, *Gille of Limerick (c. 1070–1145): Architect of a Medieval Church* (Dublin: Four Courts Press, 2001); Flanagan, *Transformation of the Irish Church*, 59–60.

Muirchertach's northern rival, Domnall Mac Lochlainn, was similarly engaged with changes in the Church, as were his successors.[93] As *rex totius Hiberniae*, his grandson, Muirchertach, granted land to a Cistercian house at Newry, County Down. He was also a generous patron to Flaithbertach Ua Brolcháin, abbot of Derry and head of the important Columban federation. The building of 'the great church of Derry' (*tempull mór Dairi*) at this time symbolised that centre's role as head of the Columban church.[94] Such was Ua Brolcháin's fame that the abbacy of Iona was offered to him in 1164 'on the advice of Somhairle, and of the men of Argyll and Innsi Gall' (*a comairli Somarlidh ocus Fer Aer[th]er-Gaidhel ocus Innsi-Gall*). It was the intervention of Muirchertach, together with the abbot of Armagh, which ensured that the offer was rejected.[95] The incident revealed the underlying belief that *Gaídil* in Ireland were ultimately different from *Gaídil* 'to the east' (*anair*).[96] Nonetheless, for ideological as well as political reasons, commonalities were often emphasised. Twelfth- and thirteenth-century Scottish kings promoted their Irish origins, acquiring 'the legitimising lustre of ancient royalty' in the process.[97] In the same way, his Irish connections were emphasised by Ragnall, son of Gofraid, king of Man in the early thirteenth century, most notably in *Baile suthach síth Emna* ('The otherworld of Emain is a fertile place'), a conventional bardic eulogy, in which his suitability for the kingship of Tara is to the fore.[98]

Collective ancestry, therefore, remained pivotal in certain circumstances and the myth of common descent served as a flexible device. The expression of sharp distinctions, when useful, between 'us' and 'them', was part of the same process of communal definition. It was for this reason that the viking as a negative type was resurrected in eleventh- and twelfth-century

93 Herbert, *Iona, Kells, and Derry*, 109–23.

94 *AU*, ii, *s.a.* 1164.

95 *AU* (Mac Airt), *s.a.* 1164: *co ro [fh]astaei comarba Patraic ocus ri Erenn, idon, Ua Lochlainn ocus maithi Cene[oi]l Eogain e.*

96 M. Herbert, 'Sea-Divided Gaels: Constructing Relationships between Irish and Scots *c.*800–1169', in Smith (ed.), *Britain and Ireland*, 87–97, at 97; S. Duffy, 'Ireland and Scotland, 1014–1169: Contacts and Caveats', in Smyth (ed.), *Seanchas*, 348–56.

97 D. Broun, *The Irish Identity of the Kingdom of the Scots* (Woodbridge: Boydell Press, 1999), 132. Matthew Hammond's important caveat should also be borne in mind: 'any pan-Gaelicism must be balanced against the understanding that peoples like the Galwegians, men of Moray, men of Argyll, seem to have seen themselves as distinct *gentes*, despite being all Gaels', 'Ethnicity and the Writing of Medieval Scottish History', *The Scottish Historical Review*, 85 (2006), 1–27, at 17. See also D. Broun, 'Becoming a Nation: Scotland in the Twelfth and Thirteenth Centuries', in Tsurushima (ed.), *Nations in Medieval Britain*, 86–103.

98 'A Poem in Praise of Raghnall, King of Man', ed. and trans. B. Ó Cuív, *Éigse*, 8 (1957), 283–301; A. Byrne, *Otherworlds: Fantasy and History in Medieval Literature* (Oxford University Press, 2016), 159–67.

Irish compositions. This northern caricature, as he appeared in a number of what are often termed pseudo-historical tracts, bore no resemblance to his Scandinavian relative who had long since been assimilated into the Irish social and political landscape. While the tenth-century king of Dublin, Amlaíb Cuarán, patronised churches and had vernacular poetry composed in his honour by one of the foremost authors of the day, Cináed ua hArtacáin, his recent ancestors were to be cast as destructive marauders in some eleventh- and twelfth-century literary texts. Defined solely by their difference in such matters as mores, weaponry and appearance, these *gaill* were deliberately set up in stark opposition to *Gaídil*. Moreover, the contrast becomes more marked as the period progresses. The eleventh-century author of the Fragmentary Annals of Ireland allows for the possibility of good and less good pagans of Scandinavian ancestry, distinguishing between *Danair* who had 'certain kinds of piety' (*cinele crabhaidh*) and *Lochlannaig* who are beyond redemption.[99] By contrast, twelfth-century examples of the genre, specifically the related texts *Cogadh Gáedhel re Gallaibh* ('The War of the Irish against Foreigners') and *Caithréim Chellacháin Chaisil* ('The Battle-triumph of Cellachán of Cashel'), can countenance only negative examples of what appears as a monochromatic, relentlessly evil viking type.[100]

Ethnic stereotyping was scarcely the preserve of the Irish, however, as the depiction by Gerald of Wales of the Irish (and elsewhere the Welsh) makes clear. Gerald's barbarian Irish, like the vikings of the *Cogadh* and *Caithréim Chellacháin Chaisil*, are distinctive in weaponry and dress. They may not be heathen, in contrast to Scandinavian *genti* (pagans), nonetheless, as Gerald echoing Bernard of Clairvaux complains, they were 'most uninstructed in the rudiments of faith'.[101] In constructing a savage Other, twelfth-century Irish authors sought to legitimise ruling dynasties by associating them with glorious ancestors who

99 *The Fragmentary Annals of Ireland*, ed. and trans. J. N. Radner (Dublin: DIAS, 1978), §235: *Uair as amhlaidh ra bhattar na Danair, ocus cinele crabhaidh aca,.i. gabhaid scalad fri fheóil ocus fri mhnáibh ar chrabhudh.* See C. Downham, 'The Good, the Bad, the Ugly: Portrayals of Vikings in "The Fragmentary Annals of Ireland"', in E. Kooper (ed.), *The Medieval Chronicle III: Proceedings of the 3rd International Conference on the Medieval Chronicle, Doorn/ Utrecht 12–17 July 2002* (Amsterdam and New York: Rodopi, 2004), 27–39.

100 CGG; *Caithréim Cellacháin Caisil: The Victorious Career of Cellachan of Cashel, or the Wars between the Irishmen and the Norsemen in the Middle of the 10th Century*, ed. and trans. A. Bugge (Oslo: J. C. Gundersens bogtrykkeri, 1905).

101 *Topographia*, 169. These accounts also bear comparison with Adam of Bremen's description of Scandinavians written in the 1070s as part of his history of the archbishopric of Hamburg-Bremen: *Gesta Hammaburgensis ecclesiae pontificum*, ed. B. Schmeidler (Hanover: Hahnsche Buchhandlung, 1917), revised version *Quellen des 9. und 11. Jahrhunderts zur Geschichte der Hamburgischen Kirche und des Reiches*, ed. W. Trillmich (Darmstadt: Wissenschaftliche Buchgesellschaft, 1961).

overthrew an almost invincible foe. In the same way, reformers and ethnographers, such as Bernard and Gerald, employed their description of a barbarian, well-nigh pagan race to justify takeover and conquest in religious and political spheres. As outsiders looking in, the perspective of Bernard and Gerald was in contrast to that of Irish writers purporting to comment on those who came to dwell in their midst. But all were writing within a broader ethnographic tradition, the influence of which is detectable in their common slant.

Lord and Subject: Commoners and Elite

That common intellectual tradition accommodated diversity.[102] Historical memory was specific even if the framework within which it was conceptualised and constructed was general.[103] As the specifics were adapted to fit ever-changing circumstances, the overarching structure required flexibility. The ideology it supported could shift in significant ways and be formed of overlapping cultural spheres. What was expressed, however, was the mentality of an elite. It is the views of kings concerned with control and continuity that are reflected, and of ecclesiastics and scholars, fellow-actors on an aristocratic stage. Some of these sophisticated literary productions may have been performed at an óenach, as the poem on Carmain suggests. As the nature of that institution continues to elude us, so too does a detailed appreciation of the life of those summoned to the 'fair'.

Although activities associated with an óenach have been misleadingly adduced in support of the existence of earlier monastic towns, the only fledgling urban settlements at the beginning of our period were the port towns founded by vikings at various points in the tenth century. The minting of the first coins in Dublin under King Sitriuc Silkenbeard marks a significant moment in the history of urbanisation, and archaeological finds from Dublin provide evidence for a thriving urban culture there in the eleventh century.[104] The development of towns in Ireland in this period undoubtedly affected the lives of many, both beyond the burgeoning settlements, as well as within.

---

102 R. Bartlett, 'Medieval and Modern Concepts of Race and Ethnicity', *Journal of Medieval and Early Modern Studies*, 31 (2001), 39–56.

103 For a highly relevant exploration of the relationship between memory and social identity: J. Fentress and C. Wickham, *Social Memory: New Perspectives on the Past* (Oxford: Blackwell, 1992).

104 Etchingham, 'Irish "Monastic Town"'; M. A. Valante, 'Re-assessing the Irish "Monastic Town"', *IHS*, 31 (1998), 1–18, and her *The Vikings in Ireland: Settlement, Trade, and Urbanisation* (Dublin: Four Courts Press, 2008), 26–30. P. Wallace, 'The Archaeology of Ireland's Viking-age Towns', in *NHI* i, 814–41; L. Simpson, 'Forty Years a-digging: A Preliminary Synthesis of Archaeological Investigations in Medieval Dublin', in S. Duffy (ed.), *Medieval Dublin I* (Dublin: Four Courts Press, 2000), 11–68.

A fertile hinterland provided foodstuffs for a growing population.[105] Goods produced and processed in commercial centres had utility outside a town's walls. Agricultural production intensified and economic prosperity reached both farmer and craftsman alike.[106]

The nature of the bond between king and subject was altered somewhat, as a result of these and other developments. A king's authority no longer revolved around a relationship of clientship alone and administrative structures increased accordingly. Royal officials became more prominent, their various duties categorised in a textual genre concerned with 'customs' (*nósa*) and 'rights' (*certa*).[107] An early twelfth-century example, *Lebor na Cert* (The Book of Rights), stems from the court of Muirchertach Ua Briain.[108] It sets out the rights and concomitant duties of particular peoples, according a central role to the king of Cashel (Ua Briain) therein. Groups such as the Norse of Dublin are given a place, reflecting an evolving political order. Subordinate kingdoms owe tribute (*cís*), emphasis on which highlights its importance in a changing world; remuneration (*tuarastal*), for what might range from food-renders to military service, was paid by a king in return. In effect, what is a system of taxation comes into being. It may be that due tax was considered at an *óenach*, as intimated in one of the stanzas quoted above; however, it is equally likely that successful kings employed tax-collectors, not dissimilar

105 J. Bradley, 'The Interpretation of Scandinavian Settlement in Ireland', in Bradley (ed.), *Settlement and Society in Medieval Ireland*, 49–78; B. Hodkinson, 'Viking Limerick and its Hinterland', in Clarke and Johnston (eds.), *Vikings in Ireland and Beyond*, 183–8; M. A. Valante, 'Dublin's Economic Relations with Hinterland and Periphery in the Later Viking Age', in Duffy (ed.), *Medieval Dublin I*, 69–83.

106 S. Lyons, 'Food Plants, Fruits and Foreign Foodstuffs: The Archaeological Evidence from Urban Medieval Ireland', in E. FitzPatrick and J. Kelly (eds.), *Food and Drink in Ireland* (= *PRIA*, 115 C [2015]), 111–66. S. Geraghty, *Viking Dublin: Botanical Evidence from Fishamble Street* (Dublin: RIA, 1996). Her analysis of plant remains from tenth-/eleventh-century Fishamble Street, Dublin, notes a preponderance of barley, but also oats and wheat. Barley and oats are the most common cereal products grown in Ireland throughout the early medieval period: F. McCormick, T. Kerr, M. McClatchie and A. O'Sullivan, *The Archaeology of Livestock and Cereal Production in Early Medieval Ireland, AD 400–1100* (Oxford: British Archaeological Reports: Archaeopress, 2014).

107 Katharine Simms has suggested that the section of a fifteenth-century Ua Conchobair inauguration ode listing the king's officers may have been written as early as the twelfth or thirteenth century: '"Gabh umad a Fheidhlimidh": A Fifteenth-Century Inauguration Ode?', *Ériu*, 31 (1980), 132–45, at 143.

108 *Lebor na Cert*, ed. and trans. M. Dillon (Dublin and London: ITS, 1962). For discussion of different aspects of the text, see Candon, '"Barefaced Effrontery"'; C. Swift, 'Royal Fleets in Viking Ireland: The Evidence of *Lebor na Cert* A.D. 1050–1150', in J. Hines, A. Lane and M. Redknap (eds.), *Land, Sea and Home: Proceedings of a Conference on Viking-period Settlement at Cardiff, July 2001* (Leeds: Society for Medieval Archaeology, 2004), 189–206; T. M. Charles-Edwards, 'Society and Politics in Pre-Norman Ireland', in *L'irlanda e gli irlandesi nell'alto medioevo, Spoleto, 16–21 aprile 2001*, Atti delle settimane LVII (Spoleto, 2010), 67–90, at 88–90.

from those described as cruel viking bailiffs in the twelfth-century pseudo-historical tract *Cogadh Gáedhel re Gallaibh*.[109] The model for the system of taxation implemented according to this text may well have been one somewhat closer to home.

Taxation and tribute lie behind the system of landholding also, and territorial units such as *trícha cét* and the smaller *baile bíataig* suggest a shift away from the community-focussed *túath* of earlier times.[110] Such developments reflect gradual changes in the structure of government and the nature of lordship, a relationship of service between king and subject becoming more structured and controlled. Military assistance formed part of this bond, as the evolution of the meaning of the term *trícha cét* makes clear. First attested as 'a force of fighting men', it came to signify the number levied in a division termed *trícha cét* and is thus intimately connected with the militarisation of Irish society.[111] It is the *trícha cét* that lies behind the post-Conquest cantred;[112] and thus a system associated with the English in actual fact continued an arrangement that had evolved in the eleventh and twelfth centuries in response to the need for a more centralised administration, as well as ready, regular access to tribute and armed forces on the part of powerful Irish kings. Thomas Charles-Edwards has observed that *Lebor na Cert*, written for Uí Briain at the beginning of the twelfth century, as already noted, embodies aspects of these changes. Failure to pay tribute or provide service on the part of a sub-king led to loss of land, highlighting the dependent nature of tenure.[113] Moreover, the growth in popularity of tracts like *Lebor na Cert* concerned with the physical manifestation of the bond between ruler and subject is in itself indicative of change.[114]

As elsewhere in the changing Europe of this period, the bond between lord and subject remained a constant, though it was scarcely, as claimed by Patrick Wormald 'almost all that was left by way of social cement'.[115] The extent to

---

109 *And luaitís fri bága bil / certa ocus cána in cóicid* 'There they would discuss with strife of speech the dues and tributes of the province': *Metrical Dindshenchas*, iii, 18–19 (lines 213–14); *CGG*, 48–51 (§XL). Swift discusses tribute and reward in the case of this text and *Caithréim Cellacháin Caisil* in her 'Royal Fleets', 194.

110 Mac Cotter, *Medieval Ireland* and for the *baile biataig*, G. Toner, '*Baile*: Settlement and Landholding in Medieval Ireland', *Éigse*, 34 (2004), 25–43.

111 For these developments see Charles-Edwards, 'Society and Politics in Pre-Norman Ireland', 87–90.

112 Mac Cotter, *Medieval Ireland*, especially 39–44.

113 Charles-Edwards, 'Society and Politics in Pre-Norman Ireland', 87–90.

114 For a discussion of the genre in general, see M. Ní Mhaonaigh, '*Nósa Ua Maine*: Fact or Fiction?', in T. M. Charles-Edwards, M. E. Owen and P. Russell (eds.), *The Welsh King and his Court* (Cardiff: University of Wales Press, 2000), 362–81, at 367–9.

115 'The West Dishes It Out' (review of Bartlett, *Making of Europe*), *London Review of Books*, 16:4 (24 February 1994).

which Ireland was affected by developments prevalent in other regions, however, is sometimes difficult to measure. In the case of population growth, for example, the increase in urbanisation which we have seen to be a feature of the eleventh century in particular was undoubtedly of significance in this regard. Yet, as Howard Clarke has noted, 'only about one fifth of the island would have had regular access to town life even at the height of the Anglo-Norman colony' around 1270, some forty years after the end of our period.[116] While population density undoubtedly increased, whether that expansion matched the steep rise suggested for Britain and other regions of Europe is impossible to say. Population growth is certainly reflected in an increase in food production, specifically cereals.[117] An improved plough with coulter appears to have been used from the tenth century and this facilitated better preparation of the soil for seed planting. A further refinement in plough design saw the addition of a mould board, but it has been suggested that implements with both coulter and mould board were not employed in Ireland until after the arrival of the English in 1169.[118] Concomitant with these changes was a decline in the significance of cattle in economic terms, arable land rather than livestock yielding more food.[119] Concern with regulation of food resources is indicated in developments in fishing in the tenth and eleventh centuries. As sources of wealth and power, fishing rights were controlled by either secular or Church authorities, and arrangements concerning them are often laid down in *nósa* texts.[120]

An aristocratic elite remained dominant, therefore, controlling new developments, as well as the commoners beneath. It encompassed lay nobility as well as ecclesiastics, with both strands of society's upper echelons undergoing

---

116 H. Clarke, 'Population', in S. Duffy (ed.), *Medieval Ireland: An Encyclopedia* (New York and London: Routledge, 2005), 384.
117 M. A. Monk, 'The Archaeobotanical Evidence for Field Crop Plants in Early Historic Ireland', in J. M. Renfrew (ed.), *New Light on Early Farming: Recent Developments in Palaeoethnobotany* (Edinburgh University Press, 1991), 315–28; N. Brady, 'Labor and Agriculture in Early Medieval Ireland: Evidence from the Sources', in A. Frantzen and D. Moffat (eds.), *The Work of Work: Servitude, Slavery and Labor in Medieval England* (Glasgow: Cruithne Press, 1994), 125–45.
118 See McCormick, Kerr, McClatchie and O'Sullivan, *Early Medieval Agriculture*, 24–5; N. Brady, 'Reconstructing a Medieval Irish Plough', in *I Jornados Internacionales sobre tecnologia agraria tradicional (Museo Nacional de Pueblo Español)* (Madrid: Ministerio de Cultura, 1993), 31–44.
119 F. McCormick, 'The Decline of the Cow: Agricultural and Settlement Change in Early Medieval Ireland', *Peritia*, 20 (2008), 209–24. I am indebted to Fiona Edmonds for discussion on this point.
120 A. O'Sullivan, 'Place, Memory and Identity among Estuarine Fishing Communities: Interpreting the Archaeology of Early Medieval Fish Weirs', *World Archaeology*, 35 (2003), 449–68; '*Nósa Ua Maine*: The Customs of the Uí Maine', ed. and trans. P. Russell, in Charles-Edwards *et al.* (eds.), *Welsh King and His Court*, 527–51, at 546–7 (§6.44).

significant change in the two hundred and fifty years under discussion here. Brian Bórama's rule retained some aspects of itinerant kingship: his circuit of the northern part of the country in the early eleventh century was designed to impose his authority through his physical presence.[121] His grandson, Tairdelbach, made his son, Muirchertach, governor of Dublin in 1075, seeking thereby to tighten control through having a deputy on site.[122] Administration from afar of what was increasingly in effect a 'capital city' remained of key significance in the following century; a crucial factor in Diarmait Mac Murchada's decision to seek military assistance in England was his loss of Dublin to a rival, Ruaidrí Ua Conchobair, in 1166.[123] The latter's brother and successor, Cathal Crobderg, who held his land under the English crown, had recourse to an organised political machine in the running of his kingdom.[124] His affairs involved intercourse with society's other aristocratic arm, the Church, whose episcopal appointments he sought to influence. Brian Bórama's brother, Marcán, as well as other members of his extended kin, held key ecclesiastical positions in Munster in his own time and that of his descendants, even in an age of a changing Church.[125] 'Reform' was also championed by Diarmait Mac Murchada, but he too had his own political interests at heart.[126]

Religious change, supported by secular authority, was a feature of Irish life in this period, and can be measured in part through the work of a series of twelfth-century synods and the foundation throughout Ireland of a considerable number of Augustinian and Cistercian houses.[127] Closely associated with it were developments in art, literature and sculpture, as represented in architectural terms by the construction in Cashel of the earliest extant Irish Romanesque monument, Cormac's chapel, in 1134.[128] The vibrancy of literary culture is manifest in a trio of vernacular manuscripts, *Lebor na hUidre* (The Book of the Dun Cow), Rawlinson B 502 and The Book of Leinster,

121 *AI*, *s.a.* 1005.3; *AU* (Mac Airt), *s.a.* 1005.7.
122 *AI*, *s.a.* 1075.2–4.
123 *AI*, *s.a.* 1166.7 and 1166.9; Flanagan, 'High-Kings with Opposition', 932–3.
124 Perros, 'Ó Conchobhair, Cathal'; Mac Shamhráin, 'Ua Conchobair, Cathal Mór Crobderg', in J. McGuire and J. Quinn (eds.), *Dictionary of Irish Biography from the Earliest Times to the Year 2002.* 9 vols. (Cambridge University Press, 2009), ix, 569–71.
125 D. Ó Corráin, 'Dál Cais – Church and Dynasty', *Ériu*, 24 (1973), 52–63; C. Etchingham, 'Episcopal Hierarchy in Connacht and Tairdelbach Ua Conchobair', *Journal of the Galway Archaeological and Historical Society*, 52 (2000), 13–29, at 24–7.
126 Byrne, 'Trembling Sod', 23.
127 See the chapter by Colmán Ó Clabaigh in this volume.
128 R. Stalley, 'Design and Function: The Construction and Decoration of Cormac's Chapel at Cashel' in Bracken and Ó Riain-Raedel (eds.), *Ireland and Europe in the Twelfth Century*, 162–75.

which span the twelfth century and preserve a wide variety of earlier and contemporary material in a number of forms.[129] The main scribe of the earliest of these codices written *c.* 1100 was also responsible for a copy of Boethius' *De re arithmetica*. Moreover, Boethius' works were being studied and glossed at Glendalough, a centre which has been associated with the second of our vernacular manuscripts, Rawlinson B 502.[130] The third, the Book of Leinster, preserves an early vernacular adaptation of *De excidio Troiae historia* ('A History of the Destruction of Troy') by Dares Phrygius, whose influence on vernacular narrative literature was extensive and profound.[131] Irish scholars were clearly immersed and engaged in the intellectual currents of their day.

Perception and Reality: Learning and its Place

As the monastic provenance of these three codices indicates, the context for this learning was ecclesiastical. Yet their wide-ranging subject matter explored concerns shared by clerics and kings. Thus, when copying a tenth-century poem by Cináed ua hArtucáin into the Book of Leinster, Finn, bishop of Kildare, updated his exemplar to bring the battles listed down to his own time. A more prolific scribe of the same manuscript, Áed mac Crimthainn, an ecclesiastical official (*comarba*) of the monastery of Terryglass, is likely to have composed a considerable part of the Book of Leinster version of a secular tale *Esnada Tige Buchet* (The Melodies of Buchet's House).[132] By the time Áed and Finn were writing, however, a process of profound cultural realignment had been set in train, as a result of which secular learning moved out of ecclesiastical establishments into the hands of professional learned families over the course of the twelfth century and into the thirteenth. The stanzas from *Óenach Carman* with which we commenced survive in the Book of Leinster, a monastic production, as does the poetic celebration of the *óenach* at Tailtiu convened by Máel Sechnaill mac Domnaill in 1005. His ascent to

129 R. Ó hUiginn (ed.), *Lebor na hUidre: Codices Hibernenses Eximii I*, (Dublin: RIA, 2015).

130 E. Duncan, '*Lebor na hUidre* and a Copy of Boethius's *De re arithmetica*: A Palaeographical Note', *Ériu*, 62 (2012), 1–23; P. Ó Néill, 'Irish Glosses in a Twelfth-Century Copy of Boethius's *Consolatio philosophiae*', *Ériu*, 55 (2005), 1–17. Rawlinson B 502 was composed in a Leinster monastery, perhaps Glendalough or Killeshin: see C. Breatnach, 'Rawlinson B 502', in Duffy (ed.), *Medieval Ireland*, 398–400.

131 B. Miles, *Heroic Saga and Classical Epic in Medieval Ireland* (Woodbridge: Boydell Press, 2011) and the essays in R. O'Connor (ed.), *Classical Literature and Learning in Medieval Irish Narrative* (Woodbridge: Boydell Press, 2014).

132 Ní Mhaonaigh, 'Literature of Medieval Ireland', 36.

power in 980 marks the beginning of our period; the death of Ragnall, king of Man, in 1229 its end. As a Manx ruler intimately associated with Ireland, Ragnall's career symbolises the extent to which any evaluation of the history of Ireland in this period must look beyond its geographical confines. His descent from his Hiberno-Norse ancestor, Amlaíb Cuarán, was deliberately recalled in a praise-poem in Irish to him. Moreover, its author equated his kingship with that of Tara. Ragnall was legitimised, as Irish kings before him, through 'the flagstone on the side of Tara' (*labra ón leic a taeib Themra*) emitting an approving noise.[133]

Ragnall's anonymous eulogist and those of his contemporaries, including Cathal Crobderg Ua Conchobair (d. 1224), formed part of a reconstituted learned order. A member of a professional poetic family, his educational context lay beyond the confines of a changed Church which had refocused its intellectual efforts on more specific ecclesiastical ends. This pronounced shift in the locus of learning is one of the most significant, and 'arguably the most certainly detectable', outcomes of 'reform'.[134] It may be compared more broadly with the decline of the eleventh-century European cathedral schools with their emphasis on education for both imperial and ecclesiastical concerns.[135] Secular learning became a feature of the court from the twelfth century, and from that point Ireland was imagined without the same level of input from the Church.

In reviewing how Ireland was perceived in the rich and varied sources of our period, I have surveyed no more than a number of pertinent themes, probing what may lie beneath. Change was undoubtedly constant though often difficult to decipher in the rich and complex textual imagery produced by professional learned classes themselves undergoing profound developments. What we know of Ireland is informed by their ideology and to gain access to her history we must negotiate their literary layers. The dual nature of what they so skilfully imaged is encompassed in the *óenach* – at once symbol and real.

---

133 'Poem in Praise of Raghnall', ed. and trans. Ó Cuív, stanza 10.
134 Etchingham, 'Review Article', 217.
135 S. C. Jaeger, *The 'Envy of Angels': Cathedral Schools and Social Ideals in Medieval Europe, 950–1200* (Philadelphia: University of Pennsylvania Press).

6

Conquest and Conquerors

COLIN VEACH

THE central Middle Ages was a period of large-scale population movement in Europe. In most instances this movement was outward from Western Europe's cultural and geographical core into its periphery. The territories acquired, and peoples conquered, were diverse. In Germany east of the Elbe, Central Europe, the western British Isles, and the Baltic Sea littoral, European colonists confronted native populations which were characterised as 'barbarians'. In territories such as Spain, Sicily and the eastern Mediterranean, Westerners encountered cultures that might appear more sophisticated than their own. The conquest and colonisation of Ireland was a small part of this Europe-wide phenomenon. Indeed, Ireland's twelfth- and thirteenth-century invaders were themselves the product of an earlier invasion of England by Duke William of Normandy in 1066. William's band of warriors was mainly drawn from northern French elite society, including Normans, Flemings and Bretons, but also had contingents from as far afield as Aquitaine. After a relatively brief period of intense conflict and bitter enmity between conquerors and conquered, the Normans (as they were collectively known) came to identify with their new environment. Consequently, the men who invaded Ireland in the late twelfth century identified themselves as 'English', because they had long seen themselves as part of the political community of England. Indeed, before they reverted to the general term *gall* (foreigner), the native Irish annals referred to the first invaders from the English king's dominions as *Sasanach* (Saxon).[1]

Historians disagree over the level of English interest in Ireland in the years preceding the invasion, but it is significant that the first English conquerors arrived by invitation. In 1166, the exiled king of Leinster, Diarmait Mac

---

1 J. Gillingham, 'Normanizing the English Invaders of Ireland', in H. Pryce and J. Watts (eds.), *Power and Identity in the Middle Ages: Essays in Memory of Rees Davies* (Oxford University Press, 2007), 85–97; H. M. Thomas, *The English and the Normans: Ethnic Hostility, Assimilation, and Identity 1066–c.1220* (Oxford University Press, 2003), 70–82.

Murchada [MacMurrough], approached King Henry II of England for help in regaining his kingdom. Irish kings had long recruited foreign troops for their domestic wars, and Diarmait had every reason to expect a positive response from Henry. Just the previous year, in 1165, Diarmait had supplied a fleet from Dublin for Henry's failed expedition to north Wales. According to a near-contemporary verse chronicle, known to historians as *The Song of Dermot and the Earl*, in 1166 Diarmait even offered to become Henry's liege man (*liges home*) for as long as he lived. However, instead of providing direct assistance, Henry granted Diarmait permission to recruit from amongst his subjects. Henry instructed the prominent Bristol burgess, Robert fitz Harding, to provide Diarmait with a base in the town, which had longstanding trading links with eastern Ireland. From Bristol, Diarmait had easy access to the lords of the southern Welsh March – inhabitants of a militarised borderland whose very existence depended upon their martial prowess. This is the energy that Diarmait sought to harness in pursuit of a return to power in Ireland.[2]

There were several potential strategies that Diarmait could follow in his recruitment drive. The most obvious was to hire mercenaries. Medieval kings frequently resorted to using mercenaries in their wars because of their battle-hardened experience, their flexible conditions of service, and – most importantly in this context – the fact that they would eventually go home. There was ample precedent for employing soldiers of fortune in Ireland, and the boatloads of Pembrokeshire Flemings who reinstalled Diarmait in his ancestral kingdom of Uí Chennselaig in 1167 seem to have been mercenaries. Another, increasingly popular, means for recruitment utilised land patronage to attract aristocratic followers. The closest precedent (at least geographically) was the Scottish king's broadening of his court, administration and military aristocracy with English and French personnel in the early twelfth century. King David I had been a 'moderniser', who sought to use foreign immigrants to impose mainstream European-style rule upon a society used to a different pattern (or patterns) of lordship. Elsewhere in Europe, the native princes of Pomerania, Silesia, Mecklenburg and Hungary recruited German and Flemish aristocrats to Europeanise, and consequently strengthen, their regimes. In each of these cases, legal and charter evidence points to a mingling of native and newcomer at the highest levels of society. Diarmait Mac Murchada has also been characterised as a moderniser; an innovator who had been driven from Leinster, at least in part, because of his attempts to establish strong centralised control over his territory. In this context, his recruitment

---

2 *Deeds of the Normans*, lines 284–315.

of the Welsh marcher barons, Earl Richard fitz Gilbert (better known as Strongbow), Robert fitz Stephen and Maurice fitz Gerald, looks remarkably like invited colonisation. The course of English involvement in Ireland was not to produce the degree of ethnic equilibrium experienced elsewhere, but this would not have been clear to Diarmait in 1166.[3]

As his comital status attests, Strongbow was a powerful transnational aristocrat from a prestigious family. He held lands in England, Wales and Normandy, and his uncle, Earl Robert of Leicester, was King Henry II's English justiciar. That said, both Gerald of Wales and William of Newburgh claim that Strongbow was in some financial difficulty, and that his trip to Ireland was an attempt to dodge his creditors.[4] It is perhaps this fact that drove Robert fitz Harding, possibly one of those creditors, to suggest that Diarmait approach the earl in the first place. An agreement was reached whereby Strongbow would help Diarmait in Ireland, and in return would marry Diarmait's daughter, Aífe, and become his heir for Leinster. The half-brothers Robert fitz Stephen and Maurice fitz Gerald were also under pressure, though their problem was the aggressive behaviour of the ascendant Welsh prince, Rhys ap Gruffudd (who was their cousin). Diarmait offered them the Norse city of Wexford in return for their service. This second wave of recruits from south Wales seems to have been under the direction of Strongbow from the very start. They began landing in May 1169, and immediately helped Diarmait to force his once-rebellious subject kings into submission. Larger numbers of soldiers arrived the following year, under Raymond 'le Gros', and captured the Norse city of Waterford that spring. By the time that Strongbow set foot in Ireland in August 1170, Leinster was more or less secure. He quickly married Aífe, and joined Diarmait, who was planning an apparent bid for the high kingship of Ireland. It was during the course of this programme of expansion that Diarmait died about 1 May 1171. His agreement with Strongbow was honoured, and the kingdom of Leinster was acquired by an English magnate.[5]

Five years on from Diarmait's initial plea for help, Strongbow's self-aggrandisement roused Henry II to action. Henry had no intention of allowing one of his barons to gain an independent kingdom in Ireland the way his great-grandfather, Duke William of Normandy, had gained England. Henry forced Strongbow to surrender his Irish possessions, and granted Leinster back to him as a fief. Henry then personally mounted an impressive

3 Bartlett, *Making of Europe*, 24–32, 82–3.
4 *Expugnatio*, 54; William of Newburgh, *Historia Rerum Anglicarum*, ed. R. Howlett (London: RS, 1884), 167–8.
5 Orpen, *Normans*, i, 141–222; Flanagan, *Irish Society*, 79–164.

expedition to Ireland to inspect his newest realm. While in Ireland, he established administrative centres in the bustling port cities of Dublin, Wexford and Waterford, all of which he retained as royal demesne. He also reinforced a pre-existing trading connection by granting the city of Dublin to his men of Bristol, permitting them to colonise and hold it on the same terms as they held Bristol.[6] Importantly, Henry received the submission of most of Ireland's native rulers. One of the only kings to refuse to submit was the man whom Henry sought to supplant, the current high king of Ireland, Ruaidrí Ua Conchobair [Rory O'Connor] of Connacht. There is reason to believe that Henry planned to launch a campaign against Connacht in the spring of 1172, but he was abruptly called away to deal with more pressing business in France. His sudden withdrawal from Ireland was symptomatic of a more general royal preoccupation with the Continent. As king of England and master of two-thirds of France, Henry had little time to spend on what contemporaries considered a political and cultural backwater. This fact was to have a lasting impact upon the nature of the conquest in Ireland. As he turned to matters in France, Henry decided to devolve much of his authority in Ireland upon his military aristocracy. Henry enticed these men to Ireland with a series of speculative grants, comprising the territories of existing Irish kingdoms. Consequently, the kingdoms of Midhe, Ulaidh, Thomond and Desmond were granted to English barons as the lordships of Meath, Ulster, Limerick and Cork. For at least the next three decades, the conquest of Ireland was driven in large part by the efforts of these provincial lords to realise their grants (see Map 7).[7]

Conquest and Colonisation

Ireland was one of the many frontier zones where Western Europe expanded at the point of the sword. Immediately preceding this period, much of the West witnessed the formation of a self-conscious knightly class, which developed a 'fellowship of arms' and adhered to an unwritten body of custom regulating the conduct of war based on mutual respect.[8] As a result, capture and ransom were at the heart of knightly behaviour on European battlefields. Such was not the case in Ireland. Gerald of Wales observes:

6 *Letters Henry II*, no. 313.
7 Frame, *Colonial Ireland*, 22–6.
8 D. Crouch, *The English Aristocracy, 1070–1272: A Social Transformation* (New Haven: Yale University Press, 2011), part 1.

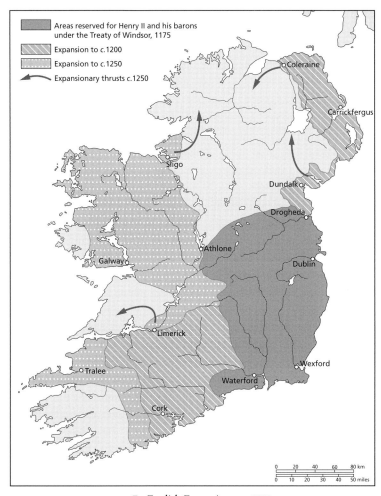

Areas reserved for Henry II and his barons
under the Treaty of Windsor, 1175

Expansion to *c.*1200

Expansion to *c.*1250

Expansionary thrusts *c.*1250

Coleraine

Carrickfergus

Sligo

Dundalk

Drogheda

Athlone

Galway

Dublin

Limerick

Tralee

Wexford

Waterford

Cork

| 0 | 20 | 40 | 60 | 80 km |

| 0 | 10 | 20 | 30 | 40 | 50 miles |

MAP 7. English Expansion to *c.*1250.

In France men choose the open plains for their battles, but in Ireland and Wales rough, wooded country; there heavy armour is a mark of distinction, here it is only a burden; there victory is won by standing firm, here by mobility; there knights are taken prisoner, here they are beheaded; there they are ransomed, here they are butchered.[9]

It should come as little surprise that different socio-economic structures produced different methods of warfare. Because land held the primary position

9 *Expugnatio*, 246; *Gir. Camb. Op.*, vi, 179–82, 209–11.

in the social and economic life of Western Europe, victory in war could be achieved by ravaging and burning the countryside, or taking castles. Consequently, the lives of knights and non-combatants (though not of infantry or archers) could be spared.[10]

Such preservation of life was incompatible with the socio-economic structure of Ireland. Although historians no longer cling to the myth of pure pastoralism, Irish wealth was still based largely on moveable commodities: livestock and men. Consequently, while other Europeans attacked land, the Irish engaged in 'hostings'. As in chivalrous warfare, this asserted the dominance of one king or lord over another by depriving the enemy of their most important economic assets, in this case livestock, captives and moveable treasure. Most battles were fought on the return trip, when the raiders were slowed down with booty. The slowest of the captives, the old, young and infirm, might consequently be slaughtered to aid escape. This level of violence was an abomination to European commentators, but was predicated upon the socio-economic base of Irish society. William of Newburgh observed the parallel with the similarly fragmented Anglo-Saxon England. So it transpired that when in May 1170 the English won their famous victory at Dún Domnaill (Baginbun, County Wexford), they eschewed their own military customs and slaughtered their captives. Once in Ireland, the English adapted their military ethos to suit the new environment.[11]

Having modified their philosophy of warfare, the English invaders were quick to import their own military technology. The ability to produce large quantities of metal armour for their troops, and arrowheads for their archers, gave the English the advantage in many of their encounters with the Irish. European-style castles, too, proved devastatingly effective in the Irish context. Perched atop earthen mounds, castles dominated their landscapes, providing commanding vantage points from which to observe – and be observed by – the native Irish. They were aggressive statements of intent, which tended to be sited as forward outposts heralding the conquest of a new region. Too strong to be quickly reduced by Irish raiding parties, they also served as bases for small rapid-strike forces of English knights who could mount their own hostings (though they would call them *chevauchés*) into native Irish territories.

---

10 J. Gillingham, 'Conquering the Barbarians: War and Chivalry in Twelfth-Century Britain', in J. Gillingham (ed.), *The English in the Twelfth Century: Imperialism, National Identity and Political Values* (Woodbridge: Boydell Press, 2000), 41–58; M. Strickland, *War and Chivalry: The Conduct and Perception of War in England and Normandy, 1066–1217* (Cambridge University Press, 1996), 180–1, 223.

11 *Chronicles of the Reigns of Stephen, Henry II and Richard I*, ed. R. Howlett, 4 vols. (London: RS, 1884–9), i, 167; *Deeds of the Normans*, lines 1474–87; *Expugnatio*, 58–64.

Once a region had been conquered, castles served as the focal points of English administration and domination.

The first lord of Meath, Hugh de Lacy, was a renowned castle builder, who was employed by the English king to fortify Leinster as well as Meath.[12] He also built castles for others as a means of attracting their service in a hostile environment. For instance, shortly after receiving his grant of Meath in 1172, Hugh endowed one of his household knights, Adam de Feipo, with land there. Adam, who was just the sort of military man Hugh needed in his new frontier lordship, lacked the resources to fortify his new estates. Consequently, Hugh built a castle for him at Skreen, demanding in return that Adam provide the heavy service of twenty knights for his territory. This compares with the twenty knights demanded by Hugh for Robert le Fleming's grant of Slane and twenty knights demanded by Strongbow for Walter of Ridelsford's grant of Uí Muiredaig in Leinster. Adam de Feipo, in turn, subinfeudated his grant, attracting his own military followers.[13] Adam's case was somewhat exceptional, because he came from de Lacy's pre-existing household. For the most part, Strongbow and de Lacy sought to use their new-found wealth to attract new followers rather than to reward their own retainers. A contemporary French verse account of the conquest preserves a list of enfeoffments in Leinster and Meath, saying that

> ... in this manner
> the country was planted
> with castles and fortified towns
> and keeps and strongholds
> so that the noble and renowned vassals
> were able to put down firm roots.[14]

This ordered process was not characteristic of other areas of settler lordship in Ireland, such as Louth and parts of Munster, yet the imagery of cultivation is evocative. It serves as a reminder that the seventeenth-century plantation was not the first royally sponsored settlement of Ireland.

Having taken steps to secure their lordships, the English conquerors needed to make them economically viable. One problem lay in securing a workforce. In Germany and Central Europe evidence exists for an entire system of recruitment, transportation and colonisation, established to

---

12 *Expugnatio*, 182–4.
13 *Chartul. St Mary's, Dublin*, i, 1–3, 96, 101–4, 156–7; ii, 21–2; *Deeds of the Normans*, lines 3094–7, 3154–5, 3174–99.
14 *Deeds of the Normans*, lines 3200–1.

support the migration of thousands of settlers to new eastern conquests.[15] Unfortunately, what evidence exists in this regard for twelfth- and early thirteenth-century Ireland is largely circumstantial. It is generally assumed that the economic incongruity between Irish society and English lordship forced the conquerors to import a workforce, and evidence survives of the conquerors' attempts to attract such labour. As in Central Europe, the conquerors created 'rural boroughs', nucleated agricultural settlements which offered prospective tenants attractive conditions of tenure and preferential legal standing relative to the native populations. This is no definitive proof that settlers came in their droves, but the durability of the English presence in Ireland has been cited as evidence that numerous English settlers populated these new boroughs and manorial villages. Had colonisation on this lower level not been so thorough, so this argument goes, English aristocrats might have Gaelicised much more quickly, or quit Ireland altogether. Furthermore, the preponderance of English place names in certain areas has been used to suggest widespread colonisation, especially when those areas show large English communities in the early-fourteenth century (when more detailed records appear). Such theories are part of a larger trend of revising upwards estimates of English immigration to the western British Isles in the twelfth and thirteenth centuries.[16]

Whatever the intensity of English colonisation, it was clearly insufficient early on. In 1175, Henry II and Ruaidrí Ua Conchobair agreed to the Treaty of Windsor, which (among other things) required the return of native Irish farmers to the lands now controlled by English lords. If any refused, then Ruaidrí was to forcibly resettle them. Gerald of Wales interprets the process positively, describing Hugh de Lacy's lordship in Meath:

> Hugh went to great trouble to conciliate those [i.e. the Irish] who had been conquered by others and forcibly ejected from their lands, and thus he restored the countryside to its rightful cultivators and brought back cattle to pastures which had formerly been deserted. So when he had won their support, he enticed them to his side still further by his mild rule and by making agreements on which they could rely, and finally, when they had been hemmed in by castles and gradually subdued, he compelled them to obey the laws.[17]

---

15 Bartlett, *Making of Europe*, 133–66.
16 K. O'Conor, *The Archaeology of Medieval Rural Settlement in Ireland* (Dublin: RIA, 1998), 41–71; S. Duffy, *Ireland in the Middle Ages* (Houndmills and Dublin: Macmillan, 1997), 83–4, 111–12; R. R. Davies, *Domination and Conquest: The Experience of Ireland, Scotland and Wales 1100–1300* (Cambridge University Press, 1990), 11–15.
17 Howden, *Gesta*, i, 103; *Expugnatio*, 190.

In the first two decades of the conquest, several lords even followed Strongbow's lead by forging marriage alliances with neighbouring royal dynasties. These marriages could calm tensions and build networks of support. Thus Hugh de Lacy (Meath) married a daughter of Ruaidrí Ua Conchobair (Connacht), and William de Burgh (Munster) a daughter of Domnall *Mór* Ua Briain [O'Brien] (Thomond). The lord of Ulster, John de Courcy, showed his lordship's maritime orientation by marrying Affrica, daughter of King Guðrøðr of the Isle of Man.[18]

While the most successful conquests thus involved a degree of accommodation with the Irish, many also involved control of the Church. Indeed, the two sometimes went hand-in-hand. Following his surprise victory over the Meic Duinn Sléibe [MacDunlevy] king of Ulaid in 1177, John de Courcy relied heavily upon the Church to consolidate his hold on the new lordship of Ulster. Monastic communities were imported from the north-west of England, southern Scotland and the Isle of Man to colonise his new territories. De Courcy also sought to co-opt the Irish of Ulster through the promotion of local saints' cults. He helped the local bishop of Down, Malachy, to convert the Meic Duinn Sléibe capital of Downpatrick into the new episcopal seat (excluding rival claims from the community at Bangor). Both men then worked together to promote the spiritual significance of Downpatrick. The bodies of Saints Patrick, Brigit and Columba were discovered at Downpatrick and translated to the cathedral, which was itself rededicated from Holy Trinity to St Patrick. John and Malachy also joined with the archbishop of Armagh in commissioning a new Life of St Patrick by Jocelin of Furness, which had the added attraction of promoting the primacy of Armagh over Dublin. Even the coins John minted in Ulster bore the inscription 'PATRICUS'.[19]

Other English lords sought to control the religious lives of their lordships, but none seem to have gone as far as John de Courcy in their identification with Ireland. The Lacy lords of Meath worked to promote their favoured bishop, Eugenius of Clonard, fashioning with him a diocese coterminous with their own secular lordship (suppressing the rival dioceses of Kells and Duleek in the process). In 1202, the seat of the new 'bishop of Meath' was even moved from Clonard to the Lacys' seigniorial capital of Trim.[20] In Leinster, Strongbow's

---

18 Davies, *Domination and Conquest*, 51–3.
19 S. Duffy, 'The First Ulster Plantation: John de Courcy and the Men of Cumbria', in Barry *et al.* (eds.), *Colony and Frontier in Medieval Ireland*, 1–27; Flanagan, 'John de Courcy, the First Ulster Plantation and Irish Church Reform', in Smith (ed.), *Britain and Ireland*, 154–78.
20 C. Veach, *Lordship in Four Realms: The Lacy Family, 1166–1241* (Manchester University Press, 2014), 248–9.

successor, William Marshal, befriended the bishop of Osraige and took steps to concentrate political and religious authority in south-western Leinster at Kilkenny.[21] In each of these instances, secular and religious authority were made to radiate from the same location. Further changes to the ecclesiastical landscape occurred throughout Ireland as imported religious orders served as the cultural glue binding the new conquests to Britain and France. In the first decades of the conquest, English lords thus sought to implement a brand of lordship sensitive to local variations and the logistics of overseas colonisation.

These early colonisers seem to have hoped to fashion for themselves in Ireland semi-independent lordships akin to those they knew in Wales. The lords of the Welsh March owed homage to the English king, but their courts were closed to royal interference. This degree of jurisdictional autonomy meant that the lord of an honour retained exclusive rights over his tenants, who could not appeal his decisions to the king's court. Consequently, the honour remained the fundamental socio-political grouping in the March, even as its importance faded in England.[22] Henry II seemingly reinforced this tendency towards marcher autonomy in Ireland by not reserving pleas of the crown in his chief grants, and, as late as 1207, William Marshal could portray himself as the sole source of authority in Leinster.[23] But appearances could be deceptive. The strength of the marcher honour also lay in its discrete boundaries. Aristocratic affinities and multiple tenancies were anathema to honorial power, and in this Ireland differed from Wales from the very beginning of the conquest. Military expertise was at a premium in conquest Ireland, forcing the great magnates to compete for the service of desirable followers. Incoming lords not only enlisted men from England, Wales and Normandy, they also recruited from each other's followings. The resulting tenurial network was vulnerable to intrigue by the crown, since the king, too, was an active participant. Henry II's son John was just the man to exploit this advantage.

Ireland in the Angevin Empire

Henry II's intervention in Ireland in 1171 changed the nature of its conquest. What was begun in the spirit of freebooting aristocratic enterprise was

21 *The Acts and Letters of the Marshal Family: Marshals of England and Earls of Pembroke, 1145–1248,* ed. D. Crouch. Camden Fifth Series (Cambridge University Press, 2015), nos. 55, 80, 82.

22 B. Holden, '"Feudal Frontiers?" Colonial Societies in Wales and Ireland 1170–1330', *Studia Hibernica,* 33 (2004/5), 61–79.

23 For instance, Meath (1172): *Cal. Gormanston Reg.*, 177; Cork (1177): G. Lyttelton, *The History of the Life of King Henry the Second and of the Age in which He Lived.* 6 vols. 3rd edn (Dublin: George Faulkner, 1777–87), vi, 406–8; *Acts and Letters of the Marshal Family*, nos. 32 and 95.

thereafter brought firmly into the realm of Angevin court politics. Strongbow was forced to reaffirm his status as Henry's man in 1171, and fought for Henry in Normandy soon thereafter in 1173–4. A number of his captains, including Miles Cogan and Robert fitz Stephen, were brought into the fold with royal grants of their own (in this case the Irish kingdom of Cork). Once Henry sent his youngest son John to take possession of Ireland in 1185 (having designated him king of Ireland in 1177), the link became even more pronounced. John's 1185 expedition to Ireland has been rightly characterised as a military and diplomatic failure. The would-be king alienated many of the island's resident elites, lost most of his army in battle or through desertion, and limped back to England, uncrowned and penniless, less than eight months after his arrival.[24] Yet in its failure, John's expedition left at least two legacies that influenced the character of the conquest for decades to come. The first was through his grants in Munster and Louth, territories which in 1185 were not as heavily colonised as Leinster, Meath and Ulster. John's expedition came in his eighteenth year.[25] It was his first taste of adult authority and offered the chance to expand his household and bestow patronage upon his friends and followers. The main recipients of that patronage in Munster were Theobald Walter (progenitor of the Butlers) and William de Burgh (progenitor of the Burkes), John's friends from his youth. Theobald was the nephew of Henry II's justiciar, Ranulf de Glanville, in whose household John spent his teenage years. Theobald's brother, Hubert Walter, was also John's companion and would eventually become archbishop of Canterbury in 1193. William de Burgh was the brother of John's chamberlain, the future English justiciar and earl of Kent, Hubert de Burgh. In Louth, John relied upon his father's trusted servants Bertram de Verdon and Gilbert Pipard to conquer the Irish kingdom of Airgialla. Consequently, the character of conquest in these new theatres owed as much to the young John's court connections as it did to local Irish conditions.[26]

The second legacy of 1185 was of mistrust between John and Ireland's established powers, English and Irish. Gerald of Wales, who was in his company, blamed John and his youthful companions for their arrogance and immaturity when dealing with those he meant to rule.[27] Having failed to overawe the

---

24 S. Duffy, 'John and Ireland: The Origins of England's Irish Problem', in S. D. Church (ed.), *King John: New Interpretations* (Woodbridge: Boydell Press, 1999), 229–34.

25 *Expugnatio*, 229.

26 S. D. Church, *King John: England, Magna Carta and the Making of a Tyrant* (Houndmills: Palgrave Macmillan, 2015), 19–28; W. L. Warren, 'King John and Ireland', in Lydon (ed.), *England and Ireland*, 27–8.

27 *Expugnatio*, 237–9.

Irish kings or his own barons, John was determined that none should grow powerful enough to overwhelm his administration. Consequently, in the late 1180s and early 1190s, John used periods of wardship over both Leinster and Meath to ignore their heirs' rights, making his own permanent (and therefore illegal) grants. King Richard forced John to reverse most of these alienations in 1194, but at least one grantee, Theobald Walter, managed to keep his lands by swearing homage to the lords of Leinster and Meath.[28] Theobald still held directly of John elsewhere, which made his loyalty to these other lords less than unconditional. John later granted a number of Meath tenants lands in western Louth, and recruited others to the royal administration. Far from being able to consolidate their lordships around discrete knightly communities, the Irish magnates thus had to compete with the king of England for the loyalty of their own tenants.[29]

At the same time as he took steps to undermine his barons in Ireland, John also sought to promote the in-built trend towards factionalism on the frontier. As in other European borderlands, the political topography of Ireland comprised overlapping and constantly shifting orbits of power. Just as Irish royal hegemonies often extended well beyond a particular power base, so too did English lordship. King-making and tribute-taking were as much a part of English conquest in Ireland as colonial settlement and administration. When hegemonies collided, the result was often warfare that took no notice of ethnicity. Alliances could be manifold, as could enmities. If the king could influence the pattern of conflict, he could perhaps direct it to his own ends. From the moment that Henry II left Ireland with Connacht unconquered, the western province emerged as Ireland's greatest prize. Indeed, the first eight decades of English involvement in Ireland could in many ways be characterised as a protracted struggle to control Connacht. Hugh de Lacy was the first magnate to enter the fray, forced as he was to carve his own lordship of Meath out of the eastern part of Ruaidrí Ua Conchobair's hegemony. His marriage to Ruaidrí's daughter around 1180 sparked rumours at the Angevin court that he sought to succeed to Connacht as Strongbow had to Leinster. Whatever Hugh's plans, Ruaidrí's usurpation by his son, Conchobar Máenmaige, in 1185, and Hugh's assassination in 1186 (leaving an underage heir), destabilised

28 *The Irish Cartularies of Llanthony Prima & Secunda,* ed. E. St J. Brooks (Dublin: IMC, 1953), 78–9, 286; *Reg. St. Thomas,* 224, 254, 270, 273; *History of William Marshal,* ed. A. J. Holden and D. Crouch, trans. S. Gregory, 3 vols. Anglo-Norman Text Society (London, 2002–7), ii, lines 9581–618.

29 B. Smith, 'Tenure and Locality in North Leinster in the Early Thirteenth Century', in Barry *et al.* (eds.), *Colony and Frontier in Medieval Ireland,* 34–5.

the situation. Connacht dynasts enlisted the help of English settlers in the resultant warfare, which only abated in 1189 when Ruaidrí's brother, Cathal Crobderg Ua Conchobair, emerged victorious. However, peace was transitory. Around 1194, John reset the dispute by making a speculative grant of the kingdom to his old friend, William de Burgh.[30]

Since arriving in Ireland in 1185, de Burgh had combined conquest, colonisation and diplomacy to achieve a position of prominence in Munster, in the process marrying a daughter of Domnall *Mór* Ua Briain, king of Thomond. When Domnall died in 1194, de Burgh was able to intrigue in the Thomond succession, convincing the warring claimants to gift him the strategic city of Limerick on the Shannon. With the path to Connacht open, John's speculative grant threatened to upset the balance of power on the island. The situation quickly came to a head in 1195 as Cathal Crobderg (himself married to a daughter of Domnall *Mór* Ua Briain) mounted an expedition against William de Burgh in Munster. John's elder brother, King Richard, then empowered the new lord of Meath, Walter de Lacy, and the lord of Ulster, John de Courcy, to mount their own expedition against the English of Munster. William was brought to heel, and a conference at Athlone sealed peace between Cathal Crobderg and Richard's representatives. In the background of the English king's deliberate undermining of his brother's policy in Ireland lay John's wider rebellion in England and France. Not for the last time, events in Ireland reflected political disputes in the wider Angevin Empire.[31]

In 1199, John succeeded his brother to become king of England and head of the Angevin Empire. Coincidentally, that year also saw the resumption of hostilities in Connacht as Cathal Crobderg was ousted from the kingship by his great-nephew, Cathal Carrach Ua Conchobair. English lords were once again drawn into the war, with William de Burgh (and seemingly King John) initially backing Cathal Carrach, and John de Courcy and the Lacy brothers, Walter and his younger brother Hugh, supporting Cathal Crobderg. The level of King John's interest in the dynastic warfare was revealed in 1201. Following their defeat at the hands of Cathal Carrach in Connacht that year, John de Courcy, Hugh de Lacy and Cathal Crobderg made their way to Walter de Lacy's lordship of Meath. The historical record is somewhat confused, but it appears that, with the connivance of his brother, Walter captured both de

---

30 H. Perros, 'Crossing the Shannon Frontier: Connacht and the Anglo-Normans, 1170–1224', in Barry *et al.* (eds.), *Colony and Frontier in Medieval Ireland*, 126.

31 *AFM*, iii, 100; *ALC*, i, 190; *AI*, 320; *Misc. Ir. Annals*, 74; *AU*, ii, 222.

Courcy and Cathal Crobderg, sending them to Dublin to be dealt with by the Irish justiciar. John de Courcy managed to escape on the way, but Cathal Crobderg was imprisoned in Dublin, where he came to terms. Once Cathal Crobderg was released from captivity, he immediately went to King John's man, William de Burgh, for aid against Cathal Carrach in Connacht.[32] The factional alignments of the Connacht wars of succession reflected earlier divisions within the settler community that had been deliberately exploited over the years by King John. The full measure of John's actions is only discernible from a wider perspective than Ireland. In 1200, Walter de Lacy married the daughter of King John's friend, William de Briouze. De Briouze had been the recipient of a spectacular outpouring of royal patronage since John's coronation the previous year, and, soon after his daughter's wedding, was granted the honour of Limerick in Ireland. Although William de Burgh's lands were excepted from the grant, his dominance in the region was threatened by a new and powerful neighbour. At the same time, however, William de Burgh's brother, Hubert, was introduced into the Briouze/Lacy ambit in the Welsh March. Hubert replaced de Briouze as sheriff of Herefordshire, and was granted custody of the Three Castles, which divided the Briouze and Lacy marcher lordships. Just after de Briouze's grant of Limerick in 1201, Hubert was given 100 knights and made Warden of the March.[33]

Having been constrained in Munster by the institution of an honour of Limerick, in 1203 William de Burgh made a second attempt to conquer Connacht. He was repulsed by Cathal Crobderg (the king he had helped install in 1201), and faced immediate censure from King John for his actions. The Irish justiciar (perhaps joined by Cathal Crobderg) marched against William, confiscated the city of Limerick, took hostages for his good behaviour, and waved him off to military service in Normandy. William was eventually put on trial late in 1204, at which point King John was busy negotiating with the king of Connacht. When William died the following year, King John had already entered into a tenurial relationship with Cathal Crobderg. Henceforth, the king of Connacht was obliged to remain loyal to King John, but at least now he was also entitled to the English king's protection.[34]

Just as King John supported Cathal Crobderg over his own baron, William de Burgh, in Connacht, so he used the Lacy brothers to remove John de

32 Howden, *Chronica*, iv, 176; *ALC*, i, 222; *Ann. Clon.*, 207; *Misc. Ir. Annals*, 82.
33 *Rot. Chart.* 84; *Rotuli de Oblatis et Finibus in Turri Londinensi Asservati*, ed. T. D. Hardy (London : Record Commission, 1835), 94, 99.
34 Perros, 'Crossing the Shannon Frontier', 130–2.

Courcy from Ulster. John de Courcy's capture in 1201 was a clear sign that the Lacy brothers were dancing to King John's tune. Roger of Howden reports that they had intended to deliver de Courcy to the English king, 'who had long wished to take him'.[35] Whatever the source of their ill-will, from 1201 John de Courcy was an outlaw. His safe conducts to court in 1202 and 1203 would have been redundant had the situation been otherwise. Consequently, when Hugh de Lacy marched against de Courcy in 1203 and 1204, he likely did so with the connivance of the king. Indeed, in 1204 Hugh's brother Walter was given a royal commission alongside the Irish justiciar, Meiler fitz Henry, to call de Courcy to the king's service and cause judgement to be taken in the royal court if he failed to appear. Just two years earlier, King Philip II of France had used King John's failure to answer a summons to court in Paris to declare his French possessions forfeit. Similarly, King John made it clear that the Lacy brothers were to have a share of de Courcy's confiscated lordship of Ulster in the event of his default. Once the sentence of default was passed (as it inevitably was), the Lacys were free to effect that judgement.[36] In a single year, 1204, King John had thus opened court proceedings against two of his magnates in Ireland. This was a reminder, if one were needed, that conquest was not always a simple matter of English versus Irish.

From Lordship to Colony

The year 1204 was profoundly important for the English community of Ireland, because it was in that year that King John lost much of his French inheritance to King Philip II. For the next decade, John's overriding concern was its recovery. In the short term, he needed to secure the loyalty of his insular possessions, especially since his defeat in Normandy deprived a number of magnates of their ancestral patrimonies. John's grant of eight cantreds of Ulster to the Lacy brothers should be seen in this context. The situation was amended the following year, when in May 1205 Hugh de Lacy was granted the entire lordship of Ulster, and belted its earl.[37] King John's creation of the earldom of Ulster was significant, and seems to have served two main purposes. Ulster had, and would continue to have, a north-eastern orientation. John thus placed his own earl in the crowded North Channel littoral which already boasted the earls of Atholl, Carrick, Caithness, Lennox,

---

35 Howden, *Chronica*, iv, 176.
36 Veach, *Lordship in Four Realms*, 116–18.
37 *Rot. Chart.*, 139–40, 151; *Rot. Litt. Pat.*, 54; *Cal. Gormanston Reg.*, 142.

Orkney, Ross and Strathearn, not to mention the king of Man and the Isles and the quasi-regal lord of Galloway. Earl Hugh was expected to dominate the northern Irish Sea. If he were successful, then the earl of Ulster would serve as a convenient counterbalance to the earl of Pembroke, William Marshal, who controlled the southern Irish Sea from Pembroke in Wales and Leinster in Ireland. Raising Ulster in the north to compete with Pembroke in the south was yet another way for the English king to play his barons against each other.[38]

Such royally backed factionalism helped John maintain control over Ireland, but it did very little to fill his coffers. With grand campaigns to mount in France, King John needed money from his insular realms. England already had an advanced administrative system geared to extracting cash for its kings. Ireland, however, was a relatively young frontier lordship, lagging well behind England in its potential. Beginning in 1204, John set about replicating in Ireland the level of control he enjoyed over his kingdom of England.[39] In that year, a new castle was constructed in Dublin, and orders were issued making it the financial, administrative and military capital of Ireland. King John then embarked on a process aimed at forging a direct relationship between his government and the local communities. This was a challenge to the established pattern of lordship on the island, and in 1207 provoked a revolt by the lords of Leinster, Meath, Limerick and Ulster. John's earlier efforts to undermine the magnates' tenurial base proved ineffective, and the magnates' forces prevailed early in 1208. King John was thus forced to backtrack on some of his policies, but William Marshal and Walter de Lacy were astute enough to realise that he still held a strong hand. Victory in Ireland meant little when the king could always attack their lands in England and Wales. Consequently, the lords of Leinster and Meath agreed to surrender the crown liberties – the quintessence of aristocratic independence – in revised charters for their lordships. Such was the price of peace after revolt.

The lord of Limerick, William de Briouze, was not so diplomatic. William refused to accept John's judgement, for which offence John confiscated the honour of Limerick, attacked his English and Welsh lands, hounded him into a hopeless rebellion, and forced him to flee for his life to Ireland. The other Irish magnates then enraged John by closing ranks to protect the fugitive Briouze family. There is even evidence that the Lacys negotiated an alliance with King

---

38 D. Crouch, 'Earls in Wales and Ireland', in D. Crouch and H. Doherty (eds.), *The Earl in Medieval Britain* (forthcoming).
39 For what follows see C. Veach, 'King John and Royal Control in Ireland: Why William de Briouze had to be Destroyed', *EHR*, 129 (2014), 1051–78.

Philip of France as they stood firm in 1209.[40] When King John mounted his expedition to Ireland in 1210, it was to complete the unfinished business of 1207 and firmly stamp his authority on the island. He marched triumphantly through the magnates' lordships, banishing the Lacy brothers and presenting charges of treason against William Marshal in Dublin. By the time he left the island, Limerick, Meath and Ulster were crown escheats, and Munster was divided into the shires of Munster and Cork (administered from the cities of Limerick and Waterford). Perhaps most importantly, John declared that English law was to run throughout Ireland. For the next 700 years, Ireland was to be jurisdictionally dependent upon England. The conquest lordship was slowly being transformed into an English colony.

As one might expect, the removal of the earl of Ulster and the lords of Meath and Limerick caused something of a shift in the focus of conquest in Ireland. The Irish justiciar was now responsible for defending these large territories. King John sought to mitigate the situation by granting lands in Ulster to members of the powerful ruling dynasty of Galloway, his close cousins. At a stroke, King John expanded his influence into western Scotland, and reinforced Ulster's North-Channel orientation.[41] In Munster, a cadet branch of the Geraldines acquired scattered lands that would later form the basis of the fourteenth-century earldom of Desmond. Their kinsmen to the north, progenitors of the lords of Kerry and knights of Glin, established holdings in Kerry and Limerick. Other minor-aristocratic families, such as the Barrys, Barretts, Cauntetons, Cogans and Prendergasts, also drove forward the conquest in Munster. One area to buck the trend was Leinster, where the only remaining magnate in Ireland, William Marshal, was resident from 1207 until 1213. His efforts at seigniorial centralisation greatly enhanced the profitability of Leinster, establishing New Ross as a trading rival to the king's city of Wexford, and turning rural Leinster into an economic powerhouse. Prior to its division in 1245, Leinster was valued at £1,716, more than all of the Marshals' other possessions combined.[42]

King John's handling of his Irish magnates had an even greater impact east of the Irish Sea. His destruction of William de Briouze showed his capacity for cruelty, and resulted in an increasingly alienated and fearful English baronage. Ironically, a number of English barons who eventually decided to

---

40 *Recueil des Actes de Philippe Auguste Roi de France, tome III, Années du Règne XXVIII à XXXVI [1er Novembre 1206–31 Octobre 1215]*, eds. M. J. Monicat and M. J. Boussard (Paris: Imprimerie Nationale, 1966), 161–2.

41 *Rot. Chart.*, 186b, 194; *Rot. Litt. Pat.*, 98; *Rot. Litt. Claus.*, i, 587, 615.

42 Orpen, *Normans*, iii, 79–80.

rebel against John in 1215, had joined John's expedition to crush the Irish magnates in 1210.[43] In 1215, John's main supporters in England included the former Irish rebels William Marshal and Walter de Lacy (newly restored to Meath). The lords of Leinster and Meath could afford to fight for John in England, because the Irish had not followed the example of the Welsh and Scots in joining the English rebellion. Once rebellion intensified in England, John moved to ensure that the Irish would not rally behind the king of Connacht. On 13 September 1215, the same day that John informed the Pope of renewed hostilities, he granted Cathal Crobderg Ua Conchobair the entire kingdom of Connacht 'during his good service'. Cathal Crobderg's charter gave him security of tenure, and the prospect of unchallenged succession for his eldest son Aed. One need only look at Cathal Crobderg's own bloody route to kingship to understand why he might have wanted that security. At the very same time, however, John granted Connacht to William de Burgh's son Richard. Having just attained his majority and possession of his Munster inheritance, Richard was poised to attack should Cathal Crobderg proceed against John.[44]

Such equilibrium came to characterise internal Irish politics for the remainder of John's reign and into the early minority of his son, King Henry III. The English rebellion drew a number of colonists across the Irish Sea, and the unsteady peace that followed convinced many to remain there. From 1216 until he was finally ousted in 1221, Ireland was ruled by the overbearing Irish justiciar, Geoffrey de Marisco. Contemporary legal opinion held that Henry III's minority government lacked the authority to remove any of King John's appointees. Consequently, there was no effective check on corruption, which was rampant. Geoffrey de Marisco rode roughshod over the rights of many absent lords, denying them possession of their lands and keeping their proceeds for himself. Despite Geoffrey's misrule, the barons of Ireland slowly regained some of the strength they had lost in 1210. In 1215, King John had rewarded Walter de Lacy's loyalty in England by restoring him to Meath. Richard de Burgh had also succeeded to his father's Munster lands and was given a dormant grant of Connacht. In 1217 the rebel Nicholas de Verdon was given possession of his lands in Louth, and Reginald de Briouze was allowed to succeed to a truncated version of his father's honour of Limerick. Perhaps most importantly, after King John's death in October 1216, William Marshal became regent of England. One of the Marshal's first acts was to regrant the

43 *Rotuli de Liberate ac de Misis et Praestitis, Regnante Johanne,* ed. T. D. Hardy (London: Eyre and Spottiswoode, 1844), 178–228.
44 *Rot. Litt. Pat.,* 182; *Rot. Chart.,* 218b–219.

Irish barons the liberties taken from them by King John and thus 'to restore the good days of their noble ancestors'.[45]

Conspicuous by its absence from the spate of restorations in Ireland was the earldom of Ulster. Both King John and William Marshal had tried to convince Hugh de Lacy to return to England in the years following his exile, but he had joined the Albigensian Crusade, and was preoccupied gaining lordships for himself in Languedoc. By the time that he decided to return from France, the mood at court had changed. On 17 September 1221, Hugh de Lacy was given a safe conduct to come to court to negotiate his restoration in Ulster. Henry III's minority government was by then under the direction of Hubert de Burgh, and was heavily influenced by William Marshal's son and heir, William. The young earl of Pembroke presided over a thriving Irish Sea trading network, and had no desire to see his dominance threatened by a revival of the earldom of Ulster. Instead of immediate restoration, Hugh was offered a pension and a cooling-off period. This was unacceptable to the hardened crusader, who refused to compromise and prepared to take his earldom by force. Hugh drew upon his family's contacts in Wales to forge alliances with the northern-Welsh prince Llywelyn ab Iorwerth of Gwynedd and Earl Ranulf of Chester. He thus created an Ulster–Gwynedd–Chester axis to rival the Marshal in Pembroke and Leinster. The seeds of discord planted in 1205 were about to bear fruit.

Hugh de Lacy's attempt to recover Ulster in 1223–4 was the first of two rebellions to span the Irish Sea in the course of a decade. The second, the rebellion of Richard Marshal in 1233–4, similarly pitted the Lacys and their allies against the Marshals and theirs. Both wars began in the Welsh March, and were transferred to Ireland in the course of the fighting. This movement of conflict across the Irish Sea was of course as natural as the movement of trade and communications. Transnational aristocrats had transnational conflicts. In 1223, William Marshal recruited heavily from Leinster for his Welsh campaigns, meaning that Leinster was relatively unprotected when Hugh invaded Ireland later that year. With the help of his half-brother, William 'Gorm' de Lacy (born of the elder Hugh's Ua Conchobair wife), Hugh secured Meath, threatened Dublin and forced the Irish justiciar to sue for peace before turning to Ulster. Hugh's invasion of Ulster was followed by score-settling, and the conflict expanded dramatically. Cathal Crobderg's son, Aed Ua Conchobair, attacked Meath and the Lacys' newest conquests in Bréifne. The Isle of Man witnessed a bloody succession dispute, and a rumour spread that the king of

---

45 *Patent Rolls ... 1216–25*, 72, 74, 132; *Rot. Litt. Claus*, i, 362b, 392b, 402b; *Foedera*, I, i, 145.

Norway was sailing to Hugh's aid. In early 1224, William Marshal was sent to Ireland as justiciar. Once there, he gathered an impressive army of Irish kings and English lords drawn from four of Ireland's five historic provinces. He even mobilised the lords of the Isles and Western Scotland for a coordinated seaborne assault. In the event, neither side was prepared to engage the other, so calmer heads prevailed. Negotiations recommenced, and once Henry III attained his majority in 1227, Hugh was restored to Ulster.[46]

Aristocratic Resurgence

Henry III's majority marked a new era of magnate dominance in Ireland. Only one month after Earl Hugh's restoration, Henry III finally activated Richard de Burgh's grant of Connacht.[47] The immediate context of the grant was a Connacht succession dispute. Cathal Crobderg had died in 1224, and had been succeeded by his son Aed. However, in 1225, Hugh de Lacy's northern ally, Aed *Méith* Ua Néill [O'Neill], deposed Aed, and installed Toirdelbach Ua Conchobair in his stead. Interestingly, Toirdelbach was William *Gorm* de Lacy's uncle, and received the backing of the Lacys in the dispute. William Marshal, on the other hand, backed Aed. With the resumption of war a very real possibility, Richard de Burgh's grant helped to refocus the colonists' energies. The Marshal's support for Aed still threatened to reignite conflict, but the latter's assassination in 1228, allegedly at the behest of the Irish justiciar and the Lacy brothers, paved the way for de Burgh's conquest of Connacht.[48]

The conquest of Connacht took place against a backdrop of wider English campaigning in Wales (1228 and 1231) and Poitou (1230). A number of the men who fought alongside Richard in Connacht also found service under Henry III in these overseas conflicts. Richard's uncle, Hubert de Burgh, was the driving force behind these other campaigns, and when they failed, so did he. In July 1232, Hubert was replaced as English justiciar by his rival, Peter des Roches. Peter had been one of King John's closest supporters, and set about restoring an intrusive style of royal rule in England and Ireland. Peter's relative, Peter de Rivallis, was put in charge of the Irish administration and granted lands to rival the greatest magnates'. When Richard de Burgh, refused to accept the consequences of English regime change by surrendering the royal castles in his charge, his lands were forfeited. Unsurprisingly, Richard's removal from

---

46 *Patent Rolls … 1225–32*, 118.
47 *C. Chart. R.*, 42.
48 *Ann. Clon.*, 232–3; *AC*, 28.

Connacht sparked more fighting in the province. The situation became such that by the middle of July 1233, Henry III was planning a royal expedition to Ireland to pacify his lordship. That expedition was halted by the rebellion of Richard Marshal.[49]

William Marshal had died in 1231, and his younger brother's rebellion was, at its core, a protest against Henry III's seemingly arbitrary rule since the return of Peter des Roches. Richard recruited heavily from Leinster, and in August 1233 launched his rebellion in the Welsh March. The situation was brought under control relatively quickly by the king, who then moved to strike the Marshal's under-defended lordship in Ireland. The parallels with 1223–4 are clear, and extended to the personnel involved. One of the rebellion's initial targets had been the marcher lordship of Ewyas Lacy, owned by the lord of Meath, Walter de Lacy. Walter was dispatched to Ireland in December 1233, and encouraged to attack Leinster in retaliation. Roger of Wendover claims that Peter des Roches and Peter de Rivallis then sent a letter in the king's name to Walter, his brother Hugh, Richard de Burgh, Geoffrey de Marisco and the Irish justiciar, Maurice fitz Gerald, in which they declared that Richard Marshal had been disinherited and banished from England. This letter then ordered its addressees to seize Richard Marshal if he were to travel to Ireland, and bring him to the king, dead or alive. If they did this, they were to divide his Irish lands and possessions amongst themselves to be held of the king in perpetuity. Wendover's testimony is corroborated by the Irish annals on several points. It should also be remembered that Hugh de Lacy had gained Ulster in similar circumstances. However, whatever the king and his counsellors wanted, it is clear that the magnates were pursuing their own private interests in Ireland.[50]

Perhaps the most important of those interests involved Richard Marshal and Richard de Burgh. The Burghs had remained at loggerheads with the Marshals ever since the Connacht crisis of the 1220s. However, what evidence exists suggests that Richard de Burgh and Richard Marshal had achieved a rapprochement in 1233, which Richard de Burgh effectively broke by siding with the king in 1234. Consequently, Richard Marshal's first offensive action in Ireland was against de Burgh. Landing in February 1234, the Marshal initially

---

49 N. Vincent, *Peter des Roches: An Alien in English Politics, 1205–1238* (Cambridge University Press, 1996), 371–5.
50 Roger of Wendover, *Flores Historiarum*, ed. H. G. Hewlett, 3 vols. (London: RS, 1886–9), iii, 72–3; B. Smith, 'Irish Politics, 1220–1245', in M. Prestwich, R. Britnel, and R. Frame (eds.), *Thirteenth Century England VIII* (Woodbridge: Boydell Press, 2001), 17.

respected a peace negotiated by his brother Gilbert the previous year. However, in mid-March he suddenly launched an attack on the city of Limerick and, in alliance with the Irish of Thomond, cut a swath of destruction through Richard de Burgh's territories in Munster and Connacht. In response, the Lacy brothers joined the Irish justiciar in besieging the Marshal's castle of Kildare. Richard Marshal's hopeless attempt to break the siege, and arrogant conduct during a parley, led directly to his death. Almost all contemporary commentators write of treachery, alleging that the Marshal was abandoned by his own guard at the crucial moment, dying some days later in captivity. Whether or not this was true, the 'murder' of Earl Richard Marshal caused a scandal at the English court, where its supposed instigators, Peter des Roches and Peter de Rivallis, were now out of favour.[51]

Despite Henry III's attempts at reconciliation, hostility remained between the government's co-conspirators and the Marshals, with Richard Marshal's brother and heir, Gilbert, pursuing with his relations a programme of 'mortal enmity' against the man he held responsible for Richard's death, the justiciar Maurice fitz Gerald. In 1235, Gilbert was implicated in the murder in London of Henry Clement, Maurice's clerk, who had boasted about his part in Earl Richard's death. Two years later, in August 1237, the Pope wrote to Ireland urging peace to be maintained between the two factions. Despite the lingering hostility, Richard de Burgh was able to capitalise on his brother Hubert's restoration to regain Connacht.[52] The territorial gold rush that followed pulled in personnel from every corner of the English colony, bringing further complexity to Ireland's tenurial network. As a result, some lesser barons, such as Maurice fitz Gerald and Walter of Ridelsford, were able to make substantial gains in the new conquest lordship, helping to direct the course of Irish politics for years to come. For instance, when Hugh de Lacy was granted extensive lands in Connacht around Sligo, he subinfeudated most of them to Maurice fitz Gerald. As earl of Ulster, Hugh made further speculative grants to Maurice in Fermanagh and Tír Conaill, and worked with him to install their preferred king in Tír Eógain. Had the two men been successful in their endeavours, the Lacy–Geraldine alliance would have dominated

---

51 D. Crouch, 'Earl Gilbert Marshal and his Mortal Enemies', *Historical Research*, 87 (2014), 397–8; Veach, *Lordship in Four Realms*, 216–17; Roger of Wendover, *Flores Historiarum*, iii, 80–1; M. J. Colker, 'The "Margam Chronicle" in a Dublin Manuscript', *HSJ*, 4 (1992), 139–40.

52 F. M. Powicke, *King Henry III and the Lord Edward. The Community of the Realm in the Thirteenth Century.* 2 vols. (Oxford University Press, 1947), ii, 740–59; *CPL, 1198–1304*, 165–6; *CPR, 1232–47*, 73.

the north of Ireland. As it happened, both men died before their vision could be realised.[53]

The Geraldines and Ridelsfords had been in Ireland since the very first adventurers arrived in 1169, and their elevation in the mid-thirteenth century coincided with the extinction of two of Ireland's most powerful dynasties. In 1241, Walter de Lacy died without a male heir. His transnational inheritance, including the lordship of Meath, was divided between the representatives of his two granddaughters. Thus the provincial lordship of Meath was eventually partitioned into the Verdon lordship of Meath, and the Geneville (or Joinville) liberty of Trim. The following year, Walter's brother Hugh also died. Although Hugh left behind at least one daughter, his earldom reverted to the crown. Finally, in 1245 Walter and Anselm Marshal, the last of five Marshal brothers, died without male heirs. The vast Marshal inheritance, including the earldom of Pembroke and lordship of Leinster, was divided among the representatives of their five sisters and co-heiresses. The families to benefit, and thus gain substantial stakes in Ireland, were Bigod, Bohun, Cantilupe, Clare, Ferrers, Hastings, Mortimer and Valence. Making matters worse, Connacht also entered a period of minority and absent rule. Richard de Burgh had died while on campaign with Henry III in Poitou in 1243. His eldest son and heir, Richard, was attached to the king's household in England, and seems to have spent the majority of his time there before his death in 1248. Richard's heir, his brother Walter, was also in the king's household, and seems to have remained in England upon reaching his majority in 1250. As a result, the conquest of Connacht was robbed of a strong central driving force.[54]

As in 1210, the removal of four of Ireland's provincial magnates facilitated royal intervention, and encouraged Irish rebellion. King Henry III was able to manipulate the marriage market to ensure that portions of Meath and Leinster went to men of his choosing. Moreover, from 1245 the Irish justiciarship of John fitz Geoffrey (a substantial English magnate and courtier from the comital family of Essex) witnessed an intensification of English court interest in western Ireland as a source of patronage. In 1247 the Irish of Connacht attacked the new English conquests in their province. Trouble spread beyond Connacht the following year, and by 1249 revolts flared up in Desmond and Leinster.[55] However, unlike the earlier period of discord, the campaigns of the late 1240s and early 1250s were carried out by the sons of

---

53 Frame, *Colonial Ireland*, 40–1.
54 Frame, *Ireland and Britain*, 46–7; Otway-Ruthven, *History of Medieval Ireland*, 100–1, 191–3.
55 *AC*, 91–3, 97–101; *AI*, 353.

Irish kings, rather than by the kings themselves. Over the past six decades, the Irish had been forced into the complicated world of English court politics. They could not afford to openly defy the English king, especially now that English courtiers eyed their territories. Consequently, the risings in Connacht were not coordinated by King Feidlim Ua Conchobair, but by his son Aed. Meanwhile, wider politics kept the lord of Connacht east of the Irish Sea. From 1253 to 1254, Walter de Burgh and the Irish justiciar, John fitz Geoffrey, campaigned in Gascony with Henry III. Events came to a head in 1255, when Aed Ua Conchobair travelled north and made common cause with Brian Ua Néill of Tír Eógain. Walter de Burgh had by that point arrived in Connacht, and the scene was set for widespread conflict. The destabilisation of Irish politics caused by the conquest of Connacht and the Lacy and Marshal partitions made concerted Irish rebellion a possibility for the first time since the Treaty of Windsor in 1175. Such was the uncertain inheritance that Henry III bequeathed to his eldest son, Lord Edward, in 1254. Henry's grant of Ireland was part of a wider package of lands to provide for Edward and his new bride, Eleanor of Castile. Within the grant, the constitutional position of Ireland was made clear for the first time since the beginning of the conquest. Ireland was granted to Edward in such a way that it was never to be alienated from the English crown. The old land of aristocratic adventure had officially become a crown dependency.[56]

It perhaps befits the often contradictory nature of the English conquest of Ireland that such a firm statement of English dominance should be made just as Irish resistance increased on the island. It is a reminder that the conquest was not a foregone conclusion, and did not proceed according to a set plan. From the moment that Henry II gave Diarmait Mac Murchada permission to recruit a fighting force in 1166, the future of English intervention in Ireland was uncertain. Had Diarmait not died in 1171, Ireland could have followed the examples of Scotland and Hungary, modernising under a strong native dynasty. Had Diarmait's son turned on Strongbow rather than allow his succession to Leinster, then the conquest might have come to an abrupt end. On the other hand, had Henry II not been called away from Ireland in the spring of 1172, then his royal army might have sought to complete the conquest. Indeed, had Henry II's vision for Ireland been realised, then it would have descended through a separate Angevin royal line under his youngest son John.

---

56 Frame, *Ireland and Britain*, 46–57. See Beth Hartland's chapter in this volume.

The future of the conquest was thus never clear to contemporaries. What began in the spirit of independent aristocratic endeavour, was quickly transformed with Henry II's involvement in 1171. Henry forced Ireland into the orbit of Angevin court politics, placing the original adventurers at an immediate disadvantage. The English king was adept at playing his barons against each other, and in Ireland that meant promoting factionalism. The western province of Connacht was often the engine house for conflict, drawing in competitors from all over the island. The resultant warfare showed that the English king was more than willing to back the native Irish over his own barons when it suited him. Indeed, from the early thirteenth century, King John issued charters to several Irish kings, bringing them into the Angevin Empire's tenurial network. That transnational web of lordship did much to determine the direction of conquest in Ireland. The priorities of the king and his magnates often lay east of the Irish Sea, and their decisions regarding Ireland were often taken in this context. That said, it is remarkable how well English lordship seems to have been grafted onto local Irish conditions, paralleling in many ways what had happened in Wales. Where possible, the English lords subinfeudated their lands among military followers. However, they were also willing to impose wider hegemonies by following the Irish model of domination and demanding tribute in cattle. The most successful lords were those who best adapted to their new environments. That adaptability would become an issue of concern for the Dublin government in the later thirteenth century thanks in part to the inflexible philosophy of government introduced by King John. Determined that Ireland should not become another Welsh March, and schooled in the household of Ranulf de Glanville at the height of the twelfth-century renaissance, King John created an incipient colony expressly tied to English law and custom. There was to be no legal accommodation with the Irish, no hybrid marcher law. The English king was to be the fount of all authority, and those in Ireland were either under his protection or outside the law. Ireland came to be ruled by an intrusive royal government with a bureaucrat's black and white view of the world, but it was a land which demanded local lordship exercised with subtlety and adaptability. The contradictions at the heart of the conquest would drive Irish history for years to come.

PART II

*

ENGLISH LORDSHIP IN IRELAND: 1200–1550

7

Angevin Ireland

NICHOLAS VINCENT

SINCE what follows is an exercise in Irish history, we had better begin with controversy and myth. The myth-maker here is Gerald of Wales. As his Irish readers have long complained, Gerald is a far from reliable witness. He none-theless dominates the history of the English conquest of Ireland to an extent not always appreciated. After him comes little save the demotic: in French, the locker-room ballad known as the 'Song of Dermot'; in Gaelic, the gore-spattered tallies of murder and cattle-rustling preserved in the Irish annals.[1] Ireland, as has frequently been pointed out, is evidentially impoverished only in comparison to England and the papacy.[2] Despite the destruction of the Irish Public Records in 1922, enough survives, much of it in the National Archives in London, to furnish the colonists with a history at least as rich as that of their Irish subjects reported in annals and poetry. Even so, Gerald, in the various editions of his *Topographia* and *Expugnatio*, remains the most vivid and quotable of reporters. Rather than surpass him, the later Middle Ages merely translated his Latin into English and Irish.[3] Rather than gather the charter evidence into coherent sequence, or complete the work of pros-opography and manorial descent begun by Orpen and Eric St John Brooks, modern historians have preferred to scratch at the itch that is Gerald. We must begin with some further scratching.

1 *Song of Dermot*, now re-edited as *Deeds of the Normans*.
2 For the sources, Connolly, *Medieval Record Sources*; Simms, *Medieval Gaelic Sources*. For their relative abundance, 'Three Exchequer Documents from the Reign of Henry III', ed. J. F. Lydon, *PRIA*, 65 C (1966), 1–2. For the most recent attempts at reconstruction, R. Frame, 'Rediscovering Medieval Ireland: Irish Chancery Rolls and the Historian', *PRIA*, 113 C (2013), 193–217.
3 A. Byrne, 'Family, Locality and Nationality: Vernacular Adaptations of the "Expugnatio Hibernica" in Late Medieval Ireland', *Medium Aevum*, 82 (2013), 101–18.

For their assistance with what follows, I am indebted to Michael Baillie, Robert Bartlett, Peter Crooks, David Crouch, Hugh Doherty, Seán Duffy, Nigel Morgan, Warwick Rodwell, Richard Sharpe, Brendan Smith and especially to Marie Therese Flanagan.

'Diarmait Mac Murchada,' Gerald informs us, 'ruler of a fifth part of Ireland ... behaved ... with grave and intolerable tyranny towards the great men of his land.'[4] What follows is a simple enough story. Having abducted the wife of King Ua Ruairc of Midhe ('since woman is always a fickle and inconstant creature'), Diarmait was chased out of Ireland (*c.*1166) and sought assistance in Aquitaine from Henry, king of England. Henry II granted him letters, recited by Gerald, soliciting support. Diarmait returned to Bristol, where after much fruitless waiting, he encountered Richard of Striguil, son of Gilbert de Clare. Richard swore to assist him in Ireland. In return, he was promised Diarmait's daughter and succession to his realm.

Impatient to revisit his native land ('where, viewed from a distance, hills and clouds seem to melt together'), Diarmait travelled to St Davids and the court of Rhys ap Gruffydd. Here he met Robert fitz Stephen, former commander of Cardigan, Rhys's prisoner for the past three years. Diarmait offered Robert and Maurice fitz Gerald the city of Wexford and two adjoining cantreds 'in fee'. He then sailed to Ireland and wintered in Ferns. In the following May (1169), Robert fitz Stephen crossed to Bannow, with 390 men carried in three ships. Joined by Diarmait and a further 500 men, Robert attacked the city of Wexford but was thrown back. Abandoning further resistance, the men of Wexford then surrendered to Diarmait, handing over hostages as a sign of their subjection. Travelling north into Osraige, the invaders obtained another victory. Presented with 200 severed enemy heads, Diarmait literally leapt for joy, clapping his hands, gnawing at the nose and cheeks of one whom he had particularly detested. So began the conquest of Ireland, a year or more before the arrival of Richard 'Strongbow', and at least two years before the intervention of King Henry II (here characterised by Gerald as 'Jupiter').[5]

Much of Gerald's story came to him from his own kinsmen, including his brother, Robert of Barry, who could still remember his tumble into the ditch at Wexford: so severe that sixteen years later his molar teeth fell out, 'and what was even more amazing, new ones immediately grew in their place'.[6] As with these miraculously regenerating molars, the problem with Gerald's history is that hardly a detail in it is entirely true. Some of the inaccuracies are factual. Thus, Diarmait seems to have encountered Henry II not in Aquitaine, as Gerald reports, but at Saumur on the Loire.[7] The letters of

---

4 *Expugnatio*, 24–5.
5 *Expugnatio*, 24–37. Henry II's personification as 'Jupiter Tonans', explicit in Gerald's 'Topographia' (*Gir. Camb. Op.*, v, 135, 149, 190), is implicit in *Expugnatio*, 90, 218.
6 *Expugnatio*, 32–5.
7 *Expugnatio*, 26, by contrast to *Deeds of the Normans*, 59 line 259, correcting *Song of Dermot*, 21.

Henry II requesting support for Diarmait are a literary invention of Gerald's rather than a product of the royal chancery. Three hundred and ninety men, of whom ninety needed horses, could hardly have been accommodated in three ships. Grants 'in fee' were unknown in Ireland, and the whole story of the promise made to Strongbow of Diarmait's daughter and inheritance seems, at best, to oversimplify, at worst entirely to distort reality.[8]

Less easily detectable, yet nonetheless just as corrosive of truth, Gerald's account is shadowed by classical archetypes intended to evoke the imperial glories of Rome. Some are explicit; others are merely implied. Thus the fickleness of women, the conquest sealed by a daughter's marriage, and even the name for the east wind that drew Diarmait back to Ireland (in a modern context, the all too blustery 'Euros') are all borrowed from Virgil's *Aeneid*, the epic telling of Rome's foundation by warriors from the east.[9] So too is the language of 'thundering' applied to Henry II as personification of Jupiter/Jove.[10] The clouds merging with hills, far from supplying evidence of Gerald's appreciation of natural beauty, come from the opening of book three of Lucan's *Bellum Civile*. Here Pompey is forced into exile from Italy at the beginning of a civil war pregnant with imperial consequence.[11] Diarmait's war dance before the severed heads of his enemies is not only barbaric but intentionally mirrors Ptolemy's treatment of the head of Pompey, as recorded by Lucan. In Gerald's telling, it stands in deliberate contradiction to Lucan's report of the magnanimity displayed in similar circumstances by Caesar.[12] Ptolemy's posterity, we should remember, was doomed to foreign conquest, Caesar's to imperial greatness.

Gerald's division of Ireland into five kingdoms, although borrowed from Irish sources, would have reminded his readers of Caesar, Josephus, Bede, Geoffrey of Monmouth or Henry of Huntingdon on the triumvirates, tetrarchies and heptarchies that presaged dissolution and foreign conquest for the peoples of Gaul, Judea, the Roman Empire or Dark Age Britain. More explicitly still, Gerald's *Topographia* was dedicated to Henry II as a work presented by 'his Sylvester': a reference not just to the prophecies of 'Merlin

---

8 *Expugnatio*, 26, 28–30 and cf. *Letters Henry II*, no. 1468. For discussion, Flanagan, *Irish Society*, 79–111; M. T. Flanagan, 'Strategies of Lordship in Pre-Norman and Post-Norman Leinster', *ANS*, 20 (1998), 109–10, 126.

9 *Expugnatio*, 22, 42–4, 60–2, 224–6 (Pompey and Caesar), 24 (Mark Antony and Troy), 62 (Alexander), 24 (fickleness), 30, 226 ('Euro/Eurus').

10 For Jupiter's thunderings, P. Hardie, *Virgil's Aeneid: Cosmos and Imperium* (Oxford University Press, 1986), 145–9.

11 *Expugnatio*, 28 ('dum inter colles et nubila vix discernitur'); Lucan, *Bellum Civile*, 3:7 ('Nubibus et dubios cernit vanescere montes').

12 Lucan, *Bellum Civile*, 8:663–710, 9:1010–1108.

Silvestris' (that Gerald claimed to interpret and had in all likelihood invented), but to the relationship between Pope Sylvester and Constantine, first of the Christian emperors of Rome.[13] The Donation of Constantine, as we shall see, was a text crucial to the conquest of Ireland. Elsewhere, Gerald's account is littered with echoes from Virgil and Lucan, all of them pointers to what was intended as a self-consciously imperial narrative. According to this, a native tyrant (Diarmait, for whom read Latinus in Virgil, Ptolemy in Lucan, Herod the Great in Josephus, or Androgeus/Vortigern in Bede/Geoffrey of Monmouth) summoned military aid from overseas, thereby condemning his already sinful and divided nation to foreign conquest.[14]

If Gerald's version of events is not to be trusted, then what was the reality of the 'Angevin' conquest of Ireland? What did England's kings hope to gain there, and what was the Irish contribution to the wider history of Plantagenet empire-building? This is no place for a narrative, expertly told elsewhere.[15] Having been haphazardly annexed to Henry II's 'empire' in 1171, Ireland was to remain a divided land, its constituent kingdoms placed under the titular authority of the Plantagenet kings, with only Connacht recognised after 1175 as a semi-independent entity ruled by native kings owing fealty (and a rent, at first of hides, hawks and hounds, only later of sterling) to Henry II and his successors.

Behind this high political facade, a visitor transported from 1171 to 1272 would have observed a wholesale transformation in Irish culture and economy, certainly in the south and east, less tangibly in Ulster and the remoter parts of the west. Over the course of a century, there was extensive building and resettlement. Towns such as Dublin, Drogheda, Wexford, Waterford, Limerick and Cork were adorned by their new colonists with parish churches, castles and public buildings, in many instances in a style directly borrowed from English models.[16] Even in the un-urbanised interior, foreign lords

---

13 Gerald, 'Topographia', second preface to the first edn (*Gir. Camb. Op.*, v, 20), and for Merlin Silvester, whose prophecies, some or all possibly invented by Gerald, loom large in the *Expugnatio*, lxi–viii, 252–6; S. Jensen, 'Merlin: Ambrosius and Silvester', in G. Barnes *et al.* (eds.), *Words and Wordsmiths* (Sydney: University of Sydney, Department of English, 1989), 45–8.

14 For classical quotations identified, *Expugnatio*, 359–60. Far more lurk as allusions. For Androgeus, *Expugnatio*, 44. For the punishment of sin, 232.

15 Standard narratives here include Orpen, *Normans*; Otway-Ruthven, *History of Medieval Ireland*; Lydon, *Lordship*; Frame, *Colonial Ireland*; Flanagan, *Irish Society*; *NHI* ii; S. Duffy, 'John and Ireland: The Origins of England's Irish Problem', in S. D. Church (ed.), *King John: New Interpretations* (Woodbridge: Boydell Press, 1999), 221–45.

16 R. Stalley, 'Three Irish Buildings with West Country Origins', *Medieval Art and Architecture at Wells and Glastonbury*, BAACT 4 (1981), 62–80; R. Stally, 'Irish Gothic and English Fashion', in Lydon (ed.), *English in Medieval Ireland*, 65–86; R. Stalley, 'Cathedral Building in Thirteenth-Century Ireland', in R. Stalley (ed.), *Irish Gothic Architecture: Construction,*

established castles, markets and more than 100 small boroughs. One of the most typical expressions of conquest, boroughs were intended to encourage the settlement of immigrants attracted not only by land hunger and the over-population of England and Wales, but by an Irish economy newly monetised and manorialised.[17] Such incomers craved the prosperity that resulted from new investment in tillage and livestock, mills and drainage, forest clearance, bridge and road building.[18]

Inevitably, comparisons have been drawn between this Irish experience and the process of conquest elsewhere: with early medieval Saxony and Christendom's eastern 'frontier', with Sicily and the Holy Land, with Wales or Scotland, and above all with England after 1066.[19] As we shall see, such comparisons distort almost as much as they illuminate. If we are to assess them objectively, let us begin with some fundamentals: with title, economy and law. Here, once again, we have no alternative but to engage with Gerald of Wales.

Laudabiliter and the Conquest of Ireland

Perhaps the greatest of Gerald's distortions is the title to Ireland that he claims was bestowed upon Henry II by the Pope. The Norman Conquest of 1066 had been widely deplored elsewhere in Europe as an act of aggression by one Christian people against another. The English conquest of Ireland evoked no such international condemnation, passing more or less unnoticed by for-eign chroniclers. Like reporters after 1066, Gerald was nonetheless aware that right was not necessarily justified by might. Certainly, he was aware that in Ireland Christians were slaughtering fellow Christians.[20] Determined to

Decay and Reinvention (Bray: Wordwell, 2012), 15–53; T. O'Keeffe, *Medieval Irish Buildings 1100–1600* (Dublin: Four Courts Press, 2015).

17 A. J. Otway-Ruthven, 'The Character of Norman Settlement in Ireland', in Crooks (ed.), *Government, War and Society*, 263–74; R. R. Davies, *The First English Empire: Power and Identities in the British Isles 1093–1343* (Oxford University Press, 2000), 137–8; H. B. Clarke, 'Planning and Regulation in the Formation of New Towns and New Quarters in Ireland, 1170–1641', in A. Simms and H. B. Clarke (eds.), *Lords and Towns in Medieval Europe* (Farnham: Ashgate, 2015), 321–54. For monetisation, D. W. Dykes, 'The Irish Coinage of Henry III', and 'King John's Irish Rex Coinage Revisited', *British Numismatic Journal*, 32 (1963), 99–116; 83 (2013), 120–33; 84 (2014), 90–100. For manorialisation, see the chapters by Murphy and Frame below.

18 A. J. Otway-Ruthven, 'The Organization of Anglo-Irish Agriculture in the Middle Ages', in Crooks (ed.), *Government, War and Society*, 275–86; Murphy and Potterton, *Dublin Region in the Middle Ages*.

19 Most notably by Bartlett, *Making of Europe*.

20 E. Van Houts, 'The Norman Conquest through European Eyes', *EHR*, 110 (1995), 832–53. *Expugnatio*, 154–6, 236, 242, 263–4.

outdo the apologists of William the Conqueror (who had alluded to a papal banner, supposedly symbolising papal approval of William's adventure), Gerald supplied a whole catalogue of justifications for Henry II's aggression. Greatest amongst these was the bull *Laudabiliter*, allegedly issued by Pope Adrian IV in 1159.[21]

In all surviving copies, *Laudabiliter* fails to employ the standard rhythmic formulae (the 'cursus') expected of the papal chancery. It perhaps originated as a genuine papal rescript sent to England in 1159, carried by John of Salisbury, not as an incitement to the invasion of Ireland but as a temporising gesture, praising the king's intentions but at the same time cautioning against their implementation. Only in the aftermath of 1171 was this letter dusted off and rewritten, almost certainly by Gerald, as an enthusiastic endorsement of conquest.[22] Not only is it now generally agreed that *Laudabiliter* was rewritten, but the circumstances in which Henry II first considered the conquest of Ireland have themselves been clarified.

By the 1150s, Ireland was known as the only major island of the British archipelago left unconquered by either Romans or Normans. Its trading contacts with Normandy, Aquitaine and above all with Bristol (principal base in the 1140s and 1150s of the adherents of the future Henry II) had long ago brought it to Henry's attention. As duke of Normandy, *c.*1150, Henry had confirmed Rouen's monopoly over Irish–Norman trade.[23] Already in 1141, King Stephen, held captive by the supporters of Henry's uncle, Robert of Gloucester, lord of Bristol, had been threatened with removal to Ireland. Writing under the patronage of Robert of Gloucester, not only had Geoffrey of Monmouth described the conquest of Ireland by Henry II's chief role model, King Arthur, as a crucial aspect of Arthur's imperial destiny, but attributed prophecies to Merlin in which, 'in the time of the eagle of the broken covenant', a king would arise to 'overthrow the walls of Ireland and turn

---

21 *Expugnatio*, 144–6; 'De Rebus a se gestis' (*c.*11), in *Gir. Camb. Op.*, i, 62–3. The only potentially independent copy, in *Diceto*, i, 300–1, was possibly copied from Gerald. For early criticism of the text, J. H. Round, *The Commune of London and Other Studies* (London: Constable, 1899), 171–200, countering K. Norgate, 'The Bull Laudabiliter', *EHR*, 8 (1893), 18–52.

22 A. Duggan, 'The Making of a Myth: Giraldus Cambrensis, "Laudabiliter", and Henry II's Lordship of Ireland', *Studies in Medieval and Renaissance History*, 3rd series 4 (2007), 107–70. Duggan's thesis resurrects a theory first advanced anonymously in 1882, in the *Analecta Juris Pontificii*: Norgate, 'The Bull', 19, 33–4.

23 A. F. O'Brien, 'Commercial Relations between Aquitaine and Ireland, *c.*1000 to *c.*1550', in J.-M. Picard (ed.), *Aquitaine and Ireland in the Middle Ages* (Dublin: Four Courts Press, 1995), 31–5; R. B. Patterson, 'Bristol: An Angevin Baronial Capital under Royal Siege', *HSJ*, 3 (1992), 171–81; *Regesta Regum Anglo-Normannorum*, 4 vols., ed. H. W. C. Davis *et al.* (Oxford University Press, 1913–70), iii, no. 729.

its forests into a plain'.[24] It is surely significant that, from the 1150s onwards, Henry II's wife, Eleanor of Aquitaine, was widely identified as the 'eagle of the broken covenant' of Merlin/Geoffrey's prophecy.[25] Even more significant was the determination of the archbishop and monks of Canterbury to maintain control over the Church in Ireland, in recent years displaying a desire to control its own newly reformed affairs independent of any 'primacy' claimed by Canterbury.[26]

In 1159, in the midst of a bid for the conquest of Toulouse, Henry toyed with the idea of claiming Ireland on behalf of his younger brother, William. But these plans were stillborn and evoked only a lukewarm response from the Pope, embodied in the original, un-doctored version of *Laudabiliter*. Twelve years later, the king tried again. This 'invasion' of 1171 was a reaction to circumstances rather than a spontaneous bid for empire. First and foremost, there was a need to curb the success of Strongbow and his companions, to reassert royal control over a conquest threatening the balance of power in the west. Second, in the aftermath of Becket's murder, there was a need to reestablish Henry's credentials as a victorious Christian king. No French-born ruler, aware of the Norman conquests after 1066 in England, Sicily, Jerusalem, and perhaps above all Scotland, could be unaware of the consequences of allowing one of his subjects to obtain the trappings of kingship, least of all in circumstances in which Henry himself was accused of being a godless tyrant. Hence the decision, made by the king, once in Ireland, to retain not only Dublin but its hinterland and the coastal towns of the south and west.[27] This ran directly contrary to previous royal policy in Wales or Scotland, 'marches' of conquest left very much to local baronial initiative.

The administration that Henry established in Ireland, under a succession of viceroys later styled 'justiciars', remained a primitive affair.[28] It nonetheless gave the king a leverage that he did not possess in either Wales or Scotland. In Ireland, from the outset the king was brought into competition with his barons, over land and prerogative wardship. This in turn was to invite yet further,

24 William of Malmesbury, *Historia Novella*, ed. E. King and K. R. Potter (Oxford University Press, 1998), 47; Geoffrey of Monmouth, *The History of the Kings of Britain*, ed. M. D. Reeve and N. Wright (Woodbridge: Boydell Press, 2007), 148–9.

25 *RHF*, xii, 419; *Diceto*, ii, 67; *Radulfi Nigri Chronica*, ed. R. Anstruther (London: Caxton Society, 1851), 98, 'A Commentary on the "Prophetia Merlini"', ed. J. Hammer, *Speculum*, 10 (1935), 29–30.

26 Flanagan, *Irish Society*, esp. chs. 1–2; Flanagan, *Transformation of the Irish Church*.

27 Flanagan, *Irish Society*, 112–24; *Expugnatio*, 88; M. T. Flanagan, 'Henry II and the Kingdom of Uí Fáeláin', in Bradley (ed.), *Settlement and Society in Medieval Ireland*, 229–39.

28 M. T. Flanagan, 'Household Favourites: Angevin Royal Agents in Ireland under Henry II and John', in Smyth (ed.), *Seanchas*, 357–80.

direct royal intervention. We thus arrive at the paradox that was medieval Ireland: a colony of intense royal administration, initially promising rich profits for the king, yet established so remotely that no king of England would incorporate it within his itinerary.

Although reporting on a conquered land, both in the *Topographia* and the *Expugnatio* Gerald offers only a handful of references to 'conquestus' or 'conquisitio'. Instead, he writes of an 'expugnatio' commanded by 'expugnatores'.[29] His scruples here extend to the titles that he bestows upon Henry II, supposedly his chief patron, equated with Caesar or Alexander, but at best described as 'triumphator', never as 'conquestor'. Gerald's choice of the term 'expugnatio' over 'conquestus/conquisitio' was deliberate. 'Expugnatio' seems to have been a term accepted, by the 1150s, for the lawful trial of arms in which one nation was defeated by another.[30] This despite the association drawn by Seneca (a favourite authority for both Gerald and Henry II) between 'expugnatio' and rape.[31] For all his deliberately barbarised portrayal of the native Irish, Gerald's description of an 'Adventus Anglorum' was intended to evoke memories of Bede's 'Adventus Saxonum': the overrunning of a corrupt Western Christian nation by stronger forces from the east. Even Ralph Niger, a confirmed critic of Henry II, allowed that Ireland was legitimately 'acquired' ('acquisierat') by Strongbow, albeit that the king then seized it from Strongbow illegitimately 'by force'.[32]

Others were less scrupulous over words. John de Courcy, for example, granting charters to the monks of Down before 1193 referred to his lordship in Ulster as the 'conquest ["conquestus"] that I acquired in Ireland'.[33] According to the 'Pembridge/Laud' Annals, in 1186, at the death of Hugh de Lacy, 'the conquest ceased'.[34] Gerald's history was itself known in medieval Ireland as

29 For references to 'conquistio/conquestus', *Gir. Camb. Op.*, v, 66, 93; *Expugnatio*, 64, 88, 120, 156, 188, 230, 246, 262, 263, 264. Besides its ubiquitous appearance in the *Expugnatio*, the word 'expugnatio' also occurs in the 'De Rebus a se gestis' and the 'Topographia', in *Gir. Camb. Op.*, i, 61, 90, v, 66 (l. 4, referring to the 'Adventus Anglorum, imminentisque conquisitionis et expugnationis gentis sue').

30 D. W. Sutherland, 'Conquest and Law', *Studia Gratiana*, 15 (1972), 35–51, esp. 47, 49, and cf. G. J. Hand, *English Law in Ireland 1290–1324* (Cambridge University Press, 1967), 176.

31 Seneca, *Controversiae* I.praef.9, whence William of Malmesbury, *Gesta Regum Anglorum*, ed. R. A. B. Mynors, R. M. Thomson and M. Winterbottom, 2 vols. (Oxford University Press, 1998–9), i, 68, 560, ii, 42 n. 3, 279 n. 5.

32 *Gir. Camb. Op.*, v, 66, 93, 108, 128 ('Adventus Anglorum'); *Radulfi Nigri Chronica*, 92.

33 'Cartae Dunenses XII–XIII Céad', ed. G. MacNiocaill, *Seanchas Ard Mhacha*, 5 (1970), 420 no. 4, 421 no. 8, and cf. S. Duffy, 'Town and Crown: The Kings of England and their City of Dublin', in M. Prestwich, R. Britnell and R. Frame (eds.), *Thirteenth Century England X* (Woodbridge: Boydell Press, 2005), 103–4. Note also the future King John's confirmation to Peter Pipard of land in Ulster 'de conquestu suo': *COD*, i, 364 no. 863/1.

34 *Chartul. St Mary's, Dublin*, ii, 305 ('et ibi cessauit conquestus').

the *Historia de Conquistione Hibernie*, and Henry II as 'Henry the Conqueror'.[35] The chancery of King John, by contrast, as late as 1215, preferred such euphemisms as 'the time when the English' (or sometimes 'the French') 'came into Ireland'. This was presumably to maintain the fiction, first popularised by Gerald, that the adventures of the 1170s and 1180s had been undertaken at the invitation and with the consent of the native Irish.[36]

For Henry himself to seek kingship in Ireland would have been to challenge that monopoly over the bestowal of kingly titles in theory claimed by Popes and emperors, both western and eastern. Even so, there was an imperative to fend off the claims to royal status advanced on behalf of Strongbow, and later of Hugh de Lacy and John de Courcy.[37] Gerald refers explicitly to Irish recognition of Henry II's 'imperium'.[38] Henry himself, by contrast, acknowledged at least a degree of inferiority towards the 'imperium' of Frederick Barbarossa and Byzantium.[39] Contemporaries who praised Henry II in terms approaching the imperial never quite dared question the uniquely imperial titles of the emperors of Rome or Constantinople.[40] Hence Gerald's use of the language of Jove/Jupiter, and the typology of 'Caesar', Julius Caesar being less than an emperor but rather greater than any king, certainly than the mere 'kinglets' ('reguli') who Gerald suggested ruled in Ireland.[41]

---

35 *Chartul. St Mary's, Dublin*, i, 138 no. 118c, 530 no. 296 ('Henricus rex conquestor Hibernie'), and see also the *Modus Tenendi Parliamentum* attributed to 'Henricus rex Anglie conquestor': P. Crooks, 'Representation and Dissent: "Parliamentarianism" and the Structure of Politics in Colonial Ireland, *c.*1370–1420', *EHR*, 125 (2010), 1–2. Cf. *Reg. St Thomas*, 419 nos. 491–2 (Hugh de Lacy as 'primus conquestor Midie').

36 *Rot. Litt. Claus.*, i, 186–6b ('quando Anglic(i) venerunt in Hyb(erniam)'); *C. Chart. R. 1226–57*, 230–1 ('aduentum Francorum in Hiberniam'); *Expugnatio*, 148.

37 Newburgh, 'Chronica', i, 239–40 (Lacy); Howden, *Chronica*, iv, 161–2 (Courcy).

38 *Expugnatio*, 232 (l. 29), and cf. 22 (l. 333); 'Topographia', in *Gir. Camb. Op.*, v, 190, and cf. *Deeds of the Normans*, 60 l. 285, referring to the barons of Henry II's 'empire'. Elsewhere, see *Expugnatio*, 26 (l. 33), 42 (Caesar), 44 (l. 28, Caesar), 60 (l. 17, Caesar), 88 (l. 6, Strongbow), 42 (l. 13, Diarmait), 124 (l. 34, Henry II), 226 (l. 155, Pompey).

39 *Letters Henry II*, nos. 1093–4, 1351, and for Henry's deference to the claims of Barbarossa, H. E. Mayer, 'Staufische Weltherrschaft? Zum Brief Heinrichs II. von England an Friedrich Barbarossa von 1157', *Festschrift Karl Pivec*, ed. A. Haidacher and H. E. Mayer (Innsbruck: Leopold-Franzens-Universitat, 1966), 265–78.

40 M. Aurell, *L'Empire des Plantagenêt 1154–1224* (St-Amand-Montrond: Éditions Perrin, 2002), 9–11; J. Gillingham, 'Expectations of Empire: Some Twelfth-and Early Thirteenth-Century English Views of What their Kings Could Do', in Duffy and Foran (eds.), *English Isles*, 56–67, and more generally, R. Folz, *L'Idée d'Empire en occident du Ve au XIVe siècle* (Paris, 1953); D. Bates, *The Normans and Empire* (Oxford University Press, 2013).

41 For Irish 'reguli', see the decrees of the Council of Cashel (1172) in *Expugnatio*, 98, and also *Gir. Camb. Op.*, v, 162, 190 (neatly combining the idea of 'reguli' with Henry II's Jupiter-like 'imperium'); *Diceto*, i, 348; Paris, *CM*, ii, 284 (1171), 529–30 (1210), iii, 196–7 (1230), iv, 57–8 (1240). According to *Deeds of the Normans*, 109, kings were as numerous in Ireland as earls in England.

In 1177, Henry acknowledged his youngest son, John, as future king of Ireland. John crossed to Waterford in 1185, but, rather than proclaim royal status, adopted the title 'son of the lord king and lord of Ireland' ('filius domini regis et dominus Hibernie'). After his accession as king of England in 1199, this was absorbed into the royal style ('By God's grace king of England, lord of Ireland, duke of Normandy and Aquitaine and count of Anjou').[42] Meanwhile, this same title, 'dominus', had been adopted both by Richard, who styled himself 'dominus Anglie' whilst king in waiting, after the death of Henry II in July 1189, and by John, claiming to rule as 'dominus Anglie' between Richard's death in April 1199 and his own coronation in May.[43] Long before this, it had been anticipated in the 1140s, in the title adopted by Matilda, Henry II's mother, as 'lady of the English' ('domina Anglorum'), following her seizure of power but before any official coronation.

That it was an exalted style is proved after 1199 both by the insertion of the title 'dominus Hibernie' in royal protocols above the king's titles as 'duke of Normandy/Aquitaine and count of Anjou', and by the choice of 'dominus Edwardus filius regis Anglie' as the principal title of the uncrowned heir-apparent, the future King Edward I, throughout the 1250s and 1260s. Henry III's decision to grant the lordship of Ireland to Edward in 1254 threatened, according to Matthew Paris, to transform the king himself into a mere 'king-let' ('regulus mutilatus').[44] Thereafter, it was as lords of Ireland that the kings of England were to rule, through to Henry VIII's reversion to the original plan for Irish kingship in 1541. In the opposite direction, we might note the tendency, already apparent in the writing of Gerald of Wales and Ralph of Diss, before 1200, to relegate the native kings of Ireland to the status of mere 'kinglets' ('reguli'), a tendency reflected in the increasing reluctance of the chancery of Henry III to acknowledge the royal titles of native Irishmen.[45]

According to Roger of Howden, petitions to the Pope to proclaim John 'king' in Ireland were eventually answered by Urban III, who in 1186 sent Henry III a

---

42 As noted by Duffy, 'John and Ireland', 235, John's charters of the 1190s occasionally combine his titles as lord of Ireland and count of Mortain, placing Mortain sometimes above (13 instances) but more often behind Ireland (27 instances).

43 A point first drawn to my attention by Stephen Church. See *Ancient Charters, Royal and Private, Prior to AD 1200*, ed. J. H. Round, PRS 10 (London, 1888), 91–2 no. 55; *CDF*, no. 112, and, for Gerald's awareness of the usage, *Gir. Camb. Op.*, i, 110.

44 Paris, *CM*, v, 450.

45 Note also Roger of Howden's exclusion of Welsh and Irish kings from a list of rulers including the king of Man and John de Courcy in Ulster: Howden, *Chronica*, iv, 161–2. For 'reguli' and royal titles withheld, Davies, *First English Empire*, 97–8; Frame, *Ireland and Britain*, 21–4; *Close Rolls 1259–61*, 64 (*CDI, 1252–1284*, no. 661); above n. 41.

crown of peacock feathers in token of John's recognition as king.[46] Scepticism has been voiced over this account, with at least one modern authority declaring that 'Popes did not send peacock-feathered crowns to anyone.'[47] The reality is more interesting, yet surprisingly unexplored. Peacock crowns had in fact long been a symbol of triumph in ancient Rome.[48] In Byzantium, a peacock crown, known as the 'tufa' (τοῦφα), was shown on coins minted for the emperor Theophilus (d. 842), and was worn by Basil II at his celebration of victories over the Bulgars in 1019.[49] This same 'tufa' was also adopted by barbarian rulers of the west, including Theudebert I of the Franks (d. 554), grandson of Clovis.[50] Most intriguingly, a 'tufa' (in Anglo-Saxon, a 'thuuf', or 'tuft of feathers') was carried in procession before King Edwin (d. 633), portrayed by Bede not only as the first of Northumbria's Christian kings but as a martyred saint whose authority extended throughout the British Isles.[51] Meanwhile, the 'phrygium' or 'crown from our head' supposedly granted by Constantine to Pope Sylvester was sometimes (erroneously) identified as a crown embellished with white peacock feathers, specifically noticed in the Donation of Constantine amongst a list of imperial regalia entrusted to the papacy immediately after Constantine's grant of papal dominion over the islands of the west.[52] Like the sandals of Pope Silvester preserved as one of the more precious relics of Dublin Cathedral, a peacock crown for Ireland would have been a peculiarly appropriate recognition of English victory, echoing not only the rhetoric of conquest but specifically the very text, the Donation of Constantine, upon which the papacy, and hence the kings of England had fashioned their claims to sovereignty.[53]

---

46 Howden, *Gesta*, i, 339; Howden, *Chronica*, ii, 306–7, 317.

47 S. Church, *King John: England, Magna Carta and the Making of a Tyrant* (Houndmills: Palgrave Macmillan, 2015), 27.

48 J. König, *Athletics and Literature in the Roman Empire* (Cambridge University Press, 2005), 78–9.

49 P. Grierson (ed.), *Catalogue of the Byzantine Coins in the Dumbarton Oaks Collection and in the Whittemore Collection*, 3 part 1 (Leo III to Michael III, 717–867) (Dumbarton Oaks: Dumbarton Oaks Research Library and Collection, 1973), 129–30; M. McCormick, *Eternal Victory: Triumphant Rulership in Late Antiquity, Byzantium and the Early Medieval West* (Cambridge University Press, 1990), 148–9, 178, 417.

50 McCormick, *Eternal Victory*, 338–9, 418.

51 *Bede's Ecclesiastical History*, 192–3, an account of Edwin subsequently adapted, without the 'tufa' but continuing to stress imperial Christian destiny, by William of Malmesbury, *Gesta Regum*, i, 68.

52 For the 'phrygium' of the Donation (*PL*, 8, col. 576), see P. E. Schramm, 'Zur Geschichte der päpstlichen Tiara', *Historische Zeitschrift*, 152 (1935), 307–12, esp. pp. 309–10. For the peacock as symbol of triumph and rebirth, H. Lother, *Der Pfau in der altchristlichen Kunst*, Studien über christliche Denkmäler 18 (Leipzig: Dieterich, 1929).

53 For the sandals, R. Ó Floinn, 'The Foundation Relics of Christ Church Cathedral and the Origins of the Diocese of Dublin', in S. Duffy (ed.), *Medieval Dublin VII* (Dublin: Four Courts Press, 2006), 95, 99–100.

After 1189, the intention remained that Richard, John's elder brother, and his posterity would inherit England. John was compensated with a maritime lordship extending from the Cotentin peninsula of Normandy, via Dorset, Devon and Cornwall to Bristol and Glamorgan, and thence via Dublin north to Lancashire. Crucial to these arrangements was John's betrothal to the heiress of the great honour of Gloucester. As John's wife, Isabella used a seal, inherited from her father, showing the winged Nike, itself denoting triumph, accompanying other imperial attributes: an eagle, a helmeted bust and two standards.[54] This was a marriage with distinctly imperial overtones. Into the 1240s Ireland itself continued to be referred to as a realm ('regnum') both in papal and royal correspondence, not least in King John's submission to the Pope after 1213, where of the 1,000 marks a year promised as tribute, 700 were to represent England, 300 the 'realm of Ireland'.[55]

Had Richard not died childless in 1199, the arrangements of 1185 might have detached Ireland from the English crown, as an estate for John and his children even more impressive than such later 'apanages' as the earldom of Cornwall or the duchy of Lancaster. Viewed in this light, John's lordship was reminiscent of (and perhaps deliberately modelled upon) the earlier sea-borne empires of Cnut in England, or the Norse kings in Ireland and the Western Isles. Throughout the 1190s, there was minimal intervention by Richard in Ireland.[56] Only after Richard's death in 1199 do we begin to receive indications – the establishment of an exchequer at Dublin, the emergence of itinerant royal justices, and of royal sheriffs beyond the immediate vicinity of Dublin – that John's dominion was being transformed into a distinctively royal affair under the direct authority of the king.[57] The Irish exchequer is

---

54 *Earldom of Gloucester Charters*, ed. R. B. Patterson (Oxford University Press, 1973), 24 and plate 31.

55 *Foedera*, i, 111–12. In general, J. Lydon, 'Ireland and the English Crown, 1171–1541', in Crooks (ed.), *Government, War and Society*, 66, citing *Rot. Chart.*, 195; *Rot. Litt. Claus.*, i, 40b. For the 'regnum Hibernie' see also (to 1246) *Expugnatio*, 88 (Dublin as 'regni caput'); *Patent Rolls 1216–25*, 191, 295; *Patent Rolls 1225–32*, 237; *Close Rolls 1231–4*, 103; *Close Rolls 1234–7*, 375; *Close Rolls 1242–7*, 432 (*CDI, 1171–1251*, nos. 286, 489, 872, 997, 1671, 1977, 2356, 2836); *Red Book of the Earls of Kildare*, 51 no. 56 ('custom of the realm').

56 C. T. Veach, 'A Question of Timing: Walter de Lacy's Seisin of Meath 1189–94', *PRIA*, 109 C (2009), 165–94; C. T. Veach, 'King and Magnate in Medieval Ireland: Walter de Lacy, King Richard and King John', *IHS*, 37 (2010), 179–202.

57 H. G. Richardson and G. O. Sayles, *The Administration of Ireland 1172–1377* (Dublin: IMC, 1963), 21–2, 25–31, 42–5. For the emergence of sheriffs, A. J. Otway-Ruthven, 'Anglo-Irish Shire Government in the Thirteenth Century', *IHS*, 5 (1946), 1–28, and literature cited in Crooks (ed.), *Government, War and Society*, 359–60.

first recorded in 1200 and after 1204, John embarked upon a great building programme at Dublin and elsewhere.[58] It was John who encouraged a gold-rush across the Shannon, by speculative awards of land in Connacht, often at the expense of pre-existing native alliances, and it was also John who began the process of playing off one great feudatory against another as a means of establishing his own supremacy as overlord.[59]

Meanwhile, by identifying Ireland as an 'island of tyrants', Gerald had deliberately bracketed it together with Sicily as a land mass placed under papal dominion, deserving conquest by a Christian prince. Yet if such claims could be entertained for Sicily or Ireland, what of the insular land mass imme-diately to the east of Ireland: Britain? Pope Alexander was clearly aware of the difficulty. In his (authentic) letters of 1172 approving Henry's conquest of Ireland, he had deliberately drawn a distinction between papal jurisdiction over islands, and the absence of any such claim over larger land masses, here rather inelegantly described as 'large and continuous land' ('terra magna et continua'). Into this latter category Britain might, or might not, be considered to fall.[60] Hence perhaps the way in which the term 'terra' came to be adopted in official circles to signify what had previously been considered the 'regnum' of Ireland, not least as a means of playing down papal claims to sovereignty. Certainly, it was as a 'terra' or 'land mass' that Henry III granted Ireland to his son, the future Edward I, in 1254.[61]

From all of this Gerald of Wales emerges as at best an only fitfully reli-able, at worst an entirely mendacious chronicler of events.[62] At the same time, even in the opening chapters of his *Expugnatio*, Gerald rehearses themes that were to remain central to Angevin rule in Ireland: the distinc-tion and toxic mistrust between native and invader; the denigration of the

---

58 Richardson and Sayles, *Administration,* 21–2, 42–4; *Rot. Litt. Pat.,* 45b (walls); *Rot. Litt. Claus.,* 6b (castle) (*CDI, 1171–1251,* nos. 226, 228).

59 Duffy, 'John and Ireland', 238–9, and more generally H. Perros, 'Crossing the Shannon Frontier: Connacht and the Anglo-Normans, 1170–1224', in Barry *et al.* (eds.), *Colony and Frontier in Medieval Ireland,* 126–33; P. Crooks, ' "Divide and Rule": Factionalism as Royal Policy in the Lordship of Ireland', *Peritia,* 19 (2005), 263–307.

60 N. Vincent, 'Beyond Becket: King Henry III and the Papacy (1154–1189)', in P. D. Clarke and A. J. Duggan (eds.), *Pope Alexander III (1159–81): The Art of Survival* (Farnham: Ashgate, 2012), 277–81.

61 *Foedera,* i, 270, 297, 308. Earlier, see *CDI, 1171–1251,* nos. 236, 505, 949, 2250, 2252, from *Rot. Litt. Pat.,* 47b (1204, 'potestatem et terram nostram Hibernie'); *Rot. Litt. Claus.,* i, 168 (1214, 'consuetudinem terre nostre Hibernie'); *Foedera,* i, 162 (a convention 'de terra Hibernie', 1220); *Close Rolls 1234–7,* 166–7 (1235, distinguishing English 'regnum' from Irish 'terra').

62 For further distortions by Gerald, see Flanagan, *Irish Society,* 232–3, 253, 266–7, 287, 298–9.

MAP 8. The Angevin Empire, *c*.1175.

native rulers as barbarian 'principes' barely deserving the title of 'king'; the way in which conquest followed an older tradition of trade and commercial exchange, not least in mercenaries; the almost immediate division of the invaders between rival clans of 'Stephanides', 'Geraldines' and 'Clarenses', and the virtual absence for large parts of the story of any direct intervention by England's kings (see Map 8).

The Nature of the Conquest

What then was the nature of the English conquest? Here too we immediately court controversy, not least in the choice of whether to describe this as an 'English' or an 'Anglo-Norman' affair. John Gillingham has deconstructed the myths from which, as recently as the nineteenth century, the adjective 'Anglo-Norman' was forged.[63] Yet even this has done little to dampen Irish enthusiasm for the term. Superficially there were resemblances between the conquests of England in 1066 and Ireland after 1169. Both were followed by wholesale distributions of estates, some of them acquired intact from their previous lords, others newly created. Both conquests were close-run affairs, in their first decades by no means assured of success.[64] As in England after 1066 and to make good their hold over Ireland, the first generation of English lords (Strongbow, Hugh de Lacy, William de Burgh) not only sought marriage to the daughters of native Irish kings but chose burial in Irish rather than English soil, Strongbow in Dublin, Hugh de Lacy, after a protracted process of translation and dispersal of his bones, in both Meath and Dublin.[65] To both England and Ireland, the conquerors brought many of the outward trappings of francophone aristocratic culture: an obsession with hunting, with the establishment of legally defined forests and deer parks, and the importation of fallow deer (ultimately from Sicily), rabbits, pheasants and other zoological exotica.[66] What the Normans achieved in England with Caen stone, adding a deliberately Norman garnish to

---

63 J. Gillingham, 'Normanizing the English Invaders of Ireland', in H. Pryce and J. Watts (eds.), *Power and Identity in the Middle Ages: Essays in Memory of Rees Davies* (Oxford University Press, 2007), 85–97.

64 Compare R. Fleming, *Kings and Lords in Conquest England* (Cambridge University Press, 1991), with MacCotter, *Medieval Ireland*; Duffy, 'John and Ireland', 226–7.

65 Marriages: G. Kenny, 'Anglo-Irish and Gaelic Marriage Laws and Traditions in Late Medieval Ireland', *JMH*, 32 (2006), 27–42; F. Verstraten Veach, 'Anglicization in Medieval Ireland: Was there a Gaelic Irish "Middle Nation"?', in Duffy and Foran (eds.), *English Isles*, 118–38, esp. 131–3, 138. Burial: *Expugnatio*, 166 (Strongbow); *Chartul. St Mary's, Dublin*, ii, 221, 276, 304, 307, 314 (Meiler fitz Henry, Hugh de Lacy, Strongbow); *Reg. St Thomas*, 348–50 no. 393 (Hugh de Lacy), and for context cf. B. Golding, 'Anglo-Norman Knightly Burials', in C. Harper-Bill and R. Harvey (eds.), *The Ideals and Practice of Medieval Knighthood* (Woodbridge: Boydell Press, 1986), 35–48.

66 Compare F. Beglane, *Anglo-Norman Parks in Medieval Ireland* (Dublin: Four Courts Press, 2015) with N. Sykes, 'Zooarchaeology of the Norman Conquest', *ANS*, 27 (2005), 185–97. For pheasants, apparently unknown in Ireland before 1169, see *Gir. Camb. Op.*, v, 56; *IPR 14 John*, 32 (also rabbits), and cf. *COD*, i, 3–4 no. 7 (hunting), 364–5 no. 863/1 (warrens); Murphy and Potterton, *Dublin Region in the Middle Ages*, 342–5, 376–80 (warrens and forests).

their newly built public monuments, the English in Ireland achieved with stone transported from Dundry near Bristol.[67]

Thanks to the Norse kings, pre-conquest Dublin already had stone walls, and Waterford the fortification known as Reginald's Tower.[68] Even so, and with the exception of round towers and such self-consciously imperial experiments as Cormac's chapel at Cashel, the conquerors of Ireland would have remarked the scarcity of building in anything save wood. According to St Bernard's 'Life of Malachy', the Irish considered Malachy's stone-built church at Down a distinctly 'French' innovation, best avoided. A monk of St Mary's, Dublin, dispatched in the 1170s to spy out a site at Dunbrody (County Wexford) granted by Hervey de Montmorency, found shelter there in a hollow oak tree, amidst a 'vast solitude' inhabited by 'wild and ferocious barbarians'.[69] For his Christmas court of 1171, Henry II was accommodated in a wooden hall constructed by his new Irish subjects, perhaps reflecting an older Irish tradition of such halls of counsel and feasting, deliberately built outside the walls of Dublin on the site where the Norse Thingmoot or public assembly had met. Thereafter, the rebuilding of Dublin Castle, in stone and at considerable expense, constituted a deliberate display of magnificence.[70] So, in general, did the campaign of castle building encouraged by King John, not least at Limerick and Athlone.[71] It is no coincidence that an image of Dublin Castle, defended by crossbowmen and with the impaled heads of (Irish) felons above its gate, was chosen c.1229 for the obverse of Dublin's city seal. The reverse showed a ship in full sail: a reminder both of the life-lines that continued

---

67 D. M. Waterman, 'Somersetshire and Other Foreign Building Stone in Medieval Ireland, c.1175–1400', *Ulster Journal of Archaeology*, 33 (1970), 63–75, at 72 noting an isolated use of Caen stone at Mellifont.

68 A. Thomas, *The Walled Towns of Ireland*, 2 vols. (Dublin: Irish Academic Press 1992), i, 151, ii, 86, 204, 212; *Expugnatio*, 66, 92, 140. For a semi-mythical account of Reginald's Tower, used in 1171 to fasten an iron boom across Waterford harbour, see A. Bugge, 'Nordisk-Sprog og Nordisk Nationalitet i Ireland', *Aarboger for Nordisk Oldkyndighed og Historie*, 2nd series 15 (Copenhagen, 1900), 329–31.

69 Bernard, 'Vita S. Malachiae' c.28, in *PL*, 182, cols. 1108–10 ('Scoti sumus, non Galli'), and for wooden churches, *ibid*. c.6.14, in *PL*, 182, col. 1083 ('opus Scoticum'); *Chartul. St Mary's, Dublin*, i, 354–7 no. 289, and cf. Davies, *First English Empire*, 119.

70 Flanagan, *Irish Society*, 200–7; S. Duffy, 'Ireland's Hastings: The Anglo-Norman Conquest of Dublin', *ANS*, 20 (1998), 81–5; Duffy, 'Town and Crown', 102; T. O'Keeffe, 'Dublin Castle's Donjon in Context', in J. Bradley, A. J. Fletcher and A. Simms (eds.), *Dublin in the Medieval World: Studies in Honour of Howard B. Clarke* (Dublin: Four Courts Press, 2009), 277–94; J. Lydon, 'Dublin Castle in the Middle Ages', in S. Duffy (ed.), *Medieval Dublin III* (Dublin: Four Courts Press, 2002), 115–27.

71 For Athlone, site of a native (wooden) castle and bridge, Perros, 'Crossing the Shannon Frontier', 117, 132–3; Duffy, 'John and Ireland', 235–6.

to connect the English colonists to their homelands, and of their essential insecurity.[72]

In 1200 and again in 1215, King John is to be found warning the lords of the Irish March they must fortify their estates on pain of confiscation. There are shades here of the law of Norman and later French-occupied Sicily, where fees and castles were forfeit to the crown after a year of non-occupancy.[73] In 1204, John commanded his justiciar to 'strengthen castles, found towns and assess rents'. By such means, and at enormous expense, the settlers established medieval ancestors to the Forts Augustus, George, Henry and William of Hanoverian Scotland or Ontario.[74]

As acts of private enterprise, towns such as Kilkenny and Drogheda were newly enclosed, each within sites of 43 hectares, more than twice the size of Dublin. By the end of Henry III's reign, the corporation of a borough such as Drogheda was superficially indistinguishable from its equivalents in Britain.[75] All of this suggests optimism on behalf of the conquerors, albeit optimism tinged with caution. Like frontier towns the world over, the Irish boroughs were segregated between settler and native quarters, at Kilkenny divided between an 'Irishtown' and an Anglo-Norman 'Hightown'.[76] It is perhaps no coincidence that Ireland boasts only two extended verse compositions written in the French language of its conquerors: the 3,457-line 'Song of Dermot', and the 218-line 'Walling of New Ross'. The first tells of pillage and mass slaughter; the second of attempts to protect an immigrant population against the feuding of settler elites happy to employ a native enemy rumoured 40,000 strong.[77]

To pay for consolidation, as in England after 1066, the conquerors turned to a combination of credit and plunder. Just as the Jews were introduced to

---

72 Duffy, 'Ireland's Hastings', 69–75.
73 *Rot. Chart.*, 98b–99; *Rot. Litt. Claus.*, i, 218b (*CDI, 1171–1251*, nos. 125, 574); J. Dunbabin, *The French in the Kingdom of Sicily, 1266–1305* (Cambridge University Press, 2011), 108, 167–8.
74 *Foedera*, i, 91 (*CDI, 1171–1251*, no. 222); For the costs of Limerick castle, noting £734 in the year 1211–12, see *IPR 14 John*, 68; K. Wiggins, *A Place of Great Consequence: Archaeological Excavations at King John's Castle, Limerick, 1990–98* (Bray: Wordwell, 2016), 3–4.
75 Thomas, *Walled Towns*, i, 39; C. Buldorini, 'The Mayors, Provosts and Bailiffs of Drogheda in the Thirteenth Century', *County Louth Archaeological and Historical Journal*, 27 (2009), 26–38; E. W. Eggerer, 'The Guild Merchant of Dublin', in S. Duffy (ed.), *Medieval Dublin VI* (Dublin: Four Courts Press, 2005), 144–9, and the precociously detailed *Dublin Guild Merchant Roll*.
76 A. Simms, 'Unity in Diversity: A Comparative Analysis of Thirteenth-Century Kilkenny, Kalkar and Sopron', in Duffy (ed.), *Princes, Prelates and Poets*, 107–23, esp. 108–9.
77 The Walling of New Ross: A Thirteenth-Century Poem in French', ed. H. Shields, *The Long Room*, 12–13 (1975–6), 24–33, esp. p. 31 lines 162–7, and cf. Thomas, *Walled Towns*, i, 39, noting an enclosed area at New Ross of 39 hectares.

England after 1066, so both Jewish and Christian financiers backed the conquest of 1169, not least Robert fitz Harding of Bristol, already in the 1150s a significant investor in Henry II's bid for the throne of England.[78] Bristol remained central to Ireland's resettlement and trade, with Dublin itself ceded to the king's men of Bristol as a colonial outpost.[79] In much the same way, in the Holy Land, the merchants of Pisa and Genoa had obtained their own quarters and a stranglehold over the trade of the newly re-Christianised cities of Acre and Damietta. It has nonetheless gone unremarked that Bristol in the 1170s lay under the authority not of the king but of William, earl of Gloucester. Only a small minority of Bristolians lived as tenants of Henry II and Robert fitz Harding, in somewhat murky circumstances, on the Somerset side of the Avon. Their acquisition of Dublin may have played no small part in alienating William, earl of Gloucester, considered untrustworthy and therefore threatened with imprisonment during the great rebellion against Henry II in 1173–4. This in turn may explain the arrangement of 1176, whereby Earl William was obliged to marry off Isabella, his eldest daughter, to John, the king's son, now promised not only Ireland but Bristol and the lion's share of the Gloucester estate, in effect disinheriting William's two younger daughters.[80]

As with the rivalry between Pisa, Genoa and Venice, Bristol was in due course obliged to compete with Chester for Irish trade.[81] In the meantime, we must assume that Bristol's ships were as crucial to the military operations of 1169–71 as the fleet of Venice proved to Constantinople and the Fourth Crusade. Two Bristolians, Aelelm brother of Hamund, and Ailward 'the young', were amongst the earliest recipients of royal charters in Ireland, granted property before 1177 in Dublin and Waterford. Two others, the brothers Robert and John L'Evesque, acquired an extensive estate in Dublin, Waterford and Cork, specifically as commanders of Strongbow's ships and shipmen.[82]

---

78 For Josce Jew of Gloucester, fined 100s. for lending money to the conquerors against the king's prohibition, PR 16 Henry II, 78. For Robert fitz Harding, Deeds of the Normans, 59–61 lines 232–7, 300–11, and R. B. Patterson, 'Robert fitz Harding of Bristol', HSJ, 1 (1989), 109–22; Flanagan, Irish Society, 116–17. For the Irish Jewry in 1232, Cal. Chart. R. 1226–57, 166–7; Close Rolls 1231–4, 102 (CDI, 1171–1251, nos. 1969, 1976).

79 Letters Henry II, no. 313, and more generally, A. Gwynn, 'Medieval Bristol and Dublin', IHS, 5 (1946–7), 275–86; G. O'Keeffe, 'The Merchant Conquistadors: Medieval Bristolians in Dublin', in S. Duffy (ed.), Medieval Dublin XIII (Dublin: Four Courts Press, 2013), 116–38; Duffy, 'Town and Crown', 100–2.

80 Letters Henry II, nos. 311–12; Patterson, 'Bristol', 174–7; Howden, Gesta, i, 124–5, 294.

81 Letters Henry II, no. 583, confirmed after 1189 by John as lord of Ireland: Chester, City Archives CH/2–3.

82 Letters Henry II, nos. 309–10; London, College of Arms ms. Vincent 59 pp. 122–3 ('magistratum totius marinagii et marinauorum meorum'); The Hungerford Cartulary, ed.

Although we have no Bayeux Tapestry for Ireland to portray the logistics of ships and ship-building, the Irish adventure involved a series of fleets, the greatest of them sufficient to transport the 500 knights with whom Henry II crossed in 1171.[83] The costs here must have been enormous. Even the limited Pipe Roll evidence for 1171–2 refers to at least 95 master mariners sent to Ireland and more than 1,000 sailors. Through to 1199, indeed, the costs of shipping represent virtually the only indication in the exchequer records that the king had any interests across the Irish Sea.[84] When King John sailed for Ireland in 1210, his fleet of at least 500 ships cost in excess of £3,800.[85] Thereafter, Ireland remained a maritime colony. Both the *Expugnatio* and the 'Song of Dermot' are shot through with references to the sea, with the 'Song' describing at least twenty-six distinct sea-crossings between Ireland, England, Wales, Normandy and Norway, using the verb 'to cross overseas' ('passer') no less than thirty-one times. Maritime vocabulary is ubiquitous here: 'mer', makes at least twenty-five appearances, while 'batel', 'eskipa', 'eschippés', 'marine', 'navire', 'nef', 'port', 'siglant', 'undes', 'mestre notimer' also feature. Appropriately, the 'Song' breaks off incomplete, with the Anglo-Norman verb 'neer': 'to drown'.[86]

Medieval kings made poor accountants. Their calculation of financial profit and loss was trumped by considerations of status and triumph. Whatever England's kings knew of Ireland before 1171 can hardly have encouraged them to expect prosperity. On the contrary, had they consulted William of Malmesbury, they would have read of Ireland's poor soil, unskilled labour and general poverty. The reality was not so squalid. Yet neither was it so prosperous as England on the eve of the conquest of 1066.[87] As in England after 1066, what there was to plunder, the invaders seized. As with England, this included treasures: books, relics and plate. More generally, it involved the pillage of natural resources. Hence the use of Irish oak, after 1200, in the rebuilding of Exeter, Salisbury and Winchester cathedrals, cut from forests

J. L. Kirby (Trowbridge: Wiltshire Record Society, 2007), 50–2 nos. 1171 80. For further examples, Frame, *Ireland and Britain*, 42–4.

83 For the relative size of the invasion forces, *Expugnatio*, 30, 50, 64, 92. The *Deeds of the Normans*, 64, 119, offers figures of 300 for Robert fitz Stephen and 4,000 for Henry II, including 400 knights.

84 *CDI, 1171–1251*, nos. 1, 2, 7–16, 20–1, 27–9, 31–2, 34–5, 40, 45, 62, 66, 72, 74, 76, 81, 83.

85 S. D. Church, 'The 1210 Campaign in Ireland: Evidence for a Military Revolution?', *ANS*, 20 (1998), 48, 51, suggesting 700 ships. Cf. the 60 ships of John's 1185 expedition (*AFM*, iii, 67; *ALC*, i, 171) and the 100 said to have been recruited for John de Courcy's 1205 bid to recover Ulster: *Cronica regum Mannie et Insularum*, ed. G. Broderick (Belfast: Manx Museum and National Trust, 1979), fo. 41r, specifying 500 ships for John in 1210.

86 *Deeds of the Normans, passim.*

87 William of Malmesbury, *Gesta Regum*, i, 738–40; B. Hudson, 'The Changing Economy of the Irish Sea Province', in Smith (ed.), *Britain and Ireland*, 39–66.

where the tallest trees, long felled in England, continued to grow.[88] There were echoes here of Geoffrey of Monmouth's report of the (entirely mythical) conquest of Ireland by King Arthur, preceded by the pillage and the transfer to Salisbury Plain of Stonehenge, imagined as the greatest of Irish stone circles.[89] Hawks were another prized resource. Rents payable in falcons are a regular feature of elite charters in Ireland after 1169, and for kings Henry II and John, both of them notorious devotees of falconry, there must have been a peculiar satisfaction in acquiring a land so rich both in raptors and their prey, not least the cranes (largest and most aggressive of the birds against which falcons were flown) on whose flesh Henry and his court feasted in Dublin at Christmas 1171.[90] We may scoff at Gerald's inventory of the native 'wonders' of Ireland; his listing of geese generated from barnacles, and bursting toads.[91] At the time, however, these were precisely the details that any conquering king would have been most anxious to learn.

From Conquest to Consolidation

In both England and Ireland, the euphoria of conquest preceded the more difficult business of consolidation. Both England and Ireland inspired Domesday surveys, England in 1086 still extant, Ireland in unknown circumstances, in a book of evidences burned before 1281 in one of the first of many losses to the Irish public records.[92] And here, appropriately enough, the distinctions between conquests begin to preponderate. England before 1066 was already a rich land, with Roman roads, many market towns, established laws, a

---

88 Information Michael Baillie and Warwick Rodwell, and cf. Murphy and Potterton, *Dublin Region in the Middle Ages*, 375–6. For Winchester, *IPR 14 John*, 16, and for the timber trade more generally, Flanagan, *Irish Society*, 48–9n.; Hudson, 'Changing Economy', 59; O'Neill, *Merchants and Mariners*, 99–102. For Irish planking used for the king's ships in 1215, *Rot. Litt. Claus.*, i, 183.

89 For Stonehenge, Geoffrey of Monmouth, *History of the Kings of Britain*, 170–5, whence Wace, *Roman de Brut*, ed. J. Weiss (University of Exeter Press, 1999), 203–7; Henry of Huntingdon, *Historia Anglorum*, ed. D. E. Greenway (Oxford University Press, 1996), 22, 576–7; *Gir. Camb. Op.*, v, 100–1; Paris, *CM*, i, 222–3.

90 *Gir. Camb. Op.*, v, 21, 34–47, 56; *Expugnatio*, 96 (crane flesh), and more generally O'Neill, *Merchants and Mariners*, 102–3; O'Brien, 'Commercial Relations', 39. For rents payable in hawks, *Letters Henry II*, no. 686 (tribute to Henry II payable in hawks and hounds); *Chartul. St Mary's, Dublin*, i, 223; *Rep. DKI*, 23 (1891), app. 3 no. 469; *Rot. Chart.*, 69; *CDF*, no. 112.

91 'Topographia' (I–II), in *Gir. Camb. Op.*, v, esp. pp. 47–9 (barnacle geese), 63 (bursting toads).

92 *CDI, 1252–1284*, no. 1879, and cf. the enfeoffments in Leinster and Meath listed in *Deeds of the Normans*, 131–5. For the destruction of a large part of the Irish chancery archive in a fire at St Mary's Dublin in 1304, see Frame, 'Rediscovering Medieval Ireland', 195.

manorial landscape maintained by generations of peasant labourers, and a bureaucracy, primitive by modern standards yet more sophisticated than anything to be found by 1066 north of the Alps. The vast capital released by conquest not only paid for a programme of cathedral and castle building, but transformed the economy of the conquerors' homeland in Normandy. In so far as England and Normandy could be compared on the eve of conquest, both were prosperous polities, England richer yet perhaps lagging behind Normandy in terms of courtesy and French polish.

Not so Ireland in the 1170s. On the contrary, the conquerors who arrived at Bannow Bay in 1169, let alone those who later crossed the Shannon or the Boyne, found themselves time-travellers to an Iron Age, closer to the world of Bede than to that of Chrétien de Troyes. In so far as the Irish Church had in the past fifty years undergone reform with the cooperation of Irish kings, it resembled the Wessex of King Edgar and tenth-century monasticism. Yet even the England of King Edgar was both monetised and manorialised. Not so Ireland. The division of Ireland between natives and Ostmen, between the north and west and the viking towns of the south and east, mirrored pre-conquest England's division between Danelaw and West Saxon hegemony. Yet even here, Wessex possessed an urban and administrative sophistication unknown in Ireland.

Most significantly perhaps, where in England the wealth of the defeated aristocracy could be easily plundered, Ireland, although in many ways a rich land, offered fewer easy pickings. Any conqueror wishing to prosper here would need to invest heavily before rewards could be reaped. Labour had to be imported from England, Wales or Galloway. Land had to be brought under cultivation. Castles, barns and mills had to be constructed, roads improved, timber felled, fields drained, ships built to export the resulting produce. And all of this against a backdrop of ongoing hostilities, with a native population never entirely pacified. As late as the 1230s, siren voices from Ireland promised King Henry III untold wealth: £20,000 of confiscated land, a new city in every cantred of Connacht, and 'greater and better rewards in Ireland than you or your father ever obtained'.[93] In a rare fit of common sense, the king refused this bait.

From the beginning, Ireland's conquerors were aware of difference. Their insecurities, first voiced by Gerald of Wales, were never entirely laid to rest. Scattered evidence from the English Pipe Rolls for 1171–2 suggests awareness, derived from Bede and his successors, that Ireland was a land of meat rather

---

93 Sayles, *Affairs*, 2–3 no. 3.

than cereals. Hence not just the supply of corn but of more than fifty hand mills, roughly three per English county, to accompany the king's expeditionary force.[94] Watermills at Waterford, built by the Ostmen, were amongst the first resources redistributed by King Henry following his arrival in Ireland. By 1200, the lowland areas of Leinster and Meath were fast being transformed into a bread-basket for the export of grain. With Bristol (and later Chester) as its Ostia, Ireland was prepared for a role not dissimilar to that of Sicily or North Africa in the affairs of imperial Rome.[95] Gerald of Wales drew particular attention to the problems of communication and transport, not least to the dangers of a pre-Roman road system. Responsibility for roads (already being described as 'via regia' as early as c.1213) and for clearing their hinterland of timber and robbers, represented one of the earliest exercises of Plantagenet public authority in Ireland, recommended by Gerald and taken up by Henry II and his successors in the prosecution of robbery.[96] The public gallows, on the banks of the Liffey, close to the Parkgate Street entrance to Phoenix Park, was already a Dublin landmark as early as the 1170s.[97] Yet even Dublin, that most anglicised of Irish cities, lay in the shadow of the nest of banditry that was the Wicklow hills. The site of William Marshal's Cistercian abbey at Duiske (Graiguenamanagh) on the Barrow south of Kilkenny, today an arcadian backwater, was described by the English-born bishop of Ossory c.1207 as 'a place of horror and vast solitude, a cave of robbers and the lair of those who lie in wait for blood'. Too much land was vulnerable to raiding and reseizure, whether by natives or by rival settlers.[98]

To secure conquered territory, as in England after 1066, there was a deliberate division of Ireland into honours and knights' fees. Yet here too there were peculiarities. Henry II's 'conquest' of Ireland was achieved following negotiations with Strongbow and native Irish kings, without any great battle. At Hastings in 1066, by contrast, a large part of the old Anglo-Saxon aristocracy had been not just defeated but slaughtered. Hastings was followed

---

94 *PR 17 Henry II*, 2, 12, 19, 34–5, 53, 82, 84, 91, 96, 113, 119, 131, 139, 148 (cf. *CDI, 1171–1251*, nos. 1, 2, 6–16).

95 *Letters Henry II*, no. 1378 (*CDI, 1171–1251*, no. 666); Hudson, 'Changing Economy', 58–9; O'Neill, *Merchants and Mariners*, 20–9; K. Down, 'Colonial Society and Economy in the High Middle Ages', *NHI* ii, 439–91.

96 *Expugnatio*, 240, 250, and for the pre-Conquest 'road' system, A. P. Smyth, *Celtic Leinster* (Dublin: Irish Academic Press, 1982). For 'via regia' at Dublin, *Chartul. St Mary's, Dublin*, i, 248–9 no. 238. For the earliest recorded criminal proceedings at Dublin (c.1192–4), see *Rotuli Curiae Regis*, ed. F. Palgrave, 2 vols. (London: Record Commission, 1835), i, 172–3 (*CDI, 1171–1251*, no. 116). For bridges and lighthouses, O'Keeffe, *Medieval Irish Buildings*, 61.

97 A. E. J. Went, 'Fisheries of the River Liffey', *JRSAI*, 83 (1953), 163–5.

98 'The Charters of the Cistercian Abbey of Duiske', ed. J. H. Bernard and C. M. Butler, *PRIA*, 35 C (1918), 23–5 no. 6 (with echoes of Deuteronomy 32:10; Jeremiah 7:11; Ezechiel 32:25); K. W. Nicholls, 'Anglo-French Ireland and After', *Peritia*, 1 (1982), 371–3.

immediately by the coronation of William I as king of England, and thereafter by a territorial and cultural revolution in which the Conqueror ruled, in theory at least, as overlord of every acre of English land, gaining far greater wealth from England than he had ever possessed as duke of Normandy. There was to be nothing like this in Ireland. Whereas in England the king was ultimate overlord of at least 3,600 men ranked as knights, Ireland owed only 425 knights' fees to the crown. Irish fees were far larger in terms of acreage (as in Normandy), and concentrated in the hands of a far smaller number of barons than their English equivalents. These barons controlled liberties more extensive than anything that existed in England by the 1170s beyond the very greatest of earldoms (Chester, Cornwall and a handful of others). In England, the Church supplied a high proportion of knights, and hence of taxation in lieu of military service. In Ireland, the Church was more or less exempt from either knight service or scutage.[99]

Moreover, whereas England enjoyed both a 'second (and even a "third") century of feudalism', in which military service was increasingly compounded into fiscal and administrative obligation, no such transformation was achieved in medieval Ireland. Here military service remained military. Power remained concentrated in the hands of a small feudal elite, never more than a dozen or so in number. These great men, in turn, commanded military followings that, although newly implanted, swiftly took on many of the attributes of native Irish lordship.[100] After 1200, few outsiders had either the ability or the inclination to break into this close-knit and closely intermarried elite. Ireland itself remained fractured between those parts drawn to the rival British regions of Severnside, Wales, Cumbria or Galloway, with no single inland frontier and with warfare endemic amongst both natives and settlers. Its colonists were themselves drawn from particular parts of England: Welsh and Wiltshire men in Leinster, Cumbrians and Somerset men in John de Courcy's Ulster, and so forth.[101]

---

99 Compare A. J. Otway-Ruthven, 'Knight Service in Ireland', and 'Royal Service in Ireland', in Crooks (ed.), *Government, War and Society*, 155–68 and 169–76, with K. Faulkner, 'The Transformation of Knighthood in Early Thirteenth-Century England', *EHR*, 111 (1996), 1–23; P. R. Coss, *The Origins of the English Gentry* (Cambridge University Press, 2003), esp. 90–2.

100 E. Curtis, 'The Clan System Among English Settlers in Ireland', in Crooks (ed.), *Government, War and Society*, 297–301, and literature cited by Crooks at 368–9; R. Frame, 'Military Service in the Lordship of Ireland 1290–1360: Institutions and Society on the Anglo-Gaelic Frontier', and K. Simms, 'Bards and Barons: The Anglo-Irish Aristocracy and the Native Culture', in Bartlett and Mackay (eds.), *Medieval Frontier Societies*, 101–26, 177–97.

101 R. R. Davies, 'Frontier Arrangements in Fragmented Societies: Ireland and Wales', in Bartlett and Mackay (eds.), *Medieval Frontier Societies*, 77–100; S. Duffy, 'The 1169 Invasion as a Turning-Point in Irish–Welsh Relations', in Smith (ed.), *Britain and Ireland*, 98–113; S. Duffy, 'The First Ulster Plantation: John de Courcy and the Men of Cumbria', in Barry *et al.* (eds.), *Colony and Frontier in Medieval Ireland*, 1–28.

Acknowledging the contrasts with England after 1066, historians of post-conquest Ireland have sought to draw comparisons not so much with England as with Norman Sicily.[102] In the sense that the Sicilian venture was a do-it-yourself affair, conducted by Norman adventurers only loosely attached to a dynasty of kings, the comparisons are worth pursuing. Even so, the differences between Sicily and Ireland remain formidable. Sicily and southern Italy were wealthy Mediterranean provinces, former parts of the Roman empire, already a melting pot of cultures, Greek and Latin, Arabic and Italian, ruled by their own resident dynasties of Norman, later Germano-Norman princes. Ireland, by contrast, was virtually never visited by its English kings, who spent less than twenty months there in the 223 years between 1171 and Richard II's return in 1394. A painting commissioned for Dublin Castle in 1243, beneath a rose window 30 feet wide, portrayed King Henry III and his Queen seated amongst their barons. This, however, showed aspiration rather than reality.[103]

In the sense that Ireland remained a land never fully conquered, comparisons could be drawn between the English in Ireland and the crusader lords of the Holy Land after 1099. Certainly, Ireland's pattern of castles and settlement, the use of rural townships, and the ever-present tension between an outnumbered settler population and a far larger indigenous majority might encourage thoughts of the Franks in Outremer.[104] Twelfth-century writers on Ireland, including Gerald of Wales, imbibed far more from the tradition of crusader narrative than has sometimes been acknowledged. Indeed, Henry II's failure to prevent the fall of Jerusalem in 1187 was an event central to Gerald's account of what went wrong for the king in Ireland.[105] Even the French verse 'Walling of New Ross' (c.1265) could be usefully compared with crusader texts such as the 'De Constructione castri Saphet' (c.1260).[106]

---

102 It is not without interest that Edmund Curtis's first book was on *Roger of Sicily and the Normans in Lower Italy, 1016–1154* (London: G.P. Putnam and Sons, 1912).

103 *Close Rolls 1242–7*, 23 (*CDI, 1171–1251*, no. 2612).

104 Compare J. Riley-Smith, 'Peace Never Established: The Case of the Kingdom of Jerusalem', *TRHS*, 5th series 28 (1978), 87–102; R. Ellenblum, *Frankish Rural Settlement in the Latin Kingdom of Jerusalem* (Cambridge University Press, 1998); R. Ellenblum, *Crusader Castles and Modern Historians* (Cambridge University Press, 2007); C. MacEvitt, *The Crusades and the Christian World of the East* (Philadelphia: University of Pennsylvania Press, 2008).

105 G. Heng, *Empire of Magic: Medieval Romance and the Politics of Cultural Fantasy* (New York: Columbia University Press, 2003); *Expugnatio*, 202–8.

106 For which, see H. Kennedy, *Crusader Castles* (Cambridge University Press, 1994), 190–8, 210–11.

Dublin's round donjon, commanded by King John in 1204, was built according to a pattern derived ultimately from the Holy Sepulchre in Jerusalem.[107] Yet Dublin was no Holy City. Nor was post-conquest Ireland ever the focus of international hopes and fears in the way that the crusader states continued to encourage eschatological expectations, and an influx of warriors, into the 1270s and beyond.

Perhaps at the very beginning of England's Irish adventure there were thoughts of using the rhetoric of Holy War, as in Spain or the Holy Land.[108] St Bernard's Life of Malachy had castigated the native Irish as 'uncouth barbarians' ('inculta … barbaries'): 'pagans at heart' ruled (in the words of the Book of Job) by 'dragons and ostriches'.[109] Deliberate echoes of this language are to be found in the letters of Pope Alexander III issued in response to Henry's invasion of 1171, congratulating Henry on bringing law to 'that barbarous and uncouth people' ('gentem illam barbaram incultam').[110] At least one of the English invaders, Miles de Cogan, is said to have urged his men on to fight 'in the name of the Cross'. Most remarkably of all, Gervase of Tilbury, writing forty or so years later, chose to present Henry's conquest as a story of forced conversion, raising Ireland from virtual paganism to Christian understanding: 'The last country to adopt the true religion, and then only under compulsion.'[111]

Had Henry II and his successors fought in Ireland with the ruthlessness and religious fervour of the crusaders in Palestine, the Teutonic knights in the Baltic, or indeed of Cromwell and his New Model Army after 1649, then the conquest might have been more bitter yet more complete. The introduction of the Templars and the Hospitallers to Ireland by both Henry II and Strongbow suggests a desire not only to reward the military orders but to capitalise on their experience of frontier lordship. Certainly, the first few years of occupancy witnessed slaughter on a scale unknown in England since the 1070s. The 3,457 lines of the 'Song of Dermot', for example, report more than

---

107 O'Keeffe, 'Dublin Castle's Donjon', 293–4.
108 As argued by M. Sheehy, *When the Normans Came to Ireland* (Cork: Mercier Press, 1998), 23–5, assuming the authenticity of *Laudabiliter*, but also stressing Alexander III's injunction to Henry (*Pontificia Hibernica*, i, 22 no. 5) that 'in remissionem tibi peccatorum … in eo quod laudabiliter incepisti … gentem illam ad cultum Christiane fidei per potentiam tuam reuoces'.
109 'Vita S. Malachiae' cc. 1, 8, 25, 27, in *PL*, 182, cols. 1075, 1084, 1105, 1108 (citing Job 30:29).
110 *Pontificia Hibernica*, i, 19 no. 5 ('gentem illam barbaram, incultam et diuine legis ignarem'), 21 no. 6 ('gentem incultam et indisciplinatam'), in turn echoed in the accounts both by Gerald (*Gir. Camb. Op.*, v, 178, 'gens nostra barbara nimis et inculta') and by Newburgh, 'Chronica', i, 166 ('populos … incultos et barbaros').
111 *Deeds of the Normans*, 102 (l. 1922); Gervase of Tilbury, *Otia Imperialia*, ed. S. E. Banks and J. W. Binns (Oxford University Press, 2002), 308–9.

4,988 deaths. Fewer than thirty of these were of English as opposed to native warriors.[112] Yet, as was widely acknowledged, and whatever their divergence from European norms, the Irish were a Christian people deserving mercy and correction rather than extermination and the sword.

During his Irish expedition of 1210, King John issued a charter commanding that the English in Ireland were to be governed by English law and custom. His intention was to strengthen the crown's control over judicial process and to prevent the greater lords from establishing their own assizes for Ireland, independent of royal authority. His charter is known only from hearsay, from 1226 onwards.[113] Had it survived, it might today be celebrated as a land-mark on the road to Magna Carta and the rule of law. Instead, it has become notorious as the origin of that apartheid between settlers and natives which ensured, by the 1290s, that an Englishman convicted of killing an Irishman was to be punished, not as a felon, but with a fine of a mere £3 10s.[114] Such segregation was perhaps not the charter's primary purpose. As with papal legislation governing relations between Christians and Jews, the intention may have been to respect Irish (cf. Jewish) legal tradition rather than to favour the English settlers. In both cases, whatever the intention, the outcome was stigma and resentment.[115]

Pre-conquest Ireland already recognised a distinction between free and unfree, just as under English common law, villeins, Jews, and in many instances women, were disbarred from pleading.[116] Similar restrictions applied to Christians and Jews living throughout the Islamic world, and across Christendom, especially in places such as Sicily or the Holy Land, in laws by which a Catholic elite was set apart from Muslims, Jews or non-Catholic Christians.[117] Certainly, similarities could be drawn between the protected sta-tus of the Ostman minority in Ireland, ghettoised and placed directly under

---

112 Browne and Ó Clabaigh (eds.), *Soldiers of Christ*; *Letters Henry II*, no. 1378; *Deeds of the Normans*, *passim*.

113 Hand, *English Law*, significantly modified by P. Brand, 'Ireland and the Literature of the Early Common Law', *Irish Jurist*, 16 (1981), 95–113, and cf. *Rot. Litt. Pat.*, 72 (*CDI, 1171–1251*, no. 329).

114 A. J. Otway-Ruthven, 'The Native Irish and English Law in Medieval Ireland', in Crooks (ed.), *Government, War and Society*, 141–54; Hand, *English Law*, 201–4.

115 Brand, 'Ireland', 96 n. 9, and cf. H. G. Richardson, 'English Institutions in Medieval Ireland', *IHS*, 1 (1939), 386–91. Cf. N. Vincent, 'Two Papal Letters on the Wearing of the Jewish Badge, 1221 and 1229', *Jewish Historical Studies*, 24 (1997), 209–24.

116 Flanagan, *Irish Society*, 183–6, and cf. Simms, *From Kings to Warlords*, 96, 100–1.

117 For Jews under Christian and Islamic law, M. R. Cohen, *Under Crescent and Cross: The Jews in the Middle Ages* (Princeton University Press, 1994). For Sicily, D. Matthew, *The Norman Kingdom of Sicily* (Cambridge University Press, 1992), 87–97, 251. For the Holy Land, J. Prawer, *Crusader Institutions* (Oxford University Press, 1980), esp. 201–14.

the crown's authority, and the protected status of England's Jews.[118] In the same way, prohibitions against the sale of arms to Irishmen followed in the tradition of papal legislation, from the 1160s onwards, forbidding arms sales to Saracens.[119] Not surprisingly, such precedents have done little to discourage the modern perception of John's 1210 legislation as precursor to the seventeenth-century penal laws: a cruel imposition upon a subject people, transforming law itself from a protection into an instrument of personalised discrimination.

Ireland's Impact upon England

We might expect the Christianity of the Irish to have protected them against the degradation elsewhere of pagans or infidels. Certainly, Ireland's fame as an island of saints had long attracted notice across the Irish Sea.[120] Henry of Sawtry (*c*.1180) was the first English reporter on St Patrick's Purgatory on Lough Derg, in an account that survives in more than fifty manuscripts, with truly international circulation.[121] Within twenty years, however, Peter of Cornwall, prior of Holy Trinity London, was writing of Loch Derg as a place of punishment and suffering: a pilgrimage destination of declining popularity, threatened by civil disorder, overtaken by more fashionable resorts such as Rome or Jerusalem. By the 1230s, recycling Henry of Sawtry, Matthew Paris transposed Patrick's Purgatory from a specifically Irish to a vaguely otherworldly setting.[122]

---

118   E. Curtis, 'The English and Ostmen in Ireland', in Crooks (ed.), *Government, War and Society*, 287–96; E. Purcell, 'The Expulsion of the Ostmen, 1169–1171: The Documentary Evidence', *Peritia*, 17–18 (2003–4), 276–94, and literature cited by Crooks (ed.), *Government, War and Society*, 368.

119   Cf. D. M. Freidenreich, 'Muslims in Western Canon Law, 1000–1500', *Christian–Muslim Relations: A Bibliographical History Volume 3 (1050–1200)*, ed. D. Thomas and A. Mallett (Leiden: Brill, 2011), 46–8.

120   J.-M. Picard, 'Early Contacts between Ireland and Normandy: The Cult of Irish Saints in Normandy before the Conquest', in M. Richter and J. M. Picard (eds.), *Ogma: Essays in Celtic Studies in Honour of Próinséas Ní Chatháin* (Dublin: Four Courts Press, 2002), 85–93; Henry of Huntingdon, *Historia Anglorum*, 28–9. For the epithet 'island of saints', recorded from the time of Marianus Scottus (*c*.1070), ubiquitous by the 1320s, see Marianus Scottus, *Chronicon*, ed. G. Waitz, Monumenta Germaniae Historica, Scriptores 5 (Hannover: MGH, 1844), 499, 544; L. Gougaud and M. Joynt, 'The Isle of Saints', *Studies: An Irish Quarterly Review*, 13 (1924), 363–80; Lydon, 'Ireland and the English Crown', 77.

121   *Manuscript Sources for the History of Irish Civilisation*, ed. R. J. Hayes, vol. 2 (Boston: G. K. Hall, 1965), 455–6, some, as in BL ms. Royal 13.B.viii, from St Augustine's Canterbury, travelling together with Gerald of Wales's Irish works.

122   *Peter of Cornwall's Book of Revelations*, ed. R. Easting and R. Sharpe (Toronto/ Oxford: Pontifical Institute of Medieval Studies, 2013), 116–41, esp. 138–41; Paris, *CM*, ii, 212–14.

The translation of relics had long been a concomitant of conquest, not least in England after 1066. By similar means, such artefacts as the 'Staff of Jesus', formerly at Armagh, found their way, after 1170, to the treasury of Christ Church Dublin.[123] In 1185, relics of SS Patrick, Brigit and Colum Cille were reportedly discovered at Down, translated to a new shrine there as a means of boosting the authority of John de Courcy, himself the dedicatee of Jocelin of Furness's Life of Patrick, responsible for striking coins marked with the single word 'Patricius'.[124] Even so, and with the exception of Irish saints noticed by Bede, or those whose relics had long been claimed by English churches, there was little or no attempt to adopt Irish men or women either into English history or English liturgy. The exceptions here, such as Glastonbury's interest in Patrick, or the discovery of the bodies of St Brendan's father, mother and brother at the Lacy manor of Ludlow in the first year of the reign of King John (1199–1200), occurred in places with very obvious connections across the Irish Sea.[125]

The first generation of conquerors contributed new chapels to Christ Church Dublin dedicated not to native saints but to the universal Virgin Mary and the very specifically English St Edmund King and Martyr.[126] Many of the invaders fought under the battle cry 'St David!', invoking a Welsh saint in their slaughter of the Irish.[127] Until the foundation in the 1190s of the new 'English' cathedral of St Patrick, the Hiberno-Norse settlement at Dublin had

123 S. J. Ridyard, '"Condigna Veneratio": Post-Conquest Attitudes to the Saints of the Anglo-Saxons', *ANS*, 9 (1986), 179–206; M. V. Ronan, 'St Patrick's Staff and Christ Church', *Dublin Historical Record*, 5 (1943), 121–9.

124 *Expugnatio*, 234–5, and for the circumstances of the 'inventio' (1185) and 'translatio' (1202), see M. T. Flanagan, 'John de Courcy, the First Ulster Plantation and Irish Church Men', in Smith (ed.), *Britain and Ireland*, 164, 175–6. For Jocelin, H. Birkett, *The Saints' Lives of Jocelin of Furness: Hagiography, Patronage and Ecclesiastical Politics* (Woodbridge: Boydell Press, 2010), esp. 141–70. For coinage, Picard, 'Early Contacts between Ireland and Normandy', 93, echoed in the Irish recoinage of 1460: Lydon, 'Ireland and the English Crown', 75.

125 *English Monastic Litanies of the Saints after 1100*, ed. N. J. Morgan, 2 vols. (Woodbridge: Henry Bradshaw Society, 2012–13), noting Benignus of Armagh, Brendan, Bridgit, Cianan of Duleek, Colum Cille, Declan of Ardmore, Forannan, Fursey, Malachy, Modwenna and Patrick, in several cases from the litany of only one monastic house, most from regular rather than secular churches. For Glastonbury, C. H. Slover, 'William of Malmesbury and the Irish', *Speculum*, 2 (1927), 268–83; R. Bartlett, 'Cults of Irish, Scottish and Welsh Saints in Twelfth-Century England', in Smith (ed.), *Britain and Ireland*, 68–77, esp. 77.

126 'Some Unpublished Texts from the Black Book of Christ Church Dublin', ed. A. Gwynn, *Analecta Hibernica*, 16 (1946), 309, and the English saints at Christ Church, *The Book of Obits and Martyrology of the Cathedral Church of the Holy Trinity … Dublin*, ed. J. C. Croswaithe (Dublin: Irish Archaeological Society, 1844), viii–xx, xxiii, xliii–xlvi

127 *Deeds of the Normans*, 72, 78, 102, 141.

no parish church dedicated to a native saint.[128] Even thereafter, St Patrick's Dublin looked more to the English present than the Irish past, not least as a centre for the dissemination of the Sarum rite.[129] The most contemporary of Irish saints' lives, St Bernard's *Vita* of Malachy of Armagh, attracted Irish patronage to Clairvaux but received little attention in England beyond a Cistercian milieu. As Gerald of Wales pointed out, since the Irish saints were confessors rather than martyrs, it was left to the English in Ireland to practise their long-established skill at martyr-making.[130]

From the 1170s onwards, the greatest such victim of Plantagenet tyranny, St Thomas of Canterbury, was enthusiastically adopted, in Dublin and elsewhere, as the patron saint not only of a victimised Church but of a nation martyred for the glory of Becket's chief persecutor, Henry II.[131] Hence the spate of miracles reported at Canterbury after 1172 involving knights returning from Ireland, uneasy that their Irish expedition had merely perpetuated the tyranny against which St Thomas had protested. Hence the first stirrings of that association between St Thomas and the wider martyrdom of Ireland still being profitably milked by the supporters of Daniel O'Connell ('a second St Thomas') as recently as the 1840s.[132]

The only medieval Irishman canonised after the English conquest of the 1170s, Laurence O'Toole [Lorcán Ua Tuathail], archbishop of Dublin (1162–80), enjoyed uneasy relations with Henry II and was portrayed both as a personal devotee of Becket's cult and, like Becket, as a defender of ecclesiastical liberty against royal tyranny. It was in and around his burial place at Eu in Normandy that the majority of Laurence's miracles were worked, and it was here too that his *Vita* was written, after the Capetian conquest of Normandy

128 A. Empey, 'The Formation and Development of Intramural Churches and Communities in Medieval Dublin in a European Context', in Bradley *et al.* (eds.), *Dublin in the Medieval World*, 249, a pattern repeated at Drogheda, p. 257n.

129 Essays by M. O'Neill and A. J. Fletcher, in J. Crawford and R. Gillespie (eds.), *St Patrick's Cathedral, Dublin: A History* (Dublin: Four Courts Press, 2009), 100–4, 122–30; Richardson and Sayles, *Administration*, 2–4.

130 Malachy occurs in only a handful of English kalendars, all of them Cistercian (information Nigel Morgan). For martyrs, *Gir. Camb. Op.*, v, 137, 174, 178–9. By contrast, the old Norse *Kongs Skuggsjo* (c.1250) interprets the lack of Irish martyrs in a positive light, as evidence that the Irish had always respected their holy men: K. Meyer, 'The Irish Mirabilia in the Norse "Speculum Regale"', *Ériu*, 4 (1910), 4.

131 Lydon (ed.), 'Three Exchequer Documents', 12; Lydon, 'Dublin Castle', 119; Duffy, 'First Ulster Plantation', 9.

132 M. Bull, 'Criticism of Henry II's Expedition to Ireland in William of Canterbury's Miracles of St Thomas Becket', *JMH*, 33 (2007), 107–29; N. Vincent, 'St Thomas of Canterbury (and of England?)', in G. Atkins (ed.), *Making and Remaking Saints in Nineteenth-Century Britain* (Manchester University Press, 2016).

in 1204, as a work highly critical of Henry II and his regime.[133] Thereafter, between St Laurence (d. 1180, canonised 1225) and Oliver Plunkett (martyred 1681, beatified in 1920, canonised in 1975), Ireland produced not a single canonised, native saint. Sanctity was too powerful a force to be attributed to the Irish (or for that matter the Welsh) under English rule.

If the English refused to learn their religion from Ireland, what other lessons or benefits were they prepared to receive? Any attempt at an answer here will remain impressionistic. Measuring by the survival rate of charters, Henry II's thirty charters for Ireland represent less than 1 per cent of the surviving total or more than 3,000. This might appear a derisory figure, until we compare it with the twenty-nine surviving charters of Henry for Wales or the mere thirty-three for the whole of Poitou and Aquitaine south of the Loire.[134] The only king of England largely indifferent to Irish affairs was Richard I.[135] Of John's surviving charters before 1199 no fewer than 108 of 369, or 29 per cent, concern Ireland.[136] As king, after 1199, John settled into a routine that each year saw between 3 and 6 per cent of the chancery charter roll given over to Irish business, a figure that remained more or less stable under Henry III, through to the 1270s.[137] Even so, it is worth noting that, in contrast to its dealings with Normandy or Gascony, the English royal chancery never established an independent series of enrolments for letters to Ireland. These instead continued to be enrolled haphazardly on the English charter, patent and close rolls.

As for the Irish contribution to Plantagenet politics, far more significant than wheat or hawks or timber was the export of warriors and warfare.[138] Summonses to the Irish to serve in Wales, Scotland and Gascony under Henry III were to culminate in the adoption into English armies of the Irish 'hobelar' or mounted infantryman: arguably the most significant new element grafted on to English warfare before the introduction of gunpowder in

133 'Vie et miracles de St Laurent', ed. C. Plummer, *Analecta Bollandiana*, 33 (1914), 121–85, esp. 144. See also the testimonials printed by M. V. Ronan, *Irish Ecclesiastical Record*, 5th series 27 (1926), 349–51, 28 (1926), 247–51, 467–80.

134 *Letters Henry II*, introduction.

135 And even here, see Veach, 'King and Magnate', 179–202.

136 For John's pre-1199 charters, N. Vincent, 'Jean, comte de Mortain: le futur roi et ses domaines en Normandie 1183–1199', in A.-M. Héricher and V. Gazeau (eds.), *1204, La Normandie entre Plantagenêts et Capétiens* (Caen: Université de Caen, 2007), 37–59.

137 Figures here based upon Charter Rolls 1–2 John, in *Rot. Chart.*

138 For Ireland's military sophistication before and after 1169, M. T. Flanagan, 'Irish and Anglo-Norman Warfare in Twelfth-Century Ireland', in T. Bartlett and K. Jeffery (eds.), *A Military History of Ireland* (Cambridge University Press, 1996), 52–75, esp. 67–8.

the fourteenth century.[139] In Ireland itself, the employment first of the followers of Strongbow and Robert fitz Stephen, and thereafter of 'galloglasses' from across the Irish Sea led to a similar military revolution, marked by the Irish adoption of arms, armour and the garrisoning of castles, all techniques if not acquired, then certainly refined in the aftermath of conquest.[140] As early as 1173, armed interventions by Strongbow, Hugh de Lacy and their fellow conquistadors were crucial in turning the scales in favour of Henry II during the great rebellion led by the king's sons. In the same way, in 1215–16, Irish support helped maintain king John's regime threatened with rebellion by the English barons.[141] Even after 1258, during the political crisis at the end of Henry III's reign, and although bitterly divided between the factions of Fitzgerald and Burgh, the Irish seem to have lent more or less united support to King Henry, fighting for him in the campaign of 1265.[142]

In financial terms, Ireland contributed significant but by no means extravagant sums. King John's 1213 census to the papacy for England and Ireland suggests a proportion of 7 to 3 for English versus Irish revenues. The real figure was perhaps closer to 10 to 1, roughly equivalent to the proportion of English chancery business devoted to Ireland.[143] Irish revenue was useful to England's kings in times of political crisis. Yet had less coin been exported to England, it is arguable that the expansion of the colony might not have juddered so rapidly to a halt, from the 1230s onwards, nor Ireland itself have suffered from those periods of want that, from 1270, seem to have contributed to the colony's instability.[144]

What is also noteworthy here is the general indifference of English chroniclers to Irish affairs. Save at moments of particular crisis, neither Roger of Wendover nor Matthew Paris devote any attention to Ireland. Indeed Matthew deliberately omits Ireland from all four of his maps of Britain.[145]

---

139 *Close Rolls 1242–7*, 254–5; *CDI, 1171–1251*, nos. 2565, 2578, 2589, 2628, 2679, 2716, 2733, 2768, 2777; J. Lydon, 'The Hobelar: An Irish Contribution to Medieval Warfare', *Irish Sword*, 2 part 5 (1954), 12–16; Frame, 'Military Service in the Lordship of Ireland', 114–15.

140 Flanagan, 'Irish and Anglo-Norman Warfare' (stressing continuity); Simms, *From Kings to Warlords* (stressing change).

141 *Expugnatio*, 120, 134; *Deeds of the Normans*, 126–9; *Diceto*, i, 375. Both King Henry III and his mother considered seeking refuge in Ireland after 1216: Frame, *Ireland and Britain*, 61. For Irish rebels in 1215, Duffy, 'John and Ireland', 244–5.

142 Frame, *Ireland and Britain*, 59–69.

143 Figures supplied by J. F. Lydon, 'Edward II and the Revenues of Ireland in 1311–12', *IHS*, 14 (1964), 53–7; Lydon (ed.), 'Three Exchequer Documents', 9–10.

144 Lydon (ed.), 'Three Exchequer Documents', 6–11, and more generally, Frame, *Ireland and Britain*, 1–13.

145 P. D. A. Harvey, 'Matthew Paris's Maps of Britain', in P. R. Coss and S. D. Lloyd (eds.), *Thirteenth Century England IV* (Woodbridge: Boydell Press, 1992), 109–21.

English monastic annalists were no more concerned with events in Ireland than their Irish counterparts with English affairs. When English visitors did report on Ireland, as was the case with Stephen of Lexington (from Laxton in Nottinghamshire), appointed in 1228 to restore discipline to the Irish Cistercians, it was in less than flattering terms. Stephen's letters describe a wilderness of rain and bestiality; a place of incomprehensible speech, where robbers lurked in every wood.[146] In particular, he noted, although the provinces of Leinster and Munster were effectively governed by their Marshal and Lacy lords, this was not true of those parts under direct royal rule. Here command was undermined by poor communication between the king in Westminster and his local justiciar.[147] All in all, this was a land divided by 'a most evil and dangerous march between English and Irish', only half of it established as a 'land of peace'.[148] This was a society of war rather than peace. Even an incomplete survey suggests that there were at least sixteen occasions in the reign of Henry III when the knight service of Ireland was collectively summoned to fight on Irish soil. It was also a place apart. As early as 1210, King John's expedition to Ireland was considered an overseas affair: a venture into foreign territory distinct from a domestic campaign fought against the Welsh or the Scots.[149]

As this should remind us, 1210 was the last expedition that an English king led to Ireland before Richard II in 1394. Much ink has been spilled over John's Irish campaigns of 1185 and 1210, assessing their relative degree of success or failure, political sophistication or morally unjustifiable brutality. Such efforts tend to reflect modern nationalist (or in the case of Lewis Warren, provocatively unionist) prejudice as much as they illuminate medieval realities.[150] By contrast, no writer has previously noticed the principal legacy of John's expeditions, not in conquest or domination, but in the king's own education in politics and warfare. John was a mere ten years old when he was promised Ireland in 1177, and still only eighteen when he took possession of his lordship

---

146 'Registrum epistolarum Stephani de Lexinton abbatis de Stanlegia et de Savigniaco', ed. B. Griesser, *Analecta Sacri Ordinis Cisterciensis*, 2 (1946), esp. 48–51, 57, 91, 93 nos. 38, 40, 52, 94–5 (language); 36 no. 31, 48–9 no. 38, 53–4 no. 44 (robbery and murder); 41 no. 34, 45–6 no. 37 (bestiality, and metaphors of rain).

147 'Registrum epistolarum Stephani de Lexinton', 78 no. 79, and 53 no. 44.

148 'Registrum epistolarum Stephani de Lexinton', 42 no. 34 ('Preualeret namque in tuto loco et terra pacis sola terre medietas … In pessima namque marchia et periculosa inter Anglicos et Hibernicos').

149 Otway-Ruthven, 'Royal Service', 173–4; Church, '1210 Campaign', 52–6.

150 See here the critiques of W. L. Warren, by S. Duffy, 'King John's Expedition to Ireland, 1210: The Evidence Reconsidered', *IHS*, 30 (1996), 1–21, and Duffy, 'John and Ireland', 221–45.

there in 1185. He reigned in Ireland for nearly forty years, more than twice as long as in England. What did he learn from the experience?

Was it here, for example, that John acquired his particular obsession with hostage-taking? Hostages were a fundamental part of Irish politics, being regularly and brutally killed in reprisal for breaches of a peace that proved impossible for either native or invading kings to maintain.[151] John's two greatest military successes, at Mirebeau in 1202 and at Carrickfergus in 1210, were both followed by the killing or prolonged incarceration of hostages in ways that jarred with English and French sensibilities and that may significantly have tipped baronial opinion against the king. It was John's difficulty in obtaining hostages that is said to have led to his withdrawal from his first Irish expedition in 1185. The disappearance of Arthur of Brittany, after 1202, one of the principal causes of the collapse of John's French 'empire', was perhaps fresh in the minds of Cathal Crobderg, king of Connacht, and Áed Méith Ua Néill, king of Cenel nEogain, both of whom, in 1210, refused to surrender sons as hostages to John.[152] Certainly, it would have been whispered amongst the barons of Ulster, in 1204 required to bring John de Courcy to obedience under a threat that the king would otherwise 'betake himself' to their hostages and fees.[153] Was it also from Ireland that John acquired his delight in head-hunting and in watching judicial duels?[154] Certainly, and by contrast to English practice, jurisdiction over ordeals and duels was regularly included in John's Irish charters as a privilege bestowed upon the greater Irish lords. It is in a case involving a murder at Dublin castle that the king is first found insisting that he attend such a duel.[155]

Above all, was it in Ireland, with its warring native kings and its clannish network of lordships, liberties and honours, that the king first perfected his

---

151 *Expugnatio*, 36, 50, 52, 92, 162–8, 298 n. 54, 342 n. 382; *Deeds of the Normans*, 53, 65–6, 74, 83, 85, 95, 111, 124, 135, and in general, Simms, *From Kings to Warlords*, 71, 96–100; Flanagan, *Irish Society*, 177–9, 182, 185, 188, 197, and from a European perspective, A. J. Kosto, *Hostages in the Middle Ages* (Oxford University Press, 2012).

152 *ALC*, i, 170–1, 243–50; *AI*, 339–40, and cf. Duffy, 'King John's Expedition to Ireland, 1210', 5, 17–20, 22–4; Duffy, 'John and Ireland', 241–2.

153 *Rot. Litt. Pat.*, 45b ('nos ad obsides vestros … capiemus'), whence *CDI, 1171–1251*, no. 225.

154 Headhunting: *Expugnatio*, 234; *Deeds of the Normans*, 72–3, 91; C. Suppe, 'The Cultural Significance of Decapitation in High Medieval Wales and the Marches', *Bulletin of the Board of Celtic Studies*, 36 (1989), 147–60. Compare *Expugnatio*, 220, where Gerald refers to the beheading of hostages on Henry II's 1165 Welsh expedition as a shameful event.

155 Grants of the 'iudicium aque et ferri et duellum [et fossam] et furcas' occur in at least ten of John's Irish charters before 1199. For example *Red Book of the Earls of Kildare*, 1; *CAL. Gormanston Reg.*, 193–4; *COD*, i, nos. 7, 12, 863. It is noticeable that, after 1199, John's charters as king tend very specifically to reserve 'all pleas pertaining to the crown': *Rot. Chart.*, 19–20b. For duels, see *Rotuli Curiae Regis*, i, 173 (*CDI, 1171–1251*, no. 116), and cf. F. M. Powicke, review in *EHR*, 39 (1924), 267, citing *Rotuli Curiae Regis*, i, 278–9.

strategy towards the English baronage of divide and rule? We find this strategy pursued in Ireland as early as the 1190s in John's dealings with Walter de Lacy and William Marshal. It was to surface again after 1199, in the playing off of Meiler fitz Henry against the Lacys and the Marshal, Hugh de Lacy against John de Courcy, William de Braose against the Geraldines and the Burghs. In each instance, war in Ireland was provoked by political game-playing at the English court. It was these disputes that drew the king himself to Ireland in 1210, in an attempt to restart the game at zero by banishing the Braose and Lacy clans. The siege of Carrickfergus in 1210 was followed by the capture of large numbers of the Anglo-Irish elite, held prisoner in England for the next five years, in some cases never released.[156]

All of this speaks of a colonial elite inheriting the traditions of their Irish forebears for whom raiding and pillage were both endemic and prestigious. It also speaks of a conquest never fully stabilised, of violence barely contained, of public order all too easily fragmenting into vendetta and pillage. Whatever investment a man like Meiler fitz Henry made in castle building or land improvement could be wasted in a few brief weeks of mayhem.[157] For all that it sought to build in stone, this remained a frontier society unprotected against its own inclination for bloodshed and dispossession.

Not everything here was unique to Ireland. Vendetta and favouritism were already familiar in the Plantagenet lands south of the Loire, ruled via a skeleton administration dependent upon English support for one or other local power-broker.[158] Yet the barons of Aquitaine rarely found a place at the centre of the king's decision making in the same way that, as early as John's reign, families such as the Lacys, Braoses and Marshals not only dominated Ireland but remained active players at the English court. When southern French lords were promoted in England, as with the Lusignans, in the 1250s, the consequences were distinctly stormy. Nor was there an exact parallel here between Ireland and Wales. In Wales there was little by way of direct royal administration against which the Marcher lords could react. In Ireland, by contrast and from the time of Henry II's first crossing, there

---

156 Duffy, 'John and Ireland', 236–41; M. T. Flanagan, 'Defining Lordships in Angevin Ireland: William Marshal and the King's Justiciar', in M. Aurell and F. Boutoulle (eds.), *Les Seigneuries dans l'éspace Plantagenêt (c.1150–c.1250)* (Bordeaux: Ausonius, 2009), 41–59, esp. 55–6, and more generally Crooks, 'Divide and Rule', 263–307, and the chapter in this volume by Veach. For 1210, http://magnacarta.cmp.uea.ac.uk/read/feature_of_the_month/Feb_2015.

157 For the effects of the war of 1207, including an attack upon New Ross, see Flanagan, 'Defining Lordships', 50–1

158 N. Vincent, 'Jean sans terre et les origines de la Gascogne anglaise', *Annales du Midi*, 123 (2011), 533–66.

was a constant and deliberate tension between royal and baronial interests. The first generation of settlers had possessed lands in Normandy, Wales and England, all of which could be used by the king to manipulate behaviour in Ireland. Indeed, the spread of a single aristocracy across England, Wales, Ireland and northern France constituted one of the most significant threads by which the Plantagenet 'empire' was stitched together.[159] The loss of Normandy in 1204, and thereafter the fraying of connections to Wales with the extinction of the dynasties of Marshal, Braose and Lacy, left the Anglo-Irish elite increasingly isolated. By the 1240s, only the Geraldines remained as a Welsh Marcher family still prominent in Ireland, and even they were increasingly insignificant in Wales. Newcomers continued to arrive, not least as a result of the partition of the Marshal and Lacy estates. Even so, as in the Holy Land from the 1240s onwards, the elite increasingly fled from estates considered too precarious. The crusader lords sought refuge in Cyprus. Irish colonists fled to England, either as absentee rentiers, or by divesting themselves of all Irish land.[160]

Tensions and hatreds distilled in Ireland continued to affect the political history of England. They led, in 1234, to the death on the Curragh of Kildare, of Richard Marshal, lord of Leinster, the first English earl to have been killed in rebellion since Earl Waltheof in 1076.[161] Historians have long sought the causes of that upsurge in political violence which, from the reign of Edward I onwards, crossed the species barrier into the higher aristocracy, paving the way to the murder, deposition and self-slaughter that characterises English elite politics in the fourteenth and fifteenth centuries. Origins here have generally been traced to the death of Simon de Montfort at Evesham in 1265, or subsequently to Edward's wars in Scotland. They might better be traced to the Curragh of Kildare. Even deeper roots might be sought in the murder of Arthur of Brittany in 1202, or the extermination of the Braose clan in 1210, both events intimately linked to Irish politics through their perpetrator, King John.

---

159 Davies, *First English Empire*, 19–20.

160 B. Hartland, 'Reasons for Leaving: The Effect of Conflict on English Landholding in Late Thirteenth-Century Leinster', *JMH*, 32 (2006), 18–26; B. Hartland, 'Absenteeism: The Chronology of a Concept', in B. Weiler, J. Burton and P. Schofield (eds), *Thirteenth Century England XI* (Woodbridge: Boydell Press, 2007), 215–29.

161 Paris, *CM*, iii, 273–9, and for the literary heroics of Wendover and Paris's narrative, N. Vincent, *Peter des Roches* (Cambridge University Press, 1996), 438–40. For the political ramifications, B. Smith, 'Irish Politics, 1220–1245', in M. Prestwich, R. Britnell and R. Frame (eds), *Thirteenth Century England VIII* (Woodbridge: Boydell Press, 2001), 13–21; D. Crouch, 'Earl Gilbert Marshal and his Mortal Enemies', *Historical Research*, 87 (2014), 393–403.

Richard Marshal's death was to have an unexpectedly dramatic impact upon the life of King Henry III. In September 1238, lying in bed at Woodstock, Henry was nearly murdered by an agent of William de Marisco. Marisco had himself been propelled into outlawry and piracy in the Bristol Channel by the recriminations that had followed the Marshal's death and the murder of Henry Clement, a Geraldine clerk, killed in 1235 within the purlieu of the royal court. All of these *crimes passionelles* were of Irish origin.[162] Ireland's contribution to political violence, as to warfare more generally, began early and lasted late. By the 1240s, both the Welsh and the Scots had largely abandoned the slaughter of women, children and high-born prisoners that had marked them out as 'barbarians' in the eyes of their French-speaking rulers. Not so the Irish, whose annals continued to wade in gore.[163]

The tendency in recent writing has been to emphasise the shared experience of medieval Ireland, Scotland and Wales, collective victims of English imperialism.[164] Yet in contesting English marginalisation of the 'Celtic fringe', historians risk conniving in the very process they deplore. Sympathy all too easily merges into partisan over-simplification. Wales, Scotland and Ireland were set apart from one another not only by geography and the chronology of their respective 'conquests', but by the roles that they played more generally in British politics. In Ireland, conquest was viewed, as Gerald demonstrates, in imperialist terms. Yet the disjunctions between English and Irish economic political development ensured that the Irish experience of the English, although just as brutal as that elsewhere, included a royal administration in many ways more precocious than anything by this time attempted in either Scotland or Wales. Although remote from the person of England's king, Ireland was in some ways far closer both to English administrative procedures and to the politics of the English royal court. Above all, as a land of peace 'never established', Ireland and its English settlers bred tensions as much among the colonisers themselves as between conquerors and natives. As with colonial history the world over, it would be naive to write of this either as a story of civilisation imposed upon remote barbarity, or of peace-loving natives corrupted by cruel foreign tyrants. Ireland's colonisation was part of a wider European experience. But the local circumstances of that experience remained distinctive. So did the response it evoked.

---

162 F. M. Powicke, 'The Murder of Henry Clement and the Pirates of Lundy Island', in F. M. Powicke, *Ways of Medieval Life and Thought* (London: Odhams, 1949), 38–68, esp. 42.

163 J. Gillingham, 'Killing and Mutilating Political Enemies in the British Isles from the Late Twelfth to the Early Fourteenth Century: A Comparative Study', in Smith (ed.), *Britain and Ireland*, 114–34, esp. 129–30.

164 Davies, *First English Empire*.

At Bannow Bay, where Robert fitz Stephen landed in 1169, memorials were soon raised to his achievement. As at the site of Hastings after 1066, the conquerors gifted land at Bannow to the monks of their (English) home-lands. A stone tower that the conquerors built there is still in use, with peculiar appropriateness, as the Hook Lighthouse.[165] In 1969, to mark the 800th anniversary of Robert's landing, a further monument was erected at nearby Baginbun. It was immediately defaced.[166] Robert's landing party was not so easily dislodged. Even so, for more than 800 years, violence, memory and politics have been entangled in Ireland in ways that neither the English nor the Irish find easy to comprehend. This essay began with controversy and misunderstanding. It must also end with them.

165 H. G. Richardson, 'Some Norman Monastic Foundations in Ireland', in J. A. Watt *et al.* (eds.), *Medieval Studies Presented to Aubrey Gwynn, S.J.* (Dublin: The Three Candles, 1961), 29–32; Canterbury Cathedral Archives Chartae Antiquae I / 231, 235–6, 239, 242; B. Colfer, 'The Tower of Hook', *Journal of the Wexford Historical Society*, 10 (1984–5), 69–78.
166 F. X. Martin, in *NHI* ii, xlix.

8

The Height of English Power: 1250–1320

BETH HARTLAND

ON 25 May 1315 Edward Bruce, heir to the throne of Scotland, landed at Larne with a force of several thousand troops. Having been joined by Domnall O'Neill [Ó Néill], the most important of the Ulster Irish lords, he was proclaimed king of Ireland. The greatest challenge to English rule in medieval Ireland had begun. Bruce's army defeated a contingent of Ulster settlers before marching south to Dundalk, which was burned in late June. Richard Burgh, earl of Ulster, pursued the attackers back into Ulster but was defeated by them at Connor in County Antrim. By early December Bruce was in Meath, where he defeated a force led by the lord of Trim, Roger Mortimer, and in the spring of 1316, having avoided defeat by a large government army at Ardscull in County Kildare, he marched into Laois and Offaly. The Scots and their Irish allies then returned to Ulster and besieged Carrickfergus castle which finally fell to them in September 1316. By Christmas of that year Edward Bruce had been joined in Ulster by his brother, King Robert I, and a force of galloglass and together they marched south early in 1317. They were menacing the outskirts of Dublin in late February and by early April were in north Munster. Their attempts to join forces there with a faction of the O'Brien [Ó Briain] dynasty failed and they retreated to Ulster. King Robert returned to Scotland and the worst of the danger was over. The capture soon after of the Isle of Man from the Scots by John of Athy cut supply and communication routes between Ulster and Scotland, and for eighteen months Edward Bruce remained in Ulster. In October 1318 he led his forces south again, but he was killed, and his army routed, by a force of local colonists at Faughart, near Dundalk. The Bruce invasion was at an end (see Map 9).[1]

---

1 S. Duffy, *Ireland in the Middle Ages* (Houndmills and Dublin: Palgrave Macmillan, 1997), 134–42; S. Duffy, 'The Bruce Brothers and the Irish Sea World, 1306–29', *Cambridge Medieval Celtic Studies*, 21 (1991), 50; *AC*, 251; J. F. Lydon, 'The Years of Crisis, 1254–1315', in *NHI* ii, 179–204; J. F. Lydon, 'The Impact of the Bruce Invasion', in *NHI* ii, 275–302.

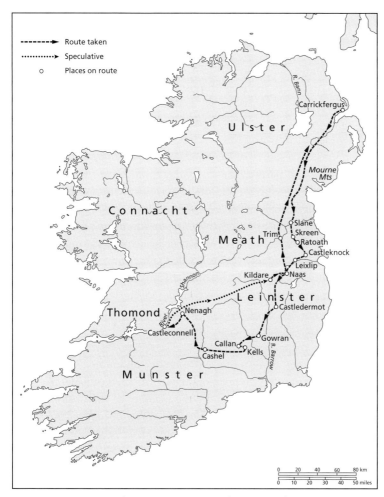

MAP 9. The Bruce Campaign, February–April 1317.

How had English rule in Ireland come to be so seriously threatened, and how had it managed to endure this trial? The period covered by this chapter begins with Henry III's decision to grant Ireland, and other parts of his domain, to his son and heir, Edward, with the proviso that these lands would be reunited to the crown when Edward acceded to the throne. As we shall see, Henry's actions complicated the nature of English rule in Ireland, but they also suggested confidence in the present and future of the Lordship as part of England's 'empire'. How did it come about that sixty years later the younger

brother of a man who was successfully leading resistance to England's claim
to rule Scotland would himself seek recognition as king of Ireland at the head
of an invading army?[2]

Such a dramatic change in fortunes encourages the search for indicators
of long-term decline in the English position in Ireland up to the early fourteenth century. The emphasis placed by historians on the ways in which the
Lordship was weakened by the exploitative nature of English governance
during the reign of Edward I has much to recommend it. The use of Ireland
by English kings as a source of men and supplies for the prosecution of their
wars elsewhere, and particularly in Scotland, did leave the Dublin government with reduced means to undertake necessary defence in the Lordship.
Such defence increasingly involved attempting to deal with attacks on the
frontiers of settled areas by Irish families, a small number of which had added
to their military muscle from the middle of the century through their importation of Scottish galloglass.[3] Undoubtedly the security situation faced by the
settlement had worsened in the second half of the thirteenth century, but it
is important not to overlook certain considerations that helped the colonists
face these dangers successfully. The Dublin government may well have found
it increasingly difficult to finance the defence of the colony, but in times of crisis the loyalty to the crown of most of the settled population could be relied
upon. In like manner, while a native resurgence undoubtedly presented serious challenges to the English position in parts of the Lordship, the factional
nature of Gaelic politics – typified by the inability of the Connacht Irish to
unite at Athenry in support of Edward Bruce in 1316, leading to their defeat at
the hands of the colonists – also helped ensure that the settlement would not
be wiped out by a native reconquest.

In attempting to assess changes in the balance of power in Ireland in this
period it is important to bear in mind that the nature of the contemporary
documentation encourages an interpretation that stresses an increase in disorder and a weakening of English control. The greater survival of evidence
generated by the administration of the Lordship from about 1290 tempts
us to imagine that problems identifiable from that point had not pertained

2 Davies, *First English Empire*, 81. See the reference to Edward as king in *Reg. Nicholas
   Fleming*, 166–7.
3 J. F. Lydon, 'Edward I, Ireland and the War in Scotland, 1303–1304', in Lydon (ed.),
   England and Ireland, 43–61; J. F. Lydon, 'Edward II and the Revenues of Ireland in 1311–
   1312 ', *IHS*, 14 (1964), 39–49; J. F. Lydon, 'An Irish Army in Scotland, 1296', *Irish Sword*, 5
   (1961–2), 188.

earlier in the century. To give an example: late in 1264 a dispute broke out between the de Burghs and the Geraldines, culminating in the capture of Richard de la Rochelle, Edward's justiciar, by Maurice fitz Maurice. Details of the affair are far from plentiful, but the Annals of Connacht recorded that 'a great part of Ireland [was] ruined between' the contending parties.[4] In 1274 Geoffrey de Geneville, justiciar of Ireland (1273–6), referred to the events of 1264 as a 'war' which had been brought to a peaceful conclusion only due to the need of Henry III and his son Edward for reinforcements from Ireland against Simon de Montfort in England.[5] The quarrel resumed under John fitz Thomas and Richard de Burgh in 1294, and the disruption caused on this later occasion is much better represented in the surviving evidence. It is perhaps only this uneven distribution of surviving documentary sources that leads to the assumption that the events of 1264 were any less serious in scale and consequence than those of thirty years later. In like manner, another source which only becomes available from the reign of Edward I – the petition – can also skew our understanding of Ireland in this period. By encouraging the sending of petitions to parliament in England, Edward I stimulated the production of documents that spoke to the less happy aspects of life in his lands. We see the impact of this on the nature of wider English political discourse in 1311 when the Lords Ordainer, who sought to address alleged shortcomings on the part of King Edward II, claimed that Ireland, Gascony and Scotland were on the point of being lost unless God improved the situation.[6]

The idea of long-term decline between 1254 and 1315 must also take into account indications that in some ways the English position in Ireland in this period was actually advancing. The strengthening of the structures of English government and administration that had begun at the start of the thirteenth century, for instance, continued after 1254. It was a sign of the depth of the foundations that had been laid that even in the midst of the Bruce Invasion, the justiciar [chief governor] still found it possible to hold crown pleas, carry out gaol deliveries, and drum up support for the government effort against the Scots in many parts of the Lordship.[7] Without doubt, Ireland was in a

---

4 Connolly, *Medieval Record Sources*; *AC*, 143.
5 Sayles, *Affairs*, 7; B. Hartland, 'Vaucouleurs, Ludlow and Trim: The Role of Ireland in the Career of Geoffrey de Geneville, *c*.1226–1314', *IHS*, 32 (2001), 466.
6 P. Brand, 'Petitions and Parliament in the Reign of Edward I', *Parliamentary History*, 23 (2004), 14–38; C. Stephenson and F. G. Marcham (eds.), *Sources of English Constitutional History* (New York and London: Harper Brothers, 1937), 193.
7 NAI KB 2/8.

pitiful state in 1318: years of bad harvests and famine reportedly led to acts of cannibalism, while Edward Bruce's scorched-earth policy certainly added to the misery. But England and much of the rest of north-west Europe were also devastated by famine in these years, and it is difficult to estimate the specific impact of the Bruce Invasion on the situation in Ireland.[8]

Lord of Ireland and King of England: Edward I

The grant to Edward, son of King Henry, of Ireland and other lands in 1254 was intended to give the future king a taste of real power, and to strengthen English authority in the assigned lands. While Edward had been granted 'all Ireland', however, the grant contained notable exceptions and reservations that caused confusion in the Lordship. The right to appoint bishops, and custody of episcopal lands during vacancies, for instance, were reserved to the king. The counties and cities of Dublin and Limerick were likewise reserved, as was Athlone and substantial lands in Connacht. These latter lands had been identified by Henry III as a suitable gift for his kinsman, Geoffrey de Lusignan.[9] Since the 1230s Ireland had proved a very useful source of patronage for the king, whose landed resources in England had been outstripped by the demands of his Savoyard and Poitevin relatives and their associates. When Henry made the grant of Ireland to Edward he still had outstanding promises to honour.[10] The dual administration of Ireland from 1254 to 1272 consequent upon Henry III's reservations caused problems from the start: Edward's attorney in Ireland, Richard de la Rochelle, for example, refused to give possession of his lands to Geoffrey de Lusignan as ordered, 'because all Ireland had … previously been assigned to Edward'.[11] There would be repeated mixups over preferment to ecclesiastical offices in the 1260s; whereas the king eventually granted Edward all the issues of Ireland, and the lands of Dublin and Limerick, he refused to loosen his grip on the profits from episcopal custodies and vacancies. A problem had been brought about that would outlive the king: both Edward I and Edward II challenged appointments to vacant sees in Ireland that had been supported by their justiciars.[12]

---

8 *AC*, 253: 'For in this Bruce's time, for three years and a half, falsehood and famine and homicide filled the country, and undoubtedly men ate each other in Ireland.'
9 *CDI, 1252–1284*, no. 326.
10 Frame, *Ireland and Britain*, 31–57.
11 *CDI, 1252–1284*, no. 364.
12 *CDI, 1252–1284*, nos. 397, 406, 975, 1433; *CPR, 1313–17*, 271; *CPR, 1317–21*, 132; *CCR, 1313–18*, 533.

In the year Edward received the grant of Ireland, 1254, it was reported that the Irish were 'over elated' because they had heard that the leading settler magnates would be travelling to serve with the king in Gascony. Edward never visited Ireland, and the Lordship was low on the list of priorities for the king and his son at the time of the grant. But settler lords who fought for the king elsewhere left lands in Ireland that were easy targets for Irish raids. The 'many evils' that were said to have arisen in Ulster in the middle of the 1250s were blamed on Ralph Pipard, who was said to have left his lands undefended while serving the king abroad. Similar complaints would be raised with increasing frequency in the decades that followed.[13] The willingness of the Irish to capitalise upon signs of confusion or weakness in the settler position in and after 1254 was enhanced by the clumsy treatment by the crown of important lords such as Feidlim O'Connor [Ó Conchobair], king of Connacht. His were the lands that Henry III had identified as a suitable gift for Geoffrey de Lusignan, and Feidlim was inclined to dispute Henry's assertion that this grant had caused him no injury.[14] The Irish king's envoys crossed to England in 1255 and apparently returned with charters that secured his position. But what really helped to restore temporary stability in Connacht at the time was the refusal of Edward's attorney in Ireland, Richard de la Rochelle, to implement the grant to de Lusignan. In 1256 the justiciar of Ireland, Alan la Zuche, secured for Feidlim a more formal grant of most of his lordship in Connacht. It was the clear-sightedness of such servants of the crown that helped ameliorate to some extent the confusions inherent in the grant of 1254, and the inability of Henry III to deal consistently and in an even-handed manner with those who relied upon his favour.[15]

As the presence of settler magnates on campaign in Gascony in 1254 demonstrates, Ireland remained part of a larger political world, and events later in the decade revealed how integrated were politics on either side of the Irish Sea.[16] In 1259 Alain mac Ruaidrí arrived in Ireland with 160 galloglass,

---

13 *CDI, 1252–1284*, nos. 357, 411–12; NLI MS 1, p. 259 (1272); TNA C 133/30/8 (1282), C 133/76/2 (1296); NAI RC 7/13/2, pp. 19–20 (1308); NAI KB 2/3, pp. 70–4 (1311); TNA SC 8/267/13333 (1319).

14 *CDI, 1252–1284*, no. 457.

15 *AC*, 113; H. Walton, 'The English in Connacht, 1171–1333' PhD thesis, University of Dublin, Trinity College (1980), 459, 464–6. In 1275 the justiciar advised the king against listening to dubious reports from Ireland: 'mout de gent passent a vus de Irlande purl or besoingnes e sont entendant a vus e a vostre consel autre chose ke verite, e sovent ont deceu le conseil nostre seingnor le roy vostre pere, ke Deus asoille, e le vostre' (Sayles, *Affairs*, 13).

16 For these links earlier in the century, see the chapter by Veach above.

representing the dowry obtained by Aed *na nGall* O'Connor on his marriage to a lady of the MacDonald [Mac Domnaill] family. The troops had come in time to support a recent initiative that spelled danger for the colony. In 1258, following successful Irish attacks on the settlers in Thomond and Ulster, Tadc O'Brien [Ó Briain] and Aed O'Connor agreed to support Brian O'Neill [Ó Néill] in his claim to the high-kingship of Ireland. The purpose of this alliance, however, may have transcended Irish concerns. In return for supporting the ambitions of O'Neill, Aengus *Mór* MacDonald, lord of Islay, expected Irish assistance against King Alexander of Scotland. Just before the battle of Downpatrick in 1260, where Aed O'Connor and Brian O'Neill were defeated by local settler forces, the justiciar had been warned not to allow persons from Scotland to be received in Ireland. Henry III, it was asserted, was seeking to prevent any confederacies between Scots and Irish which could be to the damage of his ally, King Alexander.[17]

The need to be aware of regional, national and supra-national concerns when considering the nature of Irish politics in this period is well illustrated when one turns to the ramifications of the dispute which erupted in the mid-1260s between two of the most powerful settler families in the Lordship, the de Burghs and the Geraldines of Offaly. The midlands and Connacht witnessed most of the fighting, but the impact of the conflict was felt as far away as County Wexford, as references to it in the contemporary poem 'The Walling of New Ross' make clear.[18] The feud would shape the politics of the Lordship throughout the rest of the thirteenth century, and drew in interested parties from further afield. King Edward I (as he was from 1272) appears to have wished to limit de Burgh influence in Munster, and so supported Maurice fitz Maurice of Offaly who forged an alliance with Edward's favourite, Thomas de Clare, the new lord of Thomond. In 1286, however, Richard de Burgh managed to secure the support of Thomas de Clare against the premier Geraldine lord, John fitz Thomas. In seeking to further his ambitions in north-west Ireland at the expense of fitz Thomas, Richard also attracted the support of powerful lords from beyond Ireland's shores. Robert Bruce, the grandfather of the future king of Scotland and of Edward Bruce, and leading lords from

---

17 The king of Norway was offered the high-kingship after Brian's death. Duffy, 'Bruce Brothers', 55–86; J. F. Lydon, 'The Scottish Soldier Abroad: The Bruce Invasion and the Galloglass', in S. Duffy (ed.), *Robert the Bruce's Irish Wars: The Invasions of Ireland, 1306–1329* (Stroud: Tempus, 2002), 89–106.

18 'Mes poure avoint de un gerre / Qe fu par entre deus barouns': K. V. Sinclair, *The Walling of New Ross: An Anglo-Norman Satirical Dit* (Stuttgart: Franz Steiner, 1995), 245.

the Hebrides undertook to support Richard, presumably by agreeing not to supply further galloglass to John fitz Thomas. Their agreement, known as the 'Turnberry Band', can only be understood when the interplay of political forces throughout Britain and Ireland in these decades is fully appreciated.[19]

The de Burgh–Geraldine feud culminated in John fitz Thomas, the future earl of Kildare, imprisoning Richard de Burgh, the earl of Ulster, in his castle of Lea in 1294. Records and annals make it clear that the resulting 'disturbance' was considerable: the justiciar and council travelled with an armed force 'to various parts of Ireland to establish the king's peace which was disturbed by the capture of Richard de Burgh'.[20] It was the capable justiciar, John Wogan, who persuaded fitz Thomas and de Burgh to settle their differences through an exchange of lands that led to a realignment of spheres of influence and ambition. In future the de Burghs would focus on Connacht while the Geraldines would concentrate on Leinster and Munster. As in the 1260s the truce that preceded this resolution was brought about in order to allow the English magnates of Ireland to contribute troops in support of the king; on this occasion as part of the Anglo-Scottish war of 1296.[21]

Governing Ireland

The king's Irish council, headed by the justiciar, had played a crucial role in resolving the long-running dispute between the de Burghs and the Geraldines. The justiciar needed the support of the magnates of Ireland to run the Lordship; their refusal to cooperate could make the task of governing almost impossible. Geoffrey de Geneville faced this situation while acting as chief governor between 1273 and 1276. He wrote to the king complaining of secret opposition to his reform measures, and Edward felt compelled in September 1274 to order the lords of Ireland to provide Geoffrey with counsel and aid.[22] The justiciar was required not only to deal effectively with potentially troublesome noblemen, but also to head the administration of the Lordship. Offices of government, based on English precedents, were established in Ireland early in the thirteenth century. An Irish exchequer is traceable from 1200, and an Irish chancery was instituted at some time between 1232 and 1244.

---

19 B. Hartland, 'English Lords in Late Thirteenth and Early Fourteenth Century Ireland: Roger Bigod and the de Clare lords of Thomond', *EHR*, 126 (2007), 342–4; S. Duffy, 'The Turnberry Band', in Duffy (ed.), *Princes, Prelates and Poets*, 124–38.
20 *AC*, 191; *CJRI, 1295–1303*, 148, 176; *IEP*, 124.
21 *CJRI, 1295–1303*, 234–6.
22 Sayles, *Affairs*, 13–14.

While modelled on the Westminster system, government in Ireland developed its own distinctive features. The Irish chancery, for instance, maintained fewer distinct classes of record than did its counterpart in England – a sensible response to the smaller volume of business generated by government in the Lordship.[23]

As in England, the development of parliament in Ireland, with representatives summoned from the counties, liberties and towns, was fuelled by the need to marshal resources for military activity.[24] The first recorded Irish parliament, which convened at Castledermot on 18 June 1264, pre-dated the famous assembly summoned by Simon de Montfort in England in January 1265. The interconnectedness of political events in England and Ireland in 1264–5 as civil war raged is beyond doubt, and Richardson and Sayles went so far as to connect the summoning of the Irish parliament of 1264 directly to the demands made at Oxford by the opponents of King Henry III in 1258.[25] Decisions about Ireland, of course, could be made by the king in consultation with his council and the English parliament. Magnates or administrators usually resident in Ireland might be present at such gatherings, as was the case in December 1289 when the affairs of the Lordship were discussed by 'Geoffrey [de Geneville] himself and others of the king's council in Ireland, who are now sitting in parliament'.[26]

The speed and self-confidence with which the Irish Lordship developed its own legislature perhaps explains why certain statutes promulgated in England in the late thirteenth and early fourteenth centuries were not published in Ireland until a later date. For instance, the Statute of Winchester of 1285 – which dealt with local policing and corporate local responsibility for bringing felons to justice – was not made law in Ireland until 1307. From at least 1236 the procedure for enacting English legislation in Ireland involved the relevant text being sent to the Dublin administration with an order for its publication. This involved proclamation of the legislation in the county and liberty courts as well as centrally in the king's court. Once the Irish parliament began to legislate, however, doubts emerged amongst officials on

23 The Irish chancery did not produce fine or charter rolls at this time: B. Hartland, 'Administering the Irish Fines, 1199–1254: The English Chancery, the Dublin Exchequer and the Seeking of Favours' in D. Crook and L. Wilkinson (eds.), *The Growth of Royal Government under Henry III* (Woodbridge: Boydell Press, 2015), 73–6.
24 J. F. Lydon, 'Parliament and the Community of Ireland', in Lydon (ed.), *Law and Disorder*, 125.
25 Frame, *Ireland and Britain*, 59–69; H. G. Richardson and G. O. Sayles, *The Irish Parliament in the Middle Ages* (Philadelphia: University of Pennsylvania Press, 1952), 58.
26 Hartland, 'Vaucouleurs, Ludlow and Trim', 463, 476.

both sides of the Irish Sea as to whether English legislation ought to pertain in Ireland.[27] It is possible that the topics covered by English legislation had already been dealt with in Ireland – the relatively poor records of Irish parliaments compared to those held in England may obscure this process. By the time the Statute of Winchester was promulgated in England in 1285 the belief in both Westminster and Dublin appears to have been that such legislation would also need to be passed by the Irish parliament. The third, fourth and tenth enactments of the Dublin parliament of 1297 (requiring freemen to be equipped with a horse and to pursue felons, and demanding the clearance of woods, improvements to the king's highways and repairs to bridges) echo the sixth, fifth and first articles of the Statute of Winchester. It had become clear by Michaelmas term 1306 that, despite initial success, the legislation of the Dublin parliament was not meeting its desired ends of minimising or eradicating financial outlay on local defence. The dispatch of the Statute of Winchester followed soon after.[28]

In matters of law Irish justices often looked to England for procedural advice. Following the death of Edward I in 1307, for example, special messengers were sent to England to consult on the question of pleas and processes in the courts of Ireland which had been postponed on account of the king's demise. The death of Edward's father, Henry III, in 1272, which occurred while his son and successor was on crusade, must have been an unnerving period for the Dublin government. It now had recourse only to the interim government in England headed by Robert Burnel. A letter from the Dublin ministers to the regents in England requested help and advice on a number of complaints presented by the countess of Ulster against the king's steward there. The justiciar of Ireland could not offer assistance in the matter, 'being occupied in improving, with God's help, the state of Connacht'.[29]

But Edward I – as he now was – had not left the Dublin government entirely without practical resources. In imitation of his late father he had long maintained household knights – that is, knights especially trusted by their lords, for whom they performed both military and administrative tasks – in Ireland.[30]

27 P. Brand, 'King, Church and Property: The Enforcement of Restrictions on Alienations into Mortmain in the Lordship of Ireland in the Later Middle Ages', *Peritia*, 3 (1984), 483–4; G. J. Hand, *English Law in Ireland, 1290–1324* (Cambridge University Press, 1967), 135–58.

28 J. F. Lydon, 'Ireland in 1297: "At Peace after its Manner"', in Lydon (ed.), *Law and Disorder*, 22–3.

29 *IEP*, 203; Sayles, *Affairs*, 4–6.

30 For what follows see B. Hartland, 'The Household Knights of Edward I in Ireland', *Historical Research*, 77 (2004), 161–77. A separate military household may also have been retained in Ireland by Henry II: *PR 25 Henry II*, 67, 88–9.

Indeed, during the period between 1254 and 1272 three small but separate households operated in Ireland; those of Henry III, the Lord Edward and the justiciar. Following Edward's accession and during his extended absence from England as he travelled back from the Holy Land, the two remaining households may have been merged with the third to form one larger establishment answerable to and retained by the king. The household of the Lord Edward in Ireland in 1270 numbered three men; that of King Edward in 1275–6 numbered ten. Small numbers, undoubtedly, but significant when viewed as what they were – a pool of responsible leaders to whom sensitive tasks could be delegated.

The expansion of the household in the 1270s coincided with what appears to have been an escalation of the danger posed to the settlement by the Irish of the Leinster mountains. The household knights, though small in number, played an important part in curbing this threat. William Cadel, knight, for instance, was employed to protect O'Dempsey [Ó Díomusaig], a midland Irish lord loyal to the English, from aggressive attacks, and also probably acted as a paymaster for an expedition against the O'Briens in south-west Ireland in 1276–7. Another household knight, Walter l'Enfaunt, participated in the 1275 expedition to Glenmalure, County Wicklow, and ensured its success by capturing the rebel chief Muirchertach MacMurrough [Mac Murchada]. Only two of the ten knights based in Ireland could be spared to serve the king in Wales in 1277, the others clearly being engaged on the military expeditions of the justiciar. Probably in response to a request for greater resources from his justiciar, Edward formally re-established a separate justiciar's household distinct from his own in the Lordship. From 1276 onwards the justiciar was obliged to retain twenty or so men-at-arms with the title justiciar's knights from his salary, thus reducing the number of royal household knights required. Walter l'Enfaunt and Nicholas Dunheved, who served Edward conspicuously throughout this period, continued to act as household knights of the king in Ireland, but most of their fellows departed within a few years.[31]

The presence of the king's household knights in Ireland served to ensure that the royal will in the Lordship was observed. The king further strengthened his say in Irish affairs by employing knights from his own household in England in positions of responsibility in the Lordship. Edward appointed

---

31 The household could also maintain impecunious but useful men such as John Fulburne, who in the mid-1280s led Welshmen on campaign in Connacht. Fulburne, recruited by Nicholas de Clere, treasurer of Ireland, as one 'in whom he confides to bring over Welshmen to the K[ing]'s service in Ireland', was trusted both by the Dublin administration and by the king: Hartland, 'Household Knights'.

no fewer than five of his former household knights to the Irish justiciarship. The promotion of these knights – James Audley, 1270–2, Robert Ufford 1268–70, 1276–81, Geoffrey de Geneville, 1273–6, William de Vescy, 1290–4 and John Wogan, 1295–1308 – to the chief governorship facilitated communications between Dublin and Westminster, and helped reassure members of the Dublin administration that the king's interest in the Lordship was not waning as other concerns absorbed more of his attention. In addition, other important offices were also given to household knights. William fitz Warin, for instance, served as seneschal of Ulster 1272–81, while Thomas de Clare was sheriff of Limerick from September 1274 to June 1276.

Edward I and the Irish

The inability of the settlers and the forces of the crown to completely defeat the Irish of Leinster, and the proximity of these enemies to the king's demesne manors and the seat of government in Dublin, explains the prominence of this issue in official records. Repairs to Dublin castle commenced in 1275, and expenditure on improving the buildings of the Dublin exchequer began in 1280. In 1306–7 the exchequer moved its money to the castle 'because of the war in Leinster'.[32] But threats to the English settlement were not confined to the vicinity of Dublin. Roscommon castle in the King's Cantreds of Connacht was a particular target for Irish attacks. In 1280 the exchequer dispatched £1,000 to the justiciar there, and arranged for it to be garrisoned – along with other Connacht castles – by a force of specially recruited Welshmen.[33] The task of defending the extensive lordships of Thomond and Connacht fell to the colonial government during periods when the heirs to these estates were children. It was necessary to relieve Bunratty castle in 1276, while Connacht regularly required the intervention of government forces until its lord, Richard de Burgh, earl of Ulster, reached his majority in 1286. The far-ranging itinerary of John de Sandford, archbishop of Dublin and keeper of Ireland between June 1288 and November 1290, demonstrated both the impressive extent of English interests in Ireland in the late thirteenth century, and the island-wide nature of the pressure being applied by the native Irish on colonial settlements at the time.[34]

---

32 *IEP*, 13, 50, 190.
33 *IEP*, 64, 109, 112; A. Thomas, 'Interconnections between the Lands of Edward I: A Welsh–English Mercenary Force in Ireland, 1284–1304', *Bulletin of the Board of Celtic Studies*, 40 (1993), 135–47.
34 *CDI, 1285–1292*, no. 599; Frame, *Ireland and Britain*, 283.

Ireland mattered to Edward I, even if his Irish 'policy' was essentially pragmatic. He was consistent in approving what was necessary to allow the continued flow of Irish resources to Scotland and Gascony. As its accounts for
1302 put it, the 'exchequer was open for auditing the account of exchange and
for the examination of clear debts of the king, so that money might be more
speedily levied for the king's war in Scotland'.[35] In line with this single-minded
approach was Edward's decision to grant pardons to settlers for crimes including homicide in return for service overseas. Such grants, along with pardons
of debt, were among the routine rewards given by Edward I to his soldiers.
Although some settler lords expressed reservations about serving abroad, the
majority were willing to travel and fight. They regarded the opportunity to
provide such service as a welcome one: it drew them close to their king, thus
allowing them to put requests to him; it gave the king a reason to grant such
requests; and it provided a means by which men who needed to prove their
loyalty could do so. Consequently the English of Ireland did not ignore a
royal request for service abroad if at all possible.[36]

Equally pragmatic was Edward I's attitude to the legal status of the native
Irish. When he asserted in 1277 that the laws of the Irish were 'detestable to
God, and so contrary to all law that they ought not to be deemed laws', he
was merely repeating what he had been told by David Mac Cerbaill, archbishop of Cashel, who had petitioned him to grant English law to the Irish.[37]
The Irish may have refused to accept the derogatory views of their law and
customs that prevailed among the English, but they also resented being
excluded from the privileges and protections offered by the common law to
the settlers. This resentment is a prominent feature of 'The Remonstrance of
the Irish princes to Pope John XXII', which was composed in 1317. From the
viewpoint of the king's government in Westminster the injustices described
in the Remonstrance could be tolerated because the victims were Irish and
therefore outside English law. Archbishop Mac Cerbaill's initiative failed not
because of Edward I, but because of the opposition of the settlers, whose
privileged legal position was threatened by the proposal.[38]

---

35 *IEP*, 164.
36 B. Hartland, 'English Rule in Ireland, *c.*1272–*c.*1315: Aspects of Royal and Aristocratic
    Lordship'. PhD thesis, Durham University (2001), 38–60.
37 *CDI, 1252–1284*, no. 1408; J. R. S. Phillips, 'David Maccarwell and the Proposal to Purchase
    English Law, *c.*1273–*c.*1280', *Peritia*, 10 (1996), 272 and n. 62; Hand, *English Law in Ireland*,
    187–213.
38 Walter Bower, *Scotichronicon*, vi, 384–403, 465–81; B. Smith, 'Keeping the Peace', in
    Lydon (ed.), *Law and Disorder*, 58.

The Remonstrance was undoubtedly a piece of propaganda designed to justify Irish support for the Scottish invasion of Ireland, but the misdeeds listed within it were not fabrications. In memorable detail it reported the actions of Peter de Bermingham, lord of Tethmoy, who in 1305 murdered the leaders of the O'Connor Falys, having first invited them to partake of a feast. When de Bermingham sent eighteen heads to Dublin as proof of his zeal, he was awarded £100 'for subduing the Irish of Offali of the *parentela* of the Oconeghors, felons of the king, and for decapitating the captains of that *progenies*'.[39] In the absence of a general grant of English law individual Irishmen paid to avail of it, and the fees which eventually accrued to the crown from such applications may have strengthened the argument of those who supported the legal status quo. Applications by Irishmen for the right to use the common law could be made directly to the king, as in the case of Dermot Ofalve, who petitioned Edward I in 1302 for a grant in consideration of his good services in the Scottish war, or indirectly as when Walter de Burgh, earl of Ulster, requested of Henry III in 1266 that Michael, son of Simon O Clercham, and his descendants be allowed to 'for ever use and enjoy all liberties and free customs which the English use in Ireland'. The argument that kings of England in this period were not instinctively opposed to the extension of English law to the Irish is strengthened by bearing in mind that when the idea was resurrected by the earl of Kildare and John de Bermingham in 1319, Edward II, like his father, initially acceded to the request.[40]

Conflict along simple lines of English versus Irish was a rarity. We have seen how the de Burgh/Geraldine rivalry disturbed the Lordship in the 1260s and 1290s, and competition within Irish dynasties for the position of king drew in settler lords in support of contending parties. Furthermore, since the reign of Henry II English kings had on occasion encouraged rivalry among colonial magnates in the Lordship. The last significant lord from England to be introduced into Ireland by the crown was Thomas de Clare, the younger brother of Gilbert, earl of Gloucester, who in the 1270s was established as lord of Thomond in south-west Ireland.[41] The lands awarded to him had

---

39 One recent commentator has described this as 'one of medieval Ireland's most notorious crimes': C. Ó Cléirigh, 'The Problems of Defence: A Regional Case-study', in Lydon (ed.), *Law and Disorder*, 46; *IEP*, 182. For another contemporary view of Peter de Bermingham, see St J. D. Seymour, *Anglo-Irish Literature: 1200–1582* (Cambridge University Press, 1929), 83–8.

40 TNA SC 8/133/6621; NAI JI 1/1, 85–6; TNA SC 8/119/5944.

41 For what follows see Hartland, 'English Lords in Late Thirteenth and Early Fourteenth Century Ireland, 318–48.

previously been held by the de Muscegros family, which had surrendered its Irish interests. The grant relieved the Dublin government of direct responsibility for a distant part of the Lordship. But it was also intended to help curb the growing power of the de Burghs in Ireland. Thomond was an area of strategic importance to the de Burgh family, straddling as it did the land route between their lordship of Connacht and their estates in east Limerick. Since Thomas de Clare, with royal approval, had married into the Offaly branch of the Geraldine family, his appearance in Thomond displeased the de Burghs. Edward I, by contrast, wrote to de Clare in 1282 applauding him for 'retaining Thomas fitz Maurice [a Geraldine] to resist the forces of some persons who strive to infringe the peace'. The support offered by the de Burghs and de Clares to different segments of the O'Brien family as they competed for influence in this part of Ireland is discussed elsewhere in this volume.[42] Ultimately, factionalism between these groups did not outweigh their loyalty to the king of England, and they united against the invading Scots after 1315.[43]

The contending impulses of faction and loyalty also prevailed among the colonists at a level below that of the greatest lords, as the history of the Barrys and Cogans of Cork at this time suggests. In April 1317 a large number of men of the surname Barry 'who had lately committed divers robberies, arson, homicides and very many other misdeeds in the lands and tenements of the kinsmen of the surname of Cogan and who kept themselves by a one and unanimous counsel as manifestly at war' came before the justiciar, a truce having been granted to them, to 'arrange how the malignity of the Scotch who at present are striving to destroy the land of Ireland and the king's lieges may be repressed'.[44]

While alliances across the native–settler divide might pertain at local level, by the late thirteenth century the official English view was that the Irish were enemies because they did not have access to English law. The Dublin parliament of 1297 ordained that the English were no longer to make unilateral truces with any Irish who were against the king's peace, since such truces allowed the Irish to focus their energies upon one settler target before moving on to another. Henceforth only the justiciar, or in his absence especially appointed magnates, could conclude such agreements. Thus it was that the citizens of Limerick and the O'Briens of Thomond came to a peace through the negotiation of the justiciar, John Wogan, in 1308.[45] The thrust of these

---

42 See the chapter on Gaelic politics by Katharine Simms.
43 Frame, *Ireland and Britain*, 71–97.
44 NAI KB 2/8, 53–9.
45 *CJRI, 1308–14*, 2–3.

and other provisions made by the parliament was to enjoin the English community to act in concert 'in order to establish peace more firmly' so that resources of both men and money be freed up for Edward I's campaigns against Scotland.

The stipulation regarding truces cut across customs developed by settler lords in their dealings with their Irish neighbours. Geoffrey de Geneville, who as lord of Trim held his lands on terms which afforded him a good deal of independence, had at an unspecified date written to his seneschal (his chief officer in his liberty) declaring that 'when the lords of franchise have truce with any of the Irish at war, upon whom the King, or his justice, or others with his banner, are not riding, they ought not to be punished'. In making this assertion de Geneville made clear that he drew on his knowledge of events in the Welsh March during the conquest of Wales when Marcher lords who made truce with the Welsh against whom Edward was campaigning were not punished. It is not hard to see why the officers of the Dublin government found dealing with de Geneville and his liberty so awkward. But de Geneville's usefulness to Edward I beyond Ireland (and in the summer of 1297 he was helping Edward circumvent the problems posed by the earls of Norfolk and Hereford in refusing to act as marshal and constable of the army by standing in as marshal for the campaign to Flanders) meant his voice did not go unheard, nor the rights of the lord of Trim undefended.[46]

Parliamentary legislation prohibiting local truces, however well intentioned, failed to show appreciation of the realities of the frontier society that Ireland had become. The record of the plea heard in 1315 before Theobald de Verdon, justiciar of Ireland, detailing the circumstances in which the settler Laghles [Lawless] family of Leinster lived, is worth citing in full:

> On hearing the complaint of Hugh Laghles, Walter Laghles, William son of Hugh Laghles, Thomas Laghles, Robert son of Hugh Laghles and others of their following and name, being Englishmen faithful to the king and in his peace, shewing that all Englishmen and other faithful subjects of the king who were wont to remain between the vale of Dublin and county of Weyseford in times past, by the malice and wantonness of the Irish of the mountains of Leinster, felons of the king, they have been expelled and removed from their fortresses, manors and houses up to the present, and many of the said faithful subjects of the king have been slain by the said Irish felons, so that the said Hugh Laghles, Walter Laghles and others of their

---

46 *Cal. Gormanston Reg.*, 9; B. Hartland, 'The Liberties of Ireland in the Reign of Edward I', in M. Prestwich (ed.), *Liberties and Identities in the Medieval British Isles* (Woodbridge: Boydell Press, 2008), 204–5, 210–11; *EHD*, iii, 477–80.

name and offspring whose manors, lands and houses lie in a certain confined and narrow part of the county namely between Newcastle McKynegan and Wykynglo where they have the sea between Wales and Ireland for a wall on one side and the mountains of Leinster and divers other places where the said Irish felons live on the other, whose malice the said Hugh, Walter and others of their name and offspring cannot resist without a greater and more suffi-cient armed force nor can they live or remain any longer in those parts except by the will of those Irishmen unless provision is quickly made for them by suitable succour, and praying the Justiciar and King's Council to assist them with such a remedy in this behalf as shall be useful and fitting as well for the king as for them, it is agreed and granted by the said Justiciar and all the council that Hugh, Walter, William, Thomas, Robert and the others of their name and offspring, Englishmen, may treat with the said Irish and parliament [i.e. parley] with them and take days with them in the manner of the marches so that by giving and granting such kind of escapes and munificence to the said Irish, until chance shall have improved the state of the land in the said marches and the king shall have ordered otherwise, provided that in every-thing else they behave themselves well and faithfully to the king's faith and peace. And if it happen that any of the name and parentage of the said Hugh Laghles and the others whomsoever offend against the peace, it is agreed and granted that Hugh, Walter, William, Thomas and Robert may take those malefactors and imprison them, so that by the fear of such imprisonment others of those parts of their name and parentage being chastened may the more be fearful of offending. And it is granted to the said Hugh, Walter, William, Thomas and Robert that they by reason of such imprisonment be not charged in the king's court nor hindered in any way.[47]

This extract from the plea rolls is remarkable not just for the evocative way in which the geopolitical reality of life in the Leinster marches is conveyed to the reader down the centuries, but also for the acceptance by the justiciar that in certain circumstances governmental norms needed to be waived. Far from imposing upon the Laghles 'clan' the enactment of 1297 against unilateral truces with the Irish, a system of authority with strong Irish elements was acknowledged and condoned. Offences against the king's peace committed by members of the Laghles name and parentage were not to be punished by officers of the crown but by leaders of the kin-group.[48] Was there a degree of recognition here that a kin-based approach to family organisation and defence was not necessarily inimical to English interests in Ireland? While in densely colonised areas of the Lordship family organisation remained

47 NAI KB 2/7, 52–4.
48 P. Connolly, 'The Enactments of the 1297 Parliament', in Lydon (ed.), *Law and Disorder*, 158.

identical to the pattern that pertained in contemporary England, in more distant frontier zones 'large lineages, clustered round the family head or heads' prevailed. In recognising the leadership of such heads, the Dublin government was 'attempting to harness power which already rested with them and, in some degree, always had done.'[49]

The flexibility of the colonial government in the light of frontier realities favoured the powerful over the more humble among the settlers. In 1302 Isabella Cadel and her servant were charged with associating with 'felons of the mountains' and of being 'spies of the country for them'. Despite having committed a felony in the eyes of the Dublin government, the women were pardoned, suffering only the forfeiture of their goods. John Wogan, the justiciar, explained that he had been swayed by 'the praiseworthy service to the King often done by William Cadel', Isabella's father. The court record glosses over the fact that Isabella was married to one of the felons, Diarmaid O'Dempsey, and that this marriage had probably been arranged by the same praiseworthy Wiliam Cadel whose service to the king, which had included protecting the O'Dempseys from the incursions of more aggressive Irish in the 1270s, had saved her. Other female spies were not so fortunate. The humble settler women convicted in 1305 of spying for the Irish enemies, for instance, did not benefit from any official recognition of the complexities of frontier life.[50]

The Dublin Parliament of 1297

Many parliaments were held in Ireland in the period covered by this chapter, but we lack records for most of them. The accident of documentary survival in part explains the prominence afforded to the Dublin parliament of 1297 in our historiography: the text of its enactments was included in the Black Book of Christ Church, and this account has been edited several times.[51] Notwithstanding such considerations, it is still the case that the 1297 parliament was a gathering of particular importance. The new justiciar, John Wogan, intended that it should strengthen the defences of the Lordship so that Irish resources could be deployed by the king elsewhere. Wogan had had

---

49 Frame, *Ireland and Britain*, 206–7. Examples of such lineages include the Talouns of Carlow 'common robbers', and the Maunsels, Ketyngs and St. Albinos of Tipperary (NAI KB 2/3, pp. 7, 8, 10–11). See also *CJRI, 1305–07*, 252. The Barrys and Cogans of County Cork have already been mentioned (above, 265).

50 *CJRI, 1295–1303*, 368; Kenny, *Anglo-Irish and Gaelic Women*, 40.

51 Connolly, 'Enactments of the 1297 Parliament', 139.

sufficient time to analyse the Irish situation and identify what from a government perspective looked like workable remedies for its many ills. Evidence
from the plea rolls that the third enactment of the parliament, which provided
that a man with land worth £20 per annum should have a horse constantly
ready in his dwelling, was being enforced in the years after 1297 demonstrates
that the legislation was intended to make a real difference.[52] Although within
ten years or so the strategy of the parliament was 'well and truly shattered',
it did succeed at least until 1306 in limiting the expenditure of the Dublin government on war within the lordship, thus freeing resources for the English
campaigns in Scotland.[53]

One reason why recognition of the importance of the parliament of 1297
is justified is that the assembly sought to address one of the key issues facing
the Lordship by the late thirteenth century: the behaviour of non-resident
lords who, it was said, denuded their Irish lands of the resources required for
their defence. Not only magnates were culpable in this regard. An inspection
carried out in 1312–13 of debts owed to the Irish exchequer from Edward I's
reign revealed that Reginald Russel and his wife Margaret, who owed money
in Waterford, had, without permission, diverted the profits of their Irish
lands to England, where they resided.[54] But it is important not to exaggerate the actions of the 1297 parliament in responding to this matter. Despite
the plentiful evidence of how transmarine landholding might be exploited
to the disadvantage of Irish revenues, there appears to have been no ground-
swell of opinion antipathetic to this model of lordship in Ireland at this time.
The single most important effect of the parliament in terms of landholding
was, rather, the very practical decision to establish the de Verdon share of the
lordship and liberty of Meath as a separate county. This alteration in status –
which reduced the financial worth of the lands to its lord – helped to convince
Theobald de Verdon that his energies would be better spent in developing his
estates in the Welsh March than in Ireland. He left one of his younger sons,
Miles, as the chief guardian of his lands in Ireland.[55] Miles, who would lead
the men of Meath in the rout of Edward Bruce at Faughart in 1318, was a
natural choice to defend the family lands.

---

52 NAI RC 7/4, 419; *CJRI, 1295–1303*, 175.
53 Lydon, 'Ireland in 1297', 22.
54 NAI RC 8/6, 311–13. Margaret was the widow of the Desmond Geraldine lord Thomas
   fitz Maurice.
55 Hartland, 'Liberties', 210–13; B. Smith, *Colonisation and Conquest in Medieval Ireland: The
   English in Louth 1170–1330* (Cambridge University Press, 1999), 94–5; M. Hagger, *The
   Fortunes of a Norman Family: The de Verduns in England, Ireland and Wales, 1066–1316*
   (Dublin: Four Courts Press, 2001), 84–123.

In reality, only a few of those who held land on both sides of the Irish Sea before 1297 divested themselves of their Irish interests in the years immediately thereafter.[56] Continental lords with Irish lands – few in number though they may have been by this time – apparently felt under no immediate pressure to sell their property in the Lordship. During the Bruce Invasion, it is true, the Dublin government had made a decision that rents could be taken as contributions to the expenses of the war from the lands of aliens and from those who exported all the profits of their Irish estates elsewhere, but this provision did not outlast the conflict.[57] In the same year that the Scottish intervention came to an end, half of the lands of Drew de Merlawe in Louth and Dublin were granted to Ralph, Count of Eu, the husband of Drew's eldest daughter.[58] In instances where a lord – whether resident or not – did decide to sell his estate in the Lordship, the buyer was likely to be a member of the colonial landowning elite, as the case of John de Cogan and John fitz Thomas demonstrates. In 1297 fitz Thomas persuaded de Cogan to undertake not to sell or alienate any of his Irish lands to anyone else but him on pain of a £20,000 penalty.[59]

Landholding ties between England and Ireland had certainly reduced in scale since the late twelfth and early to mid-thirteenth centuries, when extensive transnational lordships had been established. But, as the large number of attorneys appointed in Ireland by English-based lords in the decades around 1300 suggests, transmarine landholding continued to tie Ireland and England together at this time. Not only did many old links survive into the fourteenth century, important new ones were formed, as the case of the Preston family suggests. The Prestons, from Lancashire, first began living and trading in Drogheda around 1300, and by the end of the 1360s had acquired the lordship of Gormanston in Meath. While servants of the crown sent from England to Ireland were prohibited from acquiring Irish land this did not stop government ministers such as John de Fressingfield (itinerant justice and keeper of the rolls and writs, 1305–6) from seeking and acquiring landed property in the Lordship.[60]

---

56 B. Hartland, 'Reasons for Leaving: The Effect of Conflict on English Landholding in Late Thirteenth-Century Leinster', *JMH*, 32 (2006), 18–26; B. Hartland, 'Absenteeism: The Chronology of a Concept', in B. Weiler, J. Burton and P. Schofield (eds.), *Thirteenth Century England XI* (Woodbridge: Boydell Press, 2007), 215–29.

57 NAI RC 8 /10, 152–5; RC 8/6, 311–13.

58 TNA C 134/59/8; *Rep. DKI 42*, 16; *CFR, 1307–19*, 368.

59 *Red Book of the Earls of Kildare*, no. 45.

60 *Cal. Gormanston Reg.*, 53–4, 66; Frame, *English Lordship*, 95; BL Add MS 6041, fol.104 LXXXXVII; P. Brand, 'A Versatile Legal Administrator and More: The Career of John of Fressingfield in England, Ireland, and Beyond', in Smith (ed.), *Ireland and the English World*, 44–54.

Financial and Military Pressures

When allowance is made for an increase from the 1290s onwards in the range and quantity of documentary evidence at our disposal produced by the colonial government, it still appears to be the case that the scale of warfare between the English and Irish, especially in Leinster, intensified in the early fourteenth century. The seneschals in charge of the military defence of the lordships that succeeded the earlier single liberty of Leinster (Carlow, Kilkenny, Wexford and, before it was made a county, Kildare) found it increasingly difficult to bring the warlike Irish to terms.[61] It is possible that the division of the Marshal liberty of Leinster into successor liberties in the hands of a number of non-resident lords, combined with a period of vacancy in the archbishopric of Dublin, created a vacuum of lordship which contributed to the revival of Irish fortunes in Leinster. The 1297 parliament perhaps had this in mind when it ordained that 'the whole community of Leinster, which once was one liberty, shall together levy, contribute and maintain war against the Irish and shall be led by one counsel, and those refusing or dissenting shall be severely punished'.[62] While troubled marchlands bordered each of the successor liberties of Leinster, the care taken by the justiciar to ensure that the seneschals of these liberties cooperated with each other helped mitigate the danger to some extent. Much of the burden of defence lay with important local tenants, who met among themselves to devise effective responses to their security concerns. In 1313–14, such a meeting at Ross was attended by the keeper (that is, governor) of Ireland, the treasurer, the chancellor, several other members of the king's council, and a number of important settlers from Wexford. Having acknowledged that the taking of fines from the Irish no longer served to restrain them, the delegates at this assembly established a system of wards designed to curtail the movements of the most dangerous enemies of the moment, the O'Bryne [Ó Broin] family.[63] Also present at the meeting was the leading Irish lord of the region, Muiris MacMurrough, who was said to be 'hostile to the said race [the O'Byrnes]'. His actions serve as a timely reminder that in an environment characterised by endless local disputes and enmities a straight fight between English and Irish was an extremely uncommon occurrence.

---

61 B. Hartland, ' "To Serve Well and Faithfully": The Agents of English Aristocratic Rule in Leinster, *c.*1272–*c.*1315', *Medieval Prosopography*, 24 (2003), 195–246.

62 Connolly, 'Enactments of the 1297 Parliament', 159.

63 NAI KB 2/4, 44–5.

Edward I expected all of the lands over which he ruled to contribute to the fulfilment of royal wishes. He could see no contradiction between those wishes and the wellbeing of the subjects entrusted to him by God. Yet in drawing men and money away from Ireland to assist in his campaigns in Flanders and Scotland, Edward undoubtedly undermined the strength of the English position in the Lordship. From its greatest landed extent in the middle of the thirteenth century, the borders of the English settlements had already begun to retreat in many parts of the country even before the Bruce Invasion of 1315. It was true that in Ulster Richard de Burgh had extended the geographical range and political depth of his power in the decades around 1300. But this only made the strongest and ablest of the surviving Irish lords, Domnall O'Neill, son of the Brian O'Neill killed at the battle of Downpatrick in 1260, more desperate and more willing to contemplate an alliance with the Scots in order to shore up his own weak position. In Leinster the Irish families which had not been absorbed into the settlement after 1170, and which retreated to the mountains in the face of superior English military technology, were resurgent from the 1270s onwards. Warding of the type established at Ross in 1313–14 was an effective defensive measure, but it was also extremely expensive; even a well-stocked treasury at the Dublin exchequer would have been unable to pay for the system over a lengthy period. The cost of Edmund Butler's expedition against the O'Byrne family in 1313, which included the establishment of wards, amounted to £1,076 17s. 10d. – one-third of recorded exchequer receipts for the same period.[64]

Edward II had insisted in 1311 that the revenues of Ireland should be spent on Ireland, but had countermanded the order within a year, and provisions were still being raised in the Lordship for the king's wars in Scotland even as Edward Bruce and his Scots invaded in 1315. It took this dire emergency for a more flexible and realistic approach to prevail: the victuals being collected at that time for the latest proposed campaign in Scotland were instead diverted by the Dublin government for use in Ireland. When Edward II's special envoy to Ireland, John de Hothum, requested £500 from the English exchequer in March 1316 to fund his needs in defending the Lordship, the money was forthcoming. The defeat of Edward Bruce at Faughart in October 1318 came not a moment too soon for the war-torn lordship of Ireland. The annals of Connacht recorded that 'there was never a better deed done for the Irish than this'.[65] For the English of Ireland this was certainly true.

---

64 *IEP*, 218, 220 n. 1.
65 'Documents on the Early Stages of the Bruce Invasion of Ireland, 1315–1316', ed. J. R. S. Phillips, *PRIA*, 79 C (1979), 265–6; *IEP*, 244; *AC*, 253.

9

Disaster and Opportunity: 1320–1450

BRENDAN SMITH

HISTORIANS of fourteenth- and early fifteenth-century Ireland are blessed in the quantity and range of documentary sources they have at their disposal. Annals, genealogies, prose tales, histories, religious and secular poetry, and legal and medical tracts were produced by the hereditary learned classes of Gaelic Ireland, which were patronised by both native and settler lords. The English crown and its Irish administration generated official documents concerned with a plethora of financial, judicial and governmental matters. Leading settler families collected and organised the charters and manorial accounts that provided legal title to their lands, as well as the means to derive profit from them. The towns did likewise, gathering together and making use of the deeds that guaranteed their liberties, and the rules by which they organised their urban communal life. Religious houses in a number of these towns kept chronicles which recorded and interpreted current events from a settler point of view. Long used to preserving and ordering the written evidence which secured its property, the Church provided a model of record-production and record-keeping for society at large, and generated other forms of writing such as episcopal registers, collections of sermons, psalters and records of diocesan visitations. Visitors from overseas, whether present in Ireland as pilgrims or as observers of military campaigns, left written accounts of their time on the island, while inquisitive foreign chroniclers recorded information about the country provided to them by its inhabitants.[1]

While the comparative abundance of written material from this period owes something to the accident of survival, it also reflects historical developments specific to the time. Gaelic Ireland appears to have produced very few manuscripts in the period 1200–1350, a situation that makes the spectacular

---

1 Simms, *Medieval Gaelic Sources*; Connolly, *Medieval Record Sources*; *Handbook and Select Calendar of Sources for Medieval Ireland*; Haren and de Pontfarcy (eds.), *The Medieval Pilgrimage to St Patrick's Purgatory*.

growth in Irish manuscript production thereafter all the more noteworthy. It is possible to link this phenomenon to the increased security enjoyed by the learned hereditary families of Gaelic Ireland from this time – a security in turn derived from the success of native lords in withstanding English territorial and cultural advance, and the growing popularity of Gaelic culture among sections of the settler population. The Irish clergy, both native and settler, were already well accustomed to corresponding with the papal curia, but the volume of such written communication increased as the fourteenth century progressed, a development given further impetus by the schism and the two papal courts thus engendered.[2] The period also saw a significant growth in the number of petitions being dispatched by the settlers to the king's parliament and council both in England and Ireland, and the use by this group of the English chancellor's equity court. Such developments testified to the appearance from the late thirteenth century of new ways of expressing grievance and seeking redress within the wider English political community. At the same time, English noble families on both sides of the Irish Sea committed themselves with unprecedented energy to the production and collection of the legal and financial records that testified to, and strengthened, their lordship. This increased volume of writing in fourteenth-century Ireland generated innovation in the matter of document production. Waterford was precocious among the towns of the British Isles in recording the business of its council in English, while the use of Italian paper rather than parchment by the registrar of the archdiocese of Armagh in compiling the register of Archbishop Milo Sweteman (1361–80) – one of the earliest uses of paper in Ireland – testifies to a similar commitment to experimentation on the part of the Church.[3]

New ideas came to Ireland in part as a result of the participation of its inhabitants in aspects of Western Christian life such as pilgrimage. Santiago de Compostela in northern Spain enjoyed renewed popularity as a pilgrimage centre from the early fourteenth century, and settler chronicles record the death in England in 1321 of Edmund Butler, father of the first earl of Ormond, while returning to Kilkenny from Santiago. A few years later Kilkenny became

---

2 J. Carney, 'Literature in Irish', in *NHI* ii, 689–98; F. Henry and G. Marsh-Micheli, 'Manuscripts and Illuminations', in *NHI* ii, 788–801. See F. J. Byrne's introduction in O'Neill, *Irish Hand*; C. Mooney, 'The Church in Gaelic Ireland 13th to 15th Centuries', in P. J. Corish (ed.), *A History of Irish Catholicism*. Vol. II. no. 5 (Dublin: Gill & Sons, 1969).

3 J. Lydon, *Ireland in the Later Middle Ages* (Dublin: Gill & Macmillan, 1973), 70–1; G. Dodd, *Justice and Grace: Private Petitioning and the English Parliament in the Late Middle Ages* (Oxford University Press, 2007); R. R. Davies, *Lords and Lordship in the British Isles in the Late Middle Ages*, ed. B. Smith (Oxford University Press, 2009), 36–42; A. Bliss, 'Language and Literature', in Lydon (ed.), *English in Medieval Ireland*, 31; *Reg. Mey*, ix.

the site of the first witch-burning in Western Europe – a pioneering expression of modernity heartily applauded by the local Franciscan chronicler. Another instance of Irish engagement with contemporary manifestations of religious enthusiasm saw flagellants process through the streets of Drogheda in the aftermath of the first outbreak of plague in 1349.[4] Gaelic Ireland and its clergy were integrated into this Christian world. Even as Nicholas Mac Cathasaigh, bishop of Clogher, (1320–56), wrote of living 'in the ends of the world' in 1353, he must have pondered just how small that world was, given that his correspondent was a Hungarian pilgrim who wished to visit the pilgrimage site of St Patrick's Purgatory in his diocese. Nicholas's successor as bishop, Brain Mac Cathmhaoil (1356–8), was appointed to his see while attending the papal curia at Avignon, while in 1373 the chapter at Clogher elected as their bishop John Ó Corcráin, at that time a monk at the Irish Benedictine community at Würzburg. John had studied canon law at Prague and in 1381 returned to his alma mater to receive a doctorate in that subject. His contemporary, Matthew Ó hEógain, son of the archdeacon of Clogher, lectured at Oxford for fourteen years, and was esteemed locally as 'the Great Master'. The contemporary annals written within the diocese of Clogher, the Annals of Ulster, note the deaths in 1348 and 1383 at Bologna of the leading theologian, John Andreae, and canon lawyer, John of Lignano.[5]

The failure of the university established at Dublin in 1320 to flourish ensured that Oxford was the destination for most students from Ireland seeking a higher education, whether of settler or native stock. In 1346 the settlers of Louth unsuccessfully petitioned the crown to arrest all native Irish scholars then at Oxford in retaliation for an attack on the county by MacMahon [Mac Mathghamhna] that had cost the lives of hundreds of English subjects. The official response that the petition was 'not reasonable' may suggest that the number of Gaelic students present at Oxford was high. Native Irish students might travel further afield for specific training. John de Kylloylac O kannin from Meath held a medical degree from the University of Montpellier in 1320, and Latin medical tracts derived from earlier Arabic copies were being translated into Irish in the middle of the century. In 1341 Edward III made 'a grant for life, in consideration of his good service to the king beyond the seas of

---

4 *Clyn*, 174, 180, 214; M. B. Callan, *The Templars, the Witch, and the Wild Irish: Vengeance and Heresy in Medieval Ireland* (Dublin: Four Courts Press, 2015); *CPL, 1342–62*, 311, 387.
5 K. Walsh, '...*In Finibus Mundi*: Late Medieval Pilgrims to St Patrick's Purgatory, Lough Derg, and the European Dimension of the Diocese of Clogher', in H. A. Jefferies (ed.), *History of the Diocese of Clogher* (Dublin: Four Courts Press, 2005), 41–69; B. Smith, 'The Late Medieval Diocese of Clogher, c.1200–1480', in Jefferies (ed.), *History of the Diocese of Clogher*, 70–80; *AU*, ii, 495; *AU*, iii, 11, 13.

the weirs of Limerick in Ireland to William Ouhynnouvan, the king's surgeon', and also granted English law to him and his descendants 'notwithstanding that he is by birth of the Irish nation'. It is likely that William had been trained on the Continent. In 1375 the same king granted permission to two Franciscans from the O'Brien [Ó Briain] foundation at Ennis to travel to Strasbourg for their education.[6]

Warfare and its Consequences

In any narrative of political developments in fourteenth- and early fifteenth-century Ireland, warfare and violent death must loom large. As far back as 1241 Emperor Frederick II had written of 'bloodstained Ireland' in a letter attributing particular characteristics to the different countries of Western Europe, and a century later the island's reputation in the wider Christian world was no less sanguinary. Even the Devil had noticed, if the testimony of the Necromancer of Toledo is to be believed. As reported by Archbishop Richard Fitz Ralph of Armagh in a sermon he preached before Pope Clement VI at Avignon in 1349, the Necromancer had asked the Devil which Christian country sent the largest number of souls to hell. On account of the prevalence of robbery and hatred among its inhabitants, the reply was 'Ireland'.[7] That Irish soil in the 1340s and 1350s was significantly more blood-soaked than that of France, however, may be doubted.

The relief expressed in Irish annals as well as settler chronicles at the defeat of the Scots and the death in battle of Edward Bruce in 1318 spoke to the weariness of a population exhausted by three years of large-scale warfare and famine. In assessing the longer-term impact of these years, the damage caused to the power of Richard Burgh, earl of Ulster, in his extensive Ulster and Connacht lordships stands out as particularly significant. Its negative consequences for English authority in the north and west of Ireland were mirrored in the south-west by the death of Richard Clare, lord of Thomond, at the hands of the O'Briens in 1318. Equally important for the future was the prominence that defeating the invasion bestowed upon Roger Mortimer, the king's lieutenant in Ireland. A substantial landowner in Leix (Laois) and

---

6 F. McGrath, *Education in Ancient and Medieval Ireland* (Dublin: Studies 'Special Publications', 1979), 171–9; *CPR, 1340–3*, 84–5; CIRCLE: PR 49 Ed III, no. 274; Sayles, *Affairs*, 186–7.

7 Smith, *Crisis and Survival*, 32–3, 42; M. Clanchy, *England and its Rulers 1066–1272* (London: Fontana Press, 1983), 257; K. Walsh, *A Fourteenth-Century Scholar and Primate: Richard FitzRalph in Oxford, Avignon and Armagh* (Oxford University Press, 1981), 288–94.

Meath, Mortimer was responsible for the establishment of three new earl-doms in Ireland between 1318 and 1329. The earldom of Louth did not survive the death of its first holder, John Bermingham, in 1329, but the earldoms of Ormond and Desmond, along with the earldom of Kildare, established in 1316, proved more durable. In 1322 Mortimer's fate appeared to have been sealed: his support for the defeated opponents of Edward II led to his forfei-ture and imprisonment in the Tower of London. Two years later, however, he escaped to the Continent, and in 1326 joined Queen Isabella in a successful invasion of England that ended Edward II's reign. Ruling in the name of the young Edward III, Mortimer had himself made earl of March, and increased his landed interests in Ireland. He was toppled by Edward III in 1330, but the new king retained a suspicion that lasted into the 1350s of those who had benefited from Mortimer's patronage. Almost two decades of tension between the crown and the new settler elite in Ireland may be traced back to the policies of Roger Mortimer.[8]

Mortimer's willingness to seek peace with Scotland in the late 1320s offered hope for the recovery of the settlement, especially in Ulster, but the death of King Robert I (Bruce) in 1329 and Mortimer's own execution the following year allowed old antagonisms to resurface. Irish resources were once again deployed by the English against the northern kingdom in 1335, and in 1337 fighting men from the Lordship were instrumental in the seizure of the Isle of Man from the Scots. The opportunity to strike at Scotland had caused Edward III to cancel at the last moment a planned expedition to Ireland in 1332, and the prospect of an Irish visit receded further from the middle of the decade as the king's attention became absorbed by the growing likelihood of war with France. Edward's interest in Ireland as a source of military sup-port, his impatience with the administrative personnel of the Lordship, and his mistrust of the beneficiaries of Roger Mortimer's largesse, grew apace. Matters came to a head during the governorships of John Morice (1341–4) and Ralph Ufford (1344–6). The king's decision in 1341 to revoke any grants made in Ireland since the death of Edward I in 1307 provoked bitter protest from the settlers. The order was withdrawn in the following year, but Edward's choice of Morice's successor in 1344 demonstrated his continued dissatisfac-tion with affairs in the Lordship. Ralph Ufford, the younger brother of the earl of Suffolk, was close to the king, and a successful soldier with experience of war in both Scotland and France. On arriving in Ireland in the summer of 1344 he campaigned to good effect against the Irish of Leinster and Ulster,

8 Frame, *Colonial Ireland*, 136–9.

but also dismissed many senior ministers in the Dublin administration and confronted the power of the settler earls. By the time Ufford died in Dublin in 1346 the earl of Desmond was an outlaw hiding among his Irish allies in Munster, while the earl of Kildare was a prisoner in Dublin castle. Edward III had made his point, and although entirely harmonious relations with the settler earls were not fully established until the 1350s, the earls of Desmond and Kildare were rehabilitated and this period of crisis in Anglo-Irish relations was at an end.[9]

Edward III's decision to appoint Ufford to the chief governorship was also part of his response to the murder in 1333 of the most important settler lord in Ireland, William Burgh, earl of Ulster. William's widow, Matilda of Lancaster, was the king's cousin and in 1343 King Edward sanctioned her marriage to Ralph Ufford. The couple travelled to Ireland together and the Dublin chronicler was of the view that Matilda, who had maintained a close interest in her claims in Ireland since her widowhood, helped shape Ufford's Irish policies. Already, in 1342, the king had arranged the marriage of Elizabeth Burgh, daughter of Earl William and Matilda, and heiress to the earldom of Ulster, to his second son, Lionel of Antwerp. Both of the betrothed parties were infants at this time, but in the midst of his confrontation with the settlers the king's decisions with regard to the Ulster inheritance illustrated his determination to ensure that the interests of the crown remained at the heart of policy-making in the colony. William Burgh's murder by some of his leading tenants had added to the political instability of a region that encompassed not only northern Ireland but also western Scotland. The death of King Robert I and the English victories of the early 1330s severely weakened the power of the Scottish monarchy in the Highlands and Islands, allowing the leading local magnate, John MacDonald [Eoin Mac Domnaill] of Islay, to secure his own position as Lord of the Isles – a title he first used in a letter to Edward III in 1336 – by playing the English and Scottish crowns off against each other. As John consolidated his power he was happy to encourage branches of his family, and other Gaelic-Scottish families, to migrate to Ireland where, in return for military service as galloglasses, they were provided with hereditary estates by leading Irish lords. Thus by the middle of the century a branch of the MacDonalds, Clan Alexander, had been settled by O'Neill [Ó Néill], king of the Irish of Ulster, at Ballygawley in Tyrone. They joined the MacSweeney [Mac Suibhne] galloglass, who had settled in Donegal two generations earlier, and by the 1370s

---

9 Frame, *Political Development of the British Isles*, 129–41; Frame, *Ireland and Britain*, 113–39.

had been followed to Ireland by the families of MacCabe [Mac Cába] and MacSheehy [Mac Síthigh].[10]

These galloglass warriors added to the fighting power of Gaelic lords as they competed with each other and with their settler rivals for local supremacy. Already by the time of the arrival of Clan Alexander settler castles from Bunratty in the south-west and Sligo in the north-west, through Roscommon, Athlone and Randon on the Shannon, and Dunamase and Lea in the midlands, to Ferns in Wexford and Arklow on the east coast, had been burned or occupied by Irish ruling families. A confederation of Leinster Irish led by the MacMurroughs threatened Dublin and in conjunction with the O'More [Ó Morda] family of Laois sought to control the main line of communication between Dublin and the settled areas of south Leinster and Munster. In Ulster, Ralph Ufford's unexpected decision following a successful campaign against the Irish in 1345 to depose the reigning O'Neill lord and replace him with his rival proved to be a disaster for the local settlers. Ufford's favoured candidate, Aed *Mór* (or *Remor*), was the son of Domnall O'Neill, who had supported the Scottish invasion of Ireland in 1315. It was Aed who settled the MacDonald galloglass in Tyrone. For the next twenty years he devoted his energies to successfully subduing most of the lesser Gaelic lordships in Ulster. By the 1370s the pressure exerted by his son and successor, Niall, on the settlers in east Ulster and Louth was intense.[11]

The response of the English to the deteriorating security situation that faced the settlement took many forms. Chief governors were expected to be militarily active, and the majority of them led campaigns against the most dangerous Irish lords, usually in Leinster and Munster. Such campaigns were expensive, as was the system of warding favoured by some governors. This involved the stationing of soldiers in areas of strategic importance, sometimes for lengthy periods of time. Money might also be spent by the government in paying favoured leaders among the native Irish to secure their support against less amenable enemies. The administration was equally content to sponsor and reward the killing by settlers of those Irish leaders who could not be bought off. In 1356 Thomas de Asteley of Wexford received the healthy sum of £12 upon producing before the Irish council the heads of five native leaders

---

10 Frame, *English Lordship*, 51, 323–4; M. Brown, *The Wars of Scotland, 1214–1371* (Edinburgh University Press, 2004), 255–73; K. Nicholls, 'Scottish Mercenary Kindreds in Ireland, 1250–1600', in S. Duffy (ed.), *The World of the Galloglass: Kings, Warlords and Warriors in Ireland and Scotland, 1200–1600* (Dublin: Four Courts Press, 2007), 86–105.

11 J. Watt, 'The Anglo-Irish Colony under Strain, 1327–99', in *NHI* ii, 352–96. See K. Simms' chapter on Gaelic politics in this volume.

'in consideration of his praiseworthy service and also of the fact that it had been proclaimed that whoever brought the head of any Irish captain to the king's court would receive an appropriate reward'. Less fortunate in pursuing this course of action was Richard Wade of Carlow. His role in the death of Donnchadh MacMurrough [Mac Murchada], leader of the Irish of Leinster, in 1375 brought down upon him the wrath of Donnchadh's successor, Art. In the following year the latter instigated the burning of Wade's house in Carlow and promised a reward of over £66 'to any Irishman or Englishman who would cut off Richard's head'. As a result of this campaign 'Richard does not dare go outside the town to attend to his husbandry and other matters without a great company', and was forced to live instead off a small stipend secured from the government.[12]

The crown accepted that the chief governor could not coordinate or lead all security initiatives within the Lordship, and was content to see local settler lords make arrangements in their own spheres of influence that helped defend the colony. The earls of Desmond, Kildare and Ormond, in similar fashion to the Dublin government, intervened in leadership disputes among the important Irish families of their districts, and entered into written agreements with some of these concerning military service and the establishment of mechanisms to resolve disputes with settlers without recourse to warfare. The great colonial lords were also expected to take the lead in curbing the lawless actions of their relatives, and of those settler families such as the Dillons and Daltons of western Meath, the Tobins (St Albinos), Keatings, Purcells and Shortalls of Tipperary and Kilkenny, the Roches, Poers and Condons (Cauntetons) of Cork and Waterford, which had developed lineage structures similar to those of the native Irish. Official support for the earls in these endeavours was signalled by appointing them keepers of the peace in the counties concerned.[13]

Just as Edward III's determination to come to Ireland in the early 1330s had waned in the light of the opportunities presented by warfare in Scotland and then France, so the temporary cessation of conflict with his neighbours in 1360 allowed the king to focus more on Irish affairs. Since the bruising encounters of the early 1340s the settler community in Ireland had used with increasing skill its ability to present petitions to the crown through its own parliament. These petitions spoke to the declining fortunes of the colony and

---

12 Frame, *Ireland and Britain*, 249–77; E. O'Byrne, *War, Politics and the Irish of Leinster, 1156–1606* (Dublin: Four Courts Press, 2003), 100–6; *IEP*, 482, 534, 536.

13 Frame, *Ireland and Britain*, 191–220; Simms, *From Kings to Warlords*, 113.

implored the king to act before it was too late. With his coffers bulging as a result of the ransom being paid by the French for the return of their captured king, and with a united political community behind him, Edward III was ready to respond. In 1352 the long-planned marriage of his son Lionel of Antwerp to Elizabeth Burgh had taken place, and in 1360 Burgh's grandmother, Elizabeth de Clare, died, bringing to Lionel yet more substantial estates in Ireland as well as in Wales and England. (It was with reference to the most important of these English estates, the honour of Clare in Suffolk, that in 1362 the king bestowed upon Lionel the additional title of duke of Clarence.) The time was now right to install Lionel both as the principal magnate in the Irish Lordship, and as representative there of the crown. On 1 July 1361 he was appointed lieutenant of Ireland by his father and crossed the Irish Sea two months later with an exceptionally large and well-financed force.[14]

Lionel left Ireland for the last time – vowing never to return – in November 1366. His wife had died in Dublin in 1363, and he had spent eight months of the following year, and a shorter part of 1365 in England. While in Ireland he campaigned vigorously and successfully against Irish lordships in Leinster, the midlands and Munster, and oversaw an increase in the amount paid by the settlers into the Irish exchequer. His decision to relocate the exchequer and judicial benches from Dublin to Carlow was a bold move designed to help bolster the fortunes of a settler town situated on the strategic land route between the colonised areas of the Dublin region on the one hand and the south coast on the other. Carlow, however, remained a dangerous frontier town subject – as the experience of Richard Wade mentioned above suggests – to Irish raids. To quote Robin Frame: 'The main result of Lionel's lieutenancy, a cynic might say, was to accustom the English government to providing, and the colonial establishment to receiving, financial assistance.'[15]

In February 1366 a parliament summoned by Lionel met at Kilkenny and passed the body of legislation that is forever associated with his name in Irish history. While the majority of the clauses of the Statute of Kilkenny outlined administrative adjustments intended to improve the operation of justice and the security situation in the Lordship, its reputation rests on its attempts to regulate relations between the settlers and the native Irish. In the eyes of the government and the settlers these matters were closely

---

14 W. M. Ormrod, 'The Protocella Rolls and English Government Finance, 1353–1364', *EHR*, 102 (1987), 622–32; P. Connolly, 'The Financing of English Expeditions to Ireland, 1361–1376', in Lydon (ed.), *England and Ireland*, 104–21.

15 Lydon, *Lordship*, 149–57; Frame, *Colonial Ireland*, 149. For a less favourable interpretation of the Carlow initiative see the chapter by Bennett in this volume.

linked: only English law could guarantee justice for English subjects, so deficiencies in the provision of the common law must be addressed lest the colonists resort to native law instead. The 1366 statute re-issued legislation relating to settler–native interactions passed in previous parliaments, but pushed this agenda to new extremes. No alliance with the Irish by marriage, fosterage or concubinage was henceforth to be entered into. Only the English language was to be used by the settlers, who were in future also to ride their horses and dress themselves in the English manner. The settlers were not to patronise Irish minstrels or entertainers. Irishmen were not to be received by religious houses in settled areas, nor were such men to be presented to cathedrals or collegiate churches. The stated purpose of the statute was to identify a path which, if followed, would provide security for the king's subjects in Ireland and restore the finances of the colony. In attempting to regulate aspects of personal behaviour, and in emphasising the need to maintain barriers between different social groups, the Kilkenny statute was in line with legislation passed in contemporary England in response to the social upheavals wrought by the plague of 1348–9. In both instances the elites which sponsored such initiatives were motivated by fear of change, and predictably failed to legislate back into existence a world that was lost. Settlers in Ireland persisted in speaking Irish, just as in England newly wealthy peasants wilfully continued to dress above their station. The frequent re-issuing of the Statute of Kilkenny over the next century and more suggests that its real function may have been to help the settlers define for themselves and others what it was to be English.[16]

The Statute of Kilkenny also sought to remedy the tensions that existed between the settlers and the king's representatives sent from England. Since both groups were subjects of the English crown, the statute insisted, they should desist from insulting each other. Mutual suspicion between the two parties, evident since at least the 1320s and particularly noticeable during the crisis of the early 1340s, was raised to a new pitch during Lionel's governorship. As the greatest of the English lords in Ireland, as well as lieutenant of the king, Lionel expected to exercise his rights of patronage to reward his friends while in the Lordship. The settlers were pleased enough when such patronage came their way, but reacted badly when its recipients were men from England. The Englishman Lionel chose as constable of Trim was forced out of office by the settlers in 1363, and in almost

16 *Stat. Ire., John–Hen.* V, 431–69; Frame, *Colonial Ireland*, 150–2; D. Green, 'The Statute of Kilkenny (1366): Legislation and the State', *Journal of Historical Sociology*, 27 (2014), 236–62; P. Morgan, 'Ranks of Society', in R. Griffiths (ed.), *The Fourteenth and Fifteenth Centuries* (Oxford University Press, 2003), 53–85.

his last act before leaving Ireland in November 1366 the king's son was forced to rescue another of the knights he had brought with him from England, Henry Ferrers, who was being besieged by a group of prominent settlers from Meath at Clonee on the Meath–Dublin border. Ferrers's 'crime' had been to marry a member of one of the leading settler families in Meath, Joan Tuyt, and attempt to recover her lands from her disgruntled neighbours and relatives.[17]

The renewal of warfare with France at the end of the 1360s ensured that spending by the crown on its overseas territories, whether Ireland or Gascony, would be subjected to closer scrutiny than before. William Windsor, who had served with Lionel in Ireland earlier in the decade, was appointed chief governor in 1369. While he received the same level of financial support from the English exchequer as had Lionel, he lacked the personal status and wealth of the duke of Clarence, and his governorship, which lasted with interruptions until 1376, was characterised by fierce conflict with the settler community. A veteran of the French wars, he intended to pursue a vigorous military policy, and expected the settlers to supply the required cash. To that end he summoned five tax-raising parliaments during his first two years in office, increased the level of customs duties, and enforced the financial penalties contained in legislation passed against absentee lords. So loudly did the settlers complain to the king about such behaviour that Windsor was recalled to London in the summer of 1372. Edward III, however, was sympathetic to William's argument that the colonists could afford to pay what he had asked of them, and reappointed him as governor in September 1373. Stalemate ensued, with the settlers remaining reluctant to contribute to the cost of their own defence, and in September 1375 the king ordered them to send elected representatives to England in the following February to discuss the government of the country. Within a few months Windsor had been stripped of office, a victim of the campaign against the king's circle conducted by the Good Parliament in London. Although his career subsequently revived and he retained land in Ireland, his period of service to the crown there was at an end. The truculence of the settlers, by contrast, remained unchallenged.[18]

---

17 Smith, *Crisis and Survival*, 47–50; J. Lydon, 'The Middle Nation', in Crooks (ed.), *Government, War and Society*, 332–52.

18 P. Crooks, 'Negotiating Authority in a Colonial Capital: Dublin and the Windsor Crisis, 1369–78', in S. Duffy (ed.), *Medieval Dublin IX* (Dublin: Four Courts Press, 2009), 131–51; P. Crooks, 'Representation and Dissent: "Parliamentarianism" and the Structure of Politics in Colonial Ireland *c*.1370–1420', *EHR*, 125 (2010), 1–34.

In ridding themselves of William Windsor the settlers demonstrated again the political skills and connections that had in the course of the 1350s persuaded Edward III of the case for a substantial investment in Ireland. The king proved remarkably sympathetic to a political community that, while it had no trouble having its voice heard, found it impossible to articulate for him in a consistent manner the problem he was supposed to solve. Up to 1357 Irish parliamentary legislation and the petitions to the council and king in England that emanated from these assemblies identified 'default of good government' as the source of the settlers' woes. In 1366 the ground shifted, with the Statute of Kilkenny pinning the blame for the Lordship's troubles on the tendency of some settlers to assimilate with the Irish. No mention of these issues was made two years later when the settlers informed the king that the root cause of all their problems was absenteeism on the part of English lords with Irish lands. While a diagnosis of the illness proved elusive, its symptoms were plain to see. The English position in many parts of Ireland came under particular pressure in these years, with Limerick being burned by O'Brien in 1370, and MacMurrough taking the constable of Carlow castle prisoner in 1373. Ulster had remained quiet in the 1360s, not least because Edward III and King David II of Scotland had developed a good working relationship. But the accession of the Stewart dynasty to the Scottish throne in the person of King Robert II in 1371 heralded a return to fraught Anglo-Scottish relations. The significant defeat inflicted on the Ulster settlers by Niall O'Neill at Downpatrick in 1374 was one consequence of this change in the political climate.[19]

Ulster remained central to the crown's thinking about its responsibilities in Ireland. In 1342 Edward III had arranged for the marriage of the heiress of Ulster to his son, Lionel, and in 1358 he determined that the sole issue of this union, Philippa, should marry Edmund Mortimer, son of the earl of March. Both parties were children at the time and the marriage was only finally celebrated in 1368, shortly before Lionel's death. In 1373 Edmund entered into his father's estate. He was now the single largest landowner in the British Isles, holding the Mortimer and Burgh inheritances, and a large portion of the ancestral Clare lands. In Ireland this accounted for the earldom of Ulster and the lordship of Connacht, the lordship of Meath/Trim, the lordship of Leix, and a portion of the lordship of Kilkenny. From the point of view of the settlers Mortimer was the ideal governor, and from as early as 1373 they had petitioned for his appointment to the role. He was finally installed as lieutenant in

---

19 *Stat. Ire., John–Hen. V*, 408, 432, 470; Otway-Ruthven, *History of Medieval Ireland*, 297–308; *AU*, ii, 551.

October 1379 and arrived in Ireland at Howth in May 1380. He concentrated initially on reversing the recent military successes of the Irish in his family estates of Ulster, Connacht and Meath, and convened a parliament at Dublin in November that granted him financial support with none of the objections that had faced Windsor. He spent most of the following year campaigning in Leinster and Munster, but died of plague, at the age of twenty-nine, at Cork on 26 December 1381.[20]

During his sojourn in Dublin, Edmund and his entourage had been embarrassed by the bishop of Cloyne who while celebrating Mass intoned the words 'eternal God, there are two in Munster who destroy us and our goods, the earl of Ormond and the earl of Desmond with their followers, whom in the end the Lord will destroy'. Since the 1350s the earls of Kildare, Desmond and Ormond had on occasion acted as chief governor of Ireland but, as the bishop's outburst suggests, many settlers believed that they devoted most of their energies to enlarging their resources at the expense of their neighbours. Furthermore, from the 1340s onwards the earls of Desmond and Ormond had been competing with increasing violence for control of the Munster lands where their lordships met, with Ormond using his closer family connections to the English royal family to gain the upper hand. Mortimer's short, successful, term as governor strengthened the belief of the settlers that their salvation lay not in the hands of their own leading men, but in the appointment of a governor from England who enjoyed both wealth and prestige. They reiterated this message in an embassy to King Richard II late in 1385, asking that he or the greatest and most trustworthy lord in England come to their aid. Richard, still only eighteen at the time, had already decided to bestow authority over Ireland on his favourite, Robert de Vere, earl of Oxford, and reinforced his position by granting him two new titles, marquis of Dublin and duke of Ireland, in December 1385 and October 1386 respectively. Before de Vere could come to Ireland he was caught up in the dispute between the king and some of his leading magnates that dominated these years, and he eventually fled from England late in 1387, never to return.[21]

---

20 Davies, *Lords and Lordship*, 45–9; D. Johnston, 'Chief Governors and Treasurers of Ireland in the Reign of Richard II', in Barry *et al.* (eds.), *Colony and Frontier in Medieval Ireland*, 97–115.

21 P. Crooks, ' "Hobbes", "Dogs" and Politics in the Ireland of Lionel of Antwerp', *HSJ*, 16 (2005), 117–48; P. Crooks, 'The "Calculus of Faction" and Richard II's Duchy of Ireland, *c.*1382–9', in N. Saul (ed.), *Fourteenth Century England V* (Woodbridge: Boydell Press, 2008), 94–115; Otway-Ruthven, *History of Medieval Ireland*, 314–15; G. Harriss, *Shaping the Nation: England 1360–1461* (Oxford University Press, 2005), 451–68.

King Richard's commitment to finding a leading English nobleman to govern Ireland remained strong, and both he and the settlers in Ireland were aware that a suitable appointee waited in the wings. This was Roger Mortimer, earl of March and Ulster, the son of Edmund Mortimer who had died in 1381. Roger, who was born in 1374 and had a strong claim to be the heir to the throne should Richard II remain childless, had been pressing to be allowed to assume responsibility for his Irish lands since 1390. The king gave him livery of these lands in March 1393, a year before his English and Welsh lands were released to him. As a seven-year-old Roger had already served as lieutenant of Ireland for a year following his father's death, and he was reappointed to the post in the summer of 1392 in succession to the king's uncle, the duke of Gloucester, who had failed to visit Ireland. Roger arrived in Ireland in early October 1394 in the company of an even greater lord; King Richard II.[22]

Richard II was the first English monarch to visit Ireland since King John in 1210, and the 5,000-man army he led across the Irish Sea was the largest fighting force that had ever made this journey. His goal was to secure recognition of his position as their sovereign from the native Irish lords, and by force or persuasion to recover from them the lands they had captured from the settlers since the time of the initial conquest. Almost all the great Irish lords submitted; some were knighted and others were encouraged to believe that they would be invited to parliament. MacMurrough even agreed to vacate Leinster with his people, and resettle on lands he conquered from Irish leaders who had failed to comply with Richard's wishes. The unrealistic nature of this promise suggests that the Irish were happy enough to go along with whatever Richard wanted, confident in the belief that upon his departure they would again be left undisturbed in their encroachment on the settlement. The king returned to England in April 1395, leaving as his lieutenant Roger Mortimer. This appointment was enough to convince Niall O'Neill, the greatest of the northern Irish lords, that Richard II did not intend to deal fairly between native and settler in Ireland, since as earl of Ulster Mortimer had already made clear his determination to reclaim the lands lost to the Irish since the murder of William Burgh in 1333. Mortimer replicated the success his father had achieved in 1380 by launching attacks on the Irish of Ulster and Meath in 1396 and 1397, but as had been the case in Edmund Mortimer's time,

---

22 K. Simms, 'The Ulster Revolt of 1404: An Anti-Lancastrian Dimension?', in Smith (ed.), *Ireland and the English World*, 141–60; R. R. Davies, *The Revolt of Owain Glyndŵr* (Oxford University Press, 1995), 38–45; A. Dunn, 'Richard II and the Mortimer Inheritance', in C. Given-Wilson (ed.), *Fourteenth Century England II* (Woodbridge: Boydell Press, 2002), 159–70.

it proved impossible to build a permanent recovery on a temporary alteration in the balance of military power. By this time Roger appears to have lost the confidence of his king, and Richard II had already decided to replace him as lieutenant and return to Ireland himself when, in June 1398, Mortimer was killed by the Irish in a skirmish in Carlow. The king's second visit to Ireland, which was intended to be lengthy, began on 1 June 1399, but lasted only until 27 July on account of Henry Bolingbroke's invasion of England. Two months was long enough to demonstrate to Richard how illusory the achievements of 1394–5 in Ireland had been. Nothing summed the situation up better than Mac Murrough's assertion at a parley with a captain of the English forces in July 1399 that he, rather than Richard, was the rightful king of Ireland.[23]

It is possible, of course, that had he been in a position to remain in Ireland King Richard would have faced down MacMurrough and reasserted the control over Irish affairs that he had achieved in 1394–5. He might even have gone on to crown his nephew, Thomas Holland, earl of Kent and duke of Surrey (d. 1400) – who was also the brother-in-law of the late Roger Mortimer – king of Ireland in Dublin in September 1399.[24] As it was, the change of dynasty effected in England in the autumn of 1399 led to few immediate or notable alterations in how Ireland was administered. This was in large part because the new king, Henry IV, showed himself anxious to continue to employ in the Lordship men who had seen service there under his predecessor. Before the end of the year John Stanley, who had first served in Ireland as lieutenant for Robert de Vere, marquis of Dublin, in 1386, was appointed as lieutenant of Ireland by the new king, while in August 1401 Stephen Scrope, who had been in the king's employment in Ireland since 1396 and who remained loyal to Richard II even to the moment of his capture at Conway castle, was appointed chief governor of the Lordship with the title of deputy lieutenant to the king's brother, Thomas of Lancaster.[25]

Henry IV's determination to minimise the disruption caused in Ireland by his usurpation was only partly successful. After a decade of uneasy peace, the renewal of conflict between England and Scotland was signalled in August 1400 by an invasion of the northern kingdom by the new English ruler, and

23 J. Lydon, 'Richard II's Expeditions to Ireland', in Crooks (ed.), *Government, War and Society*, 216–31; D. Johnston, 'The Interim Years: Richard II and Ireland, 1395–1399', in Lydon (ed.), *England and Ireland*, 175–95; N. Saul, *Richard II* (New Haven and London: Yale University Press, 1997), 270–92.

24 M. Bennett, 'Richard II and the Wider Realm', in A. Goodman and J. L. Gillespie (eds.), *Richard II: The Art of Kingship* (Oxford University Press, 1999), 187–204. See also Bennett's comments in his chapter in this volume.

25 Otway-Ruthven, *History of Medieval Ireland*, 339–43.

the naval battle fought in Strangford Lough in the same year between the Scots and the constable of Dublin castle may be considered part of that campaign. With the Mortimer estates again devoid of leadership as a result of Roger Mortimer's death in 1398, and his son and heir Edward – who was aged six at the time of his father's demise – the focus of plots to overthrow the Lancastrian king, Meath, Connacht and especially Ulster were particularly susceptible to internal unrest and Irish attack in the first decades of the fifteenth century. The danger to the English position in the Lordship was exacerbated by the sudden reduction in the amount of financial support the crown was able to afford it. Henry IV brought with him to the throne of England the substantial estates of the duchy of Lancaster, and the view of the English political community was that these family resources should be used in place of more general taxation in pursuit of royal policy. The consequence for the government of Ireland was summed up in a message from the Irish council to the king in August 1402: Thomas of Lancaster, the king's lieutenant and fourteen-year-old son, the council informed his father, 'had not a penny in the world'.[26]

Lancaster returned to England in November 1403, leaving Stephen Scrope as his deputy. It was indicative of the loss of discipline and purpose that characterised the governance of the Lordship in these years that in February 1404 Scrope left Ireland without warning and without identifying a replacement as the crown's representative. Colonial leaders quickly convened at Castledermot and appointed the earl of Ormond to govern the country. He succeeded in repairing some of the damage inflicted in the summer of that year by the Irish of Ulster on colonial settlements in Antrim and Down. It was fortunate for the English position both in Ulster and in adjoining parts of Louth and Meath that at this juncture the power of the O'Neills was reduced as the family entered a period of internal strife over succession to its headship.[27]

Despite – or perhaps on account of – having been brought to Ireland by Richard II as a hostage for his father in 1399, and having been knighted there by the king, Henry of Monmouth, who succeeded his father as Henry V in 1413, did not regard the Lordship as a policy priority. His determination to regain and extend the English position in France, however, did have implications for the government of Ireland. As Elizabeth Matthew has demonstrated, support from the English exchequer to chief governors of Ireland under

26 H. Castor, *The King, the Crown, and the Duchy of Lancaster: Public Authority and Private Power, 1399–1461* (Oxford University Press, 2000), 25–38; F. C. Hingeston (ed.), *Royal and Historical Letters during the Reign of Henry IV*, i (London: RS, 1860), 73–6.
27 Simms, 'Ulster Revolt of 1404', 141–60.

Henry V was cut to half of what it had been under his father. This made it more likely that the wealthiest settler lords, such as the earls of Ormond and Kildare, would be called upon with increased frequency to represent the crown in the Lordship. James Butler, fourth earl of Ormond (1390–1452), who served as chief governor on numerous occasions from the age of seventeen in 1408, to his death at the age of sixty-two in 1452, succeeded in increasing the routine revenues reaching the Irish exchequer in Dublin during his terms of office, and revivified the practice whereby individuals required to contribute military service when a campaign was proclaimed could substitute personal attendance with a money payment known as scutage. It is noticeable that during periods when lieutenants sent from England governed the Lordship, exchequer receipts dropped sharply.[28]

The most important of these English governors was John Talbot, Lord Furnival (*c*.1387–1453), from 1442 earl of Shrewsbury and from 1446 also earl of Waterford. Talbot had inherited Irish interests and estates in Louth, Meath and Wexford, and served as chief governor on several occasions between 1414 and 1447. With his brother, Richard Talbot (d. 1449), who was elected archbishop of Dublin in 1417 and who also served as chief governor a number of times, John Talbot became involved in a feud with the earl of Ormond that lasted from 1414 to 1447. Desperate for funds to sustain his governorship, in 1417 Talbot confiscated Ormond's lands in Ireland for non-payment of debts at the Irish exchequer accrued in the middle of the previous century. In retaliation Ormond, when he gained leadership of the Irish administration in 1420, dismissed the men appointed by Talbot. For three decades the parties contended with each other, bringing charges of misgovernment against their opponents before the king, indulging in acts of violence, and forming alliances with settler and native lords designed to undermine the rule of the other party. A marriage alliance between Butler's daughter and Talbot's son in 1444–5 significantly reduced tensions, and from the early 1430s both sides had in any case learned to tread more carefully as they sought the favour of the figure they realised would someday acquire great power in Ireland: Richard, duke of York. Through both his parents Richard was descended from Edward III, and through his mother he had inherited the Mortimer lands and claims in Ireland. He was granted livery of his estates in 1432 and after years of service as the king's lieutenant in France was appointed to the same position in Ireland in

---

28 E. Matthew, 'The Financing of the Lordship of Ireland under Henry V and Henry VI', in T. Pollard (ed.), *Property and Politics: Essays in Later Medieval History* (Gloucester: Alan Sutton, 1984), 97–115.

1447. His arrival in July 1449 at Howth – where, in 1380, his great-grandfather, Edmund Mortimer, had landed – meant not only that the Lordship now had a governor of unusual prestige and authority, but also that it would be closely involved in the political turmoil in England that within four years would lead to the outbreak of civil war.[29]

Social Change

What underlying trends and patterns can be identified in this narrative of the political history of fourteenth- and early fifteenth-century Ireland? Settler petitions to the crown bemoaning a decline of English power on the island had a basis in reality. In comparison with the thirteenth century the geographical range of military campaigns led by the chief governor was reduced, with no such operations being conducted west of the Shannon after the Bruce invasion. Areas of north Munster and south Leinster which had in the previous century been indisputably part of the English settlement became frontier or march zones as the fourteenth century progressed. Increasingly, towns such as Waterford and Limerick were permitted to make local truces with neighbouring Irish lordships, and were allowed to retain for the purposes of their own defence payments that would previously have been made to the Irish exchequer. In Connacht and Ulster, officials of the successors to the great Burgh lordship succeeded in collecting small amounts of rent from settler tenants into the late fourteenth century, but from the 1340s onwards routine government contact with these provinces virtually ceased. The common law system no longer operated as a matter of course in such areas, which in turn contributed to a significant reduction in the revenues received at the Dublin exchequer. Whereas it was not unusual for £6,000 per annum to be collected by the exchequer at the beginning of the century, fifty years later £2,000 or even less was the normal annual receipt. By the 1440s this figure might on occasion dip as low as £300.[30]

Against this backdrop of territorial and governmental retreat it became more common after the Bruce invasion for fears to be expressed that Ireland

---

29 A. Cosgrove, *Late Medieval Ireland, 1370–1541* (Dublin: Helicon Limited, 1981), 29–51; Otway-Ruthven, *History of Medieval Ireland*, 348–81; Ellis, *Ireland in the Age of the Tudors*, 51–9; P. Crooks, 'Factions, Feuds and Noble Power in Late Medieval Ireland', *IHS*, 35 (2007), 425–54.

30 R. Frame, 'The Defence of the English Lordship, 1250–1450', in T. Bartlett and K. Jeffery (eds.), *A Military History of Ireland* (Cambridge University Press, 1996), 76–98; R. Frame, 'Ireland', in *NCMH*, vi, 375–87; B. Smith, 'Late Medieval Ireland and the English Connection: Waterford and Bristol, *ca*. 1360–1460', *Journal of British Studies*, 50 (2011), 553.

was on the point of being lost to the English crown. In 1332 and again in 1347 juries in Munster accused the first earl of Desmond, Maurice fitz Thomas, of conspiring to have himself declared king of Ireland, while a century later in 1450 Richard, duke of York, wrote to his brother-in-law the earl of Salisbury that 'I had rather be dead than that [it] be chronicled … that Ireland was lost by my negligence.' There was more than a hint of hysteria in such rhetoric, but it should be remembered that in 1401–2 Owain Glyn Dŵr had written to the native lords of Ireland urging them to throw off the shackles of English rule and assist his efforts to do the same in Wales, and that in 1405 a French naval force did land at Milford Haven in order to help him achieve this goal. The well-informed and reflective author of the *Libelle of Englyshe Polycye*, writing in the 1430s, chose his words carefully when he advised the English council 'To kepen Yreland that it be not loste / For it is a boterasse and poste / Undre England and Wales is another'.[31]

In reality, the threat to English rule in Ireland was less daunting. The most successful native lords of the period might pay their poets to identify them as the rightful rulers of all Ireland, but on a day-to-day basis were prepared to settle for domination of much smaller areas. The growing power of some Irish lordships was related to the longevity of their rulers and the stability of their succession patterns at this time. Although disputed on occasion, the lordship of the O'Neills in Ulster remained from 1345 to 1403 in the hands of Aed *Mór*, his son and his grandson. Three generations of the same family in direct line of descent held the MacCarthy [Mac Carthaig] lordship of Desmond between 1325 and 1428, while Mahon O'Brien and his son Brian were lords of Thomond from 1360 to 1400. English attempts to counter the threat posed by these resurgent dynasties exacerbated the regional character of Irish politics. The chief governor concentrated his efforts on securing the position of Dublin and the river valleys leading to the south, while the battles and truces conducted by the earls of Kildare, Ormond and Desmond, could be portrayed as contributing to the defence of the English position in more distant parts of Leinster and Munster.[32]

The revival of native Irish lordship and the retreat of English dominance had wide social and economic consequences. Warfare, as well as plague, lay behind much of the population movement discernible at this time. The

---

31 B. Smith, 'The British Isles in the Late Middle Ages: Shaping the Regions', in Smith (ed.), *Ireland and the English World*, 10–12.

32 R. Frame, 'Lordship Beyond the Pale: Munster in the Later Middle Ages', in R. Stalley (ed.), *Limerick and South-West Ireland: Medieval Art and Architecture* (Leeds: BAACT, 2011), 5–18; *NHI* ix, 212, 219, 221.

arrival and settlement of galloglass from western Scotland has already been mentioned, and expansionist Irish lords were responsible for the displacement of both native and settler groups from their homelands. In 1338 O'Connor [Ó Conchobair] took advantage of fighting among the Burghs [Burkes] of Connacht to conquer land in Sligo. As a result, the territories 'were emptied and devastated and their lordship was assumed by their native Gaels, after their Galls [settlers] had been expelled'. In 1346 the Kilkenny chronicler recorded the death of Tadhg O'Carroll [Ó Cearbhaill], who had 'killed, exiled and ejected from his lands of Ely O'Carroll [part of north Munster] those of the nation of de Barry, de Milliborne, de Brit and other English of the neighbourhood, and he took and occupied their lands and castles, being an oppressive tyrant to all faithful subjects nearby'. Similarly, in 1404 an Irish annalist reported that 'the Galls were driven from the whole province [of Ulster east of the Bann], and the North was burned … Downpatrick … and Coleraine were despoiled and demolished'. In south Ulster the pressure of the O'Neills on the lesser family of O'Hanlon [Ó hAnluain] encouraged the latter to expel the O'Rogan [Ó Rudacáin] family from its lands. The O'Rogans responded by relocating among the settlers in Louth. Among the settlers, the achievement of hegemony in their lordships by the earls of Ormond and Desmond was also accompanied by the uprooting of lesser families such as the Barrys and Poers. In 1381–2 Munster settlers petitioned the crown for help in ending a dispute between the Geraldines and the Barrys – distantly related families, of course – which had destroyed Munster and led to large numbers of settlers fleeing Ireland for Bristol and Cornwall. Economic opportunity and warfare at home led to levels of emigration from Ireland to England that were high enough to prompt discriminatory legislation in Bristol and more general attempts to return migrants from Ireland to the Lordship.[33]

Geographical mobility among the settlers was also the result of government policy. The relocation of the exchequer and judicial benches to Carlow involved journeys to that town, rather than to Dublin, for many officers of the crown. The decision of the chief governor as to where parliament would be convened, or a military campaign conducted, dictated the travel patterns of elected representatives and soldiers. Settlers from Louth complained bitterly about being forced to appear before William Windsor at Limerick in the early 1370s,

---

33 AC, 281; Clyn, 240; Misc. Ir. Annals, 173; Smith, Crisis and Survival, 32, 192; Smith, 'Late Medieval Ireland', 546–65; P. Fleming, 'Identity and Belonging: Irish and Welsh in Fifteenth-Century Bristol', in L. Clark (ed.), The Fifteenth Century VII: Conflicts, Consequences and the Crown in the Late Middle Ages (Woodbridge: Boydell and Brewer, 2007), 175–93.

though they were happy to join Edmund Mortimer in an attack on Donegal in 1380. Richard II's first visit to the Lordship witnessed Irish and settler lords undertaking long journeys to offer their submissions. Brian O'Brien, lord of Thomond, appeared before the king at Dundalk in March 1395, and a month later was at Waterford, in the company of O'Connor Don [Ó Conchobair Donn] from Roscommon and William Burgh and Walter Bermingham from Galway, to bid farewell to the departing king as he boarded ship. The pull of lordship might involve the short- or long-term relocation of influential men from Ireland to England and beyond. In 1358 the earl of Ormond took with him on a visit to his mother in Surrey Edmund O'Kennedy [Éamonn Ó Ceinnéidigh], who was then in his custody. Ormond had been present at the siege of Calais in 1347, as had the earl of Kildare, and in 1396 the Leinster lords Donnchadh O'Byrne [Ó Broin] and Tadhg O'Carroll – who had been at Rome on pilgrimage earlier the same year – were at Calais in the entourage of Richard II as he prepared to marry Isabel of France. In 1419 John Talbot captured Donnchadh MacMurrough, king of Leinster, and sent him to the Tower of London, where he remained until 1427, while in 1434 a later chief governor, Thomas Stanley, captured the leading Ulster lord Niall O'Donnell during a raid by the latter on Meath and imprisoned him on his estates in the Isle of Man where he died in 1439.[34]

Involvement in Ireland retained the potential to enhance the careers of servants of the crown from beyond the Lordship's confines. At the end of the century the Basque knight Janico Dartas, who had fought for the English in France since the 1360s, came to Ireland with Richard II and in addition to receiving a substantial grant of land in Dublin from the king, also married into a settler family. Chief governors such as John Darcy, Thomas Rokeby and William Windsor acquired Irish estates, and might use their powers of patronage to the advantage of their friends. Windsor, for instance, appointed his neighbour from Westmorland, James Pickering, as chief justice of the Irish bench. Pickering, who lacked any legal education and was loathed by the settlers for his alleged dishonesty, went on to represent Westmorland in the English parliament and even served as Speaker of the Commons in 1378. In similar fashion, John Stanley, chief governor on four occasions between 1386 and 1414, introduced several fellow-Cheshiremen into the upper reaches of the colonial administration at Dublin. For the king's most able administrators

---

34 J. Lydon, 'William of Windsor and the Irish Parliament', in Crooks (ed.), *Government, War and Society*, 90–105; Otway-Ruthven, *History of Medieval Ireland*, 331–3; Frame, *Ireland and Britain*, 148; O'Byrne, *War, Politics and the Irish of Leinster*, 111, 118, 122; *AC*, 477, 481.

service in Ireland might constitute one of many postings overseas. Robert Wikeford, archbishop of Dublin between 1376 and 1390, and Irish chancellor on three occasions between 1376 and 1384, had served on diplomatic missions to Brabant and Flanders before being appointed as constable of Bordeaux between 1373 and 1375. Thomas Cranley, archbishop of Dublin between 1397 and 1417, and Irish chancellor and chief governor on several occasions during this time, had been chancellor of Oxford and had acted as an envoy for Richard II in Paris and Rome before his appointment to Dublin.[35]

Within the settler community social advance was also possible in a period when pressure on absentee lords to sell their Irish lands brought valuable estates on to the market. The earl of Ormond's purchase of the Despenser portion of the lordship of Kilkenny in 1393 did not signal a great rise in his personal status but other transactions, such as the acquisition of the St Amand lordship of Gormanston on the Meath coast by Robert Preston, chief justice of the Irish bench, in 1362, or the purchase by John Bellew later in the same decade of the lordship of Dundalk and its associated castle of Roche from the Furnival family, were instances of notable upward social mobility. A common characteristic of the successful settler families of fourteenth-century Ireland was the care they took to build and maintain close links with the major towns in their localities. The Butlers fostered friendly relations with the elites of Kilkenny and Waterford, the Prestons built up their property-holdings in Drogheda, while the Bellews forged alliances with important Dundalk families such as the Dowdalls and Whites.[36]

The long-running dispute between John Talbot and James Butler, earl of Ormond, between the 1410s and 1440s coincided with and invigorated a process by which leading families in the counties of Dublin, Kildare, Meath and Louth came to assume more power within the Lordship as a whole. The Plunket family, for instance, had provided seneschals of the liberty of Trim and keepers and justices of the peace in Meath and Louth in the fourteenth century, and family members had also held high judicial office in the Lordship. An increase in their prominence was signalled by the appointment of Nicholas Plunket as treasurer of Ireland in 1427 and Christopher Plunket as deputy lieutenant in 1433. In like manner, the appointment of Richard

---

35 S. Walker, 'Janico Dartasso: Chivalry, Nationality and the Man-at-Arms', *History*, 84 (1991), 31–51; M. Bennett, *Community, Class and Careerism: Cheshire and Lancashire Society in the Age of Sir Gawain and the Green Knight* (Cambridge University Press, 1983), 199–200, 215–19; P. Crooks, 'State of the Union: Perspectives on English Imperialism in the Late Middle Ages', *Past and Present*, 212 (2011), 1–40. For accounts of the individuals named see *ODNB*.

36 *COD*, ii, 213–19; Smith, *Crisis and Survival*, 61, 65, 68.

fitz Eustace as Irish chancellor in 1427 marked a new high point for a family which had a long tradition of service as sheriffs and justices of the peace in Kildare. In the following year such families received a further boost when the Irish parliament agreed to provide them with government subsidies in order to build new castles for themselves, generally in the form of tower-houses. Members of this elite group of families had long been accustomed to receive individual summonses to attend the Irish parliament, and from the 1460s their elevated status within the settler community was recognised by the crown by the bestowal upon them of the title 'baron' by letters patent.[37]

In imitation of practices becoming widespread in England from the late thirteenth century, settler lords in Ireland made increasing use of legal devices designed to ensure that land was transmitted to male descendants only. Such devices were popular in the most peaceful parts of the colony, but were seen by contemporaries to have particular importance in frontier zones of the Lordship where partition of estates among female heirs had the potential to weaken the English military position. Despite this, the fourteenth century did not see the status of settler women as landowners in the Lordship significantly reduced. On the deaths of their husbands widowed ladies continued to receive back the dower they had brought to the marriage, as well as continuing to enjoy for life the marriage portion bestowed upon them at the time of their union.[38] The role high-status women played in the political life of fourteenth- and early fifteenth-century Ireland has left little impression on contemporary records. Occasional mention is made of the piety of individuals who endowed religious foundations, but those women who are named usually appear in more negative contexts. Following his account of the murder of William Burgh, earl of Ulster, in 1333, for instance, the Kilkenny chronicler continues: 'This evil, as usual, was said to be committed by reason of a woman, namely Gyle de Burgh, wife of lord Richard Mandeville, because he imprisoned her brother Walter de Burgh and others'. Matilda of Lancaster attracted the particular ire of the Dublin chronicler. He blamed her for inciting her husband, Ralph Ufford, to various misdeeds during his time as chief governor, and gloated at 'the horrible pain of heart' she felt as she accompanied her dead husband's remains from Ireland to England in 1346. The

---

37 CIRCLE: PR 5 Ric II, no. 207, PR 12 Ric II, no. 4, PR 2 Hen IV, no. 17, CR 6 Hen VI, no. 25, CR 12 Hen VI, no. 1 (Plunket); PR 29 Edw III, no. 15, PR 51 Edw III, no. 3, CR 5 Hen VI, no. 32 (Fitz Eustace); Smith, *Crisis and Survival*, 124–5; H. G. Richardson and G. O. Sayles, *The Irish Parliament in the Middle Ages* (Philadelphia: University of Pennsylvania Press, 1952), 127–35, 176–9.
38 Kenny, *Anglo-Irish and Gaelic Women*, 52–66.

records of the Irish chancery reveal that in 1393 Úna, the wife of the greatest Ulster lord, Niall Óc O'Neill, travelled to Drogheda, accompanied by twelve men and women, to negotiate with the chief governor and his council for the release of her son, Brian, who was then a hostage for the good behaviour of his father. This incident is not noted in the Gaelic annals, which for the most part mention women only in the context of the peaceful deaths of those of high birth, their generosity to the Church, or their patronage of men of learning. The violent death during an O'Connor raid on O'Rourke [Ó Ruairc] of the latter's wife, Derbil, in 1367 was sufficiently unusual to merit inclusion in the annals, while an account of a dispute among branches of the O'Farrell [Ó Feargall] family in 1387 notes that the wives of defeated opponents were taken prisoner by the victors.[39]

Ireland Imagined

The impression gleaned from the written sources relating to Ireland from the fourteenth and early fifteenth centuries is that commentators and officials yearned for a simplicity and stability that was not to be found in the fast-changing country about which they wrote. The appeal of the contemporary dualities of 'Gael' and 'Gall', 'loyal English subjects' and 'Irish enemies', 'land of peace' and 'land of war', outweighed the failure of such labels to capture the complexity of relations and identities on the island. The recourse to intermediate categories such as 'Saxain', 'rebel English', 'middle nation' and 'the march' added not clarity but further scope for confusion to the situation. The preamble to the Statute of Kilkenny of 1366, with its evocation of the 'good old days' when the superiority of English power and culture was acknowledged by the Irish, and everyone knew their place, represented more than hollow rhetoric to at least some of those who drafted and read it. There was a fantasy element to the way in which the crown viewed the situation in Ireland. The warding of Irish marches, as if they were equivalent to the Anglo-Scottish borders, represented an expensive if short-lived triumph of theory over experience. Similarly naive were the beliefs – encouraged by the settlers – that by military means Ireland could quickly be returned to profit, and that in an age of massive population decline throughout Western Europe a new wave of colonists from England could be lured across the sea to settle lands reconquered from the Irish. Edward III's willingness to expend

---

39 *Clyn*, 210, 242; *Chartul. St Mary's, Dublin*, ii, 385, 388; Kenny, *Anglo-Irish and Gaelic Women*, 30–3, 72–6.

considerable energy in the 1360s in a futile attempt to force the archbishops of Armagh and Dublin to settle their dispute about primacy over the Irish Church along the lines of the earlier Canterbury–York agreement in England demonstrated the degree of abstraction that might characterise royal policy in Ireland.[40]

Fanciful plans for the present were complemented and sometimes encouraged by appeals to a distant, mythical past. In 1421 the Irish parliament petitioned King Henry V to seek the Pope's authorisation for a crusade against the native Irish. The bearers of the petition were briefed to remind their sovereign that King Arthur's conquest of Ireland, as set out in Gerald of Wales's writings, proved that 'from first to last, the right of our lord the king to Ireland is good'. Earlier, in the 1390s, Roger Mortimer, earl of March and Ulster, had also viewed his Irish commitments and ambitions in Arthurian terms; a perspective which, with its evocation of authority over the entire British Isles and beyond, may have unsettled his lord and cousin, King Richard II. In Ulster Mortimer was confronted by Niall Óc O'Neill who, in thrall to a different corpus of myths, and despite his wealth and power, went barefoot in imitation of his hero, Cú Chulainn. A generation earlier the O'Kelly [Ó Ceallaig] lord of east Galway had paid his court historian to compose a list of the ruling families of Ireland that simply ignored the presence of settler lordships on the island. In this frontier environment cultural assimilation between native and settler – and reaction against it – produced a world that defied easy categorisation. Some native lords might prefer to go barefoot; others lived in the substantial castles they had captured from the colonists. The third earl of Desmond, Gerald fitz Maurice, chief governor of Ireland between 1367 and 1369, had attended the Kilkenny parliament of 1366 that prohibited the use of the Irish language among the settlers, and their patronage of the Gaelic learned classes. Gerald was also the most prolific amateur poet in the Irish language in the Middle Ages, and at his death in 1398 was hailed by the Irish annals as 'a cheerful and courteous man, who excelled all the English, and many of the Irish, in the knowledge of the Irish language, poetry and history, and of other learning'.[41]

---

40 J. Lydon, 'The Problem of the Frontier in Medieval Ireland', in Crooks (ed.), *Government, War and Society*, 317–31; Cosgrove, *Late Medieval Ireland*; *CCR, 1364–9*, 181; *Reg. Sweteman*, 23–4, 25–6, 45, 128.

41 E. Matthew, 'Henry V and the Proposal for an Irish Crusade', in Smith (ed.), *Ireland and the English World*, 161–75; D. Johnston, *Iolo Goch: Poems* (Llandysul: Gomer Press, 1993), 82–9; M. E. Giffin, 'Arthur, and Brutus in the Wigmore Manuscript', *Speculum*, 16 (1941), 109–20; K. Simms, 'The Barefoot Kings: Literary Image and Reality in Later Medieval Ireland', in E. Boon, A. J. McMullen and N. Sumner (eds.), *Proceedings of the*

To what extent was it the case – as the career of the third earl of Desmond might suggest – that behind an official rhetoric of native–settler antagonism lay a hidden Ireland of cultural compromise and easy social intercourse? No single answer can be given: location, time-period, and social background determined the answer in each instance. Archbishop Richard Fitz Ralph of Armagh's reference to 'the traditional and inborn hatred' between the two nations in the 1340s reflected his own experience of growing up in Dundalk in the era of the Bruce invasion as a member of that stratum of society that provided the county with its sheriffs and other office-holders. Almost a century later in 1432 Magnus MacMahon decorated the perimeter of his fortress of Carrickmarcross with the skulls of the settlers of Louth he had killed in a recent raid, to the 'terror and loathing' of those who visited the site. A kinder, gentler, Ireland may well have existed in parts of Munster in the later fourteenth and fifteenth centuries, at least for men of the rank of a Geraldine earl or a MacCarthy lord, and even in Louth Rudraige Mac Mahon, brother of the bloodthirsty Magnus, and later lord of Airgialla, married Alice White, a member of a leading Louth settler family. The archbishop of Armagh, in seeking a papal dispensation for their marriage in 1426, wrote that as a result of the union between the couple – who already had several children together – 'probably peace will be strengthened between the English and the Irish'. Some minor Gaelic lords and poets objected to leading Irish princes copying English ways, while the resentment felt by many colonists in heavily settled but vulnerable areas towards those of their leaders who adopted native customs was intense. In June 1329 at Braganstown, near Ardee, John Bermingham, earl of Louth, and scores of his relatives were massacred by a local settler force led by the grandees of the county, including its sheriff. They objected to Bermingham's policy of billeting his Irish foot-soldiers, or kerne, in their midst, regarding it as the introduction of a native practice that threatened their liberty. The kerne were lynched at Ardee the night before the attack on the earl, and during their assault on Braganstown the settlers sought out and murdered the party of native Irish musicians employed by Bermingham to entertain him in his house. The reputation of the leader of this musical company, Maolruanaigh O'Carroll, as the best timpanist and harpist of his generation ensured mention of his death not only in the Irish annals, but also

Harvard Celtic Colloquium 30, 2010 (Cambridge, MA, and London: Harvard University Press, 2011), 1–21; Simms, *Medieval Gaelic Sources*, 25–6, 58; *AU*, ii, 553; *AFM*, iv, 761.

in the settler chronicle composed at Kilkenny. His skills cut no ice with the English of Louth.[42]

The frontier bred both cultural accommodation and violence, and made demands on local military resources that to some extent distanced Ireland from England in a period when the latter was primarily concerned with war in France and Scotland. From the late 1330s onwards the call on fighting men and supplies from Ireland to support England's wars was reduced in comparison with the preceding half-century. But there were important moments and points of contact between the Lordship and the military enterprises of England's rulers. Henry V's successful campaign in Normandy after 1418 was aided by a large Irish force assembled at Waterford by the fourth earl of Ormond and transported to France in ships sent from Bristol. The earl's son, James Butler (d. 1461), later earl of Wiltshire and Ormond, served in France in 1441 with a force raised from both his English and Irish estates. Among the men from England chosen by King Edward III to act as chief governor of Ireland were several who had fought in France, such as Amaury de St Amand (justiciar 1357–9) who had served at Crécy and Calais in 1346–7, and Robert Ashton (justiciar 1372–3) who was admiral of the west when war with France resumed in 1369. No peasant revolts occurred in the Lordship, despite the operation of the Statute of Labourers after 1351 and constant complaints about the failure of chief governors to pay for the resources they extracted from local communities for military campaigns. But it was also the case that large areas of England, such as the North and the South West, were untouched by the rising of 1381. An occasional heretic was unearthed on the island, but Lollardy appears not to have crossed the Irish Sea. Ireland was seen as sufficiently distant and different to serve as a place of exile for the royal judges caught up in the defeat of Richard II by his noble opponents in 1386–8. That crisis, which brought England close to civil war, barely touched Ireland, and no earl from Ireland died in the noble bloodletting experienced in England between 1397 and 1403. For the political elite, Ireland was a safer place to be than England, as suggested by the fact that no settler earl died a violent death on the island between 1333 and 1468.[43]

---

42 Walsh, *Fourteenth-Century Scholar*, 289; Smith, *Crisis and Survival*, 124, 126–9; B. Smith, *Colonisation and Conquest in Medieval Ireland: The English in Louth 1170–1330* (Cambridge University Press, 1999), 114–21.

43 Smith, 'Late Medieval Ireland', 554; M. Brown, *Disunited Kingdoms: Peoples and Politics in the British Isles 1280–1460* (Harlow: Pearson, 2013), 199–210; B. Williams, 'Heresy in Ireland in the Thirteenth and Fourteenth Centuries', in Duffy (ed.), *Princes, Prelates and Poets*, 339–51; Crooks, 'State of the Union', 27–8; M. Bennett, *Richard II and the Revolution of 1399* (Stroud: Sutton Publishing, 1999), 23–33, 82–208; Frame, *Political Development of the British Isles*, 198–9.

But Ireland was not separating from England. Irish parliaments might make life difficult for ministers of the crown working in the Lordship, but statutes passed in English parliaments were adopted in Ireland without complaint. In 1353 the Ordinance of Staples at a single stroke extended trading privileges to the 'ports of Newcastle, Chichester, Exeter, Bristol, Carmarthen, Dublin, Waterford, Cork and Drogheda', while in 1412 Drogheda was elevated to the status of a county, following similar grants to Bristol in 1373, York in 1396, Newcastle in 1400, Norwich in 1404 and Lincoln in 1409.[44] The crown was careful to arrange marriages for settler comital families that tied them to the magnate class in England, and in the case of James Butler, first earl of Ormond, to facilitate a marriage in 1328 to a cousin of the king. Between 1360 and 1399 the crown poured money into maintaining the English position on the island on a scale not seen at any other time in the Middle Ages. The persistence of warfare and the arrival and frequent recurrence of plague after 1349 undoubtedly hurt the economy, but the sharp fall in revenues received at the Irish exchequer in the course of the century did not signal a more general economic collapse. From the point of view of the government of the Lordship the real problem as the fifteenth century progressed was not a decline in the wealth of Ireland, but a failure to extract a level of taxation from its inhabitants that bore much relation to their increasing prosperity. The century-and-more discussed here constituted a period in which Ireland was thoroughly integrated into larger political, religious and economic worlds. Its complex, conflict-ridden, history at this time is better understood when seen in these broader contexts, but can never be fully appreciated unless its unique character is also kept in view.[45]

---

44 *Statutes of the Realm,* i, 333; P. J. P. Goldberg, *Medieval England: A Social History, 1250–1550* (London: Hodder Arnold, 2004), 36–7.

45 Frame, *Colonial Ireland,* 154–63; R. Frame, 'The Wider World', in R. Horrox and W. M. Ormrod (eds.), *A Social History of England, 1200–1500* (Cambridge University Press, 2006), 435–53; P. Brand, 'Irish Law Students and Lawyers in Late Medieval England', *IHS,* 32 (2000), 161–73; V. Davis, 'Irish Clergy in Late Medieval England', *IHS,* 32 (2000), 145–60; Fleming, 'Identity and Belonging', 175–93; Smith, *Crisis and Survival,* 39–42, 167–74.

10

The Political Recovery of Gaelic Ireland

KATHARINE SIMMS

IN the early twentieth century Eoin Mac Neill lamented some historians' 'peculiar obsession of mind that makes Ireland appear a sort of hotel, in which the important people are always distinguished visitors, and the permanent residents, when they are not under orders, are occupied with quarrelling children and other household worries in the garret or the basement'. Mac Neill's own biases are well known, but the point he was making has a certain continuing relevance.[1] Even after the emotional pressures of the 1916 rising and the War of Independence had died down, a new generation of historians striving after objectivity concentrated on administrative records of a kind that the Gaelic chieftains notoriously failed to keep. Consequently the narrative focus for the fourteenth and fifteenth centuries was on the weakness of the shrinking Anglo-Irish colony, yielding chapter titles such as: 'The Ebbing Tide'; 'The Problem Of Decline'; 'A Colony In Retreat'.[2] Yet it was arguably what took place among the Irish-speaking majority of the inhabitants during this period that exercised a more formative influence on both the political and cultural history of the island thereafter.

The 'ebbing tide' of English government, distracted by the Hundred Years War, and weakened by economic depression and pestilence, allowed the Gaelic Irish to enjoy an uneven recovery of influence. They won isolated military victories, some Gaelic-Irish and Anglo-Irish lordships achieved territorial expansion over formerly colonised regions now lying waste and

---

1 E. MacNeill, *Phases of Irish History* (Dublin, 1919; repr. Port Washington, NY, and London: Kennikat Press, 1970), 349; J. A. Watt, 'Approaches to the History of Fourteenth-Century Ireland', in *NHI* ii, 303–5; S. Harrison, 'Re-fighting the Battle of Down: Orpen, Mac Neill and the Irish Nation-State', in M. Brown and S. Harrison (eds.), *The Medieval World and the Modern Mind* (Dublin: Four Courts Press, 2000), 171–82.

2 Simms, *Medieval Gaelic Sources*; Otway-Ruthven, *History of Medieval Ireland*, ch. 8; Lydon, *Lordship*, ch. 6; S. Duffy, *Ireland in the Middle Ages* (Houndmills and Dublin: Macmillan, 1997), ch. 6.

depopulated, and many chieftains regained independence from royal or baro-nial control. At the same time, greater integration took place between the ruling classes of Gaelic and Anglo-Norman descent. These developments led in turn to an atmosphere of optimism and self-confidence among the Gaels which expressed itself in a drive to enhance the chieftains' ancestral pres-tige and underpin their territorial claims through renewed patronage of the bardic classes, the traditional schools of poets, historians and judges, who had previously been in decline. The interaction of aristocratic ambition and bardic teaching produced a heady ideology extolling nobility of blood, war-rior virtues, the duty to restore a lost high-kingship of Tara and, of course, generous patronage of the learned classes. One positive result was the re-transcription and thus preservation of an extensive Dark Age literature and legal corpus in Old Irish which now forms a significant contribution to the general European cultural heritage. By the fifteenth century aristocrats of Anglo-Norman descent were actively patronising the same movement, and their participation in this revivalist culture paved the way for the emergence of a common bond, religiously, politically and socially, between 'Old English' and 'Old Irish' in the seventeenth century.[3]

The Anglo-Irish parliament's repeated warnings during this period that the king's lordship in Ireland was on the point of being lost for lack of defence against Irish enemies *and* English rebels hints at the complexity of this Gaelic recovery. It varied from place to place both in territorial extent and in political structure, and the same weaknesses of central government that allowed some Irish chiefs to expand their influence also provided opportunities for aggran-disement to leaders of Anglo-Norman descent. Let us consider each province in turn, commencing with Leinster.

Leinster

Leinster after the advent of the Anglo-Normans should be understood in its modern sense, as including counties Meath, Westmeath, Longford and Louth.[4] As well as some of the most fertile and heavily colonised parts of

---

3 K. Simms, 'Bards and Barons: The Anglo-Irish Aristocracy and the Native Culture', in Bartlett and MacKay (eds.), *Medieval Frontier Societies*, 177–97.

4 This was in effect a reversion to the 'greater Leinster' of proto-historic times. See A. S. Mac Shamhráin, *Church and Polity in Pre-Norman Ireland: The Case of Glendalough* (Maynooth: An Sagart, 1996), map at 58. In the poem 'To Art Mac Murchadha Caomhanach' (ed. L. MacKenna, *The Irish Monthly*, 56 (1928), 98–101) (d. 1416), verses 6 and 8 praise Leinster for containing the rivers Boyne and Barrow, the sites of Tara and Dublin.

Ireland, it contained the mountains of Dublin and Wicklow and the midland bogs, where, for example: 'in those areas of Laois which did not attract large-scale settlement the Anglo-Normans contented themselves with exercising overlordship over the pre-existing population groups in exchange for annual tribute', thus preserving the authority of hereditary chiefs, ready-made leaders for revolt when the opportunity presented itself.[5] However in the midlands, Empey has concluded:

> by about 1360 the force of the Gaelic resurgence was spent, and ... a stalemate had been reached. What had been achieved in effect by this time was the recovery by the indigenous Irish septs of the lordship of the territories from which they never had been expelled, and of which they had always been the major occupiers of the soil. They could not – and perhaps never tried to – roll back the tide of Anglo-Norman settlement. Certainly they burned and raided frontier towns, but it is significant that they never occupied them. It is one thing to expel a garrison from an isolated castle, but quite another to shift an armed and determined tenant class. The Anglo-Normans, for their part, seem to have abandoned any serious effort to recover the north [of Ossory] after 1350. This does not mean that a new age of reconciliation had dawned – raiding was very much a way of life in the marches – but that the lines of population and settlement ... became fixed.[6]

Ó Cléirigh agrees with this suggested date for a turning-point in the expansion of the midland chiefs, confronted from the later fourteenth century onwards by the rising power of the earls of Ormond and Kildare, but argues:

> a profound change had occurred in the region's political structures. The earls of Kildare exercised control over the Irish through a mixture of persuasion, which could involve the drawing up of personal indentures of service and the making of marriage alliances, and the application of brute force. These methods were very successful, but were markedly different to the feudal lordship operating under English law originally envisaged by Strongbow and created by the Marshals.[7]

---

5 C. Ó Cléirigh, 'The Impact of the Anglo-Normans in Laois', in P. G. Lane and W. Nolan (eds.), *Laois: History and Society* (Dublin: Geography Publications, 1999), 171. Surviving but tributary chieftainships can also be posited for the Irish of Longford, Westmeath and Offaly: K. O'Conor and C. Parker, 'Anglo-Norman Settlement in County Longford', in M. Morris and F. O'Farrell (eds.), *Longford: History and Society* (Dublin: Geography Publications, 2010), 76. On Mac Gillapatricks and O'Brennans, see C. A. Empey, 'County Kilkenny in the Anglo-Norman Period', in W. Nolan and K. Whelan (eds.), *Kilkenny: History and Society* (Dublin: Geography Publications, 1990), 89. Orpen notes the same pattern in other parts of Ireland: *Normans*, ii, 326–8.

6 Empey, 'County Kilkenny', 91.

7 Ó Cléirigh, 'Impact of the Anglo-Normans', 178.

The situation in east Leinster was more complex. Much of Dublin and Wicklow had been reserved as a series of royal manors, or manors endowing the archbishopric of Dublin, and the former bishopric and abbacy of Glendalough, annexed to the archbishopric by the mid-thirteenth century. Established before immigration from England was fully underway, they incorporated numbers of Irish and Ostman free tenants, in addition to Irish serfs, side by side with English and Welsh newcomers. When the O'Byrne [Ó Broin] and O'Toole [Ó Tuathail] chiefs and their followers expanded their territory from the mountains down into the coastal plain, it was at the expense of these original inhabitants as well as the colonists.[8] This area south of Dublin, for which a succession of chief governors coming from England found themselves directly responsible, formed a contrast both with absentee lordships elsewhere, whose weakened or neglected defences gave Irish neighbours an opportunity for expansion, and with strong resident Anglo-Irish lordships where a single ruling family could construct a network of personal relationships and alliances over generations to reinforce their authority. The proximity of the Dublin mountains to the seat of English government in Ireland posed a special problem. Royal hostings against the king's enemies in Leinster between 1290 and 1360 far outnumbered the total of expeditions to every other part of Ireland in the same period. It was not until strong resident lords in Leinster, the Butlers and FitzGeralds, began to monopolise the central administration in the course of the fifteenth century that the Irish of the Dublin and Wicklow mountains were effectively controlled.[9]

Serious trouble in Leinster post-dated the mid-thirteenth-century revolts of the Irish chiefs in the west, and has been assigned to different causes: famine in 1269, followed in 1271 by a prolonged archiepiscopal vacancy, bringing church tenants of Glendalough and south Dublin under the harsher jurisdiction of royal officials. The unrest became a serious political and military threat when the O'Toole and O'Byrne leaders combined their forces, and were joined in 1274–5 by Muirchertach MacMurrough [Mac Murchada] from north Wexford, styled in the Irish annals 'king of Leinster' (*rí Laigen*). Muirchertach's capture in 1275 was avenged in 1276 when his brother Art MacMurrough defeated a royal army at Glenmalure. The brothers were eventually assassinated in 1282,

---

8 Murphy and Potterton, *Dublin Region in the Middle Ages*, 76–85 (with maps); L. Simpson 'Anglo-Norman Settlement in Uí Briúin Cualann, 1169–1350', in K. Hannigan and W. Nolan (eds.), *Wicklow: History and Society* (Dublin: Geography Publications, 1994), 193–204, 225.
9 Frame, *Ireland and Britain*, 249–50, 280.

but in 1295 the succeeding chief, Muiris MacMurrough, promised to keep the peace on behalf of himself and his followers, Murchad O'Byrne and Fáelán O'Toole, an indication that his claim to be overlord of the Irish leaders in north Leinster was recognised by the Dublin government.[10]

At that period it is arguable that the greater threat to Dublin came from O'Byrne leaders, and that the government was encouraging the historic claims of MacMurrough as a way of controlling them. It is not impossible that the early rise of the O'Byrne dynasty to prominence had been fostered by their landlords, the Butlers of Ormond.[11] However, like the tale of the genie released from the bottle, the Irish of Wicklow speedily became emancipated from the guidance of their erstwhile patrons. The government's only hope lay in a policy of 'divide and rule'. In return for his continuing cooperation against O'Byrne, the government awarded Muiris MacMurrough an annual fee of 40 marks. The payment was continued to his successors, and significantly no MacMurrough rode out to war during the Bruce invasion. In 1328 a temporary breach occurred when the Dublin annals say Domnall MacMurrough was chosen as king by *all* the Leinster Irish, and had ordered his standard to be raised within two miles of Dublin as a preliminary to making a circuit of all Ireland. However, he was rapidly captured, and after two years of imprisonment, Domnall resumed his predecessors' alliance with the government, yielded a hostage and received the annual reward of 40 marks, raised to an annual 80 marks after his participation in Edward III's expedition to Scotland in 1335. Frame has argued that from 1309 to the end of Rokeby's justiciarship in 1357 while the Dublin government did not succeed in preventing the Irish of Wicklow and north Wexford from rebelling, by a combination of military action, rewards and diplomacy, it did manage to prevent them from joint action in such numbers as would seriously threaten the seat of government itself. Nevertheless, their constant war of attrition had done much to alter the balance of power. Castlekevin, once a key fortress in the ring of military wards containing the Irish of the Wicklow mountains, was finally captured by the O'Tooles in 1343 and never reoccupied. The O'Tooles settled the Powerscourt area, while the O'Byrnes took over much of the coastal plain south of Bray. With their expansion into a more extensive and fertile

---

10   E. O'Byrne, 'Cultures in Contact in the Dublin Marches, 1170–1400', in S. Duffy (ed.), *Medieval Dublin V* (Dublin: Four Courts Press, 2004), 122–3; Frame, *Ireland and Britain*, 241–8; *CJRI, 1295–1303*, 61.

11   Frame, *Ireland and Britain*, 269–70. E. O'Byrne, *War, Politics and the Irish of Leinster, 1156–1606* (Dublin: Four Courts Press, 2003), 62–4; O'Byrne, 'Cultures in Contact', 127–8.

territory, the Wicklow Irish became correspondingly stronger and more difficult to control.[12]

The threat from the MacMurrough chiefs was even more serious, because they were spreading from north Wexford into the Carlow area, on the one hand endangering the colony's line of communication down the valley of the River Barrow, which linked the seat of government at Dublin with the south of Ireland, and on the other raising the possibility of concerted action by the Irish of west and east Leinster, perhaps even the western chiefs' recognition of MacMurrough as provincial king. Such considerations prompted the at first sight bizarre decision in 1361 to move the Irish exchequer down to Carlow, where money due from local government officials could be more easily collected, and money paid out for military expeditions against the Irish would have a shorter distance to be transported.[13] In 1354 we are told that Muirchertach MacMurrough 'calling himself king or prince of Leinster, despite the peace made between him and the justiciar in the king's name ... entered into various confederacies, alliances and conspiracies with certain great and powerful Irish against the lord king' before being captured and executed. The pattern of Muirchertach's career, first assisted to power by the Dublin government, receiving the now customary stipend of 40 or 80 marks for his military service, then ultimately executed for rebellion, was repeated for his successors Art MacMurrough Kavanagh [Mac Murchada Caemánach] the elder (d. 1359) and Diarmait *Lámderg* ('D. Red-hand') MacMurrough (d. 1367).[14]

The reign of Art *Óc* ('A. the Younger') MacMurrough Kavanagh (king 1377–1416/17) marked a high-point in the power and prestige of the dynasty. A son of Art MacMurrough the elder, Art *Óc* rose to power in opposition to Art son of Diarmait *Lámderg*, the candidate backed by the Dublin government. His mother was a daughter of Pilib O'Byrne, while his son and probably a daughter married into the same family.[15] The O'Byrne dynasty's return to

---

12 Frame, *Ireland and Britain*, 270–6. O'Byrne, *War, Politics and the Irish of Leinster*, 66–8; Simpson, 'Anglo-Norman Settlement', 222–4.

13 See S. Doran, 'Lords of the River Valleys: Economic and Military Lordship in the Carlow Corridor, *c.* 1200–1350 – European Model in an Irish Context', in Doran and Lyttleton (eds.), *Lordship in Medieval Ireland*, 100; P. Connolly, 'The Financing of English Expeditions to Ireland, 1361–1376', in Lydon (ed.), *England and Ireland*, 109; R. Frame, 'Two Kings in Leinster: The Crown and the MicMhurchadha in the Fourteenth Century', in Barry *et al.* (eds.), *Colony and Frontier in Medieval Ireland*, 165. The exchequer returned to Dublin at the end of the fourteenth century.

14 Frame, *Ireland and Britain*, 272; 'Lord Chancellor Gerrard's Notes of his Report on Ireland', ed. C. McNeill, *Analecta Hibernica*, 2 (1931), 246; *AC*, 311; Frame, 'Two Kings in Leinster', 166–7.

15 E. O'Byrne, 'MacMurrough, Art (*c.*1357–1416/17)', in S. Duffy (ed.), *Medieval Ireland: An Encyclopedia* (New York and London: Routledge, 2005), 304–5; A. P. Smyth, *Celtic Leinster*

influence during his reign was shown in the submissions to Richard II in 1395 when both Gerald O'Byrne and Art *Óc* MacMurrough bound themselves to forfeit 20,000 marks to the papal camera in the event of a breach of their oaths, whereas O'Toole was bound by a mere £1,000.[16] This unity of purpose removed one major weakness of earlier uprisings in east Leinster. In addition to the by now customary payment of 80 marks from the Irish exchequer, Art was able from time to time to force payments of protection-money or 'black-rent' from Carlow and Wexford counties, the black-rent from Wexford becoming a regular tribute paid to his successors into the sixteenth century at a rate of £40 (or 60 marks) a year. Another strength was Art's use of allies and mercenary soldiers from Leinster west of the River Barrow and from Munster. Among the hostages he offered Richard II when submitting to him in 1395 was an O'More [Ó Mórda] of Laois, while he was more loosely associated by his sister's marriage to Murchad O'Connor Faly [Ó Conchobair Failge] of Offaly, and his daughter Sadb's marriage to Finnán MacGillapatrick [Mac Gilla Pátraic] of north Ossory.[17]

Even more significant for future developments were marriage connections with the Anglo-Irish. Art himself married Elizabeth le Veel (or Calf), heiress to the barony of Norragh in County Kildare, and thereafter claimed his right to her lands, and indeed the title of 'baron', with varying success, depending on whether the Dublin government felt it was possible or politic at the time to refuse him. However, it does not appear that Elizabeth bore him any children to continue this claim.[18] By contrast, when Art's son and successor, Donnchad, married Avelina Butler, sister of James, the fourth or 'White' earl of Ormond, the marriage produced offspring and a lasting connection with the Butler family, reinforced by the further marriage of Domnall *Riabach* ('D. the Swarthy') MacMurrough's daughter Sadb to James son of

(Blackrock: Irish Academic Press, 1982), 105–7; Frame, 'Two Kings', 168; O'Byrne, *War, Politics and the Irish of Leinster*, 104.

16 H. Long, 'Three Settlements of Gaelic Wicklow 1169–1600: Rathgall, Ballinacor and Glendalough', in K. Hannigan and W. Nolan (eds.), *Wicklow: History and Society* (Dublin: Geography Publications, 1994), 242; J. F. Lydon, 'Medieval Wicklow – a Land of War', in Hannigan and Nolan (eds.), *Wicklow: History and Society*, 178; E. Curtis, *Richard II in Ireland, 1394–5, and the Submissions of the Irish Chiefs* (Oxford University Press, 1927), 77–8, 80.

17 *SP, Henry VIII*, ii part III, section 1, p. 9; Frame, 'Two Kings', 170; Curtis, *Richard II in Ireland*, 31, 166–7; O'Byrne, *War, Politics and the Irish of Leinster*, 104, 107.

18 E. Curtis and E. St John Brooks, 'The Barons of Norragh, County Kildare', *JRSAI*, 65 (1935), 89–91; O'Byrne, *War, Politics and the Irish of Leinster*, 109–10. Mac Murchada styled himself both 'king' and 'baron' in an inscription on the shrine of the Book of Moling, dated to 1402: T. K. Abbott, 'Note on the Book of Mulling', *Hermathena: A Dublin University Review*, 8 no. 17 (1891), 89–90.

Edmund fitz Richard Butler on or before 1460, these becoming ultimately parents of Piers Butler (d. 1539), later earl of Ossory and Ormond.[19] The 'White Earl' after his marriage to the daughter and heiress of the fifth earl of Kildare controlled both his own and his wife's vast lands and often combined this with authority as chief governor of Ireland. Although Domnall *Riabach* MacMurrough and his immediate successors continued to style themselves proudly 'kings of Leinster', they were very much junior partners when allied to the Butlers. After the earls of Kildare recovered their lands and began to dominate the administration in the later fifteenth century, the MacMurrough chiefs and the rest of the Irish of Leinster and Meath figure unequivocally in the Kildare rental as tribute-paying vassals, although not in a hostile light. As a mark of his favour the ninth earl of Kildare on coming into his inheritance in 1513 presented both Sir Piers Butler and MacMurrough with a chief horse each, and hackneys for their wives.[20]

Munster

In contrast with east Leinster, where a succession of short-term chief governors of Ireland wielded authority over the chieftains, but lacked any continuity of personal contact before the rise of the Geraldines, fourteenth- and fifteenth-century Munster was dominated by two great resident Anglo-Irish lords, the earls of Desmond and Ormond. Gaelic chieftains in Munster also expanded their territory and influence, but interestingly this was sometimes in cooperation with royal government, which saw them as a counterweight to Gaelic and Anglo-Irish rebels, in particular the rebellious first earl of Desmond. This situation however, and the territorial expansion that accompanied it, was concentrated in a prolonged period of instability in the fourteenth century, described by A. F. O'Brien as a time of transition, during which the great Anglo-Irish lords of Munster struggled with the Dublin government over who should have decisive direction of affairs in their area. Once this was decided in the earls' favour by the mid-fifteenth century, they

19 *AFM*, iv, 980–1, where the Irish text makes clear that the translation should have described Gormlaith Caemánach as 'the daughter of Mac Murrough and *of* the Earl's own sister'. *COD*, iii, nos. 85, 226, 230–1, 302.

20 D. Beresford, 'Butler, James (*c*.1390–1452), 4th earl of Ormond', in J. McGuire and J. Quinn (eds.), *Dictionary of Irish Biography*. 9 vols. (Cambridge University Press, 2009), ii, 126–7; E. Curtis, 'Some Further Medieval Seals out of the Ormond Archives, Including That of Donal Reagh MacMurrough Kavanagh, King of Leinster', *JRSAI*, 7 (1937), 75–6; *Crown Surveys of Lands, 1540–41*, 235–6, 319.

became a force of stability in the province, and acquired considerable control over their Gaelic neighbours.[21]

The pattern of a Gaelic king appealing to the Dublin government for support against a local lord is already seen during the Bruce invasion. In the long succession struggle between rival O'Brien [Ó Briain] factions in Thomond, Richard de Clare, lord of Thomond, had favoured the Clann Briain *Ruaid* ('descendants of Brian the Red-haired'), whereas the Clann Taidc were backed by his neighbours the de Burghs in Connacht and the Butlers of Ormond. When Muirchertach O'Brien of Clann Taidc obtained the upper hand with the support of his de Burgh and Butler allies, Clann Briain *Ruaid* appealed to the invading Scots army. Naturally King Muirchertach gave his support to the allied forces aiding the Dublin government to resist the Scots. In 1317 when the retreat of the Bruce brothers northwards reduced the threat posed by Clann Briain *Ruaid*, the remarkable fourteenth-century O'Brien saga, *Caithréim Thoirdhealbhaigh*, tells us that Richard de Clare petitioned parliament for them to be pardoned. In response, Muirchertach O'Brien came to Dublin under Butler escort to argue against de Clare and, apparently having a good command of English and French, was able to press his case without an interpreter: 'a good instrument to a foreigner's prejudice indeed he was, for of various tongues he skilled to the extent that in any controversy he could fluently speak them to oppose the Gall'.[22]

While Muirchertach was in Dublin, his younger brother Diarmaid delivered a crushing defeat to the Clann Briain *Ruaid* at the Battle of Corcomroe (1317), confirming Muirchertach's hold on the kingship. Nevertheless, Richard de Clare attempted to limit the extent of Muirchertach's power by grants of territory to his kinsman and *tánaiste*, Mathgamain (mac Domnaill *Connachtaig* – 'son of D. the Connacht-man') O'Brien, a former supporter of Clann Briain *Ruaid*. In the resulting conflict de Clare was killed in the Battle of Dysert O'Dea (1318). The battle itself was not a decisive O'Brien victory,

---

21 Frame, *Ireland and Britain*, 198; Nicholls, *Gaelic and Gaelicized Ireland*, 189; A. F. O'Brien, 'Politics, Economy and Society: The Development of Cork and the Irish South-Coast Region c. 1170 to c. 1583', in P. O'Flanagan and C. G. Buttimer (eds.), *Cork: History and Society* (Dublin: Geography Publications, 1993), 112; A. Nic Ghiollamhaith, 'Kings and Vassals in Later Medieval Ireland: The Uí Bhriain and the MicConmara in the Fourteenth Century', in Barry *et al.* (eds.), *Colony and Frontier in Medieval Ireland*, 210–12; A. F. O'Brien, 'Medieval Youghal: The Development of an Irish Seaport Trading Town c.1200–1500', *Peritia*, 5 (1986), 360–2.

22 '*ro bo maith in seol aimlesa allmaraigh in t-árdrígh, uair rob eolach é a nilbérlaib re [a] nimluad na naghaid in gach imresain*' – *Caithréim Thoirdhealbhaigh*, i, 93; ii, 86. Note the Irish text styles Muirchertach 'high-king' – though a few lines further on it makes clear this refers to kingship of Thomond, not of Ireland.

but Lord Richard was succeeded by an underage male heir, Thomas, who died in 1321, leaving the Thomond lordship to absentee heiresses. In practice this ensured independence for the area later known as County Clare until 1542, when Thomond was surrendered to Henry VIII to be re-granted to Murchad O'Brien as an earldom.[23]

O'Brien independence was not secured without a struggle, however. At the death of the young de Clare heir, Maurice fitz Thomas, future first earl of Desmond, was granted temporary joint custody with his ally Maurice de Rochefort of the de Clare lands in Ireland, and resisted the royal government's attempts to dislodge him thereafter, seizing Bunratty castle by force in 1325, cutting out the tongue and gouging out the eyes of the English king's constable there.[24] Like his late friend Richard de Clare, Maurice supported the Clann Briain *Ruaid* candidate for the kingship of Thomond, Brian *Bán* ('B. the White-haired') O'Brien. Brian *Bán* could not unseat Muirchertach, but he developed an independent power-base in Duharra, east of the Shannon on the Limerick–Tipperary border, founding a cadet O'Brien dynasty, whose head was styled Mac Uí Briain Ara. The poem *Port oireachais Ara Chliach*, addressed to Brian *Bán*'s grandson, states that this area, part of the historic pre-Norman Thomond, had been more recently reclaimed by Domnall son of Brian *Ruaid* (Brian *Bán*'s father), when he was banished from the County Clare area by King Toirdelbach *Mór* ('T. the Great', d. 1306) of Clann Taidc. From this base Brian *Bán* not only raided Thomond, but throughout the 1320s ravaged Limerick, Cork and Waterford in company with Maurice fitz Thomas, who was asserting disputed territorial claims in the area, and in 1330 extended his activities into Tipperary, still in collusion with fitz Thomas, now earl of Desmond. King Muirchertach O'Brien's chief vassal, Mac Con MacNamara [Mac Conmara], had been slain in battle against Brian *Bán* in 1328, and his successor switched his allegiance to Brian *Bán* and the earl of Desmond, so that royal expeditions mounted by Rokeby against Thomond in the mid-fourteenth century name MacNamara, not O'Brien, as the enemy.[25]

23 Orpen, *Normans*, iv, 88–97; G. A. Hayes-McCoy, *Irish Battles: A Military History of Ireland* (London: Longmans, 1969), 35–47; Nicholls, *Gaelic and Gaelicized Ireland*, 184–6.

24 A. F. O'Brien, 'The Territorial Ambitions of Maurice fitz Thomas, First Earl of Desmond, with Particular Reference to the Barony and Manor of Inchiquin, co. Cork', *PRIA*, 82 C (1982), 65–9; G. O. Sayles, 'The Rebellious First Earl of Desmond', in J. A. Watt, J. B. Morrall and F. X. Martin (eds.), *Medieval Studies Presented to Aubrey Gwynn S.J.* (Dublin: The Three Candles, 1961), 205; Nic Ghiollamhaith, 'Kings and Vassals', 210.

25 *A Bardic Miscellany: Five Hundred Poems from Manuscripts in Irish and British Libraries*, ed. D. McManus and E. Ó Raghallaigh. (Dublin: Department of Irish, Trinity College Dublin, 2010), 541–4; Sayles, 'Rebellious First Earl', 204–6, 210–11; O'Brien, 'Territorial Ambitions'; O'Brien, 'Politics, Economy and Society', 112–14.

All that changed with the succession of Muirchertach's grandson Brian *Sreamach* ('B. the Blear-eyed') in 1369. Brian defeated and captured Gerald, the young third earl of Desmond, at the Battle of Monasternenagh, County Limerick, (1370), imprisoning him in the O'Brien palace near Ennis for the next eighteen months, while MacNamara burned the city of Limerick. Although the formidable governor William Windsor quelled the outbreak, imposed fines on the chieftains, and in 1374 bribed a number of the vassal chiefs of Thomond to support Brian's uncle Toirdelbach *Máel* ('the Bald') as king instead, Brian *Sreamach* soon expelled his rival and resumed power.[26] He also drove out another uncle, Tadc, who founded a separate chieftainship in the Comeragh mountains, County Waterford, his descendants being styled Ó Briain Cumarach.[27] Another lasting O'Brien colony was established east of the Shannon in Carrigogunnell, County Limerick, by a nephew of Brian *Sreamach* called Brian *Dub* ('B. the Black-haired').[28] Meanwhile in March 1378 Brian *Bán*'s son, Murchad *na Raithnige* ('M. of the Bracken') O'Brien, scourge of the Butler lordship, caused panic by bringing his armies into Leinster to join the insurgent O'Byrnes and MacMurroughs, and had to be paid 100 marks to go away again.[29]

Incidents like this, however, gave O'Brien of Thomond and the earl of Ormond good reason to unite against their common enemy. From the time of the fourth earl of Ormond (1404–52) to the Battle of Knockdoe (1504) a three-way alliance can be seen between the MacWilliam Burkes of Clanrickard, O'Brien of Thomond and the earls of Ormond. The only major Thomond rebellion in the fifteenth century came in the reign of Tadc *an Chomad* ('T. of Coad') O'Brien (1459–66). In 1463 he sent messengers to Henry O'Neill

---

26 Earl Gerald composed a number of poems in Irish during this captivity, indicating that he was quite well treated, and O'Brien genealogies state that Brian *Sreamach*'s fourth wife was a daughter of the earl of Desmond, though whether this was Gerald's daughter or sister is not made clear. 'Duanaire Gearóid Iarla', ed. G. Mac Niocaill, *Studia Hibernica*, 3 (1963), 7–59: nos. 6, 7, 20, 26; *Caithréim Thoirdhealbhaigh*, i, 176; ii, 187. Nicholls: *Gaelic and Gaelicized Ireland*, 185.

27 *Caithréim Thoirdhealbhaigh*, i, 176; ii, 187. Note that O'Grady has wrongly inserted 'Brian' in the translation (ii, 187) where the Irish text here and elsewhere reads 'Tadg'. See also *An Leabhar Muimhneach*, ed. T. Ó Donnchadha (Dublin: IMC, 1940), 334, 391. A descendant may have been the mysterious second Brian O'Brien, chief of Thomond, who submitted to Richard II at Waterford in April 1395, just as the king was returning to England. The list of vassals has some of the same surnames as the sub-chiefs of Brian O'Brien prince of Thomond, but their Christian names are different: M. V. Ronan, 'Some Medieval Documents', *JRSAI*, 67 (1937), 230; compare Curtis, *Richard II in Ireland*, 180.

28 *Caithréim Thoirdhealbhaigh*, i, 176; ii, 187; *An Leabhar Muimhneach*, 347.

29 Otway-Ruthven, *History of Medieval Ireland*, 311–12. Murchad *na Raithnige*'s exploits are celebrated in verses 43–5 of the poem *Port oireachais Ara Chliach*. See *Bardic Miscellany*, no. 387.

[Ó Néill], the prince of Ulster, and symbolically accepted his leadership by receiving *tuarastal* or 'wages' from the northern chief. Then in 1466 he brought a great army across the Shannon southwards, and, say the annals, 'conquered the country of the Clan-Williams (the Burkes) all and the county of Lymbrick, it being made sure to him from the Earl ... and the townsmen or Citizens of Lymbrick gave 60 markes yearely to him forever' – they add that the Irish of Desmond and 'Iar-mond' (south and west Munster) submitted to him and he had bribed the 'old Irish of Linster, so that they were working his comming to Tara', but he died suddenly in his own house immediately after this triumphant campaign.[30] Significantly, this occurred when the deputy lieutenant of Ireland was Thomas, seventh earl of Desmond, whose line had repeatedly supported Mac Uí Briain Ara against O'Brien of Thomond and against the earls of Ormond, and who had recently crushed the Butler–Lancastrian party in Ireland at the Battle of Piltown, following the execution of the fifth earl and the exile of the sixth earl of Ormond during the Wars of the Roses. The fact that Tadc *an Chomad* had earlier formed a pact with O'Neill, whose wife Gormlaith Caemánach was a daughter of MacMurrough Kavanagh and a niece of the fourth earl of Ormond, suggests an abortive 'Butlerine League', having parallels with the Geraldine League which followed the execution of Silken Thomas and his five uncles in 1535. In spite of his sudden death, one enduring result of Tadc *an Chomad*'s campaign was that into the sixteenth century County Limerick continued to pay a 'black-rent' of 60 marks (£40) yearly to O'Brien of Thomond, and an equal sum to Mac Uí Briain Ara, as the price of enjoying relative peace.[31]

Although the FitzGerald earls took their title from 'Desmond' ('south Munster'), by the fourteenth century their landed estates were rather in the north and east of the province – the Irish of Desmond had driven the settlers out of west Cork and south Kerry in the uprisings of the mid-thirteenth century. At that point the MacCarthy [Mac Carthaig] dynasty split between the descendants of Domnall *Got* ('D. the Stammerer'), father of the rebel leaders, Fingen 'of Ringrone' and Cormac 'of Mangerton', and the main line of MacCarthy *Mór*, descended from Domnall *Ruad* ('D. the Red-haired', d. 1303) son of Cormac *Finn* ('C. the Fair-haired'). Domnall *Ruad* had been defeated

---

30 K. Simms, ' "The King's Friend": O'Neill, the Crown and the Earldom of Ulster', in Lydon (ed.), *England and Ireland*, 225–7; 'The Annals of Ireland from the Year 1443 to 1468 ... by ... Duald MacFirbis', ed. J. O'Donovan, in *The Miscellany of the Irish Archaeological Society 1* (Dublin, 1846), 104–25.

31 An abortive alliance because O'Neill accepted Edward IV's livery in the same year as his bestowal of *tuarastal* on O'Brien; *SP, Henry VIII*, ii, part III, section 1, 9.

by Fingen 'of Ringrone', while fighting on the Anglo-Irish side in the Battle of Callan (1261), but was reinstated as king of the Irish of Desmond after Cormac 'of Mangerton' was slain in 1262. Domnall *Máel*, son of Domnall *Got* (the younger brother of Fingen and Cormac), founded the line of MacCarthy *Cairbrech* ('of Carbery') in West Cork, who remained subsequently resistant to the control of either MacCarthy *Mór* or the earls of Desmond.[32]

Domnall *Ruad*'s grandson and successor, Diarmaid Óc ('D. the younger') 'of Tralee', became rebellious during the Bruce invasion (1315–18), and made attacks on the settlers in north Kerry before being treacherously done to death in the Franciscan friary at Tralee in 1325.[33] It is in this context that we find Maurice fitz Thomas supporting a rival MacCarthy candidate, Diarmaid (mac Diarmada) MacCarthy (d. 1356), just as he had supported Brian *Bán* O'Brien against King Muirchertach of Thomond. 'Macdermot' MacCarthy (as he was known in English-speaking circles) then joined Brian *Bán* and Maurice fitz Thomas in repeatedly ravaging the English settlements in Munster in pursuit of fitz Thomas's territorial claims. This gave Cormac MacCarthy, who succeeded his brother Diarmaid 'of Tralee' as king of Desmond, an ideal opportunity to win the favour of the Dublin government by taking up arms against 'Macdermot' and the earl of Desmond. In 1352 he was rewarded for his assistance to Sir Thomas de Rokeby by a grant of additional lands with which he endowed his younger sons. His second son, Diarmaid, received the territory of Muskerry to the east of Desmond, and founded the line of the MacCarthy barons of Muskerry, who continued to expand eastwards until in the later fifteenth century they acquired Blarney castle, near Cork, from the Lombard family. Cormac's third son Eogan founded the line of the MacCarthy lords of Coshmang, to the north of his father's kingdom. The rebellious Diarmaid 'Macdermot' MacCarthy continued to be protected by the first earl of Desmond after the latter had made peace with the royal government, and he became ancestor of the Mac Donnchada MacCarthy lords of Duhallow in north Cork. When King Cormac died in 1359 he was succeeded by his eldest son Domnall, who also enjoyed a long and relatively peaceful reign, and the kingship, or principality, of the Irish of Desmond passed in unbroken succession from father to son thereafter to 1508. During this period the earls of Desmond claimed and intermittently succeeded in exacting tribute from the Irish of Desmond. The only chief of the MacCarthy dynasty

---

32 Nicholls, *Gaelic and Gaelicized Ireland*, 187–90; D. Ó Murchadha, 'The Battle of Callan, A.D. 1261', *Journal of the Cork Historical and Archaeological Society*, 66 (1961), 105–15.

33 O'Brien, 'Politics, Economy and Society', 108; Nicholls, *Gaelic and Gaelicized Ireland*, 188; *AI*, 434–5.

who exacted 'black-rent' from English settlers was the MacCarthy lord of Muskerry, who in 1515 was receiving an annual payment of £40 (60 marks) from County Cork.[34]

Connacht

Connacht presents a very different picture from either Leinster or Munster. Here by the mid-fourteenth century lords of Anglo-Irish descent dominated, but they were not the legal owners of the land, leading to friction and a distancing from royal government. The arrangement which completed the conquest of Connacht in 1235 had given Richard de Burgh twenty-four cantreds, reserving five cantreds nearest the royal castle of Athlone (in County Roscommon and east County Galway) to the English king, but farmed out to the titular 'king of Connacht', Feidlim son of Cathal Crobderg O'Connor [Ó Conchobair] (d. 1265).[35] Even this diminished kingdom was whittled down by confiscation and settlement of its southern parts in punishment for the rebellious activities of Feidlim's son, Aed (d. 1274), known as Aed *na nGall* 'of the Foreigners', because he was one of the first chiefs in Ireland to import Scottish mercenaries, or 'galloglass' (*gallóclaig*, 'foreign warriors').[36] Like MacCarthy chiefs under pressure from the FitzGerald lords in Munster, the O'Connor dynasty by the end of the thirteenth century was splitting into mutually hostile branches: the Clann Muirchertaig *Muimnig* ('descendants of M. the Munsterman' – i.e. fostered in Munster), whose claims to the shrunken 'kingship of Connacht' were supported by the FitzGerald lords of Sligo; Clann Briain *Luignig* ('descendants of B. the Leyney-man') in north Sligo, later to achieve the title 'Ó Conchobair Sligig' ('O'Connor Sligo'); and the main royal line, then represented by King Aed son of Eógan O'Connor (reigned 1296–1309).[37]

---

34 Nicholls, *Gaelic and Gaelicized Ireland*, 188–90; *SP, Henry VIII*, ii, part III, section 1, p. 9.

35 Orpen, *Normans*, iii, 158–89; F. Verstraten, 'Both King and Vassal: Feidlim Ua Conchobair of Connacht, 1230–65', *Journal of the Galway Archaeological and Historical Society*, 55 (2003), 18.

36 S. Duffy, 'The Pre-history of the Galloglass', in S. Duffy (ed.), *The World of the Galloglass: Kings, Warlords and Warriors in Ireland and Scotland, 1200–1600* (Dublin: Four Courts Press, 2007), 15–20; A. Woolf, 'A Dead Man at Ballyshannon', in Duffy (ed.), *World of the Galloglass*, 83–5; W. H. D. Sellar, 'Hebridean Sea-Kings: The Successors of Somerled, 1164–1316', in E. J. Cowan and R. A. McDonald (eds.), *Alba: Celtic Scotland in the Medieval Era* (East Linton: Tuckwell Press, 2000), 206–7.

37 K. Simms, 'A Lost Tribe – the Clan Murtagh O'Conors', *Galway Archaeological and Historical Society Journal*, 53 (2001), 3–9. The clans' eponymous ancestors, Muirchertach *Muimnech* and Brian *Luignech*, had been sons of the twelfth-century high-king, Toirdelbach *Mór* Ua Conchobair (d. 1156). The main royal line descended from Toirdelbach's youngest son, Cathal Crobderg (d. 1224); see *NHI* ix, table 28, p. 158.

In 1298 the bitter struggle between Richard ('the Red Earl') de Burgh, lord of Connacht and earl of Ulster, and the Geraldine leader John fitz Thomas of Offaly over the lordship of Sligo was settled by an exchange of territories, which removed the Geraldine interest from Connacht completely. Consequently, Clann Muirchertaig and Clann Briain Uí Chonchobair were left without the support of their former Anglo-Irish patrons. King Aed son of Eogan was confirmed in possession of the three remaining 'King's Cantreds' held at farm from the royal government, while the 'Red Earl' seems to have permitted him to spread his influence northwards into the former Sligo lordship, where the head of Clann Briain *Luignig* enjoyed authority as Aed's deputy-chief, or *tánaiste*.[38] A poem lamenting Aed's death in 1309 indicates that he occupied a house in Sligo town. Earlier he had erected a palace in the style of a moated grange at Cloonfree, County Roscommon, burned down by Clann Muirchertaig in 1306. A noted patron of bardic poetry, this king also showed himself influenced by English culture.[39] He was slain in battle against his Clann Muirchertaig rival, Aed *Breifnech* ('A. the Breifne-man') O'Connor, in 1309. Aed son of Eogan's hold on the kingship had depended both on the approval of the 'Red Earl' of Ulster, and on the support of MacDermott [Mac Diarmada], chief of Moylurg (north Roscommon), foster-father to his young son and heir, Feidlim. Following Aed son of Eogan's death, the 'Red Earl' built a castle in Sligo in 1310 to replace the earlier Geraldine one. His cousin and representative in Connacht, Sir William *Liath* de Burgh, bribed Seonac MacQuillin [Mac Uigilin], the Welsh mercenary commander serving Clann Muirchertaig, to assassinate the new king Aed *Breifnech* and switch his allegiance to the de Burghs, unwarrantably billeting his 200 men in the 'King's Cantreds'.[40]

38 Otway-Ruthven, *History of Medieval Ireland*, 205–7, 210–11, 214; *AC*, 212–15.
39 'An Elegy on the Death of Aodh Ó Conchobhair (†1309)', ed. D. McManus, *Ériu*, 51 (2000), 82; *AC*, 209–11; E. C. Quiggin, 'O'Conor's House at Cloonfree', in E. C. Quiggin (ed.), *Essays and Studies Presented to William Ridgeway* (Cambridge University Press, 1913), 333–52; *Dioghluim Dána*, ed. Láimhbheartach Mac Cionaith (Dublin: ITS, 1938), no. 119; 'Poem to Cloonfree Castle', ed. and trans. L. McKenna, *The Irish Monthly*, 51 (1923), 639–45; T. Finan and K. O'Conor, 'The Moated Site at Cloonfree, Co. Roscommon', *Journal of the Galway Archaeological and Historical Society*, 54 (2002), 72–87; K. Simms, 'Native Sources for Gaelic Settlement: The House Poems', in P. J. Duffy, D. Edwards and E. Fitzpatrick (eds.), *Gaelic Ireland: Land, Lordship and Settlement* (Dublin: Four Courts Press, 2001), 251–2.
40 Unwarrantably, because although in 1305 the earl of Ulster asked for the farm of the King's Cantreds to be transferred from O'Connor to himself 'or another Englishman' (*CJRI, 1305–07*, 133–4), royal officials still regarded the O'Connor kings as responsible for the farm in 1310–11 – *Rep. DKI 39*, 27; *AC*, 214–23. On the MacQuillin mercenary commanders see K. Simms, 'Gaelic Warfare in the Middle Ages', in T. Bartlett and K. Jeffery (eds.), *A Military History of Ireland* (Cambridge University Press, 1996), 108–10.

Faced with this imminent takeover, Maelruanaid MacDermott of Moylurg mustered his forces to overawe the other sub-chiefs and escorted his foster-son Feidlim O'Connor to Carn Fraich (Carnfree near Tulsk, County Roscommon), the traditional inauguration site of the O'Connor kings. There he enacted an elaborate enkinging ceremony 'in the manner remembered by the old men and recorded in the old books; and this was the most splendid kingship-marriage ever celebrated in Connacht down to that day'. The deliberately enhanced ceremony gave a prominent role to MacDermott, reflecting the relative strength of his family now that the area under O'Connor's rule was so shrunken, while the sub-kingdom of Moylurg remained intact. MacDermott chiefs continued to exercise a major influence as king-makers and inaugurators of the O'Connor kings into the fifteenth century, providing a parallel with the inflated role of the MacNamara sub-chiefs vis-à-vis the O'Brien kings of Thomond.[41] The ceremony's appeal to immemorial tradition, even if this was a tradition adjusted to reflect MacDermott's increased influence, also pointed to a desire to assert independence from the de Burghs, and even from the English king, should he agree to transfer the 'King's Cantreds' to the de Burghs. Reviving the O'Connor dynasty's claim to be provincial kings of all Connacht has a parallel in the decision of *all* the Irish of Leinster, as we are told, to elect Domnall MacMurrough Kavanagh as their king in 1328. In practice, however, the rivalry of the new head of Clann Muirchertaig, Ruaidri son of Cathal *Ruad* O'Connor, forced Feidlim to come to terms with the 'Red Earl'. In 1315 Feidlim brought his forces to join the earl's expedition into Ulster to confront the newly landed army of Edward Bruce. As had happened in Thomond, the discarded dynastic segment (in this case Clann Muirchertaig), appealed to Bruce for support, and Ruaidri son of Cathal *Ruad* took advantage of Feidlim's absence in Ulster to seize the kingship, aided by 'many galloglasses'.[42]

The 'Red Earl' was soundly defeated by Edward Bruce at the Battle of Connor, and what was perhaps of even more consequence for Connacht, his cousin Sir William *Liath* de Burgh was captured and taken back to Scotland. MacDermott deserted the powerless earl and made a temporary alliance with Ruaidri son of Cathal *Ruad* and Tadc O'Kelly [Ó Cellaig], king of Uí Maine in east Galway. From a praise-poem it appears that Tadc O'Kelly hoped for great things from the weakening of the English colony during the Bruce

---

41 *AC*, 222–5; Simms, *From Kings to Warlords*, 29–30; Nic Ghiollamhaith, 'Kings and Vassals'.
42 Cathal *Ruad* ('the Red-haired'), father of Aed *Brefnech* and Ruaidri, had been Clann Muirchertaig 'king of Connacht' 1280–8. *NHI* ix, 158.

wars – to burn Dublin, fetter its knights, ruin Limerick, drive the English from Waterford and leave the de Burgh stronghold of Loughrea (County Galway) without stone or timber.[43] However Feidlim with the assistance of Clann Briain *Luignig* Uí Chonchobair of Sligo began to make headway against Clann Muirchertaig, and regained MacDermott's support. On 24 February 1316 Feidlim, with the help of his Irish allies and de Bermingham of Athenry, defeated and killed his rival, Ruaidri son of Cathal *Ruad* O'Connor. He then re-united the Irish chiefs of Connacht under his authority, including many from outside the north Roscommon area, such as Tadc O'Kelly of Uí Maine, O'Rourke [Ó Ruairc] of Breifne, O'Hara [Ó hEdra], O'Dowd [Ó Dubda], MacDonogh [Mac Donnchada] and Magnus O'Connor the *tánaiste* (these four from the Sligo area), and together they attempted to annihilate the English settlements. When news came that Sir William *Liath* de Burgh had returned from his captivity in Scotland and was rallying the settlers for a counter-blow, Feidlim was joined by more allies: Ó Maelsechlainn of Westmeath, O'Farrell [Ó Feargall] of Longford and the Clann Briain *Ruaid* O'Brien from Thomond. William de Burgh won a great victory at Athenry over the allied Irish in August 1316, and both King Feidlim and Tadc O'Kelly were decapitated, but Kenneth Nicholls has pointed out that much land recovered by the Irish during this uprising was not subsequently resettled, especially in the east Galway and Roscommon areas.[44]

The continuing Bruce war meant that both sides in Connacht were in some disarray and Aed O'Donnell [Ó Domnaill], king of Tír Conaill, used the opportunity to extend his lordship into the territory of Carbury in north Sligo. To strengthen resistance in this northern border area, Sir William *Liath* de Burgh supported Cathal son of Domnall O'Connor of the Clann Briain *Luignig* or Sligo branch as 'king of Connacht' from 1318 to Sir William's own death in February 1324. The following October, Toirdelbach O'Connor, younger brother of the King Feidlim slain at Athenry, killed Cathal son of Domnall and seized the kingship for himself. This apparently took place with the support of the 'Red Earl', Richard de Burgh, since just a month earlier, 15 September 1324, the earl had granted Toirdelbach a charter of jurisdiction over O'Rourke's kingdom of Breifne (the County Leitrim area) where the Clann Muirchertaig Uí Chonchobair had taken refuge, and Toirdelbach bound himself to behave towards the earl as his father, Aed son of Eogan,

---

43 *AC*, 230–7; *Bardic Miscellany*, no. 447.
44 Nicholls, *Gaelic and Gaelicized Ireland*, 170–1; *AC*, 242–9.

had best borne himself.[45] Far from constituting a bulwark of opposition to the southward expansion of O'Donnell, king of Tír Conaill, Toirdelbach married Aed O'Donnell's daughter Derbail, and O'Donnell was subsequently described at his death in 1333 as 'having taken the hostages' of Carbury.[46]

Walter de Burgh, lord of Mayo, the eldest son and heir of Sir William *Liath*, violently opposed both Toirdelbach O'Connor and his brother Cathal, even in 1330 being wrongly rumoured to have slain Toirdelbach, hoping, as the Annals of Connacht allege, 'to seize the kingship of Connacht for himself'.[47] Toirdelbach O'Connor, however, retained the favour of the young earl of Ulster, William de Burgh, Richard's grandson (known as 'the Brown Earl'), who arrived from England to take up his inheritance in the autumn of 1328. Toirdelbach served with Muirchertach O'Brien, king of Thomond, in the earl's expedition against Brian *Bán* O'Brien that year. His enemy Walter de Burgh was eventually arrested in November 1331 by order of the 'Brown Earl' and imprisoned in the castle of Northburgh in Inishowen, where he starved to death the following year. Immediately war broke out in Connacht between Walter's brother Edmund *Albanach* ('E. the Scotsman')[48], the new MacWilliam Burke of Mayo, and Edmund 'the earl's son', a younger son of Earl Richard de Burgh, assisted by the Clanrickard of Galway.[49] In Ulster, Walter's brother-in-law Sir Richard de Mandeville joined the feud by assassinating the 'Brown Earl' himself in May 1333 and fleeing to raise rebellion among the Ulster Irish. The legal ownership of the two provinces of Ulster and Connacht now passed to Earl William's baby daughter, Elizabeth de Burgh, an absentee ward

45 *Report on the Manuscripts of Lord De L'Isle and Dudley*, ed. C. L. Kingsford *et al.* 6 vols. (London: Historical Manuscripts Commission, 1925–66), i, 32–3. Simms, ' "The King's Friend" ', 215.

46 *AC*, 258–9, 272–3. Simms, 'Lost Tribe', 13. At p. 21 n. 48 in this article I speculated that the problem in positing an early date for Toirdelbach's marriage to Derbail daughter of Aed O'Donnell would be solved if the annals' record of the death of Findguala daughter of O'Brien *wife* of Toirdelbach in 1335 (*AC*, 274–5) referred instead to his *mother*. In fact this is substantiated by the last two verses of the poem *An tú a-rís a ráith Temrach*, in compliment to Aed son of Eogan's wife Findguala daughter of O'Brien (Quiggin, 'O'Conor's House', 350–1, verses 51–2).

47 *AC*, 264–9. Jurors reporting the activities of the rebellious first earl of Desmond also spoke of Walter's ambition to be king of Connacht – Sayles, 'Rebellious First Earl', 211; 'The Legal Proceedings against the First Earl of Desmond', ed. G. O. Sayles, *Analecta Hibernica*, 23 (1966), 12–14.

48 Edmund *Albanach* was apparently so called because he had been sent to Scotland as hostage for the release of his father Sir William *Liath* de Burgh following the Battle of Connor – Orpen, *Normans*, iv, 182 n.

49 *AC*, 262–71. The de Burghs or Burkes of Clanrickard (Clann Ricard or 'descendants of Richard') who occupied the Galway area are traced by Kenneth Nicholls to Richard *le Hore* (the grey-haired) de Burgh, see *Gaelic and Gaelicized Ireland*, 171–2; *NHI* ix, tables 38, 40, pp. 170, 172. Richard *le Hore* flourished in 1327 see Sayles, *Affairs*, 126–7.

of the king, and the ministers who should have taken control of her lands were faced with rebellion from major Anglo-Irish tenants in both areas.[50]

In the early years of chaos and internecine warfare among the de Burghs or Burkes, Toirdelbach O'Connor made territorial gains. In 1336 he captured and destroyed the 'great castle of Mac Costello', and in 1337 established a stronghold (*foslongport*) at Athleague to defend himself 'against Edmund Burke', that is, almost certainly, against Edmund *Albanach*. However in 1338 Edmund *Albanach* captured and drowned his opponent Edmund 'the [Red] earl's son', and gradually made himself master of the province of Connacht, even obtaining a pardon from the English king for his past crimes in 1340. In 1342 and again in 1350 Edmund *Albanach*, or MacWilliam Burke, as he became known, exercised a decisive voice in appointing which O'Connor was to be styled 'king of Connacht' and rule the north Roscommon area attached to that title, no farm being now paid for these lands to the English king. Indeed Otway-Ruthven has commented that after 1347 'Connacht seems to have been effectively outside the sphere of the Dublin government: in the second half of the century seneschals or sheriffs continued to be appointed, but there is nothing to suggest that the government could in fact control them.'[51]

The continuing hostility between the Clanrickard Burkes of Galway and the MacWilliam Burkes of Mayo fostered succession disputes among the various branches of the O'Connor dynasty, as disappointed candidates for kingship appealed to the 'Upper' or 'Southern' MacWilliam (Mac Uilliam *Uachtar*) of Galway or the 'Lower' or 'Northern' MacWilliam (Mac Uilliam *Íochtar*) of Mayo for military support. The increasingly landless Clann Muirchertaig Uí Chonchobair declined in importance in the late fourteenth century and vanished from the political stage early in the fifteenth.[52] After 1384 the main O'Connor dynasty and their associated lands became split in two between the claimants Toirdelbach *Ruad* ('the Red-haired', d. 1426), grandson of Feidlimid (d. 1316), ancestor of the line of O'Connor Roe [Ó Conchobair *Ruad*], who became subordinate allies to MacWilliam Burke of Mayo; and Toirdelbach *Óc* or *Donn* ('T. the Younger' or 'the Brown-haired', d. 1406), grandson of Feidlimid's younger brother Toirdelbach (d. 1345), ancestor of the line of O'Connor Don [Ó Conchobair Donn], who became similarly allies of the MacWilliam of Clanrickard. The late fifteenth century even

50 Otway-Ruthven, *History of Medieval Ireland*, 250–5.
51 *AC*, 76–9; *CPR, 1338–40*, 440; Otway-Ruthven, *History of Medieval Ireland*, 270.
52 Simms, 'Lost Tribe', 19.

saw a prolonged succession struggle within the O'Connor Roe line itself.[53] As a result, the most significant and comparatively independent chief of the name in the later medieval period was the O'Connor of Sligo, descended from Brian *Luignech*. From a base in Cairbre (barony of Carbury Drumcliff, north County Sligo), this branch had expanded in the fourteenth century to occupy Sligo castle and town, to collect the burgage-rents and cockets of the port and to dominate the other chiefs in the south and west of the later County Sligo: MacDonogh, O'Hara and O'Dowd. These Sligo lords occupied a strategic borderland between the expansionist powers of O'Donnell of Tír Conaill and MacWilliam Burke of Mayo. In the later fourteenth and early fifteenth century, the O'Connor chiefs of Sligo, then sometimes styled by the temporary designation Mac Domnaill meic Muirchertaig, tried to secure a degree of independence from their two nearest neighbours by intermittent submission to the Great O'Neill of Tír Eogain, but from 1470 to 1539 successive MacWilliam Burke and O'Donnell rulers competed to assert their overlordship, repeatedly laying waste this border area in the process.[54]

Ulster

Ulster west of the Upper and Lower River Bann together with what was then known as Breifne or 'the Rough Third of Connacht' (*Gairbthrian Connacht* – modern counties Leitrim and Cavan) formed the greatest single expanse of territory remaining under the rule of Irish chieftains, being sometimes styled in official circles *Magna Irecheria*, 'the Great Irishry'.[55] Here the memory persisted of Brian O'Neill's claim to be 'king of the kings of Ireland'; a claim which had ended with his defeat and death at the Battle of Down in 1260. The close proximity of independent Scotland across the North Channel, which led to ties of fosterage and intermarriage between the two Gaelic aristocracies and the importation of heavy-armed mercenary footsoldiers or galloglass

---

53 Nicholls, *Gaelic and Gaelicized Ireland*, 174; *NHI* ix, 158–9, tables 28, 29a and b; K. Simms, 'Gabh umad a Fheidhlimidh – a Fifteenth-Century Inauguration Ode?, *Ériu*, 31 (1980), 134–6.

54 Curtis, *Richard II in Ireland*, 214; Simms, *From Kings to Warlords*, 110; *AFM*, iv, 838–9, 846–7, 888–9; 'Agreement between Ó Domhnaill and Tadhg Ó Conchubhair Concerning Sligo Castle (23 June 1539)', ed. M. Carney, *IHS*, 3 (1942/3), 282–3; *AC*, 598–9.

55 Cavan was not accounted part of the Ulster province until the early seventeenth century – see B. Cunningham, 'The Anglicisation of East Breifne: The O'Reillys and the Emergence of County Cavan', in R. Gillespie (ed.), *Cavan: Essays on the History of an Irish County* (Blackrock: Irish Academic Press, 1995), 61–2, 70–2; *CJRI, 1305–07*, 134; Otway-Ruthven, *History of Medieval Ireland*, 215 n. 69; Nicholls, *Gaelic and Gaelicized Ireland*, map at 218.

from the Western Isles, further stiffened native resolve.[56] King Robert (Bruce) had sent insinuating propagandists into the province even before his brother Edward had landed a Scots army at Larne in May 1315 which remained till his death at the Battle of Faughart in 1318, devastating the 'Red Earl's lands east of the Bann more thoroughly than English settlements elsewhere in Ireland.[57]

Richard de Burgh, the 'Red Earl', who spent much of his career outside Ireland, controlled affairs in Ulster largely through seneschals drawn from the de Mandeville family, and these in turn had close political ties with Brian O'Neill's rival and enemy, Aed *Buide* ('A. the Yellow-haired') O'Neill (d. 1283), his brother Niall (d. 1291), son Brian II (d. 1296) and grandson Henry (d. 1347), whom they successively supported as kings of Tír Eogain in opposition to the rebellious Brian of the Battle of Down's son Domnall (d. 1325), provoking the latter to collaborate with Edward Bruce's invasion in 1315. Domnall put his name to the striking 'Remonstrance of the Irish princes to Pope John XXII'. A many-layered document in support of Bruce, it contained an early brand of nationalism foreshadowing the somewhat later Scottish 'Declaration of Arbroath', together with grievances of the southern Irish who had petitioned the English king for full rights under English common law, and echoes of clerical disputes which may suggest its author was the recently disappointed Franciscan candidate for the archbishopric of Armagh.[58] Personal to Domnall, however, is the insistence that as legitimate heir to the kingship of all Ireland, he was fully entitled to pass on his claim to sovereignty to Edward Bruce, while retaining for himself the title *rex Ultonie*, 'king of Ulster'. Already in 1296 the contemporary Annals of Inisfallen had stated that Domnall took over 'the kingship of the province of Ulster' (*rigi Cughid Ulad*) rather than

---

56 Orpen, *Normans*, iii, 268–78; *Close Rolls, 1259–61*, 64; S. Duffy, 'The Bruce Brothers and the Irish Sea World, 1306–29', *Cambridge Medieval Celtic Studies*, 21 (1991), 56, 67, 72, 74–5. It was not until the fifteenth and sixteenth centuries that employment of hereditary mercenary commanders of Scottish extraction, 'galloglass families', spread beyond Ulster (including Cavan) and north Connacht into the rest of Ireland – see G. A. Hayes-McCoy, *Scots Mercenary Forces in Ireland (1565–1603)* (Dublin and London: Burns, Oates and Washbourne, 1937), 36; K. Nicholls, 'Scottish Mercenary Kindreds in Ireland, 1250–1600', in S. Duffy (ed.), *The World of the Galloglass: Kings, Warlords and Warriors in Ireland and Scotland, 1200–1600* (Dublin: Four Courts Press, 2007), 95–6, 101–2, 104.

57 Duffy, 'The Bruce Brothers', 64–5, 83–4; A. Müller, 'Conflicting Loyalties: The Irish Franciscans and the English Crown in the High Middle Ages', *PRIA*, 107 C (2007), 87; G. H. Orpen, 'The Earldom of Ulster, part I', *JRSAI*, 43 (1913), 46; J. F. Lydon, 'The Impact of the Bruce Invasion', in *NHI*, ii, 294–6.

58 K. Simms, 'Relations with the Irish', in Lydon (ed.), *Law and Disorder*, 69–72; Walter Bower, *Scotichronicon*, vi, 38–46; J. R. S. Phillips, 'The Remonstrance Revisited: England and Ireland in the Early Fourteenth Century', in T. G. Fraser and K. Jeffery (eds.), *Men, Women and War: Papers Read before the XXth Irish Conference of Historians, Held at Magee College, University of Ulster, 6–8 June 1991. Historical Studies XVIII* (Dublin: Lilliput Press, 1993), 20.

merely 'kingship of Tír Eogain' when he defeated Brian II O'Neill at the Battle of Creeve.[59] Brief assertions of provincial kingship are also found in Connacht during the short reign of Feidlim O'Connor (d. 1316), in Leinster in 1327 with Domnall MacMurrough Kavanagh, and more convincingly with Art *Óc* MacMurrough (d. 1416/17). In Ulster, however, it was followed by a steady acquisition of real dominion by successive O'Neill kings over the surrounding lesser chieftains.

Their rise to power was not immediate. The forces of the 'Red Earl' banished Domnall O'Neill from Tír Eogain in the aftermath of Edward Bruce's defeat and death, installing Henry, grandson of Aed *Buide* O'Neill as king in his stead.[60] Although the annals state that Domnall subsequently recovered kingship, it seems he was confined to the western end of Tír Eogain where he died in 1325. His son and successor Aed *Remor* ('A. the Fat', d. 1364) was recorded in 1333 holding Tír Eogain jointly with Henry O'Neill as tenants of William de Burgh the 'Brown Earl' of Ulster, and indeed a revised report informs us that Henry paid the full annual rent 'to have the whole lordship of Tír Eogain' although he bore only half the quota of billeted mercenaries the earl had allotted to O'Neill territory, and both 'half-kings' were summoned to aid Edward III's war against the Scots in 1335.[61] By then, however, the anglophile Henry O'Neill had been implicated in the rebellion of his de Mandeville patrons that followed their assassination of the 'Brown Earl' in May 1333. At first this brought him an important territorial gain. In 1338 the terms of a general peace settlement included a grant to Henry of a large stretch of war-wasted lands within the Ulster earldom for an annual rent of 100 cows. Subsequent events show these lands were located in the south and centre of the modern County Antrim, where Henry's descendants, known as the Uí Néill of Clann Aeda Buide (or 'O'Neills of Clandeboy'), displaced not only some English settlements, but the local east Ulster chieftain O'Flynn or O'Lynn [Ó Floinn Líne].[62] Then in 1345 the justiciar Ralph Ufford, second

---

59 *AI*, 388–9.
60 Frame, *English Lordship*, 133–4, queries whether Richard de Burgh himself took part in this expedition.
61 G. H. Orpen, 'The Earldom of Ulster, part IV', *JRSAI*, 45 (1915), 141; TNA C 47/10/20/14; K. Simms, 'Tír Eoghain North of the Mountain' in G. O'Brien (ed.), *Derry and Londonderry: History and Society* (Dublin: Geography Publications, 1999), 164. K. Simms, 'Late Medieval Tír Eoghain', in C. Dillon and H. A. Jefferies (eds.), *Tyrone: History and Society* (Dublin: Geography Publications, 2000), 144.
62 *CCR, 1337–9*, 329; J. Hogan, 'The Irish Law of Kingship, with Special Reference to Ailech and Cenél Eoghain', *PRIA*, 40 C (1932), 226–7; S. Ó Ceallaigh, *Gleanings from Ulster History* (Cork University Press, 1951), 49; K. Simms, 'The Medieval Chieftains in County Antrim: Irish, English, Scots and Welsh', in C. J. Donnelly and J. Ó Neill (eds.), *Antrim: History and Society* (Dublin: Geography Publications, forthcoming).

husband of the widowed countess of Ulster, brought an army northwards to restore the authority of the crown and safeguard his wife's and step-daughter's rights. He deposed Henry O'Neill 'king of Ulster', and gave the kingship to Aed *Remor* O'Neill, after taking a hostage for his good behaviour. In subsequent generations Aed's successor, the ruler of all Tír Eogain, was known to the English as 'the Great O'Neill' (*Magnus Oneyl, Le Grand Onel*) while Henry's heir in eastern Ulster was styled 'O'Neill Boy', 'O'Neill of Clandeboy' or 'of Clannaboy'.[63]

Already in 1337 Aed *Remor* had been acknowledged as overlord by chieftains in Fermanagh and Monaghan, while a prolonged succession struggle among the O'Donnell rulers of Tír Conaill (Donegal) allowed first Aed, then his son Niall *Mór* ('N. the elder', d. 1397) O'Neill to intervene repeatedly as king-makers, ultimately promoting the accession of Toirdelbach *an Fhína* ('T. of the Wine') O'Donnell (king 1380–1422), a son-in-law of Niall *Mór*. All the Red Earl's settlements west of the Lower Bann had been lost in the uprising that followed the murder of his grandson Earl William, those in Derry falling under O'Neill's sub-chief O'Kane [Ó Catháin], while Inis Eogain (Inishowen peninsula) was gradually annexed by O'Donnell's sub-chief O'Doherty [Ó Dochartaig]. Aed *Remor*'s chief interest was to assert lordship over all the Irish of the northern province, as implied by the title '*rex Hibernicorum Ultonie*' ('king of the Irish of Ulster'), engraved on his seal.[64] His frequent border wars with the English of Louth related mainly to their support for Henry O'Neill chief of Clann Aeda Buide and his son and successor, Brian O'Neill Buide. However a succession struggle at the outset of the reign of Niall *Mór* O'Neill (king 1364–97) saw the Clann Aeda Buide brought back under his leadership, followed by an alliance with Art *na Madmann* Magennis [Mág Aengusa] ('Art of the Battle-routs', d. 1383) of County Down. An aggressive drive against English settlements east of the Bann and against what was now the Mortimer earldom of Ulster was marked by a great O'Neill–Magennis victory over the colonists at Downpatrick in 1374. The vigorous counter-attack by Edmund Mortimer as king's lieutenant in 1380 was nullified by his premature death in December 1381, leaving his underage son Roger as heir to his vast territories.

63 R. Frame, 'The Justiciarship of Ralph Ufford: War and Politics in Fourteenth-Century Ireland', *Studia Hibernica*, 13 (1973), 25–6; Frame, *Ireland and Britain*, 143; Clyn, 230–1. The fragmentary 'Annals of Lecan' describe Henry Ó Néill as *rí cóigeadh Uladh*, 'king of the province of Ulster', in his death-notice under the year 1347. See the appendix to the introduction to *AFM, i* by Kenneth Nicholls; K. Simms, 'The Ulster Revolt of 1404: An Anti-Lancastrian Dimension?', in Smith (ed.), *Ireland and the English World*, 149, 159 n. 37.
64 W. Reeves, 'The Seal of Hugh O'Neill', *Ulster Journal of Archaeology*, 1st series, 1 (1853), 255–8.

Niall *Mór* O'Neill resumed laying waste the earldom, assisted now by his son Niall *Óc* ('N. the Younger' d. 1403) and grandson Brian (d. 1404).[65]

Negotiations during the first expedition of Richard II to Ireland 1394–5 indicated that Niall *Óc*, however unrealistically, wished to be officially recognised as overlord of all the Irish of Ulster, holding this position directly from the king, which would confine Roger Mortimer's earldom to the remaining English settlements along the coast of Antrim and Down. O'Neill had already usurped the de Burghs' institution of the 'Bonaght of Ulster', whereby a quota of mercenary soldiers was billeted on every chief in Ulster ready to serve the earl in time of war. Aed *Remor* had even employed the same mercenary commander, Stephen MacQuillin, after the death of Earl William, while Niall *Mór* and Niall *Óc* billeted out galloglass led by the Clann Alexander MacDonald [Mac Domnaill]. Roger Mortimer indignantly opposed O'Neill's proposals both on the lordship of the Irishmen and the 'Bonaght of Ulster'. As king's lieutenant he led an Anglo-Irish force including the earls of Ormond and Kildare to attack O'Neill in 1396 and reassert control over the province. Once again, the earl's premature death in 1398 removed an obstacle to O'Neill expansion.[66]

However the fifteenth century witnessed significant changes. Niall *Óc* O'Neill, described by the annals as 'arch-king of Ulster and … a man who the [learned] companies and pilgrims of Ireland thought would take the kingship of Ireland' died in 1403, followed in a few months by his eldest son and heir, Brian *Óc*.[67] A succession struggle ensued between Niall's nephew, Domnall *Boc* ('D. the Generous'), and his own younger son Eogan. This lasted until Domnall's assassination in 1432, and meanwhile the Clann Aeda Buide Uí Néill broke away from their allegiance and created an independent lordship east of the Bann. In the west Niall *Garb* II O'Donnell (d. 1439) enlarged his borders at the expense of Tír Eogain and led the two O'Neill claimants and the other Ulster chiefs on a series of raids into Louth and east of the Bann apparently as part of a sworn confederation against the English king and the earl of Ulster. To contain this threat the young Edmund Mortimer, earl of March and Ulster, was sent to Ireland in 1424 as king's lieutenant. He was in the process of negotiating peace terms with the Ulster chieftains, invited to celebrate Christmas with him in his castle at Trim, when his unexpected

---

65 Simms, 'Late Medieval Tír Eoghain', 144–6; Simms, 'Ulster Revolt of 1404', 143–8.
66 Simms, 'Gaelic Warfare', 108–10; Curtis, *Richard II in Ireland*, 145–6, 223–4. On the Clann Alexander, and their leader Eoin *Máel* MacDonald, 'constable of the Irish of Ulster', see Nicholls, 'Scottish Mercenary Kindreds', 97–9; Otway-Ruthven, *History of Medieval Ireland*, 335–6; D. Johnston, 'The Interim Years: Richard II and Ireland, 1395–1399', in Lydon (ed.), *England and Ireland*, 180–2.
67 *AU*, iii, 50–3.

death gave the new justiciar, John Talbot, the opportunity to arrest all the Ulster rulers except the canny Niall *Garb* O'Donnell, who had sent his brother Nechtain to represent him. The chieftains were then gradually released in the course of 1425, each under a separate agreement negotiated by James, fourth earl of Ormond, as king's lieutenant. The treaty with Eogan son of Niall Óc O'Neill in effect recognised his claim (rather than that of Domnall *Boc*) to rule Tír Eogain in exchange for his abandoning any sworn confederation of the Ulster Irish against the king and Mortimer's heir, Richard, duke of York. This arrangement was consolidated by the subsequent death of Domnall *Boc* O'Neill in 1432, and the capture in battle of Niall *Garb* O'Donnell in 1434, leading to his eventual death in prison on the Isle of Man in 1439.[68]

The broad pattern for the rest of the fifteenth century was a division of the northern province into three main areas of influence. Following Niall *Garb*'s capture Nechtain O'Donnell blocked Eogan O'Neill's attempt to impose his rule on Tír Conaill. Nechtain's death in 1452 was followed by a fierce succession struggle between his own sons and the sons of Niall *Garb*, until Aed *Ruad* ('A. the Red-haired', d. 1505) son of Niall *Garb* O'Donnell rose to power in 1461, initially in alliance with Henry son of Eogan O'Neill (d. 1489), ruler of Tír Eogain, but soon shaking off this dependence and extending his power over the chiefs of Sligo, west Breifne (Leitrim), and even western Fermanagh, hitherto part of O'Neill's following.[69]

East of the Bann, the O'Neills of Clann Aeda Buide not merely continued to assert their independence of the Great O'Neill, but strove to acquire overlordship of Magennis who ruled in south Down (diocese of Dromore), MacQuillin of the Route in north Antrim and the remaining English settlers in the Ards and Lecale (County Down), calling themselves 'lords of Trian Congail', that is, of 'Congal's Third [of the province of Ulster]' (i.e. Ulster east of the Upper and Lower Bann). Under pressure from Niall Óc O'Neill's attacks in the 1390s, the seneschal of Ulster, Edmund Savage, had formed an alliance with the MacDonalds of the Isles, marrying off his ward, Marjorie Bisset, heiress to the Glens of Antrim, to Eoin *Mór* MacDonald, younger brother of the Lord of the Isles. The followers of MacDonald began a steady migration into the Glens of Antrim thereafter, while subsequent wars

68 K. Simms, 'Niall Garbh II O'Donnell, King of Tír Conaill, 1422–39', *Donegal Annual*, 12 (1977), 7–21; Simms, 'Late Medieval Tír Eoghain', 150–2.

69 E. O'Byrne, 'O'Donnell (Ó Domhnaill) Aodh Ruadh (1429–1505)', in J. McGuire and J. Quinn (eds.), *Dictionary of Irish Biography*. 9 vols. (Cambridge University Press, 2009), vii, 366–7; K. Simms, 'Medieval Fermanagh', in E. M. Murphy and W. J. Roulston (eds.), *Fermanagh: History and Society* (Dublin: Geography Publications, 2004), 94, 98–9; Simms, *From Kings to Warlords*, 113.

between Scotland and England made them very unreliable allies for the Ulster colonists.[70] The inflow of Scots into the Glens of Antrim differed significantly from the Scottish mercenaries or 'galloglass' (*gallóclaig*) who arrived in the second half of the thirteenth and opening decades of the fourteenth century. These earlier migrants from the Hebrides fought under the leadership of their own nobility, but the basis of their contract of service was normally mercenary. From the mid-fourteenth century onwards, their aristocratic leaders became attached to particular Irish dynasties, were granted lands and intermarried with the local aristocracy. Irish sources by the late fourteenth century no longer refer to home-grown galloglass as *Albanaig* or 'Scotsmen'.[71]

Eoin *Mór* MacDonald (d. 1427), in contrast to these mercenary captains, not only acquired his lordship of the Glens through his wife's inheritance, but in an indenture in 1403 duly acknowledged himself a vassal of Henry IV of England for his Irish lands. He retained his Scottish title of Lord of Dunivaig, and took part in the Battle of Harlaw in 1411 against the earl of Mar, in support of his elder brother Domnall's claim to the earldom of Ross.[72] Control of Ross became a key issue in the Scottish crown's attempts to extend its authority over the Western Highlands and Islands, leading to the downfall of the lordship of the Isles in 1499. At the same time, the preoccupation of Eoin MacDonald, fourth Lord of the Isles (1449–94), with his Scottish estates and especially the earldom of Ross left the Antrim ruler, Eoin *Mór*'s son and successor Domnall *Ballach* MacDonald (d. 1476/81), Lord of Dunivaig and the Glens, as the leading figure in the Hebrides. He may have been involved with the earls of Douglas and Crawford in a mutually defensive bond concluded in 1445/6 against all enemies, not excluding the Scottish king.[73] He was certainly

---

70 S. Kingston, *Ulster and the Isles in the Fifteenth Century: The Lordship of the Clann Domhnaill of Antrim* (Dublin: Four Courts Press, 2004), 50–1, esp. nn. 105–6; Simms, 'Ulster Revolt of 1404', 145–6, 151–6.

71 A. Cathcart, 'Scots and Ulster: The Late Medieval Context', in W. P. Kelly and J. R. Young (eds.), *Scotland and the Ulster Plantations: Explorations in the British Settlements of Stuart Ireland* (Dublin: Four Courts Press, 2009), 62. An exception was the involvement of the MacDonald *gallóglaig* in the O'Donnell succession dispute *c*.1290: Sellar, 'Hebridean Sea Kings', 200. On the galloglass families and their employers see Nicholls, 'Scottish Mercenary Kindreds'; W. McLeod, *Divided Gaels: Gaelic Cultural Identities in Scotland and Ireland c. 1200–c.1650* (Oxford University Press, 2004), 40–6, 49, 225, 227; K. Simms, 'Images of the Galloglass in Poems to the MacSweeneys', in Duffy (ed.), *World of the Galloglass*, 110. See also Kingston, *Ulster and the Isles*, 56.

72 Kingston, *Ulster and the Isles*, 36, 50–1.

73 N. MacDougall, 'Achilles' Heel? The Earldom of Ross, the Lordship of the Isles and the Stewart Kings, 1449–1507', in E. J. Cowan and R. A. McDonald (eds.), *Alba: Celtic Scotland in the Medieval Era* (East Linton: Tuckwell Press, 2000), 257, 250, 255–8; S. Boardman, 'The Tale of Leper John and the Campbell Acquisition of Lorn', in Cowan and McDonald (eds.), *Alba: Celtic Scotland in the Medieval Era*, 235–8; Kingston, *Ulster*

party to the Treaty of Ardtornish/Westminster (February 1462) between Eoin MacDonald, earl of Ross and fourth Lord of the Isles, and Edward IV of England at a time when England and Scotland were still on hostile terms. By 1464 the earl of Ross had submitted to the Scottish crown and the following year attacked Domnall *Ballach*'s lands in Antrim, killing his son Angus.[74] It has been suggested that the later distinctive power-group of Clan Donald South, combining the southern Isles with the Glens of Antrim, had its origins as early as the 1460s. Trusted neither by the English nor the Scottish crowns, the Scots in the Glens remained firmly a part of the Hebridean community. The castle of Carrickfergus was described in 1468 as 'a garrison of war ... surrounded by Irish and Scots, without succour of the English for sixty miles'.[75]

In mid-Ulster the Great O'Neill, as the English called successive rulers of Tír Eogain, fought hard to retain dominance over the whole province. In pursuit of this aim both Eogan and his son Henry began, after the treaty with Ormond in 1425, to rely increasingly on the help of the colonists' troops, contributed either by local magnates in Meath, or by the Dublin government. This assistance came with a price. Henry was given Ormond's niece, Gormlaith Cáemánach, in marriage, and when he attempted to divorce her in 1452 in order to marry Nechtain O'Donnell's widow, Ormond brought an army northwards to force Henry to take Gormlaith back. After his inauguration as 'prince of the Irish of Ulster' in 1455, Henry made no more hostile raids against the Pale, although it seems the annual 'black-rent' or protection-money from Dundalk and surrounding districts, initiated during the raids led by Niall *Garb* II O'Donnell in 1423, continued to be paid. In 1515 it was noted that County Louth or 'Uriell' was accustomed to pay £40 to the Great O'Neill, while the barony of Lecale in south Down paid £40 either to the chief of Clann Aeda Buide or to the Great O'Neill, whichever of them was more powerful at the time.[76] Henry son of Eogan O'Neill's greatest period of influence came during the succession struggles among the O'Donnells in 1452–64, a period which also saw the temporary eclipse of the Butler dynasty. As noted earlier, in 1463 Tadc *an Chomad* O'Brien entered into a subordinate alliance with Henry O'Neill by accepting symbolic 'wages', or *tuarastal*, from him. If this was a move to consolidate a faction

and the Isles, 59, 67–9; 79–82; *Acts of the Lords of the Isles*, ed. J. Munro and R. W. Munro (Edinburgh: Scottish History Society, 1986), 68–9.

74 Boardman, 'Tale of Leper John', 237, 241; MacDougall, 'Achilles' Heel?', 255–6; Kingston, *Ulster and the Isles*, 82, 106–7; *Acts of the Lords of the Isles*, 111–16.

75 MacDougall, 'Achilles' Heel?', 257; *CPR, 1467–77*, 161; Simms, 'Medieval Chieftains in County Antrim'.

76 *SP, Henry VIII*, ii part III, section 1, p. 9.

among former Butler adherents it failed. In the same year Henry was offered and accepted a grant of livery from Edward IV, forty-eight yards of scarlet cloth and a chain of gold. Thereafter in 1464 Thomas fitz James FitzGerald, seventh or 'Great Earl' of Desmond, victor over the Butlers at Piltown and now justiciar, received submissions from Aed *Ruad* O'Donnell and his ally MacWilliam Burke of Mayo in Dublin.[77] After Tiptoft's strange execution of the 'Great Earl' of Desmond in 1468, leadership of the colony passed to the earls of Kildare, and they continued the policy of alliance with, and influence over, O'Neill of Tír Eogain. By now the greatest danger to the hegemony of the Great O'Neill came not from his neighbours but from junior branches within his own dynasty, and once again his authority was maintained with the help of Anglo-Irish troops. In 1480 Henry's eldest son and heir, Conn *Mór* ('C. the elder'), married Eleanor FitzGerald, sister of Gerald, eighth earl of Kildare. It is noteworthy that when the Butlers were restored to favour under the Tudors, and Sir James of Ormond was appointed Treasurer of Ireland, in 1493 Conn *Mór* was assassinated by his younger brother Henry *Óc* ('H. the younger') O'Neill, a son of Gormlaith Cáemánach, and thus great-nephew of the 'White Earl' of Ormond. When Kildare was reinstated, he brought an army northwards in 1498 to avenge Conn's death and protect the interests of his own nephews, the sons of Conn *Mór*.[78] Even in central and western Ulster the initiative was passing from Gaels to Anglo-Irish magnates. There was undoubtedly a political resurgence in Gaelic Ireland in the fourteenth and fifteenth centuries, but it neither fundamentally weakened the English grip on the island, nor encouraged the crown to incorporate Gaelic lords in the political community of the Lordship.

---

77 *AC*, 520–1; Simms, ' "The King's Friend" ', 225–6.
78 Simms, 'Late Medieval Tír Eoghain', 152–4.

11

Continuity and Change: 1470–1550

CHRISTOPHER MAGINN

THE reign of Henry VIII looms large in the history of Ireland in the period 1470 to 1550. Henry was king of England for nearly four decades (1509–47) and in those years Ireland's centuries-old relationship with England was redefined. Henry VIII set in motion a process, often referred to by historians as the 'Tudor conquest of Ireland', which saw the steady (and often violent) integration of Ireland into an expanding English state. The crown's destruction of the once-dominant FitzGerald earls of Kildare, its introduction of a new religion and establishment of the state-sponsored Church of Ireland, the king's acceptance of the native Irish as his subjects and his creation of some of their leaders as English peers, and the erection of Ireland into a Tudor kingdom can all be traced to this pivotal reign.

Henry's reign, however, straddles a historiographical fault-line which commonly separates the study of medieval Irish history from the study of early modern Irish history. The year at which historians have affixed the end of medieval Ireland varies, though it is almost invariably located in early Tudor times. Philip Wilson, writing in 1913, located 'the beginnings of modern Ireland' c.1515; a decade later, Edmund Curtis ended his enormously influential history of medieval Ireland in 1513, at the death of Gerald fitz Thomas FitzGerald, eighth earl of Kildare, 'a date when the second English conquest (the 'Tudor Reconquest') became imminent'.[1] A generation later, A.J. Otway-Ruthven chose to conclude her detailed history of medieval Ireland in 1495, during the government of Sir Edward Poynings who introduced legislation which supposedly marked 'a clear watershed between medieval Ireland and the Tudor period'; while Brendan Bradshaw, in an examination of Tudor parliaments, argued that the emergence of an active national parliament in

---

1 P. Wilson, *The Beginnings of Modern Ireland* (Dublin: Maunsel, 1912); E. Curtis, *A History of Medieval Ireland from 1086 to 1513* (Dublin: Maunsel and Roberts, 1923; 2nd edn London: Methuen and Co., 1938), v (quotation).

Henry VIII's reign represented a sure marker of 'the beginnings of modern Ireland'.[2] Yet it was the appearance shortly thereafter of the early modern volume of Oxford's seminal *A New History of Ireland* which most clearly delineated between the two historiographical periods. Beginning its account in 1534, the volume identified the Kildare rebellion as the end of one epoch and the opening 'of an era of direct rule [i.e. from London] that was to last till 1921'.[3] But its publication (as volume three) more than a decade before what was designated as the series' (second) medieval volume, covering the years 1169–1534, meant that the two volumes looked and read very differently. The medieval volume was longer – over 1,000 pages – boasted more contributors and interspersed amid its narrative more thematic chapters than the previous (though chronologically later) volume.[4] After the 1534 watershed, moreover, English subjects resident in Ireland, those men and women whose ancestors had settled there following Henry II's conquest, were generally referred to as the 'Old English', but were labelled 'Anglo-Irish' in the medieval volume. *A New History of Ireland* thus established 1534 as the beginning of early modern Ireland and inadvertently made more definite the discontinuity which existed between the study of Ireland's medieval and early modern periods.[5]

It is a discontinuity that, it would seem, is reflected in the source material. The written evidence upon which historians base their interpretations of Ireland's past – the vast preponderance of it generated by the English administration in Ireland and England – changes dramatically in Henry VIII's reign. Not only does the quantity of source material available to historians steadily increase, the nature of the evidence itself is transformed: chancery, parliamentary and exchequer rolls, inquisitions and treasurers' accounts – sources typically in formulaic Latin or Norman French – give way to what are broadly known as State Papers, the more diverse (and often more colourful) corpus of letters, maps, descriptive accounts and political tracts written by prominent, and some less prominent, Tudor officials in a form of English that is generally more accessible to modern English-speakers. The evidence, however, can be easily misinterpreted if two factors are not taken into account. The first is that the destruction in 1922 of the Four Courts, then the home of the Public Record Office of Ireland, destroyed a swathe of documentary material from Ireland's history. The chance survival of

---

2 Otway-Ruthven, *History of Medieval Ireland* (quotation, 408); B. Bradshaw, 'The Beginnings of Modern Ireland', in B. Farrell (ed.), *The Irish Parliamentary Tradition* (Dublin: Gill & Macmillan, 1973), 68–87.
3 *NHI* iii, xl.
4 *NHI* ii.
5 N. Canny, 'Early Modern Ireland: An Appraisal Appraised', *IESH*, 4 (1977), 56–65.

a greater quantity of court rolls for the later fifteenth and early sixteenth centuries can give the false impression that the institutions of English administration in Ireland which generated these materials ceased to function during Henry VIII's reign.[6] Second, the decision made by the Record Commission in the nineteenth century to begin the State Papers, Ireland series at the start of Henry VIII's reign had the effect of making 1509 – or perhaps 1515 the year ascribed to the first 'State Paper' to be transcribed and published *in extenso* – appear as the dawn of a new age of documentation rather than what it was: the continuation, evolution and broadening of an older one.[7]

Historians interested in the years between 1470 and 1550 are fortunate in being able to call upon both traditional court rolls and other 'medieval' material, as well as 'early modern' State Papers in developing their arguments. The mastery of both kinds of evidence allows historians the freedom to move easily on either side of 1534.[8] Exaggerated respect for this historiographical divide has led early modernists to over-emphasise the significance and novelty of the changes which occurred in the reign of Henry VIII; medievalists, meanwhile, seldom tread beyond 1534, and so have not attempted to reconcile the 'revolutionary' events of King Henry's reign with the intellectual, political and social patterns that had developed in Ireland by the sixteenth century. This chapter

---

6 H. Wood, 'The Public Records of Ireland before and after 1922', *TRHS*, 13 (1930), 17–49. See also R. Dudley Edwards and M. O'Dowd (eds.), *Sources for Early Modern Irish History, 1534–1641* (Cambridge University Press, 1985).

7 *SP, Henry VIII*, ii, 1; *CSPI, 1509–1573*. The commencement in the year 1515 of both the Carew manuscripts and the patent rolls further contributes to the appearance of a new beginning in documentation: *Carew, vol 1: 1515–1574*; *CPRI*. The letters and papers of the first Tudor were published separately and grouped (ironically) with those of Richard III: *Letters and Papers*. Working from the other chronological side of this, the Irish Record Commission concluded their calendar of the Exchequer Memoranda rolls in 1509: M. C. Griffith, 'The Irish Record Commission, 1810–30', *IHS*, 7 (1950–1), 1–28. See also S. G. Ellis, 'From Medieval to Early Modern: The British Isles in Transition?' in R. Hutton (ed.), *Medieval or Early Modern? The Value of a Traditional Historical Division* (Cambridge: Cambridge Scholars Press 2015), 10–28.

8 See, for example, D. B. Quinn, 'Tudor Rule in Ireland in the Reigns of Henry VII and Henry VIII, with Special Reference to the Anglo-Irish Financial Administration'. PhD thesis, University of London (1934); D. B. Quinn, 'Parliaments and Great Councils in Ireland, 1461–1586', *IHS*, 3 (1942–3), 60–77. Nicholls, *Gaelic and Gaelicised Ireland*; K. W. Nicholls, 'A Calendar of Salved Chancery Pleadings Concerning County Louth', *Journal of the County Louth Archaeological Society*, 17 (1972), 250–60. Nicholls and Quinn, it should be observed, contributed to both the early modern and the medieval volumes of *NHI*. See also: S. G. Ellis, *Tudor Ireland: Crown, Community and the Conflict of Cultures, 1470–1603* (London: Longman, 1985); Ellis, *Ireland in the Age of the Tudors*; E. O'Byrne, *War, Politics and the Irish of Leinster, 1156–1606* (Dublin: Four Courts Press, 2003); A. McCormack, *The Earldom of Desmond: the Decline and Crisis of a Feudal Lordship, 1463–1583* (Dublin: Four Courts Press, 2005). Compare also the chronological boundaries of R. W. Dudley Edwards and M. O'Dowd (eds.), *Sources for Early Modern Irish History* with D. Edwards and B. Donovan (eds.), *British Sources for Irish History, 1485–1641* (Dublin: IMC, 1997).

will seek to restore the continuity which existed between the first half of the sixteenth century and the later fifteenth century. This will allow the reign of Henry VIII to be considered in a more expansive chronological sweep: from the brief 'readeption' of Henry VI in 1470 during the Wars of the Roses to the decision, taken eighty years later, in 1550, by the government of King Henry's son and successor, Edward VI, to alter the policies pursued under Henry VIII which had sought to integrate Ireland and its inhabitants into an English state through the agreed extension of Tudor rule. In this way, the pivotal developments of the reign of Henry VIII will be shown to have been less of a break with the past and a good deal less novel than historians have supposed, rooted as they were in the ideas and relationships which had developed in the late medieval period (see Map 10).

The Kildare Ascendancy

In November 1470 Thomas fitz Maurice FitzGerald, seventh earl of Kildare, convened the parliament of Ireland at Dublin. Parliament was the legislative organ of the king of England's Lordship of Ireland, an occasion and a venue where his leading English subjects resident in Ireland could gather together as a political community to make laws and vote subsidies for the upkeep of the Lordship's defences.[9] Kildare was the Lordship's governor, acting on behalf of a king who was based in England. Only Edward IV, the king in whose name the parliament sat and in whose name Kildare governed, was no longer king. He had abandoned the throne in October, fleeing England in the face of an invasion. This was the latest in a series of dynastic wars fought between the noble houses of York and Lancaster which a decade earlier had seen the feeble-minded Lancastrian Henry VI deposed in favour of Edward IV, son of Richard, duke of York. Ireland had already featured prominently in this struggle for the crown: first as a stronghold for the Yorkists and then as a bridgehead used to launch the invasion of England which ultimately won for them the throne.[10] In 1470, however, the thrust of the Lancastrian attack which put Henry VI back in power – his 'readeption' – had come from France. That Kildare continued to hold parliament in Edward's name, when he must surely have been aware that Henry VI was now king, reveals something of

9 S. G. Ellis, 'Parliament and Community in Yorkist and Tudor Ireland', in A. Cosgrove and
   J. McGuire (eds.), *Parliament and Community: Historical Studies XIV* (Belfast: Appletree
   Press, 1983), 43–68; B. Smith, 'Keeping the Peace', in Lydon (ed.), *Law and Disorder*, 57–65.
10 Ellis, *Ireland in the Age of the Tudors*, 56–68.

MAP 10. Lordships of Ireland, c.1520.

the tendency of nobles to temporise when they suddenly found themselves on the losing side of this perilous dynastic struggle. But it was the decision of the new regime to continue the earl as governor, and the subsequent decision taken by Edward IV – who swept back into power in April 1471, bringing the 'readeption' (and then the life of Henry VI) to an end – to do the same, which reveals a great deal more about the English crown's relationship to Ireland and conditions there.

The appointment of leading noblemen and landowners to govern themselves on the crown's behalf was a basic principle of English society, and in this respect its choice of Kildare as governor of Ireland was unremarkable. But 'self-government at the king's command' does not adequately describe the relationship which developed in the decades after 1470 between the earls of Kildare and the crown, at one level, and between the earls and the inhabitants of Ireland at another.[11] The Kildares dominated government and society in the Lordship for three successive generations; for nearly sixty-five years they exercised a degree of influence on government and society unknown elsewhere in the English territories. So complete was Kildare authority that Irish historians have employed the concept of 'aristocratic autonomy' to denote the period 1460–96 that preceded a 'Kildare ascendancy' which then lasted until 1534.[12] Ascendant in these years the earls most certainly were; autonomous they were not – the crown replaced them as governor on multiple occasions in this period: 1475–9, 1492–6, 1520–2 and 1526–32. But the concept of 'aristocratic autonomy' speaks to both the sweeping powers which successive kings were prepared to grant to the earls of Kildare prior to the settlement reached in 1496 between the first Tudor king, Henry VII, and Gerald fitz Thomas FitzGerald, the eighth earl, and the indispensability of Kildare power to the operation of royal government in Ireland throughout this period: the crown could not maintain effective control over its Lordship for more than a few years without an earl of Kildare as governor.

How had this situation arisen? Always a territory of secondary importance, the crown accorded Ireland a lower priority still as Henry VI and his Yorkist successors, Edward IV and Richard III, struggled to establish, and to maintain, control in England. Not until the mid-1490s – the occasion of Poynings's expedition – was a king in a strong enough position in England to intervene in Ireland in any meaningful way. By then, however, the Kildares had already come to dominate the Lordship's government. In the king's absence, the governor of Ireland was permitted to wield vice-regal authority. He headed an executive and civil administration which, though modelled on and subordinate

---

11 A. B. White, *Self-Government at the King's Command* (Minneapolis: University of Minnesota Press, 1933).

12 Curtis, *History of Medieval Ireland*, 309–36, where this phenomenon is expressed anachronistically as 'Aristocratic Home Rule'; D. B. Quinn, 'Aristocratic Autonomy, 1460–94', in *NHI* ii, 591–618.

to Westminster, was institutionally separate from its English counterpart.[13] Earlier in the century there had been several high-ranking noble families in Ireland vying for the far-reaching power that came with this unique office.[14] But with the young FitzGerald earl of Desmond locked in a prolonged succession dispute and the Butler earls of Ormond under attainder until 1475, and then absent at court for more than three decades thereafter, the earls of Kildare were free to monopolise the office of governor (and with it to place their adherents in many lesser posts in the administration) without arousing serious noble opposition. The crown could always entrust the government to another local figure, such as a high-ranking cleric or a lesser peer. But in this period only an earl of Kildare was possessed of the necessary military strength to govern Ireland in the king's name economically and effectively.

Ireland in the late fifteenth century was an unstable border region that had for generations seen low-intensity fighting between the English crown and its subjects in Ireland on the one hand, and independent Irish lords – 'Irish enemies' – and some nativised settler lords and lineages – 'English rebels' – on the other. The governor functioned as military commander in a conflict which by the late fifteenth century had already lasted longer than the Hundred Years War. The wars in Ireland were typically fought along the frontiers of areas which in earlier centuries had undergone intensive English settlement, and where English law, culture and economic organisation continued to predominate.[15] By 1470 royal authority, which had once embraced two-thirds of the island, was regularly felt only in the four shires around Dublin, in parts of the shires of Munster, and in pockets around several isolated walled towns in the west and north-east. Beyond, lay what Englishmen generally referred to as the 'Irishry' – or the 'land of war' – areas inhabited by a different people, the 'wild Irish'. The earldom of Kildare was strategically situated in Leinster near to the heart of the administrative and cultural centre of English rule in Ireland. Here, a concentration of lesser peers, market towns and robust county communities looked to the earls as their natural leaders. The seventh earl's decision to marry his heir to the daughter of the important County Kildare peer Roland Eustace, baron of Portlester, was a reflection of the

13 Ellis, *Ireland in the Age of the Tudors*, 80–1; S. G. Ellis, *Reform and Revival: English Government in Ireland, 1470–1534* (Woodbridge: Royal Historical Society, Boydell Press, 1986), 12–48.
14 M. C. Griffith, 'The Talbot–Ormond Struggle for Control of the Anglo-Irish Government, 1414–47', *IHS*, 2 (1940–1), 376–97; P. Crooks, 'Factions, Feuds and Noble Power in Late Medieval Ireland', *IHS*, 35 (2007), 425–54.
15 S. G. Ellis, *Tudor Frontiers and Noble Power: The Making of the British State* (Oxford University Press, 1995), 23–7.

FitzGeralds' position in this, the 'Englishry'.[16] But the Kildare earldom also encompassed the marches which separated areas of English settlement from the province's independent Irish lordships. This meant that Kildare, at once the royally appointed governor, the Lordship's leading peer and a marcher lord in his own right, could combine the resources at the disposal of his office – which consisted of a standing military retinue and the power to employ the county militias of the shires around Dublin – and his own militarised tenantry to defend the king's subjects and maintain order in what was a violent land. The earls' ability to exert their influence across the military frontier, by building up an affinity among the Irish, enhanced Kildare power still further.[17]

That the Kildares could exert influence in the Irishry while at the same time being the principal leaders of the king's war against the Irish gives some indication of the complicated nature of relations between the English and Irish of Ireland by this time.[18] The earls of Kildare were products of a nuanced frontier society, and moved easily in the Irish political and cultural environment. They fostered their children with Irish lords far distant from their earldom, employed Irish poets and physicians and counted among their military retainers large numbers of Irish soldiers. They were fluent in the Irish language and sufficiently at ease with Irish (Brehon) law to avail of the services of Irish judges. The delicacy of this balance of day-to-day familiarity during an official state of war in a violent society is captured in the Irish annals where it is recorded that in 1492 Conn O'Connor 'was slain by the people of the earl of Kildare on account of a stroke of a pole he gave the earl in playing'. The earls also married their daughters to leading Irish lords. In 1479 the seventh earl's daughter, Eleanor, was wed to the premier Irish lord in Ulster, Conn O'Neill. The marriage won for the earl of Kildare an important ally and opened the way for an extension of his influence into an area largely untouched by English power or settlement.[19]

But the marriage was illegal under English law. English subjects were forbidden to intermarry with any of 'the Irish nation' who were, in constitutional terms, non-subjects, in effect illegal aliens squatting on territory that rightfully belonged to the crown. So, in 1480, the parliament of Ireland altered O'Neill's legal status, making him 'of free estate and condition in law as

16 G. Power, *A European Frontier Elite: The Nobility of the English Pale in Tudor Ireland, 1496–1566* (Hannover: Wehrhahn Verlag, 2012), 47–62.

17 Ellis, *Tudor Frontiers*, 126.

18 Nicholls, *Gaelic and Gaelicized Ireland*, 31; C. Maginn, 'Gaelic Ireland's English Frontiers in the Late Middle Ages', *PRIA*, 110 C (2010), 173–90.

19 Ellis, *Ireland in the Age of the Tudors*, 108–10; *AU*, iii, 359; Ellis, *Tudor Frontiers*, 135–6.

the king's liegeman, and that he and his issue engendered by ... Elianor be adjudged English and of English condition, and may plead and be impleaded as the king's liegeman in all courts as if he had been the king's subject'.[20] English nationality was open only to those of English (paternal) blood and condition, of free birth and born within territories under the king of England's allegiance: Lady Eleanor FitzGerald met these criteria; Conn O'Neill did not.[21] An Irishman could become an English subject through a special legal dispensation, or, as in O'Neill's case, through an act of parliament. By contrast, Irishness was impossible to attain by those who lacked an Irish father. Irishmen (the elite at least) consistently distinguished between themselves, *Gaedhil* [Gaels], the English of Ireland, *Gaill* [foreigners], and Englishmen from England, *Sasanaigh* [Englishmen]. An Englishman, whether a *Gall* or a *Sasanach*, could never be made (or become) a *Gaedheal*, regardless of the extent of their assimilation to native ways. Historians have debated whether the English of Ireland, the *Gaill*, should be understood as a 'middle nation', a people who were neither English nor Irish, or as an English people inhabiting a region in a wider English state and thus possessed of a regional English identity. What is beyond doubt is that the view prevailed in both Ireland and England that a state of war existed between the English and the Irish.[22]

In 1474 the parliament of Ireland, held by the seventh earl of Kildare, informed King Edward of the 'myserable state and desolacyon' of his land and his 'tru' subjects; they implored their king to relieve and rescue them from 'the kynges Iryssh ennemys and Englysh rebelx', and also from 'Scottes' – 10,000 of whom, it was claimed, had lately settled in Ulster – 'orels they may not long endure under his obeysaunce or ligeaunce or by distresse to depart owt of the land'. 'The realme of England', the king was famously reminded, 'is bound to the defense of his land of Irland by resoun that it ys oon of the membres of his moost noble corone and eldest member therof'.[23] Grim though this depiction was, it was explained that Ireland was recoverable. If the king would send over an army to assist his subjects in their wars, then together they could recover the cities, towns and castles built by Englishmen since 'the furst conquest', which had been lost, and use them to hold English

20 *Stat. Ire., 12–22 Edw. IV*, 787.
21 R. Griffiths, 'The English Realm and Dominions and the King's Subjects in the Later Middle Ages', in J. Rowe (ed.), *Aspects of English Government and Society in Later Medieval England: Essays in Honour of J. R. Lander* (Toronto University Press, 1986), 83–105.
22 J. F. Lydon, 'The Middle Nation', in Crooks (ed.), *Government, War and Society*, 332–52; A. Cosgrove, 'The Writing of Irish Medieval History', *IHS*, 27 (1990–1), 101–11; Ellis, *Tudor Frontiers*, 141.
23 Bryan, *Gerald FitzGerald*, 18–22.

ground until such a time as the king chose to conquer the rest. Seen in this light the parliamentary address to Edward IV can be read as a sign of resilience on the part of the English of Ireland, offering hope of an English recovery in the Lordship. By then the Yorkist dynasty looked secure: the Lancastrians had been vanquished and King Edward, still in his early thirties, was father to two healthy sons. The king also showed interest in Ireland, having dispatched royal commissioners with a small military retinue to examine the Lordship's defences in 1473. In Ireland, meanwhile, the reorganisation of the defences of the four shires round Dublin begun earlier in the century was beginning to show results. Successive parliaments had ordered the digging of dykes and ditches and offered subsidies for the construction of fortifications – tower houses and castles – to defend the frontiers of what had developed as a region of Ireland distinct even from other English areas. The core of this region, the 'maghery', was becoming increasingly insulated from Irish raids with the result that economic conditions there steadily improved, as land once vulnerable to raiding was put under cultivation. In 1477, the boundaries of the maghery and the exposed march were exactly defined; so settled had conditions become that a decade later the Irish parliament passed a statute which made illegal in the maghery 'coign and livery', an Irish practice whereby a lord quartered troops on the country. In effect, a *cordon sanitaire* was being established around the maghery where more stable economic and political conditions began to develop.[24]

This recovery was directly linked to the growth of Kildare power. In the two decades after 1480, Earl Gerald consolidated his family's control of the Kildare marches and extended Kildare authority into the Irish districts of south Leinster. He recaptured castles, built new tower houses and, in the process, expropriated Irish clansmen and made clients of those he could not. Kildare also campaigned beyond Leinster in these years, making his influence felt deep into Irish Ulster.[25] The earl proceeded in this way principally to further his own interests, the interests of his family and those of his many adherents. But his interests tended to coincide with those of his community and those of the crown, and from the crown's perspective, Kildare rule was a cheap and effective means of governing Ireland. Subventions from England ceased and the overall position of the Lordship vis-à-vis the king's enemies showed

---

24 Ellis, *Ireland in the Age of the Tudors*, 71; S. G. Ellis, 'Region and Frontier in the English State: Co. Meath and the English Pale, 1460–1542', in H. V. Holm, S. Laegreid and T. Skorgen (eds.), *The Borders of Europe: Hegemony, Aesthetics and Border Poetics* (Aarhus University Press, 2012), 62–4.
25 *AU*, iii, 273, 283, 291, 355, 357.

signs of stabilisation. The royal claim to lordship over the entire island of course remained, and occasionally generated suggestions for a general conquest. Such a project was proposed by the English of Ireland in 1474, and by the king himself in 1494 and 1506.[26] Kings of England were not prepared to commit to the expenditure required to bring about a conquest that would, in any event, raise difficult questions regarding the legal and constitutional position of the majority of the Lordship's population – what was to become of Irishmen once they were conquered? The crown preferred to allow a situation to develop in which Kildare not only governed Ireland's English subjects in its name, but also served as the de facto intermediary between the crown and the Irish polity. The greatest threat to this complex of lordship and vassalage that stretched from London to the Leinster Mountains and beyond – what has been called a 'two-tiered suzerain–vassal' arrangement – came not from Irishmen or from Kildare, who together comprised the lower tier, but from the crown at the very top.[27]

Ireland under the First Tudor

Richard III's usurpation of the throne in 1483 opened a new chapter in the dynastic struggle that, a decade earlier, appeared to have been decided so conclusively in favour of the Yorkists. Richard, and Henry VII after him, were too uncertain of their position in England to risk upsetting political arrangements in Ireland and so continued Kildare in office. But when in 1487 there appeared in Ireland a boy who claimed to be Edward, earl of Warwick, the last remaining male claimant of the House of York and thus rightful heir to the throne, Kildare was forced to make a choice between York and Tudor. This time he did not temporise: in May he saw the boy crowned Edward VI, 'king of England, France and Ireland', in Dublin; he presided over a parliament, held in Edward VI's name, which confirmed the new king's title and his own position as governor; he then furnished his king with a large force of Irish kerne to aid him in his bid to seize the English throne.[28] For Kildare, the battle of Stoke, fought in June 1487 following the Yorkist invasion of England, threatened to undo all that he and his family had built in Ireland: his Irish levies were massacred, the Yorkist

---

26 C. Maginn and S. G. Ellis, *The Tudor Discovery of Ireland* (Dublin: Four Courts Press, 2015), 125, 132–3.

27 C. Maginn, *'Civilizing' Gaelic Leinster: the Extension of Tudor Rule in the O'Byrne and O'Toole Lordships* (Dublin: Four Courts Press, 2005), 5–13.

28 Ellis, *Ireland in the Age of the Tudors*, 83–5.

forces routed, and the true identity of his 'king' – Lambert Simnel, the son of an Oxford organ maker – exposed.[29]

Kildare looked certain to join the many noblemen who had been ruined by the Wars of the Roses. But Henry VII showed himself to be an exceedingly cautious king. Rather than risk a confrontation in a remote territory of which he had little knowledge, he sought to rehabilitate the earl. To that end, the king dispatched his trusted councillor Richard Edgecombe in 1488 to secure recognition for the Tudor regime from the English political nation and most especially from Kildare. The earl swore allegiance to King Henry but in a remarkable display of confidence in his position he refused to be bound over in a bond for his future loyalty. Instead, Kildare was pardoned and received a collar of the king's livery which, it was said, he wore throughout Dublin.[30] This cleared the way for the earl and many of Ireland's leading temporal nobility to come before Henry VII at Greenwich the following year. Here, the king interviewed the lords so as to understand why they had supported the Yorkist pretender, reputedly chiding them, 'My masters of Ireland, you will crown apes at length'. The king allowed Kildare and the rest to return to the Lordship to govern it in his name, just as the earl had done in the name of Richard III and Edward IV before him. But when in November 1491 another pretender appeared and found support in Ireland – this time Perkin Warbeck presented as Edward IV's son Richard, duke of York – the king acted vigorously. He dispatched a small force to bolster royal authority in Kilkenny and Tipperary and, in May 1492, replaced Kildare as governor. Though Kildare did not, on this occasion, support the Yorkist pretender, who subsequently sailed to the Continent in search of aid from the royal houses of Europe, the earl had not done enough in the king's eyes to prove his loyalty in what Henry VII regarded as the most serious threat to his fledgling dynasty to that time.[31]

Kildare has traditionally been portrayed as a territorial magnate fiercely protective of his (and perhaps his country's) independence from the crown. This, after all, was the man who led the nobility that had defiantly told Edgecombe that 'they wuld become Irish every [one] of them' rather than be bound over in one of the king's bonds and who resisted the king's efforts

---

29 M. Bennett, 'Lambert Simnel', in *ODNB*; P. Haigh, *The Military Campaigns of the Wars of the Roses* (Stroud: Sutton Publishing, 1995), ch. 19.

30 W. Harris (ed.), *Hibernica, or, Some Ancient Pieces relating to the History of Ireland*. 2 vols. (Dublin, 1747, 1750), i, 59–77; Ellis, *Ireland in the Age of the Tudors*, 86.

31 *Carew, vol 6: Book of Howth and Miscellaneous*, 190 (quotation); J. Ware, *The Antiquities and History of Ireland* (Dublin: A Crook, 1705), 15; Ellis, *Ireland in the Age of the Tudors*, 87–8.

to strengthen the rival Butler interest in Ireland.[32] Over the next three years, however, the earl worked with the crown to see a greater assertion of royal authority in Ireland. It began in 1493 with Kildare entering into a bond of 1,000 marks for his future loyalty to King Henry and continued with his decision later that year to heed the king's summons to court. Far from being a reluctant magnate dragged from his distant territories to come before the king, Kildare was said to have gone to court 'with great retinue and splendour'.[33] What is more, the earl stayed in England for a full year so as to advise the king on Ireland, which had become a critical theatre in his ongoing efforts to secure the Tudor territories against the Yorkist threat. By early 1494, Kildare was joined at court by a number of other prominent figures in the Irish government. It was the most important, and perhaps the largest, gathering in England of the political community of Ireland in over a century. Henry VII used this opportunity to compose the differences between the FitzGeralds and the Butlers and, through Kildare, to try to reach an accommodation with the earl of Desmond who had come out in support of Warbeck. But Kildare and the leaders of Ireland's English political community also made use of the king's sustained interest in Ireland. They prevailed upon him to initiate a policy which would bring about a lasting political settlement. In August, Henry VII wrote to the king of France that on the advice of the principal nobles and religious of Ireland he intended to put his country in order, especially the 'Irlandois sauvaiges' who were henceforth to live under the same law as the English and the Irish who had adopted the English tongue.[34]

Thus came to Ireland Sir Edward Poynings in October 1494. He was to govern as the deputy of the three-year-old Prince Henry, whom the king had appointed as his lord lieutenant of Ireland, an honorific title by then reserved for the king's family. Poynings was an experienced military commander, having lately served as deputy-lieutenant of Calais, and a trusted member of King Henry's inner circle.[35] Poynings knew nothing of Ireland, but Kildare and James Ormond – the illegitimate son of John Butler, sixth earl of Ormond – returned with him and were there to advise him. Poynings's mission was twofold: to reform aspects of the Lordship's administration, notably the parliament and finance, and to campaign against the king's enemies and rebels. The parliament of Ireland was set to

---

32 Bryan, *Gerald FitzGerald*; Curtis, *History of Medieval Ireland*, 337; Harris (ed.), *Hibernica*, i, 65; S. G. Ellis, 'Henry VII and Ireland, 1491–1496', in Lydon (ed.), *England and Ireland*, 240.
33 *AU*, iii, 369.
34 Maginn and Ellis, *Tudor Discovery*, 124–5; A. Conway, *Henry VII's Relations with Scotland and Ireland, 1485–1498* (Cambridge University Press, 1932), 61–2; Ellis, 'Henry VII and Ireland', 242.
35 S. G. Ellis, 'Sir Edward Poynings', in *ODNB*.

meet in December to address the former. Poynings, meanwhile, marched north against the Ulster Irish. His army numbered only 653 men, but backed by Kildare and Ormond, who were to use their influence to defend the borders of the four shires, Poynings's small force could, in theory at least, invade the Irishry. What drew Poynings north is unclear, but the campaign was overshadowed by his spectacular falling out with Kildare. The earl had used his influence to induce two Irish lords to submit to Poynings, such was the way Kildare exercised power in Ireland and one of the keys to his success. But Poynings, ignorant of the nuances of power and society in Ireland, saw only a king's subject, whose loyalty to the regime had been questioned before, in secret communication with 'Irish enemies'. Poynings was a strongman of the Tudor regime who was sent to Ireland to make war on the Irish and to defend the king's interests, not to induce submissions. Kildare was eventually arrested, attainted of treason and sent to England. In response, the earl's brother raised rebellion and several Irish and English lords came out in support of Warbeck. Any hope of a military conquest of the Irish faded as Poynings campaigned to stamp out rebellion and to hold English areas against Warbeck who had blockaded Waterford by sea. Poynings broke the blockade in August 1495, but Warbeck escaped: the pretender travelled unmolested through Connaught and Ulster en route to Scotland, revealing once again the weakness of Tudor authority in Ireland.[36]

Poynings' parliament, meanwhile, opened at Drogheda in December 1494. It is ironic that this parliament should be forever associated with Poynings. Poynings merely presided over the parliament which introduced a legislative programme, composed of forty-nine acts, likely conceived in England with the input of the leaders of Ireland's political community. The legislation strengthened the king's authority, most especially chapter 9 – known to history as Poynings' Law – which enacted that no parliament could be held in Ireland without the king's prior authorisation and that all bills which were to be put before future Irish parliaments must first be approved by the king's council in England.[37] The extraordinary longevity of Poynings' Law, and the procedural and political difficulties to which it was to give rise, can distract from the act's immediate intention which was to prevent a pretender like Warbeck from using the parliament of Ireland to legitimise a *coup d'état*, as Kildare had done on Simnel's behalf only seven

---

36 G. O. Sayles, 'The Vindication of the Earl of Kildare from Treason in 1496', *IHS*, 7 (1951), 39–47.

37 Conway, *Henry VII's Relations with Scotland and Ireland*, 201–19; Ellis, *Ireland in the Age of the Tudors*, 92–5.

years before. The legislation also represented a singular achievement for the English of Ireland: their king was now obliged to give regular regard to the needs of his subjects in Ireland. Other acts confirmed most of the provisions of the Statute of Kilkenny (1366), made it treason to incite the Irish against the governor and required that ditches be made about the four shires, described in the parliamentary roll as the 'English Pale'. This reference to a Pale in Ireland – almost certainly related to the near contemporary description of the fortified ring around Calais as the English Pale where Poynings was previously stationed – entered official parlance and became in centuries thereafter the common term to describe the region around Dublin.[38]

But this first Tudor intervention in Ireland had come at a cost. Despite far-reaching efforts to raise revenue and cut administrative costs in 1495–6, the king had spent approximately £18,000 on Ireland, chiefly on the army, in a little more than two years after August 1494.[39] With Poynings's legislation in place, with the rebellion all but broken and with Warbeck having again drifted away from Ireland, Henry VII restored Kildare as governor in August 1496. The previous year the English parliament had reversed the earl's attainder and, in the run-up to his reappointment, Kildare, by then a widower, married the king's cousin, for which he received cash and lands in England. Before the king's council Kildare swore to defend Ireland from enemies and rebels, to observe Poynings's Law, to bury the hatchet with the Butlers and to govern the king's land justly and impartially. He left his son, Gerald, behind at court as a pledge of his future good behaviour. In return, Kildare was appointed governor for ten years and received a grant of any crown lands that he could recover from the Irish. The two-tiered suzerain–vassal arrangement in Ireland was thus restored and strengthened, with a personal bond having at last been forged between Henry VII and Earl Gerald. Kildare power reached its zenith over the next two decades, ushering in a period of stability and prosperity not witnessed in a century. The two-tiered suzerain–vassal arrangement was allowed to continue and its effectiveness, particularly in the English Pale, ensured that it survived the deaths of Henry VII, in 1509, and Earl Gerald, in 1513.[40]

---

38 Ellis, 'Parliament and Community', 43–68; J. F. Lydon, *Ireland in the Later Middle Ages* (Dublin: Gill & Macmillan, 1973), 261; Ellis, *Ireland in the Age of the Tudors*, 74–5.
39 Ellis, 'Henry VII and Ireland', 244–7.
40 Conway, *Henry VII's Relations with Scotland and Ireland*, 226; Sayles, 'Vindication of the Earl of Kildare', 43; Ellis, *Ireland in the Age of the Tudors*, 96–7; Maginn, 'Civilizing' Gaelic *Leinster*, 13–14.

Henry VIII's Intervention in Ireland

The young Henry VIII had little interest in Ireland. His sights were fixed firmly on the reconquest of France and the national and international glory that he knew would come with that oft-attempted undertaking of English kings. It was a measure of Henry VII's success that his son could afford to ignore Ireland in this way and follow in the footsteps of Henry V. In 1513, with Henry VIII campaigning in France, the government of Ireland was entrusted to the king's boyhood companion, Gerald fitz Gerald FitzGerald, the new ninth earl of Kildare. Like his father, Earl Gerald – Gearóid Óg as the Irish knew him – campaigned regularly (and generally successfully) beyond Leinster. And like his father, he did so to maintain Kildare hegemony and to strengthen royal authority. Increasingly by the early sixteenth century, however, the former endeavour was perceived by some in Ireland to have overshadowed the latter. It was not difficult to portray Kildare as a warlord who operated with scant regard for the king's laws and purely in his own interests. The very things that had made the earls so successful – their regular interaction with the Irish, their retention of a standing force of Irish troops and their tendency to billet their soldiers and retainers on the country ('coign and livery' as it was known) – were all strictly forbidden by English law. There was also the glaring fact that after nearly half a century of Kildare hegemony the war against the Irish had yet to be won. Large sections of the country remained beyond royal control and the steady influx of Irish tenants into English areas meant that it appeared as if the Englishry was being over-run by the Irish. So the belief that Ireland needed to be conquered or 'reformed', as it was often put, a belief often expressed by the English of Ireland and by Henry VII in 1494, retained its essential vitality as a social and political aspiration into the reign of Henry VIII. Yet with Kildare fulfilling his basic duties as governor at little cost to the crown, and with the new king having jumped with both feet into the labyrinthine world of European war and diplomacy, the prospect of Ireland's reform seemed remote.[41]

Thus the fact that calls for Ireland's reform increased sharply over the next two decades, as evidenced by the appearance of a spate of written political tracts, which sought reform, and the fact that the discussion of reform coincided with a period of more frequent royal engagement with Ireland, seems strange. In an effort to explain this, it has been argued that a group of reformers

---

41 S. G. Ellis, 'Tudor Policy and the Kildare Ascendancy in the Lordship of Ireland', *IHS*, 20 (1977), 235–60; Maginn and Ellis, *Tudor Discovery*, 121, 125–6, 130–1.

emerged from the Pale as a political force in the decade following Henry VIII's accession. The sons of increasingly prosperous and self-confident gentry, these early Tudor reformers allegedly sought through the medium of written tracts describing the past and present state of Ireland to impress upon the young king and his councillors the precarious position of his English subjects. So informed, the king of England would, it was hoped, reform the Lordship in the manner which they had prescribed and in the process limit Kildare power.[42] But, as we have seen, the concept of reform was not new, and Ireland's reform was not the aspiration of the Pale gentry alone. What may have occasioned this more concentrated push for reform was the occasional interest in Ireland of Thomas Wolsey, one of Henry's most prominent councillors. In 1514 the English-born archbishop of Armagh, John Kite, arrived in Ireland. Kite wrote to Wolsey explaining that he had assured the English of Ireland that the king's coming was imminent and that he was himself convinced that 'the kyng is as moche bound to reforme this land as to mayntayn the goode ordre & justice off England'.[43] The possibility that the crown had finally committed to Ireland's reform, and that Henry VIII might come to Ireland in person to see it through, as Kite let on, may account for the reform tracts written around 1515. It was then that Kildare came to court to discuss his father's estate and legislation for a forthcoming parliament and that two more political treatises describing the steady decay of the king's lordship were proffered to the king and his council.[44] But the king was unmoved by the tracts (if he read them at all) and their generally implicit criticisms of Kildare rule: the earl was returned as governor, his position strengthened by a number of royal grants. No royal visit to Ireland materialised and no reforms were begun.

Wolsey, for his part, does not appear to have backed any substantial royal intervention in Ireland until 1519 when King Henry, in one of his 'spasmodic fits of reforming energy', identified Ireland among the matters which he 'intendeth in his own person to debate with his Council and to see reformation done'.[45] By then, there were more direct complaints against Kildare's

---

42 B. Bradshaw, *The Irish Constitutional Revolution of the Sixteenth Century* (Cambridge University Press, 1976), 32–57 (quotations, 33, 268).

43 F. Fitzsimons, 'Cardinal Wolsey, the Native Affinities and the Failure of Reform in Henrician Ireland', in D. Edwards (ed.), *Regions and Rulers in Ireland, 1100–1650* (Dublin: Four Courts Press, 2004), 84; Maginn and Ellis, *Tudor Discovery*, 31 (quotation), 137, 140, 144.

44 Maginn and Ellis, *Tudor Discovery*, 31–2, 135–45.

45 J. J. Scarisbrick, *Henry VIII* (London: Eyre & Spottiswoode, 1968), 119 (quotation); Ellis, 'Tudor Policy', 239 (quotation), 239; G. Walker, 'The Expulsion of the Minions of 1519 Reconsidered', *Historical Journal*, 32 (1989), 1–16.

methods of government coming from the Butler interest following the earl's failure in 1516 to secure the earldom of Ormond for his client (and brother-in-law) Piers Butler against the claims of Thomas Boleyn, grandson of the seventh earl of Ormond and one of the king's favourites. (Piers was made first earl of Ossory in 1528, and eventually secured the title earl of Ormond in 1538.) His interest in Ireland piqued, Henry VIII summoned Kildare to court for discussions. Kildare was detained in London for the next two years as Henry's council, led by Wolsey, sought to get to the bottom of the charges of maladministration levelled at the earl. In his stead, Henry sent over as governor of Ireland one of his best generals, Thomas Howard, earl of Surrey. Surrey's expedition (1520–2) has been called a 'reconnaissance in force', for he came with too few soldiers and insufficient administrative support to achieve much beyond assessing the state of the Lordship so as to inform the king how Ireland's reform might be achieved.[46]

Time spent in Ireland had taught Surrey that the only way to reform the Lordship was to conquer the Irish polity. He explained to Wolsey and Henry that a well-equipped and adequately financed army of 6,000 men would be necessary to accomplish this end in a reasonably expeditious time frame. But the king was not prepared to pay for what Surrey admitted 'wolbe a mervellous charge'.[47] Instead, Henry showed himself open to a peaceful engagement with the Irish whom he deemed to be 'rebels', his recalcitrant subjects in other words, rather than 'enemies' who were beyond his authority. This possibility was especially attractive in light of the fact that a number of Irish lords had submitted to Surrey and recognised Henry as their king. Cormac Óg MacCarthy went so far as to seek to hold his lands of the crown and requested that he be elevated to the peerage.[48] Surrey also came away from Ireland firm in the belief that Kildare had actively frustrated his government by inducing Irishmen to attack him. Surrey's complaints against Kildare, fed to an extent by officials in the Irish government linked to the Butler family and seized upon by Wolsey in council, ensured Earl Gerald's continued detention in England. By contrast, Surrey wrote to Wolsey that Piers Butler 'hath a true English hert' and was 'the man of moost experience of the feautes of warre of this country'. But what neither Surrey nor Wolsey fully appreciated was the extent to which the Irish polity, most especially in

---

46 Ellis, *Reform and Revival*, 157–8; Ellis, *Ireland in the Age of the Tudors*, 118.
47 *SP Hen. VIII*, ii, 62 (quotation), 72–5.
48 C. Maginn, 'The Gaelic Peers, the Tudor Sovereigns, and English Multiple Monarchy', *Journal of British Studies*, 50 (2011), 570–1; C. Maginn, *William Cecil, Ireland, and the Tudor State* (Oxford University Press, 2012), 32–4.

Leinster, had divided between Geraldine and Butler factions. The decision, in 1522, to appoint Piers Butler as Surrey's replacement only emboldened the Butlers, and placed them on a collision course with the Geraldines. Kildare having rehabilitated himself through his marriage at court was sent back to Ireland in 1523. It was hoped that he would use his influence to control his adherents, but his presence only undermined Piers's administration. To restore order, the crown had no choice other than to reappoint Kildare as governor; yet a powerful Butler interest was now a force in Ireland and for the next decade a Geraldine–Butler feud dominated the Lordship's politics.[49]

Left to his own devices it is probable that Kildare would have overcome the Butler challenge to Geraldine hegemony. It was a measure of the continued potency of Kildare power and the effectiveness of his government that the earl secured reappointment as deputy in 1532 following a five-year period in which the crown governed first through Lord Delvin, then Piers Butler, earl of Ossory, and then a 'secret council' before the appointment of an outsider, the English-born soldier William Skeffington. But Ireland was no longer an obscure region of the English state whose politics were scarcely understood at the English court. Wolsey regularly devoted his attention to Ireland, and Thomas Cromwell, his successor as chief minister to Henry VIII, continued his predecessor's efforts to enhance royal power in the Lordship. And like Wolsey, Cromwell did so by establishing contacts and clients in Ireland outside (and so in all instances opposed to) the Kildare affinity.[50] All that Cromwell learned of Ireland suggested that Kildare was an impediment to reform. A report, drawn up for Cromwell in 1533, captured the sentiment: 'thErle of Kyldare, by the continuaunce of the Kingis auctoritie in him and his fader, hath banded himself on suche wise, that if the Kinge make any other Deputie but him, all the lande shalbe disordered; so as the Kinge must depende upon his pleasur, and not he upon the Kingis'.[51] A decade earlier such accusations would not have aroused any urgency in England, but the crisis surrounding Henry VIII's break with Rome had altered the political landscape. At this potentially hazardous juncture the king demanded, and Cromwell worked to achieve, compliance throughout the Tudor territories. The revolutionary ecclesiastical and constitutional changes, which

49 *SP Hen. VIII*, ii, 58; D. Edwards, *The Ormond Lordship in County Kilkenny, 1515–1642: The Rise and Fall of Butler Feudal Power* (Dublin: Four Courts Press, 2003), 152–3; Maginn, 'Civilizing' Gaelic Leinster, 14–15; Fitzsimons, 'Cardinal Wolsey', 106–12.

50 B. Bradshaw, 'Cromwellian Reform and the Origins of the Kildare Rebellion, 1533–4', *TRHS*, 27 (1977), 69–93; S. G. Ellis, 'Thomas Cromwell and Ireland, 1532–40', *Historical Journal*, 23 (1980), 497–519.

51 *SP Hen. VIII*, ii, 176.

Cromwell had carefully guided through the English parliament in 1533, needed to be extended to Ireland. Kildare, by all accounts, was unfit to oversee such an essential undertaking. The king summoned the earl and other officials in the Irish government to court in September 1533; the following month it was determined, on the advice of Cromwell and the Irish council, that an Englishman should replace Kildare as governor.[52]

It is difficult to know the extent to which Kildare appreciated the political changes afoot in the Tudor government. At the time of his summons to court, the king had also moved to establish more effective control of the administrative organs in the far north and Wales.[53] Before Kildare left Ireland in spring 1534, he secured leave to appoint his son Thomas, Lord Offaly, vice-deputy. In this way, the earl might maintain control in his absence. In England, however, Kildare was vulnerable. There, Cromwell had outflanked Thomas Howard, now duke of Norfolk, Kildare's ally at court and Cromwell's chief competitor for the king's ear; in May, Skeffington, whom Kildare had humiliated upon his recovery of office, was designated to succeed him as deputy. Kildare secreted a message to Offaly, urging his son to stay clear of the council in Ireland, for to engage the councillors would only result in his being sent over to England where he would be executed. But there was another option open to Kildare's son. The history of the Kildare's relationship with the Tudors was not forgotten. In the report presented to Cromwell referenced above, the author relates an exchange which was said to have taken place between one of the earl's kinsmen and the ninth earl's half-brother Thomas FitzGerald. The former allegedly chided him for his refusal to join the earl in his efforts to disrupt royal government in the later 1520s, reminding him:

> Thou shalt be the more estemed in Irelande, to take parte against the kinge; for what haddest thou have been, if thy fader had not doon so? What was he sett by, until he crowned a Kinge here; … resisted Ponengis and all Deputies … wold suffer no man to rule here … but himself? Than the Kinge regarded him, made him Deputie.

The young heir to the Kildare earldom must also have been aware of his family's history of selective disobedience to the crown and the benefits it had brought them. Indeed his father had already, before his departure, begun transferring the king's ordnance from Dublin Castle into Geraldine stores. With his old and ailing father detained indefinitely in England, Offaly chose

---

52 D. B. Quinn, 'Henry VIII and Ireland, 1509–34', *IHS*, 12 (1961), 320, 330, 337, 341.
53 Ellis, *Ireland in the Age of the Tudors*, 135–6.

to employ the strategy which had secured for his father and grandfather the king's favour in Ireland.[54]

On 11 June 1534, Offaly resigned from office in spectacular fashion. He entered Dublin at the head of a complement of horsemen – they wore jackets embroidered with silk which earned Offaly his famous sobriquet 'Silken Thomas' – and denounced Henry VIII as a tyrant before the council. This most public act of defiance was probably meant to force the king to reconsider his decision to replace Kildare – Offaly made no effort to seize control of Dublin; he waited for a response from London. When the king imprisoned Kildare in the Tower, Offaly unleashed a full-scale rebellion. In the wake of England's break from Rome, Offaly aligned his rebellion with religious conservatism, and so also with the interests of the Holy Roman Emperor, the secular defender of Europe's Catholic faith. But Offaly badly misjudged Henry VIII and miscalculated the king's reaction. In fairness to him, Henry VIII had yet to exhibit the ruthlessness which he was to display in the final years of his reign. As late as October, Kildare – as Offaly then was following his father's death in the Tower – was still open to the possibility of securing from the king a pardon and a lifetime appointment as governor. But, facing the real possibility of war against a Catholic coalition, Henry VIII could not allow this brazen challenge to his authority to go unpunished. He dispatched Skeffington to Ireland as governor with 2,500 soldiers, and the English parliament attainted Kildare and his adherents. Having failed to take Dublin, or any other major city, the rebellion disintegrated in the face of Skeffington's army. The rebels made a stand at Kildare's castle at Maynooth in March 1535, but a combination of Skeffington's use of artillery and his promise to pardon the castle's defenders resulted in its surrender; Skeffington's slaughter of the rebel garrison – remembered as the 'pardon of Maynooth' – was, perhaps, a manifestation of the royal intolerance of dissent in these dangerous times. Earl Thomas escaped to the Irishry, and for five months mounted raids on the Pale with his Irish allies and the remnants of the FitzGerald connection. But Kildare's agents at Rome and in Spain failed to secure military support for what the rebels represented as a Catholic crusade against heresy. Unwilling to fight on with exclusively Irish support, Kildare opened up negotiations with the Irish council. He surrendered in August in the expectation that his life would be spared.[55]

---

54 *SP Hen. VIII*, ii, 175 (quotation); S. G. Ellis, 'The Kildare Rebellion and the Early Henrician Reformation', *Historical Journal*, 19 (1976), 807–30.
55 M. Ó Siochrú, 'Foreign Involvement in the Revolt of Silken Thomas, 1534–5', *PRIA*, 96 C (1996), 49–66.

The Making of the Kingdom of Ireland

There is evidence to suggest that contemporaries, not unlike modern historians, saw the end of the Kildare rebellion as a watershed moment. The Irish council reported that the ease (and the ferocity) with which the English army had humbled the mighty Geraldines had left the leaders of the Irish polity in more fear than they had been since the Conquest. In the rebellion's immediate aftermath, Cromwell received a number of written proposals, urging him to use the opportunity to convince the king to begin the oft-mooted general reformation of Ireland. Less than two decades later, one political commentator could look back on the arrival of Skeffington as the point at which the crown ceased 'to lett the realme of Yrlande remayne under the governa[u]nce of the lordes of the same' for the sake of 'avoydinge of chardge'.[56] Indeed, Cromwell had been pursuing a deliberate policy of political and administrative centralisation, what has been called in an Irish context 'unitary sovereignty'; Kildare's removal from power only served to advance this policy.[57] Even so, for King Henry and Cromwell, the rebellion and the myriad possibilities its suppression presented only distracted from a more immediate need: to extend to Ireland the revolutionary ecclesiastical legislation lately passed in England. The longer-term matter of how to govern Ireland effectively and cheaply, and without the support of the family which had dominated the Lordship's politics for half a century and more, would have to wait.

Ireland's parliament was convened in May 1536 for the purpose of enacting the reformation bills. The English parliament was legally empowered to introduce the legislation in the Lordship, but securing local consensus for the king's revolution was a hallmark of Cromwell's *modus operandi*. The Reformation legislation, the centrepiece of which made King Henry 'the only supreme head in earth of the whole church of Ireland', passed; but there was sustained opposition to other aspects of the royal legislative programme, notably the bills to dissolve monasteries and introduce a land tax to help offset some of the expenses incurred by the king in suppressing Kildare's rebellion.[58] Leonard Grey, former marshal of the army and Kildare's brother-in-law, had succeeded to the office of deputy following Skeffington's death late in 1535. It was he who presided over the Irish Reformation Parliament. But it was he who also

---

56 Ellis, *Ireland in the Age of the Tudors*, 145; TNA SP 61/4/72, fo. 240 (quotation).
57 Bradshaw, *Irish Constitutional Revolution*, ch. 5.
58 B. Bradshaw, 'The Opposition to the Ecclesiastical Legislation in the Irish Reformation Parliament', *IHS*, 16 (1968–9), 285–303; G. A. Hayes-McCoy, 'The Royal Supremacy and Ecclesiastical Revolution, 1534–47', in *NHI* iii, 56 (quotation).

had to find a means to govern Ireland while the wrangling over legislation continued. As the parliament moved from Dublin to Kilkenny to Cashel and then on to Limerick, Grey campaigned, ranging to the banks of the Shannon where he destroyed the bridge O'Brien had built to carry his power toward Limerick. The crown was ultimately forced to modify or abandon much of its legislative programme in the Reformation Parliament, which was eventually dissolved in December 1537; but in the meanwhile Grey had shown himself unafraid to assert royal authority anywhere in the Lordship through his bold and skilful use of artillery. To the Butler faction, Grey's methods resembled those once used by Kildare; his personal relationship with the FitzGeralds and his ability to employ what remained of the Kildare connection to his own advantage seemed only to underscore the comparison.[59]

But Grey's government had in fact alienated a cross-section of interests in Ireland in ways that the earls of Kildare never had. Opposition from Piers Butler, earl of Ossory (and from January 1538 earl of Ormond), and his adherents was to be expected; yet Grey also lost the support of the Pale nobility and the council, and the combination of his successful campaigning deep into the Irishry and his conclusion of a number of burdensome indentures with individual lords led to the formation in 1539 of a confederation of Irish lords – the so-called 'Geraldine League' – which sought Grey's recall and the restoration of the FitzGerald heir who was then in their care. Blame for this wave of political instability may easily be placed on Grey. He was an underfunded and inexperienced governor who was also intemperate and bellicose. But his difficulty may also be seen to be symptomatic of Ireland's polities, English and Irish, readjusting to the absence of the stabilising influence of Kildare power at a time when royal government, preoccupied with enforcing religious reform in England, was committed to no clear policy for the Lordship. Royal commissioners were dispatched to Ireland in September 1537 with the purpose of enquiring into abuses in government and the state of English rule more generally. The king's refusal to spend, however, meant that the commissioners' recommendations were conservative: the army was reduced, Grey was left in office and the administrative reform of English areas was to be given precedence over any 'general reformation'. So Grey governed Ireland in the only way he knew how. In August 1539 he routed the Irish confederates near the Pale's border and then campaigned in Desmond, collecting submissions from several Irish lords along the way; by 1540, he could point to the twenty-seven indentures that he had concluded with Irish, and a handful of

---

59 *SP Hen. VIII*, iii, 32.

English, lords. These successes had won for Grey the support of his patron Thomas Cromwell who was by then fighting to retain his influence with the king against a challenge from religious conservatives on the council.[60]

Yet there were limits to what sporadic military campaigning (however successful) might achieve. The Irish confederation did not disintegrate after its defeat. Rather it began to assume the characteristics of a national movement, with Irish lords from across the country pledging themselves to a confederation which only gained in strength after the Geraldine heir's departure for the Continent. In 1539 Pope Paul III had styled Conn *Bacach* O'Neill – one of the confederation's leaders – 'our noble king of our realm of Ireland'. Henry VIII had, according to the Pope, forfeited his right to the sovereignty of Ireland when he broke with Rome. King Henry's Erastian settlement and his very right to rule over Ireland were now being challenged. The seriousness of the situation was not lost on members of the Lordship's government. Articles of complaint were drawn up against Grey; and the English-born bishop of Meath, Edward Staples, declared that 'the common voice of the Irishry is that the king's supremacy is maintained only by power' and suggested that Henry be 'recognised King of Ireland'. But, however much a change of political tack may have appeared necessary to some, there is no evidence to indicate that Henry VIII was contemplating a change of policy, or leadership, in Ireland. It took the sudden destruction at court of Thomas Cromwell in June 1540, and with him his client Lord Deputy Grey, to create the opportunity for a new departure in the Anglo-Irish relationship.[61]

Anthony St Leger succeeded Grey as governor that summer. St Leger had been one of the commissioners sent to Ireland in 1537 and was an experienced administrator, whose 'attemperaunce, moderation, discreation, and uprightnes', the king was sure, would stand him in good stead in Ireland; he was also a client of Norfolk who had been chiefly responsible for Cromwell's overthrow and was now chief in the king's counsels.[62] St Leger did not, to judge either by the instructions given him or his initial campaigning, arrive in Ireland with a fully formed strategy for government. But within a year it was evident that his administration had struck a new tone in the Anglo-Irish relationship. By then, Irish lords were submitting to St Leger in large numbers

---

60 Maginn, 'Civilizing' Gaelic Leinster, 56–7; Power, European Frontier Elite, 83–92; Maginn, *William Cecil*, 39; TNA, SP 60/8/37; TNA, SP 60/9/1.

61 C. Maginn, 'Whose Island? Sovereignty in Late Medieval and Early Modern Ireland', *Éire-Ireland*, 44 (2009), 234; C. Maginn, 'Edward Staples', in *ODNB* (quotation); C. Brady, *The Chief Governors: The Rise and Fall of Reform Government in Tudor Ireland, 1536–1588* (Cambridge University Press, 1994), 24.

62 Bryson, 'Anthony St Leger', in *ODNB*; *SP Hen. VIII*, iii, 229 (quotation).

and entering into detailed written indentures as proof of their willingness to acknowledge Henry VIII as their sovereign lord, to abjure papal authority, to hold their land of the crown by knight's service and to abandon Irish customs. One such Irish lord, Turlough O'Toole, was sent to court to submit before the king who, impressed by the scene, declared that all Irish lords should do likewise.[63] St Leger had also reconciled distant and recalcitrant lords to his government like the earl of Desmond and Burke of Clanrickard and was authorised to offer peerages to certain Irish lords: Barnaby MacGilpatrick became the first Irishman ever to receive an English peerage and took his seat in the House of Lords as Lord Fitzpatrick, the first baron of Upper Ossory. St Leger's first year as governor was capped off when in summer 1541 Henry VIII was proclaimed king of Ireland by a parliament which for the first time in its history welcomed Irish lords into its confines.[64]

These developments were all signs of a new departure in the Anglo-Irish relationship – seen by Brendan Bradshaw as constituting a 'constitutional revolution' – but it is important to emphasise that none of the elements which St Leger pursued were new. The intellectual and political impulse for St Leger's conciliatory engagement with the Irish polity, for instance, may be traced to Henry's communications with Surrey two decades earlier. Here the king, probably unknowingly, was already bridging the constitutional gap which existed between 'English subjects' and 'Irish enemies' by referring to the majority of the latter as 'our … Irische rebelles' – it was not long before the king's taxonomy rubbed off on Tudor officials.[65] The implication of course was that as rebels Irish lords were the king's subjects rather than non-subjects and beyond royal control. Still, formidable legal, social and cultural differences separated the Irish from the English. Grey's efforts in the 1530s to conclude written indentures with Irishmen and to have them hold their land of the king by feudal tenure may be seen as a means of accommodating Irish lords within English law and culture; St Leger adopted a similar strategy after 1540. Raising Irishmen to the peerage, meanwhile, was suggested as far back as 1515 and in 1520 Surrey had found himself confronted with Irish lords seeking English titles in return for their loyalty. Even the act which erected Ireland into a kingdom, the centrepiece of St Leger's strategy in Ireland, was first suggested to him during his stint as a royal

---

63 Maginn, 'Civilizing' Gaelic Leinster, 65–76; C. Maginn, '"Surrender and Regrant" in the Historiography of Sixteenth-Century Ireland', Sixteenth Century Journal, 38 (2007), 955–74.
64 McCormack, Earldom of Desmond, 75–7; Maginn, 'Gaelic Peers', 571–2; Bradshaw, Irish Constitutional Revolution, 3.
65 SP Hen. VIII, ii, 60 (quotation), 69, 93, 188–9.

commissioner. Nevertheless, it was St Leger who gathered all of these disparate ideas together and fashioned them into a new political policy for Ireland, something which historians generally label 'surrender and regrant' after one of the principal features of a submitting lord's indenture: his surrender of lands belonging to his extended kinship group in return for a regrant of the same lands to him by letters patent.[66]

There were some reservations in both English and Irish circles about the revolutionary implications of St Leger's policy. Henry VIII objected to the financial responsibilities that kingship would entail, and balked at handing over crown lands in Ireland without remuneration. In Ireland, the earl of Ormond – from August 1539 James son of Piers Butler – resented St Leger's intrusion and became the head of a faction which worked to dislodge the governor from power; and an anonymous Irish poem was composed berating those lords who would abandon Irish ways and allow 'foreigners' to divide up Irish land.[67] But the success of St Leger's government could not be gainsaid. The 'Geraldine League' disintegrated as Irish and English lords from across Ireland flocked to submit to St Leger. In 1542, O'Neill, the greatest of Irish lords, travelled to court where he submitted before the king and where he was created the earl of Tyrone; the following year two more great lords – O'Brien and MacWilliam Burke – came before King Henry to join the peerage of Ireland as earls. By 1544 St Leger could draw on hundreds of Irish troops to serve in Henry VIII's wars in Scotland and France. Sir Thomas Cusack, the lord chancellor and one of the most strident supporters of St Leger and his methods, could remark 'those who would not be brought under subjection with 10,000 men, cometh to Dublin with a letter'.[68] Perhaps a more impressive, though much less spectacular, feature of St Leger's success was his ability to secure the backing of the English of Ireland and the growing number of English-born officials serving in Ireland who had very little to gain from 'surrender and regrant'. He was able to rise above the traditional Geraldine / Butler allegiances by creating in Irish government what has been called a 'King's party'. Helping to bind the 'party' together, it is true, was St Leger's liberal leasing of (deliberately undervalued) crown land to those who supported him, but the English of Ireland were also responding to that which

---

66 Maginn, 'Gaelic Peers', 569–71; Murray, *Enforcing the English Reformation in Ireland*, 128.
67 A. Bryson, 'The Ormond–St Leger Feud, 1544–6', *IHS*, 38 (2012), 187–212; B. Ó Cuív, 'A Sixteenth-Century Political Poem', *Éigse*, 15 / 4 (1974), 261–76.
68 Maginn, 'Gaelic Peers', 572–3; D. G. White, 'Henry VIII's Irish Kerne in France and Scotland', *Irish Sword*, 3 (1957–8), 213–25; Ellis, *Ireland in the Age of the Tudors*, 156 (quotation).

they had long sought after and that which St Leger had achieved: the crown's sustained interest in Ireland and their own closer integration into the English state.[69]

Central to the entire enterprise, however, was King Henry. It was the sheer force of his personality and imperious reputation that had made St Leger's actions possible; the old king, moreover, seems to have been committed to St Leger and the new policy for Ireland which he embodied. So Henry's death in January 1547 held the potential to alter the political environment within which St Leger had been allowed to flourish. It is a measure of his success that he held on as governor well into Edward VI's reign; but when a rebellion erupted in south Leinster and then spread to the midlands St Leger's enemies who, following the death of Piers Butler, earl of Ormond, in January 1539, had regrouped around John Alen and the vice-treasurer, William Brabazon, used it as an opportunity to attack the government. At the court of the boy king the allegations against the governor resonated where once they were brushed aside: St Leger was replaced, in May 1548, by the English privy councillor and soldier Edward Bellingham.[70] But there was more to St Leger's fall than his failure to contain rebellion and his lack of protection at court. His real difficulty lay in the deficiencies arising from the policy that he had introduced. The legal, economic and cultural transformation of Irishmen into English subjects exhibiting English ways would take time – perhaps a generation and more: until this process was complete St Leger's enemies might always point to the governor's shortcomings. On the other side of this, the rebellion which erupted in 1547 was caused by the tensions within clans which 'surrender and regrant' had created. In the new dispensation, individual Irish lords and their heirs were invested with lands which under Irish law rightfully belonged collectively to the clan. This frequently led the now politically marginalised clansmen to challenge the settlement concluded with the crown. And there is also evidence which suggests that some English resented the crown's new relationship with the Irish. In 1543 the Tipperary and Kilkenny gentry had petitioned the king:

> beseching [you] ... to haue suche eye and respect to yo[u]r ... approvid subiect[e]s as the oonly submyssion of others newly reconcilid w[i]t[h]oute

---

69 Brady, *Chief Governors*, 30–40.
70 D. G. White, 'The Reign of Edward VI in Ireland: Some Political, Social and Economic Aspects', *IHS*, 14 (1964–5), 197–211; C. Maginn, 'A Window on Mid-Tudor Ireland: The "Matters" against Lord Deputy St. Leger, 1547–8', *Historical Research*, 78 (2005), 465–82; A. Bryson, 'Sir Anthony St Leger and the Outbreak of the Midland Rebellion, 1547–8', *PRIA*, 113 C (2013), 251–77.

further proff of ther hart[e]s & s[er]uice be not the meane to elivate them in power and streinthe that therby p[er]ill myghte growe to yo[u]r Ma[ies]ties faithfull subiect[e]s.[71]

The 'Act for kingly title' and the wider strategy of which it was a part could not erase centuries of antagonism and war – whether we view it as real or as partly an English legal and cultural construct – between English and Irish in Ireland. In short, making Ireland into a kingdom in the image of England in the conciliatory manner espoused by St Leger would take decades and require the unswerving commitment of the king of England. But the new Edwardian regime was not prepared to wait. The willingness of Protector Somerset to increase military expenditure in Ireland, principally on the establishment of forts manned by garrisons of English soldiers beyond the western and southern extremities of the Pale, to complement and expedite St Leger's strategy allowed Tudor officials in England and Ireland once again to envision the reform of Ireland in more traditionally war-like terms. The subsequent decision taken by John Dudley, earl of Warwick, who overthrew Somerset in late 1549, to curtail royal expenditure in Ireland by reappointing St Leger only served further to muddle the character and aims of English government in the new Tudor kingdom.[72]

The Ireland of 1550 was a different place than the country whose future eighty years earlier hinged on the latest manifestation of dynastic strife in England. The Wars of the Roses, and the instability they periodically wrought in Ireland, were by then a distant memory. The Tudors had ushered in not only dynastic stability but also a sustained period, especially evident under Henry VIII, of political centralisation around the crown in which the English territories were settled within the Tudor monarchy. Edward VI, the third Tudor to occupy the throne, wielded more power in Ireland than any English king since the thirteenth century. Ireland, once a frontier region remote from the centre of English power, was by 1550 a kingdom with a Protestant church, its people were Tudor subjects and its government was more closely controlled from London than at any time in the 300-year history of the Anglo-Irish relationship. Ireland, it appeared, had in these years exited one era and entered another. But, as this chapter has shown, these changes were often deeply rooted in what had come before. It is only by looking broadly at what was an eighty-year period of accumulated change that the differences between the Ireland of 1470 and 1550 are evident. The extent of change which

71 NLI, Ormond MS D 2410.
72 Brady, *Chief Governors*, 33–40; White, 'Reign of Edward VI', 209–10.

had occurred must not be exaggerated. Ireland may have been a kingdom by 1550, but it bore little resemblance to the other Tudor kingdom: royal authority in Ireland was barely felt outside of Leinster where life carried on much as it had in 1470 (and before); the Church of Ireland had yet to put down firm roots; several of the 'surrender and regrant' settlements were breaking down; and the constitutional status of Irishmen as subjects of the crown remained ambiguous – nearly twenty Irishmen are known to have received grants of English liberty in 1550 alone.[73] It may be argued, then, that Ireland was a kingdom only in name by the middle of the sixteenth century. It remained to be seen whether, and how, the Tudor crown, the driving force of change in Ireland since the late fifteenth century, would make the drastic changes introduced over the previous two decades felt throughout the island.

73 *CPRI*, 199, 200–1, 203–4, 207, 209–10, 213, 215–16.

12

Late Medieval Ireland in a Wider World

MICHAEL BENNETT

THE extent to which late medieval Ireland was connected to the wider world was forcefully illustrated by the arrival of bubonic plague in summer 1348. In Kilkenny, Friar John Clyn had already heard reports of its alarming advance through Christendom and had access to continental prophecies that informed his sense of its apocalyptic significance. Since the plague did not reach Bristol until August, around the time it arrived in Ireland, it appears likely that it arrived directly from the Continent, probably from Bordeaux with its regular trade with Irish ports. The appalling mortality that Clyn recorded before signing off, around June 1349, to 'any one of the race of Adam who might escape the pestilence', did not bring more than a temporary halt to trade and travel. As the plague moved inland, Archbishop Fitz Ralph of Armagh emerged to deliver a sermon associating the scourge with the sins of the Irish, both English and Gaelic, and urging them to live peaceably together. By summer he was on his way to the papal curia at Avignon. In his report on the plague he observed that it had most impact on Ireland's coastal areas. He may not have been as well informed about the situation in the interior, as the plague certainly caused many deaths among the Gaels. Still, it is widely assumed that the pestilence had a disproportionate impact on the English population and contributed to a shift in the demographic balance in Ireland toward the native Irish. It is a reminder of the complex interplay of indigenous agencies and exogenous forces in Irish history.[1]

Ireland's Connections with England and Beyond

It has long been a truism in world history that, in pre-modern times, the sea posed less serious barriers to communication than the land. (The rats that

---

1 B. Gummer, *The Scourging Angel. The Black Death in the British Isles* (London: Vintage, 2010), 71–5.

scurried ashore in 1348 rapidly introduced the plague to the coastal areas but found it hard going as the rivers and roads gave way to boggy causeways and forest-tracks.) Ireland was part of a larger maritime world. To the east, the Irish Sea was a zone of trade and cultural contact in its own right. The northern neck linked northern Ireland closely with the Isle of Man, south-west Scotland and the Western Isles. Further south, the sea connected Ireland with north-west England, Wales and the Severn Estuary. Nor was Britain the only area accessible by water. From the earliest times, Ireland's position on Europe's Atlantic rim provided links with Brittany, the Bay of Biscay and the Hispanic Peninsula, and the island's marginality became less evident as a result of Europe's increasing focus on the Atlantic from the fifteenth century onwards. It is scarcely surprising, then, that the history of Ireland, though often appropriately inward-looking, has also been markedly extro-vert. Ireland's long subjection to the English crown, and the colonisation that sustained it, have generally precluded an exclusively insular approach to Irish history. From this perspective it is tempting to regard the later Middle Ages as a period of relative autonomy in Ireland. After all, the fourteenth and fif-teenth centuries were marked by the decline of the English Lordship and the resurgence of Gaelic Ireland. Interestingly, too, the period is not so obviously characterised, as in earlier centuries, by themes of *peregrinatio* or, as in later centuries, large-scale emigration.

Building on scholarship that has shown the value of a British or archipe-lagic approach, this chapter explores the value of an even broader framework in the history of Ireland and its peoples.[2] Demographic decline, for example, had a major impact on politics, the economy, society and culture of Ireland. The attenuation of the English Lordship was accompanied by the retreat of cereal production in Ireland accentuated by changing patterns of demand else-where in north-west Europe. Another external development was the revival of Plantagenet ambitions in France, which had broad implications for Ireland and its position in a larger 'dynastic empire'. The period in any case cannot be regarded simply as one of English disengagement. It was punctuated by phases of forceful intervention. The English state and its facsimile in Dublin, English and Anglo-Irish political culture, and new models of lordship, English and Gaelic, all developed over the period, often in ways that were mutually constitutive. To repeat: Ireland was part of a wider world and its history was shaped by this reality. In addition to close relations with south-west Scotland

2 Frame, *Political Development of the British Isles*; Frame, *Ireland and Britain*; Davies, *First English Empire*.

and the Western Isles, it had longstanding commercial and cultural connections with Bordeaux and the Hispanic Peninsula. The Irish needed salt, wine and oil, and went as pilgrims to Santiago de Compostela. The Gaelic Church was unusually dependent on the papacy – Avignon from 1309 until the 1370s and later Rome – and its mendicant orders, so important in Irish culture, were especially closely involved in broader developments in Christendom. But, in addition to its formal sovereignty over Ireland, the geographical position, greater size, political cohesion and wealth of England meant that it exercised considerable gravitational pull. Among the English of Ireland a sense of dependence on England was accompanied by resilience and resourcefulness. Some counterpoise to the influence of England resulted from a significant shift in Europe's focus towards the Atlantic in the late fifteenth century – evident in Ireland with the expansion of the fisheries and trade on the west coast – and from the new economic vitality of the Gaelic interior. Although it is tempting to see the Gaelic world as being more enclosed, it arguably became more rather than less engaged with a wider world at this time. Many cultural developments, even the most distinctively Gaelic, can only be fully appreciated in a broader framework.

If the sea provided the most expeditious means of transporting goods, and indeed transmitting the plague, it is important to recognise that Ireland's access to continental Europe was nonetheless largely mediated physically by England. Two fourteenth-century narratives relating to travel to and from Ireland indicate a distinct preference among travellers for keeping time at sea as short as possible. In 1323 two Irish friars set out for the Holy Land. Their itinerary took them across the Irish Sea to Holyhead, along the coast to Chester, then through the heart of England to London, Canterbury and Dover. In his account of the pilgrimage Friar Simon was so impressed by what he saw in England that he exhausted his superlatives long before he and his companion crossed the English Channel.[3] The route is described in reverse in the account of a pilgrimage to St Patrick's Purgatory, Lough Derg, by the Catalan knight Ramon de Perellós in 1397–8. A well-travelled man of the world, Perellós was impressed but by no means overwhelmed by the sights in Canterbury and London. Seeking out Richard II in his country retreat outside Oxford proved more of an adventure. The king alerted him to the dangers of his quest and provided letters of introduction to the earl of March in Dublin. From this time on, Perellós was travelling further and further beyond the

---

3 *Itinerarium Symonis Semeonis ab Hybernia ad Terra Sanctam*, ed. M. Esposito. Scriptores Latini Hiberniae, 4 (Dublin: DIAS, 1960), 25–7.

world with which he was familiar. Each stage of the journey brought him to a new threshold and new set of warnings about the danger ahead. St Patrick's Purgatory itself was the entrance to the netherworld.[4]

The narratives give expression to the paradigm of civilisation and barbarism that underpinned English rule in Ireland. They suggest, though, more a spectrum than a clear divide. The friars began their pilgrimage in Clonmel, an English enclave in a largely Gaelic-speaking area. After a rough crossing to Anglesey, they travelled by land to Chester, where they were comforted by the sight of Irish ships at anchor. In Lichfield, Simon was stunned by the cathedral, the beauty of its decoration and the loftiness of its towers. Even so, he was unprepared for the English capital: the bridge laden with people and riches; the grandeur of St Paul's and the height of its spire; Westminster Abbey, the seat of kings; and the impregnable Tower of London. Perellós's journey provides a counter-narrative of wonder. After near shipwreck on the Irish Sea, he perhaps appreciated the ordinariness of Dublin. The earl of March, however, reminded him that he was about to pass through 'the lands of savage, ungoverned people whom no man should trust'. At Drogheda, Archbishop Colton of Armagh likewise warned him that he could not assure his safety in the lands of King O'Neill. It was as if the Gaelic heartland was doubly or trebly insulated. Perellós found the Irish king helpful, but unable to protect him in the lands of his O'Donnell enemies. After reaching Lough Derg, Perellós was rowed out to the island, and entered St Patrick's Purgatory to face the terrors of the night. Returning the way he came, he spent Christmas as the guest of King O'Neill, presenting him as a hearty, larger-than-life figure, not unlike the genial, but potentially dangerous, castellans of Arthurian romance. Back in England, he was reluctant to shake off the spell of myth and romance. At Dover castle, he made a point of inspecting a relic reputed to be the head of Sir Gawain.

The itineraries reflect a preference among travellers between London and Dublin for the route through Chester. Though further from the English capital than Bristol, Chester offered direct access to Dublin and, as the route hugged the coast of North Wales and involved only a short deep-sea crossing, it was more attractive to landlubbers. Travel by sea was greatly feared. Many people made wills preparatory to crossing the Irish Sea. Fearing shipwreck in a storm off the north coast of Devon, a Dubliner confessed his involvement in forging deeds to property in Bridgwater that proved his undoing when he

---

4 D. Carpenter, 'The Pilgrim from Catalonia/Aragon: Ramon de Perellós, 1397', in Haren and de Pontfarcy (eds.), *Medieval Pilgrimage to St Patrick's Purgatory*, 99–119.

made a safe landfall.[5] Travel across land, of course, was by no means risk-free. Richard II provided Perellós with an escort to Chester in 1397, and the Irish parliament complained in 1428 about attacks on Irishmen on the road between Chester, Coventry and Oxford. In comparison with other parts of Europe, however, England was a safe place to travel. In addition, travel over land was generally more convenient and flexible. It allowed the travellers to call on friends, deliver letters and catch up with news, conduct business and see sights. The Florentine Antonio di Giovanni Mannini combined a visit to St Patrick's Purgatory with business in Dublin in 1412. In returning from the Purgatory in 1431, Ghillebert de Lannoy travelled through Chester to London, calling on the Dowager Queen Katherine at Pleshey.[6] The travel narratives further document Ireland's openness to the larger world. They do suggest, however, that Ireland's links with continental Europe were often mediated, culturally as well as physically, by England.

The first age of conquest in Ireland was long past when Perellós enjoyed King O'Neill's hospitality over Christmas 1397. The population growth, economic development and state-building that had fuelled Norman and English expansionism in the British archipelago had come to an end a century earlier. The English colony in Ireland, which had contributed money and men to Edward I's wars of conquest, was on the frontline of the collapse of the Edwardian empire. Edward Bruce's invasion in 1315 largely destroyed the English position in northern Ireland and proved ruinous to the Lordship politically and economically. Ireland, like England, experienced the poor harvests and murrains that afflicted cattle in the earlier decades of the fourteenth century. The arrival of bubonic plague hit the settler population, mainly located in ports and fortified towns, harder than the more dispersed and remote population of the Gaelic interior. There was a double blow to the Lordship in that demographic collapse in England undermined the tax-base of the English crown and created opportunities for returning colonists. Tidal metaphors seem irresistible: islands too often find themselves subject to wider ebbs and flows.

The English Lordship in Ireland around 1300 is best understood in an archipelagic framework. Edward I's 'British' empire was bound together by an

5 B. Donovan and D. Edwards, 'British Sources for Irish History before 1485: A Preliminary Handlist of Documents Held in Local and Specialised Repositories', *Analecta Hibernica*, 37 (1998), 199.
6 M. Haren, 'Two Hungarian Pilgrims', in Haren and de Pontfarcy (eds.), *Medieval Pilgrimage to St Patrick's Purgatory*, 120; C. Potvin (ed.), *Oeuvres de Ghillebert de Lannoy, voyageur, diplomate et moraliste* (Louvain: Lefever, 1878), 169–73.

Anglo-French aristocracy with property interests in England, the Welsh and Scottish marches, and Ireland. Personal foibles and dynastic happen-chance played some part in the decline. The few kings who had the ambition and capacity of Edward I found theatres of war and conquest in France rather than Ireland. Dynastic misfortunes and political mistakes led to a high turn-over in aristocratic families, the partition of inheritances, confiscations of estates, and the loss of land on a contracting frontier. The decline in revenues from land and the increase in transaction costs prompted many landowners to see consolidation in England as the wisest course. Though it created space for the Butler earldom of Ormond, the Geraldine earldoms of Kildare and Desmond, and a number of baronies, this shake-out reduced the number of magnates involved in the maintenance of the Lordship. The loss of popu-lation meant that Anglo-Ireland lacked critical mass at all levels of society. One consequence was the loss of French as a spoken language in the colony and the early emergence of Middle English as a literary vernacular. Despite the revelation of the English Lordship's vulnerability in 1315, the English of Ireland were not lacking in assurance. Still, there was disappointment when Edward III's plans for a major expedition were abandoned to meet chal-lenges in Scotland and France. Even before the Black Death, the viability of the Lordship was compromised by the revival of Gaelic power in southern Leinster, and the loss of secure lines of communication with Kilkenny and Cork as the bridge over the Barrow at Leighlin became less defensible. The MacMurrough, Gaelic kings of Leinster were able to extend their influence and prestige by both traditional means and by securing concessions from the colonial government. It was a recipe for insecurity, misunderstanding and volatility.[7]

Edward III's claim to the crown of France was another factor in England's relative disengagement with Ireland. The refocusing of English military power and resources on the Continent, along with commitments in relation to Scotland, had some tendency to redefine relations between England, the English colony and Gaelic Ireland. Most basically, it had an impact on the Irish economy, enlarging the market for Irish commodities and services. The demand for ships and provisions significantly expanded the field of enterprise and opportunity. Though not on the scale of the Welsh, Irish soldiers served in Edward III's war in Scotland and France. A large force, including a company of hobelars under Domnall MacMurrough, was raised

---

7 R. Frame, 'Two Kings in Leinster: The Crown and the MicMhurchadha in the Fourteenth Century', in Barry *et al.* (eds.), *Colony and Frontier in Medieval Ireland*, 173–4.

in Ireland for an attack on Scotland in 1335. The king's bonding with the aristocracy in war included the mentoring of the young earls of Ormond and Kildare. In so far as they were motivated by personal glory and dynastic aggrandisement rather than national advantage, the Plantagenets could be more generous in their dealings with local elites and in the patronage of local cultures. The personal and dynastic dimension to Edward III's empire-building informed the creation of fiefdoms for his sons, including the duchy of Aquitaine for Edward, the Black Prince, and the possibility of Ireland for his third son Lionel. Edward III's loosely 'imperial' style of kingship of the 1340s to 1360s may explain the increasing tendency in Ireland to acknowledge the status of Gaelic lords as chiefs of their nations and even some forbearance in their use of royal titles.

After making peace with France in 1360 Edward III was able to respond to Anglo-Irish appeals for a major expedition. He sent his son Lionel, duke of Clarence, with a large force paid for by the English parliament. Lionel's wife, Elizabeth de Burgh, was titular countess of Ulster and lady of Trim, providing him with his own resources in Ireland. The young prince presided over the introduction of measures that were bold and ideological. The transfer of the capital from Dublin to Carlow, with the aim of securing communications with the south, was less a practical proposition than a measure of desperation. Another initiative was more clearly ideological. The Statute of Kilkenny of 1366 drew on earlier measures to shore up the English colony by prohibiting assimilation with the Gaelic Irish. The statute was complemented by moves in England, which received statutory expression in 1380, to compel holders of land and office in Ireland to reside in Ireland. The English government even requested the Pope in 1381 not to promote Irish clerks who did not speak English.[8] Overall, it is hard to assess the success of the Statute of Kilkenny and the measures against absentees, the latter often becoming a means of raising money from fines and licences. They certainly must have served to firm up identities and sharpen identity politics. After the duke of Clarence's departure in 1366, though, Ireland saw a succession of governors who lacked the prestige and resources to maintain the Lordship. Most of them were English knights who had learned their trade in the French wars. The most enterprising and energetic was Sir William Windsor, whose exactions and corrupt practices generated resentment and opposition.

---

8 J. A. Watt, 'The Papacy and Ireland in the Fifteenth Century', in R. B. Dobson (ed.), *The Church, Politics and Patronage in the Fifteenth Century* (Gloucester: Sutton Publishing, 1984), 135–6.

The reign of Richard II saw major interventions in Ireland that, though responding to problems identified in the colony, reflected political developments in England and the king's own projections.[9] Edmund Mortimer, earl of March, who had married Clarence's daughter and heiress, had the prestige and resources to help to stabilise the colony. After his early death in 1381, the wardship of his son and control of the inheritance were taken over by a consortium of English magnates. Richard II's interest in Ireland was nourished by frustrations in England and lofty conceptions of his *imperium*. In October 1385 he granted Ireland as a palatinate to his favourite Robert de Vere, according him the title of marquis of Dublin. In 1386 he was created duke of Ireland, and, according to a contemporary chronicle, a crown was in prospect.[10] A political crisis in England, in which the new duke was the first casualty, led to Richard's subjection to conciliar rule and the attainder of key advisors.[11] After the restoration of his authority in 1389, though, Richard appointed Sir John Stanley, De Vere's deputy, as justiciar of Ireland. Over the next two years he commanded a large force comprising men from north-west England and a sizeable number of Gaels. In 1393 Richard allowed Roger Mortimer, earl of March, to enter his inheritance and sent him to Ireland as lieutenant. His own expedition to Ireland in 1394–5 was a major enterprise. He succeeded in reducing Art MacMurrough, king of Leinster, to obedience and securing the submission of other kings and chieftains. The policy of bringing the Gaelic kings into direct relationship with the king and using them to win over lesser chieftains was novel and, if sustained over time, may have met with the success of similar moves by the Scottish kings in the Highlands. Richard planted English nobles and royal retainers in Ireland. He saw his close friend Thomas Mowbray, earl of Nottingham, established at Carlow. Janico Dartasso, a Navarrese squire, who loyally served Richard and his father for thirty years, gained a wife and estate near Dublin that attached his family to the Lordship for a century or more. Roger Coly, another retainer, was encouraged to build a castle at 'Coly's town' near Cork.[12]

9 M. Bennett, 'Richard II and the Wider Realm', in A. Goodman and J. L. Gillespie (eds.), *Richard II: The Art of Kingship* (Oxford University Press, 1999), 202–4.

10 *Thomæ Walsingham Historia Anglicana 1272–1422*, ed. H. T. Riley, 2 vols. (London: RS, 1863–4), ii, 148.

11 P. Crooks, 'The "Calculus of Faction" and Richard II's Duchy of Ireland, *c*.1382–9', in N. Saul (ed.), *Fourteenth Century England V* (Woodbridge: Boydell Press, 2008), 95–6.

12 S. Walker, 'Janico Dartasso: Chivalry, Nationality and the Man-at-Arms', *History*, 84 (1991), 31–51; TNA C 1 / 68 / 71; *Handbook and Select Calendar of Sources for Medieval Ireland*, 140.

Richard returned to England with his reputation greatly enhanced. Philippe de Mézières, who penned a letter calling on him to marry the daughter of a French princess and lead Christendom on crusade, hailed him as 'King of Great Britain ... and Lord of Great Ireland'.[13] The renewal of hostilities in Ireland, culminating in Mortimer's death in a skirmish in summer 1398, led to his return in force in 1399. By this stage he had executed or exiled the English nobles who had usurped his regality in the late 1380s and had the resources to pursue his ambitions. His creation of five new dukedoms, his elevation of the earldom of Chester to a principality, and his acceptance of William Scrope's right to use the title king of Man, seem of a piece with his Irish creations in 1385–6. With another Mortimer minority providing scope as well as need for change, he had in mind a new settlement in Ireland, planning, according to one chronicler, to make his nephew Thomas Holland, king of Ireland.[14] He took the regalia to Ireland and it was rumoured that he planned to tyrannise England from Chester, Wales and Ireland. Walsingham claims that Richard had delusions of grandeur and was drawn to prophecies of an imperial destiny. Extant in a book of model letters, written by a royal clerk in the mid-1390s, is a fantasy about his conquest of Ireland leading on to his recovery of the Holy Land. It reflects a prophetic tradition that was still being mobilised in Ireland in 1515.[15]

Ireland in the Anglo-Zone

In summer 1399 Richard II returned from Ireland to face a kingdom in revolt. Henry of Bolingbroke led a coalition that forced Richard to abdicate and raised him to the throne as Henry IV. The new regime seems to have had little cause for concern about its position in Ireland. There is no evidence of loyalist sentiment to Richard, the only king since John to visit the country. The officials and clerks in Dublin and the Anglo-Irish lords, who had seen him at close quarters, presumably shared the reservations of their English counterparts. Richard's advancement of favourites and indulgence of the Gaelic kings cannot have endeared him to the Anglo-Irish. Sir John Stanley, a key figure in the military establishment in Ireland, was an early defector to Henry's

13 Philippe de Mézières, *Letter to King Richard II: A Plea Made in 1395 for Peace between England and France*, ed. G. W. Coopland (Liverpool University Press, 1975), 101.

14 *The Chronicle of Adam Usk 1377–1421*, ed. C. Given-Wilson (Oxford University Press, 1997), 76–7.

15 BL Harleian MS. 3988, fos. 39–41; M. Bennett, *Richard II and the Revolution of 1399* (Stroud: Sutton Publishing, 1999), 73–4; *SP, Henry VIII*, ii part III, 30–1.

cause. Janico Dartasso, who won respect by being the last to remove Richard's badge, was soon making himself useful to the new order. Henry's immediate concerns in Ireland were the safe return of his eldest son, the future Henry V, a captive in Trim castle, and the royal treasure. He reappointed Stanley as lieutenant in 1399 and then in 1401 granted the office to his second son Thomas of Lancaster, duke of Clarence. There was little hope, however, that the English parliament would provide the resources for a major expedition. The rebellion of Owain Glyn Dŵr in Wales was a major distraction. His appeal to Gaelic chiefs to make common cause, though it went unheeded, would have caused additional concern.

If the new reign was characterised by a narrowing of horizons, and a lack of interest in Ireland, it also disclosed the cultural convergence between the English in Ireland and the English in England. The sense of a need to defend their language and legal status made the Anglo-Irish precocious in the expression of their Englishness and in advancing their rights. Given backbone by facsimiles of English institutions in Church and state, they developed a political identity that, notwithstanding the inevitable factionalism and local rivalries, was surprisingly robust.[16] During the middle decades of the fourteenth century, when the English parliament grew in institutional strength, the Irish parliament did likewise. The Anglo-Irish proved effective lobbyists. In prosecuting Sir William Windsor, they helped to set the scene for the parliamentary revolt in England in 1376. The two-way traffic of clerks and lawyers pursuing a common *cursus honorum* in Dublin and Westminster helped to develop a common literary and political culture. Walter Brugge, the earliest known owner of *Piers Plowman,* had his copy with him in Trim in 1396. Thomas Cranley, archbishop of Dublin, bought books in Chester and Liverpool en route to Ireland in 1408.[17] Some readers had interests that were reformist, even constitutionalist. An annotation of the *Modus tenendi parliamentum*, dateable to 1409, states that it would be preserved at Cashel, in the centre of the country, for the people of Ireland. James Young, a notary of Dublin, who translated the *Secreta secretorum* in the early 1420s, added thinly veiled reflections on Richard II's failings. The layout and illustration of a local copy of *Piers Plowman* served to highlight the poem's anti-authoritarianism and reformism.[18]

---

16 Frame, *Ireland and Britain*, 147–8.
17 New College, Oxford, MSS. 112 and 122.
18 P. Crooks, 'Representation and Dissent: "Parliamentarianism" and the Structure of Politics in Colonial Ireland *c.*1370–1420', *EHR*, 125 (2010), 30; H. Kerby-Fulton and D. L.

There was a common disposition in Dublin and Westminster, too, towards policies to shore up the Lordship in Ireland by limiting emigration and compelling Irish residents in England to return. Initially the focus of legislative concern was with absentee landowners and office-holders. The constraints on Anglo-Irish families with interests on both sides of the Irish Sea, however, led some to cut their losses in Ireland. After Sir Leonard Carew's death in France in 1368, for example, his heirs made some effort to make good their claims in Ireland but gave up the struggle, at least for a time, around the 1430s.[19] The legislative concern was soon extended to broader population flows. Observing that 'husbandry and tillage' were in decay because of the loss of labour, the Irish parliament in 1410 ruled that ships found to be carrying labourers or servants to England without licence would suffer confiscation. Though deriving some advantage from immigrant labour, the English lords and commons needed little urging to pass laws restricting Irish immigrants. The Glyn Dŵr rebellion prompted severe measures against the Welsh, and Gaels may have been caught in the crossfire. Hostile references to 'wild Irish', however, may not have been narrowly ethnic. Anglo-Irish immigrants were probably young, unruly and easily stigmatised. An act of 1413 ordered the removal of all Irish from England to strengthen the Lordship and suppress disorder in England. Although there were group exemptions, generally for professional and propertied men, no distinction was made between Gaels and Anglo-Irish.[20]

The accession of Henry V marked a new expansionary phase. In prosecuting his grandfather's claims to the French crown, he seemed to be reviving the older-style Plantagenet empire. At the council of Constance his legates secured the status of England as one of the four nations of the Roman obedience by stressing the multiplicity of peoples and languages subject to the English crown. It may have been this 'imperial' projection that inspired his summons of a company of Gaelic hobelars and foot soldiers to the siege of Rouen in 1418 that was well publicised in France.[21] The terms of the Treaty of Troyes in 1420 and Henry VI's succession as king of France in 1422 likewise suggest a Plantagenet conception of empire. Although the war in France also had the character of a national enterprise, especially in Normandy, the English parliament was reluctant to grant subsidies for a war that was not so

---

Despres, *Iconography and the Professional Reader: The Politics of Book Production in the Douce Piers Plowman* (Minneapolis: University of Minnesota Press, 1999), 56–67.

19 TNA SC 8/227/11346.
20 A. Cosgrove, 'The Emergence of the Pale 1399–1447', in *NHI* ii, 553.
21 *The Chronicles of Enguerrand de Monstrelet*, ed. T. Johnes, 2 vols. (London: Longman, 1840), i, 104.

clearly in defence of the realm. The English in Ireland may have gone cool on the war in France more quickly than their cousins in England. The earl of Ormond, who served in the French wars, was concerned about the decline in royal expenditure on the Lordship and critical of measures taken by Sir John Talbot, the lieutenant, to fund his operations. The king's appointment of Ormond as lieutenant in 1420 allowed a further scaling back of English expenditure. It was Ormond's view, reported in the 1430s, that with the money spent in one year in France he would be able, in a few years, to reconquer Ireland (see Map 11).[22]

The parlous state of the Lordship of Ireland reflected a broader malaise in England, where Henry VI and his ministers presided over a bankrupt regime, bitter factional rivalries, and the collapse of the English position in France. English lieutenants, including Edmund Mortimer, whose death in Ireland in 1425 brought an end to his house in the male line, were sent out with limited resources. The economical solution remained the appointment of an Irish magnate as lieutenant, but a local appointee tended to provoke jealousy, factionalism and jobbery. The animosity between Ormond, who often stood in for absentee governors, and a faction attached to the Talbot interest was a running sore in the Lordship into the 1440s. The turnover of English lieutenants at least broadened awareness of Ireland in English governing circles. The administration in Dublin had some success in keeping the king, council and parliament aware of the plight of Ireland. In 1435 Sir Thomas Stanley presented the council's report on the dire state of Ireland and an appeal for a royal expedition to save the Lordship, reportedly reduced to the four obedient counties and a few enclaves in the south and west, hemmed in by Irish enemies and English rebels, and surrounded by seas infested by foreign pirates. The *Libelle of English Policy*, written in the late 1430s, stressed Ireland's desperate plight, detailed its strategic importance and economic potential, and reported Ormond's boast that it could be reconquered. The author, who may have been Anglo-Irish, presented Ireland and England as having common interests, claimed that he was writing another book specifically about Ireland, and declared himself 'sore of heart' at the thought of its loss.[23]

The Anglo-Irish proved well able to air their concerns in the English capital. Given the importance of English law to their identity, they were distressed

22 *The Libelle of Englyshe Polycye. A Poem on the Use of Sea-Power 1436*, ed. G. Warner (Oxford University Press, 1926), 39.

23 *Libelle of Englyshe Polycye*, lines 711–12; M. Bennett, 'The Libelle of English Policy: The Matter of Ireland' in *The Fifteenth Century XV Writing, Records and Rhetoric*, ed. Linda Clark (Woodbridge: Boydell, 2017), 10–11.

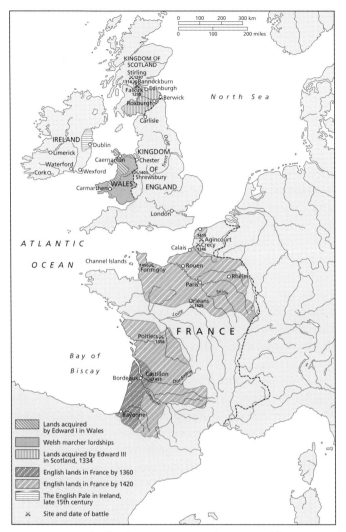

MAP 11. England and its Dominions in the Later Middle Ages.

by moves to exclude Irish students from the Inns of Court.[24] A broader cause of offence was the classification of Irish residents in England as aliens in a new tax in 1439–40. The earl of Ormond and others lobbied the English government to secure acknowledgement in spring 1442 that loyal Irish were

24 P. Brand, 'Irish Law Students and Lawyers in Late Medieval England', *IHS*, 32 (2000), 161–73.

denizens not aliens. Dr Thomas Chace, an English clerk serving as chancellor of Ireland, travelled to London to secure reassurances regarding Irish access to the law schools. Though united on some points, the Anglo-Irish lobby was divided in its attitude to Ormond's reappointment as lieutenant. Archbishop Talbot and his allies drew up articles of impeachment against him. Given the bad blood in the colony, the council in Dublin took the line that an English lord, properly resourced, would be the best candidate. Ormond organised a stout response to the charges and secured the lieutenancy in February 1442. Alarmed by the outcome, the chancellor and treasurer of Ireland fled to England. Thomas FitzGerald, prior of Kilmainham, accused Ormond of treason. In 1445 Londoners relished the spectacle of preparations at Smithfield for a judicial duel between the ageing Irish earl and the pugnacious prior. A marriage between the families brought some closure to the feud between Talbot and Ormond, who died under house arrest shortly afterwards.

The licences issued to men born in Ireland to remain in England in 1394 and the alien subsidy returns of 1440–3 provide valuable data on the Irish in England in the later Middle Ages.[25] The 500 or so men who obtained licences in 1394 were probably a mere fraction of the Irish in England. They did not include the men who served in Ireland or the absentees who did not seek a licence or have it recorded. Henry Chrystede, based in Bristol, was among the former. As a young man in Ireland he had been taken prisoner by a Gaelic chieftain and, while in captivity, he married a Gaelic woman and learned the language. After his return to England, he and his family continued to speak Gaelic at home. He served as an interpreter for Richard II in 1394–5 and as the source of Froissart's account of Ireland.[26] The alien subsidy rolls of the early 1440s hold the promise of a more comprehensive picture. In his study of the returns, Bolton identified only some 706 Irish. After making an allowance for missing returns, including from important centres like Coventry and Oxford, he proposed a 'conservative' estimate of 1,000. For a number of reasons, however, the estimate seems extremely conservative. The implication that the Irish represented only 8 per cent of the foreign taxpayers surely suggests a very significant and systemic under-reportage of the Irish. The returns probably did not capture the migrants who were in transit, in household service or in temporary employment in England. The Anglo-Irish would also have been less visible to the authorities than other aliens and may often have been

25 J. L. Bolton, 'Irish Migration to England in the Late Middle Ages: The Evidence of 1394 and 1440', *IHS*, 32 (2000), 1–21.
26 B. Smith, 'Late Medieval Ireland and the English Connection: Waterford and Bristol, ca. 1360–1460', *Journal of British Studies*, 50 (2011), 565.

able to persuade the collectors that, as denizens, they were exempt. In any case, the records provide mere snapshots of a mobile and fluid community. Robert Sygn, a native of Kilmallock, Limerick, came to England as a page of Sir William Windsor, married, and settled down. In 1410 he claimed exemption from the need for a licence for absence from Ireland on the grounds that he had been living in Yorkshire for forty years.[27] Many of the Anglo-Irish who settled in England from the late fourteenth century would have had children and grandchildren, who, though indisputably English, would have retained Irish connections and perhaps a sense of Anglo-Irish identity. The Carews in Devon, who gave up paying fees for Irish lands that brought no return, were by no means alone in holding on to the memories of their ancestors in Ireland and title deeds to their estates.

The records nonetheless provide important information. The Irish settled mainly in the western counties, presumably reflecting immigration through Bristol, Chester and other western ports. Apart from the Irish in London, they were thin on the ground in the eastern half of England. For some of the tax-payers, details of occupation are given. There were fewer Irish clergymen in England in the 1440s than in 1394. A large number of Irish contributors to the alien subsidy were retailers and craftsmen in small towns and villages. Some of the Irish who were simply described as householders were men of some substance. The database, now digitised online, will allow more analysis and produce new insights.[28] Henry May, a prominent Irish-born merchant of Bristol, paid the alien tax but a number of his known associates seem not to have done. John Chevir, who is listed in the alien subsidy roll as a householder in Dowgate ward, London, was almost certainly the lawyer of that name who was a member of Lincoln's Inn and who disclosed details of the earl of Ormond's case to his brother in Dublin in 1442.[29] Another intriguing case is Nicholas Lacy, listed in 1440 as an Irish householder at Bodenham, Herefordshire, the seat of Sir Walter Devereux, and in 1443 as married to an English woman and living elsewhere. He can probably be identified with Nicholas Lacy (alias Lassy) of Chester who was granted an allowance from the cocket of Drogheda in 1444 and who in a draft petition to Henry VI, sought, as a reward for his services in writing tracts for the 'weal of the realm', a grant in freehold tenure of the lands that the Lacy family had conquered in Ireland.[30]

27 K. W. Nicholls, 'Gaelic Society and Economy in the High Middle Ages', in *NHI* ii, 527.
28 'England's immigrants 1330–1450': www.hrionline.ac.uk/englandsimmigrants.
29 *PKCI*, 287; *CPR, 1441–6*, 3.
30 Oxford, Bodleian Library MS. Lyell 32, fos. 28r–28v; Bennett, '*Libelle of English Policy*', 11–15.

The English of Ireland proved resilient. Though the challenges to the colony were real, they were by no means terminal. It would be a mistake to assume that the Gaelic princes and chiefs were intent on the destruction of the Lordship. Often enough at war among themselves, they were eager to do deals with the authorities in Dublin and English magnates. In extending their sway over parts of the colony, they did not seek to displace the men working the land. They needed their agricultural expertise, and their access to markets and money. The Anglo-Irish, too, recognised their dependence on the native Irish to deliver important commodities from the interior – fish, horses and cattle, hides and linen – and to provide other services in the labour-strapped colony. Even in Louth, one of the 'four obedient counties', there was a great deal of routine accommodation and assimilation in the century after the Black Death.[31] At a time when England seemed to close doors, the Anglo-Irish were generally able to avail themselves of opportunities there and draw advantage from the connection. Richard duke of York, who took up the lieutenancy of Ireland in 1449, brought new hope. A prince of the blood, he was also, as heir of the Mortimers, one of their own. 'It shall never be chronicled', he declared in 1450, 'that Ireland was lost by my negligence.'[32] A political crisis prompted his return to England in the same year and factional rivalry and civil war led to his seeking refuge in Ireland in 1460 and using it as platform from which to launch a bid for the English crown. Over the next thirty years Ireland was frequently drawn into the bitter conflict in England and occasionally found itself in the eye of the storm. Overall, though, it was a period when English Ireland, itself quite fragmented, held aloof and looked for leadership closer to home.

During the governorship of the 'great' earl of Kildare, the Anglo-Irish community around Dublin bunkered down. A defensible line, the Pale, was created that excluded the less defensible western parts of the four loyal counties. The institution of the Fraternity of St George perhaps helped to stabilise the Anglo-Irish community. The linkage between Dublin and Chester, and their respective out-ports, remained important. There were still profits to be made from the transport and provisioning of officials and soldiers crossing the Irish Sea. The merchants of Dublin and the Pale, moreover, proved resourceful in seeking out new opportunities. They were well placed to build connections in England for the purposes of trade, sharing market information, and building capacity. Transnational partnerships made it easier to exploit differences in

---

31 Smith, *Crisis and Survival*, 183–7.
32 Cosgrove, 'Emergence of the Pale', 561.

market conditions, exchange rates and regulatory regimes between the two countries. The volume of Irish trade with north-west England was increasing, with wool and linen in demand in the midlands, especially Coventry, and northern England. Irish merchants found it convenient to become freemen of Chester, a status that eased their way elsewhere in England. Merchants from Chester and northern England likewise took up residence, temporarily or otherwise, in Irish towns, and established their own guild specifically in Dublin. A remarkable illustration of the scale of networking and the level of trust between Anglo-Irish and English merchants is an alleged conspiracy by some eighty of them to export to Ireland 200 ounces of silver each, produce counterfeits of English royals, and pass them off in Chester. About three-quarters were Anglo-Irish, mainly from Dublin and Drogheda. The English group included merchants from Wigan, Manchester, Stockport and Bradford, all developing as centres of textile manufacture, as well as Chester.[33]

The Anglo-Irish of the port-enclaves of southern and western Ireland looked to their own interests in trade with England and Europe. The bond between Waterford, commanding a river-system that carried goods in and out of a large hinterland, and Bristol, a major supplier of Ireland's needs and entrepôt for the trans-shipment of its commodities, was particularly strong. Henry May, an Irish-born Bristol merchant, traded extensively with Spain and Portugal, and had kinsmen and partners based in London and elsewhere. Needless to say, the merchants found the vicissitudes of English politics challenging. Prospering through the patronage of the Lancastrian earls of Ormond, May came to grief in the early 1460s. The city of Waterford proved politically adept. Timely support for Edward IV brought the city new privileges. More generally, the men of Waterford did what it took to secure their business interests, including capturing a London-owned ship that had carried pilgrims from New Ross to Santiago.[34] Walter Lincoln, a leading Bristol merchant, who imported fish from Ireland, brought wine and other goods from Gascony and Spain, and even dabbled in Icelandic trade, was probably a native of Waterford. At his death in 1484 he held Waterford's new charter for safe-keeping in his Bristol home. His Irish affiliation is further suggested by the concern in his will that his property in Waterford should remain in his family and that his anniversary would be celebrated forever in the cathedral, according to the city's custom.[35] Waterford again demonstrated its ability to pick

---

33 TNA CHES 25/15, mm. 30d–31.
34 *CPR, 1476–85*, 78–9; Smith, 'Late Medieval Ireland', 546–65.
35 W. Childs, 'Irish Merchants and Seamen in Late Medieval England', *IHS*, 32 (2000), 37–42; TNA C 1/65/215; *Handbook and Select Calendar of Sources for Medieval Ireland*, 138;

winners by its stout support for the Tudor regime in 1487 when Kildare and other notables in Dublin welcomed the Yorkist pretender Lambert Simnel and arranged his coronation as 'Edward VI'.[36]

Ireland Inside Out

The narrative of Perellós gives the impression of a Gaelic heartland that was doubly insulated. The theme is that of the knight passing through a series of thresholds of escalating danger. If the narrative echoes themes of chivalric romance, it was grounded in a reality constructed by the two cultures of medieval Ireland. The topography of Ireland lent a hand and the Gaels cultivated its impenetrability. The English likewise set boundaries culturally as well as physically. In colonising the lowlands and controlling the main river crossings, estuaries and harbours, the strategy was to contain the Irish in their fastnesses and, ultimately, to coax or starve them into submission. If the strategy were ever realisable, it became unviable in the later Middle Ages. After all, the Irish controlled much of the coastline of Munster, Connacht and Ulster. Gaelic chiefs owned ships – MacCarthy had his own admiral in 1404 – and engaged in trading, raiding and naval warfare.[37] Ulster's proximity to western Scotland and the Isles provided unmediated lines of communication and supply. Even in Leinster, the corner of Ireland most exposed to English power, it took the largest army ever brought across the Irish Sea to regain control of the vital link between Dublin and southern Ireland and to bring Art MacMurrough to terms in 1394–5. As observers reported, it was a matter of boxing him into his heartland, capturing his cattle and making it impossible for him to be re-provisioned by sea.[38] Even then, the achievement proved transitory. In any case there was no clear frontier between English and Gaelic Ireland. Between the English Lordship – itself an archipelago of enclaves – and an expanding sphere of Gaelic lordship and predation, there were frontier zones, characterised by varying degrees of assimilation, accommodation and violence. The legislative measures seeking to limit cultural contact and assimilation may have helped firm up the Englishry in their heartlands. In most

M. Carus-Wilson, *The Overseas Trade of Bristol in the Later Middle Ages* (Bristol: Bristol Record Society, 1937), 120, 248, 252, 254, 256, 276, 280, 283; TNA PROB 11/7/77.

36 M. Bennett, *Lambert Simnel and the Battle of Stoke* (Gloucester: Sutton Publishing, 1987), 66–7, 126–7.

37 *AFM*, iv, 781.

38 Lydon, 'Richard II's Expeditions to Ireland', in Crooks (ed.), *Government, War and Society*, 227–8.

parts of Ireland, even in the parts of the 'obedient counties', they seemed neither practicable nor even desirable to peoples that were, to some degree, interdependent.

The Gaelic world was more self-contained than the English. Economically, it was more self-sufficient. The Gaels were proud of their way of life and had a more limited range of needs. Their social and political organisation had sources of instability, especially inheritance customs that created tensions within and between elite families.[39] Though the Irish annals show limited interest in the outside world, there were cultural developments that can only be understood in relation to wider influences. Irish military culture developed in the wars against and alongside the English, notably in respect of castle-building, and through the settlement of galloglass, Norse-Scots mercenaries, and the use of 'redshanks', lightly armed Scots warriors.[40] The Gaelic renaissance, as with all renaissances, was no mere resurrection of the old culture. The writing down of bardic poetry and orally transmitted knowledge involved selection and adaptation. The revival owed a great deal of its impetus to the sense of Ireland being the *fons et origo* of Gaelic culture in the broader Gaelic world that included western Scotland. The very fact that the revival took place in the wider zone led to the working out of a simpler and more generally serviceable vernacular.[41] The Gaelic bards were also responding to the stimulus of continental literary trends, paralleling and drawing on French and English themes and styles. Many important works were produced at the points of intersection between the various cultures, especially the households of Gaelic princes and Anglo-Irish magnates, many of which were ethnically and culturally mixed. The practice of hostage-taking on both sides of the frontier often involved some cultural transmission.

The Christian religion likewise connected Ireland with the wider world. Ireland's very insularity and introversion can perhaps be associated with distinctive patterns of travel and engagement with the world. A relatively tight society, in which the higher ranks over-produced themselves, not least through the recognition of illegitimate children, necessarily produced tensions and blocks to ambition that were often resolved by withdrawal or exile, temporary or otherwise. Similar pressures pushed young men into the Church. In Gaelic Ireland many of the benefices were quasi-hereditary. During the fifteenth century Irish priests found church livings in English-speaking areas,

---

39 Nicholls, 'Gaelic Society', 397–8.
40 K. Simms, 'Gaelic Warfare in the Middle Ages', in T. Bartlett and K. Jeffery (eds.), *A Military History of Ireland* (Cambridge University Press, 1996), 112–15.
41 J. Carney, 'Literature in Irish, 1169–1534', in *NHI* ii, 704.

often opening up avenues of migration for lay kinsmen.[42] More striking is the number of Gaelic clerks, many the sons of priests, who studied at Oxford. In 1365 John O'Ferrall and five Gaelic companions raised a loan of six marks in Oxford by pledging a commentary on the decretals. Successful churchmen, like John Ó Gráda, archbishop of Tuam, presumably supported the studies of kinsmen. Some went on to study at continental universities. Matthew alias Macrobius O'Driscol [Ó hEidirsceóil] pursued higher studies at Vienna prior to his first benefice in Cork in 1394.[43] The Irish Church had close relations with the papal curia, and the bishops of the Gaelic dioceses generally obtained their sees by papal provision. At the beginning of the Schism some bishops in western Ireland briefly held to Avignon before following their colleagues into the Roman fold.[44]

Traditions of *peregrinatio* were deep and broad on both sides of the cultural divide. The reputation of St Patrick's Purgatory was still on the rise in the fourteenth century. Gaelic pilgrims also made their way to the major shrines in Dublin. Santiago de Compostela, in distant Galicia, was popular in Ireland, with large groups, women as well as men, sailing from Irish ports. Margaret O'Carroll [Mairgréag Ó Cearbhaill], celebrated for her patronage and piety, set out with a large company in 1445. Irish pilgrims were also commonly found on the road to Rome or seeking passage in Venice for the Holy Land. Margery Kemp met up with a broken-backed Irish beggar in Venice with whom she travelled to Rome. In 1335 the erection of the great cross in the market place in Kilkenny inspired many people to be branded with the sign of a cross as token of their intent to go to the Holy Land.[45] In 1413 Christian Oferagaid, a veteran of five pilgrimages to Rome, likewise set out as a pilgrim from Louth to the Sepulchre of Christ.[46] Among the Irish clergy, the friars were indefatigable travellers and had strong international links. As men of learning and popular preachers, they represented the major agents for the transmission of European culture to rural Ireland. The most striking evidence for the religious vitality of Ireland is its embrace of monastic reform and a series of new foundations. In 1474, for example, Aed *Ruad* O'Donnell and his mother Finola O'Connor [Ní Chonchobair] were responsible for founding the influential

42 S. Booker, 'Irish Clergy and the Diocesan Church in the "Four Obedient Shires" of Ireland, *c*. 1400–*c*. 1540', *IHS*, 39 (2014), 186–95.

43 BL Royal MS. 10 E V–VI; Watt, *Church and the Two Nations*, 210–11; A. B. Emden, *A Biographical Register of the University of Oxford to A.D. 1500*, 3 vols. (Oxford University Press, 1957–9), ii, 1394.

44 Watt, 'Papacy and Ireland', 138–9.

45 *Clyn*, 218.

46 Smith, *Crisis and Survival*, 136.

Observant Franciscan house at Donegal.[47] A larger sense of the cultural impact of the order is the impressive list of books available, including recent sermon collections from Italy, in the friary library at Youghal.[48]

A shift of Europe's focus to the Atlantic rim underpinned the Gaelic renaissance. The remarkable increase in the value of the fisheries around the coast of Ireland was an early sign of this epoch-making shift. Fish had long been a major Irish export, but the movement of shoals of herring southwards filled nets on a scale previously unimaginable and provided a huge boost to the Irish economy. The native Irish were not able to take the lead in the exploitation of the new fisheries, but there were opportunities for the coastal communities that provisioned, or preyed on, the visiting fishing fleets. Around 1450 a Bristol merchant engaged in fishing off the Atlantic coast captured a Spanish vessel but then lost the prize to men from Kinsale who had the nerve to offer the goods for sale in Bristol.[49] The increasing volume of shipping stimulated the expansion of Ireland's trade. Irish commodities, old and new, found their way out through a greater range of ports and ships. Irish woollen cloth known as 'serge' was well regarded; Gaelic Irish mantles were a fashion statement in some circles; and Irish linen cloth brought good prices. Exports brought to the west coast of Ireland salt, wine and more precious commodities from the wider world. A boat arriving in Ballyshannon carried the plague that caused great mortality in Fermanagh, Tyconnell and Ulster in 1478.[50]

Economic developments in the late fifteenth century turned Ireland inside out, and accentuated its centrifugal tendencies. They weakened the agricultural core of the English colony relative to the pastoral economy of Gaelic Ireland and provided a stimulus to maritime trade, especially along the Atlantic rim.[51] Ulster gained strength from its links across the northern channel to southwest Scotland and the Western Isles. Along the western and south-western coast, new opportunities were realisable through strategic collaboration between the Anglo-English and the Gaels. The Anglo-Irish on the eastern seaboard, increasingly divided into enclaves, looked more to England. There is little evidence of a narrowing of the gap between the two stock cultures. The Gaels and English continued to be set apart by language, dress and lifestyles. More remarkable perhaps is the religious divide. The Church

---

47 Hall, *Women and the Church*, 61.

48 C. Ó Clabaigh, *The Franciscans in Ireland 1400–1534* (Dublin: Four Courts Press, 2002), 158–80.

49 Carus-Wilson, *Overseas Trade of Bristol*, 93–4.

50 O'Neill, *Merchants and Mariners*, 67; J. Hardiman, *The History of the Town and County of Galway* (Dublin: Folds, 1820), 70–6; *AFM*, iv, 1107.

51 K. Down, 'Colonial Society and Economy in the High Middle Ages', *NHI* ii, 490.

authorities operated a double standard, treating clerical concubinage and illegitimacy more indulgently in Gaelic Ireland than in the Lordship. The Observant movement strengthened the Gaelic embrace of monasticism, while the English focus remained on the parish, guilds and chantries. Gerald fitz Thomas FitzGerald, earl of Kildare, deputy almost continuously from 1477 to 1513, had some success in managing the complex politics of a divided Ireland. Combining private wealth and public authority, he patronised both cultures, built a network of allies and dependants among both nations, and was able to deliver a measure of stability and order at modest cost. His prestige and political skills, however, could not mask the deep divisions and the centrifugal tendencies that prevented the economic and political integration necessary for even minimally effective and consensual government.

New Worlds

In the decades around 1500 the trends that encouraged English disengagement from Ireland and allowed greater scope for Irish agency were less marked and even beginning to go in reverse. Population recovery, economic growth and state-building in England were to have adverse implications for the neighbouring island. It is by no means the case, however, that in terms of its relations with England the sixteenth century merely picked up on where the thirteenth century ended. The intervening period witnessed developments that in the long run served to build England's capacity for empire. The shift away from agriculture towards pastoralism meant that the Irish economy lacked ballast, and even the capacity to feed itself, with a terrible famine in 1491. The boom in trade in the late fifteenth century was largely in raw materials for the more advanced economies of Western Europe, including England. The experiences of two centuries of conflict and accommodation, response and counter-response, obviously shaped subsequent relations between the English government and the peoples of Ireland. The growth of a body of discourse about Ireland is particularly notable. The thread of alarmism about the plight of the colony, the dangers of assimilation and degeneracy, and the barbarism of the native Irish, remained potent. It was accentuated by concerns in England about the use of Ireland by autocratic kings, ambitious magnates and foreign powers to undermine its independence and subvert its liberties. Even more important, perhaps, was a growing body of writing from the fourteenth century onwards that served colonial ends: letters advising absentee landlords on conditions in Ireland; reports on the state of the Lordship and recommendations for action; and a poem proposing remedies for Ireland's ills, including a new city in the centre of Ireland at Athlone, built on both sides of the Shannon, with a university to teach the liberal arts, canon and civil law, and the common law.[52] The mapping of Ireland, its objectification in discourse and analysis, helped to forge a distinctly modern colonial relationship.

The known world was becoming larger around 1500. Improvements in communications, however, were making Europe smaller. In 1491 Henry VII had intelligence of Perkin Warbeck's arrival in Cork in a matter of days. The growth of commerce obviously encouraged the flow of news and information, drawing Ireland, even its inner recesses, more firmly into the European system. Antonio di Giovanni Mannini was one of many Italians who did business in Ireland. Early in 1412, he sent papers, including an account of his visit to St Patrick's Purgatory, to a colleague in London who forwarded them to Florence, where they arrived less than seven weeks later.[53] Ireland was stitched surprisingly closely into the fabric of Christendom, given the profile of the Irish as pilgrims, 'Rome-runners', and supporters of Observant monasticism. The links with the wider world are often only fleetingly revealed. A lawsuit in the early fifteenth century reveals that Donatus O'Grada, a Benedictine monk in Vienna, had given up his vows and returned home to County Clare to take over the hereditary coarbship (guardianship of church lands) of the parish of Tuamgrancy.[54] Though many religious institutions went unreformed in Gaelic Ireland, St Patrick's Purgatory itself was closed down by papal order after claims made by a Dutch pilgrim, a canon of Eymstadt.[55] Apart from pilgrimages by sea to Santiago, Ireland's contact with the Continent mainly involved travel through England. The fact that several Irish bishops died in London suggests that it was common to have a layover and conduct business in the English capital on the way to and from Rome. In making his pilgrimage to Rome in 1512, Aed the son of Aed *Ruad* O'Donnell spent sixteen weeks in London both on his way and on his return.[56] He would have had the chance to consult William Tynbygh, prior of Charterhouse and reputedly the holiest man in London at this time. A Dubliner, he had found his way to the Holy Land around 1470. Imprisoned by the Saracens and despairing of his life, he recalled the picture of St

---

52 TNA E 30/1536; Frame, *English Lordship,* 35–6; Bryan, *Gerald FitzGerald,* 17–22; BL, Add. MS. 4792, fols. 99r–110v, at fol. 107v; Bennett, *'Libelle of English Policy',* 17–2.
53 Haren, 'Two Hungarian Pilgrims', 120.
54 J. A. Watt, 'Gaelic Polity and Cultural Identity', *NHI* ii, 366–7.
55 M. Haren, 'The Close of the Medieval Pilgrimage: The Papal Suppression and its Aftermath', in Haren and de Pontfarcy (eds.), *Medieval Pilgrimage to St Patrick's Purgatory,* 190–5.
56 *AFM,* v, 1313, 1315.

Catharine in his father's chapel and prayed to her for his deliverance. While he slept that night, he was miraculously transported home to Ireland. He immediately resolved to give up the world and fearing his family's opposition fled to London and became a Carthusian monk.[57]

Ireland still remained at the edge of the old world. The Irish were presumably among the first to note the movement of herring into the seas surrounding the British archipelago and to become aware of the expanding Atlantic frontier. There can only have been a few degrees of separation between the Lynches of Galway and Christopher Columbus: in 1492 Leonard Lynch sued a Genoese merchant for the cost of 6,000 bales of linen cloth and in 1493 James Lynch FitzStephen had a close friendship with a merchant in Cadiz who sent his son to stay with him in Galway.[58] Generally, Ireland was close to the end of the line in terms of news and novelties. *Mandeville's Travels*, a European bestseller since the 1360s, was not translated into Gaelic until 1475. Still, the men of Ulster were treated to at least one exotic spectacle in 1472. For some obscure reason, Edward IV sent a camel to Ireland, presumably one of the camels brought to England by the patriarch of Antioch in 1466. Pilgrims to St Patrick's Purgatory brought news of the outside world. In 1516 a French knight brought ordnance as a gift for O'Donnell that was subsequently used in an attack on Sligo.[59] Irish travellers likewise provided their compatriots with windows on the world. A Gaelic contemporary of Prior Tynbygh was arguably the greatest Irish intellect since Richard Fitz Ralph. Maurice O'Fihely, a Franciscan from Galway or Cork, studied at Oxford before moving on to pursue a doctorate in theology at Padua. A champion of the philosophy of Duns Scotus, he was appointed archbishop of Tuam in 1506 but remained in Italy until 1512, when after the fifth Lateran council he headed home but died at Galway before he could reach his see. Most interesting in terms of Ireland's place in the history of the printed book is his collaboration with printers in Venice. He edited the works of Duns Scotus for publication and he himself was the first living Irish author to appear in print. In seeing his *Enchiridion Fidei* through the press in Venice in 1505, he was obviously thinking of his homeland when he drafted the dedication to 'the serene prince' the earl of Kildare.[60]

---

57 L. Hendriks, *The London Charterhouse, its Monks and its Martyrs* (London: Kegan Paul, 1889), 69–71.

58 O'Neill, *Merchants and Mariners*, 67; Hardiman, *History of the Town and County of Galway*, 70–6.

59 *AFM*, v, 1335; C. L. Scofield, *Life and Reign of Edward IV*, 2 vols. (London: Cass, 1967), i, 400: Haren, 'Close of Medieval Pilgrimage', 200.

60 S. F. Brown, 'Ó Fithcheallaigh, Muiris (d. 1513), *ODNB*.

PART III

RELIGION, ECONOMY AND CULTURE: 1000–1550

13

The Church, 1050–1460

COLMÁN Ó CLABAIGH

FROM the early eleventh century Irish ecclesiastics were drawn into greater contact with their colleagues in England and elsewhere in Europe. Several pilgrimages to Rome by high-ranking religious and secular figures are recorded from the late tenth century onwards. By the late eleventh century a community of Irish monks, the monastery of the Holy Trinity of the Scots, existed in Rome where it catered for the needs of pilgrims and maintained an Irish presence in the city. After six centuries of silence regular correspondence between Ireland and the papacy recommenced, a development that reflected the confidence with which the reforming See of Peter asserted its authority across Europe. This is evident in the exhortation addressed by Gregory VII to Tairdelbach Ua Briain sometime between 1074 and 1085 in which he invoked apostolic authority to urge the reform of Irish Church affairs.[1] Irish pilgrim traffic through Central Europe led to the establishment of a number of monastic foundations in German-speaking lands. By the early eleventh century Cologne hosted two Irish Benedictine communities, and recent research indicates that Dúnán (Donatus), the first bishop of Dublin, had been a monk in one of these houses. The foundation relics of Dublin's newly erected Holy Trinity Cathedral included a significant number that had been brought from Cologne, and the cathedral's surviving martyrology contains many entries commemorating saints venerated in Cologne and Metz. The most important of these Irish foundations formed a congregation known as the *Schottenklöster*, discussed below.

Links with England through the Hiberno-Norse settlements at Dublin, Limerick and Waterford provided another important external point of contact, particularly as most of the early bishops of these cities sought episcopal consecration at the hands of successive archbishops of Canterbury to whom they swore canonical obedience as suffragans.[2] The earliest recorded

---

1 *Pontificia Hibernica*, i, 7–8.
2 Flanagan, *Transformation of the Irish Church*, 6–7.

occurrence of this practice was in 1074 when the bishop-elect of Dublin, Gilla Pátraic, was consecrated by Archbishop Lanfranc who, in 1085, also ordained his successor, Donngus Ua hAingliu. St Anselm, Lanfranc's successor in Canterbury, continued the practice and in 1096 ordained Samuel Ua hAingliu as bishop of Dublin and Máel Isú Ua hAinmire as the first known bishop of Waterford/Lismore. All three had been monks in English Benedictine houses before their consecrations: Donngus at Christ Church priory, Canterbury; his nephew Samuel at St Albans; while Máel Isú had been a monk at Winchester. Both Lanfranc and Anselm took a keen interest in Church affairs through-out Ireland and Britain, partly to promote reform, and partly to bolster their cause in the dispute with the archbishops of York over the ecclesiastical primacy of England. In 1072 Lanfranc informed Pope Alexander II that his predecessors had formerly exercised 'primacy over the church of York, over the whole island called Britain, as well as over Ireland'. The surviving letters of both archbishops to Irish secular and ecclesiastical leaders demonstrate their interest in ecclesiastical reform. Writing to Tairdelbach Ua Briain, king of Munster, in 1074 Lanfranc expressed concern about irregularities in the celebration of baptism and the conduct of episcopal consecrations. He also condemned the excessive number of Irish bishops and their willingness to confer holy orders in return for payment as well as a general laxity concerning sexual ethics, which he excoriated as a 'law of marriage which is rather a law of fornication'.[3] The relative ease with which divorces occurred and Gaelic propensity for marriages within the forbidden degrees of kindred would cause reformers concern throughout the twelfth century and for the rest of the Middle Ages.

St Anselm's Irish correspondents included Gillebertus (or Gille), the first bishop of Limerick from c.1106, and the first papal legate in Ireland. Little is known of his background or education, although he had spent time in Rouen where he and Anselm had met. His treatise *De uso ecclesiastico* or *De statu ecclesiae* survives in two twelfth-century English manuscripts and a number of later copies and was essentially a handbook on liturgical procedure and the right ordering of ecclesiastical and secular hierarchies.[4] He resigned his legatine commission in 1140 on grounds of old age and was succeeded by Máel Máedóc Ua Morgáir [hereafter St Malachy], the most influential of the twelfth-century reformers and the best documented because of his friend-ship with St Bernard of Clairvaux, his counsellor, correspondent and eventual

---

3 Watt, *Church and the Two Nations*, 4–7.
4 Flanagan, *Transformation of the Irish Church*, 54–91.

hagiographer. Malachy was born into a hereditary clerical family and received his initial monastic formation from Imar Ua hÁedacáin, the ascetic abbot of the monastery of Sts Peter and Paul at Armagh, being ordained a priest when he was twenty-five. After further training with Máel Isú Ua hAinmire, the monk-bishop of Waterford at his monastery in Lismore, he initiated a controversial reform of the monastic community of Bangor. In 1124 he was appointed bishop of Connor but three years later was forced into exile and returned to Lismore where he met Cormac Mac Carthaig, the exiled king of Desmond, who later became an important ally in the cause of Church reform. Although Bishop Cellach of Armagh designated him his successor before his death in 1129, Malachy's attempts to gain possession of the see did not succeed until 1134. He resigned this position in 1137 in favour of Abbot Gilla Meic Liag of Derry in order to promote concord and took up the bishopric of Down. In 1139 he journeyed to Rome to seek the approval of Pope Innocent II for the Irish reform programme, to be signified by the granting of palls or *pallia* – ecclesiastical vestments symbolic of metropolitan authority – to the archbishops of Cashel and Armagh. En route he visited the monastery of Clairvaux, then at the height of its fame under its charismatic abbot, St Bernard. In Rome the pope appointed him legate to Ireland but declined his request for *pallia* and instructed that a general synod be convened to formally request them. On the return journey Malachy left four of his entourage at Clairvaux to receive monastic formation as the nucleus of the first Cistercian foundation in Ireland. He also visited the abbey of St Nicholas of Arrouaise in Flanders, taking copies of the community's legislation and observances in order to introduce this form of the Augustinian canons regular to Ireland. In 1148, with the support of a synod held at Inis Pádraig, County Dublin, he again travelled to the Continent seeking papal endorsement. He died while visiting Clairvaux and Bernard immediately began to promote his cult, a process that culminated in Malachy's canonisation by Pope Clement III in 1190.

The efforts of reforming bishops and papal legates were augmented by legislation promulgated at ecclesiastical gatherings known as synods. The annals indicate that at least eleven such meetings were held between 1101 and 1179. Very little of the legislation enacted has survived but three synods were particularly influential in transforming the structures of the Irish Church. The eight decrees that survive from the Synod of Cashel (1101) provide the first documentary evidence for the reformers' programme and echo concerns expressed at the Council of Clermont in 1095. The Cashel synod sought to curb lay interference in ecclesiastical affairs and to regulate marital practice with regard to consanguinity and affinity. The synod was presided over by Muirchertach Ua Briain, king of Munster, who also donated the royal complex at Cashel to the Church. The Synod of Ráith Bressail (1111) saw the reorganisation of the Church into two ecclesiastical provinces each consisting of twelve dioceses with metropolitan sees established at Armagh and Cashel. It is possible that Gillebertus of Limerick's treatise, with its emphasis on hierarchy and ecclesiastical jurisdiction, was compiled in connection with this gathering. In 1152 the Synod of Kells endorsed the work of the earlier reformers but adapted their structures to contemporary political realities. Meeting first at Kells and then at the newly established Cistercian foundation at Mellifont, County Louth, it re-ordered the Irish dioceses into four provinces and erected additional metropolitan sees at Tuam and Dublin. It also endeavoured to secure the payment of tithes and to extirpate concubinage and simony. The gathering was presided over by Cardinal John Paparo who, as papal legate, confirmed its decrees and conferred the *pallia* on the four archbishops.[5]

The erection of Dublin as a metropolitan see ended its suffragan relationship with Canterbury, a relationship that had endured for well over a century. Awareness of this impending development may have lain behind King Stephen's refusal to allow Cardinal Paparo to pass through England en route to Ireland in 1150. Canterbury's desire to reassert its authority over the Hiberno-Norse dioceses that had formerly recognised its authority provides a plausible context for the papal bull *Laudabiliter* granted to Henry II in 1155 by the English-born pope, Adrian IV. Obtained at the behest of the distinguished English cleric John of Salisbury, it granted Henry the right to enter Ireland for the correction of vices, the expansion of the Church's bounds and the increase of religion. It also specified that one penny should be paid to the See of Peter from each household in Ireland. Although much debate surrounds the integrity of the surviving text of this bull, it remained the foundational document of the English Lordship of Ireland until 1541. The king, beset with difficulties elsewhere in his realms, decided not to act on the privilege until 1171 when he visited Ireland in an attempt to assert his authority over his Anglo-Norman subjects who had conquered large areas of the country and whose loyalty he had good cause to suspect.

The eleventh and twelfth centuries also witnessed an explosion of church building in Ireland as stone structures gradually began to replace earlier wooden models, although sometimes retaining some of the original wooden features such as corner projections known as antae and tapering lintelled

---

5 Flanagan, *Transformation of the Irish Church*, 34–6.

doorways. Originally simple rectangular structures, many of these churches gradually developed a bicameral arrangement with a nave area reserved for the laity and a chancel or sanctuary for the high altar and the clergy. This was an architectural expression of the developing cult of the Eucharist found elsewhere in Europe.[6] Continental and English contacts facilitated the introduction of the Romanesque and Gothic styles of architecture in the twelfth and early thirteenth centuries, both of which developed distinctively Irish idioms. Many of the early Romanesque churches were erected at centres associated with the reform movement, and the stone-vaulted, stone-roof examples found at St Flannan's Oratory, Killaloe, and Cormac's Chapel in Cashel were influential in disseminating motifs and techniques in Munster.[7] The influence of the Anglo-Normans found architectural expression in major ecclesiastical building projects such as St Thomas's Abbey in Dublin or in the refurbishment or replacement of existing structures such as the cathedrals in Cashel, Dublin, Kilkenny, Killaloe and Waterford.

More significant was the expansion of the parochial network in Ireland. Although this has generally been seen as an Anglo-Norman development, current scholarship demonstrates that the colonisers often adopted pre-existing Gaelic territorial divisions as the basis of their manors and parishes. Recent analysis of the surviving remains of parochial churches in the western, Gaelic dioceses of Killaloe and Kilfenora provides evidence for widespread construction of new churches and refurbishment of older ones in the late twelfth and thirteenth centuries. Even in the heartland of the colony, P. J. Duffy notes that 78 per cent of parish names in Meath and 70 per cent of those in Dublin were pre-Anglo-Norman in origin and suggests that the conquerors were 'inheritors rather than creators of ecclesiastical structures'.[8] The erection of parishes led to a rapid rise in the construction of parish churches and chapels, often in a simple Early English Gothic style. Some evidence survives for the presence of parochial and trade guilds, almost exclusively from the towns and parishes of the colony, but only one set of medieval churchwardens' accounts survives, for the parish of St Werburgh in Dublin, dating to the late fifteenth

---

6 T. Ó Carragáin, *Churches in Early Medieval Ireland: Architecture, Ritual and Memory* (New Haven and London: Yale University Press, 2010), 19–26, 87, 175–84.

7 R. Gem, 'Saint Flannán's Oratory at Killaloe: A Romanesque Building of *c*.1100 and the Patronage of King Muirchertach Ua Briain', in Bracken and Ó Riain-Raedel (eds.), *Ireland and Europe in the Twelfth Century*, 95; Ó Carragáin, *Churches in Early Medieval Ireland*, 288–91.

8 P. J. Duffy, 'The Shape of the Parish', in E. Fitzpatrick and R. Gillespie (eds.), *The Parish in Medieval and Early Modern Ireland: Community, Territory and Building* (Dublin: Four Courts Press, 2006), 44; Flanagan, *Transformation of the Irish Church*, 84–91.

and sixteenth centuries.[9] This is particularly regrettable, as analysis of such records has shed much light on the grass-roots practice of religion in England and on the Continent.

Throughout the thirteenth century the diocesan structures introduced in the twelfth century continued to develop and expand with the consolidation of cathedral chapters, prebends and benefices in the various dioceses. Although sketchy, the surviving ecclesiastical sources indicate that many dioceses possessed an effective if rudimentary bureaucracy. Ecclesiastical discipline was enforced by Church courts and diocesan and provincial synods, and a small amount of synodal legislation survives, much of it deriving from legislation circulating in England. Both the archbishops of Armagh and Dublin conducted visitations of their own dioceses and of their suffragan sees, although the only visitation report to survive is that concerning the diocese of Derry compiled by Archbishop John Colton in 1397. In all, seven registers survive from the medieval archdiocese of Armagh containing material for the period from 1361 to 1535, although there are significant gaps in what remains. A much smaller amount of material is extant for the dioceses of Dublin, Limerick, Ossory, Clogher and Derry. The probate of wills also came under ecclesiastical jurisdiction although only one volume of the proceedings of a consistorial court survives from Dublin dating to the mid-fifteenth century.[10]

The most significant source for Irish ecclesiastical affairs is the medieval papal registers. From the twelfth century onwards, the papacy became increasingly involved in Irish ecclesiastical affairs, and the Vatican and Roman archives contain a vast amount of material, much of it still to be accessed, relating to Ireland. Unlike England, where royal injunctions against approaching the papal court for mediation operated, Gaelic Ireland was amenable to such interaction and the papal records are replete with references to disputed episcopal elections, appointments to benefices, the granting of indulgences and, particularly, dispensations from the canonical impediment to ordination resulting from the candidate's illegitimacy. This was especially the case after the transfer of the papal court to Avignon in the early fourteenth century rendered it more accessible to Irish petitioners. Papal intervention in Irish affairs in the thirteenth and fourteenth centuries was generally supportive of Church reform, but later involvements were less constructive as a financially compromised papal court exploited every possible source of revenue. This was particularly true during

---

9 C. A. Empey, 'The Layperson in the Parish: The Medieval Inheritance, 1169–1536', in R. Gillespie and W. G. Neely (eds.), *The Laity and the Church of Ireland, 1000–2000: All Sorts and Conditions* (Dublin: Four Courts Press, 2002), 7, 25–6, 28–9.

10 Connolly, *Medieval Record Sources*, 38–49.

the Great Schism (1378–1417), which divided the Latin Church into first two and eventually three camps, each supporting the claims of rival pontiffs. The Irish Church, like that in England, sided with Pope Urban VI and his successors in the Roman obedience, although some pockets of support for Clement VII and the Avignon line emerged in the ecclesiastical provinces of Tuam and Armagh as well as among the Augustinian canons and Franciscan friars.

Very little evidence survives to show how medieval Irish clerics were trained. It is likely that most secular priests received their training by apprenticeship to another cleric and some may have received theological formation in the *studia* or schools operated by the various mendicant orders for their own members.[11] That basic catechetical competence was expected is evident in Archbishop George Cromer's instruction to his clergy in 1526 that they each acquire a copy of the text known as the *Ignorantia Sacerdotum* or face payment of a hefty fine. This clerical handbook, compiled in 1281 by Archbishop John Pecham of Canterbury, contained expositions of the creed, the ten commandments, the seven deadly sins, seven corporal works of mercy and other basic tenets that were regarded as the minimum that a pastorally effective priest needed to communicate to his parishioners. In 1533 Primate Cromer devoted a full day of the Armagh diocesan synod to a public reading of the text.[12] Medieval Ireland did not possess a university and attempts to establish one in Dublin in 1320 and 1485 and in Drogheda in 1465 were unsuccessful. Only a small number of clerics could afford to study at foreign schools and universities of which Oxford was the most popular destination. The medieval university's student body was divided into northern and southern 'nations' and Irish students were included in the latter, participating enthusiastically in the riots and fracas that characterised medieval student life. The medieval city's 'Irishman's Street' and the presence of Drogheda Hall, a residence for clerics from the archdiocese of Armagh, were testimony to the presence of Irish students. Richard Fitz Ralph, later archbishop of Armagh, had the most distinguished career of all the Irish in medieval Oxford, becoming chancellor of the university for two years in 1332.

The decree of the second Synod of Cashel in 1172, that the Church in Ireland should adopt the practices of the English Church, meant that the use of Sarum eventually became the dominant liturgical form in medieval Ireland and most of the surviving service-books derive from this tradition. The

11 Ó Clabaigh, *Friars in Ireland*, 271–6.
12 H. A. Jefferies, 'Diocesan Synods and Convocations in Armagh on the Eve of the Tudor Reformations', *Seanchas Ardmhacha*, 16 (1995), 122–4.

exercise of royal prerogative on ecclesiastical appointments in the Lordship also led to a gradual anglicisation of the Irish episcopate. Many of the English-born men appointed as bishops were university-educated, and played a key role in the administration of the Anglo-Norman colony. Their clerical status theoretically provided the crown with administrators who were talented, celi-bate, literate and incorruptible, but in practice not all royal civil servants were of the highest calibre. Archbishop Alexander Bicknor of Dublin, for instance, was convicted of massive peculation of crown revenues during his tenure as treasurer of Ireland in the first three decades of the fourteenth century.[13] Although this fluctuated over time, Watt has noted that of the thirty-two Irish dioceses, English or Anglo-Irish bishops usually controlled the ten wealthiest sees; thirteen were held by Gaelic candidates, with the remaining nine oscil-lating between the two nations or 'tongues'.

The Irish Church was recognised as comprising two ethnic groups, the *ecclesia inter Hibernicos* and the *ecclesia inter Anglicos*, and antagonism between them bedevilled Church life well into the early modern period. The Bruce invasion of 1315–18, which corresponded with the Great European Famine, proved particularly divisive among the clergy. In 1315 King Edward II wrote to Edmund Butler, the justiciar of Ireland, expressing concern about the support given to the invaders by Irish clergy and friars. In 1317, at the king's behest, Pope John XXII wrote to the archbishops of Dublin and Cashel ordering them to silence those clerics who had sided with the invaders and undermined his authority with their preaching. Later that year Domhnall O'Neill, king of Tír Eoghain, responded with a strongly worded Remonstrance on behalf of the Gaelic lords which detailed atrocities committed by the English, and accused them of failing to maintain the conditions of *Laudabiliter*. Although Pope John XXII did not accede to the request that on these grounds the English be deprived of their right to rule Ireland, he did instruct Edward II to attend more carefully to the rights of his Irish subjects. In 1324 the king sent an embassy to the papal court at Avignon to secure papal approbation for a pro-posed restructuring of the Irish Church. The king demanded that Irish clergy be instructed to preach loyalty to the crown and that all those spreading dis-sension be punished. He also called for a papal condemnation of the practice of excluding English candidates from Irish religious houses because of their racial background. The most radical proposal however was that dioceses with an income of less than £60 would be united to larger ones, each having its

---

13 J. F. Lydon, 'The Case against Alexander Bicknor, Archbishop and Peculator', in Smith (ed.), *Ireland and the English World*, 105–6.

episcopal seat in a royal city. This would have reduced the number of Irish dioceses from thirty-four to ten, ensured their financial viability and rendered the bishops more susceptible to royal control. Although the petition received a favourable hearing from the pope, it did not succeed and the issues that it articulated continued to colour Irish Church affairs for the rest of the Middle Ages.[14]

The unsettled nature of society in the first half of the fourteenth century also found expression in the persecution of individuals suspected of witchcraft and heresy. The trial of the Irish Knights Templar in 1310 revealed little of a heterodox character, although one Franciscan witness was suspicious of a Templar who had refused to look up at the elevation of the host during Mass at the Templar preceptory in Clontarf.[15] In the same year Philip de Braybrook, an Augustinian canon of Holy Trinity priory, Dublin, was accused of heresy. The English Franciscan bishop of Ossory Richard Ledred was the main agent in the most notorious of the Irish witchcraft trials, that of Dame Alice Kyteler of Kilkenny. Ledred had spent time at the papal court in Avignon and was influenced by Pope John XXII's preoccupation with the occult. Dame Alice, a wealthy matron of Flemish extraction, had married four husbands and was accused of working sorcery to advance the interests of William Outlaw, the son of her first marriage. The case became embroiled in Ledred's disputes with members of Kilkenny's mercantile elite and led to the bishop's imprisonment for a brief period. While Dame Alice escaped the flames by fleeing to England, her servant, Petronilla of Meath, was less fortunate and was executed in Kilkenny in 1324. In 1353, another Franciscan, Roger Craddock, bishop of Waterford, presided over the heresy trial and execution of two members of the MacNamara [Mac ConMara] family at Bunratty, County Clare.[16]

The advent of plague in 1348–9 and its recurrence thereafter proved as much a watershed in Irish Church and society as elsewhere in the West. The clergy were particularly hard hit and the Franciscan chronicler Friar John Clyn of Kilkenny described how 'those confessing and the confessor were together led to the grave'. A sense of panic gripped the population and Clyn recorded large numbers of pilgrims wading in the waters of St Mullins's well in Carlow to ward off the pestilence as well as the

---

14 Watt, *Church and the Two Nations*, 36–40, 186–9, 196–7. See Beth Hartland's chapter in this volume.

15 H. Nicholson, 'A Long Way from Jerusalem: Templars and Hospitallers in Ireland, c.1172–1348', in M. Browne and C. Ó Clabaigh (eds.), *Soldiers of Christ: The Knights Templar and the Knights Hospitaller in Medieval Ireland* (Dublin: Four Courts Press, 2015), 10.

16 M. B. Callan, *The Templars, the Witch, and the Wild Irish: Vengeance and Heresy in Medieval Ireland* (Dublin: Four Courts Press, 2015).

circulation of an apocalyptic text known as the 'Cedar of Lebanon'.[17] Archbishop Fitz Ralph of Armagh received permission sometime before January 1351 to dispense sixty candidates for ordination from canonical irregularities including illegitimacy, presumably in order to fill the benefices in his diocese left vacant by the plague. After the initial outbreak the plague became endemic in Ireland and major outbreaks are recorded by the annalists throughout the fourteenth century with children proving particularly susceptible to the onslaught.[18] As was the case in contemporary England and Europe, more morbid preoccupations found expression in art. These included *transi* or cadaver tomb effigies such as those found in Beaulieu, County Louth, Castledermot friary, County Kildare and that of Mayor James Rice, in Waterford Cathedral. Wall paintings and sculptures representing St Sebastian, an early Christian martyr invoked for protection against pestilence, also became widespread (see Map 12).

Monasticism and Religious Life

Early Irish monasteries were largely unaffected by the Benedictine tradition although the continental foundations associated with St Columbanus (d. 615) played a seminal role in transmitting the Rule of St Benedict in Northern Italy and France.[19] In the ninth century the ascetic reform movement known as the *Céle Dé* adopted some Benedictine liturgical practices but the Rule does not appear as the normative legislation in any foundation in Ireland before the eleventh century. As noted above, contacts with England led Hiberno-Norse candidates to join Benedictine monasteries in centres like Worcester and Winchester with some returning as bishops of the newly established Hiberno-Norse sees. A community of Benedictine monks served the cathedral in Dublin until their expulsion by Bishop Samuel in 1096. The most significant of these Irish continental foundations were the *Schottenklöster*, based primarily in German-speaking lands. These originated in 1076 when Muireadhach Mac Robhartaig (d. 1088), an Irish pilgrim and eventual anchorite, settled on the outskirts of Regensburg in Bavaria. In 1090 his disciples established the Benedictine monastery of St James in the city, and this became the motherhouse of a congregation of Irish Benedictine abbeys. Expansion began in the 1130s during the abbacy of Christianus Mac Carthaig and by 1231

---

17 *Clyn*, 250.
18 Smith, *Crisis and Survival*, 40–1.
19 D. Ó Cróinín, 'A Tale of Two Rules', in M. Browne and C. Ó Clabaigh (eds.), *The Irish Benedictines: A History* (Dublin: Columba Press, 2005), 15–24.

MAP 12. Ecclesiastical Provinces and Diocesan Centres in Ireland established at Synods between 1101 and 1152.

the congregation numbered ten monasteries, mostly concentrated in southern and eastern Germany but with outliers in Vienna and Kiev. At least two priories were established in Ireland, at Cashel and Roscarbery, to raise funds and train novices for the continental houses. Originally drawing recruits from the north of Ireland, the congregation's centre of recruitment shifted to

Munster in the twelfth century and the monks and nuns of the *Schottenklöster* maintained close links with the Ua Briain and Mac Carthaig dynasties. These contacts served as a conduit for the circulation of ideas, texts and personnel between Ireland and Germany, and the surviving historical, theological, liturgical and hagiographical material from the *Schottenklöster* is of tremendous importance for the study of twelfth-century Irish intellectual culture.[20]

The transformation of the Irish Church wrought by the twelfth-century reformers also influenced Irish monastic life. Although a small number of Benedictine houses existed in Ireland by the mid-twelfth century, the orders most favoured by the reformers were the Augustinian canons and canonesses and the Cistercians. Whereas clergy living in community had been a feature of monastic life since the time of St Augustine (d. 430), a revival of this lifestyle developed among groups of clerics in Italy and southern France in the early eleventh century. These adopted Augustine's monastic rule as the basis for their observance, receiving official sanction in 1059 from Pope Gregory VII and the Lateran synod in Rome. The movement spread throughout Europe, and the Augustinian canons and canonesses became an important vehicle of monastic and Church reform. As clerics, the canons were more disposed to pastoral engagement than monks and were often engaged by bishops to evangelise marginal communities or to establish parishes in newly settled or recently conquered territories. Some groups however, often under Cistercian influence, adopted a more contemplative lifestyle that was indistinguishable from that of monks. The movement's expansion across Europe led to the emergence of regional variations with distinctive observances, some of which expanded beyond their original localities. While the regular canons and canonesses were the most numerous of all the religious orders in medieval Ireland with approximately 120 foundations, their emergence and expansion is obscure and the dates of their early foundations mostly conjectural. Although strongly promoted by figures like Sts Malachy and Lorcán Ua Tuathail [hereafter Laurence O'Toole], their introduction into Ireland cannot be attributed to a single individual.

The most significant groups were the congregations of St Nicholas of Arrouaise, St Victor of Paris and Premontré. The Arroasian canons emerged from a group of hermits in Flanders that adopted a conventual lifestyle *c*.1097 and expanded rapidly in the Netherlands, Poland, England and Ireland during the rule of Abbot Gervase (1121–47). St Malachy, already familiar with

---

20 D. Ó Riain-Raedel, 'Cashel and Germany: The Documentary Evidence', in Bracken and Ó Riain-Raedel (eds.), *Ireland and Europe in the Twelfth Century*, 176–8; Flanagan, *Transformation of the Irish Church*, 10–14.

the canonical lifestyle through contact with the Augustinian community at Guisborough in Yorkshire, visited Arrouaise en route to Rome in 1140 and secured copies of their constitutions and liturgical texts for use in Ireland. The Victorine canons followed the customary of the abbey of St Victor in Paris, founded in 1113 and noted for its scholarly activity. Their principal Irish house was the abbey of St Thomas the Martyr on the outskirts of Dublin, founded in 1177 at the behest of Henry II in reparation for his role in the murder of Archbishop Thomas Becket. This community adopted Victorine observances *c.*1192 and became one of the wealthiest monastic foundations in Ireland. Eventually the congregation numbered nine foundations in Ireland, all of Anglo-Norman origin. The surviving texts and manuscripts from St Thomas's abbey suggest that it participated in the lively intellectual culture that characterised the Victorine tradition. The Premonstratensian canons were founded at Premontré near Laon in France in 1120 by Norbert of Xanten. Their earliest foundation in Ireland was at Carrickfergus, which was established by Dryburgh abbey in Scotland sometime before 1183. In the thirteenth century, another seven houses were established in the west of Ireland and the order eventually possessed ten conventual houses. A letter written *c.*1211 by Abbot Gervase of Premontré to Walter, abbot of Vicoigne, suggests that the Irish canons were regarded with a mixture of bemusement and irritation by their French confrères. It requested that its recipient would respond as generously as his means allowed to the demands of Brother Isaac, a canon of Holy Trinity abbey, Tuam, and counselled patience with him as one 'not accustomed to the cloistral customs and the rigour of our order'. The community at Premontré had previously hosted and clothed three of Isaac's colleagues who had come to transcribe copies of the order's liturgical and legislative texts.[21] Despite the paucity of sources it is clear that the regular canons played a significant role in advancing monastic reform. They made a significant contribution to hagiography and many of the *vitae* of the early Irish saints and liturgical calendars owe their composition or preservation to their efforts.

Female religious communities have only recently attracted critical scholarly attention.[22] Tracy Collins has identified 114 medieval Irish nunnery sites, of which sixty-five were founded or flourished between 1140 and 1540.[23] Of these, six have been classified as Cistercian, eight as Augustinian, four as

---

21 Gwynn and Hadcock, *Medieval Religious Houses: Ireland*, 206; M. Clyne, 'Archaeological Excavations at Holy Trinity Abbey, Lough Key, Co. Roscommon', *PRIA*, 105 C (2005), 24.

22 Hall, *Women and the Church*, 63–211.

23 T. Collins, 'Timolin: A Case Study of a Nunnery Estate in Late Medieval Ireland', *Anuario de Estudios Medievales*, 44/1 (2014), 54–5.

Franciscan and forty as Arroasian – although such classifications are problematic as little survives to show what was distinctive about each community's observance and lifestyle. The predominance of the Augustinian canonesses and particularly those of the Arroasian tradition is noteworthy. This is in contrast to the situation in England, where female communities mostly followed the Rule of St Benedict and also in Wales and Scotland, where most nunneries were classified as Cistercian. The chief house of the canonesses was the foundation at Clonard, County Meath, which was established c. 1144. This was credited with having thirteen daughter houses in 1195 but went into decline and in 1383 the abbacy was transferred to the community at Odra, also in Meath. The O'Connor foundation at Kilcreevanty, County Galway, had emerged as the motherhouse of the canonesses in Connacht by 1223–4. The monastery at Killone, County Clare was another royal foundation, this time patronised by the O'Brien family who also supplied a number of the community's abbesses. Other important foundations included the monasteries of St Mary de Hogges (f. c.1146) and Grace Dieu (f. c.1190) near Dublin and the house of St John the Baptist, Cork, (f. 1297) where the nuns conducted schools for girls.

The twelfth century also saw the emergence of anchorites or religious recluses attached to parochial and monastic churches in many of the towns and cities of the colony. The 1306 will of John de Wynchedon, a wealthy Cork merchant, lists four such recluses at various churches in the city and there is contemporary evidence for their presence at sites in Dublin, Waterford, Fore and Cashel.[24]

Although numerically far fewer than the regular canons and canonesses, the origins and expansion of the Cistercians in Ireland can be traced in greater detail, on account of the writings of St Bernard, the references to the Irish houses that occur in the order's general statutes from 1190 onwards, and the survival of the letter book of Abbot Stephen of Lexington detailing his visitation of the Irish houses in 1228. As noted above, the visits by Malachy to Clairvaux in 1139–40 provided the context for the foundation of the first Irish house at Mellifont, County Louth, in 1142. The contingent of Irish monks left in Clairvaux to receive monastic training formed the nucleus of the new foundation along with some French companions. Differences of opinion over observance led to the withdrawal of the French monks and the recall to Clairvaux of the founding abbot Gilla-Críst Ua Conairche for further

---

24 C. Ó Clabaigh, 'Anchorites in Late Medieval Ireland', in L. Herbert McAvoy (ed.), *Anchoritic Traditions of Medieval Europe* (Woodbridge: Boydell Press, 2010), 165–6.

training. Despite this the monastery flourished, receiving extensive support from Donnchad Ua Cerbaill who donated the site on the banks of the River Mattock and the border of his kingdom of Airgialla. The location of a religious house on a territorial boundary characterised many foundations in twelfth- and thirteenth-century Ireland as it did elsewhere in Europe. In addition to the spiritual benefits believed to accrue from endowing a monastery, the pragmatic considerations of its location often helped consolidate the patron's control over frequently contested areas. Mellifont experienced rapid growth and within ten years had established seven daughter houses. By 1170, the community numbered 100 monks and 300 laybrothers and by the early thirteenth century its filiation network consisted of twenty daughter houses. The monastic complex was built on a scale previously unknown in Ireland and was referred to in Gaelic sources as *An Mhainistir mhór* – the great monastery. Through it and their other foundations the Cistercians exercised enormous influence on the development of medieval Irish architecture and are frequently credited with being the pioneers of Gothic architecture in Ireland.[25]

The Anglo-Norman presence in Ireland after 1169 had a profound effect on monastic and religious life. In addition to endowing Cistercian and Augustinian foundations, they also introduced the Knights Templar and the Knights Hospitaller into Ireland. Initially these orders were based in the southeast of the island in the area around the Hook Peninsula and Waterford. The preceptory of the Knights Templar at Clontarf, north of Dublin, remained their principal Irish foundation until the order's suppression in 1310. The Knights Hospitallers' headquarters were at Kilmainham, close by Dublin, and the prior of Kilmainham played a leading role in the administration of the colony until the dissolution of the monasteries in the sixteenth century. Both orders were granted extensive lands and privileges throughout Ireland but recruited their members almost exclusively from the ranks of the colonists. Their manors provided their subsistence as a well as the 'responsions' or financial contributions that both orders made to support the crusading and hospitaller activities of their confrères in the Levant.[26] The Trinitarians, a group dedicated to the redemption of Christian slaves, established a single foundation at Adare, County Limerick, *c.*1226 and the Order of the Holy Cross

---

25 R. Stalley, *Cistercian Monasteries of Ireland* (London and New Haven: Yale University Press, 1987), 92–103.
26 M. Browne and C. Ó Clabaigh (eds.), *Soldiers of Christ: The Knights Templar and the Knights Hospitaller in Medieval Ireland* (Dublin: Four Courts Press, 2015), *passim*.

(*Fratres cruciferi* or Crutched Friars) established seventeen priory-hospitals by the early thirteenth century.

As was the case elsewhere in Europe, monasteries in Ireland formed an integral part of the colonisation process and the new foundations were deployed to consolidate the colonists' grip on their newly conquered territories. John de Courcy's endowment of religious communities after his conquest of the Dál Fiatach kingdom of Ulaid in 1177 provides a representative example. He established his *caput* at Down, the traditional burial place of St Patrick, and installed there a community of Benedictine monks from Chester that constituted the cathedral chapter for the rest of the Middle Ages. He also established smaller Benedictine houses at Nendrum and Ards, staffing them with monks from Cumbria and Somerset respectively. His patronage extended to the Cistercians as well. The monastery at Inch was granted to the community of Furness in Cumbria in 1180 or 1188 as an act of reparation for his earlier destruction of Erenagh abbey, while in 1193 his wife, Affreca, established Grey abbey, a daughter house of Homcultram, also in Cumbria. The Augustinian priory of St Thomas the Martyr was established before 1183 and de Courcy staffed it with Augustinian canons from Carlisle.[27] He also established a community of Crutched Friars in Downpatrick who administered the priory-hospital of St John the Baptist.

One of the principal attractions of the new orders for Irish Church reformers was the manner in which their governmental structures appeared to guarantee the maintenance of high standards of observance and discipline. Central to this were the institutions of the general chapter and regular visitation. The daily chapter meeting (so called because it included a daily reading of a chapter of the monastic rule) was a feature of Benedictine monasticism that was adopted by other religious communities. It provided the main disciplinary mechanism for governing a religious community and from the tenth century the term came to describe the regular meetings of religious superiors that sought to maintain uniformity of observance within the monasteries of their region. The annual chapter of the Cistercians at Citeaux in Burgundy was initially attended by all abbots of the order but as the order spread concessions were made to those from foreign countries for whom this obligation proved too onerous. In 1190 the Irish abbots were ordered to attend every four years, with the caveat that there were always to be Irish representatives present

---

27 C. Ó Clabaigh, 'The Benedictines in Medieval and Early Modern Ireland', in M. Browne and C. Ó Clabaigh (eds.), *The Irish Benedictines: A History* (Dublin: Columba Press, 2005), 107–13.

at the gathering. Despite this, Irish absenteeism remained a perennial problem.[28] The Irish Arroasian canons were also obliged to send representatives to their general chapter at Arrouaise and they proved even more reluctant to do so than the Cistercians. In 1200, Pope Innocent III ordered the archbishops of Armagh and Tuam to ensure that the Irish canons fulfilled this obligation but later references in the order's statutes indicate that this was ineffective.[29] In Ireland, St Mary's abbey, Louth, functioned as the motherhouse of the Arroasian canons, and chapters of the Irish superiors were held there in 1242 and 1325.[30] The Irish Benedictines of the *Schottenklöster* held their first recorded general chapter at Regensburg in 1211 and this became a regular feature. The survival of a late thirteenth- or early fourteenth-century copy of the *Liber Ordinis* or customary of St Victor in TCD MS 97 indicates that the community at St Thomas's abbey were familiar with the order's observances but there is no evidence of their participation in its general chapter. In contrast, the superiors of the Irish Knights Hospitallers regularly attended both provincial and general chapters and the decisions taken at the Irish gatherings were recorded in the mid-fourteenth-century *Registrum de Kilmainham*.[31]

The colonists' establishment of new Cistercian foundations introduced rival affiliations to that of Mellifont and her daughter houses. These new foundations were in most cases staffed by English monks, and the fact that they often maintained higher standards of discipline than were to be found in pre-conquest houses fused racial antipathy with issues of monastic observance. This exacerbated an already fraught relationship between the order's general chapter and the Mellifont filiation in Ireland that reached crisis point between 1216 and 1230 and was known in a contemporary phrase as the 'Mellifont conspiracy'. From 1216 onwards various attempts at visitations of the Gaelic houses were rebuffed and in 1227 the abbots of Mellifont and five of her daughter houses were deposed for rebelling against the authority of the order. The dispute was resolved in part by the visitation conducted by Abbot Stephen of Lexington in 1228. His letter book, detailing his struggles, presents a picture of almost complete institutional collapse. Writing to Pope Gregory IX in 1228, Abbot Stephen asserted that 'in the monasteries of Ireland our restraint and rule is scarcely observed in anything apart from the

---

28 Stalley, *Cistercian Monasteries*, 15–16.

29 *Pontificia Hibernica*, i, 112–13.

30 Gwynn and Hadcock, *Medieval Religious Houses: Ireland*, 186.

31 TCD MS 97, fols. 102–47, 149; *Registrum de Kilmainham: Register of Chapter Acts of the Hospital of Saint John of Jerusalem in Ireland, 1326–1339 under the Grand Prior, Sir Roger Outlawe*, ed. C. McNeill (Dublin: IMC, 1932), *passim*.

habit, for there is no due service in choir, or silence in the cloister, discipline in the chapter, community meals in the refectory or monastic quiet in the dormitory'.[32] To counter this Abbot Stephen disbanded the Mellifont filiation, imposed French and English abbots on a number of the Irish houses, dismissed nuns from the vicinity of the monasteries, and insisted that all monks be able to confess in either Latin or French. Despite this, tensions within the communities remained high and in 1230 members of the Cistercian community at Fermoy, County Cork, reputedly murdered their English abbot. The Mellifont filiation was restored in 1274.[33]

The arrival of the mendicant friars in Ireland in the thirteenth century brought the Irish Church into contact with one of the most vital movements within medieval Christianity. The Dominicans established their first foundations at Dublin and Drogheda in 1224 and the Irish Franciscan province was erected in 1230. The Carmelites are first mentioned in 1271 and the Augustinian friars made their first foundation in 1282. All of these orders were founded from England and the Irish Dominicans, Carmelites and Augustinians formed a division of their English mother provinces for most of the pre-Reformation period. The friars initially gravitated to the towns and boroughs of the colony where linguistic and cultural affinity with the colonists assured them of appreciative congregations and guaranteed support for their mendicant lifestyle. However some important foundations were also established in Gaelic areas in the thirteenth century and in this early phase the friars were noteworthy for their ability to transcend ethnic and cultural boundaries. Franciscan and Dominican friaries were established at Ennis, Armagh and Roscommon while the register of the Dominican priory at Athenry, County Galway, established in 1241 by Meiler de Bermingham, shows that this ostensibly Anglo-Norman foundation enjoyed substantial support from the local Gaelic aristocracy and recruited novices from both ethnic groups. English friars also spent time in Ireland: the Athenry community maintained a room for the 'English bachelors' who taught in the friars' theological school while the *Liber Exemplorum*, a late thirteenth-century collection of preachers' tales, was compiled by a Franciscan from Warwickshire active in the south-east of Ireland.[34]

The mendicant movement emerged at a time of intellectual ferment and pastoral renewal in the Church. The Fourth Lateran Council (1215) revolutionised Catholic pastoral practice and both the Dominicans and Franciscans

---

32 Stephen of Lexington, *Letters from Ireland, 1228–1229*, ed. and trans. B. O'Dwyer (Kalamazoo: Cistercian Publications Inc., 1982), 183–4.
33 Stalley, *Cistercian Monasteries*, 17–20.
34 For this, and what follows: Ó Clabaigh, *Friars in Ireland*, 1–52, 143–68, 290.

were charged by successive popes with putting its renewal programme into practice. In addition to their activities as preachers and confessors, the friars produced an entire corpus of thelogical and pastoral material designed to aid other clerics in their pastoral ministry. Each friary acted as a nodal point on a sophisticated educational and communications network that meant texts, ideas and personnel circulated freely and effectively between houses and provinces. In Ireland, too, each order developed a network of *studia* or schools in which young friars and occasionally other clerics received their philosophical and theological formation. More promising students were sent abroad for higher studies to each order's advanced *studia*, and Irish friars are recorded as both studying and teaching in Bologna, Cambridge, Milan, Oxford, Paris and Strasbourg. The mendicants also provided the teaching staff for the short-lived University of Dublin established by Archbishop Alexander Bicknor in 1320.

The friars' pastoral success, widespread lay support and papal privileges and immunities brought them into conflict with the older monastic orders and the secular clergy who perceived them as threats to their established rights and prerogatives. Although this was a feature of mendicant life throughout Europe, its Irish manifestation was particularly contentious. Between the mid-fourteenth and mid-fifteenth centuries a succession of four Oxford-educated, Anglo-Irish clerics waged a campaign against the friars. The most influential of these critics was the archbishop of Armagh, Richard Fitz Ralph (d. 1360), who, despite close childhood and familial associations with the Franciscan community in his native Dundalk, devoted the last decade of his life to agitating for their suppression. His anti-mendicant work *Defensio Curatorum* enjoyed widespread circulation, and the polemics generated on both sides of the dispute constituted the principal Irish contribution to medieval theology.

Tensions between natives and settlers were particularly pronounced among the mendicants. In 1291 sixteen friars were killed during a dispute between Gaelic and Anglo-Irish Franciscans at a chapter meeting in Cork. The campaign of Edward Bruce in Ireland between 1315 and 1317 further polarised the friars and earned a papal condemnation for those members who supported him. A plausible case has recently been made for identifying the author of the 1317 'Remonstrance of the Irish princes' as Friar Michael Mac Loclainn, lector of the Franciscan *studium* in Armagh. The document denounced the Cistercian monks of Granard for hunting and killing members of the Gaelic population without compunction and accused Friar Simon le Mercer, a Franciscan, of asserting that it was no more a sin to kill an Irishman than to kill a dog and that he would not hesitate to celebrate Mass after so doing. In the latter half of the fourteenth century, separatist tendencies among the Anglo-Irish Augustinians and Dominicans erupted in a number of violent conflicts. In 1379 eight Anglo-Irish Augustinian friars from Dublin were implicated in the murder of another friar, Richard Dermot, in the city's Augustinian priory. In 1380 the attempts of an English Dominican, Friar John of Leicester, to assert his authority as head of the Irish Dominican vicariate occasioned an armed riot in Dublin during which the friars on both sides were discovered to be wearing chain mail under their habits.

No new Cistercian monasteries or Augustinian abbeys were established after 1272, and by 1300 the first wave of mendicant expansion had peaked with only a small number of foundations made after that date. The Kilkenny chronicler, Friar John Clyn, recorded the deaths as a result of plague of twenty-five Franciscans in Drogheda and twenty-three in Dublin before Christmas 1348, which probably constituted the majority of each community. The community of Crutched Friars at Tyone, County Tipperary, was reduced to two members in 1365 as a result of the pestilence, while membership of the Augustinian nunnery at Lismullin, County Meath, dropped by 43 per cent between 1348 and 1367. Conventual life all but collapsed in many Cistercian and Augustinian monasteries. The disappearance of the lay brothers in Cistercian houses deprived them of their labour force and meant that the land was rented out, while speculation on the wool trade led some Cistercian monasteries in the south-east to the verge of bankruptcy.

The promise of rejuvenation lay in the emergence of the Observant movement among the mendicant friars at the end of the fourteenth century. Within each institution the Observants promoted rigorous discipline and strict adherence to the rule and constitutions as antidotes to the lax observance known as 'Conventualism'. On the Continent, Observants received papal and conciliar permission to elect their own superiors, thus forming a hierarchical structure within each order, nominally subordinate to the Conventual or unreformed authorities. In Ireland this was particularly attractive to Gaelic friars, who, by becoming Observants, could legitimately withdraw from the jurisdiction of the Anglo-Irish and English friars who had governed them since the thirteenth century. The movement first emerged in Ireland in 1390 at the Dominican priory in Drogheda and increased in influence throughout the fifteenth century with a distinct Observant congregation emerging by 1503. Franciscan reformers were active by 1417, establishing an Irish Observant vicariate in 1458–60. The Augustinian Observants made their first foundation at Banada, County Sligo, in 1423 and by 1517 the movement numbered eight houses. Many of the older mendicant foundations also adopted the reform, sometimes at the behest of their founders' descendants. In 1464 the earl of Kildare and various cadet branches of the FitzGeralds established an Observant Franciscan foundation at Adare, County Limerick. In Limerick the Franciscan community became Observant in 1534 as a result of lobbying from the city's mayor and aldermen.

The Franciscans in particular were keen promoters of the 'Third Order' among their lay followers. This was intended for zealous lay people who continued in their normal secular occupations while adopting a rigorous life of prayer and charitable activity. In Gaelic territories it provided a lay spiritual outlet comparable to the guilds and confraternities that flourished in the towns and cities. The Third Order or Tertiary Rule also provided the canonical basis for communities of professed religious and between 1426 and 1540 forty-nine communities of Franciscan tertiaries and one of Dominicans were founded in Ireland. These Third Order houses were concentrated in the Gaelic areas of Connacht and Ulster and their members engaged in educational and pastoral work. During this second wave of expansion, only the Franciscan movement had any impact on female religious life, with six houses of the Order of St Clare being listed in 1316. A later list gives three foundations tentatively identified as Carrick-on-Suir, County Tipperary, Youghal, County Cork, and Fooran, County Westmeath. In 1511 Walter Lynch established a house for the 'Poor nuns of St Francis' near St Nicholas church in Galway where his daughter was a member of the community.[35]

Religion and Society

The predominantly clerical authorship of both primary sources and subsequent historiography has meant that the religious lives of the medieval Irish laity have been somewhat neglected, and much of the work on lay-folk that has been conducted has focused on the experiences of the elite and the literate. Regardless of their social status, all Christians had to be baptised. The importance of this rite of initiation is attested in the *vitae* of early Irish saints that continued to be transcribed and re-edited in the later Middle Ages. The compiler of the *Liber Exemplorum* included three exempla illustrating the efficacy of the sacrament as an agent of spiritual and corporal healing in his collection. In one of these, a woman is healed from breast cancer after receiving

---

35 Ó Clabaigh, *Friars in Ireland, passim.*

a kiss from a newly baptised neophyte.[36] Because of its fundamental importance, clerics were at pains to ensure that the sacrament was performed correctly using water and invoking the orthodox Trinitarian formula for baptism. Roger Howden, in his account of the second Synod of Cashel (1172), claimed that it was the Irish practice for the father of a new-born child to subject it to a threefold immersion in water, unless it was the son of a wealthy man, in which case it was baptised in milk. This custom allegedly persisted until the sixteenth century when the chronicler Richard Stanihurst recorded it. Other irregularities were equally bizarre: in 1627 the Roman authorities had to condemn forcefully the practice of baptising infants in beer, which had been justified on account of a supposed shortage of water in Ireland.[37] Concern for the proper administration of the sacrament led the synod to insist that children be brought to the baptismal church to be baptised by the priest 'in the name of the Father and of the Son and of the Holy Spirit'.

This concern for correct practice found architectural expression in the construction of baptismal churches in some of the early Irish monastic foundations in the late twelfth and early thirteenth centuries. Tomás Ó Carragáin suggests that the Holy Trinity church at Glendalough, County Wicklow, and the church of St John the Baptist at Kilmacduagh, County Galway, served this function. In the latter case, a small window in the south-west corner of the church would have illuminated the baptismal font. Although holy wells such as those at St Mullins, County Carlow, and St Doulagh's well, County Dublin, may have continued in use as baptismal places throughout the Middle Ages, the parish church became the normal location for infant baptisms.[38] The possession of a baptismal font was one of the prerogatives of parochial churches, even where other subsidiary chapels existed in the parish. In 1186 a decree of the Synod of Dublin insisted that each church have an immoveable font constructed of stone or timber and lined with lead with a drain to enable the baptismal water and chrism to flow into the ground. In 1453 the provincial Synod of Cashel meeting in Limerick decreed that each parish church was to possess a stone font of which approximately one hundred examples survive from medieval Ireland.[39]

36 *Friars' Tales: Thirteenth-Century Exempla from the British Isles*, ed. D. Jones (Manchester University Press, 2011), 73–4.
37 S. Ryan, 'Windows on Late Medieval Devotional Practice: Máire Ní Mháille's "Book of Piety" (1513) and the World behind the Texts', in Moss et al. (eds.), *Art and Devotion in Late Medieval Ireland*, 11.
38 T. Ó Carragáin, *Churches in Early Medieval Ireland*, 205–6.
39 Moss, (ed.), *Art and Architecture of Ireland*, 324–6.

The spectre of death in childbirth lay behind the widespread devotion to figures like Sts Anne, Catherine, and Margaret of Antioch, whose intercession was held to be particularly efficacious for pregnant women. The relics of Holy Trinity Cathedral in Dublin included the Virgin Mary's belt. This was probably some form of 'birthing girdle' that was worn by a woman in childbirth. Festivities associated with the birth of children frequently occasioned clerical censure. The compiler of the *Liber Exemplorum* recounts a tale of demonic possession during one such celebration and in 1536 the Corporation of Galway ordered women not to hold banquets after giving birth but to confine their entertainments to a select group of female companions.[40] A woman was re-integrated into the life of the community by being 'churched' forty days after giving birth. In 1198, Pope Innocent III, in response to a query from the archbishop of Armagh, decreed that women could freely enter churches immediately after childbirth if they so wished but instructed that those who wished to abstain from doing so for a time were not to be criticised. The 'churching' commenced at the door of the church before proceeding to one of the altars within, where the ceremony concluded. This may explain the presence of an image of St Catherine of Alexandria, one of the saints invoked in childbirth, above the west doorway of the Augustinian priory at Clontuskert, County Galway, as well as the effigy of a female donor over that at St Ruadhan's priory, Lorrha, County Tipperary.

For most people the regeneration from sin occasioned by baptism did not last past childhood and necessitated recourse to the sacrament of penance or confession to restore right relationships with God and with neighbour. Although the Irish monastic tradition had made a major contribution to the development of the theology of penance in the earlier Middle Ages, it was the pastoral programme outlined in the decree *Omnis Utriusque Sexus* of the Fourth Lateran Council (1215) that had the most enduring influence in Ireland as elsewhere in the Latin Church. This decree imposed an obligation on each Catholic to receive the Eucharist at least annually. This in turn implied an obligation to confess one's sins and receive absolution before doing so. To implement this programme, Pope Innocent III and his successors turned to the newly established Dominican and Franciscan friars who responded enthusiastically and developed an entire corpus of pastoral literature devoted to assisting their confrères and the secular clergy in the ministry as preachers and confessors. These works, known as Lateran literature, included model

---

40 *Friars' Tales*, 138; C. Tait, 'Safely Delivered: Childbirth, Wet-Nursing, Gossip-Feasts and Churching in Ireland *c.*1530–1690', *IESH*, 30 (2003), 18.

sermons and preaching aids, theological textbooks and manuals designed to equip a priest when hearing confessions.

Although compiled between 1491 and 1526, the library catalogue of the Franciscan friary at Youghal, County Cork, contains copies of the most significant of these confessors' handbooks including the *Summa de Casibus Conscientiae* of the Catalan Dominican friar Raymond of Peñafort (d. 1275); the early fourteenth-century *Summa Aestesana* of the Italian Franciscan Aestasanus of Asti; and some of the pastoral works of Jean Gerson (d. 1429), chancellor of the University of Paris, whose reputation as a confessor earned him the soubriquet 'the Consoling Doctor'. TCD MS 250, a fifteenth-century Franciscan manuscript, contains copies of two of the most influential examples of this genre, the *Summa Confessorum* and the *Confessionale*, both by Dominican friar John of Freiburg (d. 1314). The importance of making a full confession formed the subject of many of the *exempla* in the *Liber Exemplorum* and in TCD MS 667, a late fifteenth-century Franciscan manuscript from Clare or Limerick. These include the stories of a cleric whose sins were erased from the devil's record after confession; a woman whose record of incest was likewise wiped clean; and the sacristan to whom the devil confided the extent of his losses through penitents' recourse to the sacrament.[41] Those guilty of causing scandal by their actions risked having public penances imposed on them up to and including excommunication. In 1410 Archbishop Fleming of Armagh instructed his suffragan, the bishop of Raphoe, to excommunicate certain unnamed miscreants in his diocese, denouncing them with 'cross erect, bell and candles' on Sundays and festivals in the churches of his dioceses and casting holy water to drive out the demons by which they were bound. The clergy were further instructed to terrify them by casting three stones in the direction of their dwellings as a sign of the eternal malediction of God. The archbishop also invoked the threat of excommunication in 1412 to compel Dalwagh Ocagaun, 'commonly called the horse-stealer,' to return the seven or eight pigs that he had stolen from one of the archbishop's tenants.[42]

The pope had the right to grant remission of all temporal punishment due for sins. This was known as a plenary indulgence and emerged first in connection with the preaching of the crusades. Initially confined to those who actually took the cross, it was later made available to those who made financial contributions to the crusading effort, and the *Liber Exemplorum* contains

41 Ó Clabaigh, *Friars in Ireland*, 294–301; TCD MS 667, 204.
42 *Reg. Nicholas Fleming*, 125–6, 208–9.

an exemplum illustrating the efficacy of the crusade indulgence. The pope alone could proclaim a Jubilee or 'Holy Year' in which a plenary indulgence was granted to pilgrims to the shrines of the apostles Peter and Paul in Rome. The Irish annals note the granting of the first Jubilee Indulgence by Pope Boniface VIII in 1300. The Annals of Ulster record several pilgrimages to Rome by high-ranking delegations from the north of Ireland including that of Thomas Maguire [Mág Uidir], lord of Fermanagh, and his entourage during the Jubilee Year of 1450. Other prelates could also grant indulgences although after the Fourth Lateran Council bishops were confined to granting indulgences of forty days, or one year for those attending the consecration of a church. Popes alone could grant longer periods and frequently did so in order to encourage pilgrimage, devotion and almsgiving. The earliest reference to a papal indulgence in an Irish context dates to 1255 and was granted to pilgrims to the shrine of Archbishop Laurence O'Toole of Dublin at Eu in Normandy. Indulgences for foreign beneficiaries were also promoted in Ireland. These included major Roman institutions such as the hospice of St Thomas the Martyr, the altar of *Ara Caeli* at the Cistercian monastery of Tre Fontane and the great pilgrim hostel of the *Santo Spirito in Sassia* near the Vatican. The confraternity of St Mary's church at Boston, Lincolnshire, likewise offered participation in the numerous indulgences conceded to it by the papacy to its supporters in Ireland, and the Observant Franciscans of Paris were able to quest for support in Ireland with the blessing of the archbishop of Armagh in 1489.

Marriage in medieval Ireland was influenced by several different and often contradictory traditions. Gaelic society's ready access to divorce facilitated consecutive marriages, particularly amongst the aristocracy, and incurred the wrath of both foreign and native clerics. Despite these fulminations, Gaelic traditions remained strong into the early modern period. The Anglo-Norman presence after 1169 meant that marriage customs more in keeping with English and continental practice became the norm in the *ecclesia inter Anglicos*. The provision of elaborate western doorways and wooden porches at medieval churches such as that at Lorrha, County Tipperary, may partly have been motivated by a desire to provide a suitable backdrop for marriages which, from the twelfth century, were supposed to be public ceremonies conducted by the priest in the presence of witnesses. Marital breakdown and divorce were the preserve of the ecclesiastical courts as the surviving material from the registers of the archbishops of Armagh indicates. The Church's position on affinity and consanguinity often proved an obstacle particularly among the aristocracy and members of the merchant classes, and the surviving papal registers contain numerous examples of dispensations from these impediments.

The increasing number of stone churches built from the eleventh century onwards indicates a concern to create a pastoral infrastructure that enabled parishioners to regularly attend the Eucharist. The addition of chancels and presbyteries to the east end of existing structures in the twelfth century shows an awareness of developments in Eucharistic theology, whereby the transcendent and miraculous nature of the Eucharistic species was highlighted. Care for proper reverence in celebrating Mass is evident in TCD MS 667, which contains instructions on what the priest must do if the host fell to the ground. The *Liber Exemplorum* likewise contains numerous miraculous stories relating to the host and the perils of unworthily receiving it. Most of these are stock stories that circulated widely in Europe but include some Irish material. One recounts the tale of the innkeeper's wife from Graiguenamanagh, County Kilkenny, who, desiring to increase the price of her wine, took the advice of a witch, and kept the host in her mouth after receiving communion at Easter. Returning home she placed it in a cask of wine but when later she went to draw it, the cask was empty. Puzzled, she took her husband's pilgrim's staff and used it to investigate the anomaly. When she withdrew it she found that the host had adhered to it and the barrel began to miraculously fill with wine. Remorseful at her sacrilege, she confessed her sin and shared her tale with a friar. Such sacramental pragmatism was not unusual: a text on the fourteen 'Merits of the Mass' spuriously attributed to St Augustine survives in some late medieval Gaelic manuscripts. These included the assertions that during Mass one did not age, that having attended Mass one would not die, lose one's sight or suffer from indigestion during that day. One's time in purgatory would also be shortened and one's business dealings would prosper.[43]

The centrality of the Eucharist was not confined to the liturgy; it formed part of the warp and weft of civic life and functioned as a factor of unity and collective identity. Oaths were sworn on the host. In 1324, when Bishop Richard Ledred was arraigned before the court in Kilkenny, he carried the host in order to identify himself with Christ during his arrest and passion. The 1498 ordinances for the Dublin Corpus Christi procession indicate that each of the city's guilds took responsibility for depicting a biblical tableau, often connected to their trade. Thus the glovers' guild depicted Adam and Eve being driven from paradise, the butchers depicted Christ's tormentors and the goldsmiths represented the Magi. As well as being a religious occasion,

---

43 *Friars' Tales*, 83; Ryan, 'Windows on Late Medieval Devotional Practice', 5.

the procession functioned as an expression of corporate identity. In Gaelic communities, shared reception of communion was one of the ways in which covenants of 'gossiprid' or pledges of association between lords and their clients were sealed. The clearest illustration of the corporate nature of the feast comes from Drogheda in 1412. The town had developed from two distinct settlements on opposite banks of the River Boyne and the rivalry between the two communities often exploded into violence. To counter this, Friar Philip Bennett, a member of the town's Dominican priory, invited representatives of both communities to attend a sermon on Corpus Christi day, 1412, in St Peter's church. He took as his theme the opening line of psalm 133, 'Behold, how good and how pleasant it is when brothers live in unity.' Expanding on this phrase with great force he effected a remarkable change in the hearts of his congregation. Afterwards, he invited them to dine in the Dominican priory. Both factions were reconciled and jointly petitioned the king for the charter of incorporation that established Drogheda as a single, united borough.[44]

The cult of the saints and the veneration of relics played an important role in the devotional life of the late medieval Irish faithful. The saints of the ancient Irish Church received new attention in the twelfth century as their *vitae* were rewritten and brought into conformity with continental and English norms. The newly introduced Augustinian canons and Cistercian monks and the Irish Benedictine monasteries on the Continent played an important role in this development and many of the surviving hagiographical collections emanate from these sources. The recent discovery of a single leaf from a twelfth-century manuscript litany of the saints from the Irish Benedictine foundation at Regensburg provides a striking illustration of the importance of these links. Not only does it include references to saints of the universal Church and to figures venerated in southern Germany, it also invokes saints from Ireland and particularly from north-east Munster. The inclusion of such obscure figures as Mochuille of Tulla, Ide of Killely and Colum of Terryglass in a litany composed in Bavaria shines a touching sidelight on the devotional life of the Irish monks of Regensburg as well as providing an oblique indication of where in Ireland they originated.[45] In addition to providing appropriate texts for use at the divine office and for devotional reading, these texts served a pragmatic end in justifying the presence of the new order on an ancient monastic site. Pádraig Ó Riain has noted that the links posited between some of the saints

44 Ó Clabaigh, *Friars in Ireland*, 294.
45 D. Ó Riain-Raedel and P. Ó Riain, 'Irish Saints in a Regensburg Litany', in Purcell *et al.* (eds.), *Clerics, Kings and Vikings*, 55–66.

commemorated in the hagiographies most likely reflect the relationships between Augustinian houses in the twelfth century.[46]

The religious orders were also responsible for introducing new saints' cults and for promoting devotion to their members and patrons who had gained reputations for sanctity. Thus St Bernard composed the *vita* of St Malachy and a liturgical office in his honour. The *vita* of Laurence O'Toole was compiled as part of his canonisation process by a canon of Eu in Normandy where the saint had died in 1180.[47] The coming of the friars in the thirteenth century also increased the number of saints proposed for veneration and provided a new model of what constituted sanctity. The liturgical calendar from the Augustinian community at Holy Trinity Cathedral, Dublin, contains the earliest Irish evidence for devotion to the mendicant saints Francis, Dominic, and Peter Martyr and the friars actively promoted the cults of their founders wherever they established a new community. The Dominican priory at Lorrha, County Tipperary, was a centre of devotion for the Dominican inquisitor St Peter Martyr, and a number of miracles that occurred there through his intercession are included in the earliest version of his *vita* compiled *c.*1270 by the Italian friar Thomas Agni.[48]

Pilgrimage to shrines within Ireland and abroad also provided a vehicle for devotion. The premier destination in Ireland was the island sanctuary of St Patrick's Purgatory, Lough Derg, which drew pilgrims from all over Europe from at least the twelfth century. The Cistercian monk Henry of Saltrey wrote a graphic account of the experiences of the Knight Owein who had witnessed the pains of the damned and the joys of the blessed within a cave there. A similar preoccupation with the details of the otherworld is evident in the *Vision of Tnugdal*, composed in the Irish Benedictine monastery at Regensburg in the mid-twelfth century and likewise giving an account of the pains of hell and the joys of heaven. Later pilgrims to Lough Derg were less impressed by their experience and in 1497 Pope Alexander VI attempted to suppress the pilgrimage following their complaints. The relic of the true cross at Holy Cross abbey, County Tipperary, attracted so many pilgrims that the Cistercian community there was able to completely rebuild the monastic complex in the mid-fifteenth century. Miraculous crucifixes at Christ Church Cathedral Dublin and the Augustinian monastery at Ballyboggan, County

46 P. Ó Riain, 'Longford Priories and their Manuscripts: All Saints and Abbeyderg', in M. Morris and F. O'Ferrall (eds.), *Longford: History and Society* (Dublin: Geography Publications, 2010), 39–50.

47 R. Sharpe, *Medieval Irish Saints' Lives: An Introduction to Vitae Sanctorum Hiberniae* (Oxford University Press, 1991), 26–38,

48 C. Ó Clabaigh, *Friars in Ireland*, 187–8.

Meath, attracted large numbers of pilgrims, as did the shrine of the Virgin Mary at Trim. Irish pilgrims also visited shrines abroad, and helped on their return to introduce foreign cults, devotions and motifs such as the *Volto Santo*, an image of Christ venerated in the Italian city of Lucca, that is depicted on the twelfth-century high crosses at Cashel, County Tipperary, and at Kilfenora and Dysert O'Dea, both in County Clare. The account of the miracles of Thomas Becket compiled by the monk William of Canterbury from 1172 onwards refers to miracles wrought by the saint in Ireland and to numerous Irish pilgrims to his shrine.[49] Carvings on a late medieval tomb frontal at the Dominican priory at Strade, County Mayo, depict a pilgrim kneeling before effigies of Sts Thomas Becket, Peter and Paul, and the Magi, indicating that he had undertaken pilgrimages to Canterbury, Rome and Cologne. The sanctuary of St James at Compostela was also a popular destination and numerous scallop shells and other pilgrim tokens from the shrine have been excavated at sites such as Tuam and Ardfert cathedrals.

Perhaps the most intriguing evidence is the account of pilgrimage to the Holy Land undertaken by two Franciscan friars, Simon Semeonis and Hugh the Illuminator, in 1323. Although their ultimate destination was Jerusalem, Friar Simon's account of the various sights seen and shrines visited as they travelled thorough England, France, Italy and sailed along the Adriatic coast stopping at Crete en route before arriving in Alexandria makes for fascinating reading. The illness and subsequent death of his companion delayed Friar Simon in Cairo for five weeks and enabled him to form some vivid impressions of Islamic society.[50]

The final destination of every Christian's pilgrimage was the heavenly Jerusalem but safe arrival there was not guaranteed. The reality of the four last things, death, judgement, hell and heaven, figured large in the religious mentalité of late medieval Ireland as it did across Europe. The desire to die well after the 'victory of unction and penance' led many aristocrats to spend their last days in the religious houses that they had patronised in life, hoping that the prayers and asceticism of their inmates would counterbalance their iniquities. Others secured guarantees of plenary indulgences at the hour of death from the papal curia or sought burial in the habit of a religious order or in a monastic cemetery. Those who could afford it endeavoured to speed their passage through purgatory by leaving resources for the celebration of Masses, trentals and anniversaries, as well as for other charitable causes.

---

49 M. Staunton and C. Ó Clabaigh, 'Thomas Becket and Ireland', in E. Mullins and D. Scully (eds.), *'Listen, O Isles, unto me': Studies in Medieval Word and Image in Honour of Jennifer O'Reilly* (Cork University Press, 2011), 90–2.
50 Ó Clabaigh, *Friars in Ireland*, 193–8. See also Michael Bennett's chapter in this volume.

Memorial effigies also secured the prayers of the faithful for the deceased, particularly those that offered indulgences.

As members of the Catholic or universal Church, Christians in Ireland shared the same fundamental elements of doctrine, confessed the same creed, received the same sacraments, acknowledged the authority of the pope, and to greater or lesser degrees were bound by the canon law of the Church. Likewise, medieval Irish devotion to the Trinity, Christ, the Virgin Mary and the saints sat easily within the broad sweep of medieval European piety. Irish pilgrims were frequent visitors to the shrines of Europe and the Holy Land; Irish preachers drew on many of the same resources as their continental counterparts; Irish clerics were subject to the same intellectual influences as their colleagues elsewhere, while Irish Hospitallers, Templars and crusaders headed eastwards to fight in Palestine. Nor was this a one-way traffic either intellectually or personally. From the middle of the fourteenth century the friars of the Servite community at Todi in Italy were confronted with the punishment reserved for sinners as depicted in the fresco of St Patrick's Purgatory painted on the wall of their choir. The shrine itself at Lough Derg was depicted on medieval maps and drew pilgrims from as far afield as Catalonia and Hungary, England and France. English, Italian and Greek clerics served as bishops of Irish dioceses, and Irish monasteries in southern Germany and Austria functioned as nodal points in a communications network that facilitated the dissemination of Irish hagiographical and theological texts. The cults of indigenous saints also remained influential throughout Ireland. Holy wells and ancient monastic sites continued as local centres of devotion. Influenced by English and continental exemplars, earlier Irish hagiographies were re-written, reliquaries refurbished and buildings rebuilt. The *oeuvre* of the Observant Franciscan friar-poet Pilib Bocht Ó hUiginn (d. 1487) illustrates the rich cross-fertilisation of native and imported themes. His work combines the complex conventions of bardic poetry with themes drawn from Franciscan and Dominican hagiography as well as from continental works such as James of Voragine's *Golden Legend*. As a member of a traditional Gaelic learned family and of a pan-European order, he integrated in himself a religious outlook that was both local and universal.

14

The Economy

MARGARET MURPHY

Scarcity and uneven survival of primary source material, particularly of those sources that allow systematic analysis of demography, standards of living, levels of urbanisation and agrarian exploitation, have hampered investigation of many aspects of the economy of medieval Ireland. In the past this has led to a fragmentation of research into specific areas and a reluctance to synthesise or attempt to place the disparate and imperfect Irish data into a wider European context.[1] More recent scholarship, however, has demonstrated both what can be done with partial evidence and how, on occasion, the employment of a comparative approach can partly offset the lacunae. In 2004 Richard Britnell produced an integrated examination of economy and society in Britain and Ireland in the medieval period.[2] Since then there have been some innovative studies bringing fresh approaches to familiar sources; Mark Hennessy's examination of the records of the 1292 Irish lay subsidy and Bruce Campbell's analysis of the early fourteenth century ecclesiastical tax being two cases in point.[3] Hennessy argues that the lay subsidy receipts are a good indication of which parts of Ireland had been integrated into a wider 'English' economic zone, while Campbell has assembled a range of economic data in order to analyse relative and absolute levels of economic development in Ireland, England, Scotland and Wales c.1290.

The increasing accessibility of sources has opened up possibilities for more systematic research on topics such as prices, wages, and spatial patterns of land-use and productive resources, while understanding of the commercial

1 For example the chapters by Glasscock, Childs and O'Neill, Down and Nicholls in *NHI* ii.
2 R. H. Britnell, *Britain and Ireland, 1050–1530* (Oxford University Press, 2004).
3 B. M. S. Campbell, 'Benchmarking Medieval Economic Development: England, Wales, Scotland and Ireland c.1290', *Economic History Review*, 61 (2008), 896–945; M. Hennessy, 'Making Ireland English in the Thirteenth Century: The Evidence of the Irish Lay Subsidy of 1292', in P. J. Duffy and W. Nolan (eds.), *At the Anvil: Essays in Honour of William J. Smyth* (Dublin: Geography Publications, 2012), 81–92.

networks of Irish ports has benefited from the publication of a selection of late-medieval Bristol's custom accounts. More generally, the adoption by historians and archaeologists of interdisciplinary approaches in their areas of scholarship has facilitated the emergence of a more integrated and sophisticated interpretation of the medieval Irish economy.[4] Research on the urban hierarchy and the role of large and small towns in local economies and wider commercial networks has been facilitated by the publication of regional and local studies, and there has been a recent shift of focus from the larger port towns to smaller inland towns such as Trim and Buttevant. The publication, since 1986, of 27 volumes in the *Irish Historic Towns Atlas* series has illuminated urban economic life, while the provisioning relationship between large towns and their hinterlands and the impact of urban demands on rural production is also receiving attention.[5] Finally, Irish economic historians have begun to engage with the relatively new discipline of environmental history to ask what impact ecological and climatic factors have had on the course of economic development.[6] This chapter attempts to show how new research can add nuance and richness to the narrative of Irish economic history. It also seeks to explore some of the themes that have been exercising economic historians in Britain and on the Continent in an Irish context.

The Economy of Early Medieval Ireland

The traditional depiction of early Ireland as an insular, pastoral and reciprocal society only introduced to trade and the market by the viking towns has undergone extensive revision in recent years. Analysis of the significant corpus of both archaeological and documentary evidence relating to imported

---

4 CIRCLE; *Bristol's Trade with Ireland and the Continent, 1503–1601: The Evidence of the Exchequer Customs Accounts*, ed. E. Jones and S. Flavin (Dublin: Four Courts Press, 2009); M. Murphy and M. Potterton, 'Investigating Living Standards in Medieval Dublin and its Region', in S. Duffy (ed.), *Medieval Dublin VI* (Dublin: Four Courts Press, 2005), 224–56.

5 M. Potterton, *Medieval Trim: History and Archaeology* (Dublin: Four Courts Press, 2005); É. Cotter (ed.) *Buttevant. A Medieval Anglo-French Town in Ireland* (Midleton: Éamonn Cotter, 2013); Murphy and Potterton, *Dublin Region in the Middle Ages*, 465–86, 498–9; M. Murphy, 'Feeding Another City: Dublin and its Region in the Later Middle Ages', in M. Davis and J. A. Galloway (eds.), *London and Beyond: Essays in Honour of Derek Keene* (London: Institute of Historical Research, 2012), 3–24; J. A. Galloway, 'The Economic Hinterland of Drogheda in the Later Middle Ages', in V. McAlister and T. Barry (eds.), *Space and Settlement in Medieval Ireland* (Dublin: Four Courts Press, 2015), 167–85.

6 B. M. S. Campbell, 'Nature as Historical Protagonist: Environment and Society in Pre-Industrial England', *Economic History Review*, 63 (2010), 281–314; J. Adelman and

goods in medieval Ireland has been important in this regard.[7] Irish kings valued the products of overseas trade such as slaves, wine, olive oil, pottery and glass and probably controlled coastal entrepôts which functioned as the starting points of regional distribution networks. In return, Ireland's exports included hides, butter and slaves. The necessity of obtaining wine for Communion meant that from an early date the monasteries established trade networks with Gaul, with the ports of Bordeaux and Nantes being particularly important in this trade. Increase in demand for imported and luxury goods has long been associated with the growth of towns and there remains lively debate around the precise nature of economic activity at the larger monasteries and the secular caputs.[8]

Ireland does seem to have been a largely cashless society at this time. There were types of commodity money (goods that had acquired functions normally ascribed to money), most notably cattle, but little evidence for the use of imported coin. Tributes were paid for the most part in agricultural goods, but a linguistic change in the documentary sources from 'gift' to 'wage' has been interpreted as a reflection of the way in which political relationships were being expressed less personally and more in economic or contractual terms as time went on. The importance of pastoral farming, and cattle in particular, to early medieval Ireland is indisputable but there is wide acceptance now that arable agriculture was always significant and that from around 800 its importance increased. The benign climate can be seen as a driver of this change. As was the case in much of Europe, the period from 800 to 1100 also saw considerable population growth in Ireland. Clarke has proposed a population of half a million for the island of Ireland *c.*1000 at a time when Dublin had 3,500 to 4,000 inhabitants, while Holm has recently claimed that Dublin

F. Ludlow, 'The Past, Present and Future of Irish Environmental History', *PRIA*, 114 C (2014), 1–33.

7 The evidence is usefully summarized in A. O'Sullivan, F. McCormick, T. R. Kerr and L. Harney, *Early Medieval Ireland AD 400–1100: The Evidence from Archaeological Excavations* (Dublin: RIA, 2014), 247–82.

8 E. Bhreathnach, *Ireland in the Medieval World, AD 400–1000: Landscape, Kingship and Religion* (Dublin: Four Courts Press, 2014), 30; D. Ó Corráin, 'Vikings in Ireland: The Catastrophe', in Clarke and Johnson (eds.), *Vikings in Ireland and Beyond*, 493. Ó Corráin quotes from the early ninth-century text 'The instructions of King Cormac' which has a list of things which are good for a king including 'bringing ships into harbour' and 'importing overseas treasure'. Etchingham has recently argued that there is less evidence for market activities at monasteries than has been supposed. C. Etchingham, 'The Organization and Function of an Early Irish Church Settlement: What was Glendalough?', in C. Doherty, L. Doran and M. Kelly (eds.), *Glendalough: City of God*

and its surroundings may well have had a Norse population of around 10,000 at a slightly later date.[9]

The viking impact on the Irish economy was significant and pre-dated the establishment of the coastal towns. Finds of weights and hack silver at long-phuirt sites such as Woodstown and Linn Duachaill have led to a revising of the view that these were primarily military camps. Following the establishment of the port towns, and especially Dublin, viking use of silver bullion spread outwards, later to be followed by Anglo-Saxon coins and later again by coins minted in Dublin. By the middle of the tenth century in some parts of Ireland a mixed coin and hack silver 'dual economy' had emerged. The role of Dublin was pivotal in several areas: its mercantile elite orchestrated the development of a substantial monetary economy and increased levels of commercialisation across a wide area (see Map 13), while its provisioning demands, along with its economic value systems, may have encouraged a move towards more intensive arable farming as a way of accumulating wealth. The precise nature of the economic relationships between the viking towns, larger monasteries and Irish magnates is an intriguing topic of investigation (see Map 13).[10]

Dublin was a major commercial hub with regular and consistent contact with Anglo-Saxon England and functioned as an integral part of the Irish Sea trading zone established by the vikings. Woods argues from the dominance of Dublin coins in the Manx hoards that Hiberno-Scandinavian coins were the de facto currency around the Irish Sea. Long before the arrival of the Anglo-Normans the vikings had incorporated Ireland into a north-west Europe trading milieu.[11]

(Dublin: Four Courts Press, 2011), 44. See also H. B. Clarke, 'Quo Vadis: Mapping the Irish "Monastic Town" ', in Duffy (ed.), Princes, Prelates and Poets, 261–78.

9 C. Doherty, 'Exchange and Trade in Early Medieval Ireland', JRSAI, 110 (1980), 74; O'Sullivan et al., Early Medieval Ireland, 179–214; H. B. Clarke, 'The Mother's Tale', in S. Booker and C. Peters (eds.), Tales of Medieval Dublin (Dublin: Four Courts Press, 2014), 52; P. Holm, 'Manning and Paying the Hiberno-Norse Dublin Fleet', in Purcell et al. (eds.), Clerics, Kings and Vikings, 67–78.

10 G. Williams, 'Viking Camps and the Means of Exchange', in Clarke and Johnson (eds.), Vikings in Ireland and Beyond, 95; A. Woods, 'The Coinage and Economy of Hiberno-Scandinavian Dublin', in S. Duffy (ed.), Medieval Dublin XIII (Dublin: Four Courts Press, 2013), 61, 66; F. McCormick and E. Murray, Knowth and the Zooarchaeology of Early Christian Ireland (Dublin: RIA, 2007), 112–15.

11 B. Hudson, Irish Sea Studies 900–1200 (Dublin: Four Courts Press, 2006), 25; Woods, 'Coinage and Economy of Hiberno-Scandinavian Dublin', 64; B. J. Graham, 'Ireland: Economy and Society', in S. H. Rigby (ed.), A Companion to Britain in the Later Middle Ages (Oxford: Blackwell, 2003), 147.

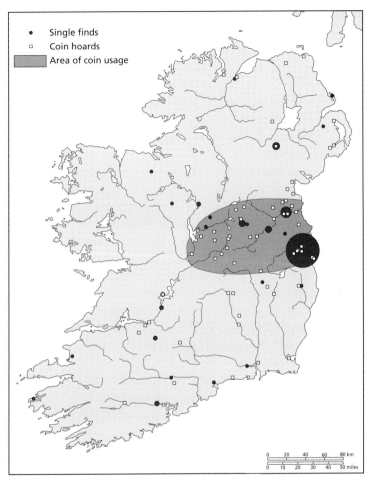

MAP 13. Area of Intensive Coin Usage, 900–1170. Source: Woods, 'Coinage and Economy of Hiberno-Scandinavian Dublin', 62.

The Rural Economy from 1100

It is now accepted that many of the agricultural innovations formerly attributed to the Anglo-Normans were already present in late twelfth-century Ireland: Gerald of Wales's comments on the inability of the Irish to properly exploit their lands, and their ignorance of markets and settled agriculture, were part of the colonial rhetoric associated with invasion and conquest. Recent research which reveals the importance of arable agriculture in early medieval Ireland and the sophistication of corn-drying kilns and milling technology helps modify his assessment. The role of the Church, especially the Cistercian order introduced into Ireland in 1142, in encouraging agrarian innovation must also be acknowledged. The Cistercian grange system, which utilised large numbers of lay brothers in the supply and processing of food and other products for the mother houses, was especially influential.[12]

The Anglo-Normans, however, were responsible for one deeply important innovation: the introduction of a commercial mind-set to agriculture. This mind-set had been forged against the backdrop of increasingly favourable economic and demographic circumstances in Europe. It stimulated a hunger for new lands, encouraged the production of surpluses for the market and underlay processes of colonisation and settlement. By the time Ireland was conquered the manor had become the key production unit through which the agrarian economy of England operated. Empey has written that in Ireland the manor was, first, a mechanism of lordship and, second, an economic institution. In truth the two functions were inextricably linked and, it can be argued, were of equal importance. In order to ensure the highest possible return from their seigneurial rights, lords (both secular and ecclesiastical) had to exploit the potential of this territorial, economic, social and legal institution to the maximum. The discussion that follows focuses on zones where a manorialism similar to that which operated in contemporary England pertained. That is, areas with significant demesne cultivation and nucleated settlements. It is recognised, however, that the units described at the time as 'manors' in Connacht and Munster, which were often vast in size and lacked major population centres, were significantly different enterprises.[13]

Sources relating to the early organisation of Irish manors, the introduction of tenants and the partitioning of landholdings are few in number. The pipe roll of 1212 describes a dozen settlements in Meath as 'manors', although the term is absent from other areas, such as Tipperary. Manorial documents start to become more plentiful from the middle of the thirteenth century, peak in

12 *Topographia*; O'Sullivan *et al.*, *Early Medieval Ireland*, 210–11; N. Brady, 'Mills in Medieval Ireland: Looking Beyond Design', in S. Walton (ed.), *Wind and Water in the Middle Ages: Fluid Technologies from Antiquity to the Renaissance* (Tempe: University of Arizona Press, 2006), 39–68; G. Stout, 'The Cistercian Grange: A Medieval Farming System', in M. Murphy and M. Stout (eds.), *Agriculture and Settlement in Ireland* (Dublin: Four Courts Press, 2015), 28–32.
13 C. A. Empey, 'Conquest and Settlement: Patterns of Anglo-Norman Settlement in North Munster and South Leinster', *IESH*, 10–13 (1983–6), 9.

the period 1280–1340 and survive in very small numbers thereafter. Extents, of varying levels of detail, survive for close to 300 manors, while the more informative manorial accounts are extant for only a handful of manors in Carlow, Kildare and Wexford.[14] Analysis of extent data shows that Irish manor centres resembled those found in Britain and on the Continent and contained the residence of the lord, various seigneurial accessories – gardens, dovecots, warrens, and the like – and the buildings used for the collection, processing and storage of agrarian products and shelter of animals. Most manors were associated with nucleated settlements, many with borough status. The manorial mill was a key resource, representing an input of capital from the lord, and typically produced for him or her an annual income of c.£3. It is notable that this was a significantly higher sum than manorial mills in England yielded. While this may to some extent reflect the larger size of Irish manors, it also attests to the strength of rural lordship in Ireland.[15]

The documents reveal that the manorial economy in medieval Ireland was founded on mixed agriculture but that cereal growing predominated to a very significant extent. Extents allow the size and balance between different land-uses on manorial demesnes to be investigated. Irish demesnes were large; those in the Dublin region were found to average 427 acres in size, making them significantly bigger than demesnes in the London region which, c.1300, averaged 180–90 acres. Much of this extra area was devoted to the growing of cereals. A number of different studies have shown that the proportion of land under arable cultivation on manors in Ireland in the thirteenth and early fourteenth centuries was very substantial, typically over 70 per cent. By the end of the thirteenth century, land-use in much of the east and south of the country closely paralleled that found across Europe where there was an almost universal trend towards the expansion of arable.[16]

---

14 *IPR 14 John.* For a discussion of the Irish manorial documents see M. Murphy, 'Manor Centres, Settlement and Agricultural Systems in Medieval Ireland, 1250–1350', in Murphy and Stout (eds.), *Agriculture and Settlement in Ireland,* 71–3. The most extensive collection of extent material is contained in *Inquisitions and Extents of Medieval Ireland,* ed. P. Dryburgh and B. Smith (London: List and Index Society, 2007). The surviving Irish accounts relate to manors held by Roger Bigod, earl of Norfolk: Ballysax (Kildare), Forth and Fennagh (Carlow) and Old Ross (Wexford). TNA SC 6/1237–9.

15 M. Murphy, 'Manor Centres', 75; English extents record an average value of £2 for manorial watermills. B. M. S. Campbell and K. Bartley, *England on the Eve of the Black Death: An Atlas of Lay Lordship, Land and Wealth, 1300–1349* (Manchester University Press, 2006), 297.

16 Murphy and Potterton, *Dublin Region in the Middle Ages,* 287–90; H. Jäger, 'Land Use in Medieval Ireland: A Review of the Documentary Evidence', *IESH,* 10 (1983), 64–5; M. Hennessy, 'Manorial Agriculture and Settlement in Early Fourteenth-Century Co. Tipperary', in Clarke *et al.* (eds.), *Surveying Ireland's Past,* 101; M. Murphy 'Rural

With some notable exceptions, extents do not reveal much about actual farming practices and for this it is necessary to rely on the small corpus of manorial accounts for the Bigod manors, supplemented by disparate sources including the mid-fourteenth-century accounts for the granges of Holy Trinity Priory in Dublin and the inventories drawn up when the properties of the Knights Templar were confiscated in 1308.[17] The significance of cereal production on Irish manorial demesnes in the late thirteenth and early fourteenth centuries is very evident from the resources devoted to ploughing and harvesting, the expenditure on the processing and storage of grain, and the income generated from sales of wheat and oats. On the Bigod manors in the 1280s, up to 70 per cent of the wheat harvest and 50 per cent of the oat harvest was marketed (see Fig. 1). In 1285–6 on the manor of Forth, County Carlow, income from sale of corn totalled £52 15s., more than five times as much as sales from pastoral products. In 1308, a substantial proportion of the value attached to the Templar manors accrued from cereals, both harvested and sown in the fields.[18]

There is compelling evidence that cereal agriculture in Anglo-Norman Ireland was producing an impressive surplus for exchange in the thirteenth and early fourteenth centuries. How had Irish agriculture become so productive? While practices that were known to increase the fertility of the soil, such as weeding, summer ploughing of the fallow, spreading dung, sanding and digging in sods taken from grassland as green manure, were employed on Irish manors, the proportion of land thus treated was never very great, and the associated labour costs were prohibitive. There is no substantial evidence for increased seeding rates or the widespread cultivation of nitrogen-fixing crops like peas, beans and vetches such as Campbell has described in parts of England. Campbell argues that intensive and productive husbandry systems were most likely to occur in areas of high economic rent – that is, areas where

Settlement in Meath, 1170–1660: The Documentary Evidence', in M. Deevy and D. Murphy (eds.), *Places Along the Way: First Findings on the M3* (Bray: Wordwell, 2009), 164; C. Dyer, 'Medieval Farming and Technology: Conclusion', in J. Langdon and G. G. Astill (eds.), *Medieval Farming and Technology: The Impact of Agricultural Change in Northwest Europe* (Leiden: Brill, 1997), 294.

17 *Account Roll of the Priory of the Holy Trinity, Dublin, 1337–1346*, ed. J. Mills (Dublin, 1891; new edn Dublin: Four Courts Press, 1996); 'Documents on the Suppression of the Templars in Ireland', ed. G. Mac Niocaill, *Analecta Hibernica*, 24 (1961), 183–226. Kevin Down made extensive use of these sources in his comprehensive survey of medieval agriculture: K. Down, 'Colonial Society and Economy in the High Middle Ages', *NHI* ii, 439–91, esp. 453.

18 TNA SC 6/1237/53; M. Murphy, 'From Swords to Ploughshares: Evidence for Templar Agriculture in Medieval Ireland', in Browne and Ó Clabaigh (eds.), *Soldiers of Christ*, 167–83.

Disposal of Wheat on Irish Manors (crannocks)

Manor	Year	Receipt	Sown	%	Transferred	%	Sold	%
Ballysax	1280–1	195	42	22	27	14	126	64
Fennagh	1283–4	141	21	15	–	–	120	85
Forth	1285–6	140	39	28	3	2	98	70
Old Ross	1287–8	78	33	42	–	–	45	58
totals		554	135	24	30	6	389	70

Disposal of Oats on Irish Manors (crannocks)

Manor	Year	Receipt	Sown	%	Fodder	%	Sold	%
Ballysax	1280–1	104	40	39	16	15	48	46
Fennagh	1283–4	168	51	30	18	11	99	59
Forth	1285–6	152	42	28	13	9	97	64
Old Ross	1287–8	165	91	55	24	15	50	30
totals		589	224	38	71	12	294	50

Figure 1. Disposal of wheat and oats on the Bigod manors in the 1280s. Source: TNA SC6.

there was high demand for land and/or good access to markets. In England this was the pattern in north-east Kent and east Norfolk, where English medieval agriculture attained its greatest peak of intensity and productivity. In Ireland, the particular circumstances of the late thirteenth century – growing urban populations combined with booming overseas demand – might be argued to have produced areas of high economic rent, but these areas do not appear to have developed very intensive practices.[19]

Increasing the volume of grain production in Anglo-Norman Ireland seems to have been a matter of extending the cultivated area, rather than adopting advanced agricultural practices. This expansion was achieved through purchase, lease and forest clearance and much of the newly acquired land was devoted to the cultivation of wheat, the most valuable and commercial crop. On the manor of Old Ross, County Wexford, the acreage under wheat increased over four-fold in the 1280s (see Fig. 2). Yields per seed and per acre remained modest on Irish manors, but in this they resembled much of

19 Digging in dung cost 1s. per acre on the Bigod manors while transporting and spreading sand could cost up to 2s. per acre. Wheat yielded around four times the seed sown ,while oats typically yielded around 2½ times the seed sown. B. M. S. Campbell, 'Economic Rent and the Intensification of English Agriculture 1086 to 1350', in Langdon and Astill (eds.), *Medieval Farming and Technology*, 238.

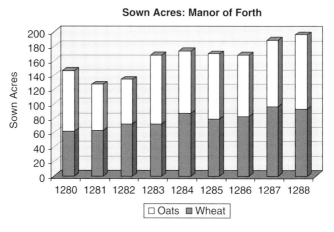

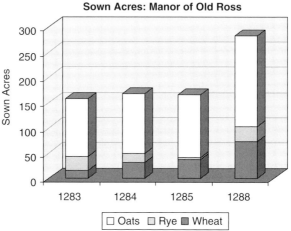

Figure 2. Increase of arable acreages in the 1280s on the manors of Forth, County Carlow, and Old Ross, County Wexford. Source: TNA SC6.

England at the same period, including counties such as Hertfordshire which formed part of the commercialised hinterland of medieval London.[20] What we do see in Ireland is the relatively early adoption of techniques which allowed more land to be cultivated. Mixed plough teams of oxen and horses increased the speed at which land could be ploughed and therefore allowed more land to be cultivated. In Ireland mixed teams of six oxen and two horses

20 B. M. S. Campbell, J. A. Galloway, D. J. Keene and M. Murphy, *A Medieval Capital and its Grain Supply: Agrarian Production and Distribution in the London Region, c.1300* (Historical Geography Research Series, 30, 1993), 126–7.

appear to have been used on the manor of Baggotrath near Dublin and in County Kildare on the manors of Rathmore and Maynooth. Such teams were the norm on the manors of the Knights Templar, where very substantial arable acreages were cultivated and quite significant levels of commercialisation were achieved.[21]

The driving forces behind the expansion of arable land were the growing opportunities for marketing along with fairly buoyant prices for grain. Some of the demand came from the growing urban population within Ireland. There are no reliable population figures for a single Irish town in this period but Campbell has proposed an urban population of 94,000 for Ireland c.1290, suggesting that 14 per cent of the population of the lordship (estimated at 0.7 million) lived in towns. A recent estimate has proposed that if Dublin had a population of 10,000, the grain output of 60,000 acres of land would have been required to supply its cereal needs. Using the same methodology suggests that an urban population of 94,000 would have required the grain output of 564,000 acres.[22]

There was also the growing external market for Irish grain. From the early days of the conquest the English kings further developed the potential of the Irish Sea area as a commercial zone, and in the thirteenth century Ireland proved to be one of the king's greatest storehouses of grain. In 1224–5 the mayor of London purchased 1,000 crannocks of wheat from the lands that had been William Marshal's and English and Scottish religious houses were permitted to take equally large quantities for their own needs or for profit.[23] Purveyance of grain for the king's armies is first mentioned in the 1240s and, from then until 1324, thousands of crannocks of Irish wheat, oats, malt, flour and meal were bought to supply the king's armies in Wales, Scotland and Gascony. The price of wheat in Ireland appears to have generally been below average English prices, although Henry III discovered in 1246 that 'corn, wine and other supplies are dearer in Ireland than the king believed'.[24] Wine was certainly cheaper in Ireland than in England. In 1306 the price of wine was

21 J. Langdon, *Horses, Oxen and Technological Innovation: The Use of Draught Animals in English Farming from 1066 to 1500* (Cambridge University Press, 1986), 51; NAI RC 8/18, 559–64; *CJRI, 1305–07*, 240–1; Murphy, 'From Swords to Ploughshares', 175–6.

22 Campbell, 'Benchmarking Medieval Economic Development', 911; Murphy and Potterton, *Dublin Region in the Middle Ages*, 482.

23 Hudson, *Irish Sea Studies*, 38–41; O'Neill, *Merchants and Mariners*, 22; Down, 'Colonial Society and Economy', 485.

24 J. F. Lydon, 'Ireland's Participation in the Military Activities of the English Kings in the Thirteenth and Early Fourteenth Centuries'. PhD thesis, University of London (1955), 192–7, 226–9; Murphy and Potterton, *Dublin Region in the Middle Ages*, 478–9; *CDI, 1171–1251*, no. 2835, p. 423.

fixed at 3*d*. a gallon, probably due to increased demand because of the war in Scotland. In 1300 in the north of England wine cost between 5*d*. and 7*d*. a gallon. In 1362 Lionel of Clarence fixed the maximum selling price of wine in Ireland at 8*d*. a gallon at a time when it was almost 13*d*. in Durham.[25]

The dominant position of arable on the demesnes and the commercial nature of cereal production may have resulted in an over-emphasis on this sector in the historical literature on the medieval Irish agricultural economy. Pastoral farming was also important and there are indications of management strategies that reflect its commercial nature. Sales of wool and cheese averaged around £70 per annum on the manor of Old Ross in County Wexford, which had a sheep flock of over 2,500 animals in 1289. Here, and on the manor of Ballysax, County Kildare, where wool sales were also significant, it is possible to identify husbandry strategies, such as employing shepherds and building sheepcotes, which recognised that keeping animals warm and healthy resulted in increased profits.[26] Wool was marketed from an early stage of the conquest. In 1213 the order of the Knights Templar were given permission to export their wool for sale. Three years later the archbishop of Dublin was able to sell fifty-one sacks of wool to merchants. This represented the clip of between 13,000 and 21,000 sheep. Some wool was needed to supply the Irish cloth industry but most was exported to Flanders where it was used for the production of cheap cloth. After 1275 Ireland followed the example of England and voted customs duties on wool, woolfells and hides to Edward 1 who appointed Italians to collect the custom. Between 1275 and 1280 the merchants of Lucca collected over £1,000 per annum from the custom.[27] The receipts from the custom suggest a high level of pastoral prosperity of the country in the south and east of Ireland, and particularly in the hinterlands of Waterford and Ross (see Map 14). The river system of the Suir, Nore and Barrow flowed through the estates of several large landholders as well as the lands of ten major Cistercian abbeys. It must also be remembered that the customs men stood no chance of assessing or drawing upon the pastoral wealth of Gaelic Ireland. The vast cattle-fines imposed upon O'Neill in the thirteenth century suggest that in Ulster, too, there was livestock aplenty (see Map 14).

25 NAI RC 8/2, 495–6; E. Gemmill, 'Prices from the Durham Obedientiary Account Rolls 1278 to 1367', in M. Allen and D'M. Coffmann (eds.), *Money, Prices and Wages: Essays in Honour of Professor Nicholas Mayhew* (Houndmills: Palgrave Macmillan, 2015), 76; NAI RC 8/28, 296–7.
26 TNA SC 6/1238/55; Murphy, 'Manor Centres', 97–8.
27 H. Wood, 'The Templars in Ireland', *PRIA*, 26 C (1906–7), 338; *CDI, 1171–1251*, 109; O'Neill, *Merchants and Mariners*, 58–65; *CDI, 1252–1284*, 195, 544–5.

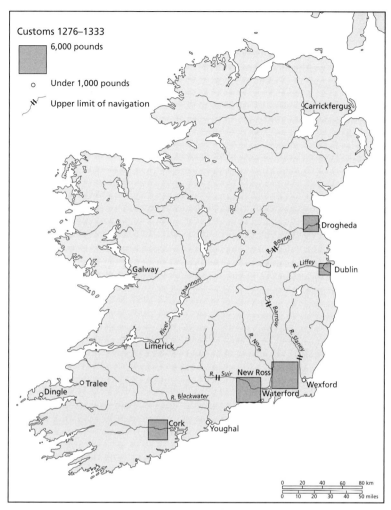

MAP 14. Customs Receipts 1276–1333. Ports and navigable rivers are shown. Source: Graham, 'The High Middle Ages', 89.

Much of the foregoing has concentrated on the demesne sector – that is the portion of the manor farmed directly by the lord – but it should be stressed that a greater proportion of land was farmed by smallholders.[28] Evidence

---

28 According to Campbell, only 25 to 30 per cent of agricultural land in medieval England was farmed by the lords. B. M. S. Campbell, *English Seigniorial Agriculture, 1250–1450* (Cambridge University Press, 2000), 26.

relating to their farming practices is much harder to find. A variety of sources, including tithe payments, lists of goods confiscated from those accused of wrongdoing, and crops handed over in return for using the manorial mill indicate that smallholders grew a greater variety of crops.[29] Dividing acreage between a number of different crops, including mixed crops and legumes, gave smallholders some protection from periodic crop failures. Their agriculture was also more mixed than that of the lords. They might possess one or two working animals, along with a few cows, sheep and pigs. The inventory of the possessions of an Irish *betagh* [unfree] tenant in 1303 provides a rare insight into the farming practices of smallholders. The sheriff of Dublin reported that Clement Ocathyll, one of the king's *betaghs*, who had been killed at Cruagh, possessed at the time of his death:

> Four cows with their calves, 16s.; an ox, 3s.; three affers (work horses) 6s. 8d.; thirty sheep, 40d. one pig, 4d., three small stacks of oats containing an estimated five crannocks; a small stack of wheat, beans and barley containing an estimated one bushel of wheat, two bushels of beans and two bushels of barley, a stack of turf worth 6s. 8d., a brass pot, 6s. 8d. and a chest worth 6d.[30]

This was clearly an individual who had a modest smallholding and was engaged in a mixture of arable and pastoral farming.

These small-scale producers may have been active in marketing their goods. Recent research suggests that peasants voluntarily engaged with the market, contradicting an earlier assumption of a subsistence peasant sector that was hostile to the market.[31] Labour services had never been required from most of the settler peasantry in Ireland, who instead paid money renders to their lords. As levels of taxation increased, the need on the part of peasants to acquire money through sale of their surpluses increased. Crops like legumes and rye may have been cultivated for family consumption, while oats and, above all, wheat were marketed. The accounts of the royal purveyors operating out of Drogheda in the early fourteenth century show many small purchases of wheat and oats, sometimes in quantities of less than a crannock (see Fig. 3). These appear to have been from smallholders and peasants. While the large lay and religious demesnes marketed large

---

29 Murphy and Potterton, *Dublin Region in the Middle Ages*, 304–5; *Account Roll of the Priory of the Holy Trinity, Dublin*, 77–83; *CDI, 1285–1292*, 293.
30 NAI RC 8/2, 314.
31 R. Grafe, 'Economic and Social Trends', in H. Scott (ed.), *Early Modern European History 1350–1750. Volume 1: Peoples and Place* (Oxford University Press, 2015), 282.

Wheat Purchases[1]

Size (crannocks)	No. of Purchases	Sum (crannocks)	% of Total
20 +	3	72	46.4
10 – <20	0	0	0
5 – <10	4	24	15.5
2 – <5	12	36.5	23.5
1 – <2	13	17.6	11.4
<1	8	5	3.2
Total	40	155.1	100

Oats Purchases[1]

Size (crannocks)[2]	No. of Purchases	Sum (crannocks)	% of Total
20 +	3	74.5	33.8
10 – <20	1	10.4	4.7
5 – <10	2	10.5	4.8
2 – <5	16	49.8	22.6
1 – <2	39	64.1	29.1
<1	13	11.2	5.1
Total	74	220.5	100.1

Figure 3. Drogheda Purveyance, May–Nov. 1314. Source: Galloway, 'Economic Hinterland of Drogheda', 175; derived from TNA E101/14/35
Note 1: Excludes quantities obtained from the Sheriff of Meath.
Note 2: In the account, purchases of oats are recorded using the large crannock of 14 pecks. Here these have been converted into 'standard' 8-peck crannocks to facilitate comparison with the statistics for wheat.

quantities of wool, it is likely that as much, or more, came from the small flocks of hundreds of peasants. A study of Scottish wool exports in the medieval period concluded that the vast bulk came from the flocks of peasant farmers.[32]

There undoubtedly were producers, large and small, who were not commercialised and this was not necessarily down to unsuccessful or unsatisfactory farming techniques. Farmers may have been pursuing a deliberate strategy of which low productivity was the logical outcome. Production for the market meant increased labour costs and increased vulnerability to market fluctuations, bad harvests and weather.

32 Galloway, 'Economic Hinterland of Drogheda', 173–7; P. G. B. McNeill and H. L. McQueen (eds.), *Atlas of Scottish History to 1707* (Edinburgh: The Scottish Medievalists and Department of Geography, University of Edinburgh, 1996), 251.

Towns, Trade, and the Urban Hinterland

The manorial system was central to the Anglo-Norman strategy of agrarian exploitation and the chartered borough was equally fundamental to their commercial intentions. A large landholder could generate profit from the sale of the surplus production of his or her demesne lands but there was also financial advantage in facilitating the marketing activities of manorial tenants. By founding a borough with marketing functions the lord could, at one stroke, attract settlers to the manor and ensure that surplus production from tenant lands was channelled into his market, with resulting profits from rents and tolls. 'The borough', it has been observed, 'was part of the mechanism by which he [the lord] abstracted the maximum profit from his lands'.[33] Borough and town foundation was therefore an aspect of economically motivated seigneurial control in Ireland, as it was in Wales, England and all over Europe where the period between 1170 and 1250 saw the greatest number of town foundations. Somewhere between 250 and 330 places in Ireland are reckoned to have had some kind of borough status. Some of these never proceeded beyond their formal enfranchisement and many more did not survive for very long. About fifty or so developed into successful commercial centres, including most of those founded by great lords on their capital manors. Smaller boroughs and markets served the needs of their immediate hinterlands as well as functioning as stepping stones to the larger markets and seaports. Much work remains to be done on the hierarchies of size, function and population of nucleated settlements in medieval Ireland. O'Brien's analysis of the 1299 list of thirty-eight market towns in Cork demonstrated that in this region the smaller market towns constituted an extensive network of commercial traffic and a vital part of the infrastructure of the agrarian and mercantile economy. There was a significant concentration of towns in mid- and east Cork, the most manorialised area. Many were situated on or at important inland routes and the fordable points of rivers.[34]

A study of the occupations pursued in towns reveals something of the social and economic complexity of these settlements. In smaller towns occupations

33 B. J. Graham, 'The High Middle Ages: c.1100 to c.1350', in B. J. Graham and L. J. Proudfoot (eds.), *A Historical Geography of Ireland* (London: Academic Press, 1993), 81.

34 G. Martin, 'Plantation Boroughs in Medieval Ireland, with a Handlist of Boroughs to c.1500', in D. Harkness and M. O'Dowd (eds.), *The Town in Ireland* (Belfast: Appletree Press, 1981), 27–8; B. J. Graham, 'Ireland: Economy and Society', 154; *CJRI, 1295–1303*, 265–6; A. F. O'Brien, 'Politics, Economy and Society: The Development of Cork and the Irish South-Coast Region c.1170 to c.1583', in P. O'Flanagan and C. G. Buttimer (eds.), *Cork: History and Society* (Dublin: Geography Publications, 1993), 94–5.

tended to relate to the provisioning and processing of agricultural produce and included bakers, millers, brewers and tanners. Medium-sized settlements might have tailors, shoemakers and potters, while larger towns had more specialised craftspeople and artisans. In the thirteenth century the provosts of the large port of New Ross included a wimpler (maker of wimples or ladies' veils), goldsmith, napper (maker of linen cloth) and gaunter (glove maker), while in the smaller settlement of Carlow the occupations of tanner, fisherman, baker, tailor and chapman are found.[35] Size cannot always be related to occupational complexity. When William, bishop of Ossory, and his entourage were assaulted by the provost and community of New Leighlin, County Carlow, in 1305 the attackers included two fishermen, three chapmen, two tanners, a mason, a potter, a smith and a cobbler.[36]

At the top of the urban hierarchy were twenty-five mercantile towns, about half of them seaports (see Map 14). The majority of these settlements had fewer than 1,000 inhabitants. Fethard, County Tipperary, might serve as an example of a successful commercial centre in an economically well-advantaged region. O'Keeffe proposed a burgess population of eighty in the thirteenth century. Postulating an equivalent number of non-burgess inhabitants and a household multiplier of five would give a population of 800.[37] Kilkenny was the most important inland town, comprising the two boroughs of High Town and Irish Town, a major ecclesiastical centre with an important castle. Its population in the late thirteenth century may have reached 4,500. Dublin, with a population of at least 10,000, possibly more, was by far the biggest urban centre while five other ports – Drogheda, Waterford, New Ross, Cork and Limerick – are each likely to have had around 2,000 inhabitants. Smaller seaports such as Dundalk, Wexford, Youghal and Galway may have reached 1,000.[38]

Commerce was an essential function of all but the smallest settlements. Grants of weekly markets and annual fairs proliferated in the course of the thirteenth century. The markets catered for the quotidian needs of urban and rural consumers while significant quantities and a wide variety of goods

35 J. S. Mills, 'Accounts of the Earl of Norfolk's Estates in Ireland, 1279–1294', *JRSAI*, 2 (1892), 50–62.
36 *CJRI, 1305–07*, 42.
37 Graham, 'High Middle Ages', 87; T. O'Keeffe, *Fethard*. Irish Historic Towns Atlas (Dublin: RIA, 2003), 2; Frame, *Colonial Ireland*, 101.
38 J. Bradley, *Kilkenny*. Irish Historic Towns Atlas (Dublin: RIA, 2000), 2, 4; J. Bradley, 'Kilkenny', in S. Duffy (ed.), *Medieval Ireland: An Encyclopedia* (New York and London: Routledge, 2005), 249–50; Campbell, 'Benchmarking Medieval Economic Development', 911–13.

could change hands at the fairs, which often went on for eight days. In June 1244 the seneschal of Meath was ordered to have retained 'all the wines, hides, wool, cloth and iron which he can find at the fair of Trim, together with 500 crannocks of wheat and 500 crannocks of oats'.[39] Murage charters are perhaps the most useful single indicator of the produce for sale in the towns of medieval Ireland. These grants of tolls to be levied on goods sold at markets and fairs contain the basic staples of grain, livestock, cloth and fuel but over time expanded to include a huge variety of commodities. They largely follow a standardised format, but on occasion do appear to reflect local specialisms which can be corroborated by other sources. Trim was notable for the sale of a wide variety of cloth, including very sought after imports like samite and diaper.[40] Commodities on which murage was chargeable in Drogheda, a centre for shipbuilding, included a number specifically related to the building or repair of boats and ships. Murage was charged on teasels in a handful of towns and might indicate an active fulling industry in or near these settlements (teasels were used to raise the nap on cloth). The 1283 murage for Kilkenny includes a toll of a farthing on every 1,000 teasels sold.[41]

Urban markets and fairs served the needs of a variety of producers and consumers. The nature of the surviving sources means that we have more information on what producers marketed than on what consumers purchased. The lack of household and kitchen accounts makes it difficult to reconstruct the consumption and shopping strategies of large households. A fragmentary account for March/April 1309 – probably for the household of Roger Mortimer and his wife Joan at Ardmulchan, County Meath – gives some insight into the patterns of purchases of a large noble household.[42] Items purchased included food, drink, animal fodder, candles and miscellaneous items, and a range of different markets were used, some near at hand including Ardmulchan and Navan, and some further away. Bread, wine, cod, herrings, oats, hay and ale were purchased at Trim about 20 km distant while assorted shellfish, including 3,000 oysters, were bought in Dublin 50 km away. There are hints that some purchases may have been made from 'door to door' salesmen – for example, 1,000 onions from a 'man of Dublin'. Dyer's study of consumers and the market in medieval

---

39 *CDI, 1171–1251*, 402.
40 A. Thomas, 'Financing Town Walls in Medieval Ireland', in C. Thomas (ed.), *Rural Landscapes and Communities: Essays Presented to Desmond McCourt* (Dublin: Irish Academic Press, 1986), 86; Potterton, *Medieval Trim*, 146, 159.
41 Galloway, 'Economic Hinterland of Drogheda', 170; *CIRCLE*: PR 4 Ed II; CR 48 Ed III; *CDI, 1252–1284*, 430.
42 *Household Accounts from Medieval England*, ed. C. M. Woolgar. 2 vols. (Oxford University Press, 1992), i, 173–7.

England revealed that geography did not always determine where consumers sourced their supplies; tastes and preferences also played a part. Noble households were more likely to build up relationships with suppliers who would visit and deliver food to them.[43] The consumption pattern of the prior of Holy Trinity Dublin reveals a liking for luxury items sourced in the Dublin market. However, rural religious houses might also consume luxuries. The survival of a fragmentary kitchen account for the priory of Kells, County Kilkenny, dated to 1382 allows a glimpse into the market activity of such a house. The Augustinian canons were buying pigs, geese, wooden bowls, and utensils. More luxurious items included figs, olive oil, pepper and saffron. These may have been sourced in Kilkenny, where a murage grant of 1283 reveals that pepper, cumin, saffron, ginger and spices were taxed as well as almonds, figs and raisins.[44]

Murage charters reveal that imported items were available in many smaller towns also. These markets served the needs of minor gentry, clergy, artisans and peasants from the countryside who would take produce into town to sell and use the opportunity to make some purchases of their own. These might include salt, metalwork, cloth, shoes, gloves, decorative items and lamp oil. The sources do not really allow us to see to what extent cash, or delayed payment or barter systems were used, or gauge how much trade took place outside of markets. The presence of the occupational name 'chapmen' in small towns such as Ratoath, Dunshaughlin and Carlow indicate that travelling salespeople were clearly important.[45]

Regional and local trade were facilitated by land, river and coastal routeways, and the murage charters frequently specify goods arriving by packhorse, cart and boat. Water transport was considerably cheaper than overland transport, especially for bulky commodities such as grain, wool, millstones and timber. While the largest medieval cart could carry 1 ton, even a small ship could carry a cargo of 10–15 tons and the boats and rafts that were used on the rivers could probably carry between 3 and 6 tons. Virtually all the important inland towns were situated on or near navigable rivers that connected them to the port towns and facilitated the movement of goods.[46] Overland carriage was also vital and the large roads leading into the major towns were well used. In 1326, on the archbishop of Dublin's manor

---

43 C. Dyer 'The Consumer and the Market in Medieval England', *Economic History Review*, 42 (1989), 305–27.
44 Murphy and Potterton, 'Investigating Living Standards', 241; *Irish Monastic and Episcopal Deeds, AD 1200–1600*, ed. N. B. White (Dublin: IMC, 1936), 10–11; *CDI, 1252–1284*, 494–5.
45 *Dublin Guild Merchant Roll*, 66, 81, 106.
46 W. Childs, 'Commerce and Trade', in *NCMH*, vii, 148; O'Neill, *Merchants and Mariners*, 108; L. Doran, 'Lords of the River Valleys: Economic and Military Lordship in the

of St Sepulchre, which was close to Dublin, six acres of meadowland were
said to be worth very little as they lay near the highway and were tram-
pled by carters.[47] Roads appear to have been of three types: the main
highways – often described as the king's ways – ran between major towns;
lesser roads linked smaller towns and boroughs; and yet smaller roads connected satellite manorial settlements to manorial centres, parish churches
and mills. The efficiency of the Irish road network in the late thirteenth century is suggested by the itinerary of the justiciar, Archbishop John Sandford.
In the summer of 1290 he left Drogheda on 14 June, travelled around the
country – stopping off in twenty-six towns and settlements – and arrived at
Ferns on 17 August. In some places, such as Athenry, Loughrea, Cashel, Cork
and Waterford, he stopped for four or five days, while other stops, such as
those at Mullingar, Rindoon, Nenagh, Kilmallock and Youghal, were for one
or two nights. We do not know the specific route Sandford followed, but can
be certain that each stage of his journey was accomplished in the course of
one day.[48] Legislation passed at the Dublin parliament of 1297 indicates that
the maintenance of safe, wide thoroughfares was the responsibility of landowners and their tenants. Neglect not only hampered commerce, but facilitated Irish malefactors who took cover in overgrown verges. The necessity
of maintaining bridges in good order was also a concern of the legislators.
Many of the new stone and timber bridges erected in the thirteenth century
were by 1297 in need of repair and replacement. Grants of pontage (the right
to levy toll on goods brought across a bridge) became common in the fourteenth and fifteenth centuries.[49]

The transport infrastructure was particularly important around the largest
urban centres, which placed considerable demands on their hinterlands for
food, fuel and building materials. It is unlikely, however, that these demands
were large enough to shape land-use and promote specialisation in the surrounding area, as has been proposed for the medieval London region.[50] There
is some evidence, nonetheless, to suggest the 'zoning' of agricultural production in response to provisioning demands. The study of Dublin's hinterland revealed some distinctive patterns of land-use which may have had an

Carlow Corridor, c. 1200–1350 – European Model in an Irish Context', in Doran and
Lyttleton (eds.), *Lordship in Medieval Ireland*, 99–129.
47 *Cal. Archbishop Alen's Register* c.*1172–1534*, ed. C. McNeill (Dublin: RSAI, 1950), 170.
48 *CDI 1285–1292*, 265–77.
49 P. Connolly, 'The Enactments of the 1297 Parliament', in Lydon (ed.), *Law and Disorder*,
159; CIRCLE: PR 4 Ed II, CR 18 Ed III, CR 48 Ed III, PR 13 Ric II.
50 Murphy, 'Feeding Another City', 3–4.

initial environmental origin but which are likely to have been emphasised and enhanced by the city's demands (see Map 15). Thus, grain needs were substantially met by the region to the north, where manors were sometimes totally grain-orientated, while demands for meat, dairy produce and wood were largely satisfied by the southern hinterland, where mixed farming predominated. Apart from crisis years, Dublin appears to have been comfortably provisioned by its hinterland (see Map 15).

Waterford was also fortunate in having a hinterland both north and south of the River Suir which provided grain and meat for its citizens along with wool and hides for overseas trade. Local woodlands provided both fuel and building materials. It was political instability that fractured the relationship between Waterford and its hinterland in the late fourteenth and fifteenth century, and necessitated imports of corn from neighbouring counties. Recent research has shown that Drogheda placed considerable demands on its hinterland for foodstuffs and fuel. There was a strong arable emphasis on the lands close to the town, which meant that even in difficult times grain would have been available. Sourcing wood for building and fuel was a problem, however, and may have placed constraints on the development of the settlement.[51]

Towns also had negative effects on their hinterlands. Finite resources such as fresh water and fuel might be drawn into the town at the expense of the countryside, while a large town might seek to stifle commercial activity in its hinterland which it perceived as competition. The fact that there were no markets within 12 km of Dublin was probably due to active lobbying by Dublin's merchants: in 1275 they complained about a market on the lands of the archbishop outside the town which was damaging their trade, and it is likely that they also successfully prevented a market from operating in Dalkey until the fifteenth century.[52] In 1290 the burgesses of Shandon, a borough on the north side of the Lee, complained that the citizens of Cork were preventing them trading as they were wont to do, and that as a result they were much impoverished. Waterford was particularly ruthless in imposing its market dominance

---

51 M. Murphy, M. Connon and J. Galloway, 'Waterford and its Hinterland: An Historical Overview', in J. Eogan and E. S. Twohig (eds.), *Cois tSiúre – Nine Thousand Years of Human Activity in the Lower Suir Valley: Archaeological Excavations on the N25 Waterford City Bypass*. NRA Scheme Monographs 8 (Dublin: The National Roads Authority, 2011), 240; Galloway, 'Economic Hinterland of Drogheda', 171.

52 Sayles, *Affairs*, 11; Murphy and Potterton, *Dublin Region in the Middle Ages*, 469; C. V. Smith, *Dalkey: Society and Economy in a Small Medieval Irish Town* (Dublin: Irish Academic Press, 1996), 51.

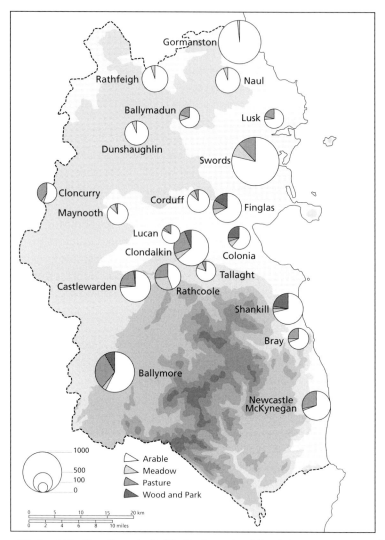

MAP 15. Land-Use Data from the Dublin Region *c.*1300. The circles represent manorial demesnes and the size reflects the acreage. Shading represents proportions of demesne acreage under different land uses. Source: Murphy, 'Feeding Another City', 13.

in both its southern and northern hinterlands. There were very few boroughs south of Waterford and none in south-east Kilkenny. In 1396 the city successfully appealed against a licence granted to the nuns of Kilculliheen, situated across the Suir opposite Waterford. This licence had given the nuns permission to buy and sell goods within their demesne, which the appeal claimed was doing 'great damage to the city of Waterford and its citizens'.[53]

Measures of Economic Prosperity

Two particular actions of the English crown facilitated trade and wealth creation in thirteenth-century Ireland. The first was the institution of a uniform and reputable coinage. Coins minted in England and at times in Scotland circulated widely in Ireland throughout this period, but a money economy was further promoted by the production of coins by the royal mint in Dublin from the early thirteenth century and in other centres, including Limerick and Waterford, by 1300. The other crucial initiative was the introduction of Italian merchant bankers into Ireland. They were already operating in England, where they were quickly becoming indispensable to the English crown, and the extension of their activities to Ireland facilitated the capital enterprises of the new settlers and promoted economic development. In Ireland they were closely connected with the collection of the papal revenues and also customs. They supervised the mint, engaged in import–export trades, acted as purveyors of supplies for the administration and the king, and lent money freely to government, clergy, aristocracy and townsmen.[54]

There have been some recent attempts to evaluate the state of Irish economic development at the end of the thirteenth century. In 1291 parliament granted Edward I permission to levy a lay subsidy of one-fifteenth in Ireland and arrangements for collection were put in place in 1292. Everyone was assessed and liable to pay this tax on moveable wealth, except the very poor. Hennessy's analysis of the returns of the subsidy show that a total of £10,000 was collected from Ireland, the vast majority of it from the east and the south of the country. The region stretching from Dublin to Louth had the highest concentration of moveable wealth, with counties Kilkenny, Carlow, Kildare, Wexford and Limerick forming a second tier and Waterford, Tipperary and Cork a further step down. The receipts of the separately recorded towns also show the economic strength of the eastern region[55] (see Fig. 4).

Hennessy interprets the lay subsidy receipts as showing the wealth and productivity of those parts of Ireland which had been integrated into a wider

53 *CPR, 1391–6*, 702; *CDI, 1285–1292*, 307.
54 M. Dolley, 'Coinage to 1534: The Sign of the Times', in *NHI* ii, 818–25; M. D. O'Sullivan, *Italian Merchant Bankers in Ireland in the Thirteenth Century* (Dublin: Alan Figgis & Co, 1962), 12, 16, 26.
55 *Parls. & Councils*, 198–9; Hennessy, 'Making Ireland English', 85–9.

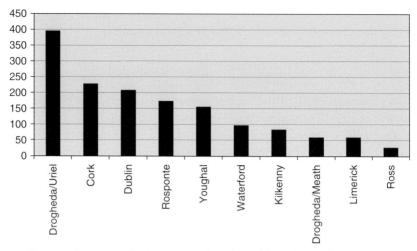

Figure 4. Summary of urban receipts from the Irish lay subsidy of 1292. Source: Hennessy, 'Making Ireland English', 81–92, fig. 4.3. Hennessy believes the Dublin receipts are artificially low as ecclesiastical wealth was not taxed and Dublin had disproportionately high level of ecclesiastical wealth.

'English' economic zone and could be successfully exploited by the crown. In contrast, Campbell has described Ireland as being only a 'modest financial asset to the crown', with its economic development far below that of England or even Scotland. While Ireland had more religious houses and was more urbanised than Scotland, the per capita ecclesiastical wealth was much smaller, the per capita money supply remained less than half that of both England and Scotland, and Ireland earned less than either England or Scotland from exports.[56]

There must be some suspicion that what our figures record is not the actual wealth of the country, but the geographical scope of English authority and the ability of the agents of the crown to turn that authority into revenue. It is difficult to believe, for instance, that parts of Munster were not far wealthier than surviving colonial and English exchequer records would lead us to believe. Negative assessments of levels of prosperity on the island must be balanced against individual examples of significant wealth creation. Some of the profits generated by Irish agriculture were immediately siphoned out of the country into the wardrobes of absentee lords, like

56 Campbell, 'Benchmarking Medieval Economic Development', 931–5.

Roger Bigod, or for repayment of debts to Italian moneylenders. A significant amount, however, was spent in Ireland, on building projects, church endowment, and also on ostentatious personal display. The array of goods and chattels which Silvester l'Ercedekne [Archdeacon] claimed was stolen from his castle of Dunohill, County Tipperary, in 1295 – wall-hangings, fine linen, silverware, and jewellery – may be unusual in its splendour but is nevertheless instructive, especially when one considers that the l'Ercedeknes were not of the top rank of settler society.[57] Even modest castles were furnished with hangings, fine linen and silverware, while their occupants possessed precious jewellery. The wealth of individual churchmen in Ireland is also eye-catching: the chattels of Stephen de Fulbourn, archbishop of Tuam, which were listed in 1288, included thirty furs and eleven pairs of silken shoes, along with a wide range of gold and silverware. In his larder were large quantities of almonds, rice, figs, raisins and dates.[58] Luxury items and gold and silverware were also a guarantee of solvency, a reserve of ready capital which could be broken into to pay debts or raise loans. In the middle of the fourteenth century, for instance, Hugh de Burgh, a former treasurer of Ireland, paid off a large debt to his apothecary with ten gold rings and a pair of silver scales with silver weights.[59]

The Fourteenth and Fifteenth Centuries

The period between c.1270 and c.1420 has long been identified as one of great socio-economic instability throughout north-west Europe, but environmental historians are now demonstrating that it was also characterised by unusually unstable climatic conditions. In most of England up to the end of the thirteenth century rising population levels and a shortage of land increased the vulnerability of its inhabitants to the shocks the fourteenth century had in store. The collapse in population, desertion of settlements and shortage of labour caused by those shocks resulted in a retreat from arable farming in many areas, and a noticeable shrinkage of urban populations. Although population densities were lower in Ireland than in England, the chronology of

57 *CJRI, 1295–1303*, 6–7.
58 *CDI 1285–1292*, 181–2. Fulbourn was suspected of having enriched himself while serving as treasurer and chief governor of Ireland. P. Connolly, 'Fulbourn, Stephen of', in *ODNB*.
59 O'Sullivan, *Italian Merchant Bankers*, 110; P. Connolly, 'The Irish Memoranda Rolls: Some Unexplored Aspects', *IESH*, 3 (1976), 69. 'There was an easy fluidity between the ornaments of a great church or the plate on a great man's table and the coin into which they could so easily be transformed': R. W. Southern, *The Making of the Middle Ages* (London: Hutchinson, 1967), 46.

demographic contraction mirrored that seen across the water. The fact that Irish resources had been so thoroughly exploited to meet the need for food, men and money of one of Europe's most belligerent nations also lessened the country's ability to withstand economic catastrophe.[60] Within the space of half a century, Europe's population halved. The Great European Famine of 1315–18 may have been the worst subsistence crisis in recorded European history, while the Black Death is almost certainly Europe's worst crisis of public health. Ireland suffered greatly during the famine and the cattle murrain which followed in its wake, and also had to face the military and political turmoil of the Bruce invasion.[61] Despite these cumulative shocks, there is some surprising evidence of economic resilience in the period between 1320 and 1340. The purveyance [compulsory purchase of foodstuffs] conducted by the crown in 1322–5 saw over 10,000 quarters of grain being acquired in County Meath, while the annual income garnered from the lordship of Trim when it was in the king's hand in the 1320s was an impressive £300. In 1344 lands in Saggart, south-west of Dublin, were said to lie waste for want of cultivators, but the grange of Clonkeen in south County Dublin, which belonged to Holy Trinity Priory, was able to marshal eighty-eight reapers to set to work on the first day of the harvest.[62]

The arrival of the Black Death in 1348–9 and the recurrence of the plague in the 1360s and 1370s resulted in substantial population decline, particularly in the urbanised areas. It has been estimated that Dublin and its region suffered a 40 per cent reduction of population through a combination of mortality and emigration.[63] However, the post-Black Death period may also have been a time of opportunity. The prosperity of some small landholders increased as they advanced from being tenants to freeholders. Women may also have found it easier to become more economically autonomous: there is evidence of a small but growing number of female merchants in Kilkenny in the late fourteenth century. Trade and exchange continued, as did the activities of the major seaports. Smith has noted that the economic dislocation caused by the plague in England led to an increased reliance on supplies from ports such as Drogheda. In 1367, during an attack on Waterford, it was

---

60 Campbell, 'Nature as Historical Protagonist', 305; Britnell, *Britain and Ireland*, 314–15.
61 Campbell, 'Nature as Historical Protagonist', 284; M. C. Lyons, 'Weather, Famine, Pestilence and Plague in Ireland, 900–1500', in E. M. Crawford (ed.), *Famine: The Irish Experience 900–1900: Subsistence Crises and Famines in Ireland* (Edinburgh: John Donald, 1989), 43, 63–4.
62 Potterton, *Medieval Trim*, 92–112; *Account Roll of the Priory of the Holy Trinity, Dublin*, 64–7.
63 M. Kelly, *The Great Dying: The Black Death in Dublin* (Stroud: Tempus, 2003), 84–92.

claimed that eighty English people from Coventry, Dartmouth and Bristol and other parts were killed.[64]

It has been calculated that the average revenue of the Irish exchequer in 1278–99 was £6,300, but that by 1368–84 it had fallen as low as £2,512.[65] Evidence suggests that government income continued to fall through the end of the fourteenth century and that the fifteenth century was even worse. While this reveals a contraction in the reach of central government, it should not be proposed as an indication of general economic decline. Indeed, there is persuasive evidence of economic recovery in the later fourteenth century and throughout the fifteenth century. It has been estimated that around 3,000 tower houses were built by Gaelic and Anglo-Irish lords across the countryside and in many of the towns in this period. These were partly erected for purposes of defence, but should be seen above all as domestic structures designed for a new class of freeholding lesser lord with significant financial resources. The production of new wealth, and the growth of opportunities for advancement were in part a result of that shrinking of central government and break-up of aristocratic estates so often identified by historians as indicators of a more general decline. The emergence of new gentry families in County Meath has been well documented, and it was these families that made their mark by constructing architecturally ambitious tower houses, endowing parish churches, and commissioning funerary monuments.[66]

While many manors and their associated nucleated settlements were deserted, there is also evidence for the persistence of the manorial economy. Empey has used early fifteenth-century extents relating to a group of small manors in south-eastern Tipperary and south-western Kilkenny to argue that 'in spite of the prevailing political and economic climate manorial society remained firmly ensconced there'.[67] The agriculture practised on these manors in many cases had changed, with a retreat from labour-intensive arable towards more pastoral farming. Traditionally seen as a result of the revival of Gaelic lordship, this move is increasingly viewed

64 T. B. Barry, 'Late Medieval Ireland: Social and Economic Transformation 1350–1550', in Graham and Proudfoot (eds.), *Historical Geography of Ireland*, 101; Kenny, *Anglo-Irish and Gaelic Women*, 19; Smith, *Crisis and Survival*, 41–2, 167–70; *The Great Parchment Book of Waterford*, ed. N. J. Byrne (Dublin: IMC, 2007), 17–19.

65 J. A. Watt, 'The Anglo-Irish Colony under Strain, 1327–99', in *NHI* ii, 366.

66 R. Sherlock, 'Tower Houses', in Moss (ed.), *Art and Architecture of Ireland*, 354–7; K. Abraham, 'Upward Mobility in Later Medieval Meath', *History Ireland*, 5 (1997), 15–20; S. G. Ellis, *Defending English Ground: War and Peace in Meath & Northumberland, 1460–1542* (Oxford University Press, 2015), 15–30.

67 C. A. Empey, 'The Anglo-Norman Community in Tipperary and Kilkenny in the Middle Ages: Change and Continuity', in Mac Niocaill, and Wallace (eds.), *Keimelia*, 460.

in the wider European context. A similar reorientation of agriculture was happening all over Europe, partly as a response to population decline but also driven by a growing demand for meat from consumers. In England, the rise in the price of wool and cattle in the late fourteenth century was accompanied by increasing sheep flocks and cattle herds. At precisely this time the institution of the 'creaght' – a combined herd of miscellaneous livestock on the move – emerged in Ireland and went on to flourish in the fifteenth century, when cattle prices rose markedly. The leaders of the creaghts were Anglo-Irish as well as Gaelic Irish, giving more substance to the theory that economic differences between the Irish and the English were becoming less marked.[68]

As the grain trade became a less attractive business option, merchants in some areas moved into trade in pastoral products. *The Libelle of Englyshe Polycye* – a tract from the 1430s that sought to influence the political and trading policies of the crown – indicates that tanned leather was a leading Irish export in the early fifteenth century, and we know that very large quantities of hides went to Gascony, Flanders and Italy later in that century. Merchants of Waterford and New Ross used small boats on the Suir, Nore and Barrow rivers to bring hides purchased in parts of Carlow and Kilkenny to these ports. Low-priced Irish cloth also became a significant export in this period, and the shaggy Irish woollen cloak, the 'fallaing' or 'faldyng', sometimes called the Waterford cloak, is listed among Ireland's chief exports in the *Libelle*. The urban merchants most likely to enter the ranks of the town oligarchies were those whose ties with the hinterlands of their towns allowed them to source agricultural products from Gaelic suppliers. In a 1468 inventory of hides held by John Blake of Galway at his death, sixteen had come from Gaelic families and one from an English family.[69] The importance of trade with the Gaelic Irish is demonstrated by the general permission granted in 1463 to Cork, Limerick, Waterford and Youghal, to buy from and sell to the Irish of their hinterlands. Much of this trade probably operated on a barter system. No coins appear to have been minted in Ireland between the late 1330s and the mid-1420s, and in the 1440s and 1450s the impact of

---

68 Britnell, *Britain and Ireland*, 43–4; M. Mate, 'Agricultural Technology in Southeast England, 1348–1540', in Langdon and Astill (eds.), *Medieval Farming and Technology*, 257; K. Simms, 'The Origins of the Creaght: Farming System or Social Unit?', in Murphy and Stout (eds.), *Agriculture and Settlement in Ireland*, 101–3.

69 *Political Poems and Songs Relating to English History, ii*, ed. T. Wright (London: Longman, 1861), 186; K. Hoare, 'The Evolution of Urban Oligarchies in Irish Towns, 1350–1534', in L. Klusakova and L. Teulieres (eds.), *Frontiers and Identities: Cities in Regions and Nations* (Pisa: Pisa University Press, 2008), 95.

the massive reduction of output from English and continental mints was no doubt also felt in Ireland.[70]

The grain-based, export-driven economy of the east coast seaports did not completely collapse. The hinterlands of Dublin and Drogheda continued to produce enough grain both to feed these towns and allow supplies to be sent to the southern ports of Wexford, Waterford, New Ross, Youghal and Cork, as well as to Ulster, Wales and England in the later fourteenth and fifteenth centuries. In the later 1400s, fears about shortages meant that there were repeated prohibitions on export of grain from Ireland. This suggests that the arable sector was still resilient, and that a covert grain trade continued. In 1471 a petition to the Dublin parliament complains of the 'gret derthe and famyn' which had befallen the King's subjects in Ireland because of 'the grete ladyng of graynes of whete, malt, ry, meslon and other graynes out of this lande into diverse parties of England, Scotland and Walys'. Dublin's growing anxiety about the city's grain supply appears to have encouraged city merchants to have a greater involvement in agriculture and it may also explain the high proportion of husbandmen who were admitted to citizenship.[71]

Not all towns survived the challenges of the fourteenth century, but many of those that did showed signs of vibrancy in the fifteenth century. Much of the evidence for fifteenth-century urban prosperity is architectural. Urban tower houses and substantial ecclesiastical buildings reveal the existence of wealthy urban elites. At Fethard, County Tipperary, several castles are mentioned *c.*1450 at the same time that the parish church acquired a new bell tower, chapel and sacristy. Carlingford in the fifteenth century experienced something of a building boom which saw the erection of a tholsel, several tower houses and a tower on the Dominican friary. The town was granted the right to mint coins in 1467 and this may be a reflection of its role as a gathering point for traded commodities from Irish areas of south Ulster, which were then channelled by sea to Dublin.[72] Some of Carlingford's wealth came from fishing, as fleets of ships regularly came to catch herring and other fish.

---

70 G. Mac Niocaill, *Na Buirgéisí.* 2 vols. (B.Á.C.: Cló Morainn, 1964), ii, 394–5; M. Dolley, 'Coinage to 1534', in *NHI* ii, 822; J. Hatcher, 'The Great Slump of the Mid-Fifteenth Century', in R. Britnell and J. Hatcher (eds.), *Progress and Problems in Medieval England: Essays in Honour of Edward Miller* (Cambridge University Press, 1996), 237–72.

71 *CARD*, I, 172; O'Neill, *Merchants and Mariners*, 20–1; G. Mac Niocaill, 'Socio-Economic Problems of the Late Medieval Town', in Harkness and O'Dowd (eds.), *The Town in Ireland*, 20–1.

72 O'Keeffe, *Fethard*, 3; H. O'Sullivan and R. Gillespie, *Carlingford.* Irish Historic Towns Atlas (Dublin: RIA, 2011), 3.

Fish had always formed part of the Irish export trade, especially to the ports of Chester and Bristol, but from the second half of the fifteenth century the arrival of the herring shoals off the south-western and western coasts gave a great stimulus to the fishing industry. O'Neill has described the advent of the herring shoals as 'the greatest single economic event' of the fourteenth and fifteenth centuries.[73]

The arrival and subsequent settlement of the Anglo-Normans in Ireland was followed by a period of considerable economic growth and development. This was founded on the products of a rapidly commercialised agricultural system and facilitated by the establishment of a comprehensive network of markets and towns in the east and south of the country. It was sustained for over a century by the introduction of a stable coinage, the maintenance of the transport infrastructure, and the activities of the Italian merchants. Levels of market involvement were high among both large and small producers and consumers. As was the case in England and on the Continent, the hinterlands of the larger towns were particularly dynamic but research on the economies of the smaller towns is beginning to reveal their vital role in sustaining commercial networks.

The crises of the fourteenth century significantly altered the demographic base of the economy. The population, which may have reached 1.3 million c.1300, probably fell by a third to a half. Continuing political instability and warfare within and outside Ireland increased the risks and costs of trade. There was profound change in the countryside, with many of the smaller towns and settlements becoming deserted, although vestiges of the manorial system survived, especially in areas where the authority of the great comital houses brought political stability. While the towns undoubtedly suffered most from the effects of the plague, they displayed considerable resilience. In the late fourteenth and fifteenth centuries the larger seaports carved out distinct economic regions within which their merchants cooperated with Gaelic and Anglo-Irish lordships. Dublin and Drogheda retained control over their arable hinterlands, allowing them to continue much as before, but the other urban survivals had to be flexible and dynamic and move to trade in other products.[74] As was the case in many other parts of Europe, smaller towns may have played a vital role in linking the production of rural areas to wider national and international markets. Continuing overseas trade, the building of tower houses and friaries, and some significant levels of urban wealth are signs of an economy which, while not booming, was still achieving a modest level of development.

73 O'Neill, *Merchants and Mariners*, 30–43, 131.
74 H. B. Clarke, 'Decolonization and the Dynamics of Urban Decline in Ireland, 1300–1550', in T. R. Slater (ed.), *Towns in Decline, AD 100–1600* (Aldershot: Ashgate, 2000), 157–92.

15

Gaelic Culture and Society

KATHARINE SIMMS

THE political changes experienced in the Gaelic lordships during the later Middle Ages were matched by considerable social and economic evolution, related to developments elsewhere in Europe. As in England and France, serfdom quietly disappeared. Personal freedom may have been one of the inducements offered to peasant settlers coming from England, with the result that after the twelfth century, the only remaining serfs bound to the soil were of native Irish descent. These had been known as *senchléithe* in the Old Irish laws, but the Anglo-Irish described them as 'betaghs', from the Irish *biatach*, a tenant yielding food-rents.[1] By the sixteenth century the normal terms for the lowest rank in society in Anglo-Ireland are 'poor husbandmen' or 'tenants-at-will'. The same expressions are used by English observers of the peasants in the Gaelic lordships. Indeed, far from being bound to the soil, Irish peasants under Gaelic rule seem to have been characterised by extraordinary mobility. Spenser speaks of some who changed landlords every year, in a fruitless quest for better terms. Sir Toby Caulfield in the early seventeenth century remarked that it was always easy to find another landlord to shelter tenants from the claims of their last one, because tenants were so scarce and in such high demand. The last surviving serfs on record were the privileged 'church serfs', the *nativi* of the Church of Armagh, the *puri homines* of St Colmán of Cloyne, or one John Neile and his wife (fl. 1531), a villein on the archiepiscopal manor of Swords, County Dublin.[2]

1 G. Mac Niocaill, 'The Origins of the Betagh', *The Irish Jurist*, new ser. 1 (1966), 292–8; L. Price, 'The Origin of the Word Betagius', *Ériu*, 20 (1966), 185–90.
2 Edmund Spenser, *A View of the State of Ireland*, ed. A. Hadfield and W. Maley (Oxford: Blackwell, 1997), 82–3; *CSPI 1608–10*, 533–4; 'A Calendar of the Reassembled Register of John Bole, Archbishop of Armagh, 1457–71', ed. A. Lynch, *Seanchas Ardmhacha*, 15 (1992), 115–16; *The Pipe Roll of Cloyne*, ed. P. McCotter and K. Nicholls (Midleton: Cloyne Literary and Historical Society, 1996), 18–19, 58–9, 86–7; *Cal. Archbishop Alen's Register c. 1172–1534*, ed. C. McNeill (Dublin: RSAI, 1950), 279; E. Curtis, 'Rental of the Manor of Lisronagh, 1333, and Notes on "Betagh" Tenure in Medieval Ireland', *PRIA*, 43 C (1935–7), 70.

These cherished their legal status as Church property because it gave them some protection against the exactions of food and billeting of mercenaries practised by lay lords on their own and neighbouring tenants, and, where this immunity was violated, they could expect Church leaders to use the weapon of excommunication in their defence.[3]

The Gaelic Recovery: Economy and Society

Ironically it was in some ways the lesser landowners who found themselves becoming 'bound to the soil'. This is because they were tied to the local lords by bonds of clientship, which obliged them to render food-tribute and labour services to their patron, even though the land they occupied was nominally their own hereditary property. The work of Bart Jaski and Colmán Etchingham has emphasised how easily in Early Irish society the life-long contract of base clientship became an inescapable burden on succeeding generations of the client's family, with lands becoming forfeit to the lord in case of a default of service.[4] The later fourteenth and fifteenth centuries increasingly saw the forfeiture of landed estates into the hands of the local chief from a depressed class of landowners who could not afford to pay labourers to work their own lands and at the same time meet the exorbitant dues and tributes demanded by their militarised overlords. However, fourteenth-century Ireland as elsewhere in Europe experienced under-population, arising from a succession of poor harvests and famine, followed by the ravages of the Black Death. In these circumstances acquiring the empty lands from a defaulting client family might render the lord little profit. Kenneth Nicholls refers to a case as late as 1547 where a MacCarthy [Mac Carthaig] and a Desmond Geraldine tried to pursue men of this class with demands for dues and services as their 'bond-men', even after these people, at least one of whom is described as a 'great gentleman', had moved away from the estates they originally occupied and gone to live on Church lands.[5] Even the forcible kidnapping of tenants was not unknown. In 1458 Archbishop John Bole received a complaint from Brian

---

3 K. Simms, 'The Archbishops of Armagh and the O'Neills, 1347–1461', *IHS*, 19 (1974), 38–55; *Pipe Roll of Cloyne*, 123–9; 'Seven Documents from the Old Abbey of Mellifont', ed. Fr C. Conway, *Journal of the County Louth Archaeological and Historical Society*, 13 (1953), 55–61.

4 C. Etchingham, *Church Organisation in Ireland AD 650 to 1000* (Naas: Laigin, 1999), 281, 447–9, 453, 472–6; B. Jaski, *Early Irish Kingship and Succession* (Dublin: Four Courts Press, 2000), 94, 106–7, 110.

5 K. W. Nicholls, *Land, Law and Society in Sixteenth-Century Ireland*. National University of Ireland. O'Donnell Lecture (Dublin, 1976), 9–13; K. W. Nicholls, 'Gaelic Society and Economy in the High Middle Ages', in *NHI* ii, 410–11, 413–14; Nicholls, *Gaelic and Gaelicized Ireland*, 41–3, 78–80.

Mac Cathmail, erenagh or steward of the Church lands of Errigalkeerogue in the modern County Tyrone, that Toirdelbach the son of the Great O'Neill [Ó Néill] had kidnapped his tenants Angelicus and his sons, and forcibly detained them so that they could not reside and cultivate the lands of the erenagh, as they were bound to do. Less violently, the sixteenth-century Shane O'Neill is said to have lured tenants from the English Pale to come and cultivate his estates by offering favourable terms.[6]

The other solution for landlords faced with a decline in population on their estates was to revert increasingly to pastoral farming. This involved much less investment of manpower, while the higher wages earned by labourers and craft workers across Europe as a result of their scarcity value enabled people of this class to buy more meat, and consequently led to a general improvement in beef prices. Ireland was no exception, though its beef consumption seems to have remained largely domestic, cattle hides being the most important export from this sector. There was a violent and lawless side to this social change. In England villagers complained when more powerful neighbours enclosed their common land and used it to graze their own herds. In Ireland wandering herds violated other people's enclosures. A number of Armagh provincial synods in the early fifteenth century ruled against persons who violently invaded Church lands with their horses and herds, grazed and destroyed the cereal crops and cut down trees and bushes. Correspondence in the archiepiscopal registers indicates the main culprits were the O'Neills [Uí Néill] and their retinues. This aggressive use of livestock was linked to the development of 'creaghts' or *caeraigechta*, amalgamated herds of cattle and sheep with their peasant owners, organised under a single leader drawn from the minor nobility, the head of the creaght. In peacetime the leaders of creaghts seem to have belonged to a particular section of society, wandering mercenary captains and their followers, or bardic poets, felons and outlaws, but in wartime whole villages became displaced with their herds under the leadership of the local landlord, and wandered into neighbouring lordships or onto the common grazing land along hill-tops or other marginal land to stay out of harm's way, or even to find alternative lands to settle. There are some signs of mercenary captains and their followers travelling with their herds of cattle in search of employment and grazing rights as early as the

---

6 PRONI Register of Archbishop John Prene vol. i, fo. 10r; 'Calendar of the Reassembled Register of John Bole', 117; N. Canny, *The Elizabethan Conquest of Ireland: A Pattern Established 1565–1576* (Hassocks: The Harvester Press, 1976), 12–13; N. Canny, 'Hugh O'Neill, Earl of Tyrone and the Changing Face of Gaelic Ulster', *Studia Hibernica*, 10 (1970), 28.

twelfth and thirteenth centuries, but the custom seems to have become far more widespread in the northern half of Ireland from the late fourteenth century onwards, when the word 'creaght' or *caeraigecht* first appears in contemporary records. As with so many other features of Irish society, this was a phenomenon found both in the Gaelic lordships and among Anglo-Irish living on the periphery of the English Pale.[7]

These developments combined to foster the growth of a semi-nomadic class of graziers, the heads of the creaghts, who owned no land themselves, but helped the chiefs to receive some profit from the extensive and underpopulated estates that fell into their hands by way of forfeiture. The creaghts either paid grazing rents – O'Neill in the early years of the seventeenth century charged a shilling per cow per year from his creaghts – or the creaght leader and his men recompensed the chief in kind by their military service.[8] One of the most successful of this new class of grazier nobility was the O'Hart family in the modern County Sligo. A member of the family is first recorded in the fifteenth century as a *mac-óclach*, or military vassal, a class equivalent to the English knight or squire. In 1584 the *Compossicion Booke of Conought* places 'Phelim O'Hart of Ardtarmon otherwise called 'O'Hart chiefe of his name' directly after Donell O'Connor Sligo [Ó Conchobair Sligech] himself among the participants to the Indenture of Sligo, yet does not subsequently list him among the landowners of the county. Nevertheless the contemporary map of Ireland by Baptiste Boazio shows the O'Hart name spread across north Sligo, dominating the area, presumably because they held extensive tracts of land there on grazing leases from the lord of that land, O Connor Sligo.[9]

Across Europe the higher wages demanded by skilled craft workers after the Black Death led to some reorganisation of the cloth trade. Large merchant houses began to by-pass town markets and guild organisations, and send out packmen to tour the rural areas selling flax or raw wool to the spinners and buying back yarn, selling yarn to the weavers and buying back

---

7   M. Kowaleski, 'A Consumer Economy', in R. Horrox and W. M. Ormrod (eds.), *A Social History of England, 1200–1500* (Cambridge University Press, 2006), 240–2; K. Simms, 'The Origins of the Creaght: Farming System or Social Unit?', in M. Murphy and M. Stout (eds.), *Agriculture and Settlement in Ireland* (Dublin: Four Courts Press, 2015); J. Thirsk, 'Enclosing and Engrossing', in J. Thirsk (ed.), *The Agrarian History of England and Wales* iv *1500–1640* (Cambridge University Press, 1967), 200–38; K. Simms, 'Nomadry in Medieval Ireland: The Origins of the Creaght or Caoraigheacht', *Peritia*, 5 (1986), 379–91.
8   *CSPI 1608–10*, 533–4; Simms, 'Nomadry in Medieval Ireland', 385–8.
9   Nicholls, *Gaelic and Gaelicized Ireland*, 80; *AC*, 442–3; Simms, *From Kings to Warlords*, 85, 90; *The Compossicion Booke of Conought*, ed. A. M. Freeman (Dublin: IMC, 1936), 120, 123–39. A reproduction of Boazio's map of Ireland forms the endpapers of J. P. Haughton (ed.), *Atlas of Ireland* (Dublin: RIA, 1979).

cloth (the *Verlagssystem*). This led to greater wealth for the countryside, and the large import–export merchants, and a decline in the prosperity of small market towns and guild-workers. There are signs of this process at work in Ireland. The large cities of Dublin, Kilkenny and Limerick flourished. Galway merchants controlled linen manufacture among Gaelic Irish in the surrounding hinterland. Dublin received a new influx of English merchants at this time, who found themselves in conflict with the city's merchant guild, but the smaller market towns in Meath, not only the more remote Fore and Mullingar, but even Kells, Trim, Navan and the County Louth port of Dundalk, dwindled away during the same period.[10] According to parliamentary legislation their walls and ditches crumbled from neglect, their merchants now wore 'huks and faldings' (Irish hoods and cloaks) and spoke Irish, and their markets were losing trade even to newly established markets in the neighbouring Irish lordships, at Cavan, Granard and Longford, and still more to the forestallers or grey merchants who travelled round the countryside buying up goods from the peasants before they reached the marketplace, agents who were acting for the great merchant houses in the cities.[11] Both Gaelic chiefs and Anglo-Irish barons sold monopoly trading rights with their subjects to the agents of particular great merchant houses who were prepared to pay well for the privilege. In 1463 the Great O'Neill delegated to the archbishop of Armagh the right to dispense letters of safe-conduct on his behalf to chosen merchants, Scottish and English, giving them the right to travel under his protection through all the lands and ports in his lordship of Ulster, a phrase that in the 1460s may well have comprehended the entire nine-county province.[12]

Another change taking place in the mid-fifteenth century which has been seen as a very important source of increased revenue to Ireland in general and especially the Gaelic lordships in the west, was a shift in the herring migrations from the West Baltic to the North Sea, Irish Sea and Atlantic. Along the west coast commercial fishing fleets were Spanish and Basque as well as English, the Irish chiefs favouring those foreigners who paid for licences to

10 H. Pirenne, *Economic and Social History of Medieval Europe*, trans. I. E. Clegg, (London: Routledge and Kegan Paul, 1936), 219; F. Braudel, *Capitalism and Material Life 1400–1600*, trans. M. Kochen (London: Weidenfeld and Nicolson, 1973), 379; E. Schubert, *Einführung in die Grundprobleme der Deutschen Geschichte im Spätmittelalter* (Darmstadt, 1992), 193; O'Neill, *Merchants and Mariners*, 66–70, 74–6.

11 *Stat. Ire., Hen. VI*, 42–5; *Stat. Ire., 12–22 Edw. IV*, 818–21; J. T. Gilbert, *History of the Viceroys of Ireland* (Dublin: James Duffy, 1865), 466.

12 Canny, *Elizabethan Conquest*, 4–6; H. F. Hore and J. Graves, *The Social State of the Southern and Eastern Counties of Ireland in the Sixteenth Century* (Dublin University Press, 1870), 83, 102, 135, 245–6; PRONI Register of Archbishop John Prene, fo. 182r–v; 'Calendar of the Reassembled Register of John Bole', 129.

fish off their coasts and to land and process their catch by salting or smoking before returning home. They did not always ask to be paid in coin, however. A report of 1560 states that O'Donnell [Ó Domnaill] was traditionally called in Spain, 'the king of the fish' and that he regularly traded fish with the Spanish merchants in exchange for wine.[13] From the late fourteenth century onwards the statute passed at the Kilkenny parliament in 1366 meant that English and Anglo-Irish merchants needed to have a royal licence to trade with the wild Irish. The commonest commodity brought by the English merchants to the unconquered north of Ireland was wine, sometimes described as 'unsaleable' or 'undrinkable among the English' (*impotabile inter Anglicos*), or beer, also bolts of cloth, iron and salt, and the return cargo was meat, hides and fish, sometimes specified as salt and fresh salmon. An oft-quoted fifteenth-century jingle claims 'Heryng of Slegoy^e [Sligo] and salmon of bame [Bann] heis made in brystowe [Bristol] many a ryche man'.[14]

While fine English cloth continued to be highly prized among the Gaelic Irish nobility, the common people experienced a sartorial revolution in the course of the fifteenth century. In 1397 the pilgrim Perellós saw the common people of Ulster wearing shaggy 'Waterford' cloaks, made of coarsely woven frieze, with tufts of raw, unspun wool inserted in the weft, but underneath they were scantily dressed in rags, 'both the women and the men show their shameful parts without any shame', as he puts it. During the fifteenth and early sixteenth century, 'Waterford' cloaks or 'fallings' became an item of Irish export – a shorter version appears as fashionable rain-wear for townswomen in Normandy. In Ireland itself by the early sixteenth century the common people were no longer dressed in rags underneath their cloaks. There was now a universal fashion for wearing long and extravagantly wide linen shirts, dyed with saffron and extending from the neck to the ankles, as described by another pilgrim to St Patrick's Purgatory, Francesco Chiericati, in 1517, and as drawn by Lucas Heere and Albrecht Dürer.[15]

13 *Stat. Ire., 1–12 Edw. IV*, 352–5; O'Neill, *Merchants and Mariners*, 30, 33–7, 131. *Carew 1515–74*, no. 229, p. 181; D. Mac Eiteagáin, 'The Renaissance and the Late Medieval Lordship of Tír Chonaill, 1461–1555', in W. Nolan, L. Ronayne and M. Dunlevy (eds.), *Donegal: History and Society* (Dublin: Geography Publications, 1995), 206–7.

14 Smith, *Crisis and Survival*, 188; G. Mac Niocaill, *Na Buirgéisi*. 2 vols. (B.Á.C.: Cló Morainn, 1964), ii, 514; M. Carus-Wilson, *The Overseas Trade of Bristol in the Later Middle Ages* (Bristol: Bristol Record Society, 1937), 86, 107; M. Carus-Wilson, *Medieval Merchant Venturers* (London: Methuen, 1967), 27; BL Cotton MS, Vesp. E IX, fo. 101r–v.

15 H. F. McClintock, 'The Mantle of St. Brigid at Bruges', *JRSAI*, 7th ser., 6 (1936), 32–40; D. Carpenter, 'The Pilgrim from Catalonia/Aragon: Ramon de Perellós, 1397', in Haren and de Pontfarcy (eds.), *Medieval Pilgrimage to St Patrick's Purgatory*, 110; O'Neill, *Merchants and Mariners*, 68–70; H. F. McClintock, *Handbook on the Traditional Old Irish*

The most obvious result of Sligo's new importance as a centre for the herring trade was the rise of an indigenous merchant family in Sligo, the O'Creans [Uí Chroiden], one of whose tombs in the Dominican priory of Sligo exceeds that of the local chieftain, O'Connor Sligo, in size and ornamentation. Seaán O'Crean (d. 1528) married the daughter of another chief, MacDermott Roe [Mac Diarmata Ruad], and maintained a public house of hospitality for the poor and sick at his own expense.[16] Sligo was the largest true town under Gaelic rule, but in the mid-fifteenth century the forward-looking chief of East Breifne, Eógan O'Reilly [Ó Raigillig], founded a market town at Cavan near his chief residence. About the same time O'Farrell [Ó Feargall] of Annaly founded less enduring markets at Granard and Longford. In every part of Ireland during the fifteenth century the erection of new buildings, principally the newly founded Observantine Franciscan friaries and the ubiquitous tower houses, testify to a surprising amount of surplus wealth in the economy at this time.[17]

All classes of society so far mentioned were rising during the fifteenth century: serfs winning their freedom, military vassals becoming large-scale graziers, or merchants accumulating enough riches to join the ranks of the nobility. However, another change which took place in society during this century involved the gradual disuse of royal titles by the Gaelic chiefs, who were henceforward normally styled lords of their land, or captains of their country, or of their surname, rather than kings. From the thirteenth century the heraldry seen in their seals had equated the status of the Irish 'kinglets' (Lat. *reguli*) with English earls or barons, rather than 'crowned kings'. The neglect of the royal title in the late fifteenth and sixteenth centuries could be associated with a change in the basis of their power, from the choice and consent of their noble followers to leadership of their own kindred, landownership

Dress (Dundalk: Dundalgan Press, 1958), 4–8, plates 1–11 and 18–20, plates 28–9; J. P. Mahaffy, 'Two Early Tours of Ireland', *Hermathena* 18 / 40 (1914), 14.

16 The O'Crean tomb is illustrated in R. F. Foster (ed.), *The Oxford Illustrated History of Ireland* (Oxford University Press, 1989), 100; discussed in B. de Breffny and G. Mott, *The Churches and Abbeys of Ireland* (London: Thames and Hudson, 1976), 89; AU, iii, 572–5. On houses of hospitality see K. Simms, 'Guesting and Feasting in Gaelic Ireland', *JRSAI*, 108 (1978), 67–100, 70–9; C. M. O'Sullivan, *Hospitality in Medieval Ireland, 900–1500* (Dublin: Four Courts Press, 2004), 120–63. On merchants in Gaelic society, see K. Simms, 'References to Landscape and Economy in Irish Bardic Poetry', in Clarke et al. (eds.), *Surveying Ireland's Past*, 156–7.

17 Nicholls, 'Gaelic Society', 404; 'Cairt ó Mhaolmhordha Ó Raighilligh, 1558', ed. G. Mac Niocaill, *Breifne*, 1 (1959), 134–5; H. G. Leask, *Irish Churches and Monastic Buildings III. Medieval Gothic: The Last Phases* (Dundalk: Dundalgan Press, 1971), 1; O'Neill, *Merchants and Mariners*, 131; T. B. Barry, *The Archaeology of Medieval Ireland* (London: Routledge, 1987), 168–98.

or command of mercenary troops. Like the other social changes in Gaelic Ireland at this time, this could be seen as a form of modernisation.[18]

The Decline and Recovery of Traditional Learning

In contrast to the fragmented and confused politics of the Gaelic lordships in the later Middle Ages, cultural developments were island-wide and uniform, thanks to the mobility and privileged status of the learned classes, the bardic poets, historians, judges and musicians. Although originating in pagan Celtic society, the upper ranks of the poetic and legal classes had been transformed by acquiring literacy in the Church schools of Early Christian Ireland and consequently they were severely affected when Irish-language learning was gradually ousted from the clerical curriculum during the twelfth-century Church reform.[19] The predominantly hereditary nature of their professions meant that training could continue in the thirteenth century by a system of apprenticeship to eminent masters of poetry, history, law, music or leechcraft. However, in the 1270s the attempt of Archbishop David Mac Cerbaill of Cashel to negotiate a purchase of full rights to English common law for all Irish freemen outside Ulster involved a condemnation of native Irish customary laws as 'detestable to God and so contrary to all law that they ought not to be called laws'. Irish clerics offered to excommunicate and place under interdict all who persisted in using Irish 'brehon' law (from Ir. *brethem*, 'a judge)'. As this proposal for general access to common law did not succeed, 'brehon' law remained in force in areas ruled by the Gaelic chieftains, but around 1300 an interesting tract by the Connacht judge Gilla na Náem mac Duinnshléibe Meic Aedagáin (d. 1309) updated the study of law by summarising the

---

18 Simms, *From Kings to Warlords*, 36–40, 94–5, 129; K. Simms, 'Changing Patterns of Regnal Succession in Later Medieval Ireland', in F. Lachaud and M. Penman (eds.), *Making and Breaking the Rules: Succession in Medieval Europe c. 1000–c. 1600/Etablir et abolir les normes: la succession dans l'Europe médiévale vers 1000–vers 1600* (Turnhout: Brepols, 2008), 167–8; F. Verstraten, 'Images of Gaelic Lordship in Ireland c.1200–1400', in Doran and Lyttleton (eds.), *Lordship in Medieval Ireland*, 70.

19 Breatnach, 'On Satire and the Poet's Circuit', in C. G. Ó Háinle and D. Meek (eds.), *Unity in Diversity: Studies in Irish and Scottish Gaelic Language, Literature and History* (Dublin: School of Irish, Trinity College Dublin, 2004), 33–4; K. Simms, 'Bardic Schools, Learned Families', in S. Duffy (ed.), *Medieval Ireland: An Encyclopedia* (New York and London: Routledge, 2005), 35–7; B. Ó Cuív (ed.), *Seven Centuries of Irish Learning* (Dublin: Stationery Office, 1961); F. Henry and G. Marsh-Micheli, 'Manuscripts and Illuminations, 1169–1603', in *NHI* ii, 783, 789–92; K. Simms, 'Literacy and the Irish Bards', in H. Pryce (ed.), *Literacy in Medieval Celtic Societies* (Cambridge University Press, 1998), 240–2; K. Simms, 'The Brehons of Later Medieval Ireland', in D. Hogan and W. N. Osborough (eds.), *Brehons, Serjeants and Attorneys* (Blackrock: Irish Academic Press, 1990), 51–7.

prescriptions of the Old Irish tracts into modern Irish and including some influence of contemporary English law.[20]

At the same time, or soon afterwards, the customary prestige of the praise-poets (*fili*) came under threat.[21] It was a main function of the court poet to legitimise a king's rule by praising his royal descent, beauty of face and form, justice, courage and generosity, and in payment the best poets received gifts of gold and jewels, fine clothing, horses and herds of cows, even grants of tax-free land. By the early fourteenth century, when every Irish chieftain owed allegiance either to the English king or one of his barons, some chiefs apparently became reluctant to lavish such wealth on traditionally qualified praise poets, and used the cheaper services of ballad-singers, male and female, to entertain their guests at feasts. To this economic pressure was added a formal ban by the Irish clergy against both composers and purchasers of praise poetry promulgated at synods held under Primates David Mag Oirechtaig (1334–46), Richard Fitz Ralph (1346–60) and John Colton (1381–1404), apparently on the grounds that such poetry encouraged sinful vanity, wasted wealth on what was essentially hot air, and diverted alms from the Church. However, by the mid-fourteenth century the resurgent power of the Irish chiefs re-awakened their interest in patronising praise-poets and historians to record their victories and genealogical and territorial claims. This sudden change was celebrated by a series of nationwide summonses of all learned classes to feast at the expense of a particular chieftain, beginning with a Christmas feast held by William O'Kelly [Ó Cellaig], chief of Uí Maine in east Galway in 1351.[22]

---

20 A. J. Otway-Ruthven, 'The Request of the Irish for English Law', *IHS*, 6 (1949), 262, 269; Otway-Ruthven, *History of Medieval Ireland*, 189; A. Gwynn, 'Edward I and the Proposed Purchase of English Law for the Irish, c.1279–80', *TRHS*, fifth series, 10 (1960), 111–27; F. Kelly, 'Giolla na Naomh Mac Aodhagáin: A Thirteenth-Century Legal Innovator', in D. S. Greer and N. M. Dawson (eds.), *Mysteries and Solutions in Irish Legal History* (Dublin: Four Courts Press, 2001), 1–14; G. Mac Niocaill, 'A propos du vocabulaire social irlandais du bas moyen age', *Études celtiques*, 12 (1968–9), 512–46; G. Mac Niocaill, 'The Interaction of Laws', in Lydon (ed.), *English in Medieval Ireland*, 105–17.

21 If the poem *A theachtaire tig ón Róimh*, 'O messenger who comes from Rome', is correctly ascribed to Gilla Brigde Mac Con Mide (d. *c.*1272) – see *The Poems of Giolla Brighde Mac Con Midhe*, ed. N. William (Dublin: ITS, 1980), 204–13, 339–44 – the Church's controversy with the poets would have begun about the same time as Mac Cerbaill's offer to excommunicate users of brehon law. However, the other poems on this theme date to the fourteenth century.

22 *Book of Magauran*, poem no. 27; *Reg. Swayne*, 11; *AFM*, iv, 685 note n.; 'An Appeal on Behalf of the Profession of Poetry', ed. and trans. B. Ó Cuív, *Éigse*, 14 (1971), 87–106; K. Simms, 'An Eaglais agus Filí na Scol', in P. Ó Fiannachta (ed.), *An Dán Díreach. Léachtaí Cholm Cille XXIV* (Maigh Nuad: An Sagart, 1994), 21–36; E. Knott, 'Filidh Éireann go haointeach', *Ériu*, 5 (1911), 163–87; Simms, 'Guesting and Feasting', 90–2; O'Sullivan, *Hospitality*, 114–16.

A direct link with the political resurgence was shown when Niall Óc O'Neill held a similar feast in 1387 in the ancient hill-fort of Emain Macha near Armagh, the imagined site of the palace of Conchobar mac Nessa, mythical king of the whole province of Ulster. The praise-poets were quick to underline the parallels between Niall Óc himself and the prehistoric king Conchobar, or his champion, Cúchullain. Identification with Ireland's heroic past even led to a passing fashion for bare feet among the Gaelic upper classes, noted in the case of both Niall Óc O'Neill and Art MacMurrough Kavanagh [Mac Murchada Caemánach].[23] The boost this new patronage gave to the learned professions themselves was demonstrated at two celebrated feasts for native 'men of art' (aes eladan), both held in 1433 by Margaret, daughter of O'Carroll [Ó Cerbaill], and wife of An Calbach O'Connor Faly [Ó Conchobair Failge], chief of Offaly, at opposite ends of her husband's extended lordship, at Killeigh in Offaly and Rathangan in County Kildare, and attended by 2,700 invited men of learning besides lesser entertainers.[24]

The first 'general summons' (gairm coitchenn) to William O'Kelly's feast in 1351 may have been inspired by William's own court poet and historian Seaán Mór Ó Dubagáin (S. 'the Great' O'Duggan, d. 1372). Like many other practitioners of Irish learning, his family were Church tenants. They claimed hereditary rights to be both archivists to the church of Clonmacnoise and court poets and historians to the chiefs of Uí Maine. Seaán began his career composing praise poetry for Tadc O'Kelly, the rebel king who was defeated and decapitated at Athenry in 1316. His nationalist sympathies appear in a long poem, Triallam timcheall na Fódla, originally intended to itemise every territory in Ireland, naming its traditional rulers, or their contemporary successors if Gaelic, but ignoring the intrusive Anglo-Irish newcomers.[25] His pupils

23 K. Simms, 'Propaganda Use of the Táin in the Later Middle Ages', Celtica, 15 (1983), 142–9; K. Simms, 'The Barefoot Kings: Literary Image and Reality in Later Medieval Ireland', in E. Boon, A. J. McMullen and N. Sumner (eds.), Proceedings of the Harvard Celtic Colloquium 30, 2010 (Cambridge, MA, and London, 2011), 1–21.

24 AC, 472–3; 'The Annals of Ireland from the Year 1443 to 1468 ... by ... Duald MacFirbis', ed. J. O'Donovan, in The Miscellany of the Irish Archaeological Society 1 (Dublin: Irish Archeological Society, 1846), 227–8; E. Fitzpatrick, 'Mairgréag-an-einigh Ó Cearbhaill, "the best woman of the Gaedhil" ', Kildare Archaeological Society Journal, 18 (1992–3), 34–5.

25 K. Simms, 'Ó Dubhagáin, Seaán Mór', ODNB; 'The Registry of Clonmacnoise', ed. J. O'Donovan, Kilkenny and the South-East of Ireland Archaeological Society Journal, 1 (1856/7), 456; A. Kehnel, Clonmacnois – the Church and Lands of St. Ciarán: Change and Continuity in an Irish Monastic Foundation (6th to 16th century) (Münster: Lit., 1995), 301; Poem 'Tairngeartaidh tréan toghbháltach', in A Bardic Miscellany: Five Hundred Poems from Manuscripts in Irish and British Libraries, ed. D. McManus and E. Ó Raghallaigh. (Dublin: Department of Irish, Trinity College, 2010), 633; The Topographical Poems of John O'Dubhagain and Giolla na naomh O'Huidhrin, ed. J. O'Donovan (Dublin: Irish Archaeological and Celtic Society, 1862).

learned to transcribe and update the prose genealogies originally compiled in pre-reform Church schools, and to study the Church calendar system that underlay the earlier annals.[26] The drive to retrieve the glories of pre-conquest Ireland led to large manuscript anthologies being compiled by the *senchaide*, or historians: the 'Book of Uí Maine', the 'Book of Ballymote', the 'Yellow Book of Lecan', the 'Great Book of Lecan', the 'Saltair of Mac Richard Butler' and so on, which preserved a far richer heritage of Dark Age literature in the vernacular for us to access today than has survived from Anglo-Saxon England, Scotland, Wales or the Continent. By this period we have unambiguous evidence for formal schools conducted through the medium of Irish, located in the homes of the masters of the various bardic arts, with students from hereditarily learned families being encouraged to study in other families' schools to increase their skills.[27]

A striking feature of late medieval Irish manuscripts is their careful imitation of pre-Norman scripts and interlaced decorative capitals, and this antiquarian art style extended to the wood-carving on the so-called 'Brian Boru harp' and the *cuir bouilli* interlace decoration of the leather book-satchel now associated with the Book of Armagh (both objects dating to the fifteenth century). Sometimes manuscript illumination shows an interesting blend of contemporary continental and native pre-Norman styles, as in the *Lebor Brecc* (compiled 1390–1410), the 'Book of Ballymote' (*c.*1390), and most successfully in the twelve folios dubbed 'the Book of the White Earl', incorporated into the slightly later 'Saltair of Mac Richard Butler' (Laud Misc. 610, and one *bifolium* in TCD MS 1436).[28]

26 J. Carney, 'The Ó Cianáin Miscellany', *Ériu*, 21 (1969), 122–47; *Catalogue of Irish Language Manuscripts in the Bodleian Library at Oxford and Oxford College Libraries*, ed. B. Ó Cuiv. 2 vols. (Dublin: DIAS, 2001), i, 217; A. Cameron (ed.), *Reliquiae Celticae*, 1 (1892). Poem '*Bliaghuin so solas a dath*' at 141–9.

27 R. A. Breatnach, 'The Book of Uí Mhaine', in *Great Books of Ireland (Thomas Davis Lectures 1964)* (Dublin: Clonmore and Reynolds, 1967), 77–89; 'Laud Misc. 610', ed. M. Dillon, *Celtica*, 5 (1960), 64–76 and *Celtica*, 6 (1963); F. Henry and G. Marsh-Micheli, 'Manuscripts and Illuminations', in *NHI* ii, 801–3; T. Ó Concheanainn, 'The Book of Ballymote', *Celtica*, 14 (1981), 15–25; W. O'Sullivan, 'Ciothruadh's Yellow Book of Lecan', *Éigse*, 18 pt 2 (1981), 177–81; Simms, 'Literacy and the Irish Bards', 249–50; K. Simms, 'Charles Lynegar, the O Luinín Family and the Study of Seanchas', in T. C. Barnard, D. Ó Cróinín and K. Simms (eds.), *A Miracle of Learning: Studies in Manuscripts and Irish Learning: Essays in Honour of William O'Sullivan* (Aldershot: Ashgate, 1998), 273–5.

28 R. Stalley, 'The Long Middle Ages: From the Twelfth Century to the Reformation', in B. de Breffny (ed.), *The Irish World* (London: Thames and Hudson, 1977), 97–8; R. Ó Floinn, 'The Norman Conquest and the Later Middle Ages', in M. Ryan (ed.), *Treasures of Ireland: Irish Art 3000 B.C.–1500 A.D.* (Dublin: National Museum of Ireland, 1983), 70–2, and catalogue nos. 86–7, pp. 178–80; Henry and Marsh-Micheli, 'Manuscripts and Illuminations', 781, 783, 789, 794–5, 798–802.

The education of the historians and lawyers was shaped by a 'backward look', which built on the inherited literature of the pre-reform Church schools. In practice, however, the decisions of the chieftains' judges and the contracts and charters drawn up by brehon lawyers for their patrons drew on a wide variety of traditions: Irish customary law ('brehon law'), civil and canon law, and an oral acquaintance with English common law. The poets and musicians, who were recruited from more diverse sources and appealed to a wider audience both Gaelic and Anglo-Irish, were more innovative. The poets illustrated their poems on occasion with apologues, or exemplary tales drawn from foreign as well as Irish literature, and the chronicler Friar John Clyn, in his account of the assassination of John de Bermingham, earl of Louth, by his Anglo-Irish tenants at Braganstown in 1329, lists among the victims in the earl's household Maelruanaid Mac Cerbaill, the best timpanist in Ireland, and his numerous following, adding 'if he were not the first inventor of the art of string music, he was the improver, teacher and director of all his predecessors, contemporaries and successors'. The Statute of Kilkenny with its ban on the entertainment of Irish poets and minstrels in Anglo-Irish houses suggests that de Bermingham was by no means alone in his liking for native Irish entertainers.[29]

The Anglo-Irish and Gaelic Culture

The most striking example of cross-cultural influence is found in the Gaelic poems of Earl Gerald 'the Rhymer' FitzGerald, third earl of Desmond (d. 1398). In the early twentieth century he was hailed by Robin Flower as having introduced the Gaelic world to the style and subject matter of the *amour courtois* poetry of twelfth-century Provence, but the more recent verdict of James Carney is that 'The approach is bardic, the ideas are bardic, but the metrical technique is amateur ... Any theory of the influence of French verse upon the Irish will not rest easily upon the figure of Gearóid Iarla ['Earl Gerald'] as revealed in his poems.'[30] Earl Gerald almost certainly received

29 F. O'Connor: *The Backward Look: A Survey of Irish Literature* (London: Macmillan, 1967). Mac Niocaill, 'Interaction of Laws', 105–17; Simms, 'Brehons of Later Medieval Ireland'; A. Gleason, 'Music', in Duffy (ed.), *Medieval Ireland: An Encyclopedia* (New York and London: Routledge, 2005), 346–8; K. Simms, 'Foreign Apologues in Bardic Poetry', in Duffy and Foran (eds.), *English Isles*, 139–50; K. Simms, 'Bards and Barons: The Anglo-Irish Aristocracy and the Native Culture', in Bartlett and Mackay (eds.), *Medieval Frontier Societies*; Clyn, 96, 194–5; *Stat. Ire., John–Hen.* V, 446–7.
30 J. Carney, 'Literature in Irish, 1169–1534', in *NHI* ii, 698 (my square brackets). Flower's view was expressed in his 'Introduction' to *Dánta Grádha*, ed. T. Ó Rathile, 2nd edn (Cork University Press, 1926), xii–xiii, and endorsed by S. Ó Tuama, 'The New Love Poetry', in B. Ó Cuiv (ed.), *Seven Centuries of Irish Learning* (Dublin: Stationery Office),

his literary training in boyhood from the master-poet of Munster, Gofraid *Finn* ('G. the Fair-haired') Ó Dálaig (d. 1387). While Earl Gerald's short, light-hearted poems on personal topics abound in casual references to the saga cycles of ancient Ireland, principally the Ulster cycle and the Fenian cycle, his mentor Gofraid *Finn* occasionally drew on continental material, both religious and classical, for illustrative anecdotes in his bardic poems. Gofraid *Finn* is celebrated for his cynical apology to the first earl of Desmond for having flattered Irish chiefs with poems foretelling their victory over the colonists, while composing poems to the colonists prophesying their final conquest of Ireland: 'You should not pay attention to it, 'tis our custom!'[31] Similarly Earl Gerald addressed a poem to the MacCarthy and O'Brien [Ó Briain] chiefs, especially Diarmait lord of Muskerry (d. 1381), in which he complained that the 'Saxons', that is, the English of England, accused him of favouring the Gaels above the colonists, so that he felt obliged to attack his dear friends and bear their retaliatory plundering, rather than be imprisoned in London by the English king. However, the message was no doubt tailored to the audience.[32]

While other fourteenth-century Irish chieftains and Anglo-Irish barons patronised bardic poets and historians, Earl Gerald was somewhat ahead of his time in his active involvement in reading and writing the language, and studying the traditional sagas and place-name lore. In the following centuries, however, other nobles followed his example. The massive late fourteenth- and early fifteenth-century manuscript anthologies chiefly served as source-books for the professional historians and their schools, but as the fifteenth century wore on, more and more of the lay nobility were literate, and later volumes such as the Saltair of Mac Richard Butler, the Roches' 'Book of Fermoy', or the Book of Mac Carthaig Riabach ('the Book of Lismore') were commissioned by lay patrons, both Gaelic and Anglo-Irish. To flatter and entertain these patrons, old sagas were re-told taking account of contemporary concerns. In the later medieval version of the 'Battle of Ventry', Finn mac

---

103–9. The assumed link between later Irish love poetry and the work of Earl Gerald has been disputed by M. Mac Craith, 'Dánta Grá', in B. Lalor (ed.), *The Encyclopedia of Ireland* (Dublin: Gill & Macmillan, 2003), 269.

31 Godfraid's influence is implied in Ó Dálaig's poem to the child Gerald: 'Historical Poems of Gofraidh Fionn Ó Dálaigh IX', ed. L. McKenna, *The Irish Monthly*, 47 (1919), 509–14; *Dioghluim Dána*, ed. L. Mac Cionaith (Dublin: ITS, 1938), no. 67 (text only). K. Simms, 'The Geraldines and Gaelic Culture', in P. Crooks and S. Duffy (eds.), *The Geraldines and Medieval Ireland: The Making of a Myth* (Dublin: Four Courts Press, 2016); K. Simms, 'Foreign Apologues', 154, 157, 160–1; 'A ráthughadh dhúibh níor dhluigh. gnáthughadh dhúin a dhéanaimh': 'Historical Poems', 513.

32 'Duanaire Gearóid Iarla', ed. G. MacNiocaill, *Studia Hibernica*, 3 (1963), 17–18, poem no. 5, verses 3–8.

Cumaill and his *Fianna* warrior-bands are criticised as if they were fifteenth-century billeted mercenaries.[33] The mid-sixteenth-century Book of Howth contained an English-language version of the 'Battle of Gabra' (the revolt of the *Fianna* against Cairbre *Lifechair*), translated from various Irish texts, one of which might have emanated from the court of MacMurrough Kavanagh. None of the presently surviving Irish recensions mentions a king of Leinster with the evocative name of Diarmait *Lámderg*.[34] In the Book of Howth version the *Fianna* brought in a Danish prince to conquer Ireland. Diarmait *Lámderg* 'the King of Leynster, being chief of Ireland' eloquently harangues the Irish troops, ending 'Behold our request and demand of God. Is it not to deliver us of our great thraldom these strangers put us to?'[35]

The fifteenth-century Butlers of Ormond became closely involved in Gaelic culture and learning. Their role as patrons of learned manuscript anthologies, the fragmentary 'Book of the White Earl' and the 'Saltair of MacRichard Butler', has been alluded to above. James, fourth earl of Ormond (d. 1452), the 'White Earl', has been described as 'strongly gaelicised'. He employed an Irish brehon (*brethem*), or professional judge of native law, Domnall Mac Flannchada, and endowed him with an estate of land within the earldom. His return to Ireland in 1447 after the settlement of his dispute with the Talbot faction was celebrated with an ode '*Aeide i nÉirinn an t-Iarla*' by the most pre-eminent bardic poet of that day, Tadc Óc Ó hUiginn.[36] The earl's younger brother Richard fostered his son Edmund with the Irish archbishop of Cashel, Richard Ó hEidigáin, and scribal comments in the margins of the 'Saltair of Mac Richard' illustrate how closely involved Edmund became with the work of its compilation. The principal scribe shared his dinner-table and on occasion slept in one bed with his patron. The team repeatedly cursed Edmund

33 C. Breatnach, 'The Historical Context of *Cath Fionntrágha*', *Éigse*, 28 (1994–5), 138–55: 142, 153–5.

34 The Irish verse account has no mention at all of the king of Leinster, and a late prose version names him as Crimthann Cúlbuide, and gives him a very minor role – *The Battle of Gabhra: Garristown in the County of Dublin*, ed. N. O'Kearney (Dublin: Transactions of the Ossianic Society, 1853). The Book of Howth translator indicates he knew more than one version of the original Irish tale, but the expression 'chief of Ireland' applied to the king of Leinster suggests he drew on a source produced under Mac Murchada patronage.

35 *Carew*, v, 2–6. A recent critique considers the speeches attributed to the various protagonists to be a feature added by the English language redactor: V. McGowan-Doyle, *The Book of Howth: Elizabethan Conquest and the Old English* (Cork University Press, 2011), 74–5.

36 Henry and Marsh-Micheli, 'Manuscripts and Illuminations', 801; A. Cosgrove, 'The Emergence of the Pale 1399–1447', in *NHI* ii, 552–3; *COD*, iii, no. 66, pp. 49–50; Simms, 'Bards and Barons', 183–8; *Aithdioghluim Dána*, ed. Lambert McKenna 2 vols. (Dublin: ITS, 1939 [text], 1940 [trans.]), poem no. 36.

for driving them to continue the work of transcribing and illustrating even on Sundays, and exclaimed that he tirelessly demanded a progress report as soon as he returned from a cattle-raid. Another fifteenth-century manuscript, BL Add. MS 30512, contains four religious poems attributed to 'Richard Butler', quite probably Edmund's father, three of them short and one containing a long catalogue of examples from scripture and the lives of saints, demonstrating that God punishes pride and requires humility even from the high-born.[37]

European Cultural Contacts

As Robin Flower realised, the poems of Richard Butler provide evidence for the influence of European social and religious developments on Irish culture. Intellectual life on the Continent of Europe was experiencing great changes in the fourteenth and fifteenth centuries, with the spread of universities and lay literacy, the renaissance of Classical culture, and pious reform movements within the Church. These last embraced both the Observantine reform of the friars' orders, including the renewal or foundation of regular and secular lay Third Orders, and the less formally organised *Devotio Moderna* ('Modern Devotion'), which also inspired literate laymen to follow a life of prayer and austerity, such as that recommended by Thomas à Kempis in his work, 'The Imitation of Christ'.[38] Gaelic Ireland received these influences by three routes, pilgrims, Churchmen and the medical profession. Ever since the appearance *c.* 1184 of the English Cistercian tract on the 'Vision of the Knight Owen' concerning Heaven, Hell and Purgatory as experienced in the cave of St Patrick's Purgatory in Lough Derg, and still more after the dramatic account of visions vouchsafed in the same place to the Hungarian war-criminal George Grissaphan in 1353, and publicised by Primate Richard Fitz Ralph, pilgrims from all over Europe made their way to this remote corner of Clogher diocese up to the end of the fifteenth century, when the cave was closed down by papal decree, following complaints about its commercialisation, although Irish pilgrims continued to pay their devotions there from the sixteenth century to the present day. It is surely no coincidence that the local ruler in this

---

37 'Laud Misc. 610', 135–55. For one of the shorter poems '*Is áille Íosa ná 'n chruinne*', see R. Flower, *Ireland and Medieval Europe*. Sir John Rhys Lecture from the Proceedings of the British Academy (London, 1929), 23–4, 34–5, and R. Flower, *The Irish Tradition* (Oxford University Press, 1947), 107–14. For two others, '*Guidhim Dia mór*' and '*Is romhaith mo leaghasa*', see 'Dhá Dhán le Risteard Buitléir', ed. G. Mac Niocaill, *Éigse*, 9 (1958), 83–8 (text only). The long poem '*Gabhaim le hollamhnacht Íosa*' ('I accept Jesus as my teacher') BL Add. MS 30512, fol. 46b, remains unpublished.
38 See the chapters by Ó Clabaigh and Lyons in this volume.

area, Tomás Óc Maguire [Mág Uidir] (d. 1480), was the most widely travelled chieftain of his day, having made pilgrimages once to Rome and twice to Santiago de Compostela. He was not the only Gaelic leader to go abroad on pilgrimage in the later Middle Ages, and his foreign travels have been seen as a reason for his enlarging and re-roofing his own parish church of Aghalurcher in a 'French' style in 1447.[39] Margaret, the daughter of O'Carroll, mentioned above as holding the two great feasts for poets in 1433, accompanied Tomás Óc Maguire on his pilgrimage to Rome in 1450, and was poetically described as a woman who lived by a rule, and was not lured by a wine-feast into neglecting the Hours (na trátha), that is, the daily monastic liturgy. Observing the Hours was a common practice among later medieval lay nobles influenced by the Devotio Moderna movement, giving rise elsewhere to magnificently illustrated liturgical books, such as the Très Riches Heures du Duc de Berry. The pious poems of Richard Butler suggest that he too was influenced by the trend for lay persons to take a more active role within the Church.[40]

Fifteenth-Century Church Reform

This lay piety had its practical side. Margaret, daughter of O'Carroll, on the day of her first great feast in 1433 'gave two chalices of gold as offerings that day on the Altar to God Almighty, and she also caused to nurse or foster two young orphans ... and she was the onely woman that has made most of pre-paring high-wayes, and erecting bridges, churches and mass-books, and of all manner of things profittable to serue God and her soule'. We are also told she was the general support and maintenance for 'philosophers, poets, guests, strangers, religious persons, souldiers, mendicants or poore orders, and to all manner and sorts of the poore in Ireland also'. The allusion to 'guests' and

---

39 Haren and de Pontfarcy (eds.), The Medieval Pilgrimage to St Patrick's Purgatory; Y. de Pontfarcy, 'Le Tractatus de Purgatorio Sancti Patricii de H. de Saltrey: sa date et ses sources', Peritia, 3 (1984), 460–80; K. Walsh, A Fourteenth-Century Scholar and Primate: Richard FitzRalph in Oxford, Avignon and Armagh (Oxford University Press, 1981), 308–11; R. Stalley, 'Irish Gothic and English Fashion', in Lydon (ed.), English in Medieval Ireland, 85–6; R. Stalley, 'Sailing to Santiago', in Bradley (ed.), Settlement and Society in Medieval Ireland, 397–420; AU, iii, 160–1; K. Simms, 'Medieval Fermanagh', in E. M. Murphy and W. J. Roulston (eds.), Fermanagh: History and Society (Dublin: Geography Publications, 2004), 77–103, at 95–7.
40 Irish Bardic Poetry, ed. O. Bergin, D. Greene and F. Kelly (Dublin: DIAS, 1970), poem no. 40, lines 95–6; J. Longnon, R. Cazelles and M. Meiss, The Très Riches Heures of Jean, Duke of Berry (New York: George Braziller, 1969); E. Duffy, 'A Very Personal Possession: Eamon Duffy Tells How a Careful Study of Surviving Books of Hours Can Tell Us Much About the Spiritual and Temporal Life of Their Owners and Much More Besides', History Today, 56/11 (Nov. 2006), 12(7).

'strangers' implies she maintained a house or houses of public hospitality at her own expense, like the Sligo merchant Seaán O'Crean (d. 1528), and other well-to-do public benefactors.[41] In a sense, these pious lay leaders of society could be seen as taking over functions traditionally performed by the institutional Church, and supplementing its shortcomings. On the Continent Geert Groote (d. 1384), a zealous Dutch deacon, founder of the mixed clerical and lay associations of the Brethren (and Sisters) of the Common Life, and a key figure in the *Devotio Moderna* movement, was also a strident critic of corrupt or sinful clergy, especially those who kept concubines. His preaching gave rise to such controversy that he was officially silenced.[42] This aspect of the movement also reached Ireland. A tract called *Riagal na Sacart*, the 'Rule of Priests', is a polemic against priests who kept concubines, which in one recension is couched in the form of a letter addressed to Magnus MacMahon [Mac Mathgamna] (d. 1443/4), lord of Fernmag (barony of Farney in Monaghan), exhorting him to arrest clerics' concubines and confiscate their goods, although leaving the priests alone, to be deposed after due process initiated by an appeal to Rome.[43]

For historical reasons clerical concubinage in Gaelic Ireland had not been viewed in quite the same light as elsewhere in Europe. Land and authority within the institutional Church prior to the twelfth-century reform had passed into the hands of Church rulers or *principes* who although wearing the *prima tonsura*, the simple clerical tonsure, and regarded as Churchmen, frequently did not take major orders, and were consequently free to marry and tended to pass on their office to their sons. Christina Harrington has argued that even in the opening years of the reform era, religious literature in Irish or Hiberno-Latin lacks the extreme 'demonization of women' and anxiety about the temptations of sex that characterised the eleventh-century Gregorian Reform. As she says,

> It should be borne in mind that many of the authors ... had close personal relations with women – because they themselves were married, or their abbot was, or their father was an ecclesiastic and their mother a cleric's wife ... Texts such as *Mé Eba Ben* (a poem in the voice of Adam's wife) and the

41 'Annals of Ireland ... MacFirbis', 227–8.
42 R. R. Post, *The Modern Devotion: Confrontation with Reformation and Humanism* (Leiden: Brill, 1968), 129–48.
43 'Riaghail na Sacart', ed. anon., *Irisleabhar Muighe Nuadhad* (1919), 73–9; K. Simms, 'The Legal Position of Irishwomen in the Later Middle Ages', *The Irish Jurist*, new series 10 (1975), 96–111: 105; C. Ó Clabaigh, *The Franciscans in Ireland 1400–1534* (Dublin: Four Courts Press, 2002), 95. The MacMahon recension comes in 'Liber Flavus Fergusiorum', RIA MS 476 pt ii (23/O/16 ii), fol. 17r.

Saltair na Rann … take up the issue of 'the female sex', but tend to betray a remarkable level of compassion for even that most culpable of women in the whole of the Christian tradition [Eve].[44]

The fact that the Norman invasion of Ireland took place before the completion of the administrative reform of the Church in the twelfth century led to a contrast in structures at a parish level between the areas fully colonised by the newcomers and those left under Gaelic control. In Gaelic areas much of the Church land remained in the hands of hereditary clerical administrators, the 'erenaghs' (*airchinnig*, 'superiors') whose claim to clerical orders might go no higher than the *prima tonsura*. Although a series of synods in the early thirteenth century appear to have transferred legal ownership of their lands to the diocesan bishops, leaving the erenaghs and their families in possession as the bishops' tenants, these hereditary Church families remained the chief recruiting pool for Irish ordained clergy and brought with them into the institutional Church inherited attitudes to clerical marriage and dynastic succession to clerical office, shown most clearly in the admiring obituaries for the wives and daughters of Fermanagh abbots, bishops and archdeacons found in the fifteenth-century Annals of Ulster.[45]

The opening years of the fifteenth century saw a new brand of Churchman gaining influence in Ireland with the spread of the Observant movement among the orders of friars, especially the Franciscans. The hereditary tendency among Irish ecclesiastics had been linked to the control of Church lands, so the Franciscans with their original determination to accept no lands at all had always been among the most idealistic section of the Irish clergy. A retreat from this position had compromised the reputation of the Conventual Franciscans. The Franciscan bardic poet Pilib Bocht Ó hUiginn (d. 1487) lamented:

> St Francis is now almost bereft of honour
> Breach of the Rule is common in his wood

---

44 S. Wood, *The Proprietary Church in the Medieval West* (Oxford University Press, 2006), 140–7; M. Holland, 'Were Early Irish Church Establishments under Lay Control?', in Bracken and Ó Riain-Raedel (eds.), *Ireland and Europe in the Twelfth Century*, 128–42; C. Harrington, *Women in a Celtic Church: Ireland 450–1150* (Oxford University Press, 2002), 192–3. My square brackets.

45 P. J. Duffy, 'The Shape of the Parish', in E. Fitzpatrick and R. Gillespie (eds.), *The Parish in Medieval and Early Modern Ireland: Community, Territory and Building* (Dublin: Four Courts Press, 2006), 41–8; J. A. Watt, '*Ecclesia inter Anglicos et inter Hibernicos*: Confrontation and Coexistence in the Medieval Diocese and Province of Armagh', in Lydon (ed.), *English in Medieval Ireland*, 46–64; K. Simms, 'Frontiers in the Irish Church – Regional and Cultural', in Barry *et al.* (eds.), *Colony and Frontier in Medieval Ireland*, 184–8, 198–200; Nicholls, *Gaelic and Gaelicized Ireland*, 106–13; C. Mooney, 'The Church in Gaelic Ireland 13th to 15th Centuries', in P. J. Corish (ed.), *A History of Irish Catholicism*. Vol. II. no. 5. (Dublin: Gill and Sons, 1969), 56–60.

A lengthy indictment lies against his children,
Were this the time to make it.[46]

However, the late fourteenth century saw the rise of groups of friars within the Conventual movement who wished to dedicate themselves to a more rigorous observance of the early Franciscan rule. While some tried to pursue their aims within Conventual houses, the movement for separate houses of Observant friars began in Ireland before 1417, though it was not until 1458–60 that these achieved the right to be separately administered under an Observant vicariate, becoming an Irish province within a fully recognised Observant Franciscan order in 1517. New friaries of both Conventual and Observant Franciscans were established across Ireland under lay patronage during the fifteenth century. In addition, houses of Dominican, Augustinian and Carmelite friars were founded, also influenced by the Observant movement to return to the ideals of their founders, but by far the greater number of the new religious communities to spring up at this time were the Third Order Franciscans, or Tertiaries.[47]

It could be argued that the lifestyle of the secular Tertiaries, as married lay people who were yet bound by modified monastic vows, was a concept that would prove attractive to hereditary erenagh families descended from the *manaig* of early medieval Ireland. In Gaelic Ireland a developed form of the Third Order was particularly successful, the Third Order Regular, small groups of mixed priests and lay brothers, less highly educated than the First Order Franciscan friars, but living a communal life under vows of poverty, chastity and obedience. Lay brothers among these regular Tertiaries similarly fitted into an Irish tradition of unordained clerics. Ó Clabaigh has drawn attention to what looks like a clear instance of a hereditary erenagh family, the Uí Máel Chairill, who gave their name to the church of Clonkeenkerrill in the diocese of Tuam, adopting the Third Order rule and continuing their hereditary hold on their family church, at some cost to the vow of celibacy, after it became a house of regular Tertiaries some time before 1438. He also noted possible examples of the same kind of connection between hereditary Churchmen and Tertiaries in Ulster in the case of the O'Moran [Ó Moráin] family in Raphoe diocese and the O'Killeen [Ó Cillín] family in Bangor, Down diocese.[48]

---

46 L. McKenna, *Philip Bocht Ó hUiginn* (Dublin: Talbot Press, 1931), 129.
47 Ó Clabaigh, *Franciscans in Ireland*, 48–9; F. X. Martin, 'The Spread of the Religious Orders 1420–1530' (Map), in *NHI* ii, 585; Gwynn and Hadcock, *Medieval Religious Houses: Ireland*, 218–305.
48 Ó Clabaigh, *Franciscans in Ireland*, 84, 96–7, 104–5.

It may well have been through the fiery preaching of the Observants that the Irish laity had their attention drawn to the discrepancy between the universal Church's rulings on celibacy of priests and the habits of their own parish clergy. The response of the O'Neill chieftains was to exact fines or 'corrections' from clerics who kept concubines. Primate Mey of Armagh sometimes tried to control and harness this zeal by authorising O'Neill princes to act on his behalf as the secular arm of the Church, and confiscate the dowries of concubines, supposedly leaving the goods of the Church untouched, but was uncertain of the wisdom of entrusting this role to men like Henry, the Great O'Neill (d. 1489):

> moved not by zeal or the intention of bringing about a salutary correction, but by his notorious coveteousness, avarice or greed, whereby at the devil's prompting he had long plotted to acquire for himself not only [the concubines'] goods but the goods of others also.[49]

However, the reforming Observants were not Ireland's only contact with the intellectual trends of fifteenth-century Europe. Inside the Irish Church hierarchy, as elsewhere in the western Church, a formal qualification in theology or civil and canon law was a normal pre-requisite for promotion to the higher positions, and the lack of a university on the island predisposed members of the more influential ecclesiastical families to go abroad for their education, to Oxford, Paris, Rome or the Holy Roman Empire, where some of the *Schottenklöster* or Irish Benedictine monasteries founded along the Rhine and the Danube in the eleventh century still drew recruits from Ireland as well as Scotland into the fourteenth and fifteenth centuries. For example the bishop of Clogher, Johannes Ó Corcráin (1373–*c*.1389), was a Benedictine monk and doctor of canon law from the monastery of St James Würzburg, and his son, Tomás Ó Corcráin, was a notary general 'by imperial authorisation', perhaps suggesting he might have received this qualification in Germany.[50]

---

49 K. Simms, 'The Concordat between Primate John Mey and Henry O'Neill, 1455', *Archivium Hibernicum*, 34 (1977), 75, 78. *Reg. Mey*, nos. 312, 354, 379. My translation – the original reads: 'non zelo aut intencione salutifere correccionis, sed intuitu notorie concupiscencie avaricie seu cupiditatis non solum earum sed ceterorum bona pro suo libito acquirenda, prout a longo, suadente diabolo, hec excogitavit': *Registrum Iohannis Mey*, no. 322. See Simms, 'Concordat', 75.

50 *Vetera Monumenta Hibernorum et Scotorum Historiam Illustrantia*, ed. A. Theiner (Romae, 1864), 349. According to Pope Clement V (13 November 1310) the monastery of St James Würzburg was bound by custom to receive religious of whatsoever Order who were Irish by birth or origin: *ibid.*, 182. '*noiteir coitchenn o udaras Imper*', *AU*, iii, 16–17 (AD

The lack of a university within Ireland also sent a number of Gaelic Irish medical students abroad to gain degrees such as Batchelor of Physic. In 1527 the death is noted of 'The Doctor' Donnchad son of Eógan Ulltach Ó Duinnshléibe, 'eminent in physic and very many other sciences (*saoi fhisici 7 andsna healadhnaibh eile d'urmór)*'.[51] Interestingly it appears this man's son (Eógan *Ulltach* son of the Doctor Donnchad) did not have a formal university degree like his father, and the annals when noting his death in 1586 are slightly defensive about this: 'this Eógan was a doctor in regard of learning, for he excelled the medical doctors of Ireland in the time in which he lived'. Stay-at-home clerical and medical students studied with individual masters in small schools (*studia particularia*), where according to Campion's description in the later sixteenth century:

> without either precepts or observation of congruity they speak Latin like a vulgar language, learned in their common Schools of Leach-craft and Law, whereat they begin children, and hold on sixteen or twenty years conning by rote the Aphorisms of Hypocrates, and the Civil Institutions, and a few other pairings of those two faculties. I have seen them where they keep schools, ten in some one chamber, groveling upon couches of straw, their books at their noses, themselves lying flat prostrate, and so to chant out their lessons by piecemeal, being the most part lusty fellows of twenty five years and upwards.[52]

These medical and clerical students, however, like the brehon lawyers and historians, also studied *filidecht*, that is, the art of reading, writing and basic metrical composition in the Irish language. This is evidenced not only by their Irish verse compositions on religious or medical topics, but by a flood of translations from Latin into Irish of medical textbooks and works of religion and piety. Such translations served not only to aid students with an imperfect grasp of Latin. In parallel with developments elsewhere in Europe, the upper classes of the laity were becoming literate in the vernacular, and, as John

---

1385). Tomás Ó Corcráin is just one example of the fact that the clergy of Clogher and other more remote parts of Ireland not only took their vows of celibacy lightly, but publicly acknowledged both partners and offspring.

51 On medieval Irish physicians with university educations see M. Dunlevy, 'The Medical Families of Medieval Ireland', in W. Doolin and O. Fitzgerald (eds.), *What's Past is Prologue: A Retrospect of Irish Medicine* (Dublin: Monument Press, 1952), 15–22; *AFM*, v, 1388–9; *AU*, iii, 564–7.

52 On *studia particularia* see H. A. Jefferies, *Priests and Prelates of Armagh in the Age of the Reformations 1518–1558* (Dublin: Four Courts Press, 1997), 75–6; Edmund Campion, *Two Bokes of the Histories of Ireland*, ed. A. F. Vossen (Assen: Van Gorcum and Comp., 1963), 25–6.

Watt observed, 'there was a vernacular literature to cater for their needs'.[53] This included not only translations of continental saints' lives and homilies, but the travels of Sir John Mandeville and Messer Marco Polo, the history of Cambrensis, tales drawing on Arthurian romance, or the Siege of Troy, the adventures of William of Palermo, Guy of Warwick and Bevis of Hampden. Chivalrous concepts like the unworthy knight who does not deserve 'the privilege nor the honour of knighthood' (*'priuiled na onoir na riderechta'*) entered the fifteenth-century Irish vocabulary, concepts that were apparently still relatively unfamiliar to Niall Óc O'Neill and Art MacMurrough Kavanagh when they were knighted in 1395.[54] A prolific scribe and translator from a medical family, William Mac an Lega worked in the mid- to late fifteenth century for both Gaelic and Anglo-Irish patrons, translating in some cases from English rather than Latin originals, prompting the notion that some of the more rural Anglo-Irish nobility found Gaelic texts easier to follow than English ones. The catalogue of the library of the Great Earl of Kildare, drawn up on or before 1500, listed twenty works in Irish and only seven in English (together with twenty-three in Latin and nine in French). However, it is significant that these Irish language titles have disappeared from a later catalogue done for the English-educated ninth earl of Kildare in 1526.[55]

Scotland and the Greater Gaeldom

Ireland's outside contacts were not only with England and the Continent. Direct cultural links with Scotland and the Isles were demonstrated in the twelfth century in 1164 when Somerled, lord of Argyll and the Hebrides, invited Flaithbertach Ó Brolcháin, the abbot of Derry, to relocate to Iona as head of a re-united Columban monastic *familia* (a move blocked by the northern high-king Muirchertach Mac Lochlainn), and in 1169 when the high-king Ruaidri Ua Conchobair endowed the lector at Armagh with ten cows a

---

53 Simms, *Medieval Gaelic Sources*, 50–60, 100–2. S. Ryan, 'Windows on Late Medieval Devotional Practice: Máire Ní Mháille's "Book of Piety" (1513) and the World behind the Texts', in Moss et al. (eds.), *Art and Devotion in Late Medieval Ireland*, 130–74; J. A. Watt, *The Church in Medieval Ireland*, 2nd edn (Dublin: Four Courts Press, 1998), 211–12. See Simms, 'Literacy and the Irish Bards', 249, 251–2.

54 Simms, *Medieval Gaelic Sources*, 87–8; G. Murphy, *The Ossianic Lore and Romantic Tales of Medieval Ireland* (Dublin: DIAS, 1955), 35–9; 'Liber Flavus Fergusiorum' (RIA, MS 476 ii, 23/0/48 II), fol. 17r col. b, line 15. See Simms, *Medieval Gaelic Sources*. Froissart: *Chronicles*, ed. and trans. G. Brereton (Harmondsworth: Penguin, 1968), 415 [*Chronicles* Bk 4, chap. 64]; see Simms, 'Barefoot Kings', 12–13.

55 *Stair Ercuil ocus a Bás*, ed. E. G. Quin (London: ITS, 1939), xiv, xxiv–xxv, xxxviii–xl; *Crown Surveys of Lands*, 312–14, 355–6; A. Byrne, 'The Earls of Kildare and their Books at the End of the Middle Ages', *The Library*, 14:2 (2013), 129–53.

year 'to instruct the youths of Ireland and Alba (Scotland) in [Latin] literature (*ar leighinn do dhénam do macaibh leighind Ereann 7 Alban archena*)'.[56] The spoken dialects of Irish and Scottish Gaelic had been gradually diverging since at least the fifth century AD, but among the first recorded uses of the literary language of Classical Early Modern Irish, developed by the Irish poetic schools towards the end of the twelfth century, were poems to Ragnall, king of Man, and to the earls of Lennox, and Classical Irish remained the common literary dialect of the Gaelic world to the first half of the sixteenth century.[57] This early communication of the newly created literary standard between the two countries is less surprising if we take it that Scottish students in the late twelfth century not only acquired Latin learning at Armagh, but also the art of poetic composition with the pre-eminent Ó Dálaig bards, two of whom, Tadc (d. 1181) and Máel Ísa Ó Dálaig (d. 1185), are each described as '*ollam Erenn 7 Alban*'– 'chief poet [*or* bardic teacher] of Ireland and Scotland'. Their kinsman Muiredach Ó Dálaig (fl. 1213) was subsequently exiled to Scotland from the court of Domnall Mór O'Donnell [Ó Domnaill], king of Tír Conaill (d. 1241), and there founded the Mac Mhuirich dynasty of pre-eminent Scottish bardic poets.[58]

After this promising beginning, we have a striking but anonymous poem addressed to Angus *Mór* MacDonald [Mac Domnaill], lord of Islay, in the second half of the thirteenth century, and no further surviving compositions of Irish poets to Scottish patrons or vice versa before the fifteenth century.[59]

---

56 Herbert, *Iona, Kells, and Derry*, 109–20; *AU*, ii, 144–5; *AFM*, ii, 1170–3. My addition in square brackets.

57 W. McLeod, *Divided Gaels: Gaelic Cultural Identities in Scotland and Ireland c.1200–c.1650* (Oxford University Press, 2004), 15; B. Ó Buachalla, '"Common Gaelic" Revisited', in C. Ó Baoill and N. R. McGuire (eds.), *Rannsachadh na Gàidhlig 2000* (Aberdeen: Clo Gaidhealach, 2002), 9. W. Gillies, 'The Lion's Tongues: Languages in Scotland to 1314', in I. Brown, T. O. Clancy, S. Manning and M. Pittock (eds.), *The Edinburgh History of Scottish Literature vol. 1. From Columba to the Union (until 1707)* (Edinburgh University Press, 2006), 58. For 'Baile suthach síth Emhna', see 'A Poem in Praise of Raghnall, King of Man', ed. and trans. B. Ó Cuív, *Éigse*, 8 (1957), 283–301; 'Saor do leannán a Leamhain', in *Aithdioghluim Dána*, poem no. 42; For 'Mairg thréigeas inn a Amhlaoimh', see 'A Poem Attributed to Muireadhach Ó Dálaigh', ed. and trans. B. Ó Cuív, in J. Carney and D. Greene (eds.), *Celtic Studies: Essays in Memory of Angus Matheson 1912–1962* (London: Routledge and Kegan Paul, 1968), 92–8. See also T. O. Clancy (ed.), *The Triumph Tree: Scotland's Earliest Poetry 550–1350* (Edinburgh University Press, 1998), 258–62.

58 *ALC*, i, 162–3, 168–9. K. Simms, 'Muireadhach Albanach Ó Dálaigh and the Classical Revolution', in Brown *et al.* (eds.), *Edinburgh History of Scottish Literature*, 83–90; W. Gillies, 'Alexander Carmichael and Clann Mhuirich', *Scottish Gaelic Studies*, 20 (2000), 1–66.

59 'Ceannaigh duain t'athar, a Aonghas': *Irish Bardic Poetry*, no. 45; W. H. D. Sellar, 'Hebridean Sea-Kings: The Successors of Somerled, 1164–1316', in E. J. Cowan and R. A. McDonald (eds.), *Alba: Celtic Scotland in the Medieval Era* (East Linton: Tuckwell Press, 2000), 207–8. A possible exception could be the address to Eoin Mac Suibne (MacSweeney): D. Meek, '"Norsemen and Noble Stewards": The Castle Sween Poem

This gap in the records presumably reflects both the increasing separation of the original galloglass families from their Scottish homeland, and stronger involvement of the Hebrides with the politics of the Scottish mainland after the transference of overlordship from Norway to the king at Edinburgh by the Treaty of Perth in 1266. Within Scotland the Gaelic language was fast dying out in the Lowlands in the course of the thirteenth century while at the same time it was spreading and replacing Norse in the Hebrides. By the later Middle Ages, Irish learned classes who had originally seen the inhabitants of the Western Isles as *Gaill* or *Gall-Gaidil* ('foreigners/Norse' or 'foreigner-Gaels') began to perceive Scotland ('Alba') as divided between Gaels or Gaelic-speakers in the Highlands and Islands as distinct from *Gaill*, or Scots/English-speakers in the Lowlands. This shrinking of the Scottish Gaelic-speaking community to the areas that were agriculturally poorest reduced the temptation for the most eminent poets and scholars from Ireland to migrate there in search of patronage, even at the court of the Lord of the Isles. The anonymous thirteenth-century poem to Angus Mór MacDonald was a polite refusal to cross the North Channel to join his household, on the specious excuse of sea-sickness, and the same weak explanation was among those offered by Ireland's greatest master-poet of the fifteenth century, Tadc Óc Ó hUiginn (d. 1448), for refusing an invitation from Alexander MacDonald, earl of Ross and third Lord of the Isles (d. 1449).[60]

Nevertheless, during the fifteenth century the establishment of the new MacDonald lordship in the Glens of Antrim, and a related worsening of relations between the Lordship of the Isles and the Scottish crown coincided with signs of increased interest among Scots of the Highlands and Western Isles in Irish literature and culture. Significantly Tadc Óc's obituary in the annals calls him 'preceptor of the schools of Ireland and Scotland in poetry and in erudition' (*oide sgol Erenn 7 Alban a ndan 7 a foghluim*), or 'chief Preceptor of the Poets of Ireland and Scotland' (*priomhoide aosa dána Ereann 7 Alban*). He is the first 'man of art' to receive such an accolade since the death of Máelruanaid Mac Cerbaill 'the most choice timpanist of Ireland and of Scotland and of the whole world' (*aenraga timpanach Erenn 7 Alban 7 in domain uile*) in 1329. The use of the phrase *oide sgol* in Tadc Óc's panegyric

in the Book of the Dean of Lismore', *Cambrian Medieval Celtic Studies*, 34 (1998), 1–50. But as Meek observed, pp. 12, 18, the internal evidence suggests the Mac Suibne patron in question was based in Ireland. *Scottish Verse from the Book of the Dean of Lismore*, ed. W. J. Watson (Edinburgh: Scottish Gaelic Texts Society, 1937), 6–13, 257–9.

60 Sellar, 'Hebridean Sea-Kings', 210; McLeod, *Divided Gaels*, 16–18, 24–8 33–5. 'Fuaras aisgidh gan iarraidh': *Aithdioghluim Dána*, no. 29.

strongly suggests that Scottish students attended the famous Ó hUiginn school of poetry in Sligo whose direction he had inherited from his elder brother, Fergal Ruad Ó hUiginn. Later teachers of this school, Brian son of Fergal Ruad (d. 1476), his son Domnall Ó hUiginn (d. 1502) and grandson Tomás (d. 1536), were also described as *oide sgol Erenn 7 Alban* in their obits.[61] Similarly the learned Roscommon historian Maílín Ó Máelchonaire (d. 1441) was described as 'principal author of the learning of Ireland and Scotland' (*primugdar odechta Ereann 7 Alpan*).[62]

There are other fragments of evidence for the coming and going of the learned classes between Scotland and Ireland, more especially Ulster and north Connacht, in the fifteenth and sixteenth centuries. Many hereditarily learned families in Scotland had Irish surnames, like Mac Muiredaig, Mac Eogain, Ó Muirgesáin, Ó Máel Chiaráin. A moving Scottish poem which became a model studied in the Irish schools of this period, cited in the bardic grammatical tracts, was Ó Máel Chiaráin's lament for his son Ferchar, a young poet who crossed to Ireland and met a violent death there at the hands of Anglo-Irish (*Goill*), for reasons that are unclear – as his father complained: 'the man had not censured you, he had not satirised you: it was not for you to wound his fair body'. Another Scot touring Ireland at this time, a certain 'Fergus', was responsible for compiling BL Add. MS 19,995, a tattered miscellaneous collection of religious poems and bardic classics of the kind cited in the grammatical tracts, but showing a particular interest in poems by the early thirteenth-century Muiredach *Albanach* and Gilla-Brigde *Albanach*.[63]

On the other side of the North Channel, the Book of the Dean of Lismore, a large miscellany of poetry compiled c.1512–42 by Seumas MacGregor [Mac Griogóir], vicar of Fortingall and Dean of Lismore, within the literary circle of the courts of the earls of Argyll and the Campbells of Glenorchy, illustrates a broad spectrum of the written literature of Gaelic Scotland after the collapse of the Lordship of the Isles, but just before the major changes brought about by the Reformation in Scotland and the development of a bitter Campbell–MacDonald feud.[64] It

---

61 *Irish Bardic Poetry*, no. 38; *AU*, iii, 258–9, 460–1; *ALC*, ii, 290–1.
62 *AC*, 440–1. The word *odecht* or *oidecht* means 'learning' in the sense of education, reinforcing the suggestion that Máeilín Ó Máelchonaire taught students from Scotland as well as Ireland.
63 McLeod, *Divided Gaels*, 69–78; MacGregor, 'Creation and Compilation', 213; Breatnach, 'Marbhna Fhearchar Í Mháoil Chíaráin', 165–84; *Catalogue of Irish Manuscripts*, 328–39; Murphy, 'Two Irish Poems', 71–9.
64 M. MacGregor, 'Creation and Compilation: The Book of the Dean of Lismore and Literary Culture in Late Medieval Gaelic Scotland', in Brown *et al.* (eds.), *Edinburgh*

contains much matter in common with later Irish miscellanies compiled for literate lay patrons – classic Irish bardic eulogies and religious poetry from the thirteenth century, heroic lays about the *Fianna*, particularly popular with galloglass families, who tended to identify with Finn and his warrior bands, and short humorous, sometimes obscene, informal verse.[65] There were also contrasts in subject-matter and style: in the range of Fenian epic poems preserved in Irish and Scottish sources; in the higher status accorded in Scotland to 'bards' or less highly educated oral praise-poets, and the fewness of the more expensive learned poets or *filid*, or courts wealthy enough to employ them, once the Lordship of the Isles was dissolved. The heyday of the Lordship had coincided with the high-point of the Gaelic political and cultural resurgence in Ireland. Ironically, in the mid-seventeenth century, when the Irish bardic schools had declined or disappeared, the temporary revival of traditional lordships during the wars of the Catholic Confederation of Kilkenny created a renewed demand for formal eulogies from learned poets, and by this time it was Scottish poets who led the field.[66]

History of Scottish Literature, 209–18. On the effects of subsequent political and religious change see McLeod, *Divided Gaels*, 194–222.

65 K. Simms, 'Images of the Galloglass in Poems to the MacSweeneys', in S. Duffy (ed.), *The World of the Galloglass: Kings, Warlords and Warriors in Ireland and Scotland, 1200–1600* (Dublin: Four Courts Press, 2007); R. Ó hUiginn, '*Fiannaigheacht*, Family, Faith and Fatherland', in S. J. Arbuthnot and G. Parsons (eds.), *The Gaelic Finn Tradition* (Dublin: Four Courts Press, 2013), 161–2; R. Ó hUiginn, '*Duanaire Finn*: Patron and Text', in J. Carey (ed.), *Duanaire Finn: Reassessments*. ITS, Subsidiary Series (London, 2003), 79–106; W. Gillies, 'Gaelic Literature in the Later Middle Ages: *The Book of the Dean* and Beyond', in Brown *et al.* (eds.), *Edinburgh History of Scottish Literature*, 219–25.

66 D. Meek, 'The Scottish Tradition of Fian Ballads in the Middle Ages', in C. G. Ó Háinle and D. Meek (eds.), *Unity in Diversity: Studies in Irish and Scottish Gaelic Language, Literature and History* (Dublin: School of Irish, Trinity College Dublin, 2004), 9–24; McLeod, *Divided Gaels*, 63–70; R. Black, 'The Genius of Cathal MacMhuirich', *Transactions of the Gaelic Society of Inverness*, 50 (1976–8), 327–65; R. Black, 'Poems by Maol Domhnaigh Ó Muirgheasáin Pts I–III', *Scottish Gaelic Studies*, 12 (1976), 104–208; 13: (1978), 46–55; 13:2 (1981), 289–301; R. Black, 'A Scottish Grammatical Tract c. 1640', *Celtica*, 21 (1990), 3–16.

16

The Structure of Politics in Theory and Practice, 1210–1541

PETER CROOKS

AMONG the many casuistries uttered at the Council of Constance – the general council of the Church that assembled between 1414 and 1418 to bring a negotiated conclusion to the Great Schism – was a startling claim concerning Ireland. The spokesman for the English nation, Thomas Polton dean of York, declared that it was well known that the world was divided into three parts, Asia, Africa and Europe; and that Europe was itself divided into four kingdoms, of which the first was Rome, the second Constantinople, the third Ireland (whose rule had since been 'translated' to the English) and the fourth Spain. By virtue of this, he claimed, 'it is apparent that the king of England and his kingdom are among the most eminent and ancient kings and kingdoms of all Europe, which prerogative the kingdom of France is not said to obtain'.[1] Polton's assertion was as opportunistic as it was tendentious, but it directs our attention to the central problematic with which this essay is concerned. What became of the 'kingdom of Ireland' after its translation to the English?

This may seem, at first glance, to be a *non sequitur*. From the accession of King John in 1199, the English royal style included a new territorial title: 'lord of Ireland' (L. *dominus Hibernie*). This was a potent, claim-making term – one that came to be understood as enhancing or augmenting the regality of English kingship itself, rather as Polton was to suggest at Constance.[2] Whatever shuffling occurred of the other elements in the royal style, *dominus Hibernie* remained a constant until a new great seal of England was engraved for Henry VIII after 1541 reflecting the change to *rex Hibernie* consequent upon the Act for the Kingly Title, passed by the Irish parliament in June 1541. The continuity in the royal style between 1199 and 1541 was, however, a patina

---

1 *Magnum Oecuminicum Constantiense Concilium* [...], ed. H. von der Hardt. 6 vols. (Frankfurt and Leipzig: Genius, 1692–1700), iv, 91.
2 *PROME*, Parliament of Richard II: Feb. 1388, item C (F. *en augmentacion de lour nouns et de lour roialte*).

overlaying deep structural change. Ireland was conquered by England in the late twelfth century at the very time when the institution of the monarchy under the Plantagenets was moving from 'law-based kingship' towards 'polity-based kingship'.[3] This development had far-reaching implications for the structuring of politics in Ireland, conceptually and institutionally. Ireland was not normally described as a 'kingdom' in the later Middle Ages, but many of the attributes of institutional growth and solidarity associated with a 'regnal' polity are to be found in its political development, especially at the level of assumptions and expectations. This presents us with something of a paradox. Even at its height, c.1300, English power in medieval Ireland was decentralised and dispersed. By the mid-fourteenth century, under the combined pressures of economic and demographic collapse and a Gaelic resurgence, 'the dispersal of authority was beginning to give way to its decomposition'.[4] All the more important, then, to explore how expectations of the king's public authority grew, and the pleas for remedy and intervention grew ever shriller, even as the capacity (or desire) of the crown to effect far-reaching change became more limited.

If English Ireland was not entirely set apart from political developments in late-medieval Europe, the politics of the Lordship also had their own distinctive flavour. Two of the most familiar and distinctive structural features of Irish politics in the centuries after the English invasion are the island's status as a lordship separate from, but dependent upon, the English crown; and the division of the island into two peoples. Historians seek to understand and explain dependency and division by describing Ireland as a classic colonial situation. The problem with the colonial paradigm is not that it is wrong, but that, by itself, it explains too much and too little. What is most interesting about Ireland as a specimen of European political ideas in action is that the characteristics of dependency and division sat awkwardly – indeed, sat *increasingly* awkwardly – in the evolving thought-world of late-medieval Europe. This was the era when the 'state' was emerging as something more than an idea and was beginning to coalesce with conceptions of nationhood. As Andrea Ruddick has shown, the kingdom of England was being conceptualised in the late Middle Ages as a defined physical space that supplied the homeland of a distinct people.[5] How, then, was one to define the

---

3 E. H. Kantorowicz, *The King's Two Bodies: A Study in Medieval Political Theology* (new edn. Princeton University Press, 1997), chs. 4–5.
4 S. Reynolds, *Kingdoms and Communities in Western Europe, 900–1300* (2nd edn. Oxford University Press, 1997), 254, 262; Frame, *Ireland and Britain*, quotation at 234.
5 A. Ruddick, *English Identity and Political Culture in the Fourteenth Century* (Cambridge University Press, 2013).

status of those of the king's English lieges who resided outside the realm yet claimed the liberties of freeborn Englishmen as their birthright? Since the king could not perform his office in person, how much of his sovereign authority devolved upon his representative in Ireland, who took an oath of office based upon the coronation oath? What were the king's duties, whether of care or correction, towards the native inhabitants of Ireland whom the settlers had displaced and disenfranchised? And finally – a question prior to all of these – by what right did the monarch of England claim to rule Ireland in the first place?

To most of these questions, there are no ready-made answers. Historians are just beginning to appreciate the sophistication and vibrancy of English political culture in the Lordship.[6] There is a distinguished, if somewhat austere, historiography of the institutions of English royal government in Ireland; but almost no aspect of the conceptual framework of English *governance* (L. *gubernaculum*) is at present well understood. The tasks of identifying the political languages or 'discourses' through which ideas were expressed; of mapping the semantic range of keywords that recur within and across those vocabularies; of probing what people thought they were doing with the language they deployed in specific political contexts; of examining how principles constrained or potentiated the political actors who invoked them; and of tracing the conceptual shifts that keywords underwent as they were redefined through 'negotiation' between crown and community, were refreshed from Europe by new conceptions of legitimate authority, and were given new significance by the changing social environment they were taken to signify – these constitute a research agenda that has scarcely been identified for late-medieval Ireland, much less begun.[7]

6 K. Kerby-Fulton and S. Justice, 'Reformist Intellectual Culture in the English and Irish Civil Service: The *Modus Tenendi Parliamentum* and its Literary Relations', *Traditio*, 53 (1998), 149–202; R. Frame, 'English Political Culture in Later Medieval Ireland', *The History Review*, 13 (2002), 1–11; R. Frame, 'Exporting State and Nation: Being English in Medieval Ireland', in L. Scales and O. Zimmer (eds.), *Power and the Nation in European History* (Cambridge University Press, 2005), 143–65; E. Matthew, 'Henry V and the Proposal for an Irish Crusade', in Smith (ed.), *Ireland and the English World*, 161–75; P. Crooks, 'Representation and Dissent: "Parliamentarianism" and the Structure of Politics in Colonial Ireland c.1370–1420', *EHR*, 125 (2010), 1–34.

7 This paragraph is influenced by several approaches to the history of language and ideas. See esp. J. G. A. Pocock, *Politics, Language and Time: Essays on Political Thought and History* (Chicago University Press, 1989), esp. ch. 1; J. G. A. Pocock, *Political Thought and History: Essays on Theory and Method* (Cambridge University Press, 2009), esp. ch. 5; M. Richter, *The History of Political and Social Concepts: A Critical Introduction* (Oxford University Press, 1994). For the political 'languages' through which ideas were expressed in late-medieval Europe, see A. Black, *Political Thought in Europe, 1250–1450* (Cambridge University Press, 1992), 7–11.

The source materials for this subject are surprisingly abundant, although many of the finest truffles have to be sniffed out in ground that may seem unpromising. Late-medieval Ireland is particularly well endowed with administrative documents of complaint. In the past, these *gravamina* were dismissed as 'wearisome and sordid' in their details, 'devoid of the enlivening interest of the great conflicts of political principle'.[8] In fact, the literature of complaint is suffused with appeals to political principle. Few, no doubt, and least of all the targets of their mud-slinging, found the complainants altogether sincere; but their sincerity is, in a sense, besides the point.[9] The literature of complaint can be read against the grain not only to demonstrate the expectations of the good ruler and the boundaries outside which the government could not stray, but also to provide a more satisfying explanation of political activity itself. Of still greater interest is the multiplicity of documents – statutes and ordinances, petitions and bills, articles of instruction and full-blown treatises – that address England's Irish problem. Taken together these texts can be thought of as constituting a specific genre of political writing: the literature of remedy.[10] Read as a genre, the literature of remedy shows a clear line of development leading to the much-studied reform treatises that appear under the early Tudors. Their didactic intent and impact is clear from the mysterious Pandarus, author of the later fifteenth-century text *Salus Populi* ('Health of the People'), whose remedies for Ireland's disease provided the basis for the famous early Tudor text, 'The State of Ireland and Plans for its Reformation' (1515):

> Let no man wonder on these conclusions,
> For when he hears the said instructions,
> If he thereof have no disdain.
> What now is wonder then shall be made plain.[11]

8 M. C. Griffith, 'The Talbot–Ormond Struggle for Control of the Anglo-Irish Government, 1414–17', *IHS*, 2 (1940–1), 376.

9 Q. Skinner, 'Some Problems in the Analysis of Political Thought and Action', in J. Tully (ed.), *Meaning and Context: Quentin Skinner and his Critics* (Oxford University Press, 1988), 97–118; Q. Skinner, *Visions of Politics I: Regarding Method* (Cambridge University Press, 2002), esp. ch. 8.

10 For 'remedy' as a contemporary term, see *Statutes of the Realm*, i, 357 (L. *remedium opportunum*); *Parls. & Councils*, no. 16 (F. [si] *remedie ne les soient le plus enhast envoiétz*).

11 TCD MS 842, fol. 34; TCD MS 581, fol. 31r. I am grateful to Michael Bennett for bringing this tract to my attention. Here and elsewhere in this chapter, quotations from original texts in Middle English have been modernised. For brief further comment, see C. Maginn and S. G. Ellis, *The Tudor Discovery of Ireland* (Dublin: Four Courts Press, 2015), 137, 139.

To develop these ideas in a relatively short space, I want to think in terms of two long-term *structures* – a term I use to refer to the institutional and ideational frameworks through which politics were transacted. The first is monarchical – centred on the normally absent figure of the king and the implications of the growing public authority of the English crown. The second is communitarian – organised around ideas of counsel and representation, corporation and resistance. These two sets of ideas were not in direct opposition, but developed in interaction with each other – a trend that John Watts has described in a European context as a 'double-layered pattern of evolution'.[12] The story should not, therefore, be unfurled as the triumph of one set of ideas over the other. It is more helpful to think of a common fund of unsyncretised political ideas that was rich and generative, and to which political actors could appeal in various ways depending on immediate needs and wider contingencies. This approach may help account for the seemingly cyclical nature of medieval Anglo-Irish interactions and confrontations. It also suggests that that there was no real contradiction in the attitude of English settlers who lobbied the king to project the harsher aspect of royal authority outwards towards the native population, even while vigorously resisting royal demands to support the military effort from their own resources.

The English Crown and the Land of Ireland

The nomenclature of the Lordship of Ireland took some time to stabilise during the first half-century of English involvement in Ireland. In letters sent to Ireland in 1204, King John refers to 'all our land and our power' in Ireland (L. *per totam terram nostrum et potestatem nostram*).[13] This phrase, 'the land of Ireland', was to become the official designation for Ireland in the English chancery for the rest of the Middle Ages, although the term 'Lordship of Ireland' was also found on the lips of contemporaries.[14] In John's reign, however, Ireland was also referred to as a kingdom (*regnum*), notably in 1210 in the register of writs that accompanied the king's order that the common law of England should

---

12 Watts, *Making of Polities*, 123–4.
13 *Rot. Litt. Pat.*, 47 (trans. *Stat. Ire. John–Hen. V*, 3). See also *Rot. Litt. Pat.*, 80, for letters of 1207 referring to the expulsion of robbers from the king's 'land of Ireland' (L. *terra Hibernie*).
14 See, e.g., *Three Prose Versions of the* Secreta Secretorum, ed. R. Steele (London: EETS, 1898), 186 ('lordshupe of Irland'); *PROME*, Parliament of June 1467, item 8 ('the reames of Englond and Fraunce, and lordship of Irlond'); 'The Voyage of Sir Richard Edgecombe', in W. Harris (ed.), *Hibernica, or, some antient Pieces relating to Ireland.* 2 vols. (Dublin: Edward Bate and Peter Wilson, 1747, 1750), i, 75.

be observed in 'in our kingdom of Ireland'.[15] Likewise, it was the 'whole kingdom of Ireland' that John surrendered to Pope Innocent III in 1213; and it was
to the 'kingdom of Ireland' that the 1216 issue of Magna Carta was sent for
observance in 1217, where it became the fundamental law of the land.[16] The
principle that Ireland should be governed by English law was frequently reiterated in the reign of Henry III, notably in letters of 1246, which state that
'for the common profit of the land of Ireland, and for the *unity* of the king's
lands … all laws and customs that are observed in the kingdom of England
should be observed in Ireland'.[17] This reference to the 'unity' of the king's
lands was an assertion of the principle of legal uniformity, not an intimation
of formal territorial union. Ireland still lay firmly outside the bounds of the
kingdom of England, and two centuries later this was still widely understood
at all social levels in England. The English shipmen who intercepted and murdered the duke of Suffolk in 1450 are said to have referred to 'another person,
then outside the realm' (Richard duke of York, then the king's lieutenant in
Ireland) whom they planned to bring into England and make king; and the
ballad of 'The Bearward and the Bear' concludes with a prayer to 'bring home
[that is, return to England from Ireland] the Master of this Game, the Duke
of York … Richard by name'.[18] As a land outside the realm, Ireland was a place
to which undesirables could be banished, as was the case with Richard II's
judges condemned to exile in Ireland in 1388, although Piers Gaveston's sentence of exile in 1311 stated explicitly that he should be exiled from 'the whole
lordship of our lord the king overseas', including Ireland.[19]

---

15 For an edition of the Irish register 'HIB', see *Early Registers of Writs*, ed. E. de Haas
    and G. D. G. Hall. Selden Society (London, 1970), 1. See also *Rot. Chart.*, 99; P. Brand,
    'Ireland and the Literature of the Early Common Law', in. P. Brand, *The Making of the
    Common Law* (London: Hambledon Press, 1992), ch. 19.
16 The text of the surrender refers twice to the kingdom of Ireland, but John is styled 'by
    grace of God king of England, lord of Ireland, duke of Normandy and Aquitaine, count
    of Anjou': *EHD*, iii, 308. For the transmission of Magna Carta, see *Patent Rolls 1216–25*, 31
    (L. *volumus quod … libertatibus regno nostro Anglie a patre nostro et nobis concessis, de gracia
    nostra et dono in regno nostro Hibernie gaudeatis*); calendared in *CDI, 1171–1251*, 115, no. 759.
17 The translation in *Stat. Ire. John–Hen. V*, 35, is 'unity of the king's dominions', but the
    Latin is clearly *pro … unitate terrarum Regis: Foedera* [O], i, 266.
18 R. Virgoe, 'The Death of William de la Pole, Duke of Suffolk', *BJRL*, 47 (1964–5), 501
    (L. *tunc extra regnum*); C. Kingsford, *English Historical Literature in the Fifteenth Century*
    (Oxford University Press, 1913), 247.
19 *The St Albans Chronicle: The Chronica Maiora of Thomas Walsingham*, i: *1376–1394*, ed.
    J. Taylor, W. R. Childs and L. Watkiss (Oxford University Press, 2003), 852; *Select Documents
    of English Constitutional History, 1307–1485*, ed. S. B. Chrimes and A. L. Brown (London:
    Adam & Charles Black, 1961), 15; trans. *EHD*, iii, 533. The wording of the latter record
    (F. *hors du roiaume Dengleterre, Descoce, Dirlaunde, et de Gales, come de tote la seignurie nostre
    seignur le roi dela la mer come de cea*) offers a rare example of 'realm' being used to refer
    to England and the king's other dominions, including Ireland, collectively.

What served to lock the realms of Ireland and England in an embrace that was to last more than eight centuries was an abstraction: the idea of 'the crown' as an impersonal institution distinct from the king. Under the influence of the Roman law concept of the fisc, legal theorists began to refer to the crown as a bundle of perpetual rights, powers, land titles and wealth that were available to the king but which should be preserved intact for his successor. This conception of the crown drew strength from the canonistic idea of inalienability, which held that the preservation of the fisc was an aspect of the public good.[20] The change in emphasis is clear in the case of Ireland. In the second preface to his *Expugnatio Hibernica*, Gerald of Wales refers to the kingdom of Ireland being 'explicitly subject to the English crown ... as if it were by a perpetual indenture and indissoluble bond'; but he also hinted that Ireland might be used to raise one of John's sons to the dignity of king. Fifty years later, a clear conceptual shift was in evidence in the charter of 1254 by which Henry III created for the Lord Edward a large *apanage*, including 'all the land of Ireland' (L. *totam terram hiberniam*). The grant included the proviso that the lands 'shall never be separated from the crown of England ... but shall remain wholly to the kings of England in perpetuity'.[21]

By 1254, Ireland was being treated as an inseparable member of the English crown. Inalienable, then; and, as a consequence, a matter of public concern to the burgeoning 'community of the realm' of England. Twice during the fourteenth century, Ireland was dragged to the centre of political controversy by the domestic enemies of the English monarch. In 1311 the Lords Ordainers charged that the crown was 'in many respects reduced and dismembered' and that the king's lands of Gascony, Ireland and Scotland were on the point of being lost. Again, in 1388, the enemies of Richard II known as the Lords Appellant claimed, without stretching the truth too far, that 'the great lordship and land of Ireland are and have been from time immemorial parcel of the crown of England and the people of that land of Ireland for all the time aforesaid have been lieges immediate to our lord the king and his progenitors'.

20 J. Dunbabin, 'Government', in J. H. Burns (ed.), *The Cambridge History of Medieval Political Thought, c.350–c.1450* (Cambridge University Press, 1988), 498–9; G. L. Harriss, *King, Parliament and Public Finance in Medieval England to 1369* (Oxford University Press, 1975), 144; E. H. Kantorowicz, 'Inalienability: A Note on Canonical Practice and the English Coronation Oath in the Thirteenth Century', *Speculum*, 29 (1954), 488–502.
21 *Expugnatio*, 262, 264; L. *Ita tamen quod predicte terre et castra omnia nunquam separentur a corona ... set integre remaneant regibus Anglie in perpetuum* (*Foedera*, i, 270; calendared in *CDI, 1252–1284*, no. 326). See J. Lydon, 'Ireland and the English Crown, 1171–1541', in Crooks (ed.), *Government, War and Society*, 66–7. See also letters patent 1292 reciting a charter of the Lord Edward (Harris, *Hibernica*, part 2, 61–2; calendared in *C. Chart. R. 1257–1300*, 416–17; *CDI, 1285–1292*, no. 1051).

That claim arose from their accusation that Richard II had planned to grant Ireland away as a *kingdom* to his favourite Robert de Vere, 'to the diminution of the honourable style of the king our lord aforesaid and in open disheri-son of his crown of the realm of England and full destruction of the loyal lieges of the king our lord and the said land of Ireland'.[22]

The accusation that Richard II intended to elevate Ireland to the status of a kingdom was inaccurate in a narrow sense. The titles that Richard II had created for de Vere were, first, 'marquis of Dublin' (1385) and then 'duke of Ireland' (1386). But the rumours that Ireland might be filleted off to create a separate kingdom did not go away, and after the Lancastrian revolution of 1399, Richard II was forced to renounce the 'kingdoms of England, France, Ireland and Scotland'.[23] A few decades later the author of the *Libelle of English Policy* (*c*.1436) pointed out that there was no other land in all Christendom comparable to Ireland in terms of size or potential wealth whose ruler went by the title, *dominus*; and, in 1460, the Irish parliament bolstered its famous claim to legislative autonomy with a clause that explicitly claimed the near-equivalence of a 'realm' and a 'land' (F. *Reaume ou terre*).[24] Rumblings of regal-ity continued to make themselves heard in the fifteenth century. In 1468, the seventh earl of Desmond was accused of plotting to make himself king of Ireland (a charge levelled at the 'rebellious' first earl of Desmond 150 years earlier).[25] The distinctions of the royal style were sometimes blundered or blurred, as in the letters issued by Edward of York shortly after his victory at Wakefield (1460) but before his inauguration in which he styles himself 'by the grace of God of Englande, Fraunce and Irlande vray and just heire' – a phrase that hinted at a triple monarchy with Ireland as the junior partner.[26] Taken together, these crumbs of evidence, which suggest that Ireland's status as a 'regnal polity' had not been altogether forgotten, must provide some background to what was otherwise an extraordinary innovation in 1487 when the pretender Lambert Simnel was crowned in Dublin as 'Edward VI' and

22 *EHD*, iii, 527; *The Westminster Chronicle, 1381–1394*, ed. L. C. Hector and B. F. Harvey (Oxford University Press, 1982), 246–9; *PROME*, Richard II: Parliament of Feb. 1388, part 2, 'Appeal of treason', article 11.

23 *The Chronicle of Adam Usk, 1377–1421*, ed. C. Given-Wilson (Oxford University Press, 1997), 76–7; *Chronicles of the Revolution, 1397–1400: The Reign of Richard II*, ed. C. Given-Wilson (Manchester University Press, 1993), 163.

24 *The Libelle of Englyshe Polycye: A Poem on the Use of Sea-Power 1436*, ed. G. Warner (Oxford University Press, 1926), lines 740–4; *Stat. Ire. Hen. VI*, 644–5.

25 *Stat. Ire., 1–12 Edw. IV*, 572–3.

26 M. C. Maxwell-Lyte, *A History of Eton College, 1440–1884* (London: Macmillan, 1889), 39. In the general Resumption of 1463, Henry VI was described as 'by reason of his crown … late in deed and not by right king of England, Ireland, Wales and their marches' (*PROME*, Edward IV: Parliament of April 1463, item 39).

issued letters patent with the style 'by the grace of God, king of England, France and Ireland' (L. *dei gratia rex Anglie, Francie et hibernie*).[27] None of this should be taken to suggest that what the king enjoyed in Ireland was anything less than a plenitude of power. Granted, the question was raised in 1329 before the king's council in England as to whether the royal prerogative was in any way diminished by virtue of the fact that 'our lord the king is named "lord of Ireland" and not "king"'; but the interrogative was surely met with a firm 'no'. The title 'lord of Ireland' provided a model for Edward III to follow in his negotiations with the French at the end of the first act of the Hundred Years War. By the terms of the Treaty of Calais (1360), Edward III was recognised as holding an enlarged duchy of Aquitaine in full sovereignty. To reflect this claim, the king hastily commissioned a new great seal with the legend: 'king of England, lord of Ireland and Aquitaine'.[28] The title 'lord' – here covering Ireland *and* Aquitaine – heralded the king's untrammelled authority recognising no superior.

The powers enjoyed by the English king as lord of Ireland are more frequently assumed than specified, so the charter of 1385 creating the marquisate of Dublin is useful in laying bare the theoretical undergirding of the king's powers as they were conceived in the late fourteenth century.[29] To endow this new creation, Richard bestowed on the new marquis his 'land and lordship of Ireland' (*terra et dominium Hibernie*) with all its appurtenances, services and 'mixed and pure *imperium*'. The three keywords here are *terra, dominium* and *imperium*. What ideological work did these words perform? In one sense, the designation 'land of Ireland' was a conventional means of subordinating Ireland to the overarching lordship of the kingdom of England, rather as Scotland was relegated to the status of a land or lordship during the conquest of Edward I. But the word had a deeper signification. David Carpenter has recently shown how the 'elemental land' functioned as a political idea in the most politically charged clauses of Magna Carta – for instance, the promise in *cap.* 39 not to proceed against freemen except by the lawful judgement of peers or by the 'law of the *land*'. Here, 'land' referred to 'an entity conterminous with the kingdom but separate and in a way older than it'.[30] Transposed to the case of Ireland, 'land' could be used to denote an entity distinct from and in some respects *prior* to the superior authority

27 NLI D 1855 (available to view on CIRCLE: PR 2 Hen VI, no. 7).
28 Sayles, *Affairs*, 146 (F. *qe nostre seigneur le roi est nome seigneur Dirlaunde e nient roy*); W. M. Ormrod, *Edward III* (New Haven and London: Yale University Press, 2012), 410, 605–6.
29 *CPR, 1385–9*, 115.
30 Davies, *First English Empire*, 27; Ruddick, *English Identity*, 220; D. Carpenter, *Magna Carta* (London: Penguin, 2015), 246–7. For later references to the 'land' of England, see the Ordinances of 1311 (*EHD*, iii, 529); and for the use of the phrase 'commonalty

expressed by the word *dominium*. As we shall see, precisely this sense of the land-as-community was current in Ireland by the fifteenth century; and the potent phrase 'law of the land' appeared in the 'Song on the Times', a Middle Hiberno-English poem from the Kildare manuscript (BL MS Harley 913) datable to the second quarter of the fourteenth century. Employing the device of an animal fable, the poem presents a dismal view of the perversion of royal justice by the evil of 'covetousness' (MHE. *coueitise*), which harms not just the individual, but the land as a whole, which (we are told) has become 'false and wicked' (MHE. *Fals and liþer is this lond*).[31]

The second keyword, *dominium*, is among the most familiar and vexing in the political vocabulary of the European Middle Ages. As a technical term in Roman law, *dominium* referred to total ownership of property, with related jurisdiction. Its potency is perhaps better conveyed by translating it as 'dominion' rather than as 'lordship'. As an element of his *dominium*, the king also exercised *imperium* within Ireland as one of the attributes of his legitimate authority. The recovery of Roman law in the eleventh century had introduced *imperium* as a technical term into the vocabulary of English law and kingship. Arising from the ideas of the Roman jurist Ulpian (d. 228), *imperium* came to be classified as both 'pure' (*imperium merum*), referring to the power to punish the wicked by the sword, and 'mixed' (*imperium mixtum*), referring to the additional power of adjudication.[32] Taken together, what this cluster of terms asserted was paramount authority recognising no superior – in a word, sovereignty.

It was a supreme authority re-affirmed by the increasingly elevated style of address employed by petitioners seeking the king's grace. In the composite monarchies of the early modern era, the principle of *aeque principaliter* ('equally important') guaranteed that the monarch ruled in each of his dominions by the local territorial title, respecting the estates, laws and customs of the territory in question.[33] It is an indicator of the tightly meshed nature of the composite monarchy of the Plantagenets that this was not the form of union that existed between Ireland and England in the later

of this *land*' (meaning England) in the reign of Edward IV, see S. B. Chrimes, *English Constitutional Ideas in the Fifteenth Century* (Cambridge University Press, 1936), 132.

31 *Poems from BL MS Harley 913: 'The Kildare Manuscript'*, ed. T. Turville-Petre. EETS, o.s. 345 (Oxford University Press, 2015), no. 33, lines 9, 17, 144, 149. On *covetise*, see J. Watts, *Henry VI and the Politics of Kingship* (Cambridge University Press, 1996), 41–3.

32 J. H. Burns, *Lordship, Kingship, and Empire: The Idea of Monarchy, 1400–1525* (Oxford University Press, 1992), ch. 2; F. Maiolo, *Medieval Sovereignty: Marsilius of Padua and Bartolus of Saxoferrato* (Delft: Eburon Academic, 2007), 153.

33 J. H. Elliott, 'A Europe of Composite Monarchies', *Past and Present*, 137 (1992), 52.

Middle Ages. When English residents of Ireland sought the king's grace, they addressed him as their *king*, and the phrase 'sovereign lord' referred to his status as monarch, not his title as 'lord of Ireland'. In 1421, for instance, the 'poor humble lieges of your land of Ireland' petitioned Henry V addressing him as 'our most excellent and most sovereign liege lord'; and in 1428 the humble lieges of Ireland addressed their 'sovereign and gracious liege lord' referring to his 'high and royal majesty, with all manner of humility and obeisance'.[34] It was with this same elevated language of obedience that Richard II received the submissions of the Irish chiefs in 1395 during his expedition to Ireland. The texts of the submissions record the chiefs' promises of humble obedience in the most abject terms. Richard II is described as 'your eminence, whose magnificent deeds redound through the whole world', and the submissions advert to his 'many realms' and 'world-famed honour'.[35] Perhaps most significant of all is the frequency and consistency with which the submissions and letters of Richard II employ the terms 'prince' (L. *princeps*) and 'majesty' (L. *maiestas*) to describe the king of England – terms derived from Roman law and reeking of all the pretensions of imperial overrule.[36] The development is all the more striking given that the language of majesty was comparatively rare in England itself, even in the late 1390s when Richard II's style of kingship was at its most autocratic. Evidently Ireland was a stage on which English kingship could give voice to full-throated rhetorical excess. But, even within Ireland, it was a rhetoric that only served within certain contexts. The smack of 'regal' lordship was primarily for the native Irish; the cosseting of 'political' lordship was a privilege claimed for themselves by the English of Ireland.[37]

---

34 *Stat. Ire. John–Henry V*, 563; *Facsimiles of National Manuscripts of Ireland* [...], ed. J. T. Gilbert. 4 pts in 5 vols. (Dublin, 1874–84), iii, plate 39 (available via CIRCLE: CR 7 Hen VI, no. 9). The style was unusually ornate for the second decade of the fifteenth century: G. Dodd, 'Kingship, Parliament and the Court: The Emergence of "High Style" in Petitions to the English Crown, *c.* 1350–1405', *EHR*, 129 (2014), 542–3.

35 N. Saul, 'Richard II and the Vocabulary of Kingship', *EHR*, 110 (1995), 868; E. Curtis, *Richard II in Ireland, 1394–5, and the Submissions of the Irish Chiefs* (Oxford University Press, 1927), 183, 206, 219.

36 *Maiestas* occurs in 5 submissions and 16 letters addressed to the king: Curtis, *Richard II in Ireland*, instruments VII, XIV, XVI; letters 1, 4–16, 19, 21. Richard II is addressed as *princeps* in 6 submissions (*ibid.*, instruments XI, XIV, XVI, XX, XXXII, XXXIV).

37 Dodd, 'Kingship, Parliament and the Court', 523, shows that of 127 common petitions addressed to Richard II in England during the 1390s, only seven employ the term 'majesty'. The distinction between 'regal' and 'political' styles of kingship is based on Fortescue's famous discussion of *dominium regale* and *dominium politicum et regale*: J. H. Burns, 'Fortescue and the Political Theory of *Dominium*', *Historical Journal*, 28 (1985), 777–97.

The King's Subjects in Ireland and their Liberties

A rather less imperious image of English royalty was commissioned by Henry III for Dublin castle in 1243. The king ordered the construction of a great hall, 120 feet in length and 80 feet in breadth, to be finished in the style of the hall at Canterbury. At the end of the hall above a dais, a mural was to be painted showing the king and his queen, Eleanor of Provence, with their baronage. As a visual expression of English royalty, this mural depicting the king sitting among his subjects – rather than seated in majesty with sword and sceptre, or in equestrian mode astride a warhorse, as he was depicted on the obverse and reverse of the great seal of England – was unusual to the point of being unique.[38] It was, perhaps, prompted by the need for a show of solidarity between king and magnates in Ireland after the murder of Richard Marshal in County Kildare in 1234, which constituted a gross breach of the expectations of royal justice and mercy. What is particularly striking in light of later developments is the narrowness of the baronial community represented. Already in the reign of King John, it is possible to detect an emergent solidarity being attributed to the king's barons and faithful subjects who were described as being *of* Ireland, rather than merely in Ireland. The idea of community is also discernible in the phrase 'all the magnates of Ireland (L. *universi magnates Hibernie*), who declared their loyalty in life or death to King John in 1213.[39] The signatories to this letter represented an elite group of twenty-seven barons. By the end of the thirteenth century, the political scene looked very different. The assemblies at which the king's representatives sought the counsel of his subjects, settled their disputes and provided redress of their grievance, were becoming a formal mechanism of government embracing a broader group of subjects. From 1264, if not earlier, these assemblies were being termed 'parliaments' in Ireland, and by the 1290s parliament included elected representatives of the boroughs and shires as well as the prelates and magnates who received their personal summons by writ. This collectivity of individuals and groups was soon found describing itself as the 'community of the land of Ireland'.[40]

---

38 J. T. Gilbert, *A History of the Viceroys of Ireland* (Dublin: James Duffy, 1865), 514; J. Watts, 'Looking for the State in Later Medieval England', in P. Coss and M. Keen (eds.), *Heraldry, Pageantry and Social Display in Medieval England* (Woodbridge: Boydell Press, 2002), 251–2.

39 *Stat. Ire. John–Hen. V*, 4; H. G. Richardson and G. O. Sayles, *The Irish Parliament in the Middle Ages* (Philadelphia: University of Pennsylvania Press, 1952), appendix 1, pp 286–7 (calendared *CDI, 1171–1251*, no. 448).

40 For the language of 'community', J. Lydon, 'Parliament and the Community of Ireland', in Lydon (ed.), *Law and Disorder*, 125–38; J. Lydon, 'William of Windsor and the Irish

Behind this commonplace lay a whole complex of political ideas arising from developments in England. Notable among them was the linkage
between taxation and consent that had been enunciated in Magna Carta
(1215) and given added force by the doctrine that what concerned all must be
approved by all (L. *Quod omnes tangit, omnibus approbetur*), which had become
a standard means by which the members of communal or corporate institutions explained their process of collective decision making – above all in the
arena through which the 'community of the realm' found representation, in
parliament. It would be a mistake, however, to think of English Ireland as a
passive recipient of these ideas. There is ample evidence that the creators and
consumers of constitutional and political writing were widespread among
the political elites of the Lordship.[41] The few surviving codices of Irish ecclesiastical institutions show a close interest in constitutional and legal matters. In
Dublin, the Augustinian Canons at Holy Trinity (Christ Church) had in their
library a codex known as the *Liber Niger*, a compendium of historical, legal
and constitutional material, the nucleus of which was an English lawyer's
collection of statutes beginning with a 1215 version of Magna Carta, which
has been annotated in a hand of the late thirteenth century. A codex from the
Cistercian house of St Mary's, Dublin, (TCD MS 11500) comprised not only
historical and mythological material with an Arthurian and Giraldian emphasis, but also a series of constitutional documents including texts of the draft
ordinances of 1310 and the letters patent issued as a prelude to the Ordinances
of 1311.[42] Ireland also boasts its share of political treatises and literary works,
adapted to suit Irish circumstances both in terms of their content and their
exploitation. Whether expressed in English constitutional language or in the
moralising and hortatory modes more typical of advice literature, the ideas
found in these sources tend to be laden with communitarian assumptions
about the proper operation of political society and English governance. The
exception that proves the rule is the royalist tract *De Quadripartita Regis Specie*.

Parliament', in Crooks (ed.), *Government, War and Society*, 90–105. For references to 'the
king and his people in Ireland', see Griffith, 'Talbot–Ormond Struggle', 395, 397.

41 M. Wilks, 'Corporation and Representation in the *Defensor Pacis*', *Studia Gratiana*,
15 (1972), 253. The two surviving library lists for medieval Ireland receive analysis
in A. Byrne, 'The Earls of Kildare and their Books at the End of the Middle Ages',
The Library, 14 (2013), 129–53; C. Ó Clabaigh, *The Franciscans in Ireland, 1400–1534*
(Dublin: Four Courts Press, 2002), appendix 1.

42 Representative Church Body Library, MS C.6. I.I, fols. 162v–165; TCD MS 11500, fol. 118r.
A facsimile reproduction is available in B. Meehan, 'A Fourteenth-Century Historical
Compilation from St Mary's Cistercian Abbey, Dublin', in S. Duffy (ed.), *Medieval Dublin
XV* (Dublin: Four Courts Press, 2016). The text is a copy of the articles that appear in the
Annales Londoniensis, reprinted in Chrimes and Brown (eds.), *Select Documents*, 8–9.

This appears to have been composed by a clerk in the Irish administration, describing himself as 'the smallest coin in the king's treasure in Ireland'. The treatise places special stress on the virtues of obedience, a view that would have found favour with Richard II in the late 1390s. This was exceptional. The general expectation of government was that it would work with the community. *Rex datur propter regnum, non regnum propter regem*, ran the chiasmus of Thomas Aquinas, putting forward a theory of mixed monarchy at the end of the thirteenth century: 'Kings are given for the sake of the kingdom, not the kingdom for the sake of the king.'[43]

The chief locus of royal power in Ireland, and consequently the chief focus of discontent, was the representative of the king himself. This officer went by many titles, the most common of which in the thirteenth century was 'justiciar' (L. *justiciarius*). A more prestigious title 'lieutenant' (L. *locum tenens*) first occurs in the fourteenth century; and, by the later fifteenth, lieutenants normally nominated deputies, giving rise to the title 'lord deputy' familiar in the early Tudor era. None of these various titles is as usefully descriptive of the function of the office as the convenient catch-all, 'chief governor' (F. *principal governour de la terre*). The governor discharged, in person or by deputy, the duty of the royal office itself to provide for the *governance* of Ireland.[44] In its origins the term 'governor' (L. *gubernator*) referred to the helmsman whose task was to guide or steer (L. *gubernare*) a ship: so it was that, for Aquinas, 'to govern is to guide that which is governed to its appointed end'. That appointed end was the common good – or, more specifically, the 'common profit' (L. *communis utilitas*) that would arise from the moral goodness of the ruler.[45] The language of 'common profit' had become increasingly prominent in English political discourse during the thirteenth century, and it was also deployed by

43 *Four English Political Tracts of the Middle Ages*, ed. J.-P. Genet (London: Camden Society, 1977); and see the important review by W. C. Jordan in *Speculum*, 54 (1979). The Angelic Doctor's phrase is cited by Sir John Fortescue (*De Laudibus Legum Angliae*, c. 37): *On the Laws and Governance of England by Sir John Fortescue*, ed. S. Lockwood (Cambridge University Press, 1997), 53.

44 *Parls. & Councils*, no. 67. The generic term 'governor' occurs also in *Parliamentary Texts of the Later Middle Ages*, ed. N. Pronay and J. Taylor (Oxford University Press, 1980), 145. The articles of instruction to Sir Gilbert Debenham (1474) refer to 'lieutenants and their deputies who had the *governance* of the same land before this time': Bryan, *Gerald FitzGerald*, 19 (emphasis added). The English parliament praised Richard II for his 'sage and supreme governance' (F. *sage et haute governance*) since his arrival in Ireland: Curtis, *Richard II in Ireland*, letter 16.

45 Lockwood (ed.), *On the Laws and Governance of England*, xix; W. M. Ormrod, ' "Common Profit" and "The Profit of the King and Kingdom": Parliament and the Development of Political Language in England, 1250–1450', *Viator*, 46 (2015), 224; M. S. Kempshall, *The Common Good in Late Medieval Political Thought* (Oxford University Press, 1999), ch. 2.

the king's chancery in Ireland, for instance in the summons of the Kilkenny parliament of 1310 for 'the common profit of the King and of the people of his land of Ireland' (F. *a commun profit du Roy e du pople de sa terre Dyrlaunde*). This formula clearly links the king's interests and those of the communities he ultimately represented, from the land of Ireland down to the local level of the shire. The 1357 Westminster ordinances for the state of Ireland were said to have been promulgated for 'the public profit' (L. *pro utilitate publica*); and, at a local level, we find the term employed again in a run-of-the-mill commission of the peace for County Wexford in 1375 that instructed the bishop of Ferns, as supervisor of the local keepers of the peace, to do all that was necessary 'for the king's comfort and the common profit of the king's faithful people' (L. *pro commodo nostro, et communi utilitate fidelis populi nostri*).[46] This set of interlinked ideas is apparent in an encomium from the Irish parliament sent to Edward IV in 1463 in support of the lord deputy, Thomas earl of Desmond, who is described, in a nice use of the metaphor of the governor-as-helmsman, as 'guiding and ruling' the land. Desmond is praised not only for his labour, manhood and strength, but also his wit, rule, wisdom and 'pollitique' – this last term suggesting his possession of the cardinal virtue of Prudence – that had brought about the peace and tranquillity of the land. By way of contrast, the evils that were understood to flow from covetousness and private interest are frequently rehearsed in grievance-laden petitions and inquisitions into ministerial misconduct. The chief governor Sir William Windsor was accused in 1378 of soliciting from the king a grant of the government of Ireland for his own profit and that of his troops, who would live upon the king's lieges for their sustenance: this, it was said, would harm not only the king's interests but also the king's faithful people of Ireland.[47]

The public nature of the chief governor's office was made manifest in the ritual that accompanied his taking of office, which remained a symbolic affair even in the increasingly bureaucratised world of late-medieval English government. The chief governor was appointed by royal letters patent that specified the extent of his competence and his term of office. To that extent, he was the king's man in Dublin. But, upon arriving in Ireland, the governor's patent was read out and he was bound through an oath, solemnly taken before the king's council in Ireland. The rolls of the Irish chancery frequently record the exact date and place of the governor's disembarkation in Ireland

---

46 *Stat. Ire., John–Hen. V*, 262–3; *Statutes of the Realm*, i, 357; CIRCLE: PR 49 Edw III, no. 278.
47 I. D. Thornley, *England under the Yorkists, 1460–1485: Illustrated from Contemporary Sources* (London: Longmans, 1920), 253–5; TNA E 368/157 (Hilary, *Recorda*), m. 24.

(a point of importance when the patent specified that his powers took effect at his first landing). The political community of the Lordship had at its disposal a counter-argument, one that lent a contractarian flavour to the relationship between governor and governed. The Irish version of the parliamentary treatise, *Modus tenendi parliamentum*, makes a twofold claim: first, that the oath is taken by the governor in the presence of the chancellor, council *and the people*; and, second, that it was only upon taking the oath that the governor was invested with the power granted to him 'and not before' (L. *sed non ante*).[48] By either interpretation, the oath-taking must have been a solemn occasion. The oath was modelled closely on the questions put to the king at his coronation. The coronation *ordo* was well known in Ireland. Indeed, it was in the annals of the Dublin Dominican that the long-lost coronation oath of Edward I was recently rediscovered, with its triplex promise to keep the peace to the clergy and people, to do justice in mercy and in truth.[49] At Edward II's coronation in 1308 a fourth question was put to the king, requiring him to promise to uphold the 'laws and rightful customs which the community of the realm shall have chosen'. It was a modified version of this oath – with the promise that 'I shall hold and guard the right laws and customs that *the people of the land of Ireland* have chosen to be kept' – that Lord Portlester used in 1462 when taking office as lord deputy. Nor were these simply constitutional niceties divorced from political realities or the prescriptions of policy. The preamble to the Westminster ordinances for the state of Ireland of 1357, which represented a considerable concession by Edward III to anti-ministerial feeling in Ireland, contains an echo of promises of the coronation oath in its admission that 'laws and *approved* customs' have not been observed through default of good rule (L. *ob defectum boni regiminis*) and that the affairs of the king and the land have been carried out unprofitably (L. *inutilitater*).[50]

It is perfectly clear that some chief governors strained against the contractarian assumptions of this framework of ideas. The clash of ideals could hardly be better illustrated than by the arrest in 1418 of Sir Christopher Preston, Lord Gormanston and the earl of Kildare during a moment of high tension with the abrasive lieutenant, Sir John Talbot. On Preston's person at the time of his arrest was found a scroll of parchment containing copies

---

48 Pronay and Taylor (eds.), *Parliamentary Texts*, 145.
49 B. Williams, 'The Lost Coronation Oath of King Edward I: Rediscovered in a Dublin Manuscript', in S. Duffy (ed.), *Medieval Dublin IX* (Dublin: Four Courts Press, 2009), 84–90.
50 Gilbert, *Viceroys*, 485; CIRCLE: PR 1 Edw IV, no. 60. For the 1308 English coronation oath, see Chrimes and Brown (eds.), *Select Documents*, 4–5 (*EHD*, iii, 525); *Statutes of the Realm*, i, 357.

of the Irish *Modus Tenendi Parliamentum,* as well as the English version of the coronation oath *and* its Irish counterpart.[51] Other governors actively cultivated the image of the good ruler. This was the subject of the treatise entitled the *Governance of Princes,* produced in 1422 at the commission of James Butler, fourth earl of Ormond (d. 1452). It was a translation, studded with Irish *exempla,* of the *Secreta Secretorum* – a 'mirror for princes' that was believed to contain the advice that Alexander the Great received from his tutor, Aristotle. The *Secreta* was an especially popular text in Ireland, having been translated in the late thirteenth century into French by Geoffrey of Waterford before being translated again, over a century later, into English.[52] The opening pages address Ormond directly as 'lieutenant of our lord, King Henry the Fifth in Ireland', clearly counting him among the 'emperors, kings and other governors of chivalry' who might benefit from its advice concerning the cardinal virtues of Prudence, Justice, Temperance and Fortitude. A key argument of the *Governance* is that 'chivalry' is maintained not only by deeds of arms, but by wisdom and by help of laws. Casting back into Irish history as presented by Gerald of Wales, Yonge discovers in the figure of Diarmait Mac Murchada, 'prince of Leinster', the perfect foil for the good ruler. Mac Murchada is presented as a cruel and intolerable tyrant who oppressed the great lords of the land and so brought about his own subjection and that of his people. Yonge follows this with a rogues' gallery of unjust rulers, from Emperor Nero to King Richard II.

The normative expectation of the English community in Ireland was that they should be ruled by English law and enjoy the liberties of the king's English subjects. But Robin Frame has detected a subtle but significant terminological shift from the late 1370s, as the English residents of Ireland began to refer with growing insistence and assurance to 'the liberties of Ireland' as opposed to the liberties of the 'king's [English] subjects in Ireland'. The change was formalised by the proceedings of Irish parliaments, which from 1402 opened with a general confirmation of the liberties

---

51 P. Crooks, 'The Background to the Arrest of the Fifth Earl of Kildare and Sir Christopher Preston in 1418: A Missing Membrane', *Analecta Hibernica,* 40 (2007), 8–9; Huntingdon Library (San Marino, CA), MS E.L. 1699, whence CIRCLE: PR 6 Hen V, no. 15.

52 *Three Prose Versions,* 121–248; J. Ferster, *Fictions of Advice: The Literature and Politics of Counsel in Late Medieval England* (Philadelphia: University of Pennsylvania Press, 1996), ch. 4; J. Monfrin, 'Sur les sources du *Secret des Secrets* de Jefroi de Waterford et Servais Copale', *Mélanges de linguistique romane et de philologie médiévale offerts à M. Maurice Delbouille.* 2 vols. (Gembloux: Duculot, 1964), ii, 509–30.

and franchises of the land of Ireland.[53] Quite what these liberties were was probably ill-defined even at the time, but their foundation stone in Ireland, as in England, was Magna Carta. It was of the great charter in the constitutional and political struggles of England in the thirteenth century that J. C. Holt stated that it had become 'a shibboleth'.[54] Exported to Ireland in 1217, Magna Carta became a shibboleth in something closer to its original, biblical sense. The liberties of Magna Carta were *English* liberties. They served to define the English settlers *against* the native Irish population. By the late thirteenth century, if not earlier, persons deemed to be 'of Irish birth and blood' commonly found it necessary to purchase from the crown an individual charter of English liberty if they wished to be 'free and quit of all Irish servitude' (L. *ab omni servitute Hibernicali liberati et quieti*).[55] Magna Carta's role as a totem of English liberty in Ireland was overtaken in the later fourteenth century by the Statute of Kilkenny (1366), which notoriously prohibited marriages and other forms of social and cultural interaction between English and Irish. The manuscript evidence for the Statute of Kilkenny is problematic (there are no surviving fourteenth-century manuscripts), but there are indications that in its original form its first clause repeated the opening clause of the 1351 Ordinances that confirmed the liberties of Holy Church and 'all the articles contained in the Great Charter of the King'. Certainly, in 1410, Magna Carta and the Statute of Kilkenny were confirmed in the same act of the Irish parliament. Magna Carta thus came to be folded into the Statute of Kilkenny to create a new set of exclusionary liberties, now described with increasing regularity as the 'liberties of the land of Ireland'.[56]

The most audacious statement of the 'ancient' liberties of Ireland was the declaration by an Irish parliament held at Drogheda before Richard, duke of York (d. 1460), that 'the land of Ireland is, and at all times has been, corporate of itself [F. *corporate de luy mesme*], by the ancient laws and customs used in the same'. Bundled into this assertion were a number of other expedients, notably the claim that Ireland was not bound by English statutes unless the

---

53 Frame, 'Exporting State and Nation', 163 n. 55; Frame, 'English Political Culture', 8; *Stat. Ire. John–Hen. V*, 504–5.
54 J. C. Holt, *Magna Carta* (3rd edn. Cambridge University Press, 2015), 348.
55 NLI MS 3, fol. 33, whence CIRCLE: PR 32 Edw III, no. 43. For thirteenth-century developments, see R. Frame, 'Ireland after 1169: Barriers to Acculturation on an "English" Edge', in K. J. Stringer and A. Jotischky (eds.), *Norman Expansion: Connections, Continuities and Contrasts* (Farnham: Ashgate, 2013), 115–41.
56 *Stat. Ire. John–Hen. V*, 376–7, 520.

Irish parliament had first specifically ratified them.[57] The validity of that claim has been the subject of much debate. Less attention has been paid to the language of incorporation that the declaration of 1460 used in staking its claim to legislative independence through an appeal to the collective memory of ancient rights. The attempt to conceptualise Ireland as a 'body politic' drew upon one of the most commonly encountered metaphors used to comprehend and explain the proper ordering of political society in the late Middle Ages. Within a short few years Sir John Fortescue was to refer to England as a *corpus mysticum* ('mystical body'), a term transposed from its original theological context to the case of undying political communities.[58] It was a key contribution of juristic thought to stress that the corporation (however described) was both a 'plurality of individuals and an abstract unitary entity perceptible only by the intellect'.[59]

While the language of incorporation was in 1460 still a comparatively recent arrival in English law, the underlying ideas had an older pedigree, expressed through many of the terms we have already encountered, notably *populus, universitas, communitas*.[60] One of the most potent of these terms in contemporary use was *res publica*. The narrative of the Alice Kyteler sorcery trial – which is so evocative of the world of litigiousness, pragmatic literacy and local government in Ireland in the first quarter of the fourteenth century – refers to royal officers as *ministri reipublicae* ('ministers of the state'), and also to the *majores reipublicae rectores* ('senior officers of the state') who sought to impede the work of the witch-hunter, Richard Ledrede, bishop of Ossory.[61] More frequently *res publica* is encountered in the documents afforcing the language of the 'common good' and refers to the collective interest (or 'common weal', as it would be termed in the vernacular of the fifteenth

---

57 *Stat. Ire. Hen. VI*, 644–5; A. Cosgrove, 'Parliament and the Anglo-Irish Community: The Declaration of 1460', in A. Cosgrove and J. I. McGuire (eds.), *Parliament and Community: Historical Studies XIV* (Belfast: Appletree Press, 1983), 25–41.

58 C. J. Nederman, 'Body Politics: The Diversification of Organic Metaphors in the Later Middle Ages', *Pensiero Politico Medievale*, 2 (2004), 59–87; Lockwood (ed.), *On the Laws and Governance of England*, 20; Kantorowicz, *King's Two Bodies*, 223–5.

59 J. Canning, *A History of Medieval Political Thought, 300–1400* (London: Routledge, 1996), 172; J. Canning, 'Law, Sovereignty and Corporation Theory', in Burns (ed.), *Cambridge History of Medieval Political Thought*, 472.

60 S. Reynolds, 'The History of the Idea of Incorporation or Legal Personality: A Case of Fallacious Teleology', in S. Reynolds, *Ideas and Solidarities of the Medieval Laity: England and Western Europe* (Farnham: Ashgate, 1995), 1–20.

61 *A Contemporary Narrative of the Proceedings against Dame Alice Kyteler Prosecuted for Sorcery in 1324*, ed. T. Wright. Camden Society, o.s. 24 (London, 1843), 13, 21, 25, 26, 35; *The Sorcery Trial of Alice Kyteler: a Contemporary Account (1324)*, ed. L. S. Davidson and J. O. Ward, trans. G. Ward (Binghamton, NY: Pegasus Press, 1993), 44, 51, 55, 56, 66.

century) of those within the polity, rather than to the polity itself (the 'commonwealth' of the early sixteenth century).[62] The very fact that this language of public authority, familiar from English government discourse, was current in Ireland is significant in itself. Even more so is the fact that this same language provided the king's subjects in Ireland – or those who claimed to speak on their behalf – with the means to describe and legitimate for themselves a separate field of political identification: the land of Ireland. Indeed, by the fifteenth century, the term 'land' was being used metonymically to refer to the collective interests of the king's lieges, as in the phrase 'the common profit of the land' in the credentials for Michael Tregury, archbishop of Dublin, who was elected as a messenger to travel to the England. It was a small step from this to employ the metaphor of the 'body politic', as when in 1476 the lord deputy William Sherwood, bishop of Meath, was 'desired by the *entire body* of this said land' (F. *par le entier corps dicest di terre*) to travel before the king in England 'for the public good and relief of this land.'[63] It was this corporate identity that was soon to achieve visual expression in the device of the three crowns – the badge of Ireland – which appears on coins issued by the Dublin mint in the reign of Richard III.[64]

The English Claim to Ireland

The claim that Ireland was 'corporate of itself' represents the apotheosis of one strand in Ireland's development as a 'regnal' polity. It was, however, only one possible use of the organological metaphor. A second usage, which had an older pedigree, was the idea that Ireland was a 'member', in the sense of a limb, of the English crown, which was itself commonly understood to symbolise England's status as a *corpus mysticum*. It was with this sense of the body politic in mind that Sir Gilbert Debenham was instructed to remind Edward IV in 1474 that 'as of very right the realm of England is bound to the defence

---

62 See, e.g., letters of 1386 that refer both to the public good and common profit (L. *rem publicam et utilitatem communem*): CIRCLE, *Patent Roll* 10 Richard II, no. 200. For the conceptual shift in English usage after 1450, see J. Watts, ' "Commonweal" and "Commonwealth": England's Monarchical Republic in the Making, *c*.1450–*c*.1530', in A. Gamberini, J.-P. Genet and A. Zorzi (eds.), *The Languages of Political Society* (Rome: Viella, 2011), 147–63.

63 *Stat. Henry VI*, 316–17 (F. *le commune profit de cest terre*); *COD*, iii, 146 (L. *pro comodo et utilitate terre predicte*); *Stat. Ire. 12–22 Edw. IV*, 464–5.

64 M. Dolley, 'Coinage to 1534', in *NHI* ii, 824; D. W. Dykes, 'The Anglo-Irish Coinage and the Ancient Arms of Ireland', *JRSAI*, 96 (1966), 111–20; M. Dolley, 'Tre Kronor – Trí Choróin: A Note on the Date of the "Three-Crown" Coinage of Ireland', *Särtryck ur Numismatiska Meddelanden*, 30 (1965), 103–12.

of Ireland by reason that it is one of the members of his most noble crown and the eldest member thereof'.[65]

The plea to the king to protect the interests of the crown with military intervention – 'as a noble and gracious prince is bound to do to his lieges', runs the petition from the great council at Kilkenny in 1360 that led to the expedition of Lionel of Antwerp – was one of the most persistent refrains in the 'literature of remedy' produced in the fourteenth and fifteenth centuries. The overarching purpose of this material was to seek the 'reformation' of Ireland, a term that implied the restoration of the country through renewed military effort to what was perceived to be its pristine condition when it was securely governed by English laws.[66] The most articulate spokesman for intervention in the first half of the fifteenth century was the author of the *Libelle of English Policy*, who urged the king to make a 'final conquest' to bring all the land under his obeisance.

> And all this world *Dominus* of name
> Should have the ground obeisant, wild and tame,
> That name and people together might accord,
> And all the ground be subject to the lord.[67]

The *Libelle* affirms the standard position that the king's *dominium* embraced the whole island of Ireland and should command the allegiance or obedience of all the island's population.[68] But he also acknowledged frankly that the reality was very different. The reach of English government in Ireland far exceeded its grasp. The contrast between the securely ruled ground and what lay beyond was cast in Manichean terms as a social chasm separating the 'wild' from the 'tame'. In other documents, the difference was expressed as a contrast between two forms of governance: 'the abominable conditions and inhuman manners of the Irish enemies of our sovereign lord the King' as against the 'the honourable conduct and orderly government of his English subjects'.[69]

---

65 The organic metaphor is explicit in the Statute of Rhuddlan (1284), which describes Wales as being 'annexed and united … to the crown of the said realm [of England], as a member of the same body': *The Statutes of Wales*, ed. I. Bowen (London: T. F. Unwin, 1908), 2; Bryan, *Gerald FitzGerald*, 22.

66 For 'reformation' in this sense, see *Stat. Ire. Hen. VI*, 356 (*F. sinon pluis hasty remedy soit ewe hors de Engleterre pur la reformacioun dicelle*).

67 Warner (ed.), *Libelle*, 38.

68 The phrasing of the Westminster ordinances (1357) is unusual in referring to 'the people through almost all of Ireland subject to the king' (L. *populus quasi per totam hiberniam nobis subjectus*), but this is a comment on the quality of royal government (L. *regimen*) in these areas, not a concession that the remainder of the island fell outside the king's lordship (*Statutes of the Realm*, i, 358).

69 *Stat. Ire. 1–12 Edw. IV*, 611.

The failure to extend 'orderly government' across the island was a public embarrassment, one that attracted comment – and some gloating – from England's rivals in Christendom. The Chronicle of Saint Denys reported in 1399 that Richard II, 'who thought of himself as one of the most powerful of western kings, was irritated because that part of Ireland which had submitted to him had now rebelled against him'.[70] As well he might be, because the incapacity to discharge the obligations that were attendant upon lordship served to undermine the claim to rightful possession itself. Within a few years the representatives of the French nation at the Council of Constance were taunting their English counterparts that although England might claim that Ireland had forty-eight dioceses, only two were obedient to the king of England.[71] The gross inaccuracy of the figures would hardly have detracted from the purpose of the argument, which was to defeat the wildly exaggerated claims to legitimate authority claimed by England's kings. The parallel with debates over the extent of imperial jurisdiction in the late-medieval West is striking. The Romans had claimed to be lords of all the world, but Nicholas of Cusa (d. 1464) came to the conclusion that the emperor is 'lord only over those who are actually subject to him and … of that part of the world over which he exercises *effective* authority'.[72] This was, in fact, only one of a number of possible angles of critique of England's *dominium* in Ireland. Another approach, famously marshalled in the Irish Remonstrance (1316), was to admit (as was prudent in a letter intended for the Pope) of the possible legitimacy of the English conquest based on the supposed papal donation of *Laudabiliter*, but to proceed to argue that the holders of *dominium* had since defaulted on their duties to abide by the terms of the grant.[73] Still another rhetorical front could be opened by accusing the English of straightforward usurpation: a line of scholastic thought, arising from Augustine's parable about the emperor and the pirate, maintained that 'subjects have no duty to obey any regime that held its power not by right but by usurpation, or commands what is wrong'.[74]

---

70 Given-Wilson (ed.), *Chronicles of the Revolution*, 110; J. Canning, *Ideas of Power in the Late Middle Ages, 1296–1417* (Cambridge University Press, 2011).
71 A. Gwynn, 'Ireland and the English Nation at the Council of Constance', *PRIA*, 45 C (1940), 199 n. 55; J. H. Mundy and K. M. Woody (eds.), *The Council of Constance: The Unification of the Church*, trans. L. R. Loomis (New York and London: Columbia University Press, 1961), 322.
72 *Nicholas of Cusa: The Catholic Concordance*, trans. P. Sigmund (Cambridge University Press, 1991), 237.
73 J. Muldoon, 'The Remonstrance of the Irish Princes and the Canon Law Theory of the Just War', *American Journal of Legal History*, 22 (1978), 321.
74 C. J. Nederman and K. Langdon Forhan (eds.), *Medieval Political Theory: A Reader. The Quest for the Body Politic, 1100–1400* (London: Routledge, 1993), 136 (Aquinas, *Summa Theologiae*).

The response from the propagandists on the English side was to generate a layered argument that could silence all objections. One avenue of apologetics that was tried but soon abandoned was the doctrine of conquest-right. 'Conquest' – with all its modern connotations of forceful military expropriation of another territory and its people – was certainly the standard term used to describe the English taking of Ireland in the later Middle Ages, as in 1454 when a letter to the duke of York stated that 'this land of Ireland was never at the point finally to be destroyed since the conquest of this land, as it is now'; and the articles of 1474 which, in requesting a royal expedition, claimed that the 'recovery' of the land would be easier than at the time of 'the first conquest thereof was obtained'.[75] By the Roman law of conquest, the victor could legitimately impose an entirely new legal and governmental dispensation upon the conquered peoples. The doctrine was known to the twelfth-century fabulist, Geoffrey of Monmouth, whose *History of the Kings of Britain* depicts the rule of the empire of King Arthur as being justified on the basis of conquest-right. Gerald of Wales later included two references to conquest snipped from the pages of Geoffrey of Monmouth and pasted into the *Expugnatio Hibernica*: the subjugation of Ireland by Gurguntius; and the conquest of King Arthur. Gerald's 'Five-fold right' of the kings of England to Ireland became a foundational text, but the idea that conquest could establish a just title was one that grated against other ideas of power, notably that empires being founded upon force were illegitimate.[76]

When, in the late thirteenth century, an English author set out a new 'Declaration' of the English title to Ireland, he undertook two important re-workings of Gerald's text. The central concern was to airbrush out of history the military conquest of Ireland. In its place a new story was pushed into the foreground of a voluntary grant by Strongbow to Henry II of Dublin and Waterford and all other Irish lands that he held by rightful inheritance. The second change was more subtle, but its implications ran deep. The author of the 'Declaration' repeated that the title of the English king arose from his succession to King Arthur (here rehearsing Gerald of Wales), but he omitted any reference to the Arthurian conquest. Instead, he emphasised that the submission of the Irish princes to Arthur had been spontaneous and

75 *Original Letters Illustrative of English History*, ed. H. Ellis. 2nd ser., 4 vols. (London: S. & J. Bentley, 1827), i, 118; Bryan, *Gerald FitzGerald*, 20. See also Steele (ed.), *Three Prose Versions*, 182 ('the conquest by king Henry the Second in Ireland'), 183–4; *The English Conquest of Ireland* […], ed. F. J. Furnivall (London: EETS, 1896), 186–7 ('Master Gerald tells no further of the conquest').
76 D. Sutherland, 'Conquest and Law', *Studia Gratiana*, 15 (1972), 45–7; Canning, *Ideas of Power*, 77–8.

voluntary.[77] The cumulative effect of elision and prolepsis was to create an argument from prescription. The English held Ireland not by conquest, nor even by papal donation (though *Laudabiliter* still served in the overall argument as the *coup de grâce*), but by a right existing since time immemorial. This proved to be a durable argument, one that came to be much prized by the colonists. A cluster of Middle-Hiberno-English texts from the first part of the fifteenth century develop the ideas still further in the vernacular. James Yonge included an elaborated version of English title to Ireland, which now stresses the spontaneous nature of the submission to Henry II, as is clear (he says) because 'the chronicles make no mention of any chivalry or war done by the king all the time that he was in Ireland'.[78]

To appreciate fully what is at stake in Yonge's argument, it is necessary to compare his insistence on the absence of 'chivalry', or feats of arms, at the time of the first coming of the English to Ireland with the strong advocacy of chivalry that Yonge provides elsewhere in his tract. Famously, Yonge urges Ormond to raise out the false Irish enemy by the root – the original meaning of the term 'eradication'.[79] The degree of emphasis he placed on martial prowess is quite unusual for a princely 'mirror'. It may in part have been urged by the fact that military activity in Ireland was a thankless task compared to the renown to be won in arms in France. As he assured his patron, the fourth earl of Ormond:

> The fourth cause why this noble earl should not have vainglory of this aforesaid prowess is the little thanks that he had of those who should have best rewarded and commended him.

But the glorification of violence and conquest was part of a wider trend associated with English chivalry more generally. That zealous advocate of the crusade, Philippe de Mézières (d. 1405) – no pacifist he! – was scornful of the English obsession with territorial conquest within Christendom, 'drunk as you are with pride and stirred up by stories of Lancelot and Gawain and worldly valour'. It is a martial image that also occurs in the Gaelic poetry fashioned for the lords of English Ireland by their Irish bards, who ornamented

77 Cambridge University Library, MS Ii.iv.5, fols. 79–81; J. R. S. Phillips, ed. 'Three Thirteenth-Century Declarations of English Rule: Over Aquitaine, Ireland and Wales', in Smith (ed.), *Ireland and the English World*, 20–43; for analysis, see W. Ullman, 'On the Influence of Geoffrey of Monmouth in English History', in C. Bauer, L. Böhm and M. Müller (eds.), *Speculum Historiale: Geschichte im Spiegel von Geschichtsschreibung und Geschichtsdeutung—Johannes Spörl aus Anlass series 60. Geburtstages dargebracht von Weggenossen, Freundun und Schülern* (Freiburg: Karl Alber, 1965), 257–76.
78 *Three Prose Versions*, 184–5.
79 *Three Prose Versions*, 164.

their battle-rolls with apologues recalling the feats of Arthur and his knights, as well as the heroes of the Irish kingly cycles.[80]

The interlacing of the language of ethnicity with the language of enmity in contemporary documents is significant in explaining how such constant warfare could be justified. Roman law made a distinction between lawful enemies in arms (L. *hostes*) and private or internal enemies of the state (L. *inimici*). It was a distinction that was respected for much of the early and high Middle Ages through the institution of 'mortal' or 'capital' enmity, which provided a legitimate means of prosecuting a grievance through private vendetta.[81] With very few exceptions, the Latin documentation from the late Middle Ages refers to Irish enemies as *inimici hibernici*. The precise valence of the term is difficult to determine. By the late Middle Ages, the language of enmity was blurring because of the growing public authority of the crown. The king's private enemies were also *ipso facto* enemies of the state. In 1311, for instance, Piers Gaveston was declared to be the 'manifest enemy of the king and his people'.[82] But the idea of mortal enmity was certainly not unknown in late-medieval Ireland. It is found, for instance, in the English vernacular document that refers to 'the wild Irishry, being mortal and natural enemies to the kings of England and English dominion'.[83] Matters were further complicated by the use of written bonds or indentures to define relations between the English king and individual chiefs. The lords who broke those bonds could be charged with 'treasonous' behaviour and suffer the full rigours of royal justice. The dilemma is apparent in a letter written by Niall Óg Ó Néill to Richard II in 1395 which expresses his concern about the implications of his submission:

> For it is openly foretold that after your departure my lord the Earl of Ulster [Roger Mortimer, earl of March] will wage bitter war against me, and if I make no resistance he will crush me without pity … on the other hand, if I resist him my rivals will say that I have become rebel and traitor to your Majesty, which, God be witness, I never intend to be.

---

80 De Mézières quote is in M. Keen, 'Chivalry and English Kingship in the Later Middle Ages', in C. Given-Wilson, A. Kettle and L. Scales (eds.), *War, Government and Aristocracy in the British Isles, c.1150–1500* (Woodbridge: Boydell Press, 2008), 262. *Aithdioghluim Dána*, ed. L. McKenna, 2 vols. (Dublin: ITS, 1939 [text], 1940 [trans.]), no. 36; *Poems on Marcher Lords*, ed. A. O'Sullivan and P. Ó Riain (Dublin: ITS, 1987) 28–33.

81 R. Bartlett, '*Mortal Enmities': The Legal Aspect of Hostility in the Middle Ages* (T. Jones Pierce Lecture, Aberystwyth, 1998).

82 Chrimes and Brown (eds.), *Select Documents*, 15 (F. *apert enemy le roi et de son poeple*).

83 *Stat. Ire. Ric. III–Hen. VIII*, 166. See also *SP, Henry VIII*, ii, part 3, 481 ('Iryshe men, our natural enymyes').

It is no coincidence that when, in 1421, the Irish parliament sent messengers to appeal to Henry V to launch a crusade in Ireland, among the arguments they presented concerning the king's title to Ireland was an additional line item: the oaths of allegiance the Irish chiefs had sworn to Richard II, and since broken.[84] This was not the first time that elements within the colony had sought to legitimate the waging of war against the Irish by employing the language of the crusade.[85] This is a useful indication of the theoretical rules of engagement. One thing that the Irish 'enemies' were not being accorded was recognition as lawful enemies in arms. The warfare prosecuted against the native chiefs was not a *bellum hostile* between princes; it was closer to *guerre mortelle*, in which no quarter might be given.[86] The language of enmity served, then, a double purpose in demonstrating the necessity for the prosecution of sustained warfare against the native population, while also proving its just cause.

Conclusion

'This men may well understand,' wrote a fifteenth-century author in Ireland as if stating a self-evident truth, 'that both by ancient right and by new, the kings of England ought to have the lordship of Ireland.'[87] The argument I have been seeking to advance is that, on the contrary, the Lordship of Ireland was not a datum. It was both a living idea and an evolving political framework. As a living idea, it represented an assertion of legitimate authority that required active defence, both intellectually and instrumentally. As a political framework, it provided the king's 'faithful English lieges of Ireland' with a separate field of identification for their political interests. For the native population,

84 R. Frame, 'Two Kings in Leinster: The Crown and the MicMhurchadha in the Fourteenth Century', in Barry *et al.* (eds.), *Colony and Frontier in Medieval Ireland*, 167–8; Curtis, *Richard II in Ireland*, letter 13; Matthew, 'Henry V and the Proposal for an Irish Crusade'.
85 For a petition of the late 1320s, see *Il Registro di Andrea Sapiti, Procutore alla Curia Avigonese*, ed. B. Bombi (Rome: Viella, 2007), part 1, no. XI, 103–5; J. A. Watt, 'Negotiations between Edward II and John XXII Concerning Ireland', *IHS*, 10 (1956), 18–20.
86 R. C. Stacey, 'The Age of Chivalry', in M. Howard, G. J. Andreopoulos and M. R. Shulman (eds.), *The Laws of War: Constraints on Warfare in the Western World* (New Haven: Yale University Press, 1994), 27–39; M. Keen, *The Laws of War in the Late Middle Ages* (London: Routledge and Kegan Paul, 1965). The idea of *guerre mortelle* or 'mortale werre' was current in fifteenth-century Ireland (*Stat. Ire. Hen. VI*, 360, 524).
87 'And þis men may vndirestand þat goyth [both] by olde right and by neve, þe kynges of Englon oȝt to hawe þe lordscheppe of Ireland': *Die Kildare Gedichte: die ältesten mittelenglischen Denkmäler in Anglo-Irischer Überlieferung*, ed. W. Heuser (Bonn: P. Hanstein, 1904), 222 (edition of Bodl., MS Laud 526).

the Lordship was, by turns, exclusionary and invasive – extruding the Irish from the ranks of its lay political society and then intruding itself again into the politics of Gaelic Ireland in reaction to pleas from the colonists to vindicate the king's title and to effect the 'reformation' of the land.

In 1541 the medieval Lordship of Ireland was, in effect, superseded. The lord deputy, Sir Anthony St Leger, wrote to Henry VIII to inform him that the Irish parliament had enacted that the king of England should 'worthelye have a nother [*sic*] Imperiall crowne'. This was the 'crown of this realm of Ireland' referred to in the Act for the Kingly Title of June 1541. The English monarch was now to be invested as 'king of Ireland', a title that would replace 'lord of Ireland' in the royal style.[88] The Act has been understood as an attempt to establish the effective sovereignty of the English monarch across the whole island of Ireland and its peoples, whether of Gaelic and English descent, after the passage of the Act of Supremacy in Ireland in 1537. But, in light of the evidence presented in this chapter, the pressing question must be: why should this have been thought necessary? What medieval English king, in his capacity as *dominus Hibernie*, claimed anything less than full sovereignty in temporals within his lordship of Ireland? The Act itself is quite clear that the kings of England, as 'lords in this land of Ireland … [held] all manner of kingly jurisdiction, power, pre-eminences, and authority royal, belonging or appertaining to the royal estate and majesty of a King'. It was (so the framers of the Act found it prudent to explain) the monarchs' *lack of naming* as kings of Ireland according to their 'true and just title, style and name', and not any deficiency in the substance of the king's lordship of Ireland, that had caused 'great occasion' amongst his Irish subjects. Both in terms of the content of its ideas and the form in which they are expressed, the Act for the Kingly Title dresses up age-old ideas in a new idiom while smuggling in innovations under the skirts of ancient custom. The Lordship of Ireland, long-since imagined to be a 'regnal' polity, is now dignified with its own imperial crown; but this Irish 'imperial crown' remains clumsily attached to the 'imperial crown' of England.[89] By this reading, the Act neatly expresses, but does not resolve, the tension in political structure that this chapter sought to survey. Yet it is surely the novel implications of the Act that are the most striking. Conceptions of political

---

88 *SP, Henry VIII*, iii, part 3, 305. Interestingly, the order of precedence within the royal style for writs issued in Ireland, as described to Henry VIII in 1541, promotes Ireland to second, and relegates France to third, place: 'Henry thEight, King of Inglande, Irelande, and of Fraunce, Defendor of the Faythe, and in Erthe Supreme Hed of the Churche of Inglande and Irelande' (*SP, Henry VIII*, iii, part 3, 308).

89 *Statutes at Large, Ireland*, i, 176 ('united and knit to the imperial crown of the realm of England').

authority, in Ireland as in England, altered markedly from the later fifteenth century. One precipitant of change was the trauma of the Wars of the Roses. A second was the growth of neo-classicist rhetoric and ideas, which emboldened and empowered those specialist administrators who sought to enforce obedience to the monarch.[90] The execution of Thomas, earl of Desmond, in 1468 by that humanistic book-collector and impaler of men, Sir John Tiptoft, was a harbinger of what the conjuncture of these trends might betoken for the older structure of politics in Ireland.

90 Watts, ' "Commonweal" and "Commonwealth" '.

17

Material Culture

RACHEL MOSS

'IN many ways the Norman invasion mark[ed] in Ireland the end of a world, and certainly the death of original artistic endeavour.'[1] This statement, made by the pioneering scholar of Irish art, Françoise Henry, summarises the opinion of several generations of scholars who saw the arrival of the Anglo-Normans as a decisive act of cultural suppression that sounded the death knell for Irish creativity. It is true that (so far as we are aware) the great heights of artistic achievement made by the hands of the *Book of Kells* scribes or the Ardagh chalice goldsmith were not to be repeated. But rumours of the total demise of artistic endeavour have been greatly exaggerated, and the impact of the 'invasion' might more accurately be seen as a catalyst for changes that were already in progress. In reality, the artistic and architectural winds of change had already started to blow almost a century before the more decisive Anglo-Norman storm reached south-eastern shores. Irish engagement with the pan-European reform of the Christian Church from the late eleventh century was probably a key instigator of this, and it is clear that regional rulers were also keen to demonstrate their potency through the commission of art works and buildings of a more cosmopolitan nature than had hitherto been the case.

Tradition and Innovation

Diocesan organisation was introduced through a series of reforming synods from the early twelfth century. During the first half of the twelfth century, as established ecclesiastical centres vied with one another for prominence, and the ultimate designation of episcopal see, secular patrons entered the fray in the architectural reshaping of churches, or in some cases of the entire

---

1 F. Henry, *Irish Art in the Romanesque Period 1020–1170 A.D.* (London: Methuen, 1970), 25.

monastic *civitas*. In the far south-west, at Ardfert, County Kerry, the modest rectangular *damliac* was extended southwards and eastwards, and its west
front transformed through the addition of a Romanesque-style arcade and
doorway more redolent of the English West Country than the south-western
tip of Ireland.[2] In the west, aspirant high king Tairdelbach Ua Conchobair set
about the remodelling of the ecclesiastical settlement at Tuam and procured
a relic of the True Cross in order to add extra weight to its, and by extension his, authority. The resulting stone crosses and fine metalwork reliquary,
now known as the Cross of Cong, exhibit hybrid features. The stone crosses
hark back to the earlier Irish tradition of large stone monuments, but take
continental crucifixes as their model. The maker of the Cross of Cong used
techniques of casting and glass gemstone manufacture long embedded in the
Irish tradition, but the form owed as much to Byzantine exemplars as it did
to the native tradition. Meanwhile in the north of the country, St Malachy
embarked on the construction of a new church at Bangor so alien to local
eyes that his biographer recorded the contemporary criticism of it: 'We are
Irish, not Gauls!'.[3]

Royal chapels built at Killaloe, close to the Ua Briain stronghold at
Kincora, and at Cashel, the Eógonacht seat of the Mac Carthaig, clearly
show the hands of craftsmen from England, presumably brought in especially.[4] The alliance of the Mac Carthaig to the trappings of European kingship was also expressed in the massive sarcophagus carved with dynamic
interlacing forms, almost certainly originally placed close to the altar inside
a church. Burial in a monumental stone sarcophagus located close to the
altar of the church was a departure for Irish royalty, reflecting practice that
was more common in continental Europe. The erection of a stone cross at
Cashel bearing the image of the Italian icon the Volto Sancto also suggests a

2 F. Moore, *Ardfert Cathedral: Summary of Excavation Results* (Dublin: Department of the
   Environment, Heritage and Local Government, 2007).
3 *Ann. Tig.* ii, 50; R. Stalley, 'The Romanesque Sculpture of Tuam', in A. Borg and A.
   Martindale (eds.), *The Vanishing Past: Studies in Medieval Art, Liturgy and Metrology presented
   to Christopher Hohler*. British Archaeological Reports, International Series III (Oxford:
   Archaeopress, 1982), 179–95; G. Murray, *The Cross of Cong: A Masterpiece of Medieval Irish
   Art* (Dublin: Irish Academic Press, 2014); H. J. Lawlor, *St. Bernard of Clairvaux's Life of St.
   Malachy of Armagh* (London and New York: Macmillan, 1920), 109–10.
4 R. Gem, 'Saint Flannán's Oratory at Killaloe: A Romanesque Building of *c*. 1100 and
   the Patronage of King Muirchertach Ua Briain', in Bracken and Ó Riain-Raedel (eds.),
   Ireland and Europe in the Twelfth Century, 74–105; R. Stalley, 'Design and Function: The
   Construction and Decoration of Cormac's Chapel at Cashel', in Bracken and Ó Riain-
   Raedel (eds.), *Ireland and Europe in the Twelfth Century*, 162–75.

deliberate emulation of the promotion of a cult that had enjoyed particular royal promotion in England in the preceding decades.[5]

By the middle of the twelfth century Irish patrons also began to broaden their sights when it came to the nature of the organisations that they chose to sponsor. Of greatest significance, in architectural terms, was the introduction of the Cistercian order to Ireland. Organised in a tight, filial network and governed by statutes that theoretically included strict governance in matters of building and decoration, the Cistercians introduced what might be described as the first international corporate brand to Ireland. With the foundation of the first Irish Cistercian house at Mellifont, on land donated by Donnchad Ua Cerbaill, king of Fernmag and Airgilla, came a French monk named Robert to advise on matters of planning and construction. Such was the success of this venture that by the end of the century the rational form of monastic planning, comprising integrated church and domestic buildings arranged around a cloister, had become the new normal.[6]

By the end of the twelfth century then, the newly arrived settlers found themselves in a place already in the throes of artistic transition and arguably not antipathetic to change. But while they may not have introduced an artistic revolution, what any expansion in population brought with it was a requirement for new buildings and the resources to finance them. As might be expected, the most immediate discernible impact of the Anglo-Normans was on settlement and the establishment of new centres of administration from which to govern. At a practical level these needed to be strategically located and well defended, and in the earliest decades of settlement this was achieved through the swift erection of earth-and-timber motte and bailey structures, typically located in contested areas, close to established centres of population, or as the focal point of newly established boroughs. Although the mottes (steep earthen mounds) and baileys (enclosed fore-works at their base) traced their origins to Normandy via England and Wales, the impact of the new settlers on the personality of the broader landscape appears to have been minimal. In small areas of Leinster, and in County Tipperary, there are traces of the nucleated settlement comprising 'castle', parish church and rectilinear streetscape that suggest the typical manorial layout of contemporary England. But elsewhere, the continuity of a more scattered pattern of

---

5 J. Bradley, 'The Sarcophagus at Cormac's Chapel, Cashel, Co. Tipperary', *North Munster Archaeological Journal*, 26 (1984), 14–35; D. Webb, 'The Holy Face of Lucca', *ANS*, 9 (1986), 227–37.

6 R. Stalley, *The Cistercian Monasteries of Ireland* (London and New Haven: Yale University Press, 1987).

settlement suggests that changes were as much the result of an expansion in population and changes in agricultural practice mirrored across Europe, as the result of a new administration.[7]

In urban areas the pattern was a little different. Civil control was maintained through the dual auspices of ecclesiastical and lay authorities, and many of the more significant building projects undertaken towards the end of the twelfth and in the early decades of the thirteenth century clearly reflect this, both in their positioning and their physical form. The town of Kilkenny provides a good example (Fig. 5).

Located at a crossing point on the western bank of the River Nore, a settlement comprising the stronghold of the kings of Osraige and two ecclesiastical enclosures was already in place when a charter for the formal establishment of a borough was issued in 1207.[8] A new castle was constructed by William Marshal I, surmounting a hill to the south-east. Facing this, on a hill further north along the river was the ancient ecclesiastical settlement dedicated to St Canice, containing at least two churches and a round tower within its circular enclosure. The churches were demolished and replaced by a stocky Gothic building, cruciform with crossing tower, its openings elaborated with richly moulded details crafted from stone imported from Dundry, near Bristol. Conversely, care was taken to retain the round tower, a precocious act of conservation that was echoed at the thirteenth-century rebuilding of other cathedrals at Cashel, Cloyne, Cork and Downpatrick. Of note at all of these places too, was the retention of the dedication to the local saint, the relationship between ancient round tower and new Gothic cathedral starkly demonstrating the cultural annexation of the Anglo-Normans also reflected in their promotion of local saints' cults and appropriation of relics at the time.

Between the two sentinels of castle and cathedral the town was laid out along the central spine of High Street, lined with narrow (20 feet wide) burgage or house plots that stretched back to the town walls to the west and river on the east. The area around St Canice's was set aside for the Irish, and became known as Irishtown. Farther south, across the small tributary of the River Nore (the River Bregagh) was an area enclosed on the west and south sides by strong stone walls and named High Town. The initial charter of High Town granted burgesses the right to draw timber from adjacent woodland for the construction of what were most likely sill-beam houses. Close to the centre of town, the parish church, St Mary's, was built and maintained by

7 T. B. Barry, *The Archaeology of Medieval Ireland* (London: Routledge, 1987).
8 J. Bradley, *Irish Historic Towns Atlas, no. 10, Kilkenny* (Dublin: RIA, 2000).

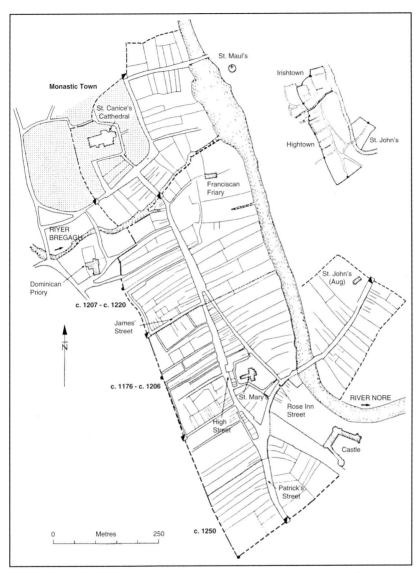

Figure 5. Plan of Anglo-Norman Kilkenny. Source: J. Bradley, *Kilkenny*. Irish Historic Towns Atlas (Dublin: RIA, 2000).

the merchants. This overlooked the main marketplace, at which, in 1335, a substantial market cross was erected. The main bridging point of the Nore was directly beneath the castle. On the east bank of the river – a safe distance from the tightly packed town – Marshal established a priory of Augustinian canons, St John's, for the relief of the poor and needy. By 1327, a hospital dedicated to St Mary Magdalen was also in place in the small suburb that grew up around the canons' foundation. In addition to these, shortly after the establishment of the mendicant orders of friars in the 1220s, houses of both the Franciscans and Dominicans were constructed on the periphery of the town; the Dominican friary immediately outside one of the western gates, and the Franciscan house close to the river in the north-eastern corner of High Town. Founded by members of the Marshall family, both foundations were staffed exclusively by friars of English origin.

Thus, by the end of the thirteenth century, the architectural topography of Kilkenny, in common with most Irish towns, demonstrated a clearly delineated set of social hierarchies. The lord and bishop occupied large stone buildings on their respective hills; the merchants of English birth, resident in stoutly built timber frame houses, enjoyed the protection of a strong, stone town wall. The key points of the town, marketplace, some gates and bridging points were overseen by the Church, also accommodated in substantial stone structures whose rooflines punctured the skyline. The Irish, in (initially) undefended Irishtown, most likely dwelt in single storey cabins, dominated by the cathedral that towered above them.

The politics of aesthetics and space were at play not just in the urban landscape, but also in buildings. Throughout the later Middle Ages churches were typically the only buildings that were publicly accessible to all strata of society. This applied not only to parish churches, but also to friary churches. With a mission to preach, and reliant on the alms of the faithful for their very survival, the houses of the mendicant friars were initially established on the peripheries of urban areas. The resident community of friars was endowed to pray for the souls of benefactors, so that before long friaries were enjoying a particularly vibrant lay patronage. By the mid-fourteenth century there were approximately ninety mendicant houses established by friars belonging to the Franciscan, Dominican, Augustinian and Carmelite orders in Ireland. Although typically 'founded' by lords, as was the case in Kilkenny, initial foundation benefactions usually consisted of the gift of a piece of land and some seed funding, with the friars then faced with raising the funds to construct and maintain buildings in perpetuity, circumstances that do much to explain the often disjointed architectural design of these buildings.[9]

The survival of a copy of a friary register from the Dominican house at Athenry is especially instructive, providing an insight into what was almost certainly the pattern of patronage in many friaries, and how this was used to visually map the changing power dynamics of the communities that they served.[10] The friary was founded in 1241 by Meiler de Birmingham close to his newly built castle at Athenry as part of the Anglo-Norman colonisation of east Connacht. Meiler provided the site and financial support, which probably funded the construction of the church, affording him and subsequent generations of Berminghams a prime burial place on the south side of the high altar. Although essentially an 'English' foundation, within the following twenty years the domestic ranges were sponsored by local Gaelic lords – Feidlimid O'Connor [Ó Conchobair] (the refectory), Conchobhar O'Kelly [Ó Ceallaig] (the chapter house), Eoghan Ó hEidhin [O' Heyne] (the dormitory), although there is no evidence that this secured them burial rights within the church.

A second phase of building was initiated during the late 1310s and early 1320s. This involved the rebuilding of the west front, the addition of the north nave aisle and transept, the insertion of a bell tower at the junction between nave and chancel and the eastern extension of the chancel by twenty feet. The work may have been prompted by damage to the friary during the 1316 battle of Athenry, or perhaps the deliberate partial dismantling of the church for strategic reasons, as happened with the Dominican friary in Dublin in anticipation of the Bruce invasion. Either way the new works reflected the altered political and social status quo in Athenry at the time. It was the victorious William *'Liath' de Burgh*, de facto Lord of Connacht, and his wife who funded the new west front and extension of the chancel. This work incorporated some particularly innovative examples of window tracery, and it is tempting to suggest that this may have accommodated at least some of the heraldic elements that had become fashionable in English glass at the time. With new east and west windows the de Burghs essentially had control over the key pictorial space of the friary. More importantly however, the eastern extension of the church allowed the movement of the high altar, and created a new, high-status area for burial. With this deft move the de Burghs were able to disenfranchise the Berminghams as 'primary' patrons

9 Ó Clabaigh, *Friars in Ireland*, 1–30.
10 'Regestum Monasterii Fratrum Praedicatorum de Athenry', ed. A. Coleman, *Archivium Hibernicum*, 1 (1912), 201–21; Moss (ed.), *Art and Architecture of Ireland*, 544–57.

22. North transept of Athenry friary, County Galway c.1320s. Photo courtesy of
Rachel Moss.

of the foundation. Perhaps as an attempt to maintain some profile within
the building a Bermingham patron started work on the north transept (Lady
Chapel) and its elaborate set of tomb recesses (Illustration 22). But following
his death this work was completed by a local burgess, and with a few exceptions, the remainder of major benefactions to the friary demonstrate that
from the 1330s the new money of the burgeoning merchant classes shouted
out the whisper of old.

The construction of a bell tower at Athenry around this time by merchant
Jacobus Lynch is echoed in Mayor Kenewreck Sherman's (d. 1349) tower at
St Saviour's Dublin, and at the Franciscan friary in Kilkenny, funded by a confraternity of local merchants in 1347.[11] Built on restricted urban sites, typically
towers were placed central to the transition between nave and chancel, neces-
sitating quite radical alterations to the church's fabric, in particular the roof.
One might question such disruption simply to accommodate the ringing of
the Mass bell, but aside from their practical uses, towers were a symbol of
status, so an important addition to the otherwise typically plain architecture
of the mendicant houses. In port towns they also functioned as navigational
aids, and the regulation of the working day through the ringing of parish

11 *Chartul. St. Mary's Abbey, Dublin*, ii, 391; *Clyn*, 242.

23. De Burgo-O'Malley Chalice and paten 1494. Reproduced courtesy of the National Museum of Ireland.

church and cathedral bells serves as a reminder of the close-knit relationship between civic and church authorities throughout the medieval period.

As all but those embellishments carved in stone have now vanished from the interiors of medieval churches, the Athenry register is particularly valuable in the picture that it paints of the more ephemeral art and liturgical paraphernalia donated to the friary during the later fourteenth and early fifteenth centuries. Gifts included vestments, variously made of silk, cloth of gold and embroidered fabric, altar clothes, candle sticks and service books, including two 'good' missals, a missal for the high altar and a missal for the friars. A number of chalices are mentioned, and it is likely that these, like the roughly contemporary de Burgo-O'Malley chalice, were engraved with their donors' names so that they would not be forgotten at the all-important moment of the chalice's elevation during the Mass (Illustration 23).[12] Some donors' international trade links put them in a position to engage with the flourishing international art market. William Butler (d. 1448), collector of customs at Galway and Sligo, thus purchased a painted and gilded altarpiece from Flanders for the friary for the significant sum of 40 marks. Similarly,

12 J. J. Buckley, *Some Irish Altar Plate* (Dublin: RSAI, 1943), 14–18.

Joanna Wffler, wife of Athenry burgess William Rider (d. 1408), and later Englishman Robert Gardiner, keeper and searcher at the ports of Galway, Cork, Kinsale and Youghal (fl. 1419), bought a sculpted tomb from 'over the sea' in which she and both husbands were ultimately interred. Joanna's patronage, which also included the total re-glazing of the east end of the church, is representative of the increased role played by women in the patronage of the arts by the early fifteenth century.[13]

Art and Memory

The primary function of the Athenry register was memorialisation. It documented who had given what, but also, significantly, where they were buried, so that their souls might be prayed for in the appropriate manner. Preoccupation with a 'good death' and shortening the soul's passage through Purgatory by inciting prayer from the living was one of the prime motivating factors behind church patronage. But in a period of sometimes dubious and untrustworthy record keeping, other verifications of one's status and rights in life were seen as important. These concerns are clearly reflected in the design and iconography of tomb sculpture during the period. Although simple tomb slabs had borne the name of the deceased in Ireland since possibly as early as the seventh century, the actual depiction of individuals in the form of carved effigies was an Anglo-Norman introduction to Ireland. Tombs created up to the mid-fourteenth century were predominantly concerned with conveying the status of the deceased. Aside from the obvious connotation of wealth attached to the ability to purchase a sculpted tomb and locate it prominently within a church, this was achieved through the costume and pose of the effigy thereon. Effigies of high-ranking ecclesiastics showed them dressed in full pontificals, with hands either raised in benediction, or awkwardly placed across the chest so as to display the episcopal ring. Knights were carved in armour, alert and youthful, and ready to spring into battle. Civilians, both men and women, were shown in their best attire, their right hand sometimes raised to grasp the tie of their cloak – a medieval gesture of nobility (Illustration 24). These images were not portraits, rather they were a readily accessible visual shorthand by which a more collective identity could

13 M. A. Lyons, 'Lay Female Piety and Church Patronage in Late Medieval Ireland', in B. Bradshaw and D. Keogh (eds.), *Christianity in Ireland: Revisiting the Story* (Dublin: Columba Press, 2002), 57–75; R. Moss, ' "Planters of Great Civilitie": Female Patrons of the Arts in Late Medieval Ireland', in T. Martin (ed.), *Reassessing the Roles of Women as 'Makers' of Medieval Art and Architecture* (Leiden: Brill, 2012), 275–308.

24. Tomb effigy of an unknown lady *c*.1300, Cashel, County Tipperary. Photo courtesy
of Rachel Moss.

be expressed. This is mirrored in the art of sigillography, with the vescia-
shaped seals of the clergy and women accommodating also identical images
in miniature, the mounted knights of circular seals of the male nobility, a similar expression adapted to its matrix. In the context of tombs, the individual
for whom the monument was initially made was a member of a larger grouping that held particular, hereditary, rights and privileges, whether ecclesiastic,
familial or corporate, and it was that, more than the death of an individual
colleague or close family member, which was being commemorated.[14]

By the late fifteenth century, funerary monuments had developed to communicate a more complex set of messages. A concern with commemorating
the status of the deceased in life remained important, and honorific effigies
were sometimes accompanied by lengthy epigraphic records of titles and
territories, or heraldic displays documenting familial alliances. Mingled with
this, though, was a range of religious imagery and symbolism that signalled

14 R. Caulfield, *Sigilla Ecclesiae Hibernicae Illustrata: The Episcopal and Capitular Seals of
the Irish Cathedral Churches Illustrated. Part I: Cashel and Emly* (Cork: H. Ridings, 1853);
W. de Gray Birch, *Catalogue of Seals in the Department of Manuscripts, British Museum. Vol.
4. Scotland and Ireland* (London: British Museum, 1895), 695–733; E. C. R. Armstrong,
Irish Seal Matrices and Seals (Dublin: Hodges, Figgis and Co., 1913).

an additional concern for the welfare of the souls of the deceased. The heartland of tomb production in the late fifteenth and early sixteenth centuries was in the earldom of Ormond, corresponding roughly to the limestone-rich counties of Kilkenny and Tipperary.[15] Here, a relatively large number of tombs made for the Butler earls of Ormond and their followers appear to be the product of two workshops: one dubbed the Ormond school and the other the O'Tunney atelier, the latter name a reference to the signatures of at least three different members of what appear to have been the same family of stonemasons. Although slightly different in style, these tombs share a preference for decorating the sides of box tombs with phalanxes of saints. One of the earliest dateable examples of the type (not the work of either school) is the Rice tomb in Waterford cathedral, commissioned by Lord Mayor James Rice *c*.1482. The two long sides of this box tomb are carved with figures of the Apostles, arranged in the order in which the phrases attributed to them appear in the text of the Apostles Creed, one of the prayers that the living were encouraged to recite for the deceased. The other prayers most commonly requested for the dead were the Ave and Pater, perhaps reflected in images of the Holy Trinity and Virgin and Child on either end of the tomb. In this instance it seems likely that the figures served as a type of mnemonic device, reminding passers-by to say a prayer for James and his wife, a request repeated epigraphically for literate viewers on the lid of the tomb.[16]

The choice of saints depicted is not, however, always that straightforward. The presence of the figure of St Lawrence on a tomb belonging to the Plunket family at Rathmore, County Meath, for example, is most likely a result of that family's particular devotion to him in a church of which he was patron saint. The figure of St James Major dressed as a pilgrim on a tomb at Kilconnell on the other hand, was probably intended as a reminder that the now anonymous deceased had expressed his piety in life by undertaking the arduous pilgrimage to the shrine of St James at Santiago di Compostela, and hoped that a prayer for intercession by that saint would have a particular potency (Illustration 25). Typically, individual saints were identified by their attributes, whether objects associated with their martyrdom, such as St Catherine holding her wheel, or some other 'prop' from their life, like St Peter holding the keys to the kingdom of heaven. The degree to which the general Irish populace was literate in this iconography is uncertain.

---

15 E. C. Rae, 'Irish Sepulchral Monuments of the Later Middle Ages: Part I: The Ormond Group', *JRSAI*, 100 (1970), 1–38; E. C. Rae, 'Irish Sepulchral Monuments of the Later Middle Ages: Part II the O'Tunney Atelier', *JRSAI*, 101 (1971), 1–39.

16 E. C. Rae, 'The Rice Monument in Waterford Cathedral', *PRIA*, 69 C (1970), 1–14.

25. Kilconnell friary, County Galway, tomb frontal. Late fifteenth century. Photo courtesy of Rachel Moss.

Instructions for liturgical pageantry make clear that the costumes worn by performers were iconographically accurate, and so may have become familiar to a broader audience in this way. However, where saints are actually labelled on tombs, it is not unusual for identifications to become muddled, such as the figure of St Dominic on a tomb at Kilconnell labelled 'SANCT DINAS', suggesting a level of ignorance, or perhaps illiteracy, at the very least on the part of the sculptor.[17]

Certain imagery would, however, have been almost instantly recognisable. By the fourteenth century a number of devotional images came to have indulgences attached to them. Those who gazed upon an image of the Mass of St Gregory, the Man of Sorrows, Arma Christi or Veronica's Veil were automatically granted remission from their time in Purgatory. As a result, these images became particularly popular, and with the introduction of the printing press, mass-produced cards bearing these images with a legend below granting remission were widely distributed.[18] A number of the tombs created by the O'Tunney atelier incorporate inscriptions that grant indulgences to those living who prayed for the souls of the deceased, a tomb at Kilcooly even specifying that this privilege had been granted by the archbishop of Cashel. For an illiterate audience, the display of indulgenced images had the same affect. A particularly fine example of this is part of a tomb preserved at Kildare Cathedral. This shows an image of the Man of Sorrows. A scroll beneath him

---

17 M. Egan-Buffet and A. J. Fletcher, 'The Dublin Visitatio Sepulchri Play', *PRIA*, 90 C (1990), 176–7.

18 F. Lewis, 'Rewarding Devotion: Indulgences and the Promotion of Images', in D. Wood (ed.), *The Church and the Arts* (Oxford: Blackwell, 1992), 179–94; R. Moss, 'Unfurling Words of Indulgence', in B. Leahy and S. Ryan (eds.), *Treasures of Irish Christianity: A People of the Word* (Dublin: Veritas, 2013), 103–7.

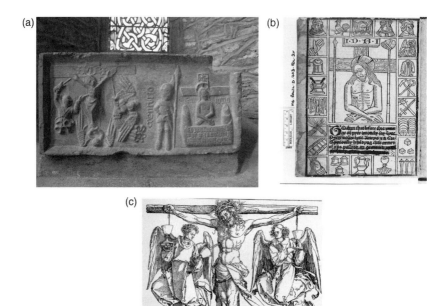

26. (a) Tomb fragment, Kildare Cathedral. Photo courtesy of Rachel Moss; (b) Woodblock print showing Man of Sorrows with indulgence beneath. © Oxford Bodl.Rawl. MSD.403 fol. 2v; (c) Albrecht Dürer Christ with three angels. Photo by The Print Collector/Getty Images.

appears to be carved with script, but on closer scrutiny the letters are not properly formed. There was no need: this direct copy of a popular wood-cut image was intended for the visually rather than the verbally literate, its meaning was clear. Other imagery on the tomb fragment also demonstrates the sculptor's access to mass-produced and widely distributed images. The composition of the crucified Christ with three angels collecting his blood in chalices is a direct derivative of Dürer's famous wood-cut Christ with the three angels; an appropriate reminder of the message of the three angels in Revelation 14: 6–13, to 'Fear God and give him glory, because the hour of his judgment has come', a message reinforced by the figure of St Michael weighing the souls on the adjacent face (Illustrations 26a, b, c).[19]

19 H. King, 'The Medieval and Seventeenth-Century Carved Stone Collection in Kildare', *Journal of the Kildare Archaeological Society*, 17 (1991), 88–9.

As the interiors of churches became ever more populated with tombs, so came the need for new ways to attract the attention of the viewer. Incentivisation through the granting of indulgences was one strategy, another was to create a complementary decorative scheme in the space surrounding the tomb. For those with sufficient means, the establishment of a chantry chapel created a suitably decorated semi-private space within the church. Typically these were formed either by the erection of timber screens in part of a side aisle, or on occasion specially constructed, like that erected by the lord treasurer Sir Roland FitzEustace, Baron Portlester, in *c.* 1482 to the south of the high altar at St Audoen's parish church in Dublin. In other cases the construction of a significant tomb prompted the refurbishment or decoration of the space immediately surrounding it. At the Cistercian monastery of Abbeyknockmoy, a new tomb was inserted into the north wall of the chancel for Malachi O'Kelly, 'king' of Ua Mhaine (d. 1401), and his wife Fionnula, daughter of O'Connor (d. 1403). The tomb itself was relatively plain, but parts of it retain traces of paint, and this, together with an eighteenth-century drawing of the tomb that shows more substantial traces of painting, suggests that originally it formed the focus of a much more substantial visual programme within the most sacred area of the church.[20]

Within the wall niche created by the O'Kelly tomb was a painted crucifixion scene with attendant figures. One of these figures, now lost, held scales – presumably St Michael weighing souls on Judgement Day. On the wall immediately to the east of the tomb is a depiction of the Three Living and Three Dead Kings (Illustration 27). This scene traces its origins to a French morality tale that dwelt on the inevitability of death. Three crowned skeletons meet three young kings out hunting and the message that they convey is inscribed beneath the scene (in translation) 'we have been as you are, you shall be as we are'. The tale itself ended with the skeletons, ancestors of the living kings, admonishing the living for not properly remembering them, so that when the living kings return home they erect a church, and have the story written on its walls. Beneath the depiction of this tale are images of the Trinity and the attempted martyrdom of St Sebastian. As one of the saints invoked for protection from plague, Sebastian's presence here served as a reminder of the near and often unexpected approach of death, and thus reinforced the message of

20 W. Fitzgerald, 'Abbey Knockmoy', *Journal of the Association for the Preservation of Memorials to the Dead in Ireland*, 10 (1917–20), 201–2; C. Moss, 'Revivalist Tendencies in the Irish Late Gothic: Defining a National Identity?' in M. Reeve (ed.), *Reading Gothic Architecture* (Turnhout and New York: Brepols, 2008), 126–7; *Misc. Ir. Annals*, 167.

27. Wall painting showing the Three Living and Three Dead Kings, Holy Trinity and attempted martyrdom of St Sebastian, Abbeyknockmoy, County Galway. © Department of Arts Heritage and the Gaeltacht.

the paintings above. Assuming that it is contemporary with the adjacent royal tomb, the subject matter would have been particularly appropriate, as plague had swept the locality in the three years leading up to Malachi's death.[21]

The paintings at Abbeyknockmoy were not only apposite to the circumstances surrounding the erection of the tomb, but are also an important indication of the cultural awareness of the O'Kelly kings. The iconography associated with Gaelic patrons, created in an apparently remote west of Ireland church, was exactly what one might expect to find in contemporary France or England. This is particularly noteworthy as, at almost exactly the same time as Malachi's tomb was erected, his kinsman Muirchertach O'Kelly, archbishop of Tuam, was involved in the commission of a *seanchas* – a manuscript compilation of tracts on classical history, topographical lore, devotional texts and genealogy. The so-called Book of Uí Mhaine (Dublin: RIA MS D ii 1) was compiled by at least ten scribes, including the renowned historian Faolán mac a'Gabhann and Ádhamh Cuisín. In common with the contemporary compilation, the Book of Ballymote (Dublin: RIA MS 23 P 12), commissioned by the MacDonough [Mac Donnchadha] of Corran in County Sligo, texts therein were adorned with illuminated initials created by a menagerie of

21 *ALC,* ii, 87, 89, 93, 97.

interlaced animals, which would not have looked out of place in an Insular manuscript of the late eleventh or early twelfth century (Illustration 28).[22]

Art and Politics in Gaelic Ireland

The composition of this type of manuscript had its roots in this earlier period, but appears to have died within about 100 years, only to be revived in the mid-fourteenth century. The revival coincided with a period of political tension and the constant shifting of frontiers, with the gradual reconquest of territory by Gaelic families. The use of the vernacular, and distinctively 'pre-Norman' ornamentation has been identified by some scholars as a conscious expression of nationalism and new-found native confidence. The degree to which Gaelic families identified themselves with the concept of an Irish 'nation' is, however, questionable. At least one *seanchas*, the Book of the White Earl/Book of Pottlerath (Oxford, Bodl. Laud. Misc MS 610), was commissioned by a patron of Anglo-Norman origin – James, fourth earl of Ormond (d. 1452), and completed by his nephew Edmund mac Richard Butler in the years immediately following his death. While these patrons had developed the ability to balance close relations with the English court with an absorption of some native custom, a statement of out-and-out nationalism seems unlikely. Rather the incentive to undertake the patronage of this type of manuscript emanated from a Renaissance-style shaping of power and self-image. Individuals emphasised their learning, pedigree and political affiliation through the collection of ancient texts, decorated in an 'antique' manner that sought to confirm their often highly dubious authenticity.[23]

A more public and arguably permanent means of expressing power and territorial control is evident in a resurgence of building at this time. The scars left by the Black Death (1348–9) and its aftermath created a new preoccupation with mortality and the afterlife. This not only had an impact on the nature of tombs and their associated imagery explored above, but also on the construction of new churches to house them. Numerous parish churches show evidence of expansion at this time, typically through the addition of side aisles to accommodate new chapels and altars, a particularly common

---

22 J. Carey, 'Book of Uí Mhaine', in B. Cunningham and S. Fitzpatrick (eds.), *Treasures of the Royal Irish Academy Library* (Dublin: RIA, 2009), 22–3.

23 C. Hourihane, *Gothic Art in Ireland 1169–1550* (London and New Haven: Yale University Press, 2003), 139–60; E. Bhreathnach, 'The *Seanchas* Tradition in Late Medieval Ireland', in E. Bhreathnach and B. Cunningham (eds.), *Writing Irish History: The Four Masters and their World* (Bray: Wordwell, 2007), 18–23.

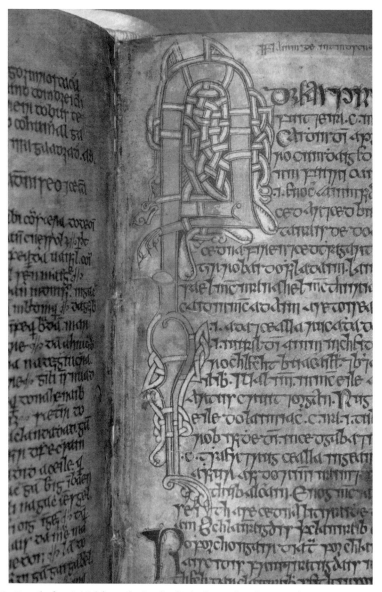

28. Detail of an initial from the Book of Uí Mhaine, late fourteenth century. Courtesy of the Royal Irish Academy, Dublin: RIA MS D ii 1 fol. 48r.

feature in urban churches. In rural areas, particularly in the east of the country, the construction of a new parish church by a local magnate was also an opportunity to enhance status and standing in society. During the latter part of the fifteenth century for example, members of the Plunket family constructed three churches (Dunsany, Rathmore and Killeen) in a very similar, one might even say 'family' style. Parishioners at Dunsany were baptised in a font emblazoned with the Plunket arms, and liturgical space outside the churches was marked by churchyard and wayside crosses on which figures of the Plunkets were carved in equal standing with the saints.[24]

More profound, though, was the investment in the foundation of new friaries that included, between 1380 and 1550, almost sixty new friaries and forty-six houses for the brothers of the Third Order Regular or tertiaries. This is in marked contrast to England and Wales, where there were there were just six new foundations of friaries during the same period and no tertiary foundations at all. Peculiar to Ireland too was the rural nature of the foundations, located predominantly in areas of the west and south-west. Sometimes these were erected close to the stronghold of their founding patrons, as for example at Kilcrea friary, County Cork, and Ardnaree, County Mayo, where Franciscan and Augustinian friaries were adjacent, respectively, to the castles of the MacCarthys and O'Dowds. The Franciscan friary at Moyne, situated close to the mouth of the Moy estuary in County Mayo, has the appearance of desolate isolation, but like Donegal and Burrishoole friaries, farther up and down the coast, it serviced merchant shipping making its way along the western coastline, as well as, doubtless, monitoring the trading interests of its patrons.[25]

The Franciscan friary at Quin, County Clare, is a particularly evocative example of a building as palimpsest of political geography (Illustration 29). Founded in 1433 by MacCon MacNamara, it was built from the rubble of a castle constructed by Thomas de Clare in the late thirteenth century as part of the Anglo-Norman attempt to take control of Thomond. Aside from the remnants of the castle's foundations, which still protrude from the corners of the friary, Quin is a classic of its type. From afar its tall slender tower, located at the transition between nave and chancel, is particularly distinctive and capped with the pronounced, elongated battlements found in many contemporary secular and religious buildings. The massing of church and conventual

24 M. O'Neill, 'The Medieval Parish Churches in Co. Meath', *JRSAI*, 132 (2002), 1–56; H. King, 'Late Medieval Crosses in County Meath, *c.*1470–1635', *PRIA*, 84 C (1984), 79–115.
25 *Carew, 1603–23*, 297; 'Brussels Ms 3947', ed. B. Jennings, *Analecta Hibernica*, 6 (1934), 12–138, 39, 43.

29. Quin friary, County Clare, late fifteenth century. Photo courtesy of Rachel Moss.

buildings is compact. The relatively small, dark integrated cloister (where the cloister arcade partly supports accommodation above, rather than being covered by a single storey lean-to roof) is located to the north of the church and transept on the south side and provided space for additional minor altars and burials. Windows are proportionately small and few, the largest being in the gables. This unnecessarily compact design, most likely deriving from the urban origins of Irish friary design, coupled with the dearth of sculptural adornment, conveys a sense of austerity that has come to exemplify late Irish Gothic, especially when contrasted with the concurrent Perpendicular style in England, in which every surface bristled with carved detail.

The same austerity is associated with the typical form of gentry-house that had begun to emerge by the mid-fourteenth century. Somewhere in the region of 3,000 so-called tower houses were constructed in Ireland. These defendable towers are unevenly distributed across the country and display distinctive regional characteristics (Illustration 30). In general terms the towers are rectangular in plan, though some, especially in the east, have additional corner turrets. Their small window openings, battlemented rooflines and stout fore-works suggest a militaristic function. Towers in east

30. Tower house, Burnchurch, County Kilkenny, late fifteenth century. Photo courtesy of Rachel Moss.

Ulster and Leinster typically have a vaulted space at either ground or first floor level, apparently used as a hall, with the more private chambers above. In south Connacht and Munster numerous examples include two superimposed vaults, with the hall located on the top storey and more private chambers below. In spite of the integration of fireplaces by the early sixteenth century, some western examples continued to have an open hearth in the centre of the upper hall, maintaining what must have been a more socially democratic reception space. Visitors from overseas were particularly disparaging of the living conditions of the Irish nobility. In the mid-seventeenth century, for example, Frenchman M. de la Boullaye le Gouz wrote with dismay:

> The castles or houses of the nobility consist of four walls extremely high, thatched with straw; but to tell the truth they are nothing but square towers without windows, or at least having such small apertures as to give no more light than there is in a prison. They have little furniture, and cover their rooms with rushes, of which they make their beds in summer and of straw in winter.

This echoed the views of a German visitor, Ludolf von Münchhausen, writing about half a century earlier who also emphasised the darkness, primitive furnishings and lack of hierarchical spatial arrangement. The 'fair wind' that whistled through the hall in which he slept also left a deep impression.[26]

These descriptions do not, however, present the full picture. Many tower houses also had halls built from organic materials adjacent to them which have not survived. These were not fortified, and so are likely to have been better lit and more commodious than the adjacent stone tower, into which a family and its retinue could retreat at time of attack. The interiors of the towers are also likely to have been more comfortable than they now appear. The most impressive, and extensive, proof of this is found in the upper storey hall of the tower house at Ardamullivan, near Gort in County Galway. Conservation work during the late 1990s and early 2000s revealed a programme of wall paintings that included the figures of individual saints on its south wall, facing abbreviated scenes of the Passion of Christ on the north wall. The Passion scenes are broken up under an arcade of shell-niches, a typical Renaissance conceit. Their positioning, all above dado level, and the apparent absence of paint below this point, suggests that timber panelling may originally have been present to dado height.[27]

For those wealthiest in society, tapestries were the preferred form of decoration. As well as the practical benefits of lining walls with heavy textiles that might help to minimise draughts, tapestries were also portable, and so could be moved between the multiple residences of the elite. A consignment of household goods sent to Greencastle in County Down during the 1330s, for example, included cendal [a type of silk] curtains with cords and eighteen tapestries from the same set, a coverlet of minerver [fur] and a crimson counterpane, six cushions of green velvet with the arms of Gloucester and Dammory, five yellow tapestries of another set powdered with green parrots and scarlet roses, two old hangings of green fretted with yellow and butterflies of the same set and a pillow of scarlet cendal with a silk border and letters of pearls.[28] References to tapestries are also made in bardic poems, which intimate (allowing for poetic licence) that at least some were stitched

---

26 R. Sherlock, 'The Evolution of the Irish Tower House as a Domestic Space', *PRIA*, 111 C (2011), 115–40; T. F. Croften Croker, *The Tour of the French Traveller M. de la Boullaye le Gouz in Ireland, 1644* (London: T. and W. Boone, 1837), 40–1; D. Ó Riain-Raedel, 'A German Visitor to Monaincha in 1591', *Tipperary Historical Journal*, 22 (1998), 223–33.

27 K. Morton, 'A Spectacular Revelation: Medieval Wall Painting at Ardamullivan', *Irish Arts Review*, 18 (2002), 104–13.

28 *The Dowdall Deeds*, ed. C. McNeill and A. J. Otway-Ruthven (Dublin: IMC, 1960), 51–3.

by the lady of the house.[29] Others were almost certainly imported from continental centres of production such as Flanders, and by the second quarter of the sixteenth century, such was the demand for such luxury goods that Flemish weavers were settled in Ireland, at Kilkenny with the aid of Margaret FitzGerald, and later in Swords, County Dublin, facilitated by Sir Henry Sidney.[30] Our relatively scant evidence of the appearance of these suggests that certain patrons in Ireland were every bit as *à la mode* as their fellow Europeans. Six large tapestries purchased to decorate the lord lieutenant's house at Kilmainham and/or Dublin castle in 1588, for example, depicted 'historical' scenes from the lives of Alexander the Great, King David, Ahab and Jezebel, Jacob and two Boscages (stylised sylvan scenes).[31]

Certainly by the end of the fifteenth century evidence from wills and inventories suggests that though spartan by modern standards, the middle gentry and mercantile classes were acquiring luxury domestic items. The will of Margaret Nugent (d. 1474), widow of Sir Thomas Newbery (eight times mayor of Dublin), even included such exotica as a cup fashioned from a coconut with silver mounts.[32] For those at the higher end of society, conspicuous consumption, together with historical scholarship, book collecting and the propagation of pedigree moved to a level beyond the simple commissioning of a *seanachas* to the shaping of individuals as Godly Renaissance princes. Gerald Óg FitzGerald, ninth earl of Kildare (d. 1534), is a prime example of this. Outwardly, his sumptuous clothing and the livery of his retinue, together with the prominence of the FitzGerald crest on various religious and infrastructural buildings, conveyed a sense of wealth and munificence. At his principal seat in Maynooth, surviving inventories indicate a significant collection of plate including luxury tableware, such as a ewer made from an ostrich egg, salt cellars decorated with dragons and maidens' heads, and various pieces imported from Germany and Spain. A surviving carved stone table incorporates classical motifs that confirm a knowledge of contemporary Renaissance design, perhaps gleaned from his travels, or his substantial collection of books.

29 *Book of Magauran*, 130–9, 339–43.
30 R. Roth, 'A Register Contayning the Pedigree of the Right Honourable Thomas, Late Earl of Ormond and a Storie of his Ancestres etc., 1616'. BL Add. MS 4792, no. 47, fols 241–65. Quoted in J. Graves and G. A. Prim, *The History, Architecture and Antiquities of the Cathedral Church of St Canice, Kilkenny* (Dublin: Hodges, Smith and Company, 1857), 248; 'Sir Henry Sidney's Memoirs of his Government in Ireland', ed. H. F. Hore, *Ulster Journal of Archaeology*, 1st ser., 5 (1857), 306.
31 'FitzWilliam Manuscripts at Milton, England', ed. C. McNeill, *Analecta Hibernica*, 4 (1932), 304.
32 *Register of the Wills and Inventories of the Diocese of Dublin 1457–1483*, ed. H. F. Berry (Dublin: RSAI, 1898), 78.

The library, documented in inventories compiled in 1518 and 1526, contained Gaelic, Latin, English and French texts, which illustrated the earl's broad interests in religion, history, philosophy, poetry and chivalric romances.[33] Many of the texts were recent, printed, productions, suggesting that the earl kept himself abreast of contemporary scholarship. But among those featured in the 1518 list was a '*Psalterium deauratum in pergameno*' [gilded parchment psalter], probably the richly illuminated Book of Hours, now MS M.105 in the Pierpont Morgan collection. This manuscript had been made in Rouen *c*. 1420–5 for Sir William Porter of Lincolnshire, and so was evidently purchased by the FitzGeralds second-hand. However, as a demonstration of the family's long-held interest in the finer things in life, notice of the obits of family members going back to the fourteenth century was retrospectively inscribed into it.[34]

In the north-west of Ireland a scholarly interest in the past was evident in the patronage dispensed by Maghnus O'Donnell, but it was manifested in a different manner.[35] In 1532 Maghnus commissioned a new Life of St Columcille compiled, it was stated, from numerous old texts and translated into modern Irish by Maghnus himself. Prefaced by a full page illustration of the saint, the manuscript is now preserved in the Bodleian Library (Rawl. MS B 514). The O'Donnell family claimed collateral ancestry with the saint, so the compilation of the text was not solely an 'historical' or pious exercise, but a propagandist one, establishing the long lineage and territorial rights of the O'Donnell family. Contained within the new Life were explicit references to relics of the saint and the reliquaries that contained them, invariably in the care of the O'Donnell family. The shrine known as the 'Cathach' contained a psalter allegedly penned by the saint. According to the Life, the reliquary protected the O'Donnells and their allies during times of battle, hence the name, meaning literally 'battler' (Illustration 31). The eleventh-century sides of the shrine, replete with Scandinavian-style ornamentation and an inscription recording the commissioning of the shrine by an O'Donnell, survive as a

---

33 C. Lennon, 'The FitzGeralds of Kildare and the Building of a Dynastic Image, 1500–1630', in W. Nolan and T. McGrath (eds.), *Kildare History and Society* (Dublin: Geography Publications, 2006), 195–211; *Crown Surveys of Lands, 1540–41*, 312–14, 355–56.

34 A. Byrne, 'The Earls of Kildare and their Books at the end of the Middle Ages', *The Library*, 14:2 (2013), 129–53; M. R. James, *Catalogue of Manuscripts and Early Printed Books from the Libraries of William Morris, Richard Bennett, Bertram Fourth Earl of Ashburnham, and Other Sources* (London: J. Pierpont Morgan, 1906), 139–45.

35 B. Bradshaw, 'Manus "the Magnificent" O'Donnell as Renaissance Prince', in A. Cosgrove and D. McCartney (eds.), *Studies in Irish History presented to R. Dudley Edwards* (Dublin: University College Dublin Press, 1979), 27–35; D. Mac Eiteagáin, 'The Renaissance and the Late Medieval Lordship of Tír Chonaill, 1461–1555', in W. Nolan, L. Ronayne and M. Dunlevy (eds.), *Donegal: History and Society* (Dublin: Geography Publications, 1995), 203–28.

31. Shrine of the Cathach. Reproduced courtesy of the National Museum of Ireland.

testament to its antiquity, and long association with the family. But the front of the shrine, in common with a number of local reliquaries, was refurbished during the late fifteenth/early sixteenth century. It is dominated by a large enthroned figure, presumably Christ, holding a book, flanked by a crucifixion scene and a bishop or abbot, probably intended to represent St Columcille, together with a number of translucent semi-precious gemstones – metaphorical windows onto the relic within. A small figure of St Francis is engraved at the side of the bishop. The O'Donnells were noted patrons of the Franciscan order, both as founders of a First Order friary adjacent to their castle and port at Donegal, but also as supporters of the Third Order Regular, with at least eleven houses established across their territory of Tír Conaill from *c.* 1450. St Columcille provided spiritual protection of the area, but the Franciscans were the foot soldiers. Another relic of the saint – his cowl – was preserved at Kilmacrennan. This was a site with strong Columban associations; it also happened to be the inauguration place of the O'Donnells and the location of a house of the Franciscan Third Order, founded by Maghnus in 1537.[36]

The O'Donnells had significant political and trade links with Scotland, and it is noteworthy that certain features of the art produced in Tír Conaill and surroundings during the later medieval period have a distinctively Scottish

36 R. Gillespie, 'Relics, Reliquaries and Hagiography in South Ulster, 1450–1550', in Moss *et al.* (eds.), *Art and Devotion in Late Medieval Ireland*, 184–201; *Manus O'Donnell: The Life of St Columcille*, ed. and trans. B. Lacey (Dublin: Four Courts Press, 1998), 100, 147, 202–3.

flavour. Grave slabs from Clonca, Doe Castle and Killybegs (all County Donegal) with dense patterning of foliage and animals betray characteristics of the so-called West Highland School of sculptors, the work of whom is associated with the Western Isles and adjacent mainland during the late fifteenth and early sixteenth centuries.[37] Perhaps the closest parallels are found between a traceried canopy of a tomb at Dungiven, County Londonderry, associated with the O'Kane family, and designs in the window of Iona Abbey, reconstructed in the second half of the fifteenth century. The Scottish flavour of art produced in Ulster towards the end of the medieval period is a reminder of the increased impact of trade on Irish material culture by the early sixteenth century. Far from presenting a unified 'national' art style, different regions absorbed the influence of those with whom they did business.

New Wealth, New Patrons

In Galway, several seventeenth-century commentators noted the 'Spanish' character of the town. This was probably somewhat overstated, especially to the eyes of a Spaniard, but certainly the town did develop a unique personality with tall town houses built from the local grey limestone and richly adorned with sculpture. Many of these survive, embedded in the later fabric of the town. The centrepiece of the urban space was the church of St Nicholas, which, in 1484, had been removed from the control of the local diocese, and with papal consent had been elevated to collegiate status. Sponsored wholly by the mercantile community, over the next 100 years the church was expanded to become one of the largest parish/collegiate churches in the country. The idea was not only to provide a fitting place for the burial and remembrance of the town's key merchant families, but also to create a public building that was worthy of a town of Galway's status as a prosperous port. Augmentation of the church building was thanks to bequests from some of the leading merchant families in the town, in particular the Lynches and Joyces, whose sculpted heraldry litters window and door surrounds, together with numerous other, now unidentifiable, merchants' marks.[38]

---

37 K. A. Steer and J. W. Bannerman, *Late Medieval Monumental Sculpture in the West Highlands* (Edinburgh: Royal Commission on the Ancient and Historical Monuments of Scotland, 1977).

38 J. Hardiman, *History of the Town and County of Galway* (Dublin: W. Folds and sons, 1820), 233–53; H. G. Leask, 'The Collegiate Church of St Nicholas, Galway', *Journal of the Galway Archaeological and Historical Society*, 17 (1936), 1–23.

Elsewhere in Ireland the *esprit de corps* of mercantile oligarchies was also making its presence felt. In the early decades of the sixteenth century the merchants of Kilkenny reconstructed the walls and three of the gates of the town, together with rebuilding the tholsel in 1513. Scrutiny of the municipal records of the period reveals an increased concern with the ordered appearance of the town and the formulation of planning regulations to ensure a 'decent and civill shewe ... adding to the bewtifying of that towne'.[39] The result was a series of miniature palazzi, elegant stone dwellings of which Rothe House, constructed for merchant John Rothe in 1594, is a well-preserved example. Ground floor and basement levels were used for retail, with separate entrances at street level, while the main room for entertaining and living was lit by a large oriel window on the first floor. Along the east coast, the absence of an adjacent source of good building stone meant that building in timber predominated well into the seventeenth century. As a result, the best indication of developments in urban architecture is to be gleaned from indirect references in administrative records. The Dublin guild records, coupled with notes of admissions to the freedom of the town, demonstrate that carpenters far outnumbered masons during the period, to the extent that with the partial collapse of Christ Church Cathedral in 1562, 'foreign' masons were granted a special dispensation to come and work in the town. During the second half of the sixteenth century it is also evident from the increased numbers of glaziers and plasterers admitted that the design of houses was changing to incorporate larger windows and at least some decorative plasterwork. Surviving illustrations of a house built a little to the north in Drogheda for merchant Nicholas Bathe in *c.*1570 give a good impression of the relative complexity and architectural elegance exhibited by least some of these houses (Illustration 32).[40]

The subtle indications of urban upward mobility in the buildings of the latter part of the sixteenth century were facilitated, in part, by the freeing up of urban plots and building materials as a result of the dissolution of the monasteries in the late 1530s. With the closure of monastic houses many towns directly petitioned the crown for their precious urban sites and buildings. In Dublin, for example, the buildings and lands of All Hallows were granted to the corporation in 1538. Over the next forty years it was used as a quarry

---

39 J. Bradley, 'The Purpose of the Pale: A View from Kilkenny', in M. Potterton and T. Herron (eds.), *Dublin and the Pale in the Renaissance c.1540–1660* (Dublin: Four Courts Press, 2011), 63.

40 H. F. Berry, 'The Dublin Gild of Carpenters, Millers, Masons and Heliers in the Sixteenth Century', *JRSAI*, 35 (1905), 321–37; *CARD*, ii, 396.

MADE·BI·NICHLAS·BATHE·IN·THE·IEARE·OF·OVRE·LORD·GOD·1570·BI·HIV·MOR·CARPENTER·

32. House of Nicholas Bathe, Drogheda c.1570. © Drogheda Municipal Art Collection, Highlanes Gallery.

for building stone to repair the city walls and the corporation's chapel of St George. It accommodated a quarantined hospital during the plague of the 1570s, and subsequently a deposit for the city's sewage, before finally, in 1591, providing the site for the first university in Ireland.[41] Individuals also benefited. Buildings were purchased for their scrap value and stripped of more valuable materials, in particular glass and much sought-after large roof timbers. Monastic estates were also plundered for their hitherto carefully managed woodland – the oaks used to construct Nicholas Bathe's house at Drogheda, for example, were allegedly procured from the great forest at Mellifont. Precious, portable items such as vestments and altar plate were recycled, in some cases probably reclaimed by their donors, but in others sold on as scrap.[42]

41 CARD, i, 445; CARD, ii, 64–5, 104.
42 R. Moss, 'Reduce, Re-use, Re-cycle: Irish Monastic Architecture c.1540–1640', in R. Stalley (ed.), Irish Gothic Architecture: Construction, Destruction and Reinvention (Dublin: Wordwell, 2012), 115–60; R. Moss, 'Continuity and Change: The Material Setting of Public Worship in the Sixteenth-century Pale', in Potterton and Herron (eds.), Dublin and the Pale in the Renaissance, 201.

Traditionally, the Acts of Suppression and Church Reform are seen as heralding the end of medieval art and architecture. Certainly, with the exception of the brief respite of Marian reform, never again was the same kind of money invested in religious art, and the iconography of devotion underwent various transformations over the following decades. With the exception of necessary repairs to cathedrals and the erection and adornment of private chapels, little was to be expended on religious architecture until the eighteenth century, by which time its character had changed utterly. Conversely though, domestic architecture, and the purchase of increasingly less utilitarian furnishings, appears to have flourished. The greater diversity of tradesmen engaged in construction has been noted in Dublin at this time, and is echoed too in the relatively large number of goldsmiths operating there during the latter part of the century. Like the Anglo-Norman invasion, this traditional end point should rather be seen as a catalyst for changes already in train. Whereas previously the Church and personal devotion had provided the predominant channel for artistic creativity in Ireland, by the mid-sixteenth century it had begun to shift more firmly in the direction of the individual and the body politic.[43]

43 H. F. Berry, 'The Goldsmiths' Company of Dublin', *JRSAI*, 31 (1901), 119–33.

18

The Onset of Religious Reform: 1460–1550

MARY ANN LYONS

WITHIN Northern Europe, Church organisation, devotional life and responses to religious reform in the late medieval and Reformation eras were far from uniform. The distinctive religious culture of late medieval Ireland, which was neither the idolatry dismissed by Protestant reformers nor the Catholicism of the Catholic Reformation, was fundamentally shaped by local circumstances and consequently found expression in very different forms and attitudes. A pronounced contrast can be identified between English and Gaelic districts, and it is within that framework that the changing nature of religion in Ireland during the period *c*.1460–*c*.1550 is best understood.[1]

Decay and Renewal

In colonised parts of the island the episcopacy failed to provide dynamic, reforming leadership during the early 1500s, partly because the nomination of bishops was the king's prerogative and those appointed to sees in the colonial heartland were expected to double as secular administrators. There were, of course, several prelates, including archbishops of Armagh, who were conscientious pastors and spiritual directors, conducting regular visitations and convening synods prescribing reforms. In Kildare diocese, Bishop Edmund Lane (1482–*c*.1522) restored St Brigid's Cathedral in Kildare, and reorganised the diocesan chapter, while Walter Wellesley (1529–39), an accomplished theologian,

---

1 D. MacCulloch, *Reformation: Europe's House Divided, 1490–1700* (London and New York: Allen Lane, 2003), 15; D. MacCulloch, 'England', in A. Pettegree (ed.), *The Early Reformation in Europe* (Cambridge University Press, 2002), 166–87; N. Tanner, *The Ages of Faith: Popular Religion in Late Medieval England and Western Europe* (London: I.B. Tauris, 2008), 54–7; F. Heal, *Reformation in Britain and Ireland* (Oxford University Press, 2003); W. I. P. Hazlett, *The Reformation in Britain and Ireland: An Introduction* (London & New York: T. & T. Clark, 2003).

was commended for his diocesan management.[2] Yet, even in the most anglicised dioceses, the bishops' control over clerical appointments and standards of pastoral service was significantly curtailed as the right to nominate clergy to more than half the benefices lay in the hands of monastic houses, cathedral chapters, lay people and corporations. Attracting suitably qualified clergy also proved challenging. Since Ireland had no university and up to two-thirds of benefices in English regions offered mere subsistence incomes of approximately £7 10s. a year, many parishes had poorly trained, badly paid priests capable of little more than a basic administration of the sacraments.

Yet, as Jefferies has shown, there is evidence that in certain dioceses, such as Armagh, the laity were satisfied with their priests' ministry.[3] Moreover, not all parishes were poor and some clearly had exceptional clerics. John Collyn (d. 1484), dean of Waterford Cathedral (1441–80), wrote at least one book (*De Sacramentis et de Arte Moriendi*), founded the chantry of St Saviour in Waterford city in 1468, raised funds to build a chantry chapel in the cathedral, and, in 1478, established a hospice to cater for twelve elderly people. The most tangible testimony to the diligence of a great many parish clergy and the support of their congregations in English districts is the significant number of churches that were newly built, extended or renovated in the decades immediately prior to the Henrician Reformation. As late as the 1530s, at least six houses (St Mary's and Christ Church in Dublin city, Grace Dieu, a convent girls' school in north Dublin, Greatconnell in County Kildare, and Kells and Jerpoint in County Kilkenny) were commended by the Irish council for their educational and social services.[4]

On the other hand, the decline in the number of new entrants to novitiates – with the exception of the Franciscans and Dominicans – can be viewed as a manifestation of a more general malaise that was steadily undermining most of the older religious orders across Western Europe – what Bradshaw termed 'the cancer of secularism'.[5] This found expression in

2 H. A. Jefferies, *Priests and Prelates of Armagh in the Age of Reformations, 1518–1588* (Dublin: Four Courts Press, 1997), part I; M. A. Lyons, *Church and Society in County Kildare c.1470–1547* (Dublin: Four Courts Press, 2000), 68–9, 99–103.

3 C. Lennon, *Sixteenth-Century Ireland: The Incomplete Conquest*. 2nd edn (Dublin: Gill & Macmillan, 2005), 120; H. A. Jefferies, *The Irish Church and the Tudor Reformations* (Dublin: Four Courts Press, 2010), 33–5, 64.

4 E. McEneaney, 'Politics and the Art of Devotion in Late Fifteenth-Century Waterford', in Moss *et al.* (eds.), *Art and Devotion in Late Medieval Ireland*, 38–9; *The Register of St Saviour's Chantry of Waterford*, ed. N. Byrne and M. Byrne (Dublin: IMC, 2013).

5 B. Bradshaw, *The Dissolution of the Religious Orders in Ireland under Henry VIII* (Cambridge University Press, 1974), 35–6; MacCulloch, *Reformation*, 89–90; Hazlett, *Reformation*, 93; E. Cameron, *The European Reformation* (Oxford University Press, 2013), 65.

a range of guises: lapsed observance of Christian asceticism, monastic piety and order rules; reduced provision of education, hospitality and alms for the poor; either lack of interest in tending to the physical maintenance of the house, or a growing fixation with asset acquisition; and a drive to appropriate the right of presentation to more and more parish benefices. In the absence of central supervision within dioceses or congregations, local families routinely supplied leading members of monastic communities and the houses were at liberty to pursue commercial interests, often in conjunction with influential laity. Enterprising abbots ran lucrative businesses, among them the Cistercian abbot of Graiguenamanagh who raised money by pawning the abbey's books and chalices. Property-rich monasteries served as joint stock enterprises for lay and clerical investors. So extensive was their property portfolio that almost 20 per cent of land in County Dublin was owned by religious orders at the time of the dissolution campaign (1539–40). As Jefferies has emphasised, secularisation was to the detriment not only of the houses themselves but also of religious practice in parishes, since these same houses held the right to present clergy to a substantial proportion of benefices in English dioceses, and many monastic churches also functioned as parish churches. In general, heads of these orders showed little concern for the quality of pastoral care provided by their appointees in these parishes and appropriated most of the parish revenues for their own use.[6]

Yet, Christian asceticism and monastic piety were far from entirely absent in English districts. They were to be found in the surviving tradition of anchoritism, and in the mendicant orders – 'the most fragrant bloom among fetid vegetation'.[7] This was particularly the case with those Franciscan, Augustinian, Dominican and, to a lesser extent, Carmelite friars who, through their adherence to the thriving Observant reform movement, were reinvigorated by a return to their founders' rules. Such clerics enthusiastically embraced one of the most vibrant intellectually driven reform currents in late medieval Western Catholicism. Although the Observant movement had less impact in English districts than in Gaelic areas, several long-established communities in towns, particularly Franciscans, became Observant. The friars, who were widely respected, also engaged with the laity in rural areas through their occasional questing visits and alms-seeking missions.[8]

6 P. J. Corish, *The Irish Catholic Experience: A Historical Survey* (Dublin: Gill & Macmillan, 1985), 55; Lennon, *Sixteenth-Century Ireland*, 122–3; Jefferies, *Irish Church*, 36.
7 Lennon, *Sixteenth-Century Ireland*, 119.
8 MacCulloch, *Reformation*, 89; Heal, *Reformation*, 55–7; Ó Clabaigh, *Friars in Ireland*.

Even more than was the case in English areas, in Gaelic Ireland political, social, economic and Church affairs were inextricably intertwined, giving rise to distinct structures, practices and attitudes. These evolved in the absence of effective enforcement by the English crown of limits on papal appointments, and were facilitated by Rome's readiness to tolerate practices such as clerical marriage and illegitimate succession among the Irish clergy. Like their counterparts in English districts, the Gaelic episcopate comprised a diverse group. Individuals can be identified who were assiduous in tending to the spiritual needs of their congregations, among them Thomas MacBrady [Mac Brádaig], bishop of Kilmore (1480–1511), who was saluted by the Four Masters as 'a luminous lamp that enlightened the laity and clergy by instruction and preaching'. However, since bishops could only function with the support of the local secular ruler, many immersed themselves in political and economic pursuits, themselves becoming secular lords. Thus, both William O'Farrell [Ó Feargall] of Ardagh (1480–1516) and Richard Barret of Killala (1513–44) combined episcopal office with the roles of secular lord and chief of their name.[9]

The Church in Gaelic Ireland also had distinctive structural features. In the provinces of Armagh and Tuam, ecclesiastical organisation centred on coarbs and erenaghs, traditional officer-holders in the Gaelic Church. Episcopally confirmed, these men, elected to the headship of the septs in which those offices were vested, linked hereditary clerical families with congregations who worshipped in local churches. In contrast to colonised parts of the island, most of Britain, and Western Europe in general, the distinctive feature of the priesthood of all ranks in late medieval Gaelic areas was its strongly hereditary character. Individuals such as John O'Grady [Ó Gráda], archbishop of Cashel (1332–45), and Maurice Maguire [Mág Uidir], archdeacon of Clogher and rector of Aghalurcher (d. 1423), founded large clerical dynasties that retained prominent diocesan and monastic offices well into the sixteenth century. Clerical marriage and hereditary succession to Church offices in fifteenth-century Gaelic Ireland were facilitated by the papacy's acceptance of both, and by the Curia's liberal granting of dispensations to sons of clergy to hold Church offices from which they were technically debarred on grounds of illegitimate birth. Gaelic Ireland was not exceptional in this regard as civil marriage was also common among the secular clergy in much of Scotland and Wales. Although clerical marriage was strictly forbidden by the Church, the failure

---

9 *AFM*, v, 1309; Lennon, *Sixteenth-Century Ireland*, 127.

of successive provincial synods to suppress the practice suggests that concubinage contracts were culturally acceptable at all levels of Gaelic society.[10]

The life of Cathal Óc MacManus Maguire (d. 1498) is emblematic of this distinctive relationship between Christianity and Gaelic Irish society. Maguire was a notable pluralist, simultaneously holding the offices of dean of Lough Erne, canon choral of both Armagh and Clogher, and parson of Inishkeen. He was married and had more than a dozen children, some of whom were certainly born after he had acquired these offices. The annalist's commendation of Maguire not only for his learning and hospitality, but as a 'gem of purity … [a] dove of heart and [a] turtle for chastity' may appear incongruous to modern readers. However, it reveals the worldview and moral lens through which Church personnel and their conduct were mediated, tolerated, accepted and at times even applauded by Gaelic society. The force of this worldview, and its efficacy in stifling attempts to reform the clergy, is evident in the case of another senior Gaelic cleric, Lochlann or Laurence O'Gallagher [Ó Gallchobhair] II, bishop of Raphoe (1442–78), the grandson of a former bishop and himself the father of at least seven sons (of whom four held benefices). Despite being denounced in 1469 for various offences (notably fornication) and suspended, he had little difficulty in securing either absolution from his metropolitan, John Bole of Armagh, or acquittal by a Roman court (1476).[11]

Ecclesiastical heredity resulted in serious disputes between clergy of various ranks in which the papacy occasionally played a complicit role. After the murder in 1461 of Bishop O'Connell [Ó Coineóil] of Killala by the sons of the late archdeacon, who had been a member of the local O'Dowd [Ó Dubhda] clan, one of the sons secured papal rehabilitation on the grounds that he and his brother had not intended to kill the bishop but only to steal his horses. In 1476 Dean O'Mohan of Elphin was killed in a dispute over the deanery. During another row between William Roche (coadjutor) and Gerald FitzGerald (bishop) in 1484 over the unification of the dioceses of Cork and Cloyne, Roche and his five sons led an army that sacked and burned the town of Cloyne. Even on the gaelicised fringes of the Pale, the bishop of Leighlin, Maurice Doran [Ó Deóradháin], was murdered in 1525 by his archdeacon,

---

10 K. Simms, 'Frontiers in the Irish Church – Regional and Cultural', in Barry *et al.* (eds.), *Colony and Frontier in Medieval Ireland*, 177–200; *CPL*, vols. xii–xviii; Heal, *Reformation*, 77. In 1447–92, 578 dispensations were granted for Ireland and Scotland compared with only eight for England, though Heal considers the latter unconvincingly low. Lennon, *Sixteenth-Century Ireland*, 127–8.

11 *AU*, iii, 429; Nicholls, *Gaelic and Gaelicized Ireland*, 98.

Maurice Kavanagh [Cáemánach], because he had chastised Kavanagh and warned him to improve his conduct.[12] As a result of warfare among clergy and their involvement in the conflicts of the laity, by the late fifteenth century there was a manifest disregard for the privileges of sanctuary and immunity claimed by the Church for its personnel and its possessions. This was the case throughout the island, but was a particular issue in Gaelic-controlled areas. Compared with the rest of the British Isles, the situation in Ireland was extreme.[13]

While Ireland's relative poverty guaranteed it immunity from one negative aspect of papal provision – the appointment of absentees – Rome's indiscriminate granting of the right to provide clergy to benefices led to an abuse which would have far-reaching consequences for the Church and for religious practice, especially in Gaelic regions. In response to mounting pressure for greater lay control in Church affairs, during the second half of the fifteenth and into the sixteenth century it became common for Rome to grant provisions to members of influential families who were barely in minor orders or, in some cases, still lay men who had declared their intention to take orders; once appointed, it was virtually impossible to have them removed.[14]

Pastoral care in Gaelic Ireland was hampered by the disorganisation and poverty of the ecclesiastical infrastructure. In contrast to the system of small, compact and relatively well-endowed parishes of the colonised east and south, and in common with the North of England, many parishes in the north and west of Ireland were large, fragmented, and often included contested boundaries which gave rise to disputes over the appropriation of payments such as tithes. As in many isolated parts of England and Scotland, large rural parishes in Gaelic districts of Ireland had numerous chapels of ease and no resident chaplains.[15] Even more so than in English areas, recruiting suitably qualified, conscientious clergy to minister in these inhospitable, poorly endowed parishes proved exceptionally challenging. As was the case with the majority of parish clergy in England, most Gaelic clerics gained their education 'according to the custom of the country' in local schools or more rarely at Oxford, Paris or Louvain. Appointments were also frequently overturned when local

12 Cameron, *European Reformation*, 62; Nicholls, *Gaelic and Gaelicized Ireland*, 101; Lyons, *Church and Society*, 57.
13 Heal, *Reformation*, 93–4; S. A. Meigs, *The Reformations in Ireland: Tradition and Confessionalism, 1400–1690* (Dublin: Gill & Macmillan, 1997), 42–5.
14 Nicholls, *Gaelic and Gaelicized Ireland*, 105.
15 MacCulloch, 'England', 177–8; Jefferies, *Priests and Prelates*, 20, 64–5; Heale, *Reformation*, 83–6; G. W. Bernard, *The Late Medieval English Church: Vitality and Vulnerability before the Break with Rome* (New Haven and London: Yale University Press, 2012), 71–2.

bishops' wishes and jurisdictions were overridden by papal provisions to benefices. Responsibility for the cure of souls typically fell to a poorly paid vicar. Some clerics alienated sections of Church land to supplement their inadequate income, while many sought papal sanction for holding two or more benefices (a practice also common in England). Others engaged in commerce or the professions, for example, teaching in local schools.[16] 'Rome-runners' seeking offices denounced sitting benefice-holders (mostly vicars) for not being ordained to the priesthood and for leaving their parishioners without a cleric to administer the sacraments. Their inherently biased testimonies convey an impression that is being challenged by evidence uncovered in recent scholarship, notably that of Henry Jefferies.[17]

If by 1400 the spiritual dynamism of the older religious orders in Ireland in general had waned, by 1500 the Cistercians in particular were in crisis. Matthew Ryan, abbot of Holy Cross in Tipperary, had grown rich through trading in wine and was, according to Corish, often his own best customer.[18] In 1498 John Troy, abbot of Mellifont, Louth, reported to the general chapter that only in Mellifont and Dublin was the Cistercian rule kept or even the habit worn. Mirroring patterns within diocesan circles, hereditary succession to abbatial appointments occurred with families such as the MacDavids, providing abbots of both Boyle and Mellifont abbeys during the fifteenth century.[19] Several Gaelic abbots were powerful secular rulers. Ruaidrí MacDermott [Mac Diarmada] (d. 1568), abbot of the Premonstratensians of Lough Key in Roscommon for sixty years, was also ruling lord of Moylurg: the Annals of Loch Cé eulogised him as a model Irish chief, praising his military exploits and plundering expeditions. In other ways, too, MacDermott exemplified advanced secularisation of the monastic order in Ireland. Married to a daughter of the lord of Clanrickard, he was succeeded at the abbey by his son, Brian. In this, he was by no means unique: the last abbots of Lisgoole in Fermanagh were Maguires who held the position by papal provision for three generations down to 1603. By the early sixteenth century there was a mercenary quality to the dealings of lay and clerical families with the monasteries, evident in the pluralism of individual religious such as Prior Glaisne Magennis [Mac Aengusa] in Iveagh (Down) who held three separate

---

16 Nicholls, *Gaelic and Gaelicized Ireland*, 99; Lennon, *Sixteenth-Century Ireland*, 129–30; Bernard, *Late Medieval English Church*, 72, 76–7.
17 *CPL*, vols. xii–xviii; Jefferies, *Irish Church*, 32.
18 In Scotland, by contrast, the Cistercians had a period of sustained renewal: Heal, *Reformation*, 49. Corish, *Irish Catholic Experience*, 55.
19 Lennon, *Sixteenth-Century Ireland*, 130–1.

priorships during the 1520s, and in simoniacal deals, such as the transfer by Abbot William O'Dwyer [Ó Duibhidhir] of Holy Cross abbey to a layman in 1534. As Colm Lennon has concluded, 'the strong impression one gets of the monastic establishment on the eve of the Reformation is that there was not much left to reform'.[20]

The Observant Movement and Lay Spirituality

The emergence in Ireland of the Observant movement within the mendicant orders in the late 1300s connected Irish friars and by extension the laity to whom they ministered with the most vibrant reform current in the late medieval Church. Unlike their forerunners and their continental contemporaries, these Observant friars, whose numbers swelled as the fifteenth century progressed, were mostly rural-based, drawn by the prospect of living their ascetic Christian life in modestly endowed houses and depending upon alms. The west and north of Ireland proved especially appealing for the new Observant foundations. Of the ninety new Dominican, Augustinian and Franciscan foundations which sprang up between 1400 and 1508, sixty-eight were in the provinces of Armagh and Tuam.[21] While all of these Observant mendicants attracted widespread following and substantial patronage among the laity, the Franciscans proved exceptionally popular. Active since the 1410s, their presence grew to the point that they established an Irish Observant vicariate in 1460 – a significant landmark in the history of religion in Ireland. Key to their success was their promotion of the 'Third Order' among their lay followers.[22] Originally intended for pious lay people influenced by the *Devotio Moderna* movement, the Third Order or Tertiary Rule also provided the canonical basis for communities of professed religious. Between 1426 and 1540, forty-nine communities of Franciscan tertiaries (and one of Dominicans) were established. These Third Order houses were concentrated in Connacht and Ulster, where their members engaged in pastoral and educational work. A vital reason for the remarkable popularity of the Franciscan movement was the fact that, uniquely, it addressed the religious enthusiasm of women: as part of the reform movement, a Franciscan nunnery, probably a Third Order foundation, was established in Galway city in 1511.[23] The Observants

20 *ALC*, ii, 397–405; Nicholls, *Gaelic and Gaelicized Ireland*, 109; Lennon, *Sixteenth-Century Ireland*, 131.
21 Lennon, *Sixteenth-Century Ireland*, 130.
22 Ó Clabaigh, *Friars in Ireland*, 302; Cameron, *European Reformation*, 48–9; MacCulloch, *Reformation*, 89; Heale, *Reformation*, 55.
23 Hall, *Women and the Church*, 91.

supplemented the work of parish clergy and were held in high esteem by the laity as confessors, preachers and moral authorities. Particularly renowned for their preaching on core elements of Christianity (namely the Eucharist, worthy reception of communion, frequent confession, good living, the life of Christ, the afterlife, purgatory, and intercession of saints especially the Virgin Mary), they were vital in providing catechesis and direction in devotional practice which were otherwise largely absent. Furthermore, through their reforming zeal and leadership, they absorbed some of the old ecclesiastical dynasties within their communities, demonstrating their compatibility with Gaelic social structures. They also spanned the politico-cultural divide, bringing together brethren of Gaelic Irish and settler origins. In addition, the Franciscans in particular exercised profound influence on lay religious practices and devotional art throughout much of Ireland in this period.[24]

The steady growth of lay influence over the Church and spiritual life, notably during the fifteenth and early sixteenth centuries, may be regarded as the most significant development in the history of religion not only in Ireland but throughout Western Europe in this period, and led to what Adrian Empey has termed 'a fundamental shift in the Church's centre of gravity'. Until recently appreciation of the magnitude of that shift has suffered on account of its proximity to the Reformation. Whilst inevitably influenced by the peculiarities of English and Gaelic society and Church organisation, the laity in Ireland, in line with contemporaries elsewhere in Europe, participated in a culture of piety that teemed with stylised rituals, time-honoured traditions and beliefs, pageantry, formulaic devotions, and a rich and diverse array of sacred and venerated objects, images and spaces. The spate of lay-sponsored parish church building, renovation and ornamentation, the sponsorship of new Observant foundations, the enthusiastic embrace of the Franciscan Third Order, the establishment of an array of lay confraternities, religious guilds and chantries, investment in funerals and funerary monuments, the symbiotic relationship between civic and religious life in cities and towns, and the popularity of pilgrimage, alms-giving, fasting and contemporary devotional and hagiographical literature, all attest to Ireland's participation in a wider European phenomenon.[25]

24 Ó Clabaigh, *Friars in Ireland*, 285–94; C. Ó Clabaigh, 'The Other Christ: The Cult of St Francis of Assisi in Late Medieval Ireland', in Moss *et al.* (eds.), *Art and Devotion in Late Medieval Ireland*, 162. For a useful survey of scholarship on the vigour of religious life in Ireland in this period, see Jefferies, *Irish Church*, 15–22.

25 C. A. Empey, 'The Layperson in the Parish: The Medieval Inheritance, 1169–1536', in R. Gillespie and W. G. Neely (eds.), *The Laity and the Church of Ireland, 1000–2000: All Sorts and Conditions* (Dublin: Four Courts Press, 2002), 46–7; E. Duffy, *The Stripping of*

Spirituality in late medieval and early modern Europe was not an abstract notion. The liturgy and sacraments provided spectacle, instruction, and a communal context for lay piety and devotion while the rite of marriage had important additional social and legal ramifications. Furthermore, ideas about God and salvation took material, concrete forms. Religious imagery and artefacts played a central role in lay piety. The dark, candle-lit setting of St Werburgh's church in Dublin closely resembled contemporary equivalents in England in that it was adorned with an image of the patron saint, had dedicated side chapels containing images of Mary and St Martin, included a roof beam that supported a great crucifix with figures of Mary and St John on either side, and was home to an Easter sepulchre light that burned in the chancel.[26] As elsewhere in Europe, relics of saints in Ireland were revered as tangible links between the earthly and heavenly worlds and were regarded as direct sources of supernatural power that could be channelled to affect daily lives – hence their use for social and political purposes ranging from swearing oaths to enhancing the fertility of land and protection in battle. The enduring popularity of shrines is illustrated by the commissioning of a new one, to St Caillín of Fenagh, in south-west Ulster, as late as 1536. The relics at Christ Church Cathedral, Dublin, drew significant numbers of pilgrims from across Ireland in the later Middle Ages, while in Gaelic areas there was a strong tradition of pilgrimage to holy sites such as wells, altars within churches, but also to prominent features of the landscape such as mountains and springs that had been the focus of pre-Christian devotion.[27]

Such visits were undertaken either as a public expression of personal piety or as penance for sins. Heneas McNichaill, for example, visited a series of venerated sites in 1541 as penance for strangling his son. Croagh Patrick in Mayo, St Patrick's Purgatory in Donegal, and to a lesser extent, Mount Brandon in Kerry and Truell in Down, were among the most popular sites. The cult of St Patrick's Purgatory, circulated widely in a rich literature that typically focused on the visions experienced by penitents, drew pilgrims from as far afield as France, Hungary, Italy and the Low Countries. Reflecting

the Altars: Traditional Religion in England, c.1400–c.1580 (New Haven and London: Yale University Press, 1992); Bernard, *Late Medieval English Church*; MacCulloch, *Reformation*, ch. 1; J. L. Halverson (ed.), *Contesting Christendom: Readings in Medieval Religion and Culture* (Lanham & Plymouth: Rowman and Littlefield, 2008), pt iv.
26 C. Walker Bynum, *Christian Materiality: An Essay on Religion in Late Medieval Europe* (New York: Zone Books, 2011); Empey, 'Layperson in the Parish', 28–9; Duffy, *Stripping of the Altars*.
27 R. Gillespie, 'Relics, Reliquaries and Hagiography in South Ulster, 1450–1550', in Moss et al. (eds.), *Art and Devotion in Late Medieval Ireland*, 184–201.

contemporary practice in Britain and continental Europe, Christ Church Cathedral in Dublin, together with many churches and monasteries throughout Ireland, held lucrative licences for special indulgences granted to pilgrims and penitents who visited their relics and altars on specific days. Miraculous statues, too, were actively promoted and generated significant revenue from pilgrims. As elsewhere, Marian devotion was strong, with statues of Mary at Navan and Trim being popular with women.[28] There was also a longstanding tradition of pilgrimage from Ireland to the most popular sites abroad – Santiago de Compostela, Rome or, more rarely, Jerusalem. The popularity of the Spanish site among the laity is borne out by the fact that a single ship carrying 400 pilgrims from Ireland returned from Santiago in 1473.[29]

Devotional works were important features of lay piety throughout Ireland, as they were throughout the Christian West. The library of Ireland's leading magnates, Gerald fitz Thomas FitzGerald (Gearóid Mór) (d. 1513), eighth earl of Kildare, and of his son, Gerald (Gearóid Óg) (d. 1534), offers a glimpse of the religious material owned by educated aristocrats in the Pale. Almost all of the earls' religious texts were in Irish. Among the ninth earl's collection were the Psalter of Cashel, the prophecies of St Berehan, the lives of various saints, the Bible, the New Testament, and the Works of Sts Anthony, Gregory, Jerome and Augustine. That his reading material also included 'The king of England's answer to Luther' and 'Sir Thomas More's book against the opinions that hold against pilgrimages' proves that he was closely following unfolding developments in continental Europe and England.[30] Original Gaelic religious prose had died by the fifteenth century. In its place there were several translations of standard works of popular medieval piety, many with a strong Franciscan influence, together with the work of religious poets such as the friar Pilib Bocht Ó hUiginn (d. 1487), acclaimed in the Annals of Ulster as 'the best and greatest religious poet in these latter times'.[31] In step with their European contemporaries, Gaelic congregations were accustomed to emotionally charged hellfire sermons and inspiring accounts of the lives of Christ and the saints. We get a glimpse of the devotional world of a Gaelic Irish woman in the 'Book of piety' commissioned by Máire Ní Mháille (d. 1522), wife of Ruaidri Mac Suibhne Fanad, a Donegal nobleman, which exuded

---

28 Moss (ed.), *Art and Architecture of Ireland*, 17–18, 191–2, 280; *Christ Church Deeds*, ed. M. J. McEnery and R. Refaussé (Dublin: Four Courts Press, 2001), no. 312; Bernard, *Late Medieval English Church*, 137, 141–2; Hall, *Women and the Church*, 29.
29 McEneaney, 'Politics and Devotion', 35, 37; Hall, *Women and the Church*, 29–30.
30 Lyons, *Church and Society*, 50, 85–6.
31 *AU*, iii, 317.

devotion *à la mode*. It featured the story of the finding of the True Cross by St Helena, an Irish version of the popular Latin Life of Mary, and the Harrowing of Hell text – all standard material possessed by the late medieval European devotee. The growing popularity among the laity of the cult of local saints is evident in Máire's possession of Lives of Patrick, Colum Cille, Catherine of Alexandria and Margaret. Máire's book also contained instruction on how to live a good life, make a good confession and attain salvation, together with bardic religious poems which served as an extension of Church sermons that could be read and reflected upon at home.[32]

That the Observant movement breathed fresh life into pious devotion in late medieval Ireland is evident in the devotion of Gaelic figures such as Máire Ní Mháille [Ó Malley] and in the presence in Ireland of recently printed works from continental Europe at a time when there was no printing in Ireland (pre-1551). The friars' library collection at Youghal contained the earliest printed edition of St Francis's writings which had recently appeared in the *Speculum minorum* (Rouen, 1509). Through their manuscript and printed material, the Franciscans also fostered throughout Ireland the cults of continental saints such as St Louis of Toulouse, St Anthony of Padua, St Louis IX, king of France, and St Elizabeth of Hungary. Each of these also features in statuary from this period. In addition, the friars at Kilcrea friary in Cork were generating illuminated books (including religious miscellanies) for secular clients in the mid-1470s.[33]

From the mid-fifteenth century to the eve of the Henrician Reformation the Church in Ireland enjoyed a remarkable and sustained period of lay benefaction. This reflected the Lordship's growing prosperity and political stability. Particularly wealthy lay individuals or couples built new parish churches in their localities. Others, of whom the most enthusiastic were the earls of Desmond and Kildare, invested in endowment of personal chantries. Thomas, seventh earl of Desmond founded a chantry college at Youghal (1464), while in 1518 Gerald, ninth earl of Kildare established a chantry college at his seat of Maynooth. In 1521 he also rebuilt the church of St Mary, which had served as the castle chapel, to accommodate the college priests, clerks and three choristers charged with celebrating Mass for the salvation of his soul, those of his

32 S. Ryan, 'Windows on Late Medieval Devotional Practice: Máire Ní Mháille's "Book of Piety" (1513)', in Moss *et al.* (eds.), *Art and Devotion in Late Medieval Ireland*, 2, 14; E. Duffy, 'Elite and Popular Religion: The Book of Hours and Lay Piety in the Later Middle Ages', in K. Cooper and J. Gregory (eds.), *Elite and Popular Religion* (Woodbridge: Boydell Press, 2006), 140–61; Heale, *Reformation*, 106–8.
33 Ó Clabaigh, 'The Other Christ', 146, 152–3; Moss (ed.), *Art and Architecture of Ireland*, 209.

family and all the dead. Beyond the Pale, in those areas where the Observant Franciscan friars were especially popular, they were the beneficiaries of often lavish bequests. At Adare in Limerick, Thomas FitzGerald, seventh earl of Kildare, and his wife, Joan, founded an Observant Franciscan friary in 1464 and donated all of the glass, a bell and two silver chalices. The O'Donnell lords of Tyrconnell, too, were especially generous: in 1474 Aed O'Donnell and his wife, Fionnuala O'Brien, established an Observant friary at Donegal which they supplied with plate, and where all principal members of the family were interred. They and families allied to them also funded several Franciscan Third Order regular houses across Tyrconnell. Margaret O'Brien, wife of Eoghan O'Rourke [Ó Ruairc] (d. 1512), like many Gaelic women, was particularly drawn to Observant Franciscan spirituality. In the only recorded instance of a woman being principal patron of a friary, she sponsored the construction of a wooden Observant Franciscan friary church at Creevelea (Dromahair) in Leitrim.[34]

The symbiotic relationship between civic and religious life that existed in urban centres across Britain and Western Europe in this period was most evident in Ireland in Dublin, Waterford, Kilkenny and Galway. In these places city life was consciously synchronised with the Church's calendar, with civic days and fairs falling on holy days. In common with English cities such as York, Kilkenny and Dublin had many craft guilds which staged mystery plays on special feasts, notably Corpus Christi, St George's Day and St Stephen's Day. That religious guilds remained popular with the laity is suggested by the fact that two of Dublin city and county's eleven religious guilds were established in this period – St Mary's in the church of St Nicholas Within (est. 1470) and the Blessed Virgin Mary and St Sythe (est. 1476). As late as 1534, confraternities were still being created. Lay confraternities were less popular in Gaelic areas, most likely because the strength of kinship ties pre-empted the creation of artificial ones and because the confraternal impulse was more commonly channelled into the Franciscan Third Order Secular.[35]

Underpinning all of this religious sentiment and observance were three priorities: maximising one's prospects of salvation; enhancing existing provisions for the 'increase of divine service'; and legitimating and reminding others of one's privileged position in society, however modest that might be.

---

34 Moss (ed.), *Art and Architecture of Ireland*, 164, 177, 206, 210, 486, 489; Ó Clabaigh, *Friars in Ireland*, 70.

35 M. Clark and R. Refaussé (eds.), *Directory of Historic Dublin Guilds* (Dublin: Dublin Public Libraries, 1993), 44–5, 32–40; Lennon, *Sixteenth-Century Ireland*, 133; Jefferies, *Church in Ireland*, 62.

A preoccupation with dying well prompted Christians in all quarters of Ireland to take steps to ensure that they expired in an optimal state of grace and had a good Christian burial. As Margaret Murphy has shown, according to their means many lay men and women throughout their lives made provision for their salvation through donations of money, missals and chalices to churches and priests on the understanding that this was 'to serve God and their souls'. Others left it until the deathbed to make arrangements to ensure that those coming after them prayed for their salvation. Having a well-lit funeral was a priority, as it was generally believed that to multiply candles was to multiply the soul's chances of salvation. Good hospitality was also important as in addition to its social function, it had a widely recognised spiritual function since the larger the crowd, the more prayers were recited. The lure of free food and alcohol was very strong for the poor, whose prayers were believed to be especially potent. Thus, in 1488, Thomas Bermingham, lord of Athenry, and his wife gave eighteen milch cows, wheat, meat, wine and other beverages for the sustenance of the poor and the religious at Athenry monastery for eight days after the burial of their son, John.[36]

Lay benefactors were preoccupied with optimising the impact of their generosity. The priorities were to ensure the maximum possible spread of donations and investment in intercessors, the greatest longevity for endowment, such as celebration of Masses, optimum visibility for the distribution of bequests, and placing as many reminders as possible in well-appointed public places so that future generations might be frequently prompted to pray for the salvation of the deceased's soul. The sound legal foundations of the Guild of St Anne's, Dublin (est. 1430) proved indispensable in enabling it to continue to fulfil its foundational brief of praying for the salvation of its founders well beyond the onset of religious reform in the mid-sixteenth century. In both Gaelic and English areas individuals sponsored the erection or maintenance of a church belfry in the hope that the call to prayer would inspire the community to remember the deceased. Others left items for use and display in their church. Sir Christopher Plunkett, Lord Dunsany (d. 1462), bequeathed to the local parish church which he founded in Meath altar vessels including a cross, two censers and a chalice, a cope of gold, two chasubles (one gold and one red satin), a chaplet (prayer beads) of pearls to adorn the statue of Mary, and sixteen service books which, through their frequent use, were to remind

---

36 M. Murphy, 'The High Cost of Dying: An Analysis of *pro anima* Bequests in Medieval Dublin', in W. J. Shiels and D. Wood (eds.), *The Church and Wealth: Studies in Church History, 24* (Oxford: Blackwell, 1987), 111–22; S. Leigh Fry, *Burial in Medieval Ireland, 900–1500* (Dublin: Four Courts Press, 1999), 93–4.

his parish congregation to pray for his soul. Less well-off testators, particularly women, conformed to the contemporary pattern of leaving personal or domestic possessions that could be converted to liturgical use. A cup from the deceased's house could be used as a chalice holding the blood of Christ; a robe might adorn a statue of the Blessed Virgin Mary; one's best bed linen might serve to cover the altar.[37]

In designing their funerary monuments, some individuals made provisions for indulgences to incentivise the living to visit their graves. A growing preoccupation with the afterlife is also evident in the increasingly common practice of depicting saints and apostles on the tombs of the laity in the south-east from the 1480s onwards. These figures acted both as protectors and as a mnemonic to the living in their prayers for the souls of the dead. In Kildare, Kilkenny and Tipperary, aristocratic and gentry couples such as the FitzEustaces, Purcells and Butlers, like their peers in England and in Gaelic regions, preferred interment away from their parish communities, often within the secluded precincts of friaries of which they were benefactors. However, there is evidence that the middle- and lower-ranking laity in English districts at least had a strong sense of identification with the local parish, the parish community, monastic houses within the parish, and in many cases, the parish church. A significant proportion of lay people in Counties Dublin and Meath, for example, opted for a form of burial that was 'public and communitarian', typically with their family and within the familiar surrounds of their cathedral, or parish church, or adjoining cemetery. Those wealthy enough to endow a chantry were usually interred in the associated chapel. Others, depending on how much they could pay, were interred in the centre of the chancel (a very rare privilege), in the nave, in the sacristy, under the church tower, in the church porch, in the church walls or in the parish cemetery. Throughout Ireland and especially in Gaelic areas, lay men and women elected to be interred in the chapels and houses of local religious orders, the Franciscans being especially popular. For instance, by the late fifteenth century, the church at the Franciscan friary in Askeaton in Limerick was such a popular place of burial that niches were inserted in the wall of the chancel to create extra space. Some opted for interment in the habit of their preferred religious order: both Éoghan *Ruad* MacSuibhne and his wife, Máire Ní Mháille, were buried in the habit of the Carmelite friars within the house at Rathmullen in Donegal that they had

---

37 Murphy, 'High Cost of Dying'; K. L. French, 'Women in the Late Medieval English Parish', in J. L. Halverston (ed.), *Contesting Christendom: Readings in Medieval Religion and Culture* (Lanham & Plymouth: Rowman and Littlefield, 2008), 156–73.

founded in 1516. The tradition was especially strong in Gaelic families such as the O'Connors of Connaught. This privileged access of wealthy lay men and women to burial places of particular spiritual potency demonstrated that the Church sanctioned their social dominance in death as in life. In spite of sermons preaching that all souls were equal after death, clearly social distinctions were perpetuated and given legitimacy by means of such discrimination in burial patterns.[38]

The Reformation: Prospects and Implementation

According to Steven Ellis, if the fate of state-sponsored religious reform had depended primarily on the condition of the pre-Reformation Church, then Ireland would have appeared ripe for success. And this despite the fact that the island was unusual in the medieval West in having no tradition of heretical activity equivalent to Lollardy in England.[39] In the early 1530s papal links with Gaelic Ireland were neither particularly strong nor positive, while lay engagement with the Church and spirituality was buoyant. The demise of traditional monasticism was well advanced and, given the differences in Church organisation and religious practices in English and Gaelic regions, there was little chance of a unified 'national' opposition to a reform movement. Henry VIII and his council, therefore, had reason to be optimistic that objections in Ireland to the religious reform would be less serious and widespread than in other parts of the realm. Contrary to the traditional view that the failure of the Reformation in Ireland was inevitable, it is now acknowledged that reformers did make progress during Henry VIII's reign (1509–47) and that of his successor, Edward VI (1547–53).

From the outset, the government sought to implement religious reform through two means; the royal prerogative and enforcement of legislation. Initially, the approach was low-key. In 1534 Lord Deputy Sir William Skeffington was instructed to resist papal provisions and jurisdiction, the earl of Ossory undertook to assist in 'reducing the people to Christian manners', and Henry's secretary, Thomas Cromwell, sent two chaplains to Ireland. The

---

38 Ó Clabaigh, *Friars in Ireland*, 84–6; Lennon, *Sixteenth-Century Ireland*, 134; C. Tait, 'Art and the Cult of the Virgin Mary in Ireland, *c*.1500–1660', in Moss *et al.* (eds.), *Art and Devotion in Late Medieval Ireland*, 172; Moss (ed.), *Art and Architecture of Ireland*, 54, 164, 171, 177, 206, 210, 211, 468, 486, 489, 494–5.

39 Ellis, *Ireland in the Age of the Tudors*, 203. Only one heresy trial is recorded in the Armagh registers: Archbishop Cromer's Register, I, fol. 109 (139) (PRONI MS DI0 4/ 2/ 11); H. A. Jefferies, 'The Church Courts of Armagh on the Eve of the Reformation', *Seanchas Ardmhacha*, 15, no. 2 (1993), 21.

ill-advised nature of this approach was exposed that summer when Thomas FitzGerald, tenth earl of Kildare, staged a rebellion which he styled a Catholic crusade against English heresy in an attempt to elicit imperial and papal backing. The Reformation, therefore, began in Ireland in an atmosphere of crisis. In formulating their appeal for papal support the FitzGeralds relied upon the advice and support of a coterie of elite clerics, mainly from St Patrick's Cathedral, Dublin. Thus, even as the Tudor administration set about preparing to introduce English ecclesiastical legislation in the Irish parliament in May 1536, Kildare's 'learned counsellors' – canon lawyers, senior Church officials and upholders of the traditional justification for the English presence in Ireland – had a well-developed understanding of how fundamental an attack the Reformation would be on the very foundations of the original *Laudabiliter* settlement which legitimated the king's lordship of Ireland. By their reasoning, if Henry VIII was willing to reject both the papal authority on which his own sovereignty over Ireland rested, and the orthodox canonical religion which he and his subjects were traditionally obliged to promote amongst the Irish, then his subjects were entitled to deny the validity of, and to rebel against, his authority.[40]

Yet opposition to the legislation was muted in comparison to England. The first set of measures, including the Acts of Supremacy, Successions and Slander, passed in the May 1536 session of the Irish parliament without much resistance, apart from that expressed by the lower clergy who constituted a third house of clerical proctors within the Irish assembly. In 1537 they were silenced through permanent expulsion from parliament on the recommendation of a commission, headed by Sir Anthony St Leger, who was dispatched by Henry VIII to deal with resistance among the Lords and Commons to certain government proposals. Chief among these was a bill to dissolve eight monasteries. As several members of the Commons held leases of monastic properties or were retainers for professional services to these communities, they vehemently resisted this proposal. However, after a delegation led by Sir Patrick Barnwell to Henry VIII's court in early 1537 received clarification on the matter, the Commons abandoned their opposition and thirteen houses were identified for closure in a bill passed that October.

Meanwhile, promotion of the royal supremacy and the assertion of the validity of Henry's marriage to Anne Boleyn proceeded slowly, partly as a result of delays in passing the legislation, and partly due to the absence of a common purpose and approach among government and ecclesiastical

---

40 Murray, *Enforcing the English Reformation in Ireland*, 83, 86–7.

officials. Although the newly appointed lord deputy, Lord Leonard Grey, exacted the Oath of Supremacy from Church and civil officials in Galway and Limerick during his military progresses in Munster and Connacht, in general his approach to promoting religious reforms was haphazard. This reflected the fact that his primary goal was ending rebellion rather than enforcing religious changes. To oversee the implementation of the reform programme in Ireland, Cromwell needed to appoint a suitable cleric to replace John Alen, archbishop of Dublin, who had been murdered by FitzGerald's followers at Artane in July 1534. As part of his strategy for simultaneous Church restructuring in England and Ireland (and indeed Scotland), he chose George Browne, an English Augustinian and world-wise civil servant, whom he had employed as an agent of the Reformation in England prior to his appointment to Dublin in January 1536. While Browne's efforts to promote the Reformation were mainly inspired by his sense of duty and service to the monarch, he bore a strong ideological attachment to the notion of royal supremacy. He set about enforcing the new religious settlement with the same rigour and using the same administrative and judicial framework that had been applied in England. However, he quickly encountered difficulties owing to the fitful nature of Henry VIII's and Cromwell's engagement with Ireland, and the limited reach of royal authority there.[41]

While the Irish parliament had proclaimed Henry supreme head of the Irish Church in May 1536, the claim was largely theoretical since the king's writ did not run far beyond English districts. The decision by Henry and Cromwell to postpone the creation of much of the administrative and judicial infrastructure used to implement the reforms in England dealt a severe blow to Browne's plans, rendering his proposed approach to reform largely inoperable. The enforced cancellation of his planned visitation of the Irish clergy because royal visitors would not be admitted to large areas of the four Irish ecclesiastical provinces marked a further significant setback for the Reformation programme. It determined that, aside from Henry VIII's exaction of new taxes from the clergy, there would be few visible signs that a national Church, subject to Henry's spiritual direction, had been established in Ireland. Browne's aggressive and authoritarian approach to promoting the king's supremacy made the challenge even more difficult. His artlessness alienated his peers who were broadly supportive of Henry's supremacy, particularly his fellow English bishop, Edward Staples of Meath,

---

41 Ellis, *Ireland in the Age of the Tudors*, 205–6; Lennon, *Sixteenth-Century Ireland*, 137; Heal, *Reformation*, 128–32; Hazlett, *Reformation*, 96.

who preferred progress by consent, education and explanation, and with whom Browne clashed in a 'battle of the sermons' during Lent 1538.[42]

Sporadic attempts since 1535 to exercise the royal supremacy gave way to a more active phase of reform in September 1537 with the passage of the last of the ecclesiastical legislation (including the Act of Succession legitimating the progeny of Henry's marriage to Jane Seymour and the Act against the bishop of Rome's power) at the closing session of the Reformation parliament. Having been chastised in July 1537 by Henry for delaying the progress of reform, Browne embarked on his inaugural visitation of the archdiocese in winter 1537. During this tour he tried to persuade his clergy to support the settlement 'by gentle exhortation, evangelical instruction' and 'threats of sharp correction'.[43] He also set about exacting the Oath of Supremacy from his clergy, imposed the new ecclesiastical taxes, introduced English versions of common prayers, and joined the expedition of Irish councillors to the Ormond lordship at Christmas 1538 to monitor James Butler's attempts to enforce conformity there. Browne preached in the approved evangelical style, complied with the English *Injunctions* that required the clergy to urge congregations to read the Bible, and criticised veneration of images, indulgences and auricular confession. In early 1538 he introduced the 'Forum of the Beads' – revised English bidding prayers which approximated to a confession of faith. In autumn of that year Cromwell dispatched to Ireland a version of the *New Injunctions*: clerics were now required to preach the Gospel quarterly and discourage superstitious practices such as pilgrimages and offerings to relics or statues. The requirement that an English Bible be provided to each parish church in Ireland had to be dispensed with owing to problems of supply and the dominance of the Irish language in large parts of the country. This evangelical phase of the Henrician Reformation drew to a close in May 1539 with the passing by the English parliament of the Act of Six Articles which reasserted the state Church's fundamental orthodoxy through its affirmation of transubstantiation, communion under one species, private Masses, auricular confession, clerical celibacy and the religious vows of poverty, chastity and obedience. Since, in Ireland, neither clergy nor laity had been exposed to zealous Protestant preachers, the Act elicited little or no reaction. Browne pragmatically altered his stance and carried on enforcing the royal supremacy.[44]

---

42 Murray, *Enforcing the English Reformation in Ireland*, 92–7; Ellis, *Ireland in the Age of the Tudors*, 207; Lennon, *Sixteenth-Century Ireland*, 38.
43 *SP, Hen. VIII*, ii, 539; Murray, *Enforcing the English Reformation in Ireland*, 106.
44 Ellis, *Ireland in the Age of the Tudors*, 208–9.

The general reaction of bishops and priests within the Pale, the earldom of Ormond and the towns where the Reformation was initially implemented was nominally conformist to the royal supremacy. Although curtailed by the studied inactivity of the primate and archbishop of Armagh, George Cromer, during these early years, Browne acquired an important ally in Richard Nangle, who was appointed by the king as bishop of Clonfert in Connacht and who had the rare merit of being able to preach in Irish. Initially, the most strident clerical opposition to the reforms came from the Observant friars, and especially the Franciscans whose recalcitrant stance was doubtless encouraged by the visit of the Franciscan General in 1534. However, towards the end of 1538 when news of the suppression of the mendicants in England had reached Ireland, their opposition began to recede. Among the laity, there appears to have been no significant opposition to the king's supremacy. Public conformity with the Act against the bishop of Rome's authority is evident in the oaths taken by the mayor and corporation of Limerick before Lord Deputy Leonard Grey in summer 1537. At that stage, little had changed in popular devotion. On Palm Sunday 1538 crowds attended the annual station and pattern at Kilmainham in Dublin. Mystery plays, chantry and confraternal devotions continued. Although the *Injunctions* paved the way for a campaign against images and shrines in winter 1538–9 and several of the most popular, including Our Lady of Trim, the Holy Cross at Ballyboggan in Westmeath, and the Baculum Jes (staff of St Patrick) in Christ Church Cathedral, were closed, there was no widespread iconoclasm, with many shrines likely to have been shielded by local patronal families.[45]

Steven Ellis contends that the dissolution of the monastic orders was vital in shaping reaction to the Henrician Reformation, since this doctrinally incidental campaign represented one of the most visible breaks with tradition.[46] While a limited number of monasteries had been suppressed following the passage of legislation in 1537, a full-scale dissolution of religious orders in all areas under crown control only began in summer 1539 and continued for approximately a year. In the preceding months, as the suppression of monasteries in England proceeded and preparations for a similar campaign were afoot in Ireland, the heads of most houses in English districts pre-empted the closures by renting out properties at low rents for long terms to local lay people. They hastily consolidated their existing ties with influential gentry, and secreted assets with them. Subsequently, some members of dissolved

---

45 Lennon, *Sixteenth-Century Ireland*, 140.
46 Ellis, *Ireland in the Age of the Tudors*, 211.

communities, such as those of the nunnery at Grace Dieu in north County Dublin, accessed these resources in order to support their clandestine communal life. The campaign which began in mid-July 1539 involved the closure of several houses in Meath and Louth. By late summer 1540, forty-two houses had surrendered and their properties were ready for redistribution. The suppression of the mendicant friaries in the east also took place during this period, with many of their premises converted for use as hospitals or municipal amenities. There is little evidence to indicate that the demise of the monasteries was much lamented. In terms of providing social and pastoral care these communities were probably missed even less than their equivalents in England. Most had long since stopped providing hospitality, education, alms or hospital care, as the foundation before the 1530s of several secular hospitals, almshouses and grammar schools in cities and towns across Leinster and Munster suggests. The overwhelming concern of those in Ireland affected by the dissolutions was how best to exploit monastic assets for public or private gain.[47]

During 1541–7 the final stage in the suppression was carried out as part of Lord Deputy Sir Anthony St Leger's policy of extending royal control into Gaelic quarters by accommodating local interests and securing the consent of local lords. By the end of Henry's reign, the campaign had accounted for about 55 per cent of Ireland's 140 or so monasteries and 40 per cent of approximately 200 mendicant communities. Within the Pale, Wexford, the earldom of Ormond and the south-western seaports, the suppression was almost entirely effective. Whereas newcomers (government or military personnel) anxious to establish themselves in Ireland were grateful to grab whatever dissolved monastic properties they could get, local landlords were more selective, seeking Church land that would consolidate and expand their existing holdings. In other regions, the property was usually granted to the local lord or his followers while in the marches of the Pale several monastic buildings were entrusted to loyal locals or newcomers charged with converting the premises for defence of the Pale. Feelings of regret or guilt on the part of the laity were typically swept away by generous grants of Church land which landowners, merchants, officials and other lay people received in return for their cooperation. Furthermore, the government usually ensured uninterrupted pastoral service by subsuming former monastic parish churches into the diocesan structure, by endowing new vicarages wherever necessary, and by intruding monks as stipendiary priests. In short, during

47 Lennon, *Sixteenth-Century Ireland*, 141–3; Ellis, *Ireland in the Age of the Tudors*, 214–15.

Henry's lifetime the state Church remained much closer doctrinally to Rome than to continental Protestantism. To those lay people more concerned with visible features of their religion than with complex theological disputation, the Church of Ireland's continuity with its predecessor was reassuring. That continuity, combined with the loyalty of the colonial population, played an important role in determining the jurisdictional success of the Henrician Reformation in Ireland.[48]

St Leger's appointment as viceroy in July 1540 opened a significant chapter in the advancement of the Reformation in Ireland as his reform project, which dominated the political scene throughout the succeeding decade and beyond, embraced and mediated all elements of the crown's religious policies. Briefly it even held out the prospect of overcoming the divide between Church and state that had hitherto hampered enforcement of the Reformation. From the outset, St Leger was anxious to bolster the crown's authority in the face of the claim, advanced by (among others) the clerical elite in Dublin during the recent crises of the FitzGerald rebellion and the Geraldine League, that Henry VIII's entitlement to rule in Ireland was conditional and ultimately dependent upon papal assent as recognised in the papal bull *Laudabiliter*. The formal enactment by the Irish parliament of the Act of Kingly Title in June 1541 was the symbolic high point of the St Leger regime's fusion of political and ecclesiastical reform. The lords, bishops and gentlemen in attendance were left in no doubt that the king's new regal status included his supreme authority within the spiritual polity of Ireland. While the clergy's acquiescence in 1541 stemmed in large part from their heightened sense of vulnerability following the recent suppression of the monasteries, it is interpreted by James Murray as reflecting a recognition that the religion now being promoted by the St Leger administration in the name of the king of Ireland was much more conservative and palatable than the aggressive evangelical version that accompanied the introduction of royal supremacy during the 1530s. This resulted in an accommodation being reached between Archbishop Browne and his former enemies, the conservative clergy of St Patrick's Cathedral and of the diocese at large; it also resulted in a more congenial atmosphere that encouraged these clerics to engage with this new monarchical ideology. As a result, Murray claims, for the first and only time in the sixteenth century, and under the auspices of St Leger's reform programme, the Tudor administration began to make real progress in establishing the Reformation within the heartland of English Ireland.[49]

48 Ellis, *Ireland in the Age of the Tudors*, 214–16.
49 Murray, *Enforcing the English Reformation in Ireland*, 134–6.

The gravitation towards a more conservative religious settlement in Ireland during the early 1540s was largely the result of Henry VIII's imposition of his own personal brand of Catholic orthodoxy on the Church of Ireland following Cromwell's fall from power in summer 1540, and the political needs that shaped St Leger's constitutional reform programme. Starting in autumn 1540, St Leger embarked upon three years of intensive negotiations with Gaelic and settler lords aimed at persuading them to recognise the sovereignty of the king (including his ecclesiastical supremacy) in return for granting them the full rights and protection accorded existing subjects in Ireland and other Tudor jurisdictions. By summer 1543 agreements had been brokered with the most important lords, and with many lesser-ranking leaders throughout the island. Mirroring the emollient St Leger's policy of concession and compromise in secular matters, and influenced by his ecclesiastical lieutenant, Bishop Staples, these agreements acknowledged local rights to Church patronage and local preferences in the selection of bishops. As with civil taxes in newly reconciled territories, there was no insistence on exacting full rents for former religious properties, and in certain parts of Connacht and Ulster, St Leger showed sensitivity to local interests by not enforcing monastic closures.[50]

Thus, by the time Henry VIII died in January 1547, the government had made good progress. The appearance of religious continuity was on the whole maintained, general conformity prevailed in English districts, and Gaelic chiefs and bishops showed a willingness to conform. St Leger's strategy had prevented the threatened alliance of political and religious dissidents in the Gaelic League and disabled a papal reaction to the government's reform programme. There was no popular protest resembling the English Pilgrimage of Grace, and when the papacy dispatched the first Jesuit missions to Ireland in 1542, O'Neill and O'Donnell ignored the two Jesuits bearing papal letters, leading to their departure after just four months.[51] Yet, any attachment to the Reformation that St Leger cultivated emerged out of the rough and tumble of politics. Its survival was entirely reliant upon 'the continuance of a stable political environment, the endurance of a doctrinally conservative religious settlement and the prolongation of St Leger's own viceroyalty'.[52] In other respects, too, the prospects for advancing the Reformation appeared uncertain. Hopes for reform through a coordinated campaign to produce a

---

50 Murray, *Enforcing the English Reformation in Ireland*, 137; Lennon, *Sixteenth-Century Ireland*, 161.
51 Ellis, *Ireland in the Age of the Tudors*, 216.
52 Murray, *Enforcing the English Reformation in Ireland*, 188.

more educated ministry, involving the foundation of a university, secular colleges and new schools, faded as the wealth appropriated from the Church was channelled into financing government. Failure to address the exceptional poverty of many dioceses which prevented recruitment of well-educated, diligent clergy was a further impediment. In addition, as Ellis has emphasised, the weakness of clerical and lay resistance to religious reform, though no less widespread than in England, reflected the slackness with which the Henrician settlement was enforced.[53]

As Murray has shown, the accession of Edward VI inaugurated a more radical and identifiably Protestant religious reform programme than had been seen before. St Leger tried but ultimately failed to absorb this into the framework of the existing religious settlement. He endeavoured to minimise religious contention and maintain the kind of consensus that existed in the 1540s, arguing that any effort to convert the indigenous population to Protestantism should be undertaken gradually, using persuasive means. However, he found it increasingly difficult to maintain that consensus for a number of reasons. First, his viceroyalties in the Edwardian reign were of short duration. Second, they were punctuated by the deputyship of Sir Edward Bellingham (April 1548–December 1549), a committed Protestant whose uncompromising approach and determination to force the pace of change diminished the trust and allegiance of religious conservatives whom St Leger had won over to the Reformation. Third, St Leger was unable to establish a working political relationship with Archbishop Browne who, as part of his campaign against the viceroy, rediscovered his enthusiasm for the Protestant religion and accused Sir Anthony of tolerating papist practices and sympathetic treatment of errant religious conservatives. By the end of his second term as viceroy in spring 1551, St Leger's settlement, which had brought religious conservatives and reformers together in the 1540s, had collapsed. The challenge of absorbing the radical doctrinal and liturgical elements of the first *Book of Common Prayer* stretched the settlement beyond the point at which it retained any meaningful continuity with its antecedents or the support of St Leger's close associate, Archbishop Dowdall of Armagh. St Leger's recall in spring 1551 and Dowdall's defection and departure for the Continent the following summer, sealed the collapse of the viceroy's settlement and of religious consensus. Yet, it did not result in dramatic religious polarisation in Ireland. Rather, the Edwardian era was marked by religious confusion and ambivalence, partly because the viceroys proceeded slowly

53 Ellis, *Ireland in the Age of the Tudors*, 216.

with implementation of the new doctrinal and liturgical changes, and partly because these changes made only a superficial impact owing to the shortness of Edward VI's reign.[54]

Whereas the Henrician Reformation of the 1530s and 1540s is regarded as marking the end of medieval religious history (and with good reason, since Church structures were externally changed at a clearly defined point), recent scholarship has warned against acceptance of such neat divisions. Nowhere is such caution more necessary than in studies of the impact of the Reformation on the majority of the population – the laity. It is clear that shifts in religious practice did not occur with the stroke of the royal pen and that in Ireland, as in England and elsewhere, people's experience of religion was in a state of flux for many years before and after 'official' dates of religious change – a reality eloquently illustrated by the need to recopy the text of the Kilkenny mystery plays in 1637 as the original was so worn from use.[55]

54 Murray, *Enforcing the English Reformation in Ireland*, 199–201.
55 Ellis, *Ireland in the Age of the Tudors*, 216–17; Lennon, *Sixteenth-Century Ireland*, 139; Murray, *Enforcing the English Reformation in Ireland*, 199; Hall, *Women and the Church*, 201.

19

Contexts, Divisions and Unities: Perspectives from the Later Middle Ages

ROBIN FRAME

THIS volume places emphasis on the need to understand Ireland in wider settings. Since the history of the island was never self-contained, to seek some aboriginal Ireland or people of Ireland, with quintessential characteristics that can be traced down the centuries, would be to pursue a will o' the wisp. Viewing Ireland in broader contexts does not threaten the integrity of 'Irish history'. When well done, it enriches the analysis by opening up comparisons and contrasts, and by encouraging careful consideration of what is or is not distinctive about the Irish past. The volume also brings regional divisions and variations to the fore: Ireland was always politically fragmented, and lacked (in practice though not in theory) a settled hierarchy of lordship. From the viking period onwards, the country was also linguistically and culturally multiple. Moreover, different parts of Ireland had different relationships with the world (or worlds) beyond. All this may seem too obvious to need stating; but it contrasts sharply with a historiographical tradition that emphasised what were regarded as age-old and distinctive features of Irish history and culture, and presented external influences (save of course for Christianity) as mostly regrettable, where they were not downright malign. At no stage between 600 and 1550 does Irish history lend itself to a narrative viewed from a single central point, yet contemporaries never doubted that there was a national story, however much they might disagree about its content and its ultimate destination. Tension between the perception of some idealised unity and the complex and shifting distribution of practical power, whether political or cultural, characterises the period.

Settings and Perceptions

Interactions with the wider scene did not, of course, produce neat clusters of changes, or map precisely on to traditional political watersheds. Commercial expansion and the beginnings of monetisation pre-dated the Anglo-Norman conquests; and the natural and man-made disasters of the fourteenth century occurred at the mid-point of the history of the Lordship of Ireland. So too, ecclesiastical reform and the cultural shifts associated with the 'twelfth-century renaissance' were affecting Church and society in Ireland long before 1170; the arrival of the Anglo-Normans complicated the process. Nor do we have to wait until 1170 to find Ireland involved in political structures that stretched beyond the island itself. The viking period had seen the development of a Dublin–York axis; this was followed in the late eleventh century by the establishment of Ua Briain lordship in Dublin, and beyond, on the Isle of Man. But such configurations of power were transient, and often involved extensions of influence outwards from Ireland. What happened from 1170 was different. It permanently removed from Irish control Dublin and north Leinster, which had become the essential hub of wider overlordship; and it made Ireland part of a political system with main centres that lay elsewhere.[1]

The regional character of Ireland's links with the exterior scene is readily apparent, though any brief description is bound to make the regions, which overlapped at the edges, appear too clear-cut. Distinctive dynamics are most obvious in the north-east, where the Solway basin, with the Isle of Man at its heart, together with the narrow waters of the North Channel, linked populations from prehistoric times. In the early Christian period this maritime zone formed a religious highway, with Iona as a crucial bridge. In the viking age it became the centre of an economic and political world extending from Dublin and Anglesey through Man and the Hebrides back to Bergen and Trondheim; a nexus of influence that persisted, though with diminishing force, into the thirteenth century. By that time, the region had been invaded by aristocrats with close, though sometimes difficult, links to the English and Scottish kings, whose direct and indirect grip tightened in the century after 1170. The influence of the two monarchies weakened markedly during the relatively intense Anglo-Scottish wars of 1296–1356, which saw not just the undermining of the earldom of Ulster but also the retreat of Scottish royal influence in the west. This created the space both for the establishment of galloglass dynasties in the north of Ireland, and for the emergence of the Lordship of the Isles, with a penumbra reaching from Antrim to Ross. When monarchical authority by fits and starts reasserted itself from the 1490s onwards, the north of Ireland again became the scene of diplomatic competition between the English and Scottish crowns.

---

1 S. Duffy, 'Ireland's Hastings: The Anglo-Norman Conquest of Dublin', *ANS*, 20 (1998), 69–85.

Further south, dynastic marriages and movements of people in both directions in the early period characterised interactions between Leinster and Wales, together with north-west England and Severnside. The viking age added to these relationships a major slave-market at Chester. During the eleventh and early twelfth centuries, Welsh rulers tapped into military support from Ireland, and when times were bad used Dublin as a refuge and springboard for recovery. A branch of the family of Gruffudd ap Cynan (d. 1147), the partly Irish king of north Wales, acquired lands in the Dublin area.[2] In one sense, the movement of troops and settlers from south Wales into south Leinster and east Munster from 1167 onwards was a redirection of a very old relationship. But the distribution of power was now quite different; the key points on the Irish coast, from Drogheda and Dublin to Wexford and Waterford, had passed into English hands. Henry III and Edward I mobilised troops and materiel from Ireland for their campaigns and castle-building in Wales. Despite rumours of a 'Celtic alliance' in the time of the Glyn Dŵr rebellion, the only practical involvement of Ireland took the form of the arrival in 1405 of an expeditionary force led by the justiciar Stephen Scrope, on Anglesey, where it recaptured Beaumaris Castle for Henry IV.

The south-west and west of Ireland also had contact with the wider world. During the 1350s, English agents of the widowed Elizabeth Burgh, lady of Clare, made their way from Kilkenny and Tipperary across the Shannon near Portumna in order to gather what profit they could from Burke cadets and other leading tenants in Galway and Mayo. Two generations later, John Banbury of Limerick (d. 1404) maintained property and other associations in his home city while pursuing a career in commerce and municipal government in Bristol, whose mayor and MP he became.[3] The Atlantic sea-lanes rendered the west particularly open to Continental connections and influences. In 1346 two groups of English nobles returning from Brittany were shipwrecked, one in Connacht and one in Desmond.[4] In 1518 Archduke Ferdinand, brother of the future Emperor Charles V, sailing from Spain to the Low Countries, found himself in Youghal. The prominence of Cork, and increasingly also the participation of smaller south-western ports such as Kinsale and Dingle, in the wine trade with Gascony is a feature of the late medieval period. At the same

---

2 M. T. Flanagan, '*Historia Gruffud vab Kenan* and the Origins of Balrothery, Co. Dublin', *Cambrian Medieval Celtic Studies*, 28 (1994), 71–94.
3 TNA SC 6/1239/31; R. Frame, 'Lordship beyond the Pale: Munster in the Later Middle Ages', in R. Stalley (ed.), *Limerick and South-West Ireland: Medieval Art and Architecture* (Leeds: BAACT, 2011), 11.
4 *Clyn*, 236–7.

time, the wealth that came by sea, particularly after the appearance of the herring shoals in the western Atlantic, was exploited by Irish lords, giving their lordships a distinctly maritime flavour.[5] The departure of John Cabot's first Atlantic expedition from Dursey Head in west Cork in 1497 symbolises the opening of new vistas.

Political fragmentation and multiple connections with Britain and the Continent existed alongside widely disseminated narratives of a coherent national past. Perhaps the most distinctive feature of early Ireland was the existence of a privileged group, the *fílid*, common to the whole island; they were custodians of law and history, and thus (in today's parlance) the creators and preservers of a national identity. Many were clergy, who 'switched codes' readily between Latin and Gaelic. Another unusual feature of Ireland that distinguished it, for instance, from contemporary England was the early emergence of a standardised written vernacular. The nature of the *literati* changed over time, as the reform of the Church in the eleventh and twelfth centuries gradually detached the more educated clergy. The poets, historians and lawyers of the later Middle Ages were primarily secular, but they remained a privileged class, with access to the whole island, together with its Scottish cultural satellite. This class shaped a body of ideas that had crystallised by 1100; it encapsulated a powerful sense of a common past and future. The eternal verities included the existence of an Irish people, the Gaels (*Gáedhil*), with an identifiable territory (Ireland, though there was the complication of Scotland), together with a distinctive language, law and history. With this was associated the belief that all newcomers, however long established, remained 'foreigners' (*Gaill*). The contemporary belief, rooted in the Bible, was that since the kingdom of heaven was one, so too an earthly people should have a single ruler. Thus actual fragmentation went hand-in-hand with a potent myth of unity.

These ideas were immutable in their outlines, but in detail infinitely malleable. The eleventh-century compilation the 'Book of Rights' contains verses setting forth the supposed duties and obligations of provincial kings in relation to their sub-kings, on the one hand, and in relation to the 'king of Ireland', on the other. It opens with material asserting the right of the kings of Cashel to be kings of Ireland, but also contains verses endorsing the

---

5 A. F. O'Brien, 'Commercial Relations between Aquitaine and Ireland, *c.*1000 to *c.*1550', in J.-M. Picard (ed.), *Aquitaine and Ireland in the Middle Ages* (Dublin: Four Courts Press, 1995), 49–72; C. Breen, 'The Maritime Cultural Landscape of Medieval Gaelic Ireland', in P. J. Duffy, D. Edwards and E. Fitzpatrick (eds.), *Gaelic Ireland: Land, Lordship and Settlement, c.1250–c.1550* (Dublin: Four Courts Press, 2001), 418–35.

suzerainty of the kings of Tara, and verses implying that other rulers such as the kings of Leinster and of Ulaid *might* hold the kingship.[6] The tension between ideal and reality is constantly visible; the ideas retained their power even in works whose content seemed to undermine them. The thirteenth-century poet Giolla Brighde Mac Con Midhe in verses addressed to Domnall *Mór* O'Donnell presented the families of O'Neill and O'Donnell as joint heirs to the kingship of Ireland, to which, he claimed, the southern dynasties had no rights. He urged upon them a duty to cooperate:

> Equal their jurisdiction throughout Ireland, equal their tribute and their tax; Equal the weight of their laws and their dominion; exactly equal is the honour due to each of them.
>
> Let them affirm brotherhood, let them have a single king, the two noble houses of Inis Fáil; as their own horses are wont to be under them, to be together is as natural to them.
>
> Whoever of us has been chosen, let us both make him our high king; the goodly assembly of nobles will bring about from our number alternation of the kingship again.

This elaborate attempt to promote unity tells its own tale. The same poet was to lament the defeat of Brian O'Neill at the hands of the Ulster colonists at the Battle of Down in 1260. He forbore to mention the awkward fact that members of the O'Donnell kindred are conspicuously absent from his list of recorded casualties, as they are from that in the Annals of Ulster.[7]

The mid-fourteenth-century Thomond history, *Caithréim Thoirdhealbhaigh* is particularly revealing in the way it operates at several levels. Written in the tradition of *Cocad Gáedel re Gallaib*, which had celebrated (and partly invented) the struggle of Brian Bórama against the vikings, it begins by presenting the narrative within the overarching theme of the conflict between *Gáedhil* and *Gaill*: 'the government of Ireland being now in the year 1172 come into Foreigners' hands; and regal dignity divorced from all and singular the clans of Milesius the Spaniard's blood'. A kingship of Ireland hovers in the background, as in the depiction of Brian O'Neill and Tadc O'Brien competing in the gifts they gave each other when they met to form an alliance at Cael Uisce in 1258. But as the story unfolds, it centres on the tussle between two branches of the O'Briens, each reliant upon the backing of 'foreigners', respectively the de Burghs and Thomas de Clare and his son Richard. The de Clares become

---

6 *Lebor na Cert*, ed. M. Dillon (London: ITS, 1962), x–xii, 5, 85, 105, 123.
7 *The Poems of Giolla Brighde Mac Con Midhe*, ed. N. Williams (Dublin: ITS, 1980), 12–15, verses 7, 10, 12, and 136–61; quotation, verses 3, 4; *AU*, ii, 328–9.

hate figures, in passages that contrast the 'nobility' of the older settlers with such newcomers, who were presumably not fluent in Irish. Thus, at the same time as it testifies to the power of established ideas, the text adds nuance to the distinction between Gael and Foreigner. It also portrays the disintegration of provincial kingship, through the intrusion of outsiders, the segmentation of the O'Brien dynasty, and the narrowing of the gap between over-kings and their vassals – in this instance the MacNamara family.[8]

The Gaelic historical tradition was counterpointed by another influential narrative, that of the English in Ireland, shaped above all by Gerald of Wales. Gerald's *Expugnatio Hibernica*, preserving versions of papal documents, told the story of the grant of Ireland to Henry II, associating it with a papally sanctioned reforming mission to root out 'corruption' and bad custom. Together with his *Topography of Ireland*, it presented copious evidence of the divergence of the Irish Church and people from twelfth-century metropolitan norms, depicting Irish society as backward and barbarous. It is difficult to exaggerate the importance of these works. They were translated into French, English and Irish, and formed the basis of what was said about Ireland in one of the most widely circulated English histories, the *Polychronicon* of the fourteenth-century Chester monk Ranulph Higden. Works by Gerald in English and Irish were in the library of the Great Earl of Kildare, while his son possessed versions in Latin and English; both owned Higden's *Polychronicon* in English.[9]

The Giraldian narrative acquired additional layers. Rather as the Normans in England had appropriated Anglo-Saxon saints, the English in Ireland took over Irish saints, a process dramatically recorded in Gerald's story of John de Courcy's 'discovery' of the bones of Patrick, Brigit and Columba at Down. The sense of English entitlement to Ireland was intensified by such appropriations, which had no necessary connection with a sense of affinity with the Gaelic tradition, any more than the Francophone Henry III's devotion to Edward the Confessor indicated susceptibility to Anglo-Saxon culture. St Patrick's Cathedral in Dublin was founded by John Comyn, a royal clerk, the first non-Irish archbishop, as a secular cathedral the canons of which could participate in the administration of the province; its prebends were later colonised by clerks working in the royal administration. Comyn's successor, Henry le Blund, a Londoner experienced in royal service, was to gain

---

8 *Caithréim Thoirdhealbhaigh*, ii, 1 (quotation), 3; A. Nic Ghiollamhaith, 'Kings and Vassals in Later Medieval Ireland: The Uí Bhriain and the MicConmara in the Fourteenth Century', in Barry *et al.* (eds.), *Colony and Frontier in Medieval Ireland*, 201–16.

9 A. Byrne, 'The Earls of Kildare and their Books at the end of the Middle Ages', *The Library: The Transactions of the Bibliographical Society*, 14 (2013), 129–53.

a reputation as an opponent of the admission of Irish clergy to high office; this did not prevent him from seeking to enhance the status of his see by promoting the canonisation of the last Irish archbishop, Lorcán Ua Tuathail (Laurence O'Toole) (d. 1180). It might almost be said that there came to be two Patricks. They confronted each other at the time of the Bruce invasion. The 1317 Remonstrance sent in the name of Domnall O'Neill to Pope John XXII set forth O'Neill's rights as heir to a supposedly unbroken line of native kings who ruled Ireland down to the coming of the English. For its authors Patrick symbolised the beginning of a continuous history of Irish spirituality, which had ended only with the arrival of the English.[10] A petition to Edward II from 'the middling people of Ireland', formulated in Dublin in 1318 in apparent awareness of the Remonstrance, bestowed upon the saint a quite different historical role. The document opens with Patrick: but here he represents the standards from which the Irish Church had later fallen away, until its rescue by the intervention of Henry II. Patrick had become the patron saint of the English in Ireland.[11]

The petition hints at a further element in the Anglo-Irish self-image when it portrays Henry II coming to Ireland, not just at the head of an army, but with 'men of law'. Law, with the rights it conveyed, was central to medieval concepts of national identity, and English law, explicitly extended to Ireland in 1210, became inextricably bound up with the identity of the settler elites. Although there were mechanisms through which English status could be acquired by Irish individuals and families, the underlying presumption was exclusionary: English law and liberties were the possession of those of Anglo-Norman descent. The emergence of a form of patriotism, associated with a sense of place, and accompanied by attachment to the inherited rights of loyal subjects, is neatly summed up in an account of events in the Dublin parliament of 1324, where Arnold le Poer, who was engaged in a bitter dispute with Richard Ledrede the English Franciscan bishop of Ossory, defended Ireland as a 'land of saints' while at the same time brandishing Magna Carta.[12]

There was, therefore, a widely known and generally accepted narrative that gave English Ireland a firm historical base. But the retreat of

---

10 Walter Bower, *Scotichronicon*, v, 384–403.
11 Sayles, *Affairs*, no. 136; R. Frame, 'Exporting State and Nation: Being English in Medieval Ireland', in L. Scales and O. Zimmer (eds.), *Power and the Nation in European History* (Cambridge University Press, 2005), 148–58.
12 *A Contemporary Narrative of the Proceedings against Dame Alice Kyteler Prosecuted for Sorcery in 1324*, ed. T. Wright. Camden Series, o.s. 24 (London: The Camden Society 1843), 17; H. G. Richardson and G. O. Sayles, *The Irish Parliament in the Middle Ages* (Philadelphia: University of Pennsylvania Press, 1952), 72–3.

government control across the fourteenth century, together with pleas for financial and military help sent to England from the 1350s onwards, made the crown acutely aware of the gap between its theoretical and actual authority in Ireland. This may have encouraged Richard II to require acts of submission in novel form from Gaelic leaders, and to have these undertakings guaranteed by financial bonds to the papacy. The 1395 acts of homage and allegiance provided the English claim to Ireland with additional confirmation; the alleged subsequent violation of these acts by leading Irish lords was cited by the settlers in 1421 as a reason why the king of England should intervene in Ireland again.[13]

Change and Continuity: After 1170, and before

The rival stories about the Irish past had a deep influence on later perceptions. They helped to direct scholarly activity into two separate channels, an effect heightened by the different character of the Gaelic and non-Gaelic sources, and the special skills required to exploit the former in particular.[14] They also served to emphasise, and arguably exaggerate, the break around 1170. Matters of continuity and change are necessarily complex, and sometimes deceptive, as discussions of the origins of urban life and structures in Ireland suggest. Important Irish ecclesiastical and royal centres had, needless to say, tended to appear at points that were favourable for communications (by water as much as by land), defence, government or economic activity; so that it would be surprising if the sites of many Anglo-Norman urban foundations did not have earlier histories. There is, however, no doubt that the later royal cities, which were all coastal and all in the southern half of Ireland, were a product of the viking period. It seems likely, too, that forms of communal organisation within them pre-dated the documentation that survives from the late twelfth century onwards. It is understandable that some have argued that the viking intervention marked a more formative phase in Irish history than the Anglo-Norman settlements. Such arguments, however, may underestimate the depth and the geographical extent of Anglo-Norman entrepreneurial activity.[15]

Although Ireland remained among the less urbanised regions of Western Europe, significant seaport and riverine towns with little earlier history were

---

13 *Stat. Ire., John–Hen. V*, 564–7.
14 Simms, *Medieval Gaelic Sources*; Connolly, *Medieval Record Sources*.
15 *Dublin Guild Merchant Roll*, xi–xii, xviii–xix; H. B. Clarke, '*Quo Vadis*: Mapping the Irish "Monastic Town" ', in Duffy (ed.), *Princes, Prelates and Poets*, 261–78.

promoted by the Anglo-Normans; the more successful included Youghal, Clonmel, Carrickfergus, Sligo and Athenry. As far afield as Kerry, there were new foundations, such as Dingle, that had a continuing, though scantily documented, history. Even where towns were founded at existing centres, they might be 'new', not merely in that they acquired a novel legal status through charters from English kings or aristocrats, but in the fact that they occupied freshly planned sites. This was true, for instance, of Dublin and Cork, and particularly clear in the case of Kilkenny, where William Marshal's town dwarfed in size an earlier settlement under the lordship of the bishop of Ossory. A similar situation might arise on a smaller scale: for instance, the seigniorial castle-borough of Antrim is accompanied in fourteenth-century records by a settlement described as 'Irish Antrim'.[16]

A similar mixture of continuity and change is apparent in the spatial organisation of lordship and settlement. The Anglo-Normans used existing territorial and political divisions when making grants, a practice anticipated by the reforming Church, in its decisions about the territorial outlines of bishoprics and rural deaneries. Just as the potential lordships of the greatest lords were understood in terms of provincial or semi-provincial regnal units, so the Irish *tricha cét* – the lesser kingdom or tribute district – was often rebranded as the 'cantred', and grants were typically expressed in terms of cantreds, half-cantreds, or groups of cantreds.[17] There is a clear parallel with the Norman England of the Domesday Book: it rested upon the shires and hundreds of the Anglo-Saxon past; these in places preserved Roman administrative units, which in turn might reflect earlier British tribal districts.[18] But the search for ultimate origins and continuities should not deflect attention from the profound changes that took place after 1170. These were most obvious in the areas of heavy settlement in the four counties around Dublin, where existing boundaries were often redrawn, and in the river valleys and coastal lowlands of south Leinster and east Munster. Here a quite different social structure was developed, with land organised around privileged borough communities and arable farming organised for the market.

Almost more striking is the evidence for remodelling in promising areas further afield. Maurice fitz Gerald, justiciar of Ireland 1232–45, participated in and benefited from the conquest of Connacht by the de Burghs. Among

---

16 J. Bradley, 'The Medieval Towns of Kerry', *North Munster Antiquarian Journal*, 28 (1986), 28–39; TNA SC 6/1239/33.

17 MacCotter, *Medieval Ireland*.

18 See, e.g., J. Campbell, *Essays in Anglo-Saxon History* (London: Hambledon Press, 1986), 121–30.

his acquisitions were 'the two cantreds of Ofecherath', an area approximately co-extensive with the bishopric of Kilmacduagh, which he was to hold 'as Yochen Ohethyin (*Eoghan Ó hEidhin*) at any time best and most fully held them', in return for the service of four knights and an annual rent of forty silver marks.[19] A remarkable clutch of surviving documents reveals his organisational energy. He was eager to develop his town of Kilcolgan, and before 1241 arranged an exchange with the bishop of Kilmacduagh, so acquiring land lying between Kilcolgan and the sea, on Galway Bay. At the same time, he obtained from Henry III a licence to hold a weekly market and annual fair at Kilcolgan, together with a grant of free chase and free warren throughout the cantreds.[20] Originally, he had allocated Ó hEidhin a half-cantred north of Kilmacduagh; in 1252 there was further reorganisation, when Ó hEidhin surrendered direct lordship over the area to Maurice, in return for two townlands, eight plough-oxen and forty marks in cash. An extent made in 1289 offers a snapshot that reminds us that men such as Maurice, who appear in the annals as warlike barons, were also acute politicians, knowledgeable in the law, skilled at deploying manpower, with a shrewd eye for landscape and profit. The extensive 'manor' of Ardrahan was valued at £95; about 55 per cent of this arose from the lord's demesnes, and 30 per cent from the rents of his main tenants, many of whom were drawn from settler families of Leinster and Munster, such as Purcell, Hacket, St Aubyn, de Valle and Caunteton. There was a castle at Ardrahan, but the burgess settlement there was valued at roughly half that of Kilcolgan, the more commercially advantageous site that Maurice had identified.

Similar sketches could be made of other outlying patches of colonial enterprise, for instance the coastal lordships of north Antrim and Derry, centred on boroughs such as Coleraine and Portrush, and exploiting the wealth of the seas and of the rivers Bann and Bush, which were developed by the de Lacy and de Burgh earls of Ulster. This area was highly profitable in the 1260s and 1270s, and remained so even in the 1350s.[21] The powerful image of late medieval colonial retreat and decomposition should not lead us to underestimate what happened between 1170 and around 1240. Though medievalists have mostly fought shy of the word, these were 'plantations' as radical as anything before 1608, and considerably more widespread than those of the Tudor

---

19 *Red Book of the Earls of Kildare*, no. 23; and for what follows, nos. 28, 48, 49, 60 and 67.
20 *CDI, 1171–1251*, no. 2550.
21 Orpen, *Normans*, iii, 278–9, 288–90; T. E. McNeill, *Anglo-Norman Ulster: The History and Archaeology of an Irish Barony* (Edinburgh: John Donald, 1980), 136–44.

period. They may not have been part of a government-organised scheme, but they were no less 'professional' for that.[22]

Harmonies and Dissonances

While traditional scholarship has tended to emphasise the differences between Irish and Anglo-Norman society, there were also underlying similarities that made them far from incompatible. For the political historian, dialogue may have been obstructed by the fact that those who wielded power in Ireland were 'kings'. As the author of the Anglo-Norman verse chronicle of the conquest put it:

> in Ireland kings were as numerous
> as counts were elsewhere,
> but whoever holds Meath and Leinster
> and Desmond and Munster
> and Connacht and Ulster,
> which the six brothers held long ago,
> whoever holds these are the chief kings
> of Ireland according to the Irish.[23]

Concentrating on their 'kingliness' (or lack, or loss, or levels, of it), can distract attention from aspects of lordship the two societies shared. Both were hierarchical, both had an aristocratic elite that supplied leadership in war and diplomacy, both had rituals of superiority and subordination with generic similarities as well as significant contrasts.

By a paradox familiar in other frontier settings, the military arena, where conflict was most obvious, was also that where accommodations and reciprocal influences can most readily be discerned. The segmentary competition endemic in Irish society enabled the Anglo-Normans to penetrate the regions they entered through alliances with native leaders, and the manpower involved in the establishment (and later the defence) of the Lordship of Ireland was always partly Irish. The challenge of the Anglo-Norman presence, the collapse of old provincial hierarchies, together with access to external manpower and the need this brought to support hired troops, profoundly affected the infrastructure of lordship in Gaelic Ireland.[24] It was equally the case that the incoming powers had little difficulty in tuning in to the idioms

22 S. Duffy, 'The First Ulster Plantation: John de Courcy and the Men of Cumbria', in Barry *et al.* (eds.), *Colony and Frontier in Medieval Ireland*, 1–27.
23 *Deeds of the Normans*, 109, lines 2189–96.
24 Simms, *From Kings to Warlords*; Nicholls, *Gaelic and Gaelicized Ireland*.

of Irish lordship. Roger Howden tells us that Henry II built a hall in Dublin in the Irish style, possibly with a view to providing a courtly venue where he received the submissions of Irish leaders, much as he was used to receiving fealty from the Welsh.[25] A generation later the sole surviving Irish exchequer Pipe Roll of John's reign shows the seneschal of Meath, then in the king's hand, receiving large cattle-tributes from Gaelic leaders; cattle were also redistributed for multiple purposes, including military wages.[26] In 1271, James Audley the justiciar of Ireland, a Cheshire man with experience in war and administration in north Wales, delivered 'robes, furs and saddles' to northern Irish leaders coming to the king's peace after the death of Walter de Burgh. This is one of many echoes of *tuarastal*, the ceremonial gifts given by an Irish overlord to a submitting vassal in order to express his superiority.[27] In English society, the holding by the king of hostages of his own greater subjects beto-kened either the collapse of conventional political relations and the onset of tyranny, as under King John, or a state of special emergency, as when hos-tages were surrendered by magnates of Ireland during the Bruce invasion. In Ireland, by contrast, the holding of hostages was a normal part of the exercise of lordship. Anglo-Norman lords and royal officials both rapidly absorbed the etiquette surrounding hostages (though they sometimes brutally disregarded it), and Dublin Castle together with other royal and seigniorial castles regu-larly housed them.[28]

Compatibility was not, however, complete. Donnchad *Cairprech* O'Brien was knighted by King John in 1210, but the next dubbing of an Irish lord for which there is clear evidence is that of Seán O'Byrne [Ó Broin] of Wicklow around 1359. Gaelic lords are conspicuously absent from the frequent accounts contained in the annals of the settlers of the knighting of members of their contingents by justiciars and colonial lords at the outset of military campaigns. Richard II's knighting of the main Irish provincial lords in 1395 was a departure, widely commented upon in English circles. That it had an impact on the recipients is suggested by a letter to the king in which Niall Óc O'Neill entitled himself 'knight by your creation'.[29]

Both societies were violent, though the nature of the violence changed over time, and the conventions governing it might differ. Slavery became

25 Flanagan, *Irish Society*, 202–3.
26 *IPR 14 John*, 36–9, 48–9, 62–3, 66–7.
27 *CDI, 1252–1284*, no. 890.
28 Frame, *Ireland and Britain*, 260–2.
29 F. Verstraten, 'Images of Gaelic Lordship in Ireland *c*.1200–*c*.1400', in Doran and Lyttleton (eds.), *Lordship in Medieval Ireland*, 52–3; E. Curtis, *Richard II in Ireland 1394–5* (Oxford University Press, 1927), 136.

rare in Ireland as elsewhere in Western Europe by around 1100, but savagery remained. Both societies were familiar with the pious warrior. John de Courcy was a prolific monastic patron. Around 1183 he endowed his Benedictine foundation of St Patrick's at Down with 'the tenth cow and every tenth animal from all my raids and from all my acquisitions and purchases of animals eastwards from the water of the Ards ... for the salvation of my soul and that of my mother, and for the souls of my ancestors and descendants, and for the souls of those who gave me counsel and help to conquer Ulster'. His extensive ecclesiastical patronage, like that of kings and nobles elsewhere in Europe, was about marking out his territory and excluding rivals as well as saving his soul.[30] Irish contemporaries behaved similarly. Domnall *Mór* Ua Briain, the king of Limerick, was at the same period founding Cistercian houses, such as Holycross and Kilcooly in Tipperary, probably to assert his influence on the eastern outskirts of his kingdom in an area that was already being occupied by the Anglo-Normans. Likewise, the lineaments of the Leinster kingdom of Diarmait Mac Murchada and the Airgialla kingdom of Donnchad Ua Cerbaill (d. 1168) can be mapped partly by the religious houses they patronised.[31]

The portrayal by twentieth-century scholars of Diarmait MacMurchada as a 'modernising' promoter of religious reform may not be incompatible with Gerald of Wales's depiction of him as a barbaric warrior in the old heroic mode, picking up the heads of his fallen enemies in order to deface them (literally) with his teeth. His delight in enemy heads is confirmed by the verse-chronicle; and Gerald's ghoulish trope recurs in *Caithréim Thoirdhealbhaigh*, which depicts handless, dying men on the battlefield trying to behead their half-dead enemies with their teeth: 'to "nose-chew" them'.[32] The settlers also hunted heads. The conventionally stylised municipal seal of the city of Dublin shows the heads of outlaws in niches above the city gate. Middle English verses celebrating Peter Bermingham's slaughter of the leaders of the O'Connor Faly family of Offaly in 1305 make sport of the leather hoods in which (it seems) their heads were delivered to the Dublin authorities. Of the one poor wretch whose life was spared, the poet remarks 'he went unhooded

---

30 'Cartae Dunenses, XII–XIII Céad', ed. G. Mac Niocaill, *Seanchas Ardmhacha*, 5 (1970), 420; M. T. Flanagan, 'John de Courcy, the First Ulster Plantation and Irish Church Men', in Smith (ed.), *Britain and Ireland*, 154–78.

31 M. T. Flanagan, *Irish Royal Charters: Texts and Contexts* (Oxford University Press, 2005), ch. 5; M. T. Flanagan, 'Strategies of Lordship in pre-Norman and post-Norman Leinster', *ANS*, 20 (1998), 108; B. Smith, *Colonisation and Conquest in Medieval Ireland: The English in Louth 1170–1330* (Cambridge University Press, 1999), 18.

32 *Expugnatio*, 36–7; *Deeds of the Normans*, 72–3, lines 777–83; *Caithréim Thoirdhealbhaigh*, ii, 103.

home'.[33] By the mid-fourteenth century the grim state rituals attendant on treason had appeared in Ireland. In 1345 the steward of the earl of Desmond, who had held Castle Island against crown forces, was drawn, hanged, beheaded, disembowelled and quartered; others in the garrison were merely drawn at the horse's tail, and hanged. Danger of this extreme punishment might extend to Irish leaders who had been unwise enough to accept the king's lordship in return for an exchequer stipend, and then failed to adhere to their agreements: two MacMurrough kings were 'drawn by the Galls' in 1354 and in 1369.[34] In 1468 state violence, at the hands of that well-educated harbinger of the Renaissance, John Tiptoft, earl of Worcester, was to claim the life of his predecessor as chief governor of Ireland, Thomas earl of Desmond.

The Church had never in practice been immune from violence, and after 1170 episodes of brutality were not the preserve of one nation. In 1323, we hear that Philip Talon and twenty-six others 'were killed by Edmund Butler, rector of Tullow [County Carlow], and the Cauntetons, who dragged them from the church; and they burnt the church of St Mullins with men, women and children and the relics of St Moling'. In 1332, 'the Irish of Leinster raided the English and burned churches; and in the church of Freynestown [County Wicklow] they burned about eighty men and women; and a certain chaplain of the church, dressed in sacred vestments, wished to leave carrying the Host, but they drove him back with their spears and burned him in that church with the rest of them'.[35] More routine, especially in the Irish areas, was the intrusion by lords, their armed retinues and their herds into church estates. Invasion of the wealth of the Church was not peculiar to Irish society, but it took distinctive forms. In 1297 the English and French kings were at loggerheads with Pope Boniface VIII over the right of secular rulers to tax the clergy, something Boniface condemned in the bull *Clericis laicos*. In Ireland, the bull was forcefully wielded by Nicholas Mac Máel Ísu, the archbishop of Armagh, but against the Gaelic lords of southern Ulster, among whose extortions was the billeting of galloglasses (*Scotici*) on the tenants of church estates.[36]

At first glance, the Church can seem more clearly divided along national lines than lay society. As Gerald of Wales's writings show, nations and national

---

33 Duffy, 'Ireland's Hastings', 70–1; *Poems from BL MS Harley 913: 'The Kildare Manuscript'*, ed. T. Turville-Petre. EETS, o.s. 345 (Oxford University Press, 2015), 73.

34 *Clyn*, 235; R. Frame, 'Two Kings in Leinster: The Crown and the MicMhurchadha in the Fourteenth Century', in Barry *et al.* (eds.), *Colony and Frontier in Medieval Ireland*, 167–8.

35 *Clyn*, 176–7; *Chartul. St Mary's, Dublin*, ii, 376.

36 Smith, *Colonisation and Conquest in Medieval Ireland*, 84, 90–1.

characteristics were part of the stock-in-trade of the educated clergy. Gerald himself had twice been denied the bishopric of St David's on account – he believed – of the fact that by ancestry he was one-quarter Welsh.[37] Arguments citing national bias were not slow to appear in Ireland. The disputed election to the see of Armagh in 1202, for instance, led Pope Innocent III to inform his legate, John of Salerno, 'that a great dispute had arisen out of that election between the Irish and the English, in which the English firmly asserted that they were wholly unwilling that any Irishman should be their archbishop; and often in [the legate's] presence certain English and Irish claimed that it would be better for that church itself and for the peace of the whole land if an Englishman were appointed to the church of Armagh'.[38] The reference to 'certain English and Irish' opposing the election of the Irish candidate should make us pause: the Irish abbot of Mellifont, for one, was of the 'English' party. The dispute may have owed less to national animosities than to the fact that the Irish candidate concerned, Echdonn, abbot of Bangor, came from within the orbit of John de Courcy, lord of Ulster, whom the king distrusted.[39] John eventually acquiesced in the appointment of Echdonn; not only that, he later countenanced his appointment as suffragan bishop of Exeter when the English Church was under interdict. Whatever mixture of motives lay behind the quarrel, the parties were sufficiently conscious of national distinctions to present events as driven by them, and to expect their interpretations to be believed by outsiders.

Echdonn's service as a suffragan in England, which can be paralleled in the careers of other Irish bishops, shows the inadequacy of a simple 'two nations' approach, particularly in the case of the higher clergy. The demands of the reforming Church created alliances and fissures that cut across the distinction between Irish and English. Communication and collaboration between Irish and English clergy had existed for decades before 1170. Everywhere in Europe the moral prescriptions of reformers were liable to collide with ingrained social habits and human frailties; but the distance between ideal and mundane reality may have seemed wider in Ireland (and Wales) than elsewhere in the West because of the existence of alternative moral codes embodied in written laws. Archbishop Nicholas Mac Máel Ísu, for instance, like several of his successors at Armagh, both Irish and English, was hostile to the

37 R. Bartlett, *Gerald of Wales, 1146–1223* (Oxford University Press, 1982), part 1.
38 *Pontificia Hibernica*, i, no. 52, at p. 118.
39 B. Smith, 'The Armagh–Clogher Dispute and the "Mellifont Conspiracy": Diocesan Politics and Monastic Reform in early Thirteenth-Century Ireland', *Seanchas Ardmhacha*, 14 (1991), 30–1.

bardic class, the purveyors of Irish secular culture. He also obtained grants of English law for kinsmen who were taking up residence in County Louth. His clashes with Edward I and the earls of Ulster over the rights of his church were not very different from those between ecclesiastical and secular authorities elsewhere in Europe. A century later, Archbishop John Colton was a crucial link in the communications between Richard II and the Gaelic lords of the north. Colton was an Englishman, once head of a Cambridge college and a former chancellor and chief governor of Ireland. In 1397 we glimpse him travelling west of the Bann with a clerical and lay household (the former mostly Irish, the latter mostly Anglo-Irish) to Ardstraw and Derry, receiving hospitality and supplies, in the form of grain as well as animal products, from Irish church tenants.[40] Churchmen had the skills to theorise about nations and nationality, and to exploit such questions when it suited them. But they were also skilled at crossing 'thresholds' of all sorts. Nor did they omit to preach peace among nations, as when Archbishop Richard Fitz Ralph of Armagh famously denounced the violence and prejudice of his Anglo-Irish audience in a sermon at Drogheda in 1349.[41] In Ireland, the ecclesiastical courts, unlike those of the king, were fully open to both nations.

In Gaelic and Anglo-Norman society, as in pre-modern Europe generally, the marriages of high-born women signified alliances or reconciliations between their families. Just as young viking males found brides in Ireland, so too young military men arriving in Leinster and Munster in the early stages of the Anglo-Norman conquest are likely to have taken Irish wives and concubines, who – together with Irish wet-nurses – will have familiarised children with Gaelic. Evidence of marriages below the topmost level of society is scarce for the late twelfth and thirteenth centuries, but these must have been common, especially beyond the core settlement areas. We know, for instance, that three daughters of Diarmait MacCarthy (? d. 1234) married men named Prendergast, Kaninges and Cosyn. Examples of marriages between settler women and Irish men (possibly a better gauge of assimilation) are not easy to find in the thirteenth century, though Aed *Buide* O'Neill (d. 1286), a protégé of the earls of Ulster, married a Nangle woman.[42] Except in cases such as the

---

40 *Acts of Archbishop Colton on his Metropolitan Visitation of the Diocese of Derry*, ed. W. Reeves (Dublin: Irish Archaeological Soc., 1850), 9–15; J. A. Watt, 'John Colton, Justiciar of Ireland (1382) and Archbishop of Armagh (1383–1404)', in Lydon (ed.), *England and Ireland*, 196–213.

41 K. Walsh, *A Fourteenth-Century Scholar and Primate: Richard FitzRalph in Oxford, Avignon and Armagh* (Oxford University Press, 1981), 284–7.

42 NAI RC 7/1, 246–7; K. Simms, 'The O Hanlons, the O Neills and the Anglo-Normans in Thirteenth-Century Armagh', *Seanchas Ardmhacha*, 9 (1978), 82.

Mac Gilla mo Cholmóc family of south Dublin, who were themselves being absorbed into colonial society, such marriages may have been more problematical. Under English law, in the absence of sons, daughters shared the inheritance, taking precedence of their fathers' brothers or remoter male kin. Given high rates of infant mortality, and the greater difficulty of rearing males, all women were potential heiresses, who might carry the inheritance outside the cultural group. Several great lords of the first generation besides Strongbow took Irish wives. These marriages have tended to be viewed through the lens of 'Gaelicisation', but that may be misleading. Aífe, daughter of Diarmait Mac Murchada, the wife of Strongbow, and Isabel their heiress who carried their inheritance in Ireland, Britain and Normandy to her husband William Marshal, seem to have been absorbed into Anglo-Norman society.[43]

After the early stages of conquest, when incoming lords sought deals with Irish provincial rulers whose networks they were entering and hoping to take over, the heads of leading families, at least in eastern Ireland, normally sought wives within colonial society, or from England. Three marriages of heads of branches of the Bermingham family make the point. In his youth John Bermingham, earl of Louth (d. 1329), had been betrothed to Matilda, one of the daughters of Richard de Burgh, earl of Ulster. This arrangement had been disrupted by the arrival of agents of the earl of Gloucester, Edward II's nephew, seeking a wife for their master. They had selected Matilda as the fairest, leaving Bermingham to console himself with Avelina, one of her sisters.[44] John's mother, the wife of Peter Bermingham, appears in the Annals of Inisfallen as a veritable Lady Macbeth: 'the foreign woman from England … used to give warning from the top of the castle of any who went into hiding, so that many were slain as a result of those warnings'. She was indeed from England, a daughter of William d'Oddingseles, a knight of Edward I who had a career in royal service in Ireland, culminating in a six-month stint as justiciar in 1294–5. By contrast the Berminghams' Connacht kinsman, Sir Richard (d. 1322), the victor of the Battle of Athenry, left a widow named in the record sources as 'Finwola'.[45]

Until the mid-fourteenth century, an Irish mother seems not to have been a bar to inheritance, though the 1317 Remonstrance complains that Irish widows of Englishmen might face obstruction in receiving their dower. Subjecting

---

43 R. Frame, 'Ireland after 1169: Barriers to Acculturation on an "English" Edge', in K. J. Stringer and A. Jotischky (eds.), *Norman Expansion: Connections, Continuities and Contrasts* (Farnham: Ashgate, 2013), 128–32.

44 *CPL, 1305–42*, 209.

45 *AI*, 394–5; Frame, *English Lordship*, 50n.

such marriages to licensing was first proposed by Dublin ministers to Edward III in 1347. The king agreed 'that no marriage take place in the future between English and Irish without special permission of the king or the justiciar'.[46] This was the gist of what was finally enacted in the 1366 Statute of Kilkenny. It seems to reflect, on the one hand, the neuroses of a once-expanding colony which now felt under threat; and on the other the increasing identification in the wider English world of political loyalty with the English language (which included the use of Latin and French for formal purposes) and a set of English cultural markers. Licences permitting marriages and other forms of contact covered by the Statute were subsequently issued, and while most of these relate to the diminishing areas where the king's writ routinely ran, there are some politically significant cases from further afield. In 1388, for instance, James, a future earl of Desmond (d. 1463) but then a younger son, was permitted to be fostered with Conchobar O'Brien, brother of Brian O'Brien of Thomond.[47]

It may be that considerations of ethnicity were relevant and clear-cut only at an upper social level, or when an inheritance fell into dispute, and by the later fifteenth century marriages across the national divide were common, even within the counties around Dublin.[48] Elsewhere, the spread among the well-born of extended lineage structures, together with the absence of interference by central government, served to reduce, and in the west of Ireland abolish, the differences in custom between Irish and English society. In culturally transitional areas, such as parts of south Leinster and Munster, landed inheritance and (in effect) family headship might be determined by the English procedure of entail, used to settle property on a sequence of male kin, thus barring female succession. Further afield, Irish customs for selecting the kin-head obtained. Women were thus less likely to become heiresses. In the north and west of Ireland, an aristocracy, still nationally differentiated by surname, inhabited a single society where serial marriage was common, with the migrations of high-born women often reflecting shifts in regional politics. The canonical norms of Christian marriage were ignored rather than rejected, as grants of dispensation make clear: unions were regularised when it became advisable to do so, sometimes on the basis of elaborate fictions.[49]

---

46 G. J. Hand, *English Law in Ireland, 1290–1324* (Cambridge University Press, 1967), 204–5; Sayles, *Affairs*, 189.

47 CIRCLE: PR 12 Ric II, no. 88.

48 S. Booker, 'Intermarriage in Fifteenth-Century Ireland: The English and Irish in the "Four Obedient Shires" ', *PRIA*, 113 C (2013), 219–50.

49 Kenny, *Anglo-Irish and Gaelic Women*; A. Cosgrove, 'Marriage in Medieval Ireland', in A. Cosgrove (ed.), *Marriage in Ireland* (Dublin: College Press, 1985), 30–3.

Widespread intermarriage, fosterage and other forms of cultural interaction, spread across many generations, can make the persistence of national distinctions in the sources seem puzzlingly out of step with social actualities. The most important influence preserving the separate nations was the belief, rooted in the Old Testament, that identity was transmitted patrilineally. This was as true in the later Middle Ages as in the viking period, and was particularly relevant in the Gaelic world where, as in Wales, genealogical learning was a major industry. It did not mean that the mother's identity was unimportant: in both English and Irish Ireland she might confer wealth and standing, though in different forms. In the Irish aristocratic world of serial marriage and legally sanctioned concubinage, the prospects of a son born to a noble mother with important political connections were normally superior to those of the child of a woman of lesser status.

Variations of Lordship: Towards the Sixteenth Century

Enduring images of late medieval Ireland, which derive their force and longevity from the contrasting nature and geographical distribution of the written evidence, revolve, on the one hand, around what Edmund Curtis dubbed 'the failure of the first conquest', and on the other, the 'Gaelic resurgence' or 'recovery', which by the fifteenth century held sway over the greater part of the island.[50] Both images should be viewed with caution. The rhetoric of colonial decline is heavily impregnated with the jeremiads of royal ministers in Dublin. 'Gaelic resurgence' accurately reflects the predominance of the Irish language across most of Ireland, and its strong presence even within the Pale. But we should beware of a sort of mission-creep, in which the ethnic epithet becomes attached to every aspect of human society, from warfare to agriculture. Over-emphasis on 'Gaelicisation' as an explanation for change may lead the unwary to conclude that in Ireland, like nowhere else on earth, cultural influences flowed in one direction only.

Single-minded reliance on 'Gaelicisation' as an explanatory tool, for instance, leaves us unequal to the task of comprehending the career and outlook of individuals such as James Butler, fourth earl of Ormond (d. 1452). Ormond was a skilled overlord of Irish leaders and an enthusiastic recipient of Gaelic praise-poetry. He can be presented as 'strongly Gaelicised'; he was

---

50 E. Curtis, *A History of Medieval Ireland from 1086 to 1513* (2nd edn. London: Methuen and Co., 1938), ch. 13.

implicitly denounced in those terms by the Talbot faction, whose members alleged in 1441 that he had 'made and ordained Irishmen (groomes and pages of his household) knights of the shire'.[51] Yet this is the same earl who was from his youth upwards closely associated with Henry V and his brothers, who served in France, spent long periods in England (where he established his son, the future earl of Wiltshire), maintained his family's association with Canterbury, and on several occasions sought to encourage increased English intervention in Ireland. It is tempting to view him as exemplifying the useful distinction that has been proposed between cultural Gaelicisation and political loyalty.[52] But that concept may fit the lesser English lineages better than it does their superiors: Ormond and his like were both culturally and politically versatile.

Investigation of the remodelling of the regional and local polities has been one of the more notable developments in the historiography of Ireland during the last generation and a half. We are now familiar with castle-dwelling (and castle-building) lords who imposed a wide range of exactions on their subjects. These mulcts, often lumped together by English observers as 'coign and livery', were sometimes described by terms traceable in early Irish law. But in their late medieval form, they arose from more recent needs, particularly that to support hired troops, from Anglo-Norman mercenaries in the early thirteenth century to household kerns and galloglass bands at a later period. Lordship in Ireland, like that on the Anglo-Scottish borders – another landscape of towers and vulnerable herds – remained predatory. A surviving elegy for Tadc O'Carroll, a minor figure based in Offaly, devotes twenty-seven of its fifty-nine verses to his cattle-raids, the geographical range of which (possibly expanded by service on campaigns with the earl of Ormond) were a confirmation of his status. Tadc, like many men of gentle birth in south-central Ireland, was buried at Holycross Abbey in Tipperary, in the fifteenth century one of the chief ornaments of the Butler sphere.[53] The military activity highlighted by the poets and annalists was not imaginary but was, no doubt, spasmodic. Disputes within and among leading families were negotiated in part by brehons, employed by Anglo-Irish as well as Irish; they were learned in Irish law, but often familiar also with canon, civil and common law and eclectic in the way they reached their judgements. The mixed inheritance is

51 *Stat. Ire., Hen. VI*, 50–3, quotation, 51.
52 E. Matthew, 'Henry V and the Proposal for an Irish Crusade', in Smith (ed.), *Ireland and the English World*, 161–75; C. Maginn, 'English Marcher Lineages of South Dublin in the Later Middle Ages', *IHS*, 34 (2004), 135–6.
53 *Poems on Marcher Lords*, ed. A. O'Sullivan and P. Ó Riain (Dublin: ITS, 1987), 45–65.

symbolised by an entry in the Annals of Connacht for 1419, which tells of the death of Donnchad O'Connor, a grandson of Domnall O'Connor, lord of Sligo, who was fatally wounded 'from a fall on the flagstone in front of Sligo castle, on the near side of the river, at the southern end of the bridge, at the cavalry sports'. Sligo, once developed by Maurice fitz Gerald, was on the way to becoming a prosperous Atlantic seaport town. We are not told whether Richard II was struck by the irony of receiving a letter from Toirdelbach O'Connor Donn dated at Roscommon, the castle-town on which his ancestor, Edward I, had expended a small fortune, which was now a power-centre for control of which Irish dynasts competed.[54]

In south-east Ireland we encounter, by contrast, what can look like a replication across the sea of English political society. Its leadership – embracing royal ministers (some born in England, some in Ireland), nobles, greater gentry (some with legal training), prosperous townsmen, and higher clergy – was politically alert and astute.[55] The appeal to Edward III from a great council at Kilkenny in 1360, which preceded the sending of Lionel of Antwerp to Ireland in the following year, employed the most up-to-date language at a time when addresses to the king were becoming more deferential and ornate. Edward was variously addressed as 'your most high lordship', 'your highness', 'noble and gracious prince', 'your excellent lordship' and 'your majesty' – an early example of a new-fangled style that was to become synonymous with kingship.[56] It was borne to Westminster by carefully chosen messengers. They included knightly representatives of the commons, among them John Lombard, who had served as sheriff and mayor of Cork: the petition was thus shown to be rooted in the wider community of the Lordship. As in England, the period saw the crystallising both of a parliamentary peerage and of a gentry class that used the fashionable English marks of social stratification, 'knight', 'esquire' and 'gentleman'. Like John Lombard, such men often held urban as well as rural property, and overlapped with the mercantile elite.[57]

We do not have to venture far from the heartlands of crown authority to find different structures and styles. In 1350 we encounter the settler Harold lineage of south Dublin choosing Walter Harold as its head, in the same manner as the chief of the O'Byrne family of Wicklow. As recently as 1328 its

54 *AC*, 448–9; Curtis, *Richard II*, 113–14.
55 P. Crooks, 'Representation and Dissent: "Parliamentarianism" and the Structure of Politics in Colonial Ireland c.1370–1420', *EHR*, 125 (2010), 1–34.
56 *Parls. & Councils*, no. 16; G. Dodd, 'Kingship, Parliament and the Court: The Emergence of "High Style" in Petitions to the English Crown, c.1350–1405', *EHR*, 129 (2014), 515–48.
57 Smith, *Crisis and Survival*, chs. 6, 7.

leading figure, Peter Harold, had used the court of common pleas to record an elaborate property settlement on the occasion of the marriage of his son to the daughter of a Dublin burgess, John Stakepoll.[58] The parliament rolls of the mid-fifteenth century contain lists of well-born miscreants on the margins of Counties Kildare and Meath. 'Christopher Cruys, gentleman' rubs shoulders with 'Walter Cruys, idleman', and we meet 'Thomas Bermingham of Carbury, brother to John Bermingham, chief of his lineage, gentleman'. Such composite addresses symbolise a society best described as 'hybrid'.[59] Moreover, it has recently been shown that the four counties of the future Pale had absorbed a significant Irish-speaking population from the surrounding lordships; such entrants, like the kinsmen of Archbishop Mac Máel Ísu several generations earlier, aimed, not at subversion, but at bettering themselves.[60]

From 1399, just after the departure of Richard II, there survives a report to England from ministers in Dublin, in which they itemised the problems of governance in Ireland as they saw them. As well as the incursions of the Irish, they picked out the profusion of liberty jurisdictions that (in theory) diminished the revenues of the crown; grants made on the collective rents of cities and other revenues, which had the same effect; the power and disobedience of the 'English lineages' (les nacions Engleis), who disrupted the peace, colluded with the Irish and were in reality no better than 'sturdy robbers' (fortz larons); and the fees and annuities given to Irish as well as English, which were beggaring the exchequer.[61] The standpoint of the authors tended to be shared by a past generation of historians, who prioritised government records and had an aversion to decentralised power, especially in the hands of aristocrats of the age of 'bastard feudalism'. But the report might equally be read as an attack on many of the social bonds and mechanisms of devolution that gave the Lordship of Ireland what stability it possessed. Practices in Ireland have parallels in Scotland, where historians have been readier to see them as constituent parts of a polity rather than agents of its dissolution.[62] It is revealing that in the 1350s

58 E. Curtis, 'The Clan System among the English Settlers in Ireland', in Crooks (ed.), *Government, War and Society*, 297–301; J. G. Smyly, 'Old Latin Deeds in the Library of Trinity College', part II, *Hermathena*, 67 (1946), no. 30.
59 *Stat. Ire., Hen. VI*, 440–3; *Stat. Ire., 1–12 Edw. IV*, 286–9.
60 S. Booker, 'Irish Clergy and the Diocesan Church in the "Four Obedient Shires" of Ireland, c.1400–c.1540', *IHS*, 39 (2014), 179–209; Smith, *Crisis and Survival*, chs. 5–7.
61 *PKCI*, 261–9.
62 J. Wormald, *Lords and Men in Scotland: Bonds of Manrent, 1442–1603* (Edinburgh: John Donald, 1985); H. L. MacQueen 'The Kin of Kennedy, "kenkynnol" and the Common Law', in A. Grant and K. J. Stringer (eds.), *Medieval Scotland, Crown, Lordship and Community: Essays Presented to G. W. S. Barrow* (Edinburgh University Press, 1993), 274–96.

Thomas Rokeby, a governor with experience of administration in northern England and occupied southern Scotland, had understood the need to use pardons as a means of keeping English marchers on side, and to award stipends to Irish lords.[63]

There may be something to be said for regarding late medieval Ireland, not as a 'failed state', or as the scene of existential conflict between those seductive abstractions 'the two nations', or 'two cultures', but rather as a fragmented polity, where the absence of a single paramount power and a single code of law demanded inventiveness. The country was a laboratory of lordship, as authorities of various sorts sought to strengthen, or indeed establish, effective political and jurisdictional hierarchies, often employing mixed customs. The result was no doubt often oppressive: it seems probable that the building of castles and towers, ecclesiastical and lay, involved something akin to forced labour. But such hierarchies also provided shelter within which individuals, kins and communities could survive, and sometimes thrive.[64]

Ireland in the fourteenth and fifteenth centuries is notable for what might be described as forms of 'bridging' lordship, with generic similarities, visible in the activities of Anglo-Irish earls, royal government and ecclesiastical authorities alike. The best-known examples are the surviving written contracts between the earls of Ormond and Kildare and lesser lords, both Gaelic and Anglo-Irish, within their orbits. Characteristically, these involved variations on a set of familiar themes: surrender of hostages; performance of military service; the duty to discipline followers and keep military bands off the backs of neighbouring Englishry; compensation for damages inflicted; and extradition of offenders to the superior lord's justice. Occasionally, there are explicit references to Irish law as when, in 1400, an agreement between the third earl of Ormond and Geoffrey O'Brennan [Ó Braonáin] stipulated that proven trespasses against the earl's people or any of the English of County Kilkenny should incur double compensation to the earl 'which is known in Irish as *keyn et ad keyn*'.[65] Deeds of this type may often have sought to document, and so strengthen, long-established patterns of interaction. They show, in the words of J. A. Watt (consciously adopting the vocabulary used by Orpen), that 'tribalism and feudalism have effortlessly coalesced'.[66] The 'law

63 R. Frame, 'Thomas Rokeby, Sheriff of Yorkshire, Justiciar of Ireland', *Peritia*, 10 (1996), 274–96.
64 C. A. Empey, 'The Sacred and the Secular: The Augustinian Priory of Kells in Ossory, 1193–1541', *IHS*, 24 (1984), 151.
65 *COD*, ii, no. 347 (2).
66 J. A. Watt, 'Gaelic Polity and Cultural Identity', *NHI* ii, 327.

of the March', denounced in mid-fourteenth-century legislation, was really a codification of the practical.

In like manner, ministers of the crown forged links with Anglo-Irish and Irish leaders which formed a set of conventions operating alongside the usual – and frequently ineffectual – mechanisms of English law and administration. Stipends were paid to Irish leaders in Leinster in return for defined services akin to those mentioned above. In 1370 Sir William Windsor made an agreement with MacNamara, who had occupied the city of Limerick after its brief capture by O'Brien. Claims by the English for future damages, Windsor accepted, would be dealt with 'according to the practice and custom of the Thomond region, that practice being called and named *Koynconhoghs*'.[67] The reference is to *cin confocuis* or kin responsibility, a concept alien to English law (which emphasised individual and neighbourhood responsibility for misdeeds), but one that had figured in the earliest surviving legislation of the Irish parliament (1278), in relation to dealings with the Irish.[68] The description of MacNamara as 'chieftain of his lineage' (*sue nacionis capitaneus*) reflects the crown's practice, developed over the fourteenth century, of engaging with and working through lineage structures among both the Irish and the settlers. In relation to the greater Irish lords, recognition came additionally to be expressed through the employment of the family name as a title. In 1375 William Windsor had sought to replace Brian *Sreamhach* O'Brien of Thomond with his more pliant uncle, Toirdelbach *Maol*. Toirdelbach's plaintive description of his failure in the role is preserved in the record of a petition heard in parliament at Castledermot in 1378. He had been 'appointed chieftain of his lineage, that is to say made "O'Brien of Thomond", by royal authority', only to be driven out, for want of the aid the king had promised him, by 'the former "O'Brien"', Brian *Sreamhach*.[69]

The search for structure and hierarchy comes into particularly clear focus in the strategies adopted by the archbishops of Armagh to identify and legitimate secular powers through whom they might work. In 1427 Archbishop John Swayne urged Art Magennis [Mág Aonghusa] 'chieftain of his lineage' to compel Ross Magennis and Colum MacCartan [Mac Artáin] 'chieftain of Kinelarty' to restore cattle that Adam Oranga, a canon of Dromore, insisted they had stolen. Swayne was prepared to gloss over Adam's allegation of Art's complicity in the theft:

> The archbishop does not believe that such things, though committed by said Art's subjects, are, or have been perpetrated against ecclesiastical liberty by

67 S. Harbison, 'William of Windsor and the Wars of Thomond', *JRSAI*, 119 (1989), 109–11.
68 Richardson and Sayles, *Irish Parliament*, 292; Hand, *English Law in Ireland*, 193, 203–4.
69 *Parls. & Councils*, no. 54.

Art's authority or command … He therefore exhorts said Art to compel his subjects, if guilty, to make condign satisfaction, lest on further complaint of Adam, the archbishop have cause of proceeding against Art, the aforesaid being true.[70]

Not for nothing had the archbishop cut his diplomatic teeth at the Roman curia in the period of the Council of Constance.[71] Endorsement of Gaelic leadership reached its peak in the attendance of Archbishop Mey at the inauguration of Henry Ó Néill in 1455, when various vassal lords 'and the successor of St Patrick went with him to Tulach-óg and he was made king there by them honourably by the will of God and men'. In Armagh diplomatic Henry remained, not a king, but 'chieftain of his lineage', though the addition of the word *principalis* may hint at his exceptional position.[72]

The distribution of power in Ireland had shifted markedly since the time of Edward I. While we should not exaggerate the range and regularity of Edwardian government, much less of Ireland was now administered regularly from Dublin, allowing new alliances to be made among leading Gaelic families. In 1250 or even 1350 contact between the native lords of Donegal and Offaly barely existed, but by 1423 it was possible for Niall *Garb* O'Donnell to marry a daughter of An Calbach O'Connor Faly.[73] Anyone familiar with the period 1250–1350 who reads the Irish annals of the late fifteenth and early sixteenth centuries will be struck by the freedom of movement enjoyed by major lords, both Irish and Anglo-Irish; the power of northern leaders such as O'Neill and O'Donnell and their direct interactions, not just with the Dublin government but at times with the English and Scottish courts; and the geographical range of military campaigns conducted by the Kildare earls as chief governors, which in the early 1500s included Antrim, Tyrone, Donegal and Galway. A convincing case has been made for some recovery of Dublin's jurisdiction and collecting-power in the late fifteenth century.[74] But crown authority was more dependent on personal networks and charisma than it had been in the late thirteenth and early fourteenth centuries. The retreat of the 'administrative model' of rule in favour of alliances and

---

70 *Reg. Swayne*, 58.
71 K. Walsh, 'The Roman Career of John Swayne, Archbishop of Armagh, 1418–39', *Seanchas Ardmhacha*, 11 (1983–4), 1–21.
72 *AU*, iv, 184–5; K. Simms, 'The Concordat between Primate John Mey and Henry O'Neill, 1455', *Archivium Hibernicum*, 34 (1977), 71–82; *Reg. Octaviani*, nos. 126, 361–2.
73 *AFM*, iv, 952–5; C. Ó Cléirigh, 'The O'Connor Faly Lordship of Offaly, 1395–1513', *PRIA*, 96 C (1996), 91–6; K. Simms, 'Niall Garbh II O'Donnell, King of Tír Conaill, 1422–39', *Donegal Annual*, 12 (1977–9), 7–21.
74 Ellis, *Ireland in the Age of the Tudors*, chs. 4, 5.

diplomacy is illustrated by the marriage around 1480 of Eleanor FitzGerald, sister of the Great Earl of Kildare, to Conn son of Henry O'Neill, and the fostering, twenty years later, of one of Kildare's sons with Aed *Ruad* O'Donnell, who collected young Henry fitz Gerald during a visit to the *Galltacht* (north Leinster).[75]

Should we, then, dismiss the formal distinctions between Irish and English as an irrelevant legal fiction? A contrast between Ireland and Wales may suggest why it would be unwise to do so. There were, of course, many straightforward reasons why the Tudors found Wales easier than Ireland to 'reduce to obedience' and absorb: it was smaller and closer to hand; large areas were in the hands of noble families based in England; there was not the complication of a frontier with Scotland. But the history of two late medieval contemporaries, both at times seen as prime enemies of the English crown, suggests an additional consideration. The careers of Art MacMurrough Kavanagh [Mac Murchada Caomanách] (d. 1416) and Owain Glyn Dŵr (d. *c.*1415–16) were pursued relatively few nautical miles apart, and both had more than one dimension. Art presented himself to the Irish as 'king of Leinster'. A praise-poem addressed to him celebrates Leinster as a realm of gold, and presents it at maximum extent, with references to Tara, the Hill of Allen, Dublin, and the Boyne as well as the Barrow, a geography that harks back to the time of his ancestor Diarmait mac Máel na mBó (d. 1072).[76] Owain also attracted the attention of the bards, who clothed him in myth and prophecy, celebrating his blood-right as a scion of the royal dynasties of Powys and Deheubarth.[77] But the difference between the worlds in which these men moved is striking. Art demanded his annual fee as 'chieftain of his lineage' from the Dublin government; he sought recognition of his marriage to Elizabeth la Veel, heiress of the Kildare barony of Norragh; he blackmailed the towns of south Leinster, but also, as a great cattle-baron, traded through them; in 1415 he sent the abbot of Duiske, a doctor of laws, as his emissary to Henry V. Glyn Dŵr's other persona reveals the additional opportunities that were available in Wales. His father, the product of a 'mixed marriage', had been steward of the rich lordship of Oswestry, which belonged to the Fitzalan earls of Arundel; Owain himself served in the earl's retinue in Scotland in 1385. He married the daughter of Sir David Hanmer, a regular on judicial commissions in Wales; he may even, like his Hanmer brother-in-law, have studied law at the Inns of

---

75 *AU*, iii, 438–9.
76 'To Art Mac Murchadha Caomhanach', ed. L. MacKenna, *The Irish Monthly*, 56 (1928), 98–101; Frame, 'Two Kings in Leinster'.
77 R. R. Davies, *The Revolt of Owain Glyndŵr* (Oxford University Press, 1995), 129–73.

Court at Westminster. He belonged, that is, to a culturally versatile Welsh squirearchy, whose members were used to building careers amid the more flexible legal and administrative systems that had developed not just in the marcher lordships but also in the royal lands. The principality was set up after 1282, when Edward I was sufficiently interested, and the English state sufficiently sophisticated, to distinguish between 'acceptable' and 'unacceptable' aspects of Welsh custom, and to sanction the continuation of the former.[78]

Nothing of the sort was ever attempted in Ireland, which had been occupied just as English common law was taking shape.[79] From the time of John, the legal distinctions between newcomers and natives grew increasingly sharp. Legal distinctions remained sufficiently real to inhibit the co-option of junior members of Irish aristocratic families into the office-holding elite of the Lordship of Ireland: there were no Irish sheriffs or keepers of the peace, let alone Irishmen in central government. Ireland thus lacked the partially assimilated gentry class that helped to facilitate the fuller incorporation of Wales into the English polity. Nor, despite the parchment schemes of Richard II, were English kings ever sufficiently authoritative and present to provide a courtly environment into which the topmost levels of Gaelic society might have been drawn, as the Scottish court and household had provided a venue where lords from diverse cultural backgrounds were woven into a single polity with a single law of property. The need for such a development, at a period when major Irish lords were doing deals on equal terms with Anglo-Irish earls and developing diplomatic ties with Scotland and the Continent, was manifest. It is implicit, for instance, in Edward IV's direct dealings with Henry O'Neill, and in Henry VIII's knighting in 1511 of Aed *Dub* O'Donnell. Aed, who was returning from a pilgrimage to Rome, 'got large donatives from the king of the Saxons; for not often did anyone that left Ireland receive an equal amount of honour as he got from the king'.[80] A decade later, Henry was to send the insignia of knighthood to Conn *Bacach* Ó Néill. But on a long view, the policy of 'surrender and regrant' was planted out on inadequately fertilised ground.

What changed in the sixteenth century was not so much the capacity of the English state: Edward I put larger armies in the field than any Tudor monarch; and he and his successors down to the 1440s projected their power on

78 *CPR, 1413–16*, 328; L. B. Smith, 'The Statute of Wales, 1284', *Welsh History Review*, 10 (1980–1), 127–54.
79 Frame, 'Ireland after 1169'.
80 K. Simms, '"The King's Friend": O Neill, the Crown and the Earldom of Ulster', in Lydon (ed.), *England and Ireland*, 224–32; *AU*, iii, 496–7.

the Continent far beyond anything Henry VIII could contemplate. Nor was there, yet, an increased capacity to move people about and organise settlements. But the contexts had shifted. Royal advisors in the time of Henry VIII were even less tolerant than those of Edward's day of administrative, legal and cultural diversity. Ireland epitomised that diversity, with its plethora of units of power, its mixed customs, and the bewildering palimpsest, in which lords with English surnames might be transmitters of Irish learning, while those with Gaelic surnames presided over lordship structures that had absorbed features of the Anglo-Norman world. This mattered the more because Ireland now typified the vulnerability of the Tudor regime. There had been worries about security in the past, as when King John's baronial enemies, who possessed Irish estates, had dealings with Philip II of France. But the only serious threat from outside had been the Bruce invasion. The instability of the English crown during the Wars of the Roses changed all that. During Henry VII's reign the Yorkist pretender, Perkin Warbeck, found backing both in Scotland and from Continental powers.

Such insecurities were increased by the Reformation. Both the twelfth-century and the sixteenth-century phase of English conquest in Ireland had a religious dimension. But their political implications could not have been more different. In 1172 Henry II, trying to recover his reputation after the murder of Thomas Becket, presented himself as a champion of Church reform, and successfully advertised his work to Pope Alexander III. From the 1530s the English crown was not an ally of reform, but its driver. The breach with Rome made Ireland a more obvious target for continental powers, and a more vulnerable one, since it complicated questions of loyalty for the Anglo-Irish elites. It can be argued that ancestry and the sense of a shared past was by 1500 a more significant element of the identity of the English of Ireland than the English language and other cultural features, which were more liable to erosion.[81] Thus the second English conquest both built upon, and challenged, the foundations of the first.

---

81 S. Booker, 'After the "Middle Nation": The English of Ireland, Gaelicisation, and Identity in the "Four Loyal Shires" of Ireland in the Fifteenth and Sixteenth Centuries'. PhD thesis, University of Dublin, Trinity College (2011), 280–2.

Bibliography

Introduction

Brendan Smith

Secondary Works

Barrow, G. W. S., 'Scotland, Wales and Ireland', in *NCMH*, iv. Part 2, 581–610.

Bartlett, R., 'Colonial Aristocracies of the High Middle Ages', in Bartlett and Mackay (eds.), *Medieval Frontier Societies*, 23–48.

'The Celtic Lands of the British Isles', in *NCMH*, v, 809–27.

Bhreathnach, E., 'Review: Medieval Irish History at the End of the Twentieth Century: Unfinished Work', *IHS*, 32 (2000), 260–71.

Broun, D., 'A Second England?: Scotland and the Monarchy of Britain in *The First English Empire*', in Duffy and Foran (eds.), *English Isles*, 84–102.

Brown, M., *Disunited Kingdoms: Peoples and Politics in the British Isles 1280–1460* (Harlow: Pearson, 2013).

Bury, J. B. (gen. ed.), *The Cambridge Medieval History*. 8 vols. (Cambridge University Press, 1911–36).

Byrne, F. J., 'The Viking Age', in *NHI* i, 609–34.

'Ireland before the Battle of Clontarf', in *NHI* i, 852–9.

'Ireland and her Neighbours, *c.*1014–*c.*1072', in *NHI* i, 862–98.

Cosgrove, A., 'The Writing of Medieval Irish History', *IHS*, 27 (1990), 97–111.

'Ireland', in *NCMH*, vii, 496–513.

Crooks, P., Green, D. and Ormrod, W. M. (eds.), *The Plantagenet Empire, 1259–1453* (Donington: Shaun Tyas, 2016).

Davies, R. R. (ed.), *The British Isles 1100–1500: Comparisons, Contrasts and Connections* (Edinburgh: John Donald, 1988).

Domination and Conquest: The Experience of Ireland, Scotland and Wales 1100–1300 (Cambridge University Press, 1990).

'In Praise of British History', in R. R. Davies (ed.), *The British Isles 1100–1500: Comparisons, Contrasts and Connections* (Edinburgh: John Donald, 1988), 9–26.

'The Peoples of Britain and Ireland 1100–1400. I. Identities', *TRHS*, 6th ser., no. 4 (1994), 1–20.

'Frontier Arrangements in Fragmented Societies: Ireland and Wales', in Bartlett and Mackay (eds.), *Medieval Frontier Societies*, 77–100.

Duffy, S., *Ireland in the Middle Ages* (Houndmills and Dublin: Macmillan, 1997).

Ellis, S., 'From Medieval to Early Modern: The British Isles in Transition?', in R. Hutton (ed.), *Medieval or Early Modern: The Value of a Traditional Historical Division* (Cambridge: Cambridge Scholars Publishing, 2015), 10–28.

Flanagan. M. T., 'High-Kings with Opposition', in *NHI* i, 899–933.

Fossier, R. (ed.), *The Cambridge Illustrated History of the Middle Ages*. 3 vols. (Cambridge University Press, 1986–97).

  'Clouds Gather in the West', in R. Fossier (ed.), *The Cambridge Illustrated History of the Middle Ages, 1250–1520* (Cambridge University Press, 1986), 17–51.

Fouracre, P. *et al.* (eds.), *The New Cambridge Medieval History*. 7 vols. (Cambridge University Press, 1995–2005).

Frame, R., *The Political Development of the British Isles 1100–1400* (Oxford University Press, 1990).

  Colonial Ireland 1169–1369, 2nd edn. (Dublin: Four Courts Press, 2012).

  'Ireland', in *NCMH*, vi, 375–87, 967–70.

  'Kingdoms and Dominions at Peace and War', in R. Griffiths (ed.), *The Fourteenth and Fifteenth Centuries* (Oxford University Press, 2003), 149–80.

Hammond, M., 'Domination and Conquest?: The Scottish Experience in the Twelfth and Thirteenth Centuries', in Duffy and Foran (eds.), *English Isles*, 68–83.

Holmes, G. (ed.), *The Oxford Illustrated History of Medieval Europe* (Oxford University Press, 1988).

Hutton, R., 'The British Isles in Transition: A View from the Other Side', in R. Hutton (ed.), *Medieval or Early Modern: The Value of a Traditional Historical Division* (Cambridge: Cambridge Scholars Publishing, 2015), 29–41.

McGuire, J. and Quinn, J. (eds.), *Dictionary of Irish Biography*, 9 vols. (Cambridge University Press and RIA, 2009).

Ó Cróinín, D. (ed.), *A New History of Ireland I: Prehistoric and Early Ireland* (Oxford University Press, 2005).

  'Ireland, 400–800', in *NHI* i, 182–234.

Orpen, G. H., 'Ireland to 1315', in *The Cambridge Medieval History VII: Decline of Empire and Papacy*, ed. J. R. Tanner, C. W. Previté-Orton and Z. N. Brooke (Cambridge University Press, 1932), 527–47.

  'Ireland 1315–c.1485', in *The Cambridge Medieval History VIII: The Close of the Middle Ages*, ed. C. W. Previté-Orton and Z. N. Brooke (Cambridge University Press, 1936), 450–65.

Pollard, M., *Dublin's Trade in Books, 1550–1800* (Oxford University Press, 1990).

Powicke, F. M., 'England: Richard I and John', in *The Cambridge Medieval History VI: Victory of the Papacy*, ed. J. R. Tanner, C. W. Previté-Orton and Z. N. Brooke (Cambridge University Press, 1929), 236–47.

Previté-Orton, C. W. and Brooke, Z. N. (eds.), *The Cambridge Medieval History VIII: The Close of the Middle Ages* (Cambridge University Press, 1936).

Ruddick, A. C., 'Gascony and the Limits of Medieval British Isles History', in Smith (ed.), *Ireland and the English World*, 68–88.

Smith, B., 'The British Isles in the Late Middle Ages: Shaping the Regions', in Smith (ed.), *Ireland and the English World*, 7–19.

  'The Frontiers of Church Reform in the British Isles, 1170–1230', in D. Abulafia and N. Berend (eds.), *Medieval Frontiers: Concepts and Practices* (Aldershot: Ashgate, 2002), 239–53.

Stenton, D. M., 'England: Henry II', in *The Cambridge Medieval History V: Contest of Empire and Papacy*, ed. J. R. Tanner, C. W. Previté-Orton and Z. N. Brooke (Cambridge University Press, 1926), 554–91.

Watts, J., 'Looking for the State in Later Medieval England', in P. Coss and M. Keen (eds.), *Heraldry, Pageantry and Social Display in Medieval England* (Woodbridge: Boydell Press, 2002), 243–68.

Wickham, C. *Framing the Early Middle Ages: Europe and the Mediterranean, 400–800* (Oxford University Press, 2005).

Websites

www.discoveryprogramme.ie/
www.heritagecouncil.ie/
www.monastic.ie/
www.ucc.ie/celt/
www.isos.dias.ie/
www.ucd.ie/mocleirigh/
https://chancery.tcd.ie/
https://discover.ukdataservice.ac.uk/catalogue?sn=5570;
www.researchcatalogue.esrc.ac.uk/grants/R000239389/read
www.cdh.ucla.edu/about/

1 Communities and their Landscapes

Edel Bhreathnach

Primary Sources

Adomnán's 'Law of the Innocents': Cáin Adomnáin, ed. G. Márkus (Glasgow: Blackfriars Books, 1997).

Adomnán's Life of Columba, ed. and trans. A. O. Anderson and M. O. Anderson (Edinburgh: Nelson, 1961; rev. by M. O. Anderson, 1991).

Airne Fíngein, ed. J. Vendryes, Mediaeval and Modern Irish Series 15 (Dublin: DIAS, 1953).

Bechbretha: An Old Irish Law-Tract on Bee-Keeping, ed. T. M. Charles-Edwards and F. Kelly. Early Irish Law Series 1 (Dublin: DIAS, 1983).

Cath Maige Muccrama, ed. M. O'Daly (Dublin: ITS, 1975).

'Coibnes Uisci Thairidne', ed. D. A. Binchy, *Ériu*, 17 (1955), 55–85.

Críth Gablach, ed. D. A. Binchy, Mediaeval and Modern Irish Series 11 (Dublin: DIAS, 1941).

Early Irish Lyrics: Eighth to Twelfth Century, ed. and trans. G. Murphy (Oxford University Press, 1956; repr. 1998).

Félire Óengusso Céli Dé: The Martyrology of Oengus the Culdee, ed. and trans. W. Stokes (London: Henry Bradshaw Society, 1905; repr. 1984).

A Medley of Irish Texts 13: Aided Néill Nóigiallaig', ed. K. Meyer, *Archiv für celtische Lexicographie*, 3 (1907), 323–4.

The Patrician Texts in the Book of Armagh, ed. L. Bieler. Scriptores Latini Hiberniae 10 (Dublin: DIAS, 1979).
Sanas Cormaic (Cormac's glossary), ed. K. Meyer (Halle and Dublin, 1913; Felinfach, 1994).
Scéla Mucce Meic Dathó, ed. R. Thurneysen, Mediaeval and Modern Irish Series 6 (Dublin: DIAS, 1935; repr. 1969).

Secondary Works

Bhreathnach, E., *Ireland in the Medieval World, AD 400–1000: Landscape, Kingship and Religion* (Dublin; Four Courts Press, 2014).
'Abbesses, Minor Dynasties and Kings *in clericatu*: Perspectives of Ireland, 700–850', in M. O. Brown and C. A. Farr (eds.), *Mercia: An Anglo-Saxon Kingdom in Europe* (London and New York: Leicester University Press, 2001), 113–25.
'Transforming Kingship and Cult: The Provincial Ceremonial Capitals in Early Medieval Ireland', in R. Schot, C. Newman and E. Bhreathnach (eds.), *Landscapes of Cult and Kingship* (Dublin: Four Courts Press, 2011), 126–48.
Bolger, T., 'Status, Inheritance and Land Tenure: Some Thoughts on Early Medieval Settlement in Light of Recent Archaeological Excavations', in C. Corlett and M. Potterton (eds.), *Settlement in Early Medieval Ireland in Light of Recent Archaeological Excavations* (Bray: Wordwell, 2011), 1–10.
Bradley, J., 'The Interpretation of Scandinavian Settlement in Ireland', in Bradley (ed.), *Settlement and Society in Medieval Ireland*, 49–78.
'An Early Medieval Crannog at Moynagh Lough, Co. Meath', in C. Corlett and M. Potterton (eds.), *Settlement in Early Medieval Ireland in Light of Recent Archaeological Excavations* (Dublin: Wordwell, 2011), 11–33.
Brady, K., 'Secrets of the Lake: The Lough Corrib Longboats', *Archaeology Ireland*, 110 (2014), 34–8.
Buckley, L. and McConway, C., 'Early Medieval Settlement and Burial Ground at Faughart Lower, Co. Louth', in C. Corlett and M. Potterton (eds.), *Death and Burial in Early Medieval Ireland in the Light of Recent Archaeological Excavations* (Bray: Wordwell, 2010), 49–59.
Byrne, F. J., *Irish Kings and High-Kings* (London: Batsford, 1973; repr. Dublin: Four Courts Press, 2001, 2004).
Carew, M., *Tara and the Ark of the Covenant* (Dublin: RIA, 2003).
Carey, J., 'Tara and the Supernatural', in E. Bhreathnach (ed.), *The Kingship and Landscape of Tara* (Dublin: The Discovery Programme, 2005), 32–48.
Charles-Edwards, T. M., *Early Irish and Welsh Kinship* (Oxford University Press, 1993).
The Early Mediaeval Gaelic Lawyer (Cambridge: Department of Anglo-Saxon, Norse, and Celtic, 1999).
(ed.), *After Rome* (Oxford University Press, 2003).
'A Contract between King and People in Early Medieval Ireland? *Críth Gablach* on Kingship', *Peritia*, 8 (1994), 107–19.
'The *Airgíalla Charter Poem*: The Legal Content', in E. Bhreathnach (ed.), *The Kingship and Landscape of Tara* (Dublin: The Discovery Programme, 2005), 100–23.
Coffey, G., 'On the Excavation of a Tumulus near Loughrea, Co. Galway', *PRIA*, 25 C (1904), 14–20.
Comber, M. and Hull, G., 'Excavations at Caherconnell Cashel, the Burren, Co. Clare: Implications for Cashel Chronology and Gaelic Settlement', *PRIA*, 110 C (2010), 133–71.

Connon, A., 'Prosopography II: A Prosopography of the Early Queens of Tara', in E. Bhreathnach (ed.), *The Kingship and Landscape of Tara* (Dublin: The Discovery Programme, 2005), 225–357.

Cotter, C., 'Cahercommaun Fort, Co. Clare: A Reassessment of its Cultural Context', *Discovery Programme Reports*, 5 (1999), 41–95.

Crawford, S., 'Special Burials, Special Buildings? An Anglo-Saxon Perspective on the Interpretation of Infant Burials in Association with Rural Settlement Structures', in K. Bacvarov (ed.), *Babies Reborn: Infant/Child Burials in Pre- and Protohistory* (Oxford: Archaeopress, 2008), 197–204.

Doyle, I. W., 'The Early Medieval Activity at Dalkey Island: A Reassessment', *Journal of Irish Archaeology*, 9 (1998), 89–103.

Eliade, M., *The Sacred and the Profane* (San Diego, Harvard and London: Harcourt, Brace & Co., 1959).

Fenwick, J. and Newman, C., 'Geomagnetic Survey on the Hill of Tara, Co. Meath, 1998–9', *Discovery Programme Reports*, 6 (2002), 1–17.

FitzPatrick, E., 'The Landscape of Máel Sechnaill's *rígdál*, 859AD', in T. Condit and C. Corlett (eds.), *Above and Beyond: Essays in Memory of Leo Swan* (Bray: Wordwell, 2005), 267–80.

Gillespie, R. F., 'An Early Medieval Settlement at Lowpark, Co. Mayo', in C. Corlett and M. Potterton (eds.), *Settlement in Early Medieval Ireland in Light of Recent Archaeological Excavations* (Bray: Wordwell, 2011), 181–211.

Gosling, P., *Archaeological Inventory of County Galway. Vol. 1: West Galway* (Dublin: The Stationery Office, 1993).

Halpin, A., 'Weapons and Warfare in Viking-Age Ireland', in Sheehan and Ó Corráin (eds.), *The Viking Age in Ireland*, 124–35.

Healy, P., *Pre-Norman Grave-Slabs and Cross-Inscribed Stones in the Dublin Region*, ed. K. Swords (Dublin: Local Studies Section, South Dublin Libraries, 2009).

Hodkinson, B., 'A Reappraisal of the Archaeological Evidence for Weaving in Ireland in the Early Christian Period', *Ulster Journal of Archaeology*, 50 (1987), 47–53.

Jaski, B., *Early Irish Kingship and Succession* (Dublin: Four Courts Press, 2000).

Kehnel, A., *Clonmacnois – the Church and Lands of St. Ciarán: Change and Continuity in an Irish Monastic Foundation (6th to 16th century)* (Münster: Lit, 1995).

Kelly, F., *A Guide to Early Irish Law*, Early Irish Law Series 3 (Dublin: DIAS, 1988).

Early Irish Farming (Dublin: DIAS, 1997).

Koch, J. T. and Carey, J., *The Celtic Heroic Age; Literary Sources for Ancient Celtic Europe and Early Ireland and Wales* (Malden, MA: Celtic Studies Publications, 1995).

Latvio, R., '*Neimed*: Exploring Social Distinctions and Sacredness in Early Irish Legal Sources', in K. Ritari and A. Bergholm (eds.), *Approaches to Religion and Mythology in Celtic Studies* (Cambridge: Cambridge Scholars Publishing, 2008), 220–42.

Mac Cana, P., *The Learned Tales of Medieval Ireland* (Dublin: DIAS, 1980).

Colmán of Cloyne. A Study (Dublin: Four Courts Press, 2004).

Mac Giolla Easpaig, D., 'Significance and Etymology of the Placename *Temair*', in E. Bhreathnach (ed.), *The Kingship and Landscape of Tara* (Dublin: The Discovery Programme, 2005), 421–48.

MacNeill, E., 'Early Irish Population-Groups: Their Nomenclature, Classification, and Chronology', *PRIA*, 29 C (1911), 59–109.

MacShamhráin, A. S., *Church and Polity in Pre-Norman Ireland: The Case of Glendalough* (Maynooth: An Sagart, 1996).

Mallory, J. P., *The Origins of the Irish* (London and New York: Thames and Hudson, 2013).

Meyer, K., 'The Expulsion of the Déssi', *Y Cymmrodor*, 14 (1901), 101–35.

'The Expulsion of the Déssi', *Ériu*, 3 (1907), 135–42.

Moisl, H., 'The Bernician Royal Dynasty and the Irish in the Seventh Century', *Peritia*, 2 (1983), 103–26.

'A Frankish Aristocrat at the Battle of Mag Roth', in M. Richter and J.-M. Picard (eds.), *Ogma: Essays in Celtic Studies in Honour of Proinséas Ní Chatháin* (Dublin: Four Courts Press, 2002), 36–47.

Moore, M., *Archaeological Inventory of County Waterford* (Dublin: The Stationery Office, 1999).

Muhr, K., 'Place-Names and the Understanding of Monuments', in R. Schot, C. Newman and E. Bhreathnach (eds.), *Landscapes of Cult and Kingship* (Dublin: Four Courts Press, 2011), 232–55.

Ní Mhaonaigh, M., 'Friend and Foe: Vikings in Ninth- and Tenth-Century Irish Literature', in Clarke *et al.* (eds.), *Ireland and Scandinavia*, 381–402.

O'Brien, E., 'Churches of South-East County Dublin, Seventh to Twelfth Century', in Mac Niocaill and Wallace (eds.), *Keimelia*, 504–24.

O'Brien, E. and Bhreathnach, E., 'Irish Boundary *Ferta*: Their Physical Manifestation and Historical Context', in F. Edmonds and P. Russell (eds.), *Tome: Studies in Medieval Celtic History and Law in Honour of Thomas Charles-Edwards* (Woodbridge: Boydell Press, 2011), 53–64.

Ó Carragáin, T., 'Church Buildings and Pastoral Care in Early Medieval Ireland', in E. FitzPatrick and R. Gillespie (eds.), *The Parish in Medieval and Early Modern Ireland: Community, Territory and Building* (Dublin: Four Courts Press, 2006), 91–123.

'The Semantics of *Síd*', *Éigse*, 17 (1978), 137–55.

Ó Crualaoich, G., *The Book of the Cailleach: Stories of the Wise-Woman Healer* (Cork University Press, 2003).

Ó Floinn, R., 'Freestone Hill, Co. Kilkenny: A Reassessment', in Smyth (ed.), *Seanchas*, 12–29.

'Patrons and Politics: Art, Artefact and Methodology', in M. Redknap, N. Edwards, S. Youngs, A. Lane and J. Knight (eds.), *Pattern and Purpose in Insular Art: Proceedings of the Fourth International Conference on Insular Art held at the National Museum and Gallery, Cardiff 3–6 September 1998* (Oxford University Press, 2001), 1–14.

'The Anglo-Saxon Connection: Irish Metalwork, AD 400–800', in J. Graham-Campbell and M. Ryan (eds.), *Anglo-Saxon/Irish Relations before the Vikings*. Proceedings of the British Academy 157 (Oxford University Press, 2009), 231–51.

Ó Lochlainn, C., 'Roadways in Ancient Ireland', in J. Ryan (ed.), *Féilsgribhinn Eoin Mhic Néill* (Dublin: Three Candles, 1940), 465–74.

Ó Muraíle, N., 'Some Early Connacht Population-Groups', in Smyth (ed.), *Seanchas*, 161–77.

'Temair/Tara and Other Places of the Name', in E. Bhreathnach (ed.), *The Kingship and Landscape of Tara* (Dublin: The Discovery Programme, 2005), 449–77.

Ó Néill, J., 'Excavation of Pre-Norman Structures on the Site of an Enclosed Early Christian Cemetery at Cherrywood, County Dublin', in S. Duffy (ed.), *Medieval Dublin VII* (Dublin: Four Courts Press, 2006), 66–88.

O'Sullivan, A., *Crannogs: Lake-Dwellings in Early Ireland* (Dublin: Country House, 2000).

O'Sullivan, A. and Boland, D., *The Clonmacnoise Bridge*. Heritage Ireland guide no. 11 (Bray: Wordwell, 2000).

O'Sullivan, A., Sands, R. and Kelly, E. P., *Coolure Demesne Crannog, Lough Derravaragh: An Introduction to its Archaeology and Landscapes* (Bray: Wordwell, 2007).

Power, P., *The Place-Names of Decies* (Cork University Press, 1952).

'Ancient Ruined Churches of Co. Waterford', *Waterford Archaeological Journal*, 4 (1898), 83–95, 195–219.

Raftery, B., *Trackway Excavations in Mountdillon Bogs, Co. Longford, 1985–1991* (Dublin: Crannóg Publication, 1996).

Ritari, K., 'Images of Ageing in the Early Irish Poem *Caillech Bérri*', *Studia Celtica Fennica*, 3 (2006), 57–70.

Rivet, A. L. F. and Smith, C., *The Place-Names of Roman Britain* (London: Batsford, 1979; repr. 1981).

Roche, H., 'Excavations at Ráith na Ríg, Tara, Co. Meath, 1997', *Discovery Programme Reports*, 6 (2002), 19–82.

Scott, B. G., *Early Irish Ironworking* (Belfast: Ulster Museum, 1990).

Seaver, M., 'Interchange: Excavations in an Early Medieval Landscape at Glebe and Laughanstown, Co. Dublin', in C. Corlett and M. Potterton (eds.), *Settlement in Early Medieval Ireland in Light of Recent Archaeological Excavations* (Bray: Wordwell, 2011), 261–87.

Stokes, W. and Strachan, J., *Thesaurus Palaeohibernicus*, 2 vols. (Cambridge University Press, 1901–2).

Stout, M., *The Irish Ringfort* (Dublin: Four Courts Press, 1997).

Townshend, C., *Easter 1916. The Irish Rebellion* (London: Allen Lane, 2005).

Waddell, J., *Archaeology and Celtic Myth: An Exploration* (Dublin: Four Courts Press, 2014).

Whitfield, N., 'The Gold Filigree Panel', in R. F. Gillespie and A. Kerrigan (eds.), *Of Troughs and Tuyères: The Archaeology of the N5 Charlestown Bypass* (Dublin: National Roads Authority, 2010), 296–303.

Websites

www.excavations.ie
www.ucc.ie/locus/
http://adminstaff.vassar.edu/sttaylor/MacDatho/
www.mappingdeathdb.ie

2 Learning, Imagination and Belief

John Carey

Primary Sources

Airne Fíngein, ed. J. Vendryes, Mediaeval and Modern Irish Series 15 (Dublin: DIAS, 1953).

Aldhelmi Opera, ed. R. Ehwald, Monumenta Germaniae Historica, Auctores Antiquissimi 15 (Berlin: Weidmann, 1919).

The Anglo-Saxon Minor Poems, ed. E. V. K. Dobie, Anglo-Saxon Poetic Records 6 (New York; Columbia University Press, 1942).

'*Apgitir Chrábaid:* The Alphabet of Piety', ed. and trans. V. Hull, *Celtica,* 8 (1968), 44–89.

Audacht Morainn, ed. and trans. F. Kelly (Dublin: DIAS, 1976).

'"Audite omnes amantes": A Hymn in Patrick's Praise', ed. and trans. A. Orchard, in D. N. Dumville (ed.), *Saint Patrick, A.D. 493–1993* (Woodbridge: Boydell Press, 1993), 153–73.

Auraicept na n-Éces: The Scholars' Primer, ed. and trans. G. Calder (Edinburgh: John Grant, 1917).

'*Baile Chuinn Chétchathaig*: Edition', ed. and trans. E. Bhreathnach and K. Murray, in E. Bhreathnach (ed.), *The Kingship and Landscape of Tara* (Dublin: The Discovery Programme, 2005), 73–84.

Bethu Phátraic, ed. K. Mulchrone (Dublin: RIA, 1939).

'*Bretha Crólige*', ed. and trans. D. A. Binchy, *Ériu,* 12 (1938), 1–77.

'"The Caldron of Poesy"', ed. and trans. L. Breatnach, *Ériu,* 32 (1981), 45–93.

Carey, J., *King of Mysteries: Early Irish Religious Writings*, rev. edn (Dublin: Four Courts Press, 2000).

Chronica Minora, i, ed. T. Mommsen, Monumenta Germaniae Historica, Auctores Antiquissimi 9 (Berlin: Weidmann, 1892).

Colgan, J., *Trias Thaumaturga* (Louvain: apud Cornelium Coenestenium, 1647; repr. Dublin: Éamonn de Búrca, 1997).

Compert Mongáin and Three Other Early Mongán Tales, ed. and trans. N. White, Maynooth Medieval Irish Texts 5 (Maynooth: Department of Old and Middle Irish, 2006).

Corpus Genealogiarum Sanctorum Hiberniae, ed. P. Ó Riain (Dublin: DIAS, 1985).

Cummian's Letter De Controversia Paschali and the De Ratione Conputandi, ed. and trans. M.Walsh and D. Ó Cróinín (Toronto: Pontifical Institute of Medieval Studies, 1988).

Dicuili Liber de Mensura Orbis Terrae, ed. and trans. J. J. Tierney, Scriptores Latini Hiberniae 6 (Dublin: DIAS, 1967).

Dioecesis Salisburgensis, ed. S. Herzberg-Fränkel, Monumenta Germaniae Historica, Necrologia Germaniae 2 (Berlin: Weidmann, 1904).

Diplomata regum et imperatorum Germaniae pars II, ed. E. Sickel (Berlin: Weidmann, 1879–84; repr. Munich, 1980).

The Early Irish Linguist: An Edition of the Canonical Part of the Auraicept na nÉces, ed. and trans. A. Ahlqvist, Commentationes Humanarum Litterarum 73 (Helsinki : Societas Scientiarum Fennica, 1982).

Echtrae Chonnlai and the Beginnings of Vernacular Narrative Writing in Ireland, ed. and trans. K. McCone, Maynooth Medieval Irish Texts 1 (Maynooth: Department of Old and Middle Irish, 2000).

'An Edition of the Pseudo-Historical Prologue to the *Senchas Már* ', ed. and trans. J. Carey, *Ériu*, 45 (1994), 1–32.

Félire Óengusso Céli Dé, ed. and trans. W. Stokes (London: Henry Bradshaw Society, 1905).

'The Finding of the *Táin* ', ed. and trans. K. Murray, *Cambrian Medieval Celtic Studies*, 41 (2001), 17–23.

First Grammatical Treatise: The Earliest Germanic Phonology, ed. and trans. E. Haugen (London: Longman, 1972).

'The First Middle Irish Metrical Tract', ed. and trans. D. Ó hAodha, in H. Tristram (ed.), *Metrik und Medienwechsel/ Metrics and Media*, ScriptOralia 35 (Tübingen: Gunter Narr, 1991), 207–44.

'The First Third of *Bretha Nemed Toísech*', ed. and trans. L. Breatnach, *Ériu*, 40 (1989), 1–40.

'A Fragment of the Book of Enoch in Latin', ed. M. R. James, *Apocrypha Anecdota*, Texts and Studies 2:3 (Cambridge University Press, 1893), 146–50.

Ford, P. (trans.), *The Celtic Poets: Songs and Tales from Early Ireland and Wales* (Belmont, MA: Ford and Baillie, 1999).

Grammaires Provençales de Hugues Faidit et de Raymond Vidal de Besaudun, ed. F. Guessard, 2nd edn (Paris: Brunsvic, 1858).

In Tenga Bithnua: The Ever-new Tongue, ed. and trans. J. Carey, Corpus Christianorum Series Apocryphorum 16 (Turnhout: Brepols, 2009).

Die irische Kanonensammlung, ed. H. Wasserschleben (Giessen: J. Ricker'sche Buchhandlung, 1874).

'An Irish Penitential', ed. and trans. E. J. Gwynn, *Ériu*, 7 (1914), 121–95.

The Irish Penitentials, ed. and trans. L. Bieler, Scriptores Latini Hiberniae 5 (Dublin: DIAS, 1963).

Jonas of Bobbio, *Vita Columbani Discipulorumque Eius*, in B. Krusch (ed.), *Passiones Vitaeque Sanctorum Aevi Merovingici*, Monumenta Germaniae Historica, Scriptores Rerum Merovingicarum 4 (Hannover and Leipzig: Hahn, 1902), 1–156.

Lebor Gabála Érenn, ed. R. A. S. Macalister, ITS, 34, 35, 39, 41, 45 (London: ITS, 1938–56).

Lebor na hUidre: Book of the Dun Cow, ed. R. I. Best and O. Bergin (Dublin: RIA, 1929).

Libri Epistolarum Sancti Patricii Episcopi, ed. L. Bieler, (Copenhagen: Librairie Gyldendal, 1950–51).

'The Lough Foyle Colloquy Texts: *Immacaldam Choluim Chille* ⅂ *ind Óclaig oc Carraic Eolairg* and *Immacaldam in Druad Brain* ⅂ *inna Banfátho Febuil ós Loch Febuil*', ed. and trans. J. Carey, *Ériu*, 52 (2002), 53–87.

'Mittelirische Verslehren', ed. R. Thurneysen, *Irische Texte*, 3: 1 (1891), 1–182.

Navigatio Sancti Brendani, ed. G. Orlandi. 2 vols. (Milan and Varese: Istituto Editoriale Cisalpino, 1968).

Navigatio Sancti Brendani abbatis, ed. C. Selmer (South Bend: University of Notre Dame Press, 1959).

O'Grady, S. H. (ed. and trans.), *Silva Gadelica*, 2 vols. (London: Williams and Norgate, 1892).

'The Old-Irish Table of Penitential Commutations', ed. and trans. D. A. Binchy, *Ériu*, 19 (1962), 47–72.

'O'Mulconry's Glossary', ed. and trans. W. Stokes, *Archiv für celtische Lexikographie*, 1 (1900), 232–324.

Passiones Vitaeque Sanctorum Aevi Merovingici, ed. B. Krusch, Monumenta Germaniae Historica, Scriptores Rerum Merovingicarum 4 (Hannover and Leipzig: Hahn, 1902).

The Patrician Texts in the Book of Armagh, ed. L. Bieler. Scriptores Latini Hiberniae 10 (Dublin; DIAS, 1979).

'The Rhymeless "Leinster Poems": Diplomatic Texts', ed. and trans. J. Corthals, *Celtica*, 24 (2003), 79–100.

'Sanas Cormaic... Edited from the Copy in the Yellow Book of Lecan', ed. K. Meyer, *Anecdota from Irish Manuscripts*, 4 (1912), 1–128.

Sancti Columbani Opera, ed. and trans. G. S. M. Walker, Scriptores Latini Hiberniae 2 (Dublin: DIAS, 1957).

'Scél Tuáin meic Chairill', ed. and trans. J. Carey, *Ériu*, 35 (1984), 93–111.

Scriptores Hiberniae Minores, Pars I, ed. R. E. McNally, Corpus Christianorum Series Latina 108B (Turnhout: Brepols, 1973).

'The Settling of the Manor of Tara', ed. and trans. R. I. Best, *Ériu*, 4 (1908–10), 121–72.

Three Irish Glossaries, ed. W. Stokes (London: Williams and Norgate, 1862).

'*Tiughraind Bhécáin*', ed. and trans. F. Kelly, *Ériu*, 26 (1975), 66–98.

Transitus Beati Fursei: A Translation of the 8th Century Manuscript, ed. and trans O. Rackham (Norwich: Fursey Pilgrims, 2007).

Two Texts on Loch nEchach, ed. and trans R. de Vries, ITS 65 (Dublin ITS, 2012).

Uraicecht na Ríar: The Poetic Grades in Early Irish Law, ed. and trans. L. Breatnach, Early Irish Law Series 2 (Dublin: DIAS, 1987).

'The Welsh-Latin Poetry of Sulien's Family', ed. and trans. M. Lapidge, *Studia Celtica*, 8/ 9 (1973–4), 68–106.

Secondary Works

Bieler, L., *Ireland Harbinger of the Middle Ages*, rev. edn. (Oxford University Press, 1966).

Bisagni, J., 'The Language and the Date of *Amrae Coluimb Chille*', in S. Zimmer (ed.), *Kelten am Rhein: Akten des dreizehnten Internationalen Keltologiekongresses*, 2 vols, Beihefte der Bonner Jahrbücher 58 (Mainz am Rhein: Philipp von Zabern, 2009), ii, 1–11.

Borsje, J., 'Monotheistic to a Certain Extent: The "Good Neighbours" of God in Ireland', in A.-M. Korte and M. de Haardt (eds.), *The Boundaries of Monotheism: Interdisciplinary Explorations into the Foundations of Western Monotheism*, Studies in Theology and Religion 13 (Leiden: Brill, 2009), 53–81.

Breatnach, L., 'Canon Law and Secular Law in Early Ireland: The Significance of *Bretha Nemed*', *Peritia*, 3 (1984), 439–59.

'The Ecclesiastical Element in the Old Irish Legal Tract *Cáin Fhuithirbe*', *Peritia*, 5 (1986), 36–52.

'Poets and Poetry', in K. McCone and K. Simms (eds.), *Progress in Medieval Irish Studies* (Maynooth: Department of Old Irish, Saint Patrick's College, 1996), 65–77.

Byrne, F. J., 'Seventh-Century Documents', *Irish Ecclesiastical Record*, 5th ser. 108 (1967), 164–82.

'Introduction', in O'Neill, *The Irish Hand*, xi–xxvii.

Carey, J., *A Single Ray of the Sun: Religious Speculation in Early Ireland*, 2nd edn. (Aberystwyth: Celtic Studies Publications, 2011).

'Origin and Development of the Cesair Legend', *Éigse*, 22 (1987), 37–48.

'Angelology in *Saltair na Rann*', *Celtica*, 17 (1987), 1–8.

'Ireland and the Antipodes: The Heterodoxy of Virgil of Salzburg', *Speculum*, 64 (1989), 1–10.

'On the Interrelationships of Some *Cín Dromma Snechtai* Texts', *Ériu*, 46 (1995), 71–92.

'Saint Patrick, the Druids, and the End of the World', *History of Religions*, 36 (1996), 42–53.

'The Three Things Required of a Poet', *Ériu*, 48 (1997), 41–58.

'Téacsanna Draíochta in Éirinn sa Mheánaois Luath', *Léachtaí Cholm Cille*, 30 (2000), 98–117.

Carney, J., *Studies in Irish Literature and History* (Dublin: DIAS, 1955).

The Irish Bardic Poet (Dublin: DIAS, 1985).

Chadwick, H. M. and N. K., *The Growth of Literature*, 3 vols. (Cambridge University Press, 1932–40).

Charles-Edwards, T. M., *Early Christian Ireland* (Cambridge University Press, 2000).

'The Social Background of Irish *Peregrinatio*', *Celtica*, 11 (1976), 43–59.

'The Church and Settlement', in P. Ní Chatháin and M. Richter (eds.), *Irland und Europa: Die Kirche der Frühmittelalter* (Stuttgart: Klett-Cotta, 1984), 167–75.

'Palladius, Prosper, and Leo the Great: Mission and Primatial Authority', in D. N. Dumville (ed.), *Saint Patrick, A.D. 493–1993* (Woodbridge: Boydell Press, 1993), 1–12.

Clancy, T. O., 'Before the Ballad: Gaelic Narrative Verse before 1200', *Scottish Gaelic Studies*, 24 (2008), 115–31.

Dumville, D. N., *A Palaeographer's Review: The Insular System of Scripts in the Early Middle Ages*, vol. 1, Institute of Oriental and Occidental Studies Sources and Materials Series 20–1 (Suita; Kansai University Press, 1999), 17–40.

'Biblical Apocrypha and the Early Irish: A Preliminary Investigation', *PRIA*, 73 C (1973), 299–338.

'The *Táin* and the Annals: A Caveat', *Éigse*, 17:1 (1977), 47–54.

'Two Approaches to the Dating of *Navigatio Sancti Brendani*', *Studi medievali*, 3rd ser., no. 29 (1988), 87–102.

'St Cathróe of Metz and the Hagiography of Exoticism', in J. Carey, M. Herbert and P. Ó Riain (eds.), *Studies in Irish Hagiography: Saints and Scholars* (Dublin: Four Courts Press, 2001), 172–88.

Emmerich, F., *Der heilige Kilian, Regionarbischof und Märtyrer* (Würzburg: A. Göbel, 1896).

Etchingham, C., *Church Organisation in Ireland AD 650 to 1000* (Naas: Laigin, 1999).

Follett, W., *Céli Dé in Ireland: Monastic Writing and Identity in the Early Middle Ages* (Woodbridge: Boydell Press, 2006).

Gougaud, L., *Christianity in Celtic Lands*, trans. M. Joynt (London: Sheed and Ward, 1932).

Harvey, A., 'Some Significant Points of Early Insular Celtic Orthography', in D. Ó Corráin, L. Breatnach and K. McCone (eds.), *Sages, Saints and Storytellers: Celtic Studies in Honour of Professor James Carney*, Maynooth Monographs 2 (Maynooth: An Sagart, 1989), 56–66.

Herren, M., 'Classical and Secular Learning among the Irish before the Carolingian Renaissance', *Florilegium*, 3 (1981), 118–57.

Hughes, K., *The Church in Early Irish Society* (London: Methuen, 1966).

Hull, E., *The Cuchullin Saga in Irish Literature* (London: David Nutt, 1898).

James, M. R., Irish Apocrypha', *Journal of Theological Studies*, 20 (1919), 9–16.

Kelly, F., *A Guide to Early Irish Law*, Early Irish Law Series 3 (Dublin: DIAS, 1988).

Koch, J. T., 'When was Welsh Literature First Written Down?', *Studia Celtica*, 20/21 (1985–6), 43–66.

'On the Origins of the Old Irish Terms *Goídil* and *Goídelc*', in G. Evans, B. Martin and J. M. Wooding (eds.), *Origins and Revivals: Proceedings of the First Australian Conference of Celtic Studies* (University of Sydney, 2000), 3–16.

Ködderitzsch, R., 'Der 2. Merseburger Zauberspruch und seine Parallelen', *Zeitschrift für celtische Philologie*, 33 (1974), 45–57.

Labitte, C., 'La *Divine Comédie* avant Dante', *Revue des Deux Mondes*, 31 (1842), 704–42.

Lapidge, M., 'Columbanus and the "Antiphonary of Bangor"', *Peritia*, 4 (1985), 104–16.

Law, V., *The Insular Latin Grammarians* (Woodbridge: Boydell Press, 1982).

Mac Cana, P., *The Learned Tales of Medieval Ireland* (Dublin: DIAS, 1980).

'Conservation and Innovation in Early Celtic Literature', *Études celtiques*, 13 (1971), 61–118.

'*Regnum* and *Sacerdotium*: Notes on Irish Tradition', *Proceedings of the British Academy*, 65 (1979), 443–79.

McCone, K., *Pagan Past and Christian Present in Early Irish Literature*, Maynooth Monographs 3 (Maynooth: An Sagart, 1990).

Towards a Relative Chronology of Ancient and Medieval Celtic Sound Change, Maynooth Studies in Celtic Linguistics 1 (Maynooth: Department of Old and Middle Irish, 1996).

'Dán agus Tallann', *Léachtaí Cholm Cille*, 16 (1986), 9–53.

MacDonald, A., 'Notes on Monastic Archaeology and the Annals of Ulster, 650–1050', in D. Ó Corráin (ed.), *Irish Antiquity: Essays and Studies Presented to M. J. O'Kelly* (Cork: Tower Books, 1981), 304–19.

McManus, D., *A Guide to Ogam*, Maynooth Monographs 4 (Maynooth: An Sagart, 1991).

MacNeill, E., *Early Irish Laws and Institutions* (Dublin: Burns Oates and Washbourne, 1935).

'Archaisms in the Ogham Inscriptions', *PRIA*, 39 C (1931), 33–53.

'De Origine Scoticae Linguae', *Ériu*, 11 (1930–2), 112–29.

Murphy, G., *Saga and Myth in Ancient Ireland* (Dublin: Three Candles, 1961).

'Bards and Filidh', *Éigse*, 2 (1940), 200–7.

Murray, K., 'Interpreting the Evidence: Problems with Dating the Early *Fíanaigecht* Corpus', in S. J. Arbuthnot and G. Parsons (eds.), *The Gaelic Finn Tradition* (Dublin: Four Courts Press, 2012), 31–49.

Ní Dhonnchadha, M., 'The Guarantor List of *Cáin Adomnáin*, 697', *Peritia*, 1 (1982), 178–215.

Ó Corráin, D., 'Irish Origin Legends and Genealogy: Recurrent Aetiologies', in T. Nyberg, P. Iørn and P. M. Sørensen (eds.), *History and Heroic Tale: A Symposium* (Odense University Press, 1985), 57–67.

'Irish Vernacular Law and the Old Testament', in P. Ní Chatháin and M. Richter (eds.), *Irland und die Christenheit* (Stuttgart: Klett-Cotta, 1987), 284–307.

'St Patrick and the Kings', in Duffy (ed.), *Princes, Prelates and Poets*, 211–20.

Ó Corráin, D., Breatnach, L. and Breen, A., 'The Laws of the Irish', *Peritia*, 3 (1984), 382–438.

Ó Cróinín, D., 'Rath Melsigi, Willibrord, and the Earliest Echternach Manuscripts', *Peritia*, 3 (1984), 17–49.

Oliver, L., *The Beginnings of English Law* (University of Toronto Press, 2002).

Ó Mainnín, M., 'Eochaid Ua Flainn agus Eochaid Ua Flannucáin: Súil Úr ar an bhFianaise', *Léann*, 2 (2009), 75–105.

O'Meara, J. J., *Eriugena* (Oxford University Press, 1988).

Ó Néill, P., 'The Date and Authorship of *Apgitir Chrábaid*: Some Internal Evidence', in P. Ní Chatháin and M. Richter (eds.), *Irland und die Christenheit: Bibelstudien und Mission* (Stuttgart: Klett-Cotta, 1987), 203–15.

Page, R. I., *Runes* (London: British Museum, 1987).

Perceval, W. K., 'The Grammatical Traditions and the Rise of the Vernaculars', *Current Trends in Linguistics*, 13 (1975), 231–75.

Renan, E., *Essais de morale et de critique* (Paris: Michel Lévy Frères, 1859).

Russell, P., 'The Sounds of a Silence: The Growth of Cormac's Glossary', *Cambridge Medieval Celtic Studies*, 15 (1988), 1–30.

Savage, J. J. H., 'The Manuscripts of the Commentary of Servius Danielis on Virgil', *Harvard Studies in Classical Philology*, 43 (1932), 77–121.

'The Manuscripts of Servius's Commentary on Virgil', *Harvard Studies in Classical Philology*, 45 (1934), 157–204.

Sharpe, R., *Medieval Irish Saints' Lives: An Introduction to Vitae Sanctorum Hiberniae* (Oxford University Press, 1991).

'Some Problems Concerning the Organization of the Church in Early Medieval Ireland', *Peritia*, 3 (1984), 230–70.

'Churches and Communities in Early Medieval Ireland: Towards a Pastoral Model', in J. Blair and R. Sharpe (eds.), *Pastoral Care before the Parish* (Leicester University Press, 1992), 81–109.

Smyth, A. P., 'The Earliest Irish Annals: Their First Contemporary Entries, and the Earliest Centres of Recording', *PRIA*, 72 C (1972), 1–48.

Stokes, W. and Strachan, J., *Thesaurus Palaeohibernicus*, 2 vols. (Cambridge University Press, 1901–2).

Swift, C., *Ogam Stones and the Earliest Irish Christians*, Maynooth Monographs Series Minor 2 (Maynooth: Department of Old and Middle Irish, Saint Patrick's College, 1997).

Thompson, E. A., *Who was Saint Patrick?* (Woodbridge: Boydell Press, 1985).

Thurneysen, R., *Die irische Helden- und Königsage bis zum siebzehnten Jahrhundert* (Halle: Niemeyer, 1921).

'Mélanges irlandais', *Revue celtique*, 6 (1883–5), 371–3.

Toner, G., 'The Ulster Cycle: Historiography or Fiction?', *Cambrian Medieval Celtic Studies*, 40 (2000), 1–20.

Vogel, L., *Vom Werden eines Heiligen: eine Untersuchung der Vita Corbiniani des Bischofs Arbeo von Freising* (Berlin: Walter de Gruyter, 2000).

Wiley, D. M., *Essays on the Early Irish King Tales* (Dublin: Four Courts Press, 2008).

3 Art and Society

Jane Hawkes

Manuscript Sources

RIA MS 12 R 33   Cathach of St Columba
TCD MS 52   Book of Armagh
TCD MS 55   Codex Usserianus Primus
TCD MS 57   Book of Durrow
TCD MS 58   Book of Kells
University of Cambridge: Corpus Christi College Library, MS 286   Augustine Gospels
Lambeth Palace Library, MS 1370   Macdurnan Gospels
Paris: Bibliothèque Nationale de France, MS lat. 12190
Milan: Biblioteca Ambrosiana, MS D. 23.   Copy of Paulus Orosius' *Chronicon*
Trier: Domschatz Codex 61 (Bibliotheksnummer 134)   Trier Gospels

Primary Sources

Adamnán's De Locis Sanctis, ed. and trans. D. Meehan. Scriptores Latini Hiberniae 3 (Dublin: DIAS, 1958).

Bede: on the Temple, ed. S. Connolly with introduction by J. O'Reilly (Liverpool University Press, 1995).

The Letters of Gregory the Great, ed. J. R. C. Martyn. 3 vols. (Toronto: Pontifical Institute of Medieval Studies, 2004).

Secondary Works

Alexander, J. J. G., *Insular Manuscripts, 6th to the 9th Century* (London: Harvey Miller, 1978).

Baker, N. G., 'The Evangelists in Insular Culture, *c.*600–*c.*800 AD'. PhD thesis, 2 vols. University of York (2011).

Bhreathnach, E., 'The Cultural and Political Milieu of the Deposition and Manufacture of the Hoard Discovered at Reerasta Rath, Ardagh, Co. Limerick', in M. Redknap, N. Edwards, A. Lane and S. Youngs (eds.), *Pattern and Purpose in Insular Art: Proceedings of the Fourth International Conference on Insular Art held at the National Museum and Gallery, Cardiff, 3–6 September 1998* (Oxford: Oxbow Books, 2001), 15–23.

Carruthers, M., *The Experience of Beauty in the Middle Ages* (Oxford University Press, 2013).

Connolly, S. and Picard, J.-M., 'Cogitosus's "Life of St Brigit" Content and Value', *JRSAI*, 117 (1987), 5–27.

Murray, G., *The Cross of Cong: A Masterpiece of Medieval Irish Art* (Dublin: Irish Academic Press, 2014).

Ó Carragáin, É., 'Recapitulating History: Contexts for the Mysterious Moment of Resurrection on Irish High Crosses', in J. Hawkes (ed.), *Making Histories: Proceedings of the Sixth International Conference on Insular Art, York 2011* (Donington: Shaun Tyas, 2013), 246–61.

Ó Floinn, R., *Irish Shrines and Reliquaries of the Middle Ages* (Dublin: Country House, 1994).

The Moylough Belt-Shrine (Bray: Wordwell, 2008).

'Patrons and Politics: Art, Artefact and Methodology', in M. Redknap, N. Edwards, A. Lane and S. Youngs (eds.), *Pattern and Purpose in Insular Art: Proceedings of the Fourth International Conference on Insular Art held at the National Museum and Gallery, Cardiff, 3–6 September 1998* (Oxford: Oxbow Books, 2001), 1–14.

O'Reilly, J., 'The Hiberno-Latin Tradition of the Evangelists and the Gospels of Mael Brigte', *Peritia*, 9 (1995), 290–309.

'Patristic and Insular Traditions of the Evangelists: Exegesis and Iconography', in A. M. Luiselli Fadda and É. Ó Carragáin (eds.), *Le Isole Britanniche e Roma in Età Romanobarbarica* (Rome: Herder Herder Editrice e Libreria, 1998), 49–94.

Rubin, E. *Experimenta Psychologica: Collected Scientific Papers in German, English and French* (Copenhagen: Munksgaard, 1949).

Ryan, M., *The Derrynaflan Hoard, I: A Preliminary Account* (Dublin: National Museum of Ireland, 1983).

4 The Scandinavian Intervention

Alex Woolf

Primary Sources

Anglo-Saxon Chronicle 5, MS C, ed. K. O'Brien O'Keeffe (Woodbridge: Boydell Press, 2000).

Íslendingabók, Landnámabók, ed. J. Benediktsson (Reykjavík: Hid islenzka fornritafelag, 1986).

Secondary Works

Abrams, L., 'The Conversion of the Scandinavians of Dublin', *ANS*, 20 (1997), 1–29.

   'Diaspora and Identity in the Viking Age', *Early Medieval Europe*, 20.1 (2012), 17–38.

   'Conversion and the Church in Viking-Age Ireland', in Sheehan and Ó Corráin (eds.), *Viking Age in Ireland*, 1–10.

Axboe, M., 'Towards the Kingdom of Denmark', *Anglo-Saxon Studies in Archaeology and History*, 10 (1999), 109–18.

Barnes, M. P., 'The Scandinavian Languages in the Viking Age', in S. Brink (ed.), *The Viking World* (London: Routledge, 2008), 274–80.

Barrett, J. H., 'What Caused the Viking Age?' *Antiquity*, 82 (2008), 671–85.

Blum, J., *Lord and Peasant in Russia: From the Ninth to the Nineteenth Century* (Princeton University Press, 1961).

Boyd, R., 'From Country to Town: Social Transitions in Viking Age Housing', in D. M. Hadley and L. ten Harkel (eds.), *Everyday Life in Viking-Age Towns: Social Approaches to Towns in England and Ireland, c.800–1100* (Oxford: Oxbow, 2013), 73–85.

Bradley, J., 'The Interpretation of Scandinavian Settlement in Ireland', in Bradley (ed.), *Settlement and Society in Medieval Ireland*, 49–78.

Brink, S., 'Law and Legal Customs in Viking-Age Scandinavia', in J. Jesch (ed.), *The Scandinavians from the Vendel Period to the Tenth Century: An Ethnographic Perspective* (Woodbridge: Boydell Press, 2003), 87–115.

   'Legal Assemblies and Judicial Structure in Early Scandinavia', in O. S. Barnwell and M. Mostert (eds.), *Political Assemblies in the Earlier Middle Ages* (Turnhout: Brepols, 2003), 61–72.

Clarke, H. B., 'Proto-Towns and Towns in Ireland and Britain in the Ninth and Tenth Centuries', in Clarke *et al.* (eds.), *Ireland and Scandinavia*, 331–80.

   'King Sitriuc Silkenbeard: A Great Survivor', in Clarke and Johnson (eds.), *Vikings in Ireland and Beyond*, 253–67.

Downham, C., *Viking Kings of Britain and Ireland: The Dynasty of Ívarr to* AD *1014* (Edinburgh: Dunedin Academic Press, 2007).

Drumbl, M. A., *Reimagining Child Soldiers in International Law and Policy* (Oxford University Press, 2012).

Duffy, S., *Brian Boru and the Battle of Clontarf* (Dublin: Gill & Macmillan, 2013).

'Irishmen and Islesmen in the Kingdoms of Dublin and Man, 1052–1171', *Ériu*, 43 (1992), 93–133.

'A Reconsideration of the Site of Dublin's Viking Thing-mót', in T. Condit and C. Corlett (eds.), *Above and Beyond: Essays in Memory of Leo Swan* (Bray: Wordwell, 2005), 351–60.

'The Royal Dynasties of Dublin and the Isles in the Eleventh Century', in S. Duffy (ed.), *Medieval Dublin VII* (Dublin: Four Courts Press, 2006), 51–65.

Dumville, D. N., *The Churches of North Britain in the First Viking Age* (Whithorn: Whithorn Trust, 1997).

Etchingham, C., *Viking Raids on Irish Church Settlements in the Ninth Century* (Maynooth: An Sagart, 1996).

Church Organisation in Ireland AD *650 to 1000* (Naas: Laigin, 1999).

Graham-Campbell, J., '"Silver Economies" and the Ninth-Century Background', in J. Graham-Campbell, S, M. Sindbæk and G. Williams (eds.), *Silver Economies, Monetisation and Society in Scandinavia,* AD *800–1100* (Aarhus University Press, 2011), 29–40.

Griffiths, D., *Vikings in the Irish Sea: Conflict and Assimilation,* AD *790–1050* (Stroud: Sutton Publishing, 2010).

Hadley, D. M. and ten Harkel, L., 'Preface', in D. M. Hadley and L. ten Harkel (eds.), *Everyday Life in Viking-Age Towns: Social Approaches to Towns in England and Ireland, c.800–1100* (Oxford: Oxbow, 2013), vii–xii.

Hårdh, B., *Silver in the Viking Age: A Regional Economic Study* (Stockholm: Almquist and Wiksell International, 1996).

Harrison, S. H., 'Beyond *longphuirt*? Life and Death in Early Viking-Age Ireland', in D. M. Hadley and L. ten Harkel (eds.), *Everyday Life in Viking-Age Towns: Social Approaches to Towns in England and Ireland, c.800–1100* (Oxford: Oxbow, 2013), 61–72.

Harrison, S. H. and Ó Floinn, R., *Viking Graves and Grave-Goods in Ireland* (Dublin: National Museum of Ireland, 2015).

Heen-Pettersen, M., 'Insular Artefacts from Viking-Age Burials from Mid-Norway: A Review of Contact between Trøndelag and Britain and Ireland', *Internet Archaeology*, 38 (2014) http://dx.doi.org/10.11141/ia.38.2.

Holm, P., 'The Slave Trade of Dublin, Ninth to Twelfth Centuries', *Peritia*, 5 (1986), 317–45.

'Manning and Paying the Hiberno-Norse Dublin Fleet', in Purcell *et al.* (eds.), *Clerics, Kings and Vikings*, 67–78.

Honwana, A., *Child Soldiers in Africa* (Philadelphia: University of Pennsylvania Press, 2006).

Hudson, B., *Viking Pirates and Christian Princes: Dynasty, Religion and Empire in the North Atlantic* (Oxford University Press, 2005).

Jesch, J., *Ships and Men in the Late Viking Age: The Vocabulary of Runic Inscriptions and Skaldic Verse* (Woodbridge: Boydell Press, 2001).

The Viking Diaspora (London: Routledge, 2015).

Kelly, E. P., 'The *longphort* in Viking-Age Ireland: The Archaeological Evidence', in Clarke and Johnson (eds.), *Vikings in Ireland and Beyond*, 55–92.

McAlister, D., 'Childhood in Viking and Hiberno-Scandinavian Dublin, 800–1100', in D. M. Hadley and L. ten Harkel (eds.), *Everyday Life in Viking-Age Towns: Social Approaches to Towns in England and Ireland, c.800–1100* (Oxford: Oxbow, 2013), 86–102.

McCormick, M., *The Origins of the European Economy: Communications and Commerce, AD 300–900* (Cambridge University Press, 2001).

'New Light on the "Dark Ages": How the Slave Trade Fuelled the Carolingian Economy', *Past and Present*, 177 (2002), 17–54.

Maund, K. L., 'Turmoil of Warring Princes: Political Leadership in Ninth-Century Denmark', *HSJ*, 6 (1994), 29–47.

Myhre, B., 'The Beginning of the Viking Age – Some Current Archaeological Problems', in A. Faulkes and R. Perkins (eds.), *Viking Revaluations* (London: Viking Society, 1993), 182–216.

Näsman, U., 'The Ethnogenesis of the Danes and the Making of a Danish Kingdom', *Anglo-Saxon Studies in Archaeology and History*, 10 (1999), 1–10.

Ní Mhaonaigh, M., *Brian Boru: Ireland's Greatest King?* (Stroud: Tempus, 2007).

Purcell, E. and Sheehan, J., 'Viking Dublin: Enmities, Alliances and the Cold Gleam of Silver', in D. M. Hadley and L. ten Harkel (eds.), *Everyday Life in Viking-Age Towns: Social Approaches to Towns in England and Ireland, c.800–1100* (Oxford: Oxbow, 2013), 35–60.

Reid, R. J., *Warfare in African History* (Cambridge University Press, 2012).

Reyna, S. P., *Wars without End: The Political Economy of a Pre-Colonial African State* (Hanover, NH: University Press of New England, 1990).

Schaps, D., 'The Invention of Coinage in Lydia, in India, and in China' *XIV International Economic History Congress* (Helsinki, 2006), session 30 www.helsinki.fi/iehc2006/papers1/Schaps.pdf.

Sheehan, J., 'The Longphort in Ireland', *Acta Archaeologica*, 79 (2008), 282–95.

'Silver', in I. Russell and M. F. Hurley (eds.), *Woodstown: A Viking-Age Settlement in Co. Waterford* (Dublin: Four Courts Press, 2014), 194–221.

Simpson, L., 'The First Phase of Viking Activity in Ireland: Archaeological Evidence from Dublin', in Sheehan and Ó Corráin (eds.), *Viking Age in Ireland*, 418–29.

'A Viking Warrior Grave from Dublin', in Clarke and Johnson (eds.), *Vikings in Ireland and Beyond*, 129–50.

Smyth, A. P., 'The Effect of Scandinavian Raiders on the English and Irish Churches: A Preliminary Reassessment', in Smith (ed.), *Britain and Ireland*, 1–38.

Valante, M. A., *The Vikings in Ireland: Settlement, Trade and Urbanization* (Dublin: Four Courts Press, 2008).

Wallace, P. F., '*Gardda* and *Airbeada*: The Plot Thickens in Medieval Dublin', in Smyth (ed.), *Seanchas*, 261–74.

Wilson, D. M., *The Vikings in the Isle of Man* (Aarhus University Press, 2008).

Woolf, A., *From Pictland to Alba, 789–1070* (Edinburgh University Press, 2007).

'Amláib Cúarán and the Gael, 941–81', in S. Duffy (ed.), *Medieval Dublin III* (Dublin: Four Courts Press, 2002), 34–42.

'The Diocese of the Sudreyar', in S. Imsen (ed.), *Ecclesia Nidrosiensis, 1153–1537* (Trondheim: Senter for middelalderstudier, 2003), 171–81.

5 Perception and Reality: Ireland *c.*980–1229

Máire Ní Mhaonaigh

Primary Sources

'Acallam na Senórach', ed. and trans. W. Stokes, in *Irische Texte mit Wörterbuch*, ed. E. Windisch and W. Stokes, 4 vols., vol. 4:1 (Leipzig: Verlag von S. Hirzel, 1900).

'Airbertach mac Cosse's Poem on the Psalter', ed. P. Ó Néill, *Éigse*, 17 (1977–8), 19–46.

'The Annals in Coton MS Titus A xxv', ed. and trans. A. M. Freeman, *Revue celtique*, 41 (1924), 301–30; 42 (1925), 283–505; 43 (1926), 358–84; 44 (1927), 336–61.

'The Ban-shenchus', ed. and trans. M. C. Dobbs *Revue celtique*, 47 (1930), 283–339; 48 (1931), 163–233; and 49 (1932), 437–89.

Caithréim Cellacháin Caisil: The Victorious Career of Cellachan of Cashel, or the Wars between the Irishmen and the Norsemen in the Middle of the 10th Century, ed. and trans. A. Bugge (Oslo: J. C. Gundersens bogtrykkeri, 1905).

Cronica Regum Mannie et Insularum, ed. G. Broderick (Belfast: Manx Museum and National Trust, 1979).

'The Death of Crimthann son of Fidach and the Adventures of the Sons of Eochaid Mugmedóin', ed. and trans. W. Stokes, *Revue celtique*, 24 (1903), 172–207.

'Echtra maic Echdach Mugmedóin', ed. and trans. M. Joynt, *Ériu*, 4 (1910), 91–111.

The Fragmentary Annals of Ireland, ed. and trans. J. N. Radner (Dublin: DIAS, 1978).

Gesta Hammaburgensis ecclesiae pontificum, ed. B. Schmeidler (Hanover: Hahnsche Buchhandlung, 1917).

Heimskringla, ed. Bjarni Aðalbjarnarson, 3 vols. Íslenzk fornrit 26–8 (Reykjavík: Hið ílenzka fornritafélag, 1941–51).

The Irish Sex Aetates Mundi, ed. and trans. D. Ó Cróinín (Dublin: DIAS, 1983).

Lebor na Cert, ed. and trans. M. Dillon (Dublin and London: ITS, 1962).

The Letters of Lanfranc, Archbishop of Canterbury, ed. and trans. H. Clover and M. T. Gibson (Oxford University Press, 1979).

Liber Ardmachanus: The Book of Armagh, ed. J. Gwynn (Dublin: Hodges Figgis & Co., 1913).

The Life of King Edward who rests at Westminster attributed to a Monk of Saint-Bertin, ed. and trans. F. Barlow (Oxford University Press, 1992).

Marianus Scottus, *Chronicon*, ed. G. Waitz, Monumenta Germaniae Historica, Scriptores 5 (Hannover, 1844).

'Mittelirische Verslehren', ed. R. Thurneysen, in *Irische Texte mit Wörterbuch*, ed. E. Windisch and W. Stokes, 4 vols., vol. 3:1 (Leipzig: Verlag von S. Hirzel, 1891), 1–82.

Nósa Ua Maine: The Customs of the Uí Maine', ed. and trans. P. Russell, in T. M. Charles-Edwards, M. E. Owen and P. Russell (eds.), *The Welsh King and his Court* (Cardiff: University of Wales Press, 2000), 527–51.

'A Poem Composed for Cathal Croibhdhearg Ó Conchubair', ed. and trans. B. Ó Cuív, *Ériu*, 34 (1983), 157–74.

'A Poem in Praise of Raghnall, King of Man', ed. and trans. B. Ó Cuív, *Éigse*, 8 (1957), 283–301.

Poetry from the Kings' Sagas 1: From Mythical Times to c. 1035, ed. D. Whaley, Skaldic Poetry of the Scandinavian Middle Ages, 1 (Turnhout: Brepols, 2012).

Quellen des 9. und 11. Jahrhunderts zur Geschichte der Hamburgischen Kirche und des Reiches, ed. W. Trillmich (Darmstadt: Wissenschaftliche Buchgesellschaft, 1961).

Sex Aetates Mundi. Die Weltzeitalter bei den Angelsachsen und den Iren. Untersuchungen und Texte, ed. H. L. C. Tristram. Anglistische Forschungen, 165 (Heidelberg, 1985).

Stephen of Lexington, Letters from Ireland, ed. B. W. O'Dwyer (Kalamazoo: Cistercian Publications, 1982).

Tales of the Elders of Ireland, trans. A. Dooley and H. Roe (Oxford University Press, 1999).

'Two Middle Irish Poems', ed. K. Meyer, *Zeitschrift für celtische Philologie*, 1 (1897), 112–13.
Vita Sancti Malachiae, in *Sancti Bernardi Opera*, ed. J. Leclercq, H. M. Rochais and C. H.
    Talbot, 8 vols. (Rome: Editiones Cistercienses, 1957–77), iii, 307–78.
Warner of Rouen, Moriuht: A Norman Latin Poem from the Early Eleventh Century, ed. and
    trans. C. J. McDonough (Toronto; Pontifical Institute of Mediaeval Studies, 1995).

Secondary Works

Ashe, L., *Fiction and History in England, 1066–1200* (Cambridge University Press, 2007).
Bartlett, R., *Gerald of Wales: A Voice of the Middle Ages* (Stroud: Tempus, 2006).
    Gerald of Wales and the Ethnographic Imagination, Kathleen Hughes Memorial Lectures,
    12 (Cambridge: Department of Anglo-Saxon, Norse, and Celtic, 2013).
    'Medieval and Modern Concepts of Race and Ethnicity', *Journal of Medieval and Early
    Modern Studies*, 31 (2001), 39–56.
Beuermann, I., *Masters of the Narrow Sea: Forgotten Challenges to Norwegian Rule in Man
    and the Isles, 1979–1266*, Acta Humaniora (Oslo: Faculty of Humanities, University of
    Oslo, 2006), 100–22.
Bhreathnach, E., 'Temoria: Caput Scotorum?', *Ériu*, 47 (1996), 67–88.
Bradley, J., 'The Interpretation of Scandinavian Settlement in Ireland', in Bradley (ed.),
    Settlement and Society in Medieval Ireland, 49–78.
Brady, N., 'Reconstructing a Medieval Irish Plough', in *I Jornados Internacionales sobre tec-
    nologia agraia tradicionale Museo Nacionale de Pueblo Español* (Madrid: Ministerio de
    Cultura, 1993), 31–44.
    'Labor and Agriculture in Early Medieval Ireland: Evidence from the Sources', in A.
    Frantzen and D. Moffat (eds.), *The Work of Work: Servitude, Slavery and Labor in
    Medieval England* (Glasgow: Cruithne Press, 1994), 125–45.
Breatnach, C., 'Rawlinson B 502', in S. Duffy (ed.), *Medieval Ireland: An Encyclopedia*
    (New York and London: Routledge, 2005), 398–400.
Broun, D., *The Irish Identity of the Kingdom of the Scots* (Woodbridge: Boydell Press,
    1999).
    'Becoming a Nation: Scotland in the Twelfth and Thirteenth Centuries', in H.
    Tsurushima (ed.), *Nations in Medieval Britain* (Donington: Shaun Tyas, 2010), 86–103.
Byrne, A., *Otherworlds: Fantasy and History in Medieval Literature* (Oxford University
    Press, 2016).
Byrne, F. J., 'The Trembling Sod: Ireland in 1169', in *NHI* ii, 1–42.
Candon, A., '"Barefaced Effrontery": Secular and Ecclesiastical Politics in Early Twelfth-
    Century Ireland', *Seanchas Ard Mhacha*, 14 (1991), 1–25.
    'Muirchertach Ua Briain: Politics and Naval Activity in the Irish Sea 1075–1119', in Mac
    Niocaill and Wallace (eds.), *Keimelia*, 397–415.
Carey, J., *A New Introduction to Lebor Gabála Érenn, The Book of the Taking of Ireland* (Dublin
    and London: ITS, 1993).
    Lebor Gabála Érenn: Textual History and Pseudo-History (Dublin and London: ITS, 2009).
    '*Lebor Gabála* and the Legendary History of Ireland', in H. Fulton (ed.), *Medieval Celtic
    Literature and Society* (Dublin: Four Courts Press, 2005), 32–48.

Casey, D. and Meehan, B., 'Brian Boru and the Book of Armagh', *History Ireland*, 22:2 (2014), 28–9.

Charles-Edwards, T. M., 'Ireland and its Invaders, 1166–1186', *Quaestio Insularis: Selected Proceedings of the Cambridge Colloquium in Anglo-Saxon, Norse, and Celtic*, 4 (2003), 1–34.

'Society and Politics in Pre-Norman Ireland', in *L'irlanda e gli irlandesi nell'alto medioevo, Spoleto, 16–21 aprile 2001*, Atti delle settimane LVII (Spoleto, 2010), 67–90.

Clancy, T. O., 'Scotland, the "Nennian" Recension of the *Historia Brittonum*, and the *Lebor Bretnach*', in S. Taylor (ed.), *Kings, Clerics and Chronicles in Scotland 500–1297: Essays in Honour of Marjorie Ogilvie Anderson on the Occasion of her Ninetieth Birthday* (Dublin: Four Courts Press, 2000), 87–107.

Clarke, H., 'Population', in S. Duffy (ed.), *Medieval Ireland: An Encyclopedia* (New York and London: Routledge, 2005), 384.

Clarke, M. 'The *Leabhar Gabhála* and Carolingian Origin Legends', in P. Moran and I. Warntjes (eds.), *Early Medieval Ireland and Europe: Chronology, Contacts, Scholarship. A Festschrift for Dáibhí Ó Cróinín* (Turnhout: Brepols, 2015), 441–79.

Connon, A., 'The *Banshenchas* and the Uí Néill Queens of Tara', in Smyth (ed.), *Seanchas*, 98–108.

Curtis, E., 'Murchertach O'Brien, High-King of Ireland and his Norman Son-in-Law, Arnulf de Montgomery, *circa* 1100', *JRSAI*, 51 (1921), 116–34.

Davies, R. R., 'The Peoples of Britain and Ireland, 1100–1400: IV, Language and Historical Mythology', *TRHS*, 6th ser., no. 7 (1997), 1–24.

Dooley, A., 'The Date and Purpose of *Acallam na Senórach*', *Éigse*, 34 (2004), 97–126.

Downey, C., 'Literature and Learning in Early Medieval Meath', in F. Ludlow and A. Crampsie (eds.), *Meath, History and Society: Interdisciplinary Essays on the History of an Irish County* (Dublin: Geography Publications, 2015), 101–34.

Downham, C., 'The Good, the Bad, the Ugly: Portrayals of Vikings in "The Fragmentary Annals of Ireland"', in E. Kooper (ed.), *The Medieval Chronicle III: Proceedings of the 3rd International Conference on the Medieval Chronicle, Doorn/Utrecht 12–17 July 2002* (Amsterdam and New York: Rodopi, 2004), 27–39.

Duffy, S., *Brian Boru and the Battle of Clontarf* (Dublin: Gill & Macmillan, 2013).

'The Bruce Brothers and the Irish Sea World, 1306–29', *Cambridge Medieval Celtic Studies*, 21 (1991), 55–86.

'Irishmen and Islesmen in the Kingdom of Dublin and Man, 1052–1171', *Ériu*, 43 (1992), 93–133.

'Ostmen, Irish and Welsh in the Eleventh Century', *Peritia*, 9 (1995), 378–96.

'The First Ulster Plantation: John de Courcy and the Men of Cumbria', in Barry *et al.* (eds.), *Colony and Frontier in Medieval Ireland*, 1–27.

'Ireland and Scotland, 1014–1169: Contacts and Caveats', in Smyth (ed.), *Seanchas*, 348–56.

Duffy, S. and Mytum, H. (eds.), *A New History of the Isle of Man*, vol. III, *The Medieval Period, 1000–1406* (Liverpool University Press, 2015).

Dumville, D. N., 'The Textual History of "Lebor Bretnach": A Preliminary Study', *Éigse*, 16 (1975/6), 255–73.

'Did Ireland Exist in the Twelfth Century?', in Purcell *et al.* (eds.), *Clerics, Kings and Vikings*, 115–26.

Duncan, E., '*Lebor na hUidre* and a Copy of Boethius's *De re arithmetica*: A Palaeographical Note', *Ériu*, 62 (2012), 1–23.

Dunning, P. J., 'Pope Innocent III and the Irish Kings', *Journal of Ecclesiastical History*, 8 (1957), 17–32.

Etchingham, C., *The Irish 'Monastic Town': Is this a Valid Concept?* Kathleen Hughes Memorial Lecture, 8 (Cambridge: Department of Anglo-Saxon, Norse and Celtic, 2010).

'Episcopal Hierarchy in Connacht and Tairdelbach Ua Conchobair', *Journal of the Galway Archaeological and Historical Society*, 52 (2000), 13–29.

'North Wales, Ireland and the Isles: The Insular Viking Zone', *Peritia*, 15 (2001), 145–87.

'Review Article: The "Reform" of the Irish Church in the Eleventh and Twelfth Centuries', *Studia Hibernica*, 37 (2011), 215–37.

Fentress, J. and Wickham, C., *Social Memory: New Perspectives on the Past* (Oxford: Blackwell, 1992).

Flanagan, M. T., 'John de Courcy, the First Irish Plantation and Irish Church Men', in Smith (ed.), *Britain and Ireland*, 154–78.

'High-Kings with Opposition, 1072–1166', in *NHI* i, 899–933.

'Strategies of Distinction: Defining Nations in Medieval Ireland', in H. Tsurushima (ed.), *Nations in Medieval Britain* (Donington: Shaun Tyas, 2010), 104–20.

'Jocelin of Furness', in C. Downham (ed.), *Jocelin of Furness: Essays from the 2011 Conference* (Donington: Shaun Tyas, 2013), 45–66.

Fleming, J., *Gille of Limerick (c. 1070–1145): Architect of a Medieval Church* (Dublin: Four Courts Press, 2001).

Garrison, M., 'Divine Election for Nations – a Difficult Rhetoric for Medieval Scholars?', in L. B. Mortensen (ed.), *The Making of Christian Myths in the Periphery of Latin Christendom (c. 100–1300)* (Copenhagen: Museum Tusculanum Press, 2006), 275–314.

Geary, P., 'Reflections on Historiography and the Holy: Center and Periphery', in L. B. Mortensen (ed.), *The Making of Christian Myths in the Periphery of Latin Christendom (c. 100–1300)* (Copenhagen: Museum Tusculanum Press, 2006), 323–9.

Geraghty, S., *Viking Dublin: Botanical Evidence from Fishamble Street* (Dublin: RIA, 1996).

Gillingham, J., 'Conquering the Barbarians: War and Chivalry in Twelfth-Century Britain', in J. Gillingham (ed.), *The English in the Twelfth Century: Imperialism, National Identity and Political Values* (Woodbridge: Boydell Press, 2000), 41–58.

Gleeson, P., 'Kingdoms, Communities and Óenaig: Irish Assembly Practices in their Northwest European Context', *Journal of the North Atlantic*, 8 (2015), 33–51.

Griffiths, D., *Vikings of the Irish Sea: Conflict and Assimilation AD 790–1050* (Stroud: History Press, 2010).

Gwynn, A., 'Brian in Armagh (1005)', *Seanchas Ard Mhacha*, 9 (1978), 38–51.

Hammond, M., 'Ethnicity and the Writing of Medieval Scottish History', *The Scottish Historical Review*, 85 (2006), 1–27.

Herbert, M., 'The Irish *Sex Aetates Mundi*: First Editions', *Cambridge Medieval Celtic Studies*, 11 (1986), 97–112.

'*Rí Érenn, Rí Alban*: Kingship and Identity in the Ninth and Tenth Centuries', in S. Taylor (ed.), *Kings, Clerics and Chronicles in Scotland 500–1297: Essays in Honour of Marjorie Ogilvie Anderson on the Occasion of her Ninetieth Birthday* (Dublin: Four Courts Press, 2000), 62–72.

'Crossing Historical and Literary Boundaries: Irish Written Culture around the Year 1000', in *Crossing Boundaries, Croesi Ffiniau: Proceedings of the XIIth International Congress of Celtic Studies 24–30 August 2003, University of Wales, Aberystwyth* (= *Cambrian Medieval Celtic Studies, 53 / 54 [2007]*), 87–101.

Hodkinson, B., 'Viking Limerick and its Hinterland', in Clarke and Johnston (eds.), *The Vikings in Ireland and Beyond*, 183–8.

Hudson, B., *Irish Sea Studies 900–1200* (Dublin: Four Courts Press, 2006).

'William the Conqueror and Ireland', *IHS*, 29 (1994), 145–58

Jaeger, S. C., *The 'Envy of Angels': Cathedral Schools and Social Ideals in Medieval Europe, 950–1200* (Philadelphia: University of Pennsylvania Press).

Johnston, E., *Literacy and Identity in Early Medieval Ireland* (Woodbridge: Boydell Press, 2013).

Leyser, K., '*Theophanu Divina Gratia Imperatrix Augusta*: Western and Eastern Emperorship in the Later Tenth Century', in A. Davids (ed.), *The Empress Theophano: Byzantium and the West at the Turn of the First Millennium* (Cambridge University Press, 2002), 1–48.

Lyons, S., 'Food Plants, Fruits and Foreign Foodstuffs: The Archaeological Evidence from Urban Medieval Ireland', in E. FitzPatrick and J. Kelly (eds.), *Food and Drink in Ireland* (= *PRIA*, 115 C [2015]), 111–66.

Mac Carthy, B., *The Codex Palatino-Vaticanus, No. 830*, Todd Lecture Series III (Dublin: RIA, 1892).

McCormick, F., 'The Decline of the Cow: Agricultural and Settlement Change in Early Medieval Ireland', *Peritia*, 20 (2008), 209–24.

McCormick, F., Kerr, T., McClatchie, M. and O'Sullivan, A., *The Archaeology of Livestock and Cereal Production in Early Medieval Ireland, AD 400–1100* (Oxford: British Archaeological Reports; Archaeopress, 2014).

Mac Shamhráin, A., 'Ua Conchobair, Cathal Mór Crobderg', in J. McGuire and J. Quinn (eds.), *Dictionary of Irish Biography from the Earliest Times to the Year 2002*, 9 vols. (Cambridge University Press and RIA, 2009), ix, 569–71.

Maund, K. L., *Ireland, Wales and England in the Eleventh Century* (Woodbridge: Boydell Press, 1991).

K. Meyer (ed.), *Bruchstücke der älteren Lyrik Irlands* (Berlin, 1919).

Miles, B., *Heroic Saga and Classical Epic in Medieval Ireland* (Woodbridge: Boydell Press, 2011).

Monk, M. A., 'The Archaeobotanical Evidence for Field Crop Plants in Early Historic Ireland', in J. M. Renfrew (ed.), *New Light on Early Farming: Recent Developments in Palaeoethnobotany* (Edinburgh University Press, 1991), 315–28.

Murray, K. 'Gill Mo Dutu Ua Casaide', in J. Carey, M. Herbert and K. Murray (eds.), Cin Chille Cúile, Texts, Saints and Places: Essays in honour of Pádraig Ó Riain (Andover, MA and Aberystwyth: Celtic Studies Publications, 2004), 150–62.

Ní Chatháin, P., 'Bede's Ecclesiastical History in Irish', *Peritia*, 3 (1984), 115–30.

Ní Mhaonaigh, M., *Brian Boru: Ireland's Greatest King?* (Stroud: Tempus, 2007).

'*Nósa Ua Maine*: Fact or Fiction?', in T. M. Charles-Edwards, M. E. Owen and P. Russell (eds.), *The Welsh King and his Court* (Cardiff: University of Wales Press, 2000), 362–81.

'The Literature of Medieval Ireland, 800–1200: From the Vikings to the Normans', in M. Kelleher and P. O'Leary (eds.), *The Cambridge History of Irish Literature, Volume I: to 1890* (Cambridge University Press, 2006), 32–73.

'A Man of Two Faces: Máel Sechnaill mac Domnaill in Middle Irish Sources', in Clarke and Johnston (eds.), *Vikings in Ireland and Beyond*, 232–52.

'*Carait tairisi*: Literary Links between Ireland and England in the Eleventh Century', in A. and N. Harlos (eds.), *Adapting Texts and Styles in a Celtic Context* (Münster: Nodos Publikationen, 2016), 265–88.

O'Connor, R. (ed.), *Classical Literature and Learning in Medieval Irish Narrative* (Woodbridge: Boydell Press, 2014).

Ó Corráin, D., 'Dál Cais – Church and Dynasty', *Ériu*, 24 (1973), 52–63.

'Nationality and Kingship in pre-Norman Ireland', in T. W. Moody (ed.), *Nationality and the Pursuit of National Independence. Historical Studies, XI* (Belfast: Appletree, 1978), 1–35.

'Historical Need and Literary Narrative', in D. Ellis Evans, J. G. Griffith and E. M. Jope (eds.), *Proceedings of the Seventh International Congress of Celtic Studies, Oxford 1983* (Oxford: Cranham Press, 1986), 141–58.

'Legend as Critic', in T. Dunne (ed.), *The Writer as Witness: Literature as Historical Evidence. Historical Studies XVI* (Cork University Press, 1987), 23–38.

'Viking Ireland – Afterthoughts', in Clarke, *et al.* (eds.), *Ireland and Scandinavia*, 421–52.

'The Church and Secular Society', in *L'irlanda e gli irlandesi nell'alto medioevo, Spoleto, 16–21 aprile 2009*, Atti delle settimane, CVII (Spoleto, 2010), 261–321.

Ó Cuív, B., 'The Irish Marginalia in Codex Palatino-Vaticanus No. 830', *Éigse*, 24 (1990), 45–67.

O'Donnell, T., Townend, M. and Tyler, E. M., 'European Literature and Eleventh-Century England', in C. A. Lees (ed.), *The Cambridge History of Early Medieval English Literature* (Cambridge University Press, 2013), 607–36.

Ó hUiginn, R., (ed.), *Lebor na hUidre: Codices Hibernenses Eximii I*, (Dublin: RIA, 2015).

Ó Macháin, P., 'Aspects of Bardic Poetry in the Thirteenth Century', in C. Breatnach and M. Ní Úrdail (eds.), *Aon don Éigse: Essays Marking Osborn Bergin's Centenary Lecture on Bardic Poetry (1912)* (Dublin: DIAS, 2015), 91–125.

Ó Néill, P., 'Irish Glosses in a Twelfth-Century Copy of Boethius's *Consolatio philosophiae*', *Ériu*, 55 (2005), 1–17.

O'Sullivan, A., 'Place, Memory and Identity among Estuarine Fishing Communities: Interpreting the Archaeology of Early Medieval Fish Weirs', *World Archaeology*, 35 (2003), 449–68.

Perros [Walton], H., 'Crossing the Shannon Frontier: Connacht and the Anglo-Normans, 1170–1224', in Barry *et al.* (eds.), *Colony and Frontier in Medieval Ireland*, 117–38.

'Ó Conchobhair, Cathal', in *ODNB*.

Power, R., 'Meeting in Norway: Norse–Gaelic Relations in the Kingdom of Man and the Isles', 1090–1270', *Saga-Book*, 29 (2005), 5–66.

Reynolds, S., 'Medieval *origines gentium* and the Community of the Realm', *History*, 68 (1983), 375–90.

Scully, D., 'Ireland and the Irish in Bernard of Clairvaux's Life of Malachy', in Bracken and Ó Riain-Raedel (eds.), *Ireland and Europe in the Twelfth Century*, 239–56.

Simms, K., '"Gabh umad a Fheidhlimidh": A Fifteenth-Century Inauguration Ode?', *Ériu*, 31 (1980), 132–45.

'An Eaglais agus Filí na Scol', in P. Ó Fiannachta (ed.), *An Dán Díreach. Léachtaí Cholm Cille XXIV.* (Maigh Nuad: An Sagart, 1994), 21–36.

Simpson, L., 'Forty Years a-digging: A Preliminary Synthesis of Archaeological Investigations in Medieval Dublin', in S. Duffy (ed.), *Medieval Dublin I* (Dublin: Four Courts Press, 2000), 11–68.

Spiegel, G. M., 'History, Historicism and the Social Logic of the Text in the Middle Ages', *Speculum*, 65 (1990), 59–86.

Stalley, R., 'Design and Function: The Construction and Decoration of Cormac's Chapel at Cashel', in Bracken and Ó Riain-Raedel (eds.), *Ireland and Europe in the Twelfth Century*, 162–75.

'Royal Fleets in Viking Ireland: The Evidence of *Lebor na Cert* A.D. 1050–1150', in J. Hines, A. Lane and M. Redknap (eds.), *Land, Sea and Home: Proceedings of a Conference on Viking-period Settlement at Cardiff, July 2001* (Leeds: Society for Medieval Archaeology, 2004), 189–206.

Swift, C., 'The Local Context of *Óenach Tailten*', *Ríocht na Midhe*, 11 (2000), 24–50.

Toner, G., '*Baile*: Settlement and Landholding in Medieval Ireland', *Éigse*, 34 (2004), 25–43.

Townend, M., 'Contextualising the *Knútsdrápur*: Skaldic Praise Poetry at the Court of Cnut', *Anglo-Saxon England*, 30 (2001), 145–79.

Tyler, E. M., 'The *Vita Edwardi*: The Politics of Poetry at Wilton Abbey', *ANS*, 31 (2009), 131–56.

Valante, M. A., *The Vikings in Ireland: Settlement, Trade, and Urbanisation* (Dublin: Four Courts Press, 2008).

'Re-assessing the Irish "Monastic Town"', *IHS*, 31 (1998), 1–18.

'Dublin's Economic Relations with Hinterland and Periphery in the Later Viking Age', in S. Duffy (ed.), *Medieval Dublin I* (Dublin: Four Courts Press, 2000), 69–83.

Wadden, P., 'Some Views of the Normans in Eleventh- and Twelfth-Century Ireland', in Duffy and Foran (eds.), *The English Isles*, 13–36.

Wallace, P., 'The Archaeology of Ireland's Viking-age Towns', in *NHI* i, 814–41.

6 Conquest and Conquerors

Colin Veach

Primary Sources

The Acts and Letters of the Marshal Family: Marshals of England and Earls of Pembroke, 1145–1248, ed. D. Crouch. Camden Fifth Series (Cambridge University Press, 2015).

Chronicles of the Reigns of Stephen, Henry II and Richard I, ed. R. Howlett, 4 vols. (London: RS, 1884–9).

History of William Marshal, ed. A. J. Holden and D. Crouch, trans. S. Gregory, 3 vols. Anglo-Norman Text Society (London, 2002–7).

The Irish Cartularies of Llanthony Prima & Secunda, ed. E. St. J. Brooks (Dublin: IMC, 1953).

Recueil des Actes de Philippe Auguste Roi de France, tome III, Années du Règne XXVIII à XXXVI [1er Novembre 1206–31 Octobre 1215], eds. M. J. Monicat and M. J. Boussard (Paris: Imprimerie Nationale, 1966).

Roger of Wendover, *Flores Historiarum*, ed. H. G. Hewlett, 3 vols. (London: RS, 1886–9).

Rotuli de Liberate ac de Misis et Praestitis, Regnante Johanne, ed. T. D. Hardy (London: Eyre and Spottiswoode, 1844).

Rotuli de Oblatis et Finibus in Turri Londinensi Asservati, ed. T. D. Hardy (London: Record Commission, 1835).

William of Newburgh, *Historia Rerum Anglicarum*, ed. R. Howlett (London: RS, 1884).

Secondary Sources

Church, S. D., *King John: England, Magna Carta and the Making of a Tyrant* (Houndmills: Palgrave Macmillan, 2015).

Colker, M. J., 'The "Margam Chronicle" in a Dublin Manuscript', *HSJ*, 4 (1992), 123–48.

Crooks, P., '"Divide and rule": Factionalism as Royal Policy in the Lordship of Ireland, 1171–1265', *Peritia*, 19 (2005), 263–307.

Crouch, D., *The English Aristocracy, 1070–1272: A Social Transformation* (New Haven: Yale University Press, 2011).

    'Earls in Wales and Ireland', in D. Crouch and H. Doherty (eds.), *The Earl in Medieval Britain* (forthcoming).

    'Earl Gilbert Marshal and his Mortal Enemies', *Historical Research*, 87 (2014), 393–403.

Davies, R. R., *Domination and Conquest: The Experience of Ireland, Scotland and Wales 1100–1300* (Cambridge University Press, 1990).

Duffy, S., *Ireland in the Middle Ages* (Houndmills & Dublin: Macmillan, 1997).

    'The First Ulster Plantation: John de Courcy and the Men of Cumbria', in Barry *et al.* (eds.), *Colony and Frontier in Medieval Ireland*, 1–27.

    'John and Ireland: The Origins of England's Irish Problem', in S. D. Church (ed.), *King John: New Interpretations* (Woodbridge: Boydell Press, 1999), 221–45.

Flanagan, M. T., 'John de Courcy, the First Ulster Plantation and Irish Church Reform', in Smith (ed.), *Britain and Ireland*, 154–78.

Gillingham, J., 'Conquering the Barbarians: War and Chivalry in Twelfth-Century Britain', in J. Gillingham (ed.), *The English in the Twelfth Century: Imperialism, National Identity and Political Values* (Woodbridge: Boydell Press, 2000), 41–58.

    'Normanizing the English Invaders of Ireland', in H. Pryce and J. Watts (eds.), *Power and Identity in the Middle Ages: Essays in Memory of Rees Davies* (Oxford University Press, 2007), 85–97.

Holden, B. '"Feudal Frontiers?" Colonial Societies in Wales and Ireland 1170–1330', *Studia Hibernica*, 33 (2004/5), 61–79.

Lyttelton, G., *The History of the Life of King Henry the Second and of the Age in which he Lived*. 6 vols. 3rd edn (Dublin: George Faulkner, 1777–87).

O'Conor, K., *The Archaeology of Medieval Rural Settlement in Ireland* (Dublin: RIA, 1998).

Perros [Walton], H., 'Crossing the Shannon Frontier: Connacht and the Anglo-Normans, 1170–1224', in Barry *et al.* (eds.), *Colony and Frontier in Medieval Ireland*, 117–38.

Powicke, F. M., *King Henry III and the Lord Edward. The Community of the Realm in the Thirteenth Century*. 2 vols. (Oxford University Press, 1947).

Smith, B., *Colonisation and Conquest in Medieval Ireland: The English in Louth, 1170–1330* (Cambridge University Press, 1999).

    'Tenure and Locality in North Leinster in the Early Thirteenth Century', in Barry *et al.* (eds.), *Colony and Frontier in Medieval Ireland*, 29–40.

'Irish Politics, 1220–1245', in M. Prestwich, R. Britnell and R. Frame (eds.), *Thirteenth Century England VIII* (Woodbridge: Boydell Press, 2001), 13–32.

Strickland, M., *War and Chivalry: The Conduct and Perception of War in England and Normandy, 1066–1217* (Cambridge University Press, 1996).

Thomas, H. M., *The English and the Normans: Ethnic Hostility, Assimilation, and Identity 1066–c.1220* (Oxford University Press, 2003).

Veach, C., *Lordship in Four Realms: The Lacy Family, 1166–1241* (Manchester University Press, 2014).

'King John and Royal Control in Ireland: Why William de Briouze had to be Destroyed', *EHR*, 129 (2014), 1051–78.

Vincent, N., *Peter des Roches: An Alien in English Politics, 1205–1238* (Cambridge University Press, 1996).

Warren, W. L., 'King John and Ireland', in Lydon (ed.), *England and Ireland*, 26–42.

7 Angevin Ireland

Nicholas Vincent

Manuscript Sources

Canterbury Cathedral Archives Chartae Antiquae

Chester, City Archives CH/2–3

London, College of Arms ms. Vincent 59

Primary Sources

Ancient Charters, Royal and Private, Prior to AD 1200, ed. J. H. Round, PRS 10 (London, 1888).

The Book of Obits and Martyrology of the Cathedral Church of the Holy Trinity ... Dublin, ed. J. C. Croswaithe (Dublin: Irish Archaeological Society, 1844).

'Cartae Dunenses, XII–XIII Céad', ed. G. Mac Niocaill, *Seanchas Ardmhacha*, 5 (1970).

'The Charters of the Cistercian Abbey of Duiske', ed. J. H. Bernard and C. M. Butler, *PRIA*, 35 C (1918), 1–188.

'A Commentary on the "Prophetia Melini"', ed. J. Hammer, *Speculum*, 10 (1935), 29–30.

Cronica Regum Mannie et Insularum, ed. G. Broderick (Belfast: Manx Museum and National Trust, 1979).

Earldom of Gloucester Charters, ed. R. B. Patterson (Oxford University Press, 1973).

English Monastic Litanies of the Saints after 1100, ed. N. J. Morgan, 2 vols. (Woodbridge: Henry Bradshaw Society, 2012–13).

Geoffrey of Monmouth, *The History of the Kings of Britain*, ed. M. D. Reeve and N. Wright (Woodbridge: Boydell Press, 2007).

Gervase of Tilbury, *Otia Imperialia*, ed. S. E. Banks and J. W. Binns (Oxford University Press, 2002).

Henry of Huntingdon, *Historia Anglorum*, ed. D. E. Greenway (Oxford University Press, 1996).

The Hungerford Cartulary, ed. J. L. Kirby (Trowbridge: Wiltshire Record Society, 2007).

'The Irish Mirabilia in the Norse "Speculum Regale"', ed. K. Meyer, *Ériu*, 4 (1910), 1–16.

Manuscript Sources for the History of Irish Civilisation, ed. R. J. Hayes, vol. 2 (Boston: G. K. Hall, 1965).

Marianus Scottus, *Chronicon*, ed. G. Waitz, Monumenta Germaniae Historica, Scriptores 5 (Hannover, 1844).

Peter of Cornwall's Book of Revelations, ed. R. Easting and R. Sharpe (Toronto/Oxford: Pontifical Institute of Medieval Studies, 2013).

Radulfi Nigri Chronica, ed. R. Anstruther (London: Caxton Society 1851).

Regesta Regum Anglo-Normannorum, 4 vols., ed. H. W. C. Davis *et al.* (Oxford University Press, 1913–70).

'Registrum epistolarum Stephani de Lexinton abbatis de Stanlegia et de Savigniaco', ed. B. Griesser, *Analecta Sacri Ordinis Cisterciensis*, 2 (1946), 1–118.

Rotuli Curiae Regis, ed. F. Palgrave, 2 vols. (London, 1835).

'Some Unpublished Texts from the Black Book of Christ Church Dublin', ed. A. Gwynn, *Analecta Hibernica*, 16 (1946), 281–337.

'Three Exchequer Documents from the Reign of Henry III', ed. J. F. Lydon, *PRIA*, 65C (1966), 1–27.

'Vie et miracles de St Laurent', ed. C. Plummer, *Analecta Bollandiana*, 33 (1914), 121–85.

'Vita St Malachiae', in *PL*, 182.

Wace, *Roman de Brut*, ed. J. Weiss (University of Exeter Press, 1999).

'The Walling of New Ross: A Thirteenth-Century Poem in French', ed. H. Shields, *Long Room*, 12–13 (1975–6), 24–33.

William of Malmesbury, *Gesta Regum Anglorum*, ed. R. A. B. Mynors, R. M. Thomson and M. Winterbottom, 2 vols. (Oxford University Press, 1998–9).

 Historia Novella, ed. E. King and K. R. Potter (Oxford University Press, 1998).

Secondary Works

Aurell, M., *L'Empire des Plantagenêt 1154–1224* (St-Amand-Montrond: Éditions Perrin, 2002).

Aurell, M. and Boutoulle, F. (eds.), *Les Seigneuries dans l'éspace Plantagenêt (c.1150–c.1250)* (Bordeaux: Ausonius, 2009).

Bartlett, R., 'Cults of Irish, Scottish and Welsh Saints in Twelfth-Century England', in Smith (ed.), *Britain and Ireland*, 68–77.

Bates, D., *The Normans and Empire* (Oxford University Press, 2013).

Beglane, F., *Anglo-Norman Parks in Medieval Ireland* (Dublin: Four Courts Press, 2015).

Birkett, H., *The Saints' Lives of Jocelin of Furness: Hagiography, Patronage and Ecclesiastical Politics* (Woodbridge: Boydell Press, 2010).

Brand, P., 'Ireland and the Literature of the Early Common Law', *Irish Jurist*, 16 (1981), 95–113.

Bugge, A., 'Nordisk-Sprog og Nordisk Nationalitet i Ireland', *Aarboger for Nordisk Oldkyndighed og Historie*, 2nd series 15 (Copenhagen, 1900), 329–31.

Buldorini, C., 'The Mayors, Provosts and Bailiffs of Drogheda in the Thirteenth Century', *County Louth Archaeological and Historical Journal*, 27 (2009), 26–38.

Bull, M., 'Criticism of Henry II's Expedition to Ireland in William of Canterbury's Miracles of St Thomas Becket', *JMH*, 33 (2007), 107–29.

Byrne, A., 'Family, Locality and Nationality: Vernacular Adaptations of the "Expugnatio Hibernica" in Late Medieval Ireland', *Medium Aevum*, 82 (2013), 101–18.

Church, S. D., 'The 1210 Campaign in Ireland: Evidence for a Military Revolution?', *ANS*, 20 (1998), 45–57.

Clarke, H. B., 'Planning and Regulation in the Formation of New Towns and New Quarters in Ireland, 1170–1641', in A. Simms and H. B. Clarke (eds.), *Lords and Towns in Medieval Europe* (Farnham: Ashgate, 2015), 321–54.

Cohen, M. R., *Under Crescent and Cross: The Jews in the Middle Ages* (Princeton University Press, 1994).

Colfer, B., 'The Tower of Hook', *Journal of the Wexford Historical Society*, 10 (1984–5), 69–78.

Coss, P. R., *The Origins of the English Gentry* (Cambridge University Press, 2003).

Crawford, J. and Gillespie, R. (eds.), *St Patrick's Cathedral, Dublin: A History* (Dublin: Four Courts Press, 2009).

Crooks, P., '"Divide and Rule": Factionalism as Royal Policy in the Lordship of Ireland', *Peritia*, 19 (2005), 263–307.

'Representation and Dissent: "Parliamentarianism" and the Structure of Politics in Colonial Ireland *c*.1370–1420', *EHR*, 125 (2010), 1–34.

Crouch, D., 'Earl Gilbert Marshal and his Mortal Enemies', *Historical Research*, 87 (2014), 393–403.

Curtis, E., *Roger of Sicily and the Normans in Lower Italy, 1016–1154* (London: G. P. Putnam's Sons, 1912).

'The Clan System Among English Settlers in Ireland', in Crooks (ed.), *Government, War and Society*, 297–301.

'The English and Ostmen in Ireland', in Crooks (ed.), *Government, War and Society*, 287–96.

Davies, R. R., 'Frontier Arrangements in Fragmented Societies: Ireland and Wales', in Bartlett and Mackay (eds.), *Medieval Frontier Societies*, 77–100.

Down, K., 'Colonial Society and Economy in the High Middle Ages', in *NHI* ii, 439–91.

Duffy, S., 'King John's Expedition to Ireland, 1210: The Evidence Reconsidered', *IHS*, 30 (1996), 1–21.

'Ireland's Hastings: The Anglo-Norman Conquest of Dublin', *ANS*, 20 (1998), 69–85.

'The First Ulster Plantation: John de Courcy and the Men of Cumbria', in Barry *et al.* (eds.), *Colony and Frontier in Medieval Ireland*, 1–28.

'The 1169 Invasion as a Turning-Point in Irish–Welsh Relations', in Smith (ed.), *Britain and Ireland*, 98–113.

'John and Ireland: The Origins of England's Irish Problem', in S. D. Church (ed.), *King John: New Interpretations* (Woodbridge: Boydell Press, 1999), 221–45.

'Town and Crown: The Kings of England and their City of Dublin', in M. Prestwich, R. Britnell and R. Frame (eds.), *Thirteenth Century England X* (Woodbridge: Boydell Press, 2005), 95–117.

Duggan, A., 'The Making of a Myth: Giraldus Cambrensis, "Laudabiliter", and Henry II's Lordship of Ireland', *Studies in Medieval and Renaissance History*, 3rd series 4 (2007), 107–70.

Dunbabin, J., *The French in the Kingdom of Sicily, 1266–1305* (Cambridge University Press, 2011).

Dykes, D. W., 'The Irish Coinage of Henry III', *British Numismatic Journal*, 32 (1963), 99–116.

'King John's Irish Rex Coinage Revisited', *British Numismatic Journal*, 83 (2013), 120–33; 84 (2014), 90–100.

Eggerer, E. W., 'The Guild Merchant of Dublin', in S. Duffy (ed.), *Medieval Dublin VI* (Dublin: Four Courts Press, 2005), 144–9.

Ellenblum, R., *Frankish Rural Settlement in the Latin Kingdom of Jerusalem* (Cambridge University Press, 1998).

Crusader Castles and Modern Historians (Cambridge University Press, 2007).

Empey, A., 'The Formation and Development of Intramural Churches and Communities in Medieval Dublin in a European Context', in J. Bradley, A. J. Fletcher and A. Simms (eds.), *Dublin in the Medieval World: Studies in Honour of Howard B. Clarke* (Dublin: Four Courts Press, 2009), 249–76.

Faulkner, K., 'The Transformation of Knighthood in Early Thirteenth-Century England', *EHR*, 111 (1996), 1–23.

Flanagan, M. T., 'Strategies of Lordship in Pre-Norman and Post-Norman Leinster', *ANS*, 20 (1998), 107–26.

'Henry II and the Kingdom of Uí Fáeláin', in Bradley (ed.), *Settlement and Society in Medieval Ireland*, 229–39.

'John de Courcy, the First Ulster Plantation and Irish Church Men', in Smith (ed.), *Britain and Ireland*, 154–78.

'Household Favourites: Angevin Royal Agents in Ireland under Henry II and John', in Smyth (ed.), *Seanchas*, 357–80.

'Irish and Anglo-Norman Warfare in Twelfth-Century Ireland', in T. Bartlett and K. Jeffery (eds.), *A Military History of Ireland* (Cambridge University Press, 1996), 52–75.

'Defining Lordships in Angevin Ireland: William Marshal and the King's Justiciar', in M. Aurell and F. Boutoulle (eds.), *Les Seigneuries dans l'éspace Plantagenêt (c.1150–c.1250)* (Bordeaux, 2009), 41–59.

Fleming, R., *Kings and Lords in Conquest England* (Cambridge University Press, 1991).

Frame, R., 'Rediscovering Medieval Ireland: Irish Chancery Rolls and the Historian', *PRIA*, 113 C (2013), 193–217.

'Military Service in the Lordship of Ireland 1290–1360: Institutions and Society on the Anglo-Gaelic Frontier', in Bartlett and Mackay (eds.), *Medieval Frontier Societies*, 101–26.

Freidenreich, D. M., 'Muslims in Western Canon Law, 1000–1500', *Christian–Muslim Relations: A Bibliographical History Volume 3 (1050–1200)*, ed. D. Thomas and A. Mallett (Leiden: Brill, 2011).

Gillingham, J., 'Killing and Mutilating Political Enemies in the British Isles from the Late Twelfth to the Early Fourteenth Century: A Comparative Study', in Smith (ed.), *Britain and Ireland*, 114–34.

'Expectations of Empire: Some Twelfth-and Early Thirteenth-Century English Views of What their Kings Could Do', in Duffy and Foran (eds.), *English Isles*, 56–67.

'Normanizing the English Invaders of Ireland', in H. Pryce and J. Watts (eds.), *Power and Identity in the Middle Ages: Essays in Memory of Rees Davies* (Oxford University Press, 2007), 85–97.

Golding, B., 'Anglo-Norman Knightly Burials', in C. Harper-Bill and R. Harvey (eds.), *The Ideals and Practice of Medieval Knighthood* (Woodbridge: Boydell Press, 1986), 35–48.

Gougaud, L. and Joynt, M., 'The Isle of Saints', *Studies: An Irish Quarterly Review*, 13 (1924), 363–80.

Grierson, P. (ed.), *Catalogue of the Byzantine Coins in the Dumbarton Oaks Collection and in the Whittemore Collection*, 3 part 1 (Leo III to Michael III, 717–867) (Dumbarton Oaks: Dumbarton Oaks Research Library and Collection, 1973).

Gwynn, A., 'Medieval Bristol and Dublin', *IHS*, 5 (1946–7), 275–86.

Hammer, J., 'A Commentary on the "Prophetia Merlini" ', *Speculum*, 10 (1935), 29–30.

Hand, G. J., *English Law in Ireland, 1290–1324* (Cambridge University Press, 1967).

Hardie, P., *Virgil's Aeneid: Cosmos and Imperium* (Oxford University Press, 1986).

Hartland, B., 'Reasons for Leaving: The Effect of Conflict on English Landholding in Leinster in Late Thirteenth-Century Leinster', *JMH*, 32 (2006), 18–26.

'Absenteeism: The Chronology of a Concept', in B. Weiler, J. Burton and P. Schofield (eds.), *Thirteenth Century England XI* (Woodbridge: Boydell Press, 2007), 215–29.

Harvey, P. D. A., 'Matthew Paris's Maps of Britain', in P. R. Coss and S. D. Lloyd (eds.), *Thirteenth Century England IV* (Woodbridge: Boydell Press, 1992), 109–21.

Heng, G., *Empire of Magic: Medieval Romance and the Politics of Cultural Fantasy* (New York: Columbia University Press, 2003).

Héricher, A.-M. and Gazeau, V. (eds.), *1204, La Normandie entre Plantagenêts et Capétiens* (Caen: Université de Caen, 2007).

Hudson, B., 'The Changing Economy of the Irish Sea Province', in Smith (ed.), *Britain and Ireland*, 39–66.

Jensen, S., 'Merlin: Ambrosius and Silvester', in G. Barnes, J, Gunn, S. Jensen and L. Jobling (eds.), *Words and Wordsmiths* (Sydney: University of Sydney, Department of English, 1989), 45–8.

Kennedy, H., *Crusader Castles* (Cambridge University Press, 1994).

Kenny, G., 'Anglo-Irish and Gaelic Marriage Laws and Traditions in Late Medieval Ireland', *JMH*, 32 (2006), 27–42.

König, J., *Athletics and Literature in the Roman Empire* (Cambridge University Press, 2005).

Kosto, A. J., *Hostages in the Middle Ages* (Oxford University Press, 2012).

Lother, H., *Der Pfau in der altchristlichen Kunst*, Studien über christliche Denkmäler 18 (Leipzig: Dieterich, 1929).

Lydon, J., 'The Hobelar: An Irish Contribution to Medieval Warfare', *Irish Sword*, 2 part 5 (1954), 12–16.

Lydon, J. F., 'Edward II and the Revenues of Ireland in 1311–12', *IHS*, 14 (1964), 39–57.

'Three Exchequer Documents from the Reign of Henry the Third', *PRIA*, 65 C (1966), 1–27.

'Ireland and the English Crown, 1171–1541', in Crooks (ed.), *Government, War and Society*, 65–78.

'Dublin Castle in the Middle Ages', in S. Duffy (ed.), *Medieval Dublin III* (Dublin: Four Courts Press, 2002), 115–27.

McCormick, M., *Eternal Victory: Triumphant Rulership in Late Antiquity, Byzantium and the Early Medieval West* (Cambridge University Press, 1990).

MacEvitt, C., *The Crusades and the Christian World of the East* (Philadelphia: University of Pennsylvania Press, 2008).

Mac Niocaill, G., 'Cartae Dunenses, XII–XIII Céad', *Seanchas Ardmhacha*, 5 (1970), 418–28.

Matthew, D., *The Norman Kingdom of Sicily* (Cambridge University Press, 1992).

Mayer, H. E., 'Staufische Weltherrschaft? Zum Brief Heinrichs II. von England an Friedrich Barbarossa von 1157', in *Festschrift Karl Pivec*, ed. A. Haidacher and H. E. Mayer (Innsbruck: Leopold-Franzens-Universitat, 1966).

Nicholls, K. W., 'Anglo-French Ireland and After', *Peritia*, 1 (1982), 370–403.

Norgate, K., 'The Bull Laudabiliter', *EHR*, 8 (1893), 18–52.

O'Brien, A. F., 'Commercial Relations between Aquitaine and Ireland, *c.*1000 to *c.*1550', in J.-M. Picard (ed.), *Aquitaine and Ireland in the Middle Ages* (Dublin: Four Courts Press, 1995), 31–80.

Ó Floinn, R., 'The Foundation Relics of Christ Church Cathedral and the Origins of the Diocese of Dublin', in S. Duffy (ed.), *Medieval Dublin VII* (Dublin: Four Courts Press, 2006).

O'Keeffe, G., 'The Merchant Conquistadors: Medieval Bristolians in Dublin', in S. Duffy (ed.), *Medieval Dublin XIII* (Dublin: Four Courts Press, 2013), 116–38.

O'Keeffe, T., *Medieval Irish Buildings, 1100–1600* (Dublin: Four Courts Press, 2015).

    'Dublin Castle's Donjon in Context', in. J. Bradley, A. J. Fletcher and A. Simms (eds.), *Dublin in the Medieval World: Studies in Honour of Howard B. Clarke* (Dublin: Four Courts Press, 2009), 277–94.

Otway-Ruthven, A. J., 'Anglo-Irish Shire Government in the Thirteenth Century', *IHS*, 5 (1946), 1–28.

    'The Native Irish and English Law in Medieval Ireland', in Crooks (ed.), *Government, War and Society*, 141–54.

    'Knight Service in Ireland', in Crooks (ed.), *Government, War and Society*, 155–68.

    'Royal Service in Ireland', in Crooks (ed.), *Government, War and Society*, 169–76.

    'The Character of Norman Settlement in Ireland', in Crooks (ed.), *Government, War and Society*, 263–74.

    'The Organization of Anglo-Irish Agriculture in the Middle Ages', in Crooks (ed.), *Government, War and Society*, 275–86.

Patterson, R. B., 'Robert fitz Harding of Bristol', *HSJ*, 1 (1989), 109–22.

    'Bristol: An Angevin Baronial Capital under Royal Siege', *HSJ*, 3 (1992), 171–81.

Perros, H., 'Crossing the Shannon Frontier: Connacht and the Anglo-Normans, 1170–1224', in Barry *et al.* (eds.), *Colony and Frontier in Medieval Ireland*, 117–38.

Picard, J.-M., 'Early Contacts between Ireland and Normandy: The Cult of Irish Saints in Normandy before the Conquest', in M. Richter and J.-M. Picard (eds.), *Ogma: Essays in Celtic Studies in Honour of Próinséas Ní Chatháin* (Dublin: Four Courts Press, 2002), 85–93.

Powicke, F. M., 'The Murder of Henry Clement and the Pirates of Lundy Island', in F. M. Powicke, *Ways of Medieval Life and Thought* (London: Odhams, 1949), 38–68.

Prawer, J., *Crusader Institutions* (Oxford University Press, 1980).

Purcell, E., 'The Expulsion of the Ostmen, 1169–1171: The Documentary Evidence', *Peritia*, 17–18 (2003–4), 276–94.

Richardson, H. G., 'English Institutions in Medieval Ireland', *IHS*, 1 (1939), 386–91.

    'Some Norman Monastic Foundations in Ireland', in. J. A. Watt *et al.* (eds.), *Medieval Studies Presented to Aubrey Gwynn, S.J.* (Dublin: The Three Candles, 1961), 29–43.

Richardson, H. G. and Sayles, G. O., *The Administration of Ireland 1172–1377* (Dublin: IMC, 1963).

Ridyard, S. J., '"Condigna Veneratio": Post-Conquest Attitudes to the Saints of the Anglo-Saxons', *ANS*, 9 (1986), 179–206.

Riley-Smith, J., 'Peace Never Established: The Case of the Kingdom of Jerusalem', *TRHS*, 5th series 28 (1978), 87–102.

Ronan, M. V., 'St Patrick's Staff and Christ Church', *Dublin Historical Record*, 5 (1943), 121–9.

Round, J. H., *The Commune of London and Other Studies* (London: Constable, 1899).

Schramm, P. E., 'Zur Geschichte der päpstlichen Tiara', *Historische Zeitschrift*, 152 (1935), 307–12.

Sheehy, M., *When the Normans Came to Ireland* (Cork: Mercier Press, 1998).

Simms, A., 'Unity in Diversity: A Comparative Analysis of Thirteenth-Century Kilkenny, Kalkar and Sopron', in Duffy (ed.), *Princes, Prelates and Poets*, 107–23.

Simms, K., 'Bards and Barons: The Anglo-Irish Aristocracy and the Native Culture', in Bartlett and Mackay (eds.), *Medieval Frontier Societies*, 177–97.

Slover, C. H., 'William of Malmesbury and the Irish', *Speculum*, 2 (1927), 268–83.

Smith, B., 'Irish Politics, 1220–1245', in M. Prestwich, R. Britnell and R. Frame (eds.), *Thirteenth Century England VIII* (Woodbridge: Boydell Press, 2001), 13–32.

Smyth, A. P., *Celtic Leinster* (Dublin: Irish Academic Press, 1982).

Stalley, R., 'Three Irish Buildings with West Country Origins', *Medieval Art and Architecture at Wells and Glastonbury*, BAACT 4 (1981), 62–80.

'Irish Gothic and English Fashion', in Lydon (ed.), *English in Medieval Ireland*, 65–86.

'Cathedral Building in Thirteenth-Century Ireland', in R. Stalley (ed.), *Irish Gothic Architecture: Construction, Decay and Reinvention* (Bray: Wordwell, 2012), 15–53.

Suppe, C., 'The Cultural Significance of Decapitation in High Medieval Wales and the Marches', *Bulletin of the Board of Celtic Studies*, 36 (1989), 147–60.

Sutherland, D. W., 'Conquest and Law', *Studia Gratiana*, 15 (1972), 35–51.

Sykes, N., 'Zooarchaeology of the Norman Conquest', *ANS*, 27 (2005), 185–97.

Thomas, A., *The Walled Towns of Ireland*, 2 vols. (Dublin: Irish Academic Press 1992).

Van Houts, E., 'The Norman Conquest through European Eyes', *EHR*, 110 (1995), 832–53.

Veach, C. T., 'A Question of Timing: Walter de Lacy's Seisin of Meath 1189–94', *PRIA*, 109 C (2009), 165–94.

'King and Magnate in Medieval Ireland: Walter de Lacy, King Richard and King John', *IHS*, 37 (2010), 179–202.

Verstraten Veach, F., 'Anglicization in Medieval Ireland: Was there a Gaelic Irish "Middle Nation"', in Duffy and Foran (eds.), *English Isles*, 118–38.

Vincent, N., *Peter des Roches* (Cambridge University Press, 1996).

'Two Papal Letters on the Wearing of the Jewish Badge, 1221 and 1229', *Jewish Historical Studies*, 24 (1997), 209–24.

'Jean sans terre et les origines de la Gascogne anglaise', *Annales du Midi,* 123 (2011), 533–66.

'Jean, comte de Mortain: le futur roi et ses domaines en Normandie 1183–1199', in A.-M. Héricher and V. Gazeau (eds.), *1204, La Normandie entre Plantagenêts et Capétiens* (Caen: Crahm, 2007).

'Beyond Becket: King Henry III and the Papacy (1154–1189)', in P. D. Clarke and A. J. Duggan (eds.), *Pope Alexander III (1159–81): The Art of Survival* (Farnham: Ashgate, 2012), 257–99.

'St Thomas of Canterbury (and of England?)', in G. Atkins (ed.), *Making and Remaking Saints in Nineteenth-Century Britain* (Manchester University Press, 2016),

Waterman, D. M., 'Somersetshire and Other Foreign Building Stone in Medieval Ireland, c.1175–1400', *Ulster Journal of Archaeology*, 33 (1970), 63–75.

Went, A. E. J., 'Fisheries of the River Liffey', *JRSAI*, 83 (1953), 163–73.

Wiggins, K., *A Place of Great Consequence: Archaeological Excavations at King John's Castle, Limerick, 1990–98* (Bray: Wordwell, 2016).

8 The Height of English Power: 1250–1320

Beth Hartland

Manuscript Sources

BL Add MS 6041   Mortimer Inventories

NAI JI 1/1   Calendar of roll of Justices Itinerant, 33–4 Edw I

NAI KB 2   Plea Rolls

NAI RC 7   Memoranda Rolls

NAI RC 8   Memoranda Rolls

NLI MS 1   Collectanea de rebus Hibernicis, compiled by Walter Harris

TNA C 133, 134   Inquisitions Post Mortem

TNA SC 8   Ancient Petitions

Primary Sources

'Documents on the Early Stages of the Bruce Invasion of Ireland, 1315–1316', ed. J. R. S. Phillips, *PRIA*, 79 C (1979), 247–70.

Sources of English Constitutional History, ed. C. Stephenson and F. G. Marcham (New York and London: Harper Brothers, 1937).

Secondary Works

Brand, P., 'King, Church and Property: The Enforcement of Restrictions on Alienations into Mortmain in the Lordship of Ireland in the Later Middle Ages', *Peritia*, 3 (1984), 481–502.

'Petitions and Parliament in the Reign of Edward I', *Parliamentary History*, 23 (2004), 14–38.

'A Versatile Legal Administrator and More: The Career of John of Fressingfield in England, Ireland, and Beyond', in Smith (ed.), *Ireland and the English World*, 44–54.

Connolly, P., 'The Enactments of the 1297 Parliament', in Lydon (ed.), *Law and Disorder*, 148–61.

Duffy, S., *Ireland in the Middle Ages* (Houndmills and Dublin: Palgrave Macmillan, 1997).

'The Bruce Brothers and the Irish Sea World, 1306–29', *Cambridge Medieval Celtic Studies*, 21 (1991), 55–86.

'The Turnberry Band', in S. Duffy (ed.), *Princes, Prelates and Poets*, 124–38.

Hand, G. J., *English Law in Ireland, 1290–1324* (Cambridge University Press, 1967).

Hagger, M., *The Fortunes of a Norman Family: The de Verduns in England, Ireland and Wales, 1066–1316* (Dublin: Four Courts Press, 2001).

Hartland, B., 'English Rule in Ireland, *c*.1272–*c*.1315: Aspects of Royal and Aristocratic Lordship'. PhD thesis, Durham University (2001).

'Vaucouleurs, Ludlow and Trim: The Role of Ireland in the Career of Geoffrey de Geneville, *c*.1226–1314', *IHS*, 32 (2001), 457–77.

'"To Serve Well and Faithfully": The Agents of English Aristocratic Rule in Leinster, *c*.1272–*c*.1315', *Medieval Prosopography*, 24 (2003), 195–246.

'The Household Knights of Edward I in Ireland', *Historical Research*, 77 (2004), 161–77.

'Reasons for Leaving: The Effect of Conflict on English Landholding in Late Thirteenth-Century Leinster', *JMH*, 32 (2006), 18–26.

'English Lords in Late Thirteenth and Early Fourteenth Century Ireland: Roger Bigod and the de Clare Lords of Thomond', *EHR*, 126 (2007), 318–48.

'Absenteeism: The Chronology of a Concept', in *Thirteenth Century England XI*, ed. B. Weiler, J. Burton and P. Schofield (Woodbridge: Boydell Press, 2007), 215–29.

'The Liberties of Ireland in the Reign of Edward I', in M. Prestwich (ed.), *Liberties and Identities in the Medieval British Isles* (Woodbridge: Boydell Press, 2008), 200–16.

'Administering the Irish Fines, 1199–1254: The English Chancery, the Dublin Exchequer and the Seeking of Favours', in D. Crook and L. Wilkinson (eds.), *The Growth of Royal Government under Henry III* (Woodbridge: Boydell Press, 2015), 72–84.

Lydon, J. F., 'An Irish Army in Scotland, 1296', *Irish Sword*, 5 (1961–2), 184–90.

'Edward II and the Revenues of Ireland in 1311–1312', *IHS*, 14 (1964), 39–49.

'Edward I, Ireland and the War in Scotland, 1303–1304', in Lydon (ed.), *England and Ireland*, 43–61.

'The Years of Crisis, 1254–1315', in *NHI* ii, 179–204.

'The Impact of the Bruce Invasion', in *NHI* ii, 275–302.

'Ireland in 1297: "At Peace after its Manner" ', in Lydon (ed.), *Law and Disorder*, 11–24.

'Parliament and the Community of Ireland', in Lydon (ed.), *Law and Disorder*, 125–38.

'The Scottish Soldier Abroad: The Bruce Invasion and the Galloglass' in S. Duffy (ed), *Robert the Bruce's Irish Wars: The Invasions of Ireland, 1306–1329* (Stroud: Tempus, 2002), 89–106.

Ó Cléirigh, C., 'The Problems of Defence: A Regional Case-study', in Lydon (ed.), *Law and Disorder*, 25–56.

Phillips, J. R. S., 'David Maccarwell and the Proposal to Purchase English Law, *c*.1273–*c*.1280', *Peritia*, 10 (1996), 253–73.

Richardson, H. G. and Sayles, G. O., *The Irish Parliament in the Middle Ages* (Philadelphia: University of Pennsylvania Press, 1952).

Seymour, St J. D., *Anglo-Irish Literature: 1200–1582* (Cambridge University Press, 1929).

Sinclair, K. V., *The Walling of New Ross: An Anglo-Norman Satirical Dit* (Stuttgart: Franz Steiner, 1995).

Smith, B., *Colonisation and Conquest in Medieval Ireland: The English in Louth 1170–1330* (Cambridge University Press, 1999).

'Keeping the Peace', in J. Lydon (ed.), *Law and Disorder*, 57–65.

Thomas, A., 'Interconnections between the Lands of Edward I: A Welsh–English Mercenary Force in Ireland, 1284–1304' *Bulletin of the Board of Celtic Studies*, 40 (1993), 135–47.

Walton, H., 'The English in Connacht, 1171–1333'. PhD thesis, University of Dublin, Trinity College (1980).

9 Disaster and Opportunity: 1320–1450

Brendan Smith

Primary Sources

Royal and Historical Letters during the Reign of Henry IV, ed. F. C. Hingeston, 2 vols. (London: RS, 1860).

Secondary Works

Bennett, M., *Community, Class and Careerism: Cheshire and Lancashire Society in the Age of Sir Gawain and the Green Knight* (Cambridge University Press, 1983).

   Richard II and the Revolution of 1399 (Stroud: Sutton Publishing, 1999).

   'Richard II and the Wider Realm', in A. Goodman and J. L. Gillespie (eds.), *Richard II: The Art of Kingship* (Oxford University Press, 1999), 187–204.

Bliss, A., 'Language and Literature', in Lydon (ed.), *English in Medieval Ireland*, 27–45.

Brand, P., 'Irish Law Students and Lawyers in Late Medieval England', *IHS*, 32 (2000), 161–73.

Brown, M., *The Wars of Scotland, 1214–1371* (Edinburgh University Press, 2004).

   Disunited Kingdoms: Peoples and Politics in the British Isles 1280–1460 (Harlow: Pearson, 2013).

Callan, M. B., *The Templars, the Witch, and the Wild Irish: Vengeance and Heresy in Medieval Ireland* (Dublin: Four Courts Press, 2015).

Carney, J., 'Literature in Irish, 1169–1534', in *NHI* ii, 688–707.

Castor, H., *The King, the Crown, and the Duchy of Lancaster: Public Authority and Private Power, 1399–1461* (Oxford University Press, 2000).

Clanchy, M., *England and its Rulers 1066–1272* (London: Fontana Press, 1983).

Connolly, P., 'The Financing of English Expeditions to Ireland, 1361–1376', in Lydon (ed.), *England and Ireland*, 104–21.

Cosgrove, A., *Late Medieval Ireland, 1370–1541* (Dublin: Helicon Limited, 1981).

Crooks, P., '"Hobbes", "Dogs" and Politics in the Ireland of Lionel of Antwerp', *HSJ*, 16 (2005), 117–48.

   'Factions, Feuds and Noble Power in Late Medieval Ireland', *IHS*, 35 (2007), 425–54.

   'The "Calculus of Faction" and Richard II's Duchy of Ireland, c.1382–9', in N. Saul (ed.), *Fourteenth Century England V* (Woodbridge: Boydell Press, 2008), 94–115.

   'Negotiating Authority in a Colonial Capital: Dublin and the Windsor Crisis, 1369–78', in S. Duffy (ed.), *Medieval Dublin IX* (Dublin: Four Courts Press, 2009), 131–51.

'Representation and Dissent: "Parliamentarianism" and the Structure of Politics in Colonial Ireland *c*.1370–1420', *EHR*, 125 (2010), 1–34.

'State of the Union: Perspectives on English Imperialism in the Late Middle Ages', *Past and Present*, 212 (2011), 1–40.

Davies, R. R., *The Revolt of Owain Glyndŵr* (Oxford University Press, 1995).

Lords and Lordship in the British Isles in the Late Middle Ages, ed. B. Smith (Oxford University Press, 2009).

Davis, V., 'Irish Clergy in Late Medieval England', *IHS*, 32 (2000), 145–60.

Dodd, G., *Justice and Grace: Private Petitioning and the English Parliament in the Late Middle Ages* (Oxford University Press, 2007).

Dunn, A., 'Richard II and the Mortimer Inheritance', in C. Given-Wilson (ed.), *Fourteenth Century England II* (Woodbridge: Boydell Press, 2002), 159–70.

Fleming, P., 'Identity and Belonging: Irish and Welsh in Fifteenth-Century Bristol', in L. Clark (ed.), *The Fifteenth Century VII: Conflicts, Consequences and the Crown in the Late Middle Ages* (Woodbridge: Boydell Press, 2007), 175–93.

Frame, R., 'Ireland', in *NCMH*, vi, 375–87.

'The Defence of the English Lordship, 1250–1450', in T. Bartlett and K. Jeffery (eds.), *A Military History of Ireland* (Cambridge University Press, 1996), 76–98.

'The Wider World', in R. Horrox and W. M. Ormrod (eds.), *A Social History of England, 1200–1500* (Cambridge University Press, 2006), 435–53.

'Lordship Beyond the Pale: Munster in the Later Middle Ages', in R. Stalley (ed.), *Limerick and South-West Ireland: Medieval Art and Architecture* (Leeds: BAACT, 2011), 5–18.

Giffin, M. E., 'Arthur, and Brutus in the Wigmore Manuscript', *Speculum*, 16 (1941), 109–20.

Goldberg, P. J. P., *Medieval England: A Social History, 1250–1550* (London: Hodder Arnold, 2004).

Green, D., 'The Statute of Kilkenny (1366): Legislation and the State', *Journal of Historical Sociology*, 27 (2014), 236–62.

Harriss, G. *Shaping the Nation: England 1360–1461* (Oxford University Press, 2005).

Henry, F. and Marsh-Micheli, G., 'Manuscripts and Illuminations, 1169–1603', in *NHI* ii, 780–815.

Johnston, D., 'The Interim Years: Richard II and Ireland, 1395–1399', in Lydon (ed.), *England and Ireland*, 175–95.

'Chief Governors and Treasurers of Ireland in the Reign of Richard II', in Barry *et al.* (eds.), *Colony and Frontier in Medieval Ireland*, 97–115.

Johnston, Daffyd, *Iolo Goch: Poems* (Llandysul: Gomer Press, 1993).

Lydon, J., *Ireland in the Later Middle Ages* (Dublin: Gill & Macmillan, 1973).

'William of Windsor and the Irish Parliament', in Crooks (ed.), *Government, War and Society*, 90–105.

'Richard II's Expeditions to Ireland', in Crooks (ed.), *Government, War and Society*, 216–31.

'The Problem of the Frontier in Medieval Ireland', in Crooks (ed.), *Government, War and Society*, 317–31.

'The Middle Nation', in Crooks (ed.), *Government, War and Society*, 332–52.

McGrath, F., *Education in Ancient and Medieval Ireland* (Dublin: Studies 'Special Publications', 1979).

Matthew, E., 'The Financing of the Lordship of Ireland under Henry V and Henry VI', in T. Pollard (ed.), *Property and Politics: Essays in Later Medieval History* (Gloucester: Alan Sutton, 1984), 97–113.

'Henry V and the Proposal for an Irish Crusade', in Smith (ed.), *Ireland and the English World*, 161–75.

Mooney, C., 'The Church in Gaelic Ireland 13th to 15th Centuries', in P. J. Corish (ed.), *A History of Irish Catholicism*, Vol. II. no. 5 (Dublin: Gill & Sons, 1969).

Morgan, P., 'Ranks of Society', in R. Griffiths (ed.), *The Fourteenth and Fifteenth Centuries* (Oxford University Press, 2003), 53–85.

Nicholls, K., 'Scottish Mercenary Kindreds in Ireland, 1250–1600', in S. Duffy (ed.), *The World of the Galloglass: Kings, Warlords and Warriors in Ireland and Scotland, 1200–1600* (Dublin: Four Courts Press, 2007), 86–105.

O'Byrne, E., *War, Politics and the Irish of Leinster, 1156–1606* (Dublin: Four Courts Press, 2003).

Ormrod, W. M., 'The Protocella Rolls and English Government Finance, 1353–1364', *EHR*, 102 (1987), 622–32.

Richardson, H. G. and Sayles, G. O., *The Irish Parliament in the Middle Ages* (Philadelphia: University of Pennsylvania Press, 1952).

Saul, N., *Richard II* (New Haven and London: Yale University Press, 1997).

Simms, K., 'The Ulster Revolt of 1404: An Anti-Lancastrian Dimension?', in Smith (ed.), *Ireland and the English World*, 141–60.

'The Barefoot Kings: Literary Image and Reality in Later Medieval Ireland', in E. Boon, A. J. McMullen and N. Sumner (eds.), *Proceedings of the Harvard Celtic Colloquium 30, 2010* (Cambridge, MA, and London: Harvard University Press, 2011), 1–21.

Smith, B., *Colonisation and Conquest in Medieval Ireland: The English in Louth 1170–1330* (Cambridge University Press, 1999).

'Late Medieval Ireland and the English Connection: Waterford and Bristol, ca. 1360–1460', *Journal of British Studies*, 50 (2011), 546–65.

'The British Isles in the Late Middle Ages: Shaping the Regions', in Smith (ed.), *Ireland and the English World*, 7–19.

'The Late Medieval Diocese of Clogher, c.1200–1480', in H. A. Jefferies (ed.), *History of the Diocese of Clogher* (Dublin: Four Courts Press 2005), 70–80.

Walker, S., 'Janico Dartasso: Chivalry, Nationality and the Man-at-Arms', *History*, 84 (1991), 31–51.

Walsh, K., *A Fourteenth-Century Scholar and Primate: Richard FitzRalph in Oxford, Avignon and Armagh* (Oxford University Press, 1981).

'...In Finibus Mundi: Late Medieval Pilgrims to St Patrick's Purgatory, Lough Derg, and the European Dimension of the Diocese of Clogher', in H. A. Jefferies (ed.), *History of the Diocese of Clogher* (Dublin: Four Courts Press, 2005), 41–69.

Watt, J. A., 'The Anglo-Irish Colony under Strain, 1327–99', in *NHI* ii, 352–96.

Williams, B., 'Heresy in Ireland in the Thirteenth and Fourteenth Centuries', in Duffy (ed.), *Princes, Prelates and Poets*, 339–51.

Websites

CIRCLE: A Calendar of Irish Chancery Letters, *c.*1244–1509 http://chancery .tcd.ie/

10 The Political Recovery of Gaelic Ireland

Katharine Simms

Manuscript Sources

TNA C 47   Chancery Miscellanea.

Primary Sources

Acts of the Lords of the Isles, ed. J. Munro and R. W. Munro (Edinburgh: Scottish History Society, 1986).

'Agreement between Ó Domhnaill and Tadhg Ó Conchubhair Concerning Sligo Castle (23 June 1539)', ed. M. Carney, *IHS*, 3 (1942/3), 282–96.

'The Annals of Ireland from the Year 1443 to 1468 … by … Duald MacFirbis', ed. J. O'Donovan, in *The Miscellany of the Irish Archaeological Society 1* (Dublin, 1846), 198–302.

A Bardic Miscellany: Five Hundred Poems from Manuscripts in Irish and British Libraries, ed. D. McManus and E. Ó Raghallaigh. (Dublin: Department of Irish, Trinity College Dublin, 2010).

Dioghluim Dána, ed. Láimhbheartach Mac Cionaith (Dublin: ITS, 1938).

'Duanaire Gearóid Iarla', ed. G. Mac Niocaill, *Studia Hibernica*, 3 (1963), 7–59.

'An Elegy on the Death of Aodh Ó Conchobhair (†1309)', ed. D. McManus, *Ériu*, 51 (2000), 69–91.

An Leabhar Muimhneach, ed. T. Ó Donnchadha (Dublin: IMC, 1940).

'The Legal Proceedings against the First Earl of Desmond', ed. G. O. Sayles, *Analecta Hibernica*, 23 (1966), 1–47.

'Poem to Cloonfree Castle', ed. and trans. L. McKenna, *The Irish Monthly*, 51 (1923), 639–45.

Report on the Manuscripts of Lord De L'Isle and Dudley, ed. C. L. Kingsford and A. Sidney, Baron de L'Isle & Dudley, 6 vols. (London: Historical Manuscripts Commission, 1925–66).

'To Art Mac Murchadha Caomhanach', ed. L. MacKenna, *The Irish Monthly*, 56 (1928), 98–101.

Secondary Works

Abbott, T. K., 'Note on the Book of Mulling', *Hermathena: A Dublin University Review*, 8 no. 17 (1891), 89–90.

Beresford, D., 'Butler, James (c. 1390–1452), 4th earl of Ormond', in J. McGuire and J. Quinn (eds.), *Dictionary of Irish Biography*. 9 vols. (Cambridge University Press and RIA, 2009), ii, 126–7.

Boardman, S., 'The Tale of Leper John and the Campbell Acquisition of Lorn', in E. J. Cowan and R. A. McDonald (eds.), *Alba: Celtic Scotland in the Medieval Era* (East Linton: Tuckwell Press, 2000), 219–47.

Cathcart, A., 'Scots and Ulster: The Late Medieval Context', in W. P. Kelly and J. R. Young (eds.), *Scotland and the Ulster Plantations: Explorations in the British Settlements of Stuart Ireland* (Dublin: Four Courts Press, 2009), 62–83.

Connolly, P., 'The Financing of English Expeditions to Ireland, 1361–1376', in Lydon (ed.), *England and Ireland*, 104–21.

Cowan, E. J. and McDonald, R. A. (eds.), *Alba: Celtic Scotland in the Medieval Era* (East Linton: Tuckwell Press, 2000).

Cunningham, B., 'The Anglicisation of East Breifne: The O'Reillys and the Emergence of County Cavan', in R. Gillespie (ed.), *Cavan: Essays on the History of an Irish County* (Blackrock: Irish Academic Press, 1995), 51–72.

Curtis, E., *Richard II in Ireland, 1394–5, and the Submissions of the Irish Chiefs* (Oxford University Press, 1927).

  'Some Further Medieval Seals out of the Ormond Archives, Including That of Donal Reagh MacMurrough Kavanagh, King of Leinster', *JRSAI*, 7 (1937), 72–6.

Curtis, E. and St John Brooks, E, 'The Barons of Norragh, County Kildare', *JRSAI*, 65 (1935), 84–101.

Doran, L., 'Lords of the River Valleys: Economic and Military Lordship in the Carlow Corridor, *c.* 1200–1350 – European Model in an Irish Context', in Doran and Lyttleton (eds.), *Lordship in Medieval Ireland*, 99–127.

Duffy, S., *Ireland in the Middle Ages* (Houndmills and Dublin: Macmillan, 1997).

  'The Bruce Brothers and the Irish Sea World, 1306–29', *Cambridge Medieval Celtic Studies*, 21 (1991), 55–86.

  'The Pre-history of the Galloglass', in S. Duffy (ed.), *The World of the Galloglass: Kings, Warlords and Warriors in Ireland and Scotland, 1200–1600* (Dublin: Four Courts Press, 2007), 1–23.

Empey, C. A., 'County Kilkenny in the Anglo-Norman Period', in W. Nolan and K. Whelan (eds.), *Kilkenny: History and Society* (Dublin: Geography Publications, 1990), 75–95.

Finan, T. and O'Conor, K., 'The Moated Site at Cloonfree, Co. Roscommon', *Journal of the Galway Archaeological and Historical Society*, 54 (2002), 72–87.

Frame, R., 'Two Kings in Leinster: The Crown and the MicMhurchadha in the Fourteenth Century', in Barry *et al.* (eds.), *Colony and Frontier in Medieval Ireland*, 155–75.

  'The Justiciarship of Ralph Ufford: War and Politics in Fourteenth-Century Ireland', *Studia Hibernica*, 13 (1973), 7–47.

Harrison, S., 'Re-fighting the Battle of Down: Orpen, Mac Neill and the Irish Nation-State' in M. Brown and S. Harrison (eds.), *The Medieval World and the Modern Mind* (Dublin: Four Courts Press, 2000), 171–82.

Hayes-McCoy, G. A., *Scots Mercenary Forces in Ireland (1565–1603): An Account of Their Service during that Period, of the Reaction, of Their Activities on Scottish Affairs, and of the Effect of Their Presence in Ireland, Together with an Examination of the Gallóglaigh Or Galloglas* (Dublin and London: Burns, Oates and Washbourne, 1937).

  Irish Battles: A Military History of Ireland (London: Longmans, 1969).

Hogan, J., 'The Irish Law of Kingship, with Special Reference to Ailech and Cenél Eoghain', *PRIA*, 40 C (1932), 186–254.

Johnston, D., 'The Interim Years: Richard II and Ireland, 1395–1399', in Lydon (ed.), *England and Ireland*, 175–95.

Kingston, S., *Ulster and the Isles in the Fifteenth Century: The Lordship of the Clann Domhnaill of Antrim* (Dublin: Four Courts Press, 2004).

Long, H., 'Three Settlements of Gaelic Wicklow 1169–1600: Rathgall, Ballinacor and Glendalough' in K. Hannigan and W. Nolan (eds.), *Wicklow: History and Society* (Dublin: Geography Publications, 1994), 237–65.

Lydon, J. F., 'The Impact of the Bruce Invasion', in *NHI* ii, 275–302.

'Medieval Wicklow – a Land of War', in K. Hannigan and W. Nolan (eds.), *Wicklow: History and Society* (Dublin: Geography Publications, 1994), 151–89.

MacDougall, N., 'Achilles' Heel? The Earldom of Ross, the Lordship of the Isles and the Stewart Kings, 1449–1507', in E. J. Cowan and R. A. McDonald (eds.), *Alba: Celtic Scotland in the Medieval Era* (East Linton: Tuckwell Press, 2000), 248–75.

McLeod, W., *Divided Gaels: Gaelic Cultural Identities in Scotland and Ireland c. 1200–c.1650* (Oxford University Press, 2004).

MacNeill, E., *Phases of Irish History* (Dublin, 1919; repr. Port Washington NY and London: Kennikat Press, 1970).

MacShamhráin, A. S., *Church and Polity in Pre-Norman Ireland: The Case of Glendalough* (Maynooth: An Sagart, 1996).

Müller, A., 'Conflicting Loyalties: The Irish Franciscans and the English Crown in the High Middle Ages', *PRIA*, 107 C (2007), 87–106.

Nic Ghiollamhaith, A., 'Kings and Vassals in Later Medieval Ireland: The Uí Bhriain and the MicConmara in the Fourteenth Century', in Barry *et al.* (eds.), *Colony and Frontier in Medieval Ireland*, 201–16.

Nicholls, K., 'Scottish Mercenary Kindreds in Ireland, 1250–1600', in S. Duffy (ed.), *The World of the Galloglass: Kings, Warlords and Warriors in Ireland and Scotland, 1200–1600* (Dublin: Four Courts Press, 2007), 86–105.

O'Brien, A. F., 'The Territorial Ambitions of Maurice fitz Thomas, First Earl of Desmond, with Particular Reference to the Barony and Manor of Inchiquin, co. Cork', *PRIA*, 82 C (1982), 59–88.

'Medieval Youghal: The Development of an Irish Seaport Trading Town *c.*1200–1500', *Peritia*, 5 (1986), 346–78.

'Politics, Economy and Society: The Development of Cork and the Irish South-Coast Region c. 1170 to c. 1583', in P. O'Flanagan and C. G. Buttimer (eds.), *Cork: History and Society* (Dublin: Geography Publications, 1993), 83–154.

O'Byrne, E., *War, Politics and the Irish of Leinster, 1156–1606* (Dublin: Four Courts Press, 2003).

'Cultures in Contact in the Dublin Marches, 1170–1400', in S. Duffy (ed.), *Medieval Dublin V* (Dublin: Four Courts Press, 2004), 111–48.

'MacMurrough, Art (*c.*1357–1416/17)', in S. Duffy (ed.), *Medieval Ireland: An Encyclopedia* (New York and London: Routledge, 2005), 304–5.

'O'Donnell (Ó Domhnaill) Aodh Ruadh (1429–1505)', in J. McGuire and J. Quinn (eds.), *Dictionary of Irish Biography*. 9 vols. (Cambridge University Press and RIA, 2009), vii, 366–7.

Ó Ceallaigh, S., *Gleanings from Ulster History* (Cork University Press, 1951).

Ó Cléirigh, C., 'The Impact of the Anglo-Normans in Laois', in P. G. Lane and W. Nolan (eds.), *Laois: History and Society* (Dublin: Geography Publications, 1999), 161–82.

O'Conor, K. and Parker, C., 'Anglo-Norman Settlement in County Longford', in M. Morris and F. O'Farrell (eds.), *Longford: History and Society* (Dublin: Geography Publications, 2010), 75–99.

Ó Murchadha, D., 'The Battle of Callan, A.D. 1261', *Journal of the Cork Historical and Archaeological Society*, 66 (1961), 105–15.

Orpen, G. H., 'The Earldom of Ulster, part I', *JRSAI*, 43 (1913), 30–46.

'The Earldom of Ulster, part IV', *JRSAI*, 45 (1915), 123–42.

Phillips, J. R. S., 'The Remonstrance Revisited: England and Ireland in the Early Fourteenth Century', in T. G. Fraser and K. Jeffery (eds.) *Men, Women and War: Papers Read before the XXth Irish Conference of Historians, Held at Magee College, University of Ulster, 6–8 June 1991. Historical Studies XVIII* (Dublin: Lilliput Press, 1993), 13–27.

Quiggin, E. C., 'O'Conor's House at Cloonfree', in E. C. Quiggin (ed.), *Essays and Studies Presented to William Ridgeway* (Cambridge University Press, 1913), 333–52.

Reeves, W., 'The Seal of Hugh O'Neill', *Ulster Journal of Archaeology*, 1st series, 1 (1853), 255–8.

Ronan, M. V., 'Some Medieval Documents', *JRSAI*, 67 (1937), 229–41.

Sayles, G. O., 'The Rebellious First Earl of Desmond', in J. A. Watt, J. B. Morrall and F. X. Martin (eds.), *Medieval Studies Presented to Aubrey Gwynn S.J.* (Dublin: The Three Candles, 1961), 203–29.

Sellar, W. H. D., 'Hebridean Sea-Kings: The Successors of Somerled, 1164–1316', in E. J. Cowan and R. A. McDonald (eds.), *Alba: Celtic Scotland in the Medieval Era* (East Linton: Tuckwell Press, 2000), 187–218.

Simms, K., 'Niall Garbh II O'Donnell, King of Tír Conaill, 1422–39', *Donegal Annual*, 12 (1977), 7–21.

'Gabh umad a Fheidhlimidh – a Fifteenth-Century Inauguration Ode?', *Ériu*, 31 (1980), 132–45.

'"The King's Friend": O'Neill, the Crown and the Earldom of Ulster', in Lydon (ed.), *England and Ireland*, 214–36.

'Bards and Barons: The Anglo-Irish Aristocracy and the Native Culture', in Bartlett and MacKay (eds.), *Medieval Frontier Societies*, 177–97.

'Gaelic Warfare in the Middle Ages', in T. Bartlett and K. Jeffery (eds.), *A Military History of Ireland* (Cambridge University Press, 1996), 99–115.

'Relations with the Irish', in Lydon (ed.), *Law and Disorder*, 66–86.

'Tír Eoghain North of the Mountain', in G. O'Brien (ed.), *Derry and Londonderry: History and Society* (Dublin: Geography Publications, 1999), 149–73.

'Late Medieval Tír Eoghain', in C. Dillon and H. A. Jefferies (eds.), *Tyrone: History and Society* (Dublin: Geography Publications, 2000), 127–62.

Native Sources for Gaelic Settlement: The House Poems', in P. J. Duffy, D. Edwards and E. Fitzpatrick (eds.), *Gaelic Ireland: Land, Lordship and Settlement* (Dublin: Four Courts Press, 2001), 246–67.

'A Lost Tribe – the Clan Murtagh O'Conors', *Galway Archaeological and Historical Society Journal*, 53 (2001), 1–23.

'Images of the Galloglass in Poems to the MacSweeneys', in S. Duffy (ed.), *The World of the Galloglass: Kings, Warlords and Warriors in Ireland and Scotland, 1200–1600* (Dublin: Four Courts Press, 2007), 106–23.

'The Ulster Revolt of 1404: An Anti-Lancastrian Dimension?', in Smith (ed.), *Ireland and the English World*, 141–60.

'The Medieval Chieftains in County Antrim: Irish, English, Scots and Welsh', in C. J. Donnelly and J. Ó Neill (eds.), *Antrim: History and Society* (Dublin: Geography Publications, forthcoming).

Simpson, L., 'Anglo-Norman Settlement in Uí Briúin Cualann, 1169–1350' in K. Hannigan and W. Nolan (eds.), *Wicklow: History and Society* (Dublin: Geography Publications, 1994), 191–235.

Smyth, A. P., *Celtic Leinster* (Blackrock: Irish Academic Press, 1982).

Verstraten, F., 'Both King and Vassal: Feidlim Ua Conchobair of Connacht, 1230–65', *Journal of the Galway Archaeological and Historical Society*, 55 (2003), 15–37.

Watt, J. A., 'Approaches to the History of Fourteenth-Century Ireland', in *NHI* ii, 303–13.

Woolf, A., 'A Dead Man at Ballyshannon', in S. Duffy (ed.), *The World of the Galloglass: Kings, Warlords and Warriors in Ireland and Scotland, 1200–1600* (Dublin: Four Courts Press, 2007), 77–85.

11 Continuity and Change: 1470–1550

Christopher Maginn

Manuscript Sources

NLI MS D   Ormond Deeds

TNA SP   State Papers, Ireland

Primary Sources

British Sources for Irish History, 1485–1641, ed. D. Edwards and B. Donovan (Dublin: IMC, 1997).

'Sources for Early Modern Irish History, 1534–1641', ed. R. W. Dudley Edwards and M. O'Dowd (Cambridge University Press, 1985).

Secondary Works

Bennett, M., 'Lambert Simnel', in *ODNB*.

Bradshaw, B., *The Irish Constitutional Revolution of the Sixteenth Century* (Cambridge University Press, 1976).

'The Opposition to the Ecclesiastical Legislation in the Irish Reformation Parliament', *IHS*, 16 (1968–9), 285–303.

'Cromwellian Reform and the Origins of the Kildare Rebellion, 1533–4', *TRHS*, 27 (1977), 69–93.

'The Beginnings of Modern Ireland', in B. Farrell (ed.), *The Irish Parliamentary Tradition* (Dublin: Gill & Macmillan, 1973), 68–87.

Brady, C., *The Chief Governors: The Rise and Fall of Reform Government in Tudor Ireland, 1536–1588* (Cambridge University Press, 1994).

Bryson, A., 'The Ormond–St Leger Feud, 1544–6', *IHS*, 38 (2012), 187–212.

'Sir Anthony St Leger and the Outbreak of the Midland Rebellion, 1547–8', *PRIA*, 113 C (2013), 251–77.

'Anthony St Leger', in *ODNB*.

Canny, N., 'Early Modern Ireland: An Appraisal Appraised', *IESH*, 4 (1977), 56–65.

Conway, A., *Henry VII's Relations with Scotland and Ireland, 1485–1498* (Cambridge University Press, 1932).

Cosgrove, A., 'The Writing of Irish Medieval History', *IHS*, 27 (1990–1), 97–111.

Crooks, P., 'Factions, Feuds and Noble Power in Late Medieval Ireland', *IHS*, 35 (2007), 425–54.

Curtis, E., *A History of Medieval Ireland from 1086 to 1513* (Dublin: Maunsel and Roberts, 1923, 2nd edn. London; Methuen and Co., 1938).

Edwards, D., *The Ormond Lordship in County Kilkenny, 1515–1642: The Rise and Fall of Butler Feudal Power* (Dublin: Four Courts Press, 2003).

Ellis, S. G., *Tudor Ireland: Crown, Community and the Conflict of Cultures, 1470–1603* (London: Longman, 1985).

Reform and Revival: English Government in Ireland, 1470–1534 (Woodbridge: Royal Historical Society, Boydell Press, 1986).

Tudor Frontiers and Noble Power: The Making of the British State (Oxford University Press, 1995).

'The Kildare Rebellion and the Early Henrician Reformation', *Historical Journal*, 19 (1976), 807–30.

'Tudor Policy and the Kildare Ascendancy in the Lordship of Ireland', *IHS*, 20 (1977), 235–60.

'Thomas Cromwell and Ireland, 1532–40', *Historical Journal*, 23 (1980), 497–519.

'Henry VII and Ireland, 1491–1496', in Lydon (ed.), *England and Ireland*, 237–54.

'Sir Edward Poynings', in *ODNB*.

'Parliament and Community in Yorkist and Tudor Ireland', in A. Cosgrove and J. McGuire (eds.), *Parliament and Community: Historical Studies XIV* (Belfast: Appletree Press, 1983), 43–68.

'Region and Frontier in the English State: Co. Meath and the English Pale, 1460–1542', in H. V. Holm, S. Laegreid and T. Skorgen (eds.), *The Borders of Europe: Hegemony, Aesthetics and Border Poetics* (Aarhus University Press, 2012), 49–70.

'From Medieval to Early Modern: the British Isles in Transition?' in R. Hutton (ed.), *Medieval or Early Modern? The Value of a Traditional Historical Division* (Cambridge: Cambridge Scholars Press 2015), 10–28.

Farrell, B. (ed.), *The Irish Parliamentary Tradition* (Dublin: Gill & Macmillan, 1973).

Fitzsimons, F., 'Cardinal Wolsey, the Native Affinities and the Failure of Reform in Henrician Ireland', in D. Edwards (ed.), *Regions and Rulers in Ireland, 1100–1650* (Dublin: Four Courts Press, 2004), 78–121.

Griffith, M. C., 'The Talbot–Ormond Struggle for Control of the Anglo-Irish Government, 1414–47', *IHS*, 2 (1940–1), 376–97.

'The Irish Record Commission, 1810–30', *IHS*, 7 (1950–1), 1–28.

Griffiths, R. A., 'The English Realm and Dominions and the King's Subjects in the Later Middle Ages', in J. Rowe (ed.), *Aspects of English Government and Society in Later Medieval England: Essays in Honour of J. R. Lander* (Toronto University Press, 1986), 83–105.

Haigh, P. A., *The Military Campaigns of the Wars of the Roses* (Stroud: Sutton Publishing, 1995).

Harris, W. (ed.), *Hibernica, or, Some Ancient Pieces relating to the History of Ireland*. 2 vols. (Dublin: Edward Bate, 1747, 1750).

Hayes-McCoy, G. A., 'The Royal Supremacy and Ecclesiastical Revolution, 1534–47', in *NHI* iii, 39–68.

Lydon, J., *Ireland in the Later Middle Ages* (Dublin: Gill & Macmillan, 1973).

'The Middle Nation', in Crooks (ed.), *Government, War and Society*, 332–52.

McCormack, A., *The Earldom of Desmond: The Decline and Crisis of a Feudal Lordship, 1463–1583* (Dublin: Four Courts Press, 2005).

Maginn, C., *'Civilizing' Gaelic Leinster: The Extension of Tudor Rule in the O'Byrne and O'Toole Lordships* (Dublin: Four Courts Press, 2005).

William Cecil, Ireland, and the Tudor State (Oxford University Press, 2012).

'A Window on Mid-Tudor Ireland: The "Matters" against Lord Deputy St. Leger, 1547–8', *Historical Research*, 78 (2005), 465–82.

'"Surrender and Regrant" in the Historiography of Sixteenth-Century Ireland', *Sixteenth Century Journal*, 38 (2007), 955–74.

'Whose Island? Sovereignty in Late Medieval and Early Modern Ireland', *Éire-Ireland*, 44 (2009), 229–47.

'Gaelic Ireland's English Frontiers in the Late Middle Ages', *PRIA*, 110 C (2010), 173–90.

'The Gaelic Peers, the Tudor Sovereigns, and English Multiple Monarchy', *Journal of British Studies*, 50 (2011), 566–86.

'Edward Staples', in *ODNB*.

Maginn, C. and Ellis, S. G., *The Tudor Discovery of Ireland* (Dublin: Four Courts Press, 2015).

Nicholls, K. W., 'A Calendar of Salved Chancery Pleadings Concerning County Louth', *Journal of the County Louth Archaeological Society*, 17 (1972), 250–60.

O'Byrne, E., *War, Politics and the Irish of Leinster, 1156–1606* (Dublin: Four Courts Press, 2003).

Ó Cuív, B., 'A Sixteenth-Century Political Poem', *Éigse*, 15 / 4 (1974), 261–76.

Ó Siochrú, M., 'Foreign Involvement in the Revolt of Silken Thomas, 1534–5', *PRIA*, 96 C (1996), 49–66.

Power, G., *A European Frontier Elite: The Nobility of the English Pale in Tudor Ireland, 1496–1566* (Hannover: Wehrhahn Verlag, 2012).

Quinn, D. B., 'Tudor Rule in Ireland in the Reigns of Henry VII and Henry VIII, with Special Reference to the Anglo-Irish Financial Administration'. PhD thesis, University of London (1934).

'Parliaments and Great Councils in Ireland, 1461–1586', *IHS*, 3 (1942–3), 60–77.

'Henry VIII and Ireland, 1509–34', *IHS*, 12 (1961), 318–44.

'Aristocratic Autonomy, 1460–94', in *NHI* ii, 591–618.

Sayles, G. O., 'The Vindication of the Earl of Kildare from Treason in 1496', *IHS*, 7 (1951), 39–47.

Scarisbrick, J. J., *Henry VIII* (London: Eyre & Spottiswoode, 1968).

Smith, B., 'Keeping the Peace', in Lydon (ed.), *Law and Disorder*, 57–65.

Walker, G., 'The Expulsion of the Minions of 1519 Reconsidered', *Historical Journal*, 32 (1989), 1–16.

Ware, J., *The Antiquities and History of Ireland* (Dublin: A. Crook, 1705).

White, A. B., *Self-Government at the King's Command* (Minneapolis: University of Minnesota Press, 1933).

White, D. G., 'Henry VIII's Irish Kerne in France and Scotland', *Irish Sword*, 3 (1957–8), 213–25.

'The Reign of Edward VI in Ireland: Some Political, Social and Economic Aspects', *IHS*, 14 (1964–5), 197–211.

Wilson, P., *The Beginnings of Modern Ireland* (Dublin: Maunsel, 1912).

Wood, H., 'The Public Records of Ireland before and after 1922', *TRHS*, 13 (1930), 17–49.

12 Late Medieval Ireland in a Wider World

Michael Bennett

Manuscript Sources

BL Add. MS. 4792   Composite volume of State Papers
BL Harleian MS. 3988   Letter of Charles VI to Richard II
  BL Royal MS. 10 E V–VI
TNA C 1   Court of Chancery: Six Clerks' Office: Early Proceedings, Richard II–Philip and Mary
TNA CHES 25   Palatinate of Chester
TNA E 30   Treasury of Receipt: Diplomatic Documents
TNA, PROB 11   Wills, 1384–1858
TNA SC 8   Ancient Petitions
New College, Oxford, MSS. 112 and 122   Books purchased by Archbishop Thomas Cranley
Oxford, Bodleian Library MS. Lyell 32   Collection concerning Royal Forests

Primary Sources

The Chronicle of Adam Usk 1377–1421, ed. C. Given-Wilson (Oxford University Press, 1997).
The Chronicles of Enguerrand de Monstrelet, ed. T. Johnes, 2 vols. (London: Longman, 1840).
Itinerarium Symonis Semeonis ab Hybernia ad Terra Sanctam, ed. M. Esposito. Scriptores Latini Hiberniae, 4 (Dublin: DIAS, 1960).
The Libelle of Englyshe Polycye. A Poem on the Use of Sea-Power 1436, ed. G. Warner (Oxford University Press, 1926).
Philippe de Mezières, *Letter to King Richard II: A Plea Made in 1395 for Peace between England and France*, ed. G. W. Coopland (Liverpool University Press, 1975).
Thomæ Walsingham Historia Anglicana 1272–1422, ed. H. T. Riley, 2 vols. (London: RS, 1863–4).

Secondary Works

Bennett, M., *Lambert Simnel and the Battle of Stoke* (Gloucester: Sutton Publishing, 1987).
Richard II and the Revolution of 1399 (Stroud: Sutton Publishing, 1999).

'Richard II and the Wider Realm', in A. Goodman and J. L. Gillespie (eds.), *Richard II: The Art of Kingship* (Oxford University Press, 1999), 187–204.

Bolton, J. L., 'Irish Migration to England in the Late Middle Ages: The Evidence of 1394 and 1440', *IHS*, 32 (2000), 1–21.

Booker, S., 'Irish Clergy and the Diocesan Church in the "Four Obedient Shires" of Ireland, *c*. 1400–*c*. 1540', *IHS*, 39 (2014), 179–209.

Brand, P., 'Irish Law Students and Lawyers in Late Medieval England', *IHS*, 32 (2000), 161–73.

Brown, S. F., 'Ó Fithcheallaigh, Muiris (d. 1513)', in *ODNB*.

Carney, J., 'Literature in Irish, 1169–1534', in *NHI* ii, 688–707.

Carpenter, D., 'The Pilgrim from Catalonia / Aragon: Ramon de Perellós, 1397', in Haren and de Pontfarcy (eds.), *Medieval Pilgrimage to St Patrick's Purgatory*, 99–119.

Carus-Wilson, M., *The Overseas Trade of Bristol in the Later Middle Ages* (Bristol: Bristol Record Society, 1937).

Childs, W., 'Irish Merchants and Seamen in Late Medieval England', *IHS*, 32 (2000), 22–42.

Cosgrove, A., 'The Emergence of the Pale 1399–1447', in *NHI* ii, 533–56.

Crooks, P., 'Representation and Dissent: "Parliamentarianism" and the Structure of Politics in Colonial Ireland *c*.1370–1420', *EHR*, 125 (2010), 1–34.

'The "Calculus of Faction" and Richard II's Duchy of Ireland, *c*.1382–9', in N. Saul (ed.), *Fourteenth Century England V* (Woodbridge: Boydell Press, 2008), 94–115.

Donovan, B. and Edwards, D., 'British Sources for Irish History before 1485: A Preliminary Handlist of Documents Held in Local and Specialised Repositories', *Analecta Hibernica*, 37 (1998), 191–220.

Down, K., 'Colonial Society and Economy in the High Middle Ages', in *NHI* ii, 439–91.

Emden, A. B., *A Biographical Register of the University of Oxford to A.D. 1500*, 3 vols. (Oxford University Press, 1957–9).

Frame, R., 'Two Kings in Leinster: The Crown and the MicMhurchadha in the Fourteenth Century', in Barry *et al.* (eds.), *Colony and Frontier in Medieval Ireland*, 155–175.

Gummer, B., *The Scourging Angel. The Black Death in the British Isles* (London: Vintage, 2010).

Hardiman, J., *The History of the Town and County of Galway* (Dublin: Folds, 1820).

Haren, M., 'Two Hungarian Pilgrims', in Haren and de Pontfarcy (eds.), *Medieval Pilgrimage to St Patrick's Purgatory*, 120–68.

'The Close of the Medieval Pilgrimage: The Papal Suppression and its Aftermath', in Haren and de Pontfarcy (eds.), *Medieval Pilgrimage to St Patrick's Purgatory*, 190–201.

Hendriks, L., *The London Charterhouse, its Monks and its Martyrs* (London: Kegan Paul, 1889).

Kerby-Fulton, K. and Despres, D. L., *Iconography and the Professional Reader: The Politics of Book Production in the Douce Piers Plowman* (Minneapolis: University of Minnesota Press, 1999).

Lydon, J. F., 'Richard II's Expeditions to Ireland', in Crooks (ed.), *Government, War and Society*, 216–31.

Nicholls, K. W., 'Gaelic Society and Economy in the High Middle Ages', in *NHI* ii, 397–438.

Ó Clabaigh, C., *The Franciscans in Ireland, 1400–1534* (Dublin: Four Courts Press, 2002).

Potvin, C. (ed.), *Oeuvres de Ghillebert de Lannoy, voyageur, diplomate et moraliste* (Louvain: Lefever, 1878).

Scofield, C. L., *Life and Reign of Edward IV*, 2 vols. (London: Cass, 1967).

Simms, K., 'Gaelic Warfare in the Middle Ages', in T. Bartlett and K. Jeffery (eds.), *A Military History of Ireland* (Cambridge University Press, 1996), 99–115.

Smith, B., 'Late Medieval Ireland and the English Connection: Waterford and Bristol, *ca.* 1360–1460', *Journal of British Studies*, 50 (2011), 546–65.

Walker, S., 'Janico Dartasso: Chivalry, Nationality and the Man-at-Arms', *History*, 84 (1991), 31–51.

Watt, J. A., 'Gaelic Polity and Cultural Identity', in *NHI* ii, 314–51.

'The Papacy and Ireland in the Fifteenth Century', in R. B. Dobson (ed.), *The Church, Politics and Patronage in the Fifteenth Century* (Gloucester: Sutton Publishing, 1984), 133–45.

Websites

'England's immigrants 1330–1450' database: www.hrionline.ac.uk/englandsimmigrants.

13 The Church, 1050–1460

Colmán Ó Clabaigh

Manuscript Sources

TCD MS 97	Customary of St Victor
TCD MS 667	*Exempla* and Romance literature

Primary Sources

Friars' Tales: Thirteenth-Century Exempla from the British Isles, ed. D. Jones (Manchester University Press, 2011).

Registrum de Kilmainham: Register of Chapter Acts of the Hospital of Saint John of Jerusalem in Ireland, 1326–1339 under the Grand Prior, Sir Roger Outlawe, ed. C. McNeill (Dublin: IMC, 1932).

Stephen of Lexington, *Letters from Ireland, 1228–1229*, ed. and trans. B. O'Dwyer (Kalamazoo: Cistercian Publications Inc., 1982).

Secondary Works

Callan, M. B., *The Templars, the Witch, and the Wild Irish: Vengeance and Heresy in Medieval Ireland* (Dublin: Four Courts Press, 2015).

Clyne, M., 'Archaeological Excavations at Holy Trinity Abbey, Lough Key, Co. Roscommon', *PRIA*, 105 C (2005), 23–98.

Collins, T., 'Timolin: A Case Study of a Nunnery Estate in Late Medieval Ireland', *Anuario de Estudios Medievales*, 44/1 (2014), 51–80.

Duffy, P. J., 'The Shape of the Parish', in E. Fitzpatrick and R. Gillespie (eds.), *The Parish in Medieval and Early Modern Ireland: Community, Territory and Building* (Dublin: Four Courts Press, 2006), 33–61.

Empey, C. A., 'The Layperson in the Parish: The Medieval Inheritance, 1169–1536', in R. Gillespie and W. G. Neely (eds.), *The Laity and the Church of Ireland, 1000–2000: All Sorts and Conditions* (Dublin: Four Courts Press, 2002), 7–48.

Gem, R., 'Saint Flannán's Oratory at Killaloe: A Romanesque Building of *c*.1100 and the Patronage of King Muirchertach Ua Briain', in Bracken and Ó Riain-Raedel (eds.), *Ireland and Europe in the Twelfth Century*, 74–105.

Jefferies, H. A., 'Diocesan Synods and Convocations in Armagh on the Eve of the Tudor Reformations', *Seanchas Ardmhacha*, 16 (1995), 120–32.

Lydon, J., 'The Case against Alexander Bicknor, Archbishop and Peculator', in Smith (ed.), *Ireland and the English World*, 103–11.

Nicholson, H., 'A Long Way from Jerusalem: Templars and Hospitallers in Ireland, *c*.1172–1348' in Browne and Ó Clabaigh (eds.), *Soldiers of Christ*, 1–22.

Ó Carragáin, T., *Churches in Early Medieval Ireland: Architecture, Ritual and Memory* (New Haven and London: Yale University Press, 2010).

Ó Clabaigh, C., 'The Benedictines in Medieval and Early Modern Ireland', in M. Browne and C. Ó Clabaigh (eds.), *The Irish Benedictines: A History* (Dublin: Columba Press, 2005), 79–121.

'Anchorites in Late Medieval Ireland', in L. Herbert McAvoy (ed.), *Anchoritic Traditions of Medieval Europe* (Woodbridge: Boydell Press, 2010), 153–77.

Ó Cróinín, D., 'A Tale of Two Rules', in M. Browne and C. Ó Clabaigh (eds.), *The Irish Benedictines: A History* (Dublin: Columba Press, 2005), 11–24.

Ó Riain, P., 'Longford Priories and their Manuscripts: All Saints and Abbeyderg', in M. Morris and F. O'Ferrall (eds.), *Longford: History and Society* (Dublin: Geography Publications, 2010), 39–50.

Ó Riain-Raedel, D., 'Cashel and Germany: The Documentary Evidence', in Bracken and Ó Riain-Raedel (eds.), *Ireland and Europe in the Twelfth Century*, 176–217.

Ó Riain-Raedel, D. and Ó Riain, P., 'Irish Saints in a Regensburg Litany', in Purcell *et al.* (eds.), *Clerics, Kings and Vikings*, 55–66.

Ryan, S., 'Windows on Late Medieval Devotional Practice: Máire Ní Mháille's "Book of Piety" (1513) and the World behind the Texts', in Moss *et al.* (eds.), *Art and Devotion in Late Medieval Ireland*, 1–15.

Sharpe, R., *Medieval Irish Saints' Lives: An Introduction to Vitae Sanctorum Hiberniae* (Oxford University Press, 1991).

Stalley, R., *Cistercian Monasteries of Ireland* (London and New Haven: Yale University Press, 1987).

Staunton, M. and Ó Clabaigh, C., 'Thomas Becket and Ireland', in E. Mullins and D. Scully (eds.), *'Listen, O Isles, unto me': Studies in Medieval Word and Image in Honour of Jennifer O'Reilly* (Cork University Press: 2011), 87–101, 340–3, 464–6.

Tait, C., 'Safely Delivered: Childbirth, Wet-Nursing, Gossip-Feasts and Churching in Ireland *c*.1530–1690', *IESH*, 30 (2003), 1–23.

14 The Economy

Margaret Murphy

Manuscript Sources

NAI RC 8   Memoranda Rolls
NLI MS 3   Collectanea de rebus Hibernicis, compiled by Walter Harris
TNA E 101   Exchequer Miscellanea
TNA SC 6   Ministers' and Receivers' Accounts

Primary Sources

Account Roll of the Priory of the Holy Trinity, Dublin, 1337–1346, ed. J. Mills (Dublin, 1891; new edn Dublin: Four Courts Press, 1996).

Bristol's Trade with Ireland and the Continent, 1503–1601: The Evidence of the Exchequer Customs Accounts, ed. E. Jones and S. Flavin (Dublin: Four Courts Press, 2009).

Calendar of Ancient Records of Dublin, ed. J. T. Gilbert *et al.* 19 vols. (Dublin, 1889–1944)

Calendar of Archbishop Alen's Register c.*1172–1534*, ed. C. McNeill (Dublin: RSAI, 1950).

Chartae, Priviligiam et Immunitates (London, 1889).

'Documents on the Suppression of the Templars in Ireland', ed. G. Mac Niocaill, *Analecta Hibernica*, 24 (1961), 183–226.

The Great Parchment Book of Waterford, ed. N. J. Byrne (Dublin: IMC, 2007).

Household Accounts from Medieval England, ed. C. M. Woolgar. 2 vols. (Oxford University Press, 1992).

Inquisitions and Extents of Medieval Ireland, ed. P. Dryburgh and B. Smith (London: List and Index Society, 2007).

Irish Monastic and Episcopal Deeds, AD *1200–1600*, ed. N. B. White (Dublin: IMC, 1936).

Political Poems and Songs Relating to English History, ii, ed. T. Wright (London: Longman, 1861).

Secondary Works

Abraham, K., 'Upward Mobility in Later Medieval Meath', *History Ireland*, 5 (1997), 15–20.

Adelman, J. and Ludlow, F., 'The Past, Present and Future of Irish Environmental History', *PRIA*, 114 C (2014), 1–33.

Barry, T. B., 'Late Medieval Ireland: Social and Economic Transformation 1350–1550', in B. J. Graham and L. J. Proudfoot (eds.), *A Historical Geography of Ireland*, (London: Academic Press, 1993), 99–122.

Bhreathnach, E., *Ireland in the Medieval World*, AD *400–1000: Landscape, Kingship and Religion* (Dublin: Four Courts Press, 2014).

Bradley, J., *Kilkenny*. Irish Historic Towns Atlas (Dublin: RIA, 2000).

'Kilkenny', in S. Duffy (ed.), *Medieval Ireland: An Encyclopedia* (New York and London: Routledge, 2005), 249–50.

Brady, N., 'Mills in Medieval Ireland: Looking Beyond Design', in S. Walton (ed.), *Wind and Water in the Middle Ages: Fluid Technologies from Antiquity to the Renaissance* (Tempe: University of Arizona Press, 2006), 39–68.

Britnell, R. H., *Britain and Ireland, 1050–1530* (Oxford University Press, 2004).

Campbell, B. M. S., *English Seigniorial Agriculture, 1250–1450* (Cambridge University Press, 2000).

'Benchmarking Medieval Economic Development: England, Wales, Scotland and Ireland *c*.1290', *Economic History Review*, 61 (2008), 896–945.

'Nature as Historical Protagonist: Environment and Society in Pre-Industrial England', *Economic History Review*, 63 (2010), 281–314.

'Economic Rent and the Intensification of English Agriculture 1086 to 1350', in J. Langdon and G. G. Astill (eds.), *Medieval Farming and Technology: The Impact of Agricultural Change in Northwest Europe* (Leiden: Brill, 1997), 225–50.

Campbell, B. M. S. and Bartley, K., *England on the Eve of the Black Death: An Atlas of Lay Lordship, Land and Wealth, 1300–1349* (Manchester University Press, 2006).

Campbell, B. M. S., Galloway, J. A., Keene, D. J. and Murphy, M., *A Medieval Capital and its Grain Supply: Agrarian Production and Distribution in the London Region, c.1300* (Historical Geography Research Series, 30, 1993).

Childs, W., 'Commerce and Trade', in *NCMH*, vii, 145–60.

Childs, W. and O'Neill, T., 'Overseas Trade', in *NHI* ii, 492–524.

Clarke, H. B., '*Quo Vadis*: Mapping the Irish "Monastic Town"', in Duffy (ed.), *Princes, Prelates and Poets*, 261–78.

'Decolonization and the Dynamics of Urban Decline in Ireland, 1300–1550', in T. R. Slater (ed.), *Towns in Decline, AD 100–1600* (Aldershot: Ashgate, 2000), 157–92.

'The Mother's Tale', in S. Booker and C. Peters (eds.), *Tales of Medieval Dublin* (Dublin: Four Courts Press, 2014), 52–61.

Connolly, P., 'The Irish Memoranda Rolls: Some Unexplored Aspects', *IESH*, 3 (1976), 66–74.

'The Enactments of the 1297 Parliament', in Lydon (ed.), *Law and Disorder*, 148–61.

'Fulbourn, Stephen of', in *ODNB*.

Cotter, É. (ed.), *Buttevant. A Medieval Anglo-French Town in Ireland* (Midleton: Éamonn Cotter, 2013).

Doherty, C., 'Exchange and Trade in Early Medieval Ireland', *JRSAI*, 110 (1980), 67–89.

Dolley, M., 'Coinage to 1534: The Sign of the Times', in *NHI* ii, 818–25.

Doran, L., 'Lords of the River Valleys: Economic and Military Lordship in the Carlow Corridor, *c*. 1200–1350 – European Model in an Irish Context', in Doran and Lyttleton (eds.), *Lordship in Medieval Ireland*, 99–127.

Down, K., 'Colonial Society and Economy in the High Middle Ages', *NHI* ii, 439–91.

Dyer, C., 'The Consumer and the Market in Medieval England', *Economic History Review*, 42 (1989), 305–27.

'Medieval Farming and Technology: Conclusion', in J. Langdon and G. G. Astill (eds.), *Medieval Farming and Technology: The Impact of Agricultural Change in Northwest Europe* (Leiden: Brill, 1997), 293–312.

Ellis, S. G., *Defending English Ground: War and Peace in Meath & Northumberland, 1460–1542* (Oxford University Press, 2015).

Empey, C. A., 'Conquest and Settlement: Patterns of Anglo-Norman Settlement in North Munster and South Leinster', *IESH*, 10–13 (1983–6), 5–31.

'The Anglo-Norman Community in Tipperary and Kilkenny in the Middle Ages: Change and Continuity', in Mac Niocaill, and Wallace (eds.), *Keimelia*, 449–67.

Etchingham, C., 'The Organization and Function of an Early Irish Church Settlement: What was Glendalough?', in C. Doherty, L. Doran and M. Kelly (eds.), *Glendalough: City of God* (Dublin: Four Courts Press, 2011), 22–53.

Galloway, J. A., 'The Economic Hinterland of Drogheda in the Later Middle Ages', in V. McAlister and T. Barry (eds.), *Space and Settlement in Medieval Ireland* (Dublin: Four Courts Press, 2015), 167–85.

Gemmill, E., 'Prices from the Durham Obedientiary Account Rolls 1278 to 1367', in M. Allen and D'M. Coffmann (eds.), *Money, Prices and Wages: Essays in Honour of Professor Nicholas Mayhew* (Houndmills: Palgrave Macmillan, 2015), 74–93.

Glasscock, R. E., 'Land and People, *c.*1300', in *NHI* ii, 205–39.

Grafe, R., 'Economic and Social Trends', in H. Scott (ed.), *Early Modern European History 1350–1750. Volume 1: Peoples and Place* (Oxford University Press, 2015), 269–94.

Graham, B. J., 'The High Middle Ages: *c.*1100 to *c.*1350', in B. J. Graham and L. J. Proudfoot (eds.), *A Historical Geography of Ireland*, (London: Academic Press, 1993), 58–98.

'Ireland: Economy and Society', in S. H. Rigby (ed.), *A Companion to Britain in the Later Middle Ages* (Oxford: Blackwell, 2003), 142–62.

Hatcher, J., 'The Great Slump of the Mid-Fifteenth Century', in R. Britnell and J. Hatcher (eds.), *Progress and Problems in Medieval England: Essays in Honour of Edward Miller* (Cambridge University Press, 1996), 237–72.

Hennessy, M., 'Manorial Agriculture and Settlement in Early Fourteenth-Century Co. Tipperary', in Clarke *et al.* (eds.), *Surveying Ireland's Past*, 99–118.

'Making Ireland English in the Thirteenth Century: The Evidence of the Irish Lay Subsidy of 1292', in P. J. Duffy and W. Nolan (eds.), *At the Anvil: Essays in Honour of William J. Smyth* (Dublin: Geography Publications, 2012), 81–92.

Hoare, K., 'The Evolution of Urban Oligarchies in Irish Towns, 1350–1534', in L. Klusakova and L. Teulieres (eds.), *Frontiers and Identities: Cities in Regions and Nations* (Pisa University Press, 2008), 87–107.

Holm, P., 'Manning and Paying the Hiberno-Norse Dublin Fleet', in Purcell *et al.* (eds.), *Clerics, Kings and Vikings*, 67–78.

Hudson, B., *Irish Sea Studies 900–1200* (Dublin: Four Courts Press, 2006).

Jäger, H., 'Land Use in Medieval Ireland: A Review of the Documentary Evidence', *IESH*, 10 (1983), 51–65.

Kelly, M., *The Great Dying: The Black Death in Dublin* (Stroud: Tempus, 2003).

Langdon, J., *Horses, Oxen and Technological Innovation: The Use of Draught Animals in English Farming from 1066 to 1500* (Cambridge University Press, 1986).

Lydon, J. F., 'Ireland's Participation in the Military Activities of the English Kings in the Thirteenth and Early Fourteenth Centuries'. PhD thesis, University of London (1955).

Lyons, M. C., 'Weather, Famine, Pestilence and Plague in Ireland, 900–1500', in E. M. Crawford (ed.), *Famine: The Irish Experience 900–1900: Subsistence Crises and Famines in Ireland* (Edinburgh: John Donald, 1989), 31–74.

McCormick, F. and Murray, E., *Knowth and the Zooarchaeology of Early Christian Ireland* (Dublin: RIA, 2007).

McNeill, P. G. B. and McQueen, H. L. (eds.), *Atlas of Scottish History to 1707* (Edinburgh: The Scottish Medievalists and Department of Geography, University of Edinburgh, 1996).

Mac Niocaill, G., *Na Buirgéisí*. 2 vols. (B.Á.C: Cló Morainn, 1964).

'Socio-Economic Problems of the Late Medieval Town', in D. Harkness and M. O'Dowd (eds.), *The Town in Ireland* (Belfast: Appletree Press, 1981), 7–21.

Martin, G., 'Plantation Boroughs in Medieval Ireland, with a Handlist of Boroughs to *c*.1500', in D. Harkness and M. O'Dowd (eds.), *The Town in Ireland* (Belfast: Appletree Press, 1981), 23–53.

Mate, M., 'Agricultural Technology in Southeast England, 1348–1540', in J. Langdon and G. G. Astill (eds.), *Medieval Farming and Technology: The Impact of Agricultural Change in Northwest Europe* (Leiden: Brill, 1997), 251–74.

Mills, J. S., 'Accounts of the Earl of Norfolk's Estates in Ireland, 1279–1294', *JRSAI*, 2 (1892), 50–62.

Murphy, M., 'From Swords to Ploughshares: Evidence for Templar Agriculture in Medieval Ireland', in Browne and Ó Clabaigh (eds.), *Soldiers of Christ*, 167–83.

'Rural Settlement in Meath, 1170–1660: The Documentary Evidence', in M. Deevy and D. Murphy (eds.), *Places Along the Way: First Findings on the M3* (Bray: Wordwell, 2009), 153–68.

'Feeding Another City: Dublin and its Region in the Later Middle Ages', in M. Davis and J. A. Galloway (eds.), *London and Beyond: Essays in Honour of Derek Keene* (London: Institute of Historical Research, 2012), 3–24.

'Manor Centres, Settlement and Agricultural Systems in Medieval Ireland, 1250–1350', in M. Murphy and M. Stout (eds.), *Agriculture and Settlement in Ireland* (Dublin: Four Courts Press, 2015), 69–100.

Murphy, M. and Potterton, M., 'Investigating Living Standards in Medieval Dublin and its Region', in S. Duffy (ed.), *Medieval Dublin VI* (Dublin: Four Courts Press, 2005), 224–56.

Murphy, M., Connon, A. and Galloway, J., 'Waterford and its Hinterland: An Historical Overview', in J. Eogan and E. S. Twohig (eds.), *Cois tSiúre – Nine Thousand Years of Human Activity in the Lower Suir Valley: Archaeological Excavations on the N25 Waterford City Bypass*. NRA Scheme Monographs 8 (Dublin: The National Roads Authority, 2011), 217–44.

Nicholls, K. W., 'Gaelic Society and Economy in the High Middle Ages', in *NHI* ii, 397–438.

O'Brien, A. F., 'Politics, Economy and Society: The Development of Cork and the Irish South-Coast Region *c*.1170 to *c*.1583', in P. O'Flanagan and C. G. Buttimer (eds.), *Cork: History and Society* (Dublin: Geography Publications, 1993), 83–154.

Ó Corráin, D., 'Vikings in Ireland: The Catastrophe', in Clarke and Johnson (eds.), *Vikings in Ireland and Beyond*.

O'Keeffe, T., *Fethard*. Irish Historic Towns Atlas (Dublin: RIA, 2003).

O'Sullivan, A., McCormick, F., Kerr, T. R. and Harney, L., *Early Medieval Ireland AD 400–1100: The Evidence from Archaeological Excavations* (Dublin: RIA, 2014).

O'Sullivan, H. and Gillespie, R., *Carlingford*. Irish Historic Towns Atlas (Dublin: RIA, 2011).

O'Sullivan, M. D., *Italian Merchant Bankers in Ireland in the Thirteenth Century* (Dublin: Alan Figgis & Co, 1962).

Potterton, M., *Medieval Trim: History and Archaeology* (Dublin: Four Courts Press, 2005).

Sherlock, R., 'Tower Houses', in Moss (ed.), *Art and Architecture of Ireland*, 354–7.

Simms, K., The Origins of the Creaght: Farming System or Social Unit?' in M. Murphy and M. Stout (eds.), *Agriculture and Settlement in Ireland* (Dublin: Four Courts Press, 2015), 101–18.

Smith, C. V., *Dalkey: Society and Economy in a Small Medieval Irish Town* (Dublin: Irish Academic Press, 1996).

Southern, R. W., *The Making of the Middle Ages* (London: Hutchinson, 1967).

Stout, G., 'The Cistercian Grange: A Medieval Farming System', in M. Murphy and M. Stout (eds.), *Agriculture and Settlement in Ireland* (Dublin: Four Courts Press, 2015), 28–68.

Thomas, A., 'Financing Town Walls in Medieval Ireland', in C. Thomas (ed.), *Rural Landscapes and Communities: Essays Presented to Desmond McCourt* (Dublin: Irish Academic Press, 1986), 65–91.

Watt, J. A., 'The Anglo-Irish Colony under Strain, 1327–99', in *NHI* ii, 352–96.

Williams, G. 'Viking Camps and the Means of Exchange', in Clarke and Johnson (eds.), *Vikings in Ireland and Beyond*, 93–117.

Wood, H., 'The Templars in Ireland', *PRIA*, 26 C (1906–7), 327–77.

Woods, A., 'The Coinage and Economy of Hiberno-Scandinavian Dublin', in S. Duffy (ed.), *Medieval Dublin XIII* (Dublin: Four Courts Press, 2013), 43–69.

15 Gaelic Culture and Society

Katharine Simms

Manuscript Sources

BL Add. MS 30512   Leabhar Uí Maolconaire
BL Cotton MS, Vesp. E IX.   Various, including Chronicle of England
RIA MS 476   *Liber Flavus Fergusiorum*
PRONI   Register of Archbishop John Prene

Primary Sources

Aithdioghluim Dána, ed. L. McKenna. 2 vols. (Dublin: ITS, 1939 [text], 1940 [trans.]).

'The Annals of Ireland from the Year 1443 to 1468 … by … Duald MacFirbis', ed. J. O'Donovan, in *The Miscellany of the Irish Archaeological Society 1* (Dublin, 1846), 198–302.

'An Appeal on Behalf of the Profession of Poetry', ed. and trans. B. Ó Cuív, *Éigse*, 14 (1971), 87–106.

The Battle of Gabhra: Garristown in the County of Dublin, ed. N. O'Kearney (Dublin: Transactions of the Ossianic Society, 1853).

'A Calendar of the Reassembled Register of John Bole, Archbishop of Armagh, 1457–71', ed. A. Lynch, *Seanchas Ardmhacha*, 15 (1992), 113–85.

'Cairt ó Mhaolmhordha Ó Raighilligh, 1558', ed. G. Mac Niocaill, *Breifne*, 1 (1959), 134–5.

Catalogue of Irish Language Manuscripts in the Bodleian Library at Oxford and Oxford College Libraries, ed. B. Ó Cuiv. 2 vols. (Dublin: DIAS, 2001).

The Compossicion Booke of Conought, ed. A. M. Freeman (Dublin: IMC, 1936).

Dánta Grádha, ed. T. Ó Rathile, 2nd edn (Cork University Press, 1926).

'Dhá Dhán le Risteard Buitléir', ed. G. Mac Niocaill, *Éigse*, 9 (1958), 83–8.

Dioghluim Dána, ed. Láimhbheartach Mac Cionaith (Dublin: ITS 1938).

'Duanaire Gearóid Iarla', ed. G. MacNiocaill, *Studia Hibernica*, 3 (1963), 7–59.

Edmund Campion, *Two Bokes of the Histories of Ireland*, ed. A. F. Vossen (Assen: Van Gorcum and Comp., 1963).

Edmund Spenser, *A View of the State of Ireland*, ed. A. Hadfield and W. Maley (Oxford: Blackwell, 1997).

Froissart: Chronicles, ed. and trans. G. Brereton (Harmondsworth: Penguin, 1968).

'Historical Poems of Gofraidh Fionn Ó Dálaigh IX', ed. L. McKenna, *The Irish Monthly*, 47 (1919), 509–51.

Irish Bardic Poetry, ed. O. Bergin, D. Greene and F. Kelly (Dublin: DIAS, 1970).

'Laud Misc. 610', ed. M. Dillon, *Celtica*, 5 (1960), 64–76 and *Celtica*, 6 (1963), 135–55.

'Marbhna Fhearchar Í Mháoil Chíaráin', ed. R. A. Breatnach, *Éigse*, 3 (1942), 165–84.

The Pipe Roll of Cloyne, ed. P. McCotter and K. Nicholls (Midleton: Cloyne Literary and Historical Society, 1996).

'A Poem Attributed to Muireadhach Ó Dálaigh', ed. and trans. B. Ó Cuív, in J. Carney and D. Greene (eds.), *Celtic Studies: Essays in Memory of Angus Matheson 1912–1962* (London: Routledge and Kegan Paul, 1968), 92–8.

'A Poem in Praise of Raghnall, King of Man', ed. and trans. B. Ó Cuív, *Éigse*, 8 (1957), 283–301.

The Poems of Giolla Brighde Mac Con Midhe, ed. N. William (Dublin: ITS, 1980).

'The Registry of Clonmacnoise', ed. J. O'Donovan, *Kilkenny and the South-East of Ireland Archaeological Society Journal*, 1 (1856/7), 444–60.

'Riaghail na Sacart', ed. anon., *Irisleabhar Muighe Nuadhad* (1919), 73–9.

Scottish Verse from the Book of the Dean of Lismore, ed. W. J. Watson (Edinburgh: Scottish Gaelic Texts Society, 1937).

'Seven Documents from the Old Abbey of Mellifont', ed. Fr C. Conway, *Journal of the County Louth Archaeological and Historical Society*, 13 (1953), 35–67.

Stair Ercuil ocus a Bás, ed. E. G. Quin (London: ITS, 1939).

The Topographical Poems of John O'Dubhagain and Giolla na naomh O'Huidhrin, ed. J. O'Donovan (Dublin: Irish Archaeological and Celtic Society, 1862).

'Two Irish Poems Written from the Mediterranean in the Thirteenth Century', ed. and trans. G. Murphy, *Éigse*, 7 (1953–5), 71–9.

    Vetera Monumenta Hibernorum et Scotorum Historiam Illustrantia, ed. A. Theiner (Romae, 1864).

Secondary Works

Barry, T. B., *The Archaeology of Medieval Ireland* (London: Routledge, 1987).

Black, R., 'The Genius of Cathal MacMhuirich', *Transactions of the Gaelic Society of Inverness*, 50 (1976–8), 327–65.

    'Poems by Maol Domhnaigh Ó Muirgheasáin Pts I–III', *Scottish Gaelic Studies*, 12 (1976), 104–208; 13 (1978), 46–55; 13:2 (1981), 289–301.

    'A Scottish Grammatical Tract c. 1640', *Celtica*, 21 (1990), 3–16.

Braudel, F., *Capitalism and Material Life 1400–1600*, trans. M. Kochen (London: Weidenfeld and Nicolson, 1973).

Breathnach, C., 'The Historical Context of *Cath Fionntrágha*', *Éigse*, 28 (1994–5), 138–55: 142, 153–5.

Breathnach, L., 'On Satire and the Poet's Circuit', in C. G. Ó Háinle and D. Meek (eds.), *Unity in Diversity: Studies in Irish and Scottish Gaelic Language, Literature and History* (Dublin: School of Irish, Trinity College Dublin, 2004), 25–35.

Breathnach, R. A., 'The Book of Uí Mhaine', in *Great Books of Ireland (Thomas Davis Lectures 1964)* (Dublin: Clonmore and Reynolds, 1967), 77–89.

de Breffny, B. and Mott, G., *The Churches and Abbeys of Ireland* (London: Thames and Hudson, 1976).

Byrne, A. 'The Earls of Kildare and their Books at the End of the Middle Ages', *The Library: The Transactions of the Bibliographical Society*, 14 (2013), 129–53.

Cameron, A. (ed.), *Reliquiae Celticae*, 1 (1892).

Canny, N., *The Elizabethan Conquest of Ireland: A Pattern Established 1565–1576* (Hassocks: The Harvester Press, 1976).

'Hugh O'Neill, Earl of Tyrone and the Changing Face of Gaelic Ulster', *Studia Hibernica*, 10 (1970), 7–35.

Carney, J., 'The Ó Cianáin Miscellany', *Ériu*, 21 (1969), 122–47.

'Literature in Irish, 1169–1534', in *NHI* ii, 688–707.

Carpenter, D., 'The Pilgrim from Catalonia / Aragon: Ramon de Perellós, 1397', in Haren and de Pontfarcy (eds.), *The Medieval Pilgrimage to St Patrick's Purgatory*, 99–119.

Carus-Wilson, M., *The Overseas Trade of Bristol in the Later Middle Ages* (Bristol: Bristol Record Society, 1937).

Medieval Merchant Venturers (London: Methuen, 1967).

Cosgrove, A., 'The Emergence of the Pale 1399–1447', in *NHI* ii, 533–56.

Curtis, E., 'Rental of the Manor of Lisronagh, 1333, and Notes on "Betagh" Tenure in Medieval Ireland', *PRIA*, 43 C (1935–7), 41–76.

Duffy, E., 'A Very Personal Possession: Eamon Duffy Tells How a Careful Study of Surviving Books of Hours Can Tell Us Much About the Spiritual and Temporal Life of Their Owners and Much More Besides,' *History Today*, 56 / 11 (2006): 12(7).

Duffy, P. J., 'The Shape of the Parish', in E. Fitzpatrick and R. Gillespie (eds.), *The Parish in Medieval and Early Modern Ireland: Community, Territory and Building* (Dublin: Four Courts Press, 2006), 33–61.

Duffy, S. (ed.), *Medieval Ireland: An Encyclopedia* (New York and London: Routledge, 2005).

Dunlevy, M., 'The Medical Families of Medieval Ireland', in W. Doolin and O. Fitzgerald (eds.), *What's Past is Prologue: A Retrospect of Irish Medicine* (Dublin: Monument Press, 1952), 15–22.

Etchingham, C., *Church Organisation in Ireland AD 650 to 1000* (Naas: Laigin, 1999).

Fitzpatrick, E., 'Mairgréag-an-einigh Ó Cearbhaill, "the best woman of the Gaedhil"', *Kildare Archaeological Society Journal*, 18 (1992–3), 20–38.

Flower, R., *Ireland and Medieval Europe*. Sir John Rhys Lecture from the Proceedings of the British Academy (London, 1929).

The Irish Tradition (Oxford University Press, 1947).

Foster, R. F. (ed.), *The Oxford Illustrated History of Ireland* (Oxford University Press, 1989).

Gilbert, J. T., *History of the Viceroys of Ireland* (Dublin: James Duffy, 1865).

Gillies, W., 'Alexander Carmichael and Clann Mhuirich', *Scottish Gaelic Studies*, 20 (2000), 1–66.

'The Lion's Tongues: Languages in Scotland to 1314', in I. Brown, T. O. Clancy, S. Manning and M. Pittock (eds.), *The Edinburgh History of Scottish Literature vol. 1. From Columba to the Union (until 1707)* (Edinburgh University Press, 2006), 52–62.

'Gaelic Literature in the Later Middle Ages: *The Book of the Dean* and Beyond', in I. Brown, T. O. Clancy, S. Manning and M. Pittock (eds.), *The Edinburgh History of Scottish Literature vol. 1. From Columba to the Union (until 1707)* (Edinburgh University Press, 2006), 219–25.

Gleason, A., 'Music', in S. Duffy (ed.), *Medieval Ireland: An Encyclopedia* (New York and London: Routledge, 2005), 346–8.

Gwynn, A., 'Edward I and the Proposed Purchase of English Law for the Irish, *c*.1279–80', *TRHS*, fifth series, 10 (1960), 111–27.

Harrington, C., *Women in a Celtic Church: Ireland 450–1150* (Oxford University Press, 2002).

Haughton, J. P. (ed.), *Atlas of Ireland* (Dublin: RIA, 1979).

Henry, F. and Marsh-Micheli, G., 'Manuscripts and Illuminations, 1169–1603', in *NHI* ii, 780–815.

Holland, M., 'Were Early Irish Church Establishments under Lay Control?' in Bracken and Ó Riain-Raedel (eds.), *Ireland and Europe in the Twelfth Century*, 128–42.

Hore, H. F. and Graves, J., *The Social State of the Southern and Eastern Counties of Ireland in the Sixteenth Century* (Dublin University Press, 1870).

Jaski, B., *Early Irish Kingship and Succession* (Dublin: Four Courts Press, 2000).

Jefferies, H. A., *Priests and Prelates of Armagh in the Age of the Reformations 1518–1558* (Dublin: Four Courts Press, 1997).

Kehnel, A., *Clonmacnois – the Church and Lands of St. Ciarán: Change and Continuity in an Irish Monastic Foundation (6th to 16th century)* (Münster: Lit., 1995).

Kelly, F., 'Giolla na Naomh Mac Aodhagáin: A Thirteenth-Century Legal Innovator', in D. S. Greer and N. M. Dawson (eds.), *Mysteries and Solutions in Irish Legal History* (Dublin: Four Courts Press, 2001), 1–14.

Knott, E., 'Filidh Éireann go haointeach', *Ériu*, 5 (1911), 163–87.

Kowaleski, M., 'A Consumer Economy', in R. Horrox and W. M. Ormrod (eds.), *A Social History of England, 1200–1500* (Cambridge University Press, 2006), 238–59.

Leask, H. G., *Irish Churches and Monastic Buildings III. Medieval Gothic: The Last Phases* (Dundalk: Dundalgan Press 1971).

Longnon, J., Cazelles, R. and Meiss, M., *The Très Riches Heures of Jean, Duke of Berry* (New York: George Braziller, 1969).

McClintock, H. F., *Handbook on the Traditional Old Irish Dress* (Dundalk: Dundalgan Press, 1958).

'The Mantle of St. Brigid at Bruges', *JRSAI*, 7th ser., 6 (1936), 32–40.

Mac Craith, M., 'Dánta Grá', in B. Lalor (ed.), *The Encyclopedia of Ireland* (Dublin: Gill & Macmillan, 2003), 269.

Mac Eiteagáin, D., 'The Renaissance and the Late Medieval Lordship of Tír Chonaill, 1461–1555', in W. Nolan, L. Ronayne and M. Dunlevy (eds.), *Donegal: History and Society* (Dublin: Geography Publications, 1995), 203–28.

McGowan-Doyle, V., *The Book of Howth: Elizabethan Conquest and the Old English* (Cork University Press, 2011).

MacGregor, M., 'Creation and Compilation: The Book of the Dean of Lismore and Literary Culture in Late Medieval Gaelic Scotland', in I. Brown, T. O. Clancy, S. Manning and M. Pittock (eds.), *The Edinburgh History of Scottish Literature vol. 1. From Columba to the Union (until 1707)* (Edinburgh University Press, 2006), 209–18.

McKenna, L., *Philip Bocht Ó hUiginn* (Dublin: Talbot Press, 1931).

McLeod, W., *Divided Gaels: Gaelic Cultural Identities in Scotland and Ireland c.1200–c.1650* (Oxford University Press, 2004).

Mac Niocaill, G., *Na Buirgéisí.* 2 vols. (B.Á.C: Cló Morainn, 1964).

'The Origins of the Betagh', *The Irish Jurist*, new ser., 1 (1966), 292–8.

'A propos du vocabulaire social irlandais du bas moyen age', *Études celtiques*, 12 (1968–9), 512–46.

'The Interaction of Laws', in J. Lydon (ed.), *English in Medieval Ireland*, 105–17.

Mahaffy, J. P., 'Two Early Tours of Ireland', *Hermathena* 18/40 (1914), 1–16.

Martin, F. X., 'The Spread of the Religious Orders 1420–1530' (Map), in *NHI* ii, 585.

Meek, D., '"Norsemen and Noble Stewards": The Castle Sween Poem in the Book of the Dean of Lismore', *Cambrian Medieval Celtic Studies*, 34 (1998), 1–50.

'The Scottish Tradition of Fian Ballads in the Middle Ages', in C. G. Ó Háinle and D. Meek (eds.), *Unity in Diversity: Studies in Irish and Scottish Gaelic Language, Literature and History* (Dublin: School of Irish, Trinity College Dublin, 2004), 9–24.

Mooney, C., 'The Church in Gaelic Ireland 13th to 15th Centuries', in P. J. Corish (ed.), *A History of Irish Catholicism.* Vol. II. no. 5. (Dublin: Gill & Sons, 1969).

Murphy, G., *The Ossianic Lore and Romantic Tales of Medieval Ireland* (Dublin: DIAS, 1955).

Nicholls, K., *Land, Law and Society in Sixteenth-Century Ireland.* National University of Ireland. O'Donnell Lecture (Dublin, 1976).

'Gaelic Society and Economy in the High Middle Ages', in *NHI* ii, 397–438.

Ó Buachalla, B., '"Common Gaelic" Revisited', in C. Ó Baoill and N. R. McGuire (eds.), *Rannsachadh na Gàidhlig 2000* (Aberdeen: Clo Gaidhealach, 2002), 1–12.

Ó Clabaigh, C., *The Franciscans in Ireland 1400–1534* (Dublin: Four Courts Press, 2002).

Ó Concheanainn, T., 'The Book of Ballymote', *Celtica*, 14 (1981), 15–25.

O'Connor, F., *The Backward Look: A Survey of Irish Literature* (London: Macmillan, 1967).

Ó Cuív, B. (ed.), *Seven Centuries of Irish Learning* (Dublin: Stationery Office 1961).

Ó Floinn, R., 'The Norman Conquest and the Later Middle Ages', in M. Ryan (ed.), *Treasures of Ireland: Irish Art 3000 B.C.–1500 A.D.* (Dublin: National Museum of Ireland, 1983), 70–2.

Ó hUiginn, R., '*Duanaire Finn*: Patron and Text', in J. Carey (ed.), *Duanaire Finn: Reassessments.* ITS, Subsidiary Series (London: ITS, 2003), 79–106.

'Fiannaigheacht, Family, Faith and Fatherland', in S. J. Arbuthnot and G. Parsons (eds.), *The Gaelic Finn Tradition* (Dublin: Four Courts Press, 2013), 151–62.

O'Sullivan, C. M., *Hospitality in Medieval Ireland, 900–1500* (Dublin: Four Courts Press, 2004).

O'Sullivan, W., 'Ciothruadh's Yellow Book of Lecan', *Éigse*, 18 pt 2 (1981), 177–81.

Ó Tuama, S., 'The New Love Poetry', in B. Ó Cuiv (ed.), *Seven Centuries of Irish Learning* (Dublin: Stationery Office 1961), 102–20.

Otway-Ruthven, A. J., 'The Request of the Irish for English Law', *IHS*, 6 (1949), 261–70.

Pirenne, H., *Economic and Social History of Medieval Europe*, trans. I. E. Clegg (London: Routledge and Kegan Paul, 1936).

de Pontfarcy, Y., 'Le *Tractatus de Purgatorio Sancti Patricii* de H. de Saltrey: sa date et ses sources', *Peritia*, 3 (1984), 460–80.

Post, R. R., *The Modern Devotion: Confrontation with Reformation and Humanism* (Leiden: Brill, 1968).

Price, L., 'The Origin of the Word Betagius', *Ériu*, 20 (1966), 185–90.

Ryan, S., 'Windows on Late Medieval Devotional Practice: Máire Ní Mháille's "Book of Piety" (1513) and the World behind the Texts', in Moss *et al.* (eds.), *Art and Devotion in Late Medieval Ireland*, 1–15.

Schubert, E., *Einführung in die Grundprobleme der Deutschen Geschichte im Spätmittelalter* (Darmstadt, 1992).

Sellar, W. H. D., 'Hebridean Sea-Kings: The Successors of Somerled, 1164–1316', in E. J. Cowan and R. A. McDonald (eds.), *Alba: Celtic Scotland in the Medieval Era* (East Linton: Tuckwell Press, 2000), 187–218.

Simms, K., 'The Archbishops of Armagh and the O'Neills, 1347–1461', *IHS*, 19 (1974), 38–55.

'The Legal Position of Irishwomen in the Later Middle Ages', *The Irish Jurist*, new series 10 (1975), 96–111.

'The Concordat between Primate John Mey and Henry O'Neill, 1455', *Archivium Hibernicum*, 34 (1977), 71–82.

'Guesting and Feasting in Gaelic Ireland', *JRSAI*, 108 (1978), 67–100.

'Propaganda Use of the *Táin* in the Later Middle Ages', *Celtica*, 15 (1983), 142–9.

'Nomadry in Medieval Ireland: The Origins of the Creaght or Caoraigheacht', *Peritia*, 5 (1986), 379–91.

'Bards and Barons: The Anglo-Irish Aristocracy and the Native Culture', in Bartlett and MacKay (eds.), *Medieval Frontier Societies*, 177–97.

'The Brehons of Later Medieval Ireland', in D. Hogan and W. N. Osborough (eds.), *Brehons, Serjeants and Attorneys* (Blackrock: Irish Academic Press, 1990), 51–76.

'An Eaglais agus Filí na Scol', in P. Ó Fiannachta (ed.), *An Dán Díreach. Léachtaí Cholm Cille XXIV* (Maigh Nuad: An Sagart, 1994), 21–36.

'Frontiers in the Irish Church – Regional and Cultural', in Barry *et al.* (eds.), *Colony and Frontier in Medieval Ireland*, 177–200.

'Literacy and the Irish Bards', in H. Pryce (ed.), *Literacy in Medieval Celtic Societies* (Cambridge University Press, 1998), 238–58.

'Charles Lynegar, the O Luinín Family and the Study of Seanchas', in T. C. Barnard, D. Ó Cróinín and K. Simms (eds.) *A Miracle of Learning: Studies in Manuscripts and Irish Learning: Essays in Honour of William O'Sullivan* (Aldershot: Ashgate, 1998), 266–83.

'Medieval Fermanagh', in E. M. Murphy and W. J. Roulston (eds.), *Fermanagh: History and Society* (Dublin: Geography Publications, 2004), 77–103.

'References to Landscape and Economy in Irish Bardic Poetry', in Clarke *et al.* (eds.), *Surveying Ireland's Past*, 145–68.

'Ó Dubhagáin, Seaán Mór', *ODNB*.

'Bardic Schools, Learned Families', in S. Duffy (ed.), *Medieval Ireland: An Encyclopedia* (New York and London: Routledge, 2005), 35–7.

'Muireadhach Albanach Ó Dálaigh and the Classical Revolution', in I. Brown, T. O. Clancy, S. Manning and M. Pittock (eds.), *The Edinburgh History of Scottish Literature vol. 1. From Columba to the Union (until 1707)* (Edinburgh University Press, 2006), 83–90.

'Images of the Galloglass in Poems to the MacSweeneys', in S. Duffy (ed.), *The World of the Galloglass: Kings, Warlords and Warriors in Ireland and Scotland, 1200–1600* (Dublin: Four Courts Press, 2007), 106–23.

'Changing Patterns of Regnal Succession in Later Medieval Ireland', in F. Lachaud and M. Penman (eds.), *Making and Breaking the Rules: Succession in Medieval Europe c. 1000–c. 1600/Etablir et abolir les normes: la succession dans l'Europe médiévale vers 1000–vers 1600* (Turnhout: Brepols, 2008), 161–72.

'The Barefoot Kings: Literary Image and Reality in Later Medieval Ireland', in E. Boon, A. J. McMullen and N. Sumner (eds.), *Proceedings of the Harvard Celtic Colloquium 30, 2010* (Cambridge, MA and London, 2011), 1–21.

'Foreign Apologues in Bardic Poetry', in Duffy and Foran (eds.), *English Isles* , 139– 50.

'The Origins of the Creaght: Farming System or Social Unit?', in M. Murphy and M. Stout (eds.), *Agriculture and Settlement in Ireland* (Dublin: Four Courts Press, 2015), 101–18.

'The Geraldines and Gaelic Culture', in P. Crooks and S. Duffy (eds.), *The Geraldines and Medieval Ireland: The Making of a Myth* (Dublin: Four Courts Press, 2016).

Stalley, R., 'Irish Gothic and English Fashion', in Lydon (ed.), *English in Medieval Ireland*, 65–86.

'Sailing to Santiago', in Bradley (ed.), *Settlement and Society in Medieval Ireland*, 397–420.

'The Long Middle Ages: From the Twelfth Century to the Reformation', in B. de Breffny (ed.), *The Irish World* (London: Thames and Hudson, 1977), 71–98.

Thirsk, J., 'Enclosing and Engrossing', in J. Thirsk (ed.), *The Agrarian History of England and Wales iv 1500–1640* (Cambridge University Press, 1967), 200–38.

Verstraten, F., 'Images of Gaelic Lordship in Ireland c. 1200–1400', in Doran and Lyttleton (eds.), *Lordship in Medieval Ireland*, 47–71.

Watt, J. A., *The Church in Medieval Ireland*, 2nd edn (Dublin: Four Courts Press, 1998).

'*Ecclesia inter Anglicos et inter Hibernicos*: Confrontation and Coexistence in the Medieval Diocese and Province of Armagh', in Lydon (ed.), *English in Medieval Ireland*, 46–64.

Wood, S., *The Proprietary Church in the Medieval West* (Oxford University Press, 2006).

16 The Structure of Politics in Theory and Practice, 1210–1541

Peter Crooks

Manuscript Sources

BL MS Harley 913   Kildare Manuscript.

Cambridge University Library, MS Ii.iv.5   Declaration of the rights of Edward I to rule Ireland etc.

Huntington Library (San Marino, California), MS E.L. 1699   *Modus Tenendi Parliamentum*

TNA E 368   Exchequer: Lord Treasurer's Remembrancer: Memoranda Rolls

NLI D 1855   Letter patent from Ormond Deeds
NLI MS 3   Collectanea de rebus Hibernicis, compiled by Walter Harris
Representative Church Body Library, MS C.6. I.I   *Liber Niger*
TCD MS 581   Historical Miscellanea
TCD MS 842   Historical Miscellanea
TCD MS 11500   Historical texts from St Mary's abbey, Dublin

Primary Sources

Aithdioghluim Dána, ed. L. McKenna. 2 vols. (Dublin: ITS, 1939 [text], 1940 [trans.]).
The Chronicle of Adam Usk, 1377–1421, ed. C. Given-Wilson (Oxford University Press, 1997).
Chronicles of the Revolution, 1397–1400: The Reign of Richard II, ed. C. Given-Wilson (Manchester University Press, 1993).
A Contemporary Narrative of the Proceedings against Dame Alice Kyteler Prosecuted for Sorcery in 1324, ed. T. Wright. Camden Society, o.s. 24 (London, 1843).
Early Registers of Writs, ed. E. de Haas and G. D. G. Hall. Selden Society (London, 1970).
The English Conquest of Ireland [...], ed. F. J. Furnivall. EETS (London, 1896).
Facsimiles of National Manuscripts of Ireland [...], ed. J. T. Gilbert. 4 pts in 5 vols (Dublin, 1874–84).
Four English Political Tracts of the Middle Ages, ed. J.-P. Genet. Camden Series (London, 1977).
Hibernica, or, some antient Pieces relating to Ireland, ed. W. Harris, 2 vols. (Dublin: Edward Bate and Peter Wilson, 1747, 1750)
Il Registro di Andrea Sapiti, Procutore alla Curia Avigonese, ed. B. Bombi (Rome: Viella, 2007).
Die Kildare Gedichte: die ältesten mittelenglischen Denkmäler in Anglo-Irischer Überlieferung, ed. W. Heuser (Bonn: P. Hanstein, 1904).
The Libelle of Englyshe Polycye. A Poem on the Use of Sea-Power 1436, ed. G. Warner (Oxford University Press, 1926).
Magnum Oecuminicum Constantiense Concilium [...], ed. H. von der Hardt. 6 vols. (Frankfurt and Leipzig: Gensius, 1692–1700).
Nicholas of Cusa: The Catholic Concordance, trans. P. Sigmund (Cambridge University Press, 1991).
On the Laws and Governance of England by Sir John Fortescue, ed. S. Lockwood (Cambridge University Press, 1997).
Original Letters Illustrative of English History, ed. H. Ellis. 2nd ser., 4 vols. (London: S. & J. Bentley, 1827).
Parliamentary Texts of the Later Middle Ages, ed. N. Pronay and J. Taylor (Oxford University Press, 1980).
Poems from BL MS Harley 913: 'The Kildare Manuscript', ed. T. Turville-Petre. EETS, o.s. 345 (Oxford University Press, 2015).
Poems on Marcher Lords, ed. A. O'Sullivan and P. Ó Riain (Dublin: ITS, 1987).
The St Albans Chronicle: The Chronica Maiora of Thomas Walsingham, i: *1376–1394*, ed. J. Taylor, W. R. Childs and L. Watkiss (Oxford University Press, 2003).
Select Documents of English Constitutional History, 1307–1485, ed. S. B. Chrimes and A. L. Brown (London: Adam & Charles Black, 1961).

The Sorcery Trial of Alice Kyteler: a Contemporary Account (1324), ed. L. S. Davidson and J. O. Ward, trans. G. Ward (Binghamton, NY: Pegasus Press, 1993).

The Statutes at Large Passed in the Parliaments Held in Ireland [...], ed. W. Ball, 13 vols. (Dublin: Boulter Grierson, 1765–1801).

The Statutes of Wales, ed. I. Bowen (London: T. F. Unwin, 1908).

Three Prose Versions of the Secreta Secretorum, ed. R. Steele (London: EETS, 1898).

'The Voyage of Sir Richard Edgecombe', in W. Harris (ed.), *Hibernica, or, some antient Pieces relating to Ireland* (2 vols., Dublin: Edward Bate and Peter Wilson, 1747, 1750).

The Westminster Chronicle, 1381–1394, ed. L. C. Hector and B. F. Harvey (Oxford University Press, 1982).

Secondary Works

Bartlett, R., *'Mortal Enmities': The Legal Aspect of Hostility in the Middle Ages* (T. Jones Pierce Lecture, Aberystwyth, 1998).

Black, A., *Political Thought in Europe, 1250–1450* (Cambridge University Press, 1992).

Brand, P., 'Ireland and the Literature of the Early Common Law', in P. Brand *The Making of the Common Law* (London: Hambledon Press, 1992), 445–63.

Burns, J. H., *Lordship, Kingship, and Empire: The Idea of Monarchy, 1400–1525* (Oxford University Press, 1992).

'Fortescue and the Political Theory of *Dominium*', *Historical Journal*, 28 (1985), 777–97.

Byrne, A. 'The Earls of Kildare and their Books at the End of the Middle Ages', *The Library: The Transactions of the Bibliographical Society*, 14 (2013), 129–53.

Canning, J., *A History of Medieval Political Thought, 300–1400* (London: Routledge, 1996).

Ideas of Power in the Late Middle Ages, 1296–1417 (Cambridge University Press, 2011).

'Law, Sovereignty and Corporation Theory', in J. H. Burns (ed.), *The Cambridge History of Medieval Political Thought, c.350–c.1450* (Cambridge University Press, 1988), 454–76.

Carpenter, D., *Magna Carta* (London: Penguin, 2015).

Chrimes, S. B., *English Constitutional Ideas in the Fifteenth Century* (Cambridge University Press, 1936).

Cosgrove, A., 'Parliament and the Anglo-Irish Community: The Declaration of 1460', in A. Cosgrove and J. I. McGuire (eds.), *Parliament and Community: Historical Studies XIV* (Belfast: Appletree Press, 1983), 25–41.

Crooks, P., 'The Background to the Arrest of the Fifth Earl of Kildare and Sir Christopher Preston in 1418: A Missing Membrane', *Analecta Hibernica*, 40 (2007), 1–15.

'Representation and Dissent: "Parliamentarianism" and the Structure of Politics in Colonial Ireland *c.*1370–1420', *EHR*, 125 (2010), 1–34.

Curtis, E., *Richard II in Ireland, 1394–5, and the Submissions of the Irish Chiefs* (Oxford University Press, 1927).

Dodd, G., 'Kingship, Parliament and the Court: The Emergence of "High Style" in Petitions to the English Crown, *c.* 1350–1405', *EHR*, 129 (2014), 515–48.

Dolley, M., 'Tre Kronor – Trí Choróin: A Note on the Date of the "Three-Crown" Coinage of Ireland', *Särtryck ur Numismatiska Meddelanden*, 30 (1965), 103–12.

'Coinage to 1534: The Sign of the Times', in *NHI* ii, 818–25.

Dunbabin, J., 'Government', in J. H. Burns (ed.), *The Cambridge History of Medieval Political Thought, c.350–c.1450* (Cambridge University Press, 1988), 477–519.

Dykes, D. W., 'The Anglo-Irish Coinage and the Ancient Arms of Ireland', *JRSAI*, 96 (1966), 111–20.

Elliott, J. H., 'A Europe of Composite Monarchies', *Past and Present*, 137 (1992), 48–71.

Ferster, J., *Fictions of Advice: The Literature and Politics of Counsel in Late Medieval England* (Philadelphia: University of Pennsylvania Press, 1996).

Frame, R., 'English Political Culture in Later Medieval Ireland', *The History Review*, 13 (2002), 1–11.

    'Two Kings in Leinster: The Crown and the MicMhurchadha in the Fourteenth Century', in Barry *et al.* (eds.), *Colony and Frontier in Medieval Ireland*, 155–75.

    'Exporting State and Nation: Being English in Medieval Ireland', in L. Scales and O. Zimmer (eds.), *Power and the Nation in European History* (Cambridge University Press, 2005), 143–65.

    'Ireland after 1169: Barriers to Acculturation on an "English" Edge', in K. J. Stringer and A. Jotischky (eds.), *Norman Expansion: Connections, Continuities and Contrasts* (Farnham: Ashgate, 2013), 115–41.

Gilbert, J. T., *History of the Viceroys of Ireland* (Dublin: James Duffy, 1865).

Griffith, M. C., 'The Talbot–Ormond Struggle for Control of the Anglo-Irish Government, 1414–47', *IHS*, 2 (1940–1), 376–97.

Gwynn, A., 'Ireland and the English Nation at the Council of Constance', *PRIA*, 45 C (1940), 183–233.

Harriss, G. L., *King, Parliament and Public Finance in Medieval England to 1369* (Oxford University Press, 1975).

Holt, J. C., *Magna Carta* (3rd edn. Cambridge University Press, 2015).

Kantorowicz, E. H., *The King's Two Bodies: A Study in Medieval Political Theology* (new edn, Princeton University Press, 1997).

    'Inalienability: A Note on Canonical Practice and the English Coronation Oath in the Thirteenth Century', *Speculum*, 29 (1954), 488–502.

Keen, M., *The Laws of War in the Late Middle Ages* (London: Routledge and Kegan Paul, 1965).

    'Chivalry and English Kingship in the Later Middle Ages', in C. Given-Wilson, A. Kettle and L. Scales (eds.), *War, Government and Aristocracy in the British Isles, c.1150–1500* (Woodbridge: Boydell Press, 2008), 250–66.

Kempshall, M. S., *The Common Good in Late Medieval Political Thought* (Oxford University Press, 1999).

Kerby-Fulton, K. and Justice, S., 'Reformist Intellectual Culture in the English and Irish Civil Service: The *Modus Tenendi Parliamentum* and its Literary Relations', *Traditio*, 53 (1998), 149–202.

Kingsford, C., *English Historical Literature in the Fifteenth Century* (Oxford University Press, 1913).

Lydon, J., 'Ireland and the English Crown, 1171–1541', in Crooks (ed.), *Government, War and Society*, 65–78.

    'William of Windsor and the Irish Parliament', in Crooks (ed.), *Government, War and Society*, 90–105.

Lydon, J. F., 'Parliament and the Community of Ireland', in Lydon (ed.), *Law and Disorder*, 125–38.

Maginn, C. and Ellis, S. G., *The Tudor Discovery of Ireland* (Dublin: Four Courts Press, 2015).

Maiolo, F., *Medieval Sovereignty: Marsilius of Padua and Bartolus of Saxoferrato* (Delft: Eburon Academic, 2007).

Matthew, E., 'Henry V and the Proposal for an Irish Crusade', in Smith (ed.), *Ireland and the English World*, 161–75.

Maxwell-Lyte, M. C., *A History of Eton College, 1440–1884* (London: Macmillan, 1889).

Meehan, B., 'A Fourteenth-Century Historical Compilation from St Mary's Cistercian Abbey, Dublin', in S. Duffy (ed.), *Medieval Dublin XV* (Dublin: Four Courts Press, 2016).

Monfrin, J., 'Sur les sources du *Secret des Secrets* de Jefroi de Waterford et Servais Copale', *Mélanges de linguistique romane et de philologie médiévale offerts à M. Maurice Delbouille*. 2 vols. (Gembloux: Duculot, 1964), ii, 509–30.

Muldoon, J., 'The Remonstrance of the Irish Princes and the Canon Law Theory of the Just War', *American Journal of Legal History*, 22 (1978), 309–25.

Mundy, J. H., and Woody, K. M. (eds.), *The Council of Constance: The Unification of the Church*, trans. L. R. Loomis (New York and London: Columbia University Press, 1961).

Nederman, C. J., 'Body Politics: The Diversification of Organic Metaphors in the Later Middle Ages', *Pensiero Politico Medievale*, 2 (2004), 59–87.

Nederman, C. J. and Langdon Forhan, K. (eds.), *Medieval Political Theory: A Reader. The Quest for the Body Politic, 1100–1400* (London: Routledge, 1993).

Ó Clabaigh, C., *The Franciscans in Ireland 1400–1534* (Dublin: Four Courts Press, 2002).

Ormrod, W. M., *Edward III* (New Haven and London: Yale University Press, 2012).

'"Common Profit" and "The Profit of the King and Kingdom": Parliament and the Development of Political Language in England, 1250–1450', *Viator*, 46 (2015), 219–52.

Phillips, J. R. S., 'Three Thirteenth-Century Declarations of English Rule: Over Aquitaine, Ireland and Wales', in Smith (ed.), *Ireland and the English World*, 20–43.

Pocock, J. G. A., *Politics, Language and Time: Essays on Political Thought and History* (Chicago University Press, 1989).

Political Thought and History: Essays on Theory and Method (Cambridge University Press, 2009).

Reynolds, S., *Kingdoms and Communities in Western Europe, 900–1300* (2nd edn, Oxford University Press, 1997).

'The History of the Idea of Incorporation or Legal Personality: A Case of Fallacious Teleology', in S. Reynolds, *Ideas and Solidarities of the Medieval Laity: England and Western Europe* (Farnham: Ashgate, 1995), 1–20.

Richter, M., *The History of Political and Social Concepts: A Critical Introduction* (Oxford University Press, 1994).

Richardson, H. G. and Sayles, G. O., *The Irish Parliament in the Middle Ages* (Philadelphia: University of Pennsylvania Press, 1952).

Ruddick, A., *English Identity and Political Culture in the Fourteenth Century* (Cambridge University Press, 2013).

Saul, N., 'Richard II and the Vocabulary of Kingship', *EHR*, 110 (1995), 854–77.

Skinner, Q., *Visions of Politics I: Regarding Method* (Cambridge University Press, 2002).

'Some Problems in the Analysis of Political Thought and Action', in J. Tully (ed.), *Meaning and Context: Quentin Skinner and his Critics* (Oxford University Press, 1988).

Stacey, R. C., 'The Age of Chivalry', in M. Howard, G. J. Andreopoulos and M. R. Shulman (eds.), *The Laws of War: Constraints on Warfare in the Western World* (New Haven: Yale University Press, 1994), 27–39.

Sutherland, D., 'Conquest and Law', *Studia Gratiana*, 15 (1972), 35–51.

Thornley, I. D., *England under the Yorkists, 1460–1485: Illustrated from Contemporary Sources* (London: Longmans, 1920).

Ullman, W., 'On the Influence of Geoffrey of Monmouth in English History', in C. Bauer, L. Böhm and M. Müller (eds.), *Speculum Historiale: Geschichte im Spiegel von Geschtsschreibung und Geschichtsdeutung Johannes Spörl aus Anlass Seines 60. Geburtstages dargebracht von Weggenossen, Freunden und Schülern* (Frieburg: Karl Alber, 1965), 257–76.

Virgoe, R., 'The Death of William de la Pole, Duke of Suffolk', *BJRL*, 47 (1964–5), 489–502.

Watt, J. A., 'Negotiations between Edward II and John XXII Concerning Ireland', *IHS*, 10 (1956), 1–20.

Watts, J., *Henry VI and the Politics of Kingship* (Cambridge University Press, 1996).

    'Looking for the State in Later Medieval England', in P. Coss and M. Keen (eds.), *Heraldry, Pageantry and Social Display in Medieval England* (Woodbridge: Boydell Press, 2002), 243–68.

    '"Commonweal" and "Commonwealth": England's Monarchical Republic in the Making, *c.*1450–*c.*1530', in A. Gamberini, J.-P. Genet and A. Zorzi (eds.), *The Languages of Political Society* (Rome : Viella, 2011), 147–63.

Wilks, M., 'Corporation and Representation in the *Defensor Pacis*', *Studia Gratiana*, 15 (1972), 251–92.

Williams, B., 'The Lost Coronation Oath of King Edward I: Rediscovered in a Dublin Manuscript', in S. Duffy (ed.), *Medieval Dublin IX* (Dublin: Four Courts Press, 2009), 84–90.

17 Material Culture

Rachel Moss

Manuscript Sources

BL Add. MS 4792, no. 47, fols. 241–65. R. Roth, 'A Register Contayning the Pedigree of the Right Honourable Thomas, Late Earl of Ormond and a Storie of his Ancestres etc., 1616'

Primary Sources

'Brussels Ms 3947', ed. B. Jennings, *Analecta Hibernica,* 6 (1934), 12–138.

The Dowdall Deeds, ed. C. McNeill and A. J. Otway-Ruthven (Dublin: IMC, 1960).

'FitzWilliam Manuscripts at Milton, England', ed. C. McNeill, *Analecta Hibernica*, 4 (1932), 287–326.

Manus O'Donnell: The Life of St Columcille, ed. and trans. B. Lacey (Dublin: Four Courts Press, 1998).

'Regestum Monasterii Fratrum Praedicatorum de Athenry', ed. A. Coleman, *Archivium Hibernicum*, 1 (1912), 201–21.

Register of the Wills and Inventories of the Diocese of Dublin 1457–1483, ed. H. F. Berry (Dublin: RSAI, 1898).

'Sir Henry Sidney's Memoirs of his Government in Ireland', ed. H. F. Hore, *Ulster Journal of Archaeology*, 1st ser., 5 (1857), 299–322.

Secondary Works

Armstrong, E. C. R., *Irish Seal Matrices and Seals* (Dublin: Hodges, Figgis and Co., 1913).

Barry, T. B., *The Archaeology of Medieval Ireland* (London: Routledge, 1987).

Berry, H. F., 'The Goldsmiths' Company of Dublin', *JRSAI*, 31 (1901), 119–33.

'The Dublin Gild of Carpenters, Millers, Masons and Heliers in the Sixteenth Century', *JRSAI*, 35 (1905), 321–37.

Bhreathnach, E., 'The *Seanchas* Tradition in Late Medieval Ireland', in E. Bhreathnach and B. Cunningham (eds.), *Writing Irish History: The Four Masters and their World* (Bray: Wordwell, 2007), 18–23.

Birch, W. de Gray, *Catalogue of Seals in the Department of Manuscripts, British Museum. Vol. 4. Scotland and Ireland* (London: British Museum, 1895).

Borg, A. and Martindale, A. (eds.), *The Vanishing Past: Studies in Medieval Art, Liturgy and Metrology presented to Christopher Hohler*. British Archaeological Reports, International Series III (Oxford: Archaeopress, 1982).

Bradley, J., *Irish Historic Towns Atlas, no. 10, Kilkenny* (Dublin: RIA, 2000).

'The Sarcophagus at Cormac's Chapel, Cashel, Co. Tipperary', *North Munster Archaeological Journal*, 26 (1984), 14–35.

'The Purpose of the Pale: A View from Kilkenny', in M. Potterton and T. Herron (eds.), *Dublin and the Pale in the Renaissance c.1540–1660* (Dublin: Four Courts Press, 2011), 51–67.

Bradshaw, B., 'Manus "the Magnificent" O'Donnell as Renaissance Prince', in A. Cosgrove and D. McCartney (eds.), *Studies in Irish History presented to R. Dudley Edwards* (Dublin: University College Dublin Press, 1979), 27–35.

Buckley, J. J., *Some Irish Altar Plate* (Dublin: RSAI, 1943).

Byrne, A. 'The Earls of Kildare and their Books at the end of the Middle Ages', *The Library: The Transactions of the Bibliographical Society*, 14 (2013), 129–53.

Carey, J., 'Book of Uí Mhaine', in B. Cunningham and S. Fitzpatrick (eds.), *Treasures of the Royal Irish Academy Library* (Dublin: RIA, 2009), 22–3.

Caulfield, R., *Sigilla Ecclesiae Hibernicae Illustrata: The Episcopal and Capitular Seals of the Irish Cathedral Churches Illustrated. Part I: Cashel and Emly* (Cork: H. Ridings, 1853).

Crofton Croker, T. F., *The Tour of the French Traveller M. de la Boullaye le Gouz in Ireland, 1644* (London: T. and W. Boone, 1837).

Egan-Buffet, M. and Fletcher, A. J., 'The Dublin Visitatio Sepulchri Play', *PRIA*, 90 C (1990), 159–241.

Fitzgerald, W., 'Abbey Knockmoy', *Journal of the Association for the Preservation of Memorials to the Dead in Ireland*, 10 (1917–20), 201–2.

Gem, R., 'Saint Flannán's Oratory at Killaloe: A Romanesque Building of *c.* 1100 and the Patronage of King Muirchertach Ua Briain', in Bracken and Ó Riain-Raedel (eds.), *Ireland and Europe in the Twelfth Century*, 74–105.

Gillespie, R., 'Relics, Reliquaries and Hagiography in South Ulster, 1450–1550', in Moss *et al.* (eds.), *Art and Devotion in Late Medieval Ireland*, 184–201.

Graves, J. and Prim, G. A., *The History, Architecture and Antiquities of the Cathedral Church of St Canice, Kilkenny* (Dublin: Hodges, Smith and Company, 1857).

Hardiman, J., *History of the Town and County of Galway* (Dublin: W. Folds and sons, 1820).

Henry, F., *Irish Art in the Romanesque Period 1020–1170 A.D.* (London: Methuen, 1970).

Hourihane, C., *Gothic Art in Ireland 1169–1550* (London and New Haven: Yale University Press, 2003).

James, M. R., *Catalogue of Manuscripts and Early Printed Books from the Libraries of William Morris, Richard Bennett, Bertram Fourth Earl of Ashburnham, and Other Sources* (London: J. Pierpont Morgan, 1906).

King, H., 'Late Medieval Crosses in County Meath, *c.*1470–1635', *PRIA*, 84 C (1984), 79–115.

'The Medieval and Seventeenth-Century Carved Stone Collection in Kildare', *Journal of the Kildare Archaeological Society*, 17 (1991), 59–95.

Lawlor, H. J., *St. Bernard of Clairvaux's Life of St. Malachy of Armagh* (London and New York: Macmillan, 1920).

Leask, H. G., 'The Collegiate Church of St Nicholas, Galway', *Journal of the Galway Archaeological and Historical Society*, 17 (1936), 1–23.

Lennon, C., 'The FitzGeralds of Kildare and the Building of a Dynastic Image, 1500–1630', in W. Nolan and T. McGrath (eds.), *Kildare History and Society* (Dublin: Geography Publications, 2006), 195–211.

Lewis, F., 'Rewarding Devotion: Indulgences and the Promotion of Images', in D. Wood (ed.), *The Church and the Arts* (Oxford: Blackwell, 1992), 179–94.

Lyons, M. A., 'Lay Female Piety and Church Patronage in Late Medieval Ireland', in B. Bradshaw and D. Keogh (eds.), *Christianity in Ireland: Revisiting the Story* (Dublin: Columba Press, 2002), 57–75.

Mac Eiteagáin, D., 'The Renaissance and the Late Medieval Lordship of Tír Chonaill, 1461–1555', in W. Nolan, L. Ronayne and M. Dunlevy (eds.), *Donegal: History and Society* (Dublin: Geography Publications, 1995), 203–28.

Moore, F., *Ardfert Cathedral: Summary of Excavation Results* (Dublin: Department of the Environment, Heritage and Local Government, 2007).

Morton, K., 'A Spectacular Revelation: Medieval Wall Painting at Ardamullivan', *Irish Arts Review*, 18 (2002), 104–13.

Moss, R., 'Revivalist Tendencies in the Irish Late Gothic: Defining a National Identity?', in M. Reeve (ed.), *Reading Gothic Architecture* (Turnhout and New York: Brepols, 2008), 123–37.

'Continuity and Change: The Material Setting of Public Worship in the Sixteenth-century Pale', in M. Potterton and T. Herron (eds.), *Dublin and the Pale in the Renaissance c.1540–1660* (Dublin: Four Courts Press, 2011), 182–206.

'"Planters of Great Civilitie": Female Patrons of the Arts in Late Medieval Ireland', in T. Martin (ed.), *Reassessing the Roles of Women as 'Makers' of Medieval Art and Architecture* (Leiden: Brill, 2012), 275–308.

'Reduce, Re-use, Re-cycle: Irish Monastic Architecture *c.*1540–1640', in R. Stalley (ed.), *Irish Gothic Architecture: Construction, Destruction and Reinvention* (Dublin: Wordwell, 2012), 115–60.

'Unfurling Words of Indulgence', in B. Leahy and S. Ryan (eds.), *Treasures of Irish Christianity: A People of the Word* (Dublin: Veritas, 2013), 103–7.

Murray, G., *The Cross of Cong: A Masterpiece of Medieval Irish Art* (Dublin: Irish Academic Press, 2014).

O'Neill, M., 'The Medieval Parish Churches in Co. Meath', *JRSAI*, 132 (2002), 1–56.

Ó Riain-Raedel. D., 'A German Visitor to Monaincha in 1591', *Tipperary Historical Journal*, 22 (1998), 223–33.

Rae, E. C., 'Irish Sepulchral Monuments of the Later Middle Ages: Part I: The Ormond Group', *JRSAI*, 100 (1970), 1–38.

'The Rice Monument in Waterford Cathedral', *PRIA*, 69 C (1970), 1–14.

'Irish Sepulchral Monuments of the Later Middle Ages: Part II the O'Tunney Atelier', *JRSAI*, 101 (1971), 1–39.

Sherlock, R., 'The Evolution of the Irish Tower House as a Domestic Space', *PRIA*, 111 C (2011), 115–40.

Stalley, R., *The Cistercian Monasteries of Ireland* (London and New Haven: Yale University Press, 1987).

'Design and Function: The Construction and Decoration of Cormac's Chapel at Cashel', in Bracken and Ó Riain-Raedel (eds.), *Ireland and Europe in the Twelfth Century*, 162–75.

Stalley, R. A., 'The Romanesque Sculpture of Tuam,' in A. Borg and A. Martindale (eds.), *The Vanishing Past: Studies in Medieval Art, Liturgy and Metrology presented to Christopher Hohler*. British Archaeological Reports, International Series III (Oxford: Archaeopress, 1982), 179–95.

Steer, K. A. and Bannerman, J. W., *Late Medieval Monumental Sculpture in the West Highlands* (Edinburgh: Royal Commission on the Ancient and Historical Monuments of Scotland, 1977).

Webb, D., 'The Holy Face of Lucca', *ANS*, 9 (1986), 227–37.

18 The Onset of Religious Reform: 1460–1550

Mary Ann Lyons

Manuscript Sources

PRONI MS DI0 4/ 2/ 11   Archbishop Cromer's Register

Primary Sources

Christ Church Deeds, ed. M. J. McEnery and R. Refaussé (Dublin: Four Courts Press, 2001).

The Register of St Saviour's Chantry of Waterford, ed. N. Byrne and M. Byrne (Dublin: IMC, 2013).

Secondary Works

Bernard, G. W., *The Late Medieval English Church: Vitality and Vulnerability before the Break with Rome* (New Haven and London: Yale University Press, 2012).

Bradshaw, B., *The Dissolution of the Religious Orders in Ireland under Henry VIII* (Cambridge University Press, 1974).

Cameron, E., *The European Reformation* (Oxford University Press, 2013).

Clark, M. and Refaussé, R. (eds.), *Directory of Historic Dublin Guilds* (Dublin: Dublin Public Libraries, 1993).

Corish, P. J., *The Irish Catholic Experience: A Historical Survey* (Dublin: Gill & Macmillan, 1985).

Duffy, E., *The Stripping of the Altars: Traditional Religion in England, c.1400–c.1580* (New Haven and London: Yale University Press, 1992).

'Elite and Popular Religion: The Book of Hours and Lay Piety in the Later Middle Ages' in K. Cooper and J. Gregory (eds.), *Elite and Popular Religion* (Woodbridge: Boydell Press, 2006), 140–61.

Empey, C. A., 'The Layperson in the Parish: The Medieval Inheritance, 1169–1536', in R. Gillespie and W. G. Neely (eds.), *The Laity and the Church of Ireland, 1000–2000: All Sorts and Conditions* (Dublin: Four Courts Press, 2002), 7–48.

French, K. L., 'Women in the Late Medieval English Parish', in J. L. Halverston (ed.), *Contesting Christendom: Readings in Medieval Religion and Culture* (Lanham & Plymouth: Rowman and Littlefield, 2008), 156–73

Gillespie, R., 'Relics, Reliquaries and Hagiography in South Ulster, 1450–1550', in Moss *et al.* (eds.), *Art and Devotion in Late Medieval Ireland*, 184–201.

Halverson, J. L. (ed.), *Contesting Christendom: Readings in Medieval Religion and Culture* (Lanham & Plymouth: Rowman and Littlefield, 2008).

Hazlett, W. I. P., *The Reformation in Britain and Ireland: An Introduction* (London & New York: T. & T. Clark, 2003).

Heal, F., *Reformation in Britain and Ireland* (Oxford University Press, 2003).

Jefferies, H. A., *Priests and Prelates of Armagh in the Age of Reformations, 1518–1588* (Dublin: Four Courts Press, 1997).

The Irish Church and the Tudor Reformations (Dublin: Four Courts Press, 2010).

'The Church Courts of Armagh on the Eve of the Reformation', *Seanchas Ard Mhacha*, 15, no. 2 (1993), 1–38.

Leigh Fry, S., *Burial in Medieval Ireland, 900–1500* (Dublin: Four Courts Press, 1999).

Lennon, C., *Sixteenth-Century Ireland: The Incomplete Conquest*. 2nd edn (Dublin: Gill & Macmillan, 2005).

Lyons, M. A., *Church and Society in County Kildare c.1470–1547* (Dublin: Four Courts Press, 2000).

MacCulloch, D., *Reformation: Europe's House Divided, 1490–1700* (London and New York: Allen Lane, 2003).

'England', in A. Pettegree (ed.), *The Early Reformation in Europe* (Cambridge University Press, 2002), 166–87.

McEneaney, E., 'Politics and the Art of Devotion in Late Fifteenth-Century Waterford', in Moss *et al.* (eds.), *Art and Devotion in Late Medieval Ireland*, 33–50.

Meigs, S. A., *The Reformations in Ireland: Tradition and Confessionalism, 1400–1690* (Dublin: Gill & Macmillan, 1997).

Murphy, M., 'The High Cost of Dying: An Analysis of *pro anima* Bequests in Medieval Dublin', in W. J. Shiels and D. Wood (eds.), *The Church and Wealth: Studies in Church History, 24* (Oxford: Blackwell, 1987), 111–22.

Ó Clabaigh, C., 'The Other Christ: The Cult of St Francis of Assisi in Late Medieval Ireland', in Moss *et al.* (eds.), *Art and Devotion in Late Medieval Ireland*, 142–62.

Ryan, S., 'Windows on Late Medieval Devotional Practice: Máire Ní Mháille's 'Book of Piety' (1513)', in Moss *et al.* (eds.), *Art and Devotion in Late Medieval Ireland*, 1–15.

Simms, K., 'Frontiers in the Irish Church – Regional and Cultural', in Barry *et al.* (eds.), *Colony and Frontier in Medieval Ireland*, 177–200.

Tait, C., 'Art and the Cult of the Virgin Mary in Ireland, *c.*1500–1660', in Moss *et al.* (eds.), *Art and Devotion in Late Medieval Ireland*, 163–83.

Tanner, N., *The Ages of Faith: Popular Religion in Late Medieval England and Western Europe* (London: I.B. Tauris, 2008).

Walker Bynum, C., *Christian Materiality: An Essay on Religion in Late Medieval Europe* (New York: Zone Books, 2011).

19 Contexts, Divisions and Unities: Perspectives from the Later Middle Ages

Robin Frame

Manuscript Sources

NAI RC 7   Record Commission Calendar of Plea Rolls
TNA SC 6   Ministers' Accounts

Primary Sources

Acts of Archbishop Colton on his Metropolitan Visitation of the Diocese of Derry, ed. W. Reeves (Dublin: Irish Archaeological Soc., 1850).

'Cartae Dunenses, XII–XIII Céad', ed. G. Mac Niocaill, *Seanchas Ardmhacha*, 5 (1970), 418–28.

A Contemporary Narrative of the Proceedings against Dame Alice Kyteler Prosecuted for Sorcery in 1324, ed. T. Wright. Camden Series, o.s. 24 (London: The Camden Society, 1843).

Lebor na Cert, ed. M. Dillon (London: ITS, 1962).

Poems from BL MS Harley 913: 'The Kildare Manuscript', ed. T. Turville-Petre. EETS, o.s. 345 (Oxford University Press, 2015).

The Poems of Giolla Brighde Mac Con Midhe, ed. N. Williams (Dublin: ITS, 1980).

Poems on Marcher Lords, ed. A. O'Sullivan and P. Ó Riain (Dublin: ITS, 1987).

'To Art Mac Murchadha Caomhanach', ed. L. MacKenna, *The Irish Monthly*, 56 (1928), 98–101.

Secondary Works

Bartlett, R., *Gerald of Wales, 1146–1223* (Oxford University Press, 1982).

Booker, S., 'After the "Middle Nation": The English of Ireland, Gaelicisation, and Identity in the "Four Loyal Shires" of Ireland in the Fifteenth and Sixteenth Centuries'. PhD thesis, University of Dublin, Trinity College (2011).

'Intermarriage in Fifteenth-Century Ireland: The English and Irish in the "Four Obedient Shires"', *PRIA*, 113 C (2013), 219–50.

'Irish Clergy and the Diocesan Church in the "Four Obedient Shires" of Ireland, *c.*1400–*c.*1540', *IHS*, 39 (2014), 179–209.

Bradley, J., 'The Medieval Towns of Kerry', *North Munster Antiquarian Journal*, 28 (1986), 28–39.

Breen, C., 'The Maritime Cultural Landscape of Medieval Gaelic Ireland', in P. J. Duffy, D. Edwards and E. Fitzpatrick (eds.), *Gaelic Ireland: Land, Lordship and Settlement, c.1250–c.1550* (Dublin: Four Courts Press, 2001), 418–35.

Byrne, A., 'The Earls of Kildare and their Books at the end of the Middle Ages', *The Library: The Transactions of the Bibliographical Society*, 14 (2013), 129–53.

Campbell, J., *Essays in Anglo-Saxon History* (London: Hambledon Press, 1986).

Clarke, H. B., '*Quo Vadis*: Mapping the Irish "Monastic Town"', in Duffy (ed.), *Princes, Prelates and Poets*, 261–78.

Cosgrove, A., 'Marriage in Medieval Ireland', in A. Cosgrove (ed.), *Marriage in Ireland* (Dublin: College Press, 1985), 25–50.

Crooks, P., 'Representation and Dissent: "Parliamentarianism" and the Structure of Politics in Colonial Ireland *c.*1370–1420', *EHR*, 125 (2010), 1–34.

Curtis, E., *Richard II in Ireland 1394–5* (Oxford University Press, 1927).

A History of Medieval Ireland from 1086 to 1513 (Dublin: Maunsel and Roberts, 1923; 2nd edn London: Methuen and Co., 1938).

'The Clan System among the English Settlers in Ireland', in Crooks (ed.), *Government, War and Society*, 297–301.

Davies, R. R., *The Revolt of Owain Glyndŵr* (Oxford University Press, 1995).

Dodd, G., 'Kingship, Parliament and the Court: The Emergence of "High Style" in Petitions to the English Crown, *c.*1350–1405', *EHR*, 129 (2014), 515–48.

Duffy, S., 'Ireland's Hastings: The Anglo-Norman Conquest of Dublin', *ANS*, 20 (1998), 69–85.

'The First Ulster Plantation: John de Courcy and the Men of Cumbria', in Barry *et al.* (eds.), *Colony and Frontier in Medieval Ireland*, 1–27.

Empey, C. A., 'The Sacred and the Secular: The Augustinian Priory of Kells in Ossory, 1193–1541', *IHS*, 24 (1984), 131–51.

Flanagan, M. T., *Irish Royal Charters: Texts and Contexts* (Oxford University Press, 2005)

'*Historia Gruffud vab Kenan* and the Origins of Balrothery, Co. Dublin', *Cambrian Medieval Celtic Studies*, 28 (1994), 71–94.

'Strategies of Lordship in pre-Norman and post-Norman Leinster', *ANS*, 20 (1998), 107–26.

'John de Courcy, the First Ulster Plantation and Irish Church Men', in Smith (ed.), *Britain and Ireland*, 154–178.

Frame, R., 'Two Kings in Leinster: The Crown and the MicMhurchadha in the Fourteenth Century', in Barry *et al.* (eds.), *Colony and Frontier in Medieval Ireland*, 155–75.

'Thomas Rokeby, Sheriff of Yorkshire, Justiciar of Ireland', *Peritia*, 10 (1996), 274–96.

'Exporting State and Nation: Being English in Medieval Ireland', in L. Scales and O. Zimmer (eds.), *Power and the Nation in European History* (Cambridge University Press, 2005), 143–65.

'Lordship beyond the Pale: Munster in the Later Middle Ages', in R. Stalley (ed.), *Limerick and South-West Ireland: Medieval Art and Architecture* (Leeds: BAACT, 2011), 5–18.

'Ireland after 1169: Barriers to Acculturation on an "English" Edge', in K. J. Stringer and A. Jotischky (eds.), *Norman Expansion: Connections, Continuities and Contrasts* (Farnham: Ashgate, 2013), 115–41.

Hand, G. J., *English Law in Ireland, 1290–1324* (Cambridge University Press, 1967).

Harbison, S., 'William of Windsor and the Wars of Thomond', *JRSAI*, 119 (1989), 98–112.

McNeill, T. E., *Anglo-Norman Ulster: The History and Archaeology of an Irish Barony* (Edinburgh: John Donald, 1980).

MacQueen, H. L., 'The Kin of Kennedy, "kenkynnol" and the Common Law', in A. Grant and K. J. Stringer (eds.), *Medieval Scotland, Crown, Lordship and Community: Essays Presented to G. W.S. Barrow* (Edinburgh University Press, 1993), 274–96.

Maginn, C., 'English Marcher Lineages of South Dublin in the Later Middle Ages', *IHS*, 34 (2004), 113–37.

Matthew, E., 'Henry V and the Proposal for an Irish Crusade', in Smith (ed.), *Ireland and the English World*, 161–75.

Nic Ghiollamhaith, A., 'Kings and Vassals in Later Medieval Ireland: The Uí Bhriain and the MicConmara in the Fourteenth Century', in Barry *et al.* (eds.), *Colony and Frontier in Medieval Ireland*, 201–16.

O'Brien, A. F., 'Commercial Relations between Aquitaine and Ireland, *c.*1000 to *c.*1550', in J.-M. Picard (ed.), *Aquitaine and Ireland in the Middle Ages* (Dublin: Four Courts Press, 1995), 31–80.

Ó Cléirigh, C., 'The O'Connor Faly Lordship of Offaly, 1395–1513', *PRIA*, 96 C (1996), 87–102.

Richardson, H. G. and Sayles, G. O., *The Irish Parliament in the Middle Ages* (Philadelphia: University of Pennsylvania Press, 1952).

Simms, K., 'The Concordat between Primate John Mey and Henry O'Neill, 1455', *Archivium Hibernicum*, 34 (1977), 71–82.

'Niall Garbh II O Donnell, King of Tír Conaill, 1422–39', *The Donegal Annual*, 12 (1977–9), 7–21.

'The O Hanlons, the O Neills and the Anglo-Normans in Thirteenth-Century Armagh', *Seanchas Ardmhacha*, 9 (1978), 70–94.

'"The King's Friend": O'Neill, the Crown and the Earldom of Ulster', in Lydon (ed.), *England and Ireland*, 214–36.

Smith, B., *Colonisation and Conquest in Medieval Ireland: The English in Louth 1170–1330* (Cambridge University Press, 1999).

'The Armagh–Clogher Dispute and the "Mellifont Conspiracy": Diocesan Politics and Monastic Reform in early Thirteenth-Century Ireland', *Seanchas Ardmhacha*, 14 (1991), 26–37.

Smith, L. B., 'The Statute of Wales, 1284', *Welsh History Review*, 10 (1980–1), 127–54.

621

Smyly, J. G., 'Old Latin Deeds in the Library of Trinity College', part II, *Hermathena*, 67 (1946).

Verstraten, F., 'Images of Gaelic Lordship in Ireland *c*.1200–1400', in Doran and Lyttleton (eds.), *Lordship in Medieval Ireland*, 47–71.

Walsh, K., *A Fourteenth-Century Scholar and Primate: Richard FitzRalph in Oxford, Avignon and Armagh* (Oxford University Press, 1981).

'The Roman Career of John Swayne, Archbishop of Armagh, 1418–39', *Seanchas Ardmhacha*, 11 (1983–4), 1–21.

Watt, J. A., 'John Colton, Justiciar of Ireland (1382) and Archbishop of Armagh (1383–1404)', in Lydon (ed.), *England and Ireland*, 196–213.

'Gaelic Polity and Cultural Identity', in *NHI* ii, 314–51.

Wormald, J., *Lords and Men in Scotland: Bonds of Manrent, 1442–1603* (Edinburgh: John Donald, 1985).

Websites

CIRCLE: A Calendar of Irish Chancery Letters, *c*.1244–1509 http://chancery .tcd.ie/

Index